KOOWON KIM, Ph.D. (2010) in Hebrew Bible and ancient Near East, University of Chicago, is Assistant Professor at Reformed Theological Seminary in Seoul, South Korea. He is a contributor to *Dictionary of the Old Testament: Wisdom, Poetry & Writings* (IVP, 2008).

Incubation as a Type-Scene in the ʾAqhatu, Kirta, and Hannah Stories

Supplements

to

Vetus Testamentum

VOLUME 145

Incubation as a Type-Scene in the ʾAqhatu, Kirta, and Hannah Stories

A Form-Critical and Narratological Study of KTU 1.14 I–1.15 III, 1.17 I–II, and 1 Samuel 1:1–2:11

By

Koowon Kim

BRILL

LEIDEN • BOSTON
2011

This book is printed on acid-free paper.

Library of Congress Cataloging-in-Publication Data

Incubation as a type-scene in the Aqhatu, Kirta, and Hannah stories : a form-critical and narratological study of KTU 1.14 i–1.15 III, 1.17 I–II, and 1 Samuel 1:1–2:11 / edited by Koowon Kim.
p. cm. — (Supplements to Vetus testamentum, ISSN 0083-5889 ; v. 145)
Includes bibliographical references.
ISBN 978-90-04-20239-9 (hardback : alk. paper) 1. Incubation (Religion) 2. Aqhat epic. 3. Keret epic. 4. Hannah (Biblical figure) 5. Bible. O.T. Samuel, 1st, I,1–II,11—Criticism, interpretation, etc. I. Kim, Koowon. II. Title. III. Series.

BL325.I5I53 2011
203'.8—dc22

2011008357

ISSN 0083-5889
ISBN 978 90 04 20239 9

PRINTED BY DRUKKERIJ WILCO B.V. - AMERSFOORT, THE NETHERLANDS

CONTENTS

LIST OF TABLES

ACKNOWLEDGMENTS

The idea for this book originated in Professor Pardee's graduate course on the ʾAqhatu story at the University of Chicago where it would then become a doctoral dissertation. I am grateful to my dissertation readers, Dr. Dennis Pardee, Dr. Theo van den Hout, Dr. David Schloen, and Dr. Jefferey Stackert, for their instruction and encouragement. Especially, my adviser, Dr. Dennis Pardee, has been a model not only of scholarly integrity but also of generosity throughout my time at the University of Chicago.

I would also like to thank my parents and parents-in-law. Without their prayers and encouragement, this study would never have been completed. Finally, I gratefully acknowledge the love and encouragement of my wife Sook Gyung Lee. Words cannot express my gratitude for her self-sacrificing love and support. I dedicate this study to her.

ABBREVIATIONS

AAeg	*Analecta Aegyptiaca*
AB	Anchor Bible
ABD	Anchor Bible Dictionary
AfO	*Archiv für Orientforschung*
AHw	Akkadisches Handwörterbuch. W. von Soden. 3 vols. Wiesbaden, 1965–1981
AJP	*American Journal of Philology*
ALASP	Abhandlungen zur Literatur Alt-Syrien-Palästinas
AMD	Ancient Magic and Divination
ANET	Ancient Near Eastern Texts Relating to the Old Testament. Edited by J. B. Pritchard. 3d ed. Princeton, 1969
AnOr	Analecta Orientalia
AnSt	*Anatolian Studies*
AOAT	Alter Orient und Altes Testament
AOS	American Oriental Series
ARM	Archives royales de Mari
ASAE	*Annales du service des antiquités de l'Égypte*
BA	*Biblical Archaeologist*
BASOR	*Bulletin of the American Schools of Oriental Research*
Ber	*Berytus*
Bib	*Biblica*
BO	*Bibliotheca Orientalis*
BOH	Bibliotheca orientalis Hungarica
BS	Biblical Seminar
BSOAS	*Bulletin of the School of Oriental and African Studies*
BZAW	Beihefte zur Zeitschrift für die Alttestamentliche Wissenschaft
CAD	The Assyrian Dictionary of the Oriental Institute of the University of Chicago. Chicago, 1956–
CBQ	*Catholic Biblical Quarterly*
CHANE	Culture and History of the Ancient Near East
CI	*Critical Inquiry*
COS	The Context of Scripture. Edited by W. W. Hallo. 3 vols. Leiden, 1997–

CSCP	Cornell Studies in Classical Philology
DMOA	Documenta et monumenta Orientis antiqui
Ebib	Études bibliques
ERE	Encyclopaedia of Religion and Ethics
ErIsr	*Eretz-Israel*
FAT	Forschungen zum Alten Testament
FOTL	Forms of the Old Testament Literature
HR	*History of Religions*
HSM	Harvard Semitic Monograph
HTR	*Harvard Theological Review*
HUCA	*Hebrew Union College Annual*
ICC	International Critical Commentary
IEJ	*Israel Exploration Journal*
Int	*Interpretation*
JAAR	*Journal of the American Academy of Religion*
JANER	*Journal of Ancient Near Eastern Religions*
JANESCU	*Journal of the Ancient Near Eastern Society of Columbia University*
JAOS	*Journal of the American Oriental Society*
JBL	*Journal of Biblical Literature*
JBR	*Journal of Bible and Religion*
JCS	*Journal of Cuneiform Studies*
JEA	*Journal of Egyptian Archaeology*
JHS	*Journal of Hellenic Studies*
JNES	*Journal of Near Eastern Studies*
JNSL	*Journal of Northwest Semitic Languages*
JOST	*Journal for the Study of the Old Testament*
JOSTSup	Journal for the Study of the Old Testament: Supplement Series
JR	*Journal of Religion*
JSS	*Journal of Semitic Studies*
KAI	Kanaanäische und aramäische Inschriften. H. Donner and W. Röllig. 2d ed. Wiesbaden, 1966–1969
NEA	*Near Eastern Archaeology*
NIB	New Interpreter's Bible
NIBCOT	New International Biblical Commentary on the Old Testament
NLH	*New Literary History*
OBO	Orbis Biblicus et Orientalis

OLP	*Orientalia lovaniensia periodica*
Or	*Orientalia*
OTL	Old Testament Library
OTS	Old Testament Studies
OtSt	*Oudtestamentische Studiën*
PAAJR	*Proceedings of the American Academy of Jewish Research*
PIBA	*Proceedings of the Irish Biblical Association*
Proof	*Prooftexts: A Journal of Jewish Literary History*
PRU	Le Palais royal d'Ugarit
RB	*Revue Biblique*
REJ	*Revue des études juives*
RSO	Revista degli studi orientali
RSOu	Ras Shamra-Ougarit
SBLDS	Society of Biblical Literature Dissertation Series
SBLRBS	Society of Biblical Literature Resources for Biblical Study
SBLTT	Society of Biblical Literature Texts and Translations
SEÅ	*Svensk exegetisk årsbok*
SEL	Studi epigrafici e linguistic
SHCANE	Studies in the History and Culture of the Ancient Near East
SO	*Sources Orientales*
TAPA	Transactions of the American Philological Association
TB	*Tyndale Bulletin*
TDOT	Theological Dictionary of the Old Testament
TUAT	Texte aus der Umwelt des Alten Testaments
UF	*Ugarit-Forschungen*
VT	*Vetus Testamentum*
VTSup	Supplements to Vetus Testamentum
WMANT	Wissenschaftliche Monographien zum Alten und Neuen Testament
WO	*Die Welt des Orients*
WTS	*Westminster Theological Journal*
ZA	*Zeitschrift für Assyriologie*
ZAW	*Zeitschrift für die alttestamentliche Wissenschaft*

CHAPTER ONE

INTRODUCTION

1. Introduction

In the historical study of religion, the term 'incubation' generally refers to the practice of sleeping, or at least passing the night, in a holy place with the object of receiving a divine revelation or divine aid in a dream.[1] The most prominent example of this in antiquity is the incubation practiced in Greece from 5th century B.C.E. well into the early Christian centuries. The purpose of the Greek incubation was primarily therapeutic and the most popular healing god was Asclepius, who had more than two hundred sanctuaries by the beginning of the Christian era. At Epidauros, for instance, a sick person would undergo purification by ritual bathing and preliminary sacrifice before being invited into the *abaton* (literally "untrodden," "inaccessible"), the sacred precinct in Asklepieion. The incubant then lay on a *clinê* or a couch and awaited a dream or vision from the god, who appeared with a caduceus (a staff around which a snake is coiled) and healed

[1] Louis H. Gray, "Incubation," in *ERE: Vol. 7*, ed. James Hastings (Edinburgh: T. & T. Clark, 1914), 206. This definition of incubation is accepted, or at least presupposed, by a large number of biblical and ancient Near Eastern scholars. According to Ehrlich, for instance, "Inkubation ist... eine Traumoffenbarung, die der Mensch an heiliger Statte erlangt" (Ernst L. Ehrlich, *Der Traum im Alten Testament*, BZAW 73 [Berlin: Töpelmann, 1953], 14). A similar view is expressed by Contenau: "L'incubation consiste, pour celui qui veut être favorisé de rêves, à passer la nuit dans un temple, où, par definition, il sera plus proche de la divinité, et plus en état de recevoir son apparition" (Georges Contenau, *La divination chez les Assyriens et les Babyloniens. Avec 13 figures, 1 carte et 8 gravures hors texte* [Paris: Payot, 1940], 171). Other definitions have been primarily influenced by the Greek form of the practice and cannot readily be applied to incubation in general. Thus the description given by Deubner in his work on incubation applies essentially to incubation in ancient Greece: "In deorum templis ad dormiendum se prosternebant, quia certis ritibus atque caeremoniis effectis animoque bene praeparato atque prorsus in res divinas converso verisimillimum erat illum per somnium appariturum esse deum in cuius templo incubant" (Ludwig Deubner, *De Incubatione Capita Quattuor Scripsit Ludovicus Deubner. Accedit Laudatio in Miracula Sancti Hieromartyris Therapontis e Codice Messanensi Denuo Edita.* [Lipsiae: B. G. Teubner, 1900], 5, cited by Ehrlich, *Traum*, p. 13 and by Margaret G. Robinson, "Dreams in the Old Testament" [Ph.D. diss., Manchester University, 1987], 256). The problem of defining incubation will be dealt with below.

the patient either by a simple touch, by performing surgery, or by administrating a healing drug.[2]

This practice of seeking dream experiences in sacred places is, however, generally believed to be much older than the Greek practice. Furthermore, the practice of incubation was never geographically confined to ancient Greece. In fact, the earliest evidence dates back to the Neolithic period. For example, figurines with deformed bodies and representations of the so-called sleeping ladies found in Neolithic temples in Malta suggest that these temples were sites of healing and reception of oracles, where through the process of incubation believers could obtain cures for the body or soul.[3] Considerable evidence has been collected to suggest the existence of similar practices in the ancient Near East,[4] Arabia,[5] India,[6] China,[7] North America,[8] etc. Surprisingly,

[2] Cf. Gary B. Ferngren and Darrel W. Amundsen, "Healing and Medicine: Healing and Medicine in Greece and Rome," in *Encyclopedia of Religion*, ed. Mircea Eliade (New York: Macmillan, 2005), 3842; Frances L. Flannery-Dailey, "Standing at the Heads of Dreamers: A Study of Dreams in Antiquity Second Temple Period" (Ph.D. diss., University of Iowa, 2000), 165; Carl A. Meier, "The Dream in Ancient Greece and Its Use in Temple Cures (Incubation)," in *The Dream and Human Societies*, ed. Gustave E. Von Grunebaum and Roger Caillois (Berkeley: University of California Press, 1966), 314ff.

[3] Evans who excavated these Maltese temples claims to have found two small rooms that could well have been used as cubicles for those practicing incubation (John D. Evans, *Malta* [London: Thames and Hudson, 1959]). Also see Dragoslav Srejović, "Neolithic Religion," in *Encyclopedia of Religion*, ed. Mircea Eliade (New York: Macmillan, 1987), 6465.

[4] See section 4 in chapter two.

[5] The practice called *istikhāra*, an Islamic incubation, consists of the recital of a special prayer with the expectation of an answering dream. Jean Lecerf, concurring with Taufy Fahd, says that this practice is short of being called incubation because it lacks the element ordinarily thought essential—the all night vigil in the sanctuary (Jean Lecerf, "The Dream in Popular Culture: Arabic and Islamic," in *The Dream and Human Societies*, ed. Gustave E. Von Grunebaum and Roger Caillois [Berkeley: University of California Press, 1966], 377; cf. Taufy Fahd, "Les songes et leur interprétation selon l'Islam," in *Les songes et leur interprétation*, ed. A.-M. Esnoul [Paris: Édition du Seuil, 1959], 125–57; Taufy Fahd, "Istikhāra," in *The Encyclopaedia of Israel* [Leiden: Brill, 1978], 4:259–60).

[6] Serenity Young, "Buddhist Dream Experience: The Role of Interpretation, Ritual, and Gender," in *Dreams: A Reader on the Religious, Cultural, and Psychological Dimensions of Dreaming*, ed. Kelly Bulkeley (New York: Palgrave, 2001), 9–28. Cf. Kimberley C. Patton, "A Great and Strange Correction: Intentionality, Locality, and Epiphany in the Category of Dream Incubation," *HR* 43 (2004): 210, footnote 40.

[7] G. Foot Moore, *History of Religions* (New York: Charles Scribner's Sons, 1922), 13. See also W. D. Wallis, "Prodigies and Portents," in *ERE: Vol. X*, ed. James Hastings (Edinburgh: T. & T. Clark, 1914), 372.

[8] See Louis H. Gray, "Incubation," 206; Anthony Shafton, *Dream Reader: Contemporary Approaches to the Understanding of Dreams* (New York: State University of

the ancient notion of physical healing through cultic dreaming continues even today. While psychoanalysts such as Carl Meier practice incubation in their laboratories,[9] orthodox Christians make pilgrimages to "holy" churches throughout the Mediterranean to seek dreams through incubation.[10] Hence, although the scholarly interest in incubation *per se* seems to have declined in recent years,[11] it comes as no surprise that this religious practice has generated significant interest among historians of religion. Kimberley C. Patton's statement seems to epitomize the significance that the subject of incubation occupies in the historical study of religion: Incubation represents "a rich nexus of cognitive, performative, locative, and theological issues in the historical study of religion."[12]

New York Press, 1995), 408; Lee Irwin, *The Dream Seekers: Native American Visionary Traditions of the Great Plains* (Norman: University of Oklahoma Press, 1994).

[9] Carl Meier pioneered the use of deliberate sleeping to produce healing dreams in psychotherapy. See Carl A. Meier, *Ancient Incubation and Modern Psychotherapy* (Evanston: Northwestern University Press, 1967).

[10] At the Cathedral at Tinos and elsewhere in modern Greece, for example, the dream incubation is widely practiced. According to a recent account (2002) reported by Nun Aemiliance of the Monastery of the Elevation of Holy Cross in Greece, the grandfather of her friend named Nun Mariam, who had suffered severe gangrene, slept in a holy place within the sanctuary of the Church of the Holy Unmercenaries Ss. Cosmos and Damian (soldier-doctors from the period of Roman persecution) in northern Greece, and was healed by them in a dream (Patton, "A Great and Strange Correction: Intentionality, Locality, and Epiphany in the Category of Dream Incubation," 217, footnote 57).

[11] A quick survey of literatures on incubation reveals this tendency. Many important studies on incubation were already undertaken either before the 20th century or at the turn of the century (for example, Alice Walton, *The Cult of Asklepios*, CSCP 3 [Ithaca: Cornell University Press, 1894]; Deubner, *De Incubatione Capita Quattuor Scripsit Ludovicus Deubner. Accedit Laudatio in Miracula Sancti Hieromartyris Therapontis e Codice Messanensi Denuo Edita.*; Mary Hamilton, *Incubation or The Cure of Disease in Pagan Temples and Christian Churches* [St. Andrews: W. C. Henderson & Son, 1906]). They usually devoted entire studies to the subject of incubation. In the past 50–60 years, however, the subject of incubation has been relegated to a subset of other topics such as dream, theophany, divination and so forth (The exception is Meier, *Ancient Incubation and Modern Psychotherapy*). This is most clearly illustrated in the divergent ways that two prestigious encyclopedias of religion, separated by a time span little short of a century, deal under the entry "incubation." *Encyclopaedia of Religion and Ethics* (1913) edited by J. Hastings treats "incubation" in a full-length article, while the entry "incubation" in Encyclopedia of Religion (2002) edited by M. Eliade simply redirects the reader to "dream" and "Asclepius" without further ado.

[12] Patton, "A Great and Strange Correction: Intentionality, Locality, and Epiphany in the Category of Dream Incubation," 194.

2. Statement of Problems

Although the subject of incubation has not been neglected in either biblical studies[13] or in ancient Near Eastern studies,[14] the interest of biblical and ancient Near Eastern scholars in incubation has been essentially of the nature of historians of religion.[15] They have almost always focused on the reconstruction of the historical details pertaining to the incubation practice. It is with that end in mind that scholars have tended to examine textual data to find allusions to the practice of incubation. But irrespective of whether the scholarly analysis of relevant texts is thoroughly philological or even literary in nature, their final goal has almost always been to get behind the written documents to some historical facts about religious practice. This history-of-religions approach to incubation has, however, had only a limited success.[16] This is exemplified, for instance, by the marked division of opinion among scholars on the issue of even whether incubation was ever practiced in ancient Israel, let alone on its historical details. Köhler says, for instance, "...there is no human process, no prayer, sacrifice or technique of any kind, whereby man could induce a divine apparition. Man is always the recipient only, never the author

[13] To name a few, Ehrlich, Resch, Gnuse, Robinson, Husser, etc. See Bibliography for full citations.

[14] To name a few, Oppenheim, Caquot, Contenau, Mouton, etc. See Bibliography for full citations.

[15] This is true of Classical studies as well. Some of the representative studies include Naphtali Lewis, *The Interpretation of Dreams and Portents* (Toronto: Samuel Stevens Hakkert, 1976) and Veit Rosenberger, *Griechische Orakel: eine Kulturgeschichte* (Darmstadt: Wissenschaftliche Buchgesellschaft, 2001).

[16] For details see the discussion on previous studies in chapters 4–6 below. Oppenheim's study should be considered an exception. In his study of an Assyrian dream book (*Zaqīqu*), he suggested almost in passing that the incubation dream is to be considered to provide a literary prototype for all accounts of ancient Near Eastern message dreams (A. Leo Oppenheim, *The Interpretation of Dreams in the Ancient Near East: With a Translation of an Assyrian Dream-Book*, TAPA 46 [Philadelphia, PA: American Philological Society, 1956], 190). He further proposed a literary paradigm according to which message dreams are to be reported. Although many scholars have since been very reluctant to admit any literary influence of the incubation practice on the account of message dreams, they have all accepted Oppenheim's literary analysis for message dreams as valid. Gnuse, for instance, applied Oppenheim's literary analysis to 1 Samuel 3 in his dissertation (Robert K. Gnuse, "The Dream Theophany of Samuel: Its Structure in Relation to Ancient Near Eastern Dreams and Its Theological Significance" [Ph.D. diss., Nashville, TN: Vanderbilt University, 1980]).

of revelation."[17] Against this attitude, others contend that the concept of seeking a response from the deity was far from unknown in ancient Israel situated as it was at the junction of international highways in ancient Near Eastern world.[18]

Several reasons may be adduced for this state of affairs in biblical and ancient Near Eastern scholarship on incubation. First, as Jean-Marie Husser points out, the texts that speak of incubation in unambiguous terms are rare before the Hellenistic period.[19] Unlike the Greek evidence, the evidence in the Hebrew Bible as well as in ancient Near Eastern texts is sparse, and what little we have is not explicit enough to permit us to arrive at any consensus as to what really happened in history.[20] Second, more importantly, the history-of-religions approach, though preoccupied with the search for possible allusions to incubation, has neglected to deal with the problem of defining incubation. The problem of definition, however, is crucial, since any positive indices to the practice of incubation depend on the preliminary definition given to it.[21] Generally speaking, scholars assume prior to their search efforts, the form that an incubation scene should take on the basis of what they already know about incubation as an actual practice, for

---

[17] Ludwig H. Köhler, *Old Testament Theology*, trans. A. S. Todd (Philadelphia, PA: Westminster Press, 1957), 103 A similar view was expressed by Resch who believed that incubation "...mit der Theologien Israels absolut unvereinbar ist" (Andreas Resch, *Der Traum im Heilsplan Gottes: Deutung und Bedeutung des Traums im Alten Testament* [Freiburg: Herder, 1964], 115).

[18] Robinson, "Dreams in the Old Testament," 99; cf. Ehrlich, *Der Traum im Alten Testament*, VI; Robert K. Gnuse, *Dreams and Dream Report in the Writings of Josephus: A Traditio-Historical Analysis* (Leiden: Brill, 1996), 233. A similar point can be made about ancient Near Eastern studies. Scholars debate whether incubation was ever practiced in the ancient Near East. Walter A. Jayne (*The Healing Gods of Ancient Civilizations* [New Haven, CT: Yale University Press, 1925], 101–3) and Eduard Thrämer ("Health and Gods of Healing," in *ERE: Vol. VI*, ed. James Hastings [New York: Charles Scribner's Sons, 1908], 6:542) assume that incubation was common in the ancient Near East. However, W. G. Lambert (*Babylonian Wisdom Literature* [Oxford: Clarendon Press, 1960], 24) and J. Bergman ("Chālam," in *Theological Dictionary of the Old Testament*, ed. J. Botterweck and H. Ringgren [Grand Rapids, MI: Eerdmans, 1977], 4:424) doubt that such was the case. Cf. Gnuse, *Dreams and Dream Report in the Writings of Josephus: A Traditio-Historical Analysis*, 46.

[19] Jean-Marie Husser, *Dreams and Dream Narratives in the Biblical World*, BS 63 (Sheffield: Sheffield Academic Press, 1999), 21.

[20] As for 1 King 3:1–5 which Ehrlich regards as "die vollständigste Inkubation im Alten Testament" (Ehrlich, *Der Traum im Alten Testament*, 19), for example, Caquot does not regard it as an incubation scene because "l'initiative de la révélation appartient pleinement à la divinité" (André Caquot, "Les songes et leur interpretation selon Canaan et Israel," *SO* 2 [1959]: 107).

[21] Husser, *Dreams and Dream Narratives in the Biblical World*, 121.

instance, incubation in Greece. Margalit, for example, insists on the presence of a chthonic deity as one of the defining features of an incubation scene.[22] Although most scholars are not as stringent as Margalit in their definition of incubation, they nonetheless operate with varying sets of definitions. This situation has contributed to a wide diversity of opinion on incubation.

I believe that the current impasse in the biblical and ancient Near Eastern scholarship on incubation may be overcome with scholars taking a more self-conscious approach to the problem of definition. To that end, I propose that at least three different levels be differentiated: namely, a) the lexical meaning of incubation, b) the religious reality referred to by the word "incubation," and c) the "incubation" motif as a literary device. Those who are interested in the subject of incubation ought to recognize that there are different levels of definition and then consciously keep these separate in their study of incubation.

a) The lexical meaning of incubation: The term incubation derives from Latin *incubāre* which means "to lie or recline in a place."[23] By the 2nd century B.C.E., this term had acquired the technical (albeit not exclusive) sense of sleeping in a temple "um durch Träume über die Zukunft überhaupt oder <von einem Kranken> über seine Krankheit von der Gottheit Belehrung zu erhalten" ("in order to receive, through dream, divine instruction concerning one's future or one's sickness").[24] The Latin verb *incubāre* was, for example, used in Titus Maccius Plautus's *Curculio* (act 1, scene 1, line 61)[25] to refer to ritual sleeping in the temple of Asclepius, the ancient Greek god of healing. The term continued to have this technical usage some five hundred years later, when the church historian Eusebius (265–339 C.E.) in his commentary on Isaiah 65:4 used *incubāre* more generally to refer to the religious rite of sleeping in a shrine to get a dream-oracle (*Isaiam Commentaria*, XVIII, 65).[26] This shows an etymological connection of the

[22] Baruch Margalit, *The Ugaritic Poem of Aqht: Text, Translation, Commentary*, BZAW 182 (New York: De Gruyter, 1989), 264.

[23] S.v. "Incubō," in *Oxford Latin Dictionary*, ed. P. G. W. Glare (Oxford: Clarendon Press, 1982).

[24] Annette von Zgoll, "Die Welt im Schlaf sehen: Inkubation von Träumen im antiken Mesopotamien," *WO* 32 (2002): 14.

[25] For the Latin text and the English translation, See the Perseus Digital Library: http://www.perseus.tufts.edu/hopper/text?doc=Perseus:text:1999.02.0037&redirect=true (accessed August 10, 2010).

[26] Emma J. Edelstein and Ludwig Edelstein, *Asclepius: A Collection and Interpretation of the Testimonies* (Baltimore, MD: Johns Hopkins Press, 1945), 143.

English term "incubation" to the practice of theurgic healing in ancient Greece.

Whereas *incubāre* is the only Latin word associated with the incubation practice, one can find several Greek words attested to in the context of the therapeutic incubation in ancient Greece. In Aristophanes's comedy *Plutus* (5th century B.C.E.), the Greek word (ἐγ)κατακλίνω was used transitively to denote laying someone down in the temple of Asclepius for a cure.[27] The inscriptional texts found in Epidaurus (from the 5th century B.C.E. to the 2nd century C.E.), however, use ἐγκαθεύδω or ἐγκατακοιμάω to refer to ritual sleeping in the temple of Asclepius.[28] But by the first century B.C.E., the term ἐγκοιμάω and its derivatives had gradually acquired the technical sense of incubation, among which ἐγκοίμησις is worth noting, not only because it is a nominal form of the verb, but also because it came to be used exclusively to refer to 'sleeping in a temple for a revelatory dream.'[29] Scholars seem to agree that the Latin term *incubāre* is a translation of the Greek term ἐγκοίμησις.[30]

All this seems to affirm the Greco-roman religious milieu in which both the Latin word *incubāre* and the Greek word ἐγκοίμησις (< ἐγκοιμάω) came to acquire their technical meaning. It would be no exaggeration, therefore, to say that the modern English term "incubation," whose historical root is in both these ancient terms, presents the practical danger of leading us to associate the term with the paraphernalia attached to Greco-Roman incubation practice. In this context,

---

[27] Aristophanes, *Plutus*, line 620: αὕτη μὲν ἡμῖν ἡπίτριπτος οἴχεται. ἐγὼ δὲ καὶ σύ γ' ὡς τάχιστα τὸν θεὸν ἐγκατακλινοῦντ' ἄγωμεν εἰς Ἀσκληπιοῦ. ("So that hussy has gone at last! But let us make haste to put Plutus to bed in the Temple of Asclepius"). Online: http://www.perseus.tufts.edu/hopper/text?doc=Perseus:text:1999.01.0039:card%3D598 (accessed August 10, 2010).

[28] Lynn R. LiDonnici, *The Epidaurian Miracle Inscriptions*, SBLTT 36 (Atlanta, GA: Scholars Press, 1995), 23, 32–3, 39, 68, 80. Stelae with these verbs include the following: a9, 25, 37, 57, 66, 76, 98, 107; b9, 39, 61, 66, 69, 83, 88, 111, 117, 120, 123; gl l, 31, 59, 65. Cf. Flannery-Dailey, "Standing at the Heads of Dreamers: A Study of Dreams in Antiquity Second Temple Period," 165, 191, footnote 223.

[29] ἐγκοίμησις is used in parallel with other divination techniques in Diodorus Siculus's *Library* 1.53: "Others encouraged him by their divinations, foretelling his successes by the entrails of the sacrifices, by their dreams in the temple, and prodigies seen in the air" (cf. G. Booth, trans., *The Historical Library of Diodorus the Sicilian* [London: W. Taylor, 1814], 58).

[30] Meier, *Ancient Incubation and Modern Psychotherapy*, 58. Also see Fritz Graf, "Incubation," in *Brill's New Pauly: Encyclopaedia of the Ancient World*, vol. 6, ed. Francis G. Gentry (Leiden: Brill, 2006), 766–67.

the words of Walter J. Ong are worth quoting: "But concepts have a way of carrying their etymologies with them forever. The elements out of which a term is originally built usually, and probably always, linger somehow in subsequent meanings, perhaps obscurely but often powerfully and even irreducibly."[31] This is the reason why the Greek concept of incubation still exerts a considerable influence on ancient Near Eastern scholarship on incubation.

b) The religious reality of incubation: As we have already seen, the religious reality of incubation neither originated with the Greeks, nor is it confined to them. Throughout human history, incubation has been practiced, wherever there was a belief in the power of a dream, whatever its origin may be, to "discuss waking life-problems."[32] And evidence shows that the practice of incubation varies from one culture to another. In the vision quest tradition known throughout Native American cultures, for example, the sleeping aspect of classical incubation is not mandatory. An incubant experienced the theophany while he was awake.[33] This variation may be explained in terms of Native American epistemology, wherein dreaming and waking vision are not distinguished.[34] Furthermore, not only could incubation occur in any place,[35] but also without any intentionality on the incubant's part.[36] Therefore, the term incubation, despite its Greco-Roman origin,

[31] Walter J. Ong, *Orality and Literacy: The Technologizing of the Word* (London: Routledge, 1982), 12.

[32] Jack Maguire, *Night and Day* (New York: Simon & Schuster, 1989), 144. A similar thought is expressed by Ehrlich, *Der Traum im Alten Testament*, 14. Shafton adds psycho-physiological reasons for the ubiquity of incubation, namely, our natural tendency/ability to incubate the dream we want (Shafton, *Dream Reader: Contemporary Approaches to the Understanding of Dreams*, 394–404). While psychoanalysts (e.g. Carl Meier) explain the therapeutic effects of incubation dream in terms of psychotherapy, ancient people ascribed the power of dream to its divine origin. The thought world of ancient Israel is no exception to this. For ancient Israelites' attitudes toward dream, see Johannes Pedersen, *Israel: Its Life and Culture*, vol. I (Atlanta, GA: Scholars Press, 1991), 134ff.

[33] Barbara Tedlock, "Sharing and Interpreting Dreams in Amerindian Nations," in *Dream Cultures: Explorations in the Comparative History of Dreaming*, ed. David Shulman and Guy G. Stroumsa (New York: Oxford University Press, 1999), 98.

[34] Considering that the Egyptian word for dream (*rswt*) is not only etymologically connected with the root meaning "to be awake" but also written with the determinative representing an opened eye (Oppenheim, *The Interpretation of Dreams in the Ancient Near East: With a Translation of an Assyrian Dream-Book*, 190), we may further assume that the Egyptian incubation account may show a similar feature.

[35] Louis H. Gray, "Incubation," 206.

[36] Oppenheim calls this kind "unintentional incubation" and gives as an example the account of the so-called Sphinx Stele, which describes the dream visited upon

should be suitably amended so as to accommodate other practices, ancient and modern, which legitimately represent the religious reality behind the term "incubation." As a matter of fact, historians of religion and modern psychoanalysts currently use the term incubation rather extensively to refer to any kind of (intentional) sleeping to produce dreams.[37]

This sort of disparity between the original lexical meaning of a word and the broader religious reality referred to by that word has already been noted by historians of religion in the case of the term *shaman*.[38] The home of the "shaman" is the Tungus-speaking people of Eastern Siberia of the seventeenth century and earlier. The Russian orthodox cleric Avvakum Petrovich was the first to use the Tungus word *saman* in a published text.[39] Tungus shamans were originally "special" individuals who communicated with spirits especially "to heal or to divine." When Swiss anthropologist Alfred Métraux applied the term *shaman* to his subjects, however, he defined *shaman*, without specifying his or her function, as "any individual" who maintains an intermittent commerce with spirits by profession.[40] Later on, Mircea Eliade in his 1951 phenomenological study, *Shamanism, Archaic Techniques of Ecstasy* made "ecstasy" the primary feature of the universal shamanism.[41] Hence, healing is not an essential characteristic of shamans in the historical study of religion any more, although the shaman's traditional vocation was analogous to that of a doctor. The semantic expansion of the term *shaman* shows in relief the need for a more flexible definition of incubation when we attempt to do justice to the practice of 'incubation' in cultures other than the Greek in general, and the cultures of the ancient Near East in particular.

Tuthmosis IV as he slept between the feet of the sacred sphinx (Oppenheim, *The Interpretation of Dreams in the Ancient Near East: With a Translation of an Assyrian Dream-Book*, 187).

[37] Cf. Louis H. Gray, "Incubation," 206–7.

[38] The following explanation of *shaman* is based on Patton, "A Great and Strange Correction: Intentionality, Locality, and Epiphany in the Category of Dream Incubation," 200–201.

[39] Avvakum Petrovich, *La vie de l'Archprêtre Avaakum, ecrite par lui-même*, trans. Pierre Pascal (Paris: Galimard, 1938).

[40] Alfred Métraux, "Le shamanisme chez les Indiens de l'Amérique du Sud tropicale," in *Acta Americana*, ed. and trans. Jeremy Narby and Francis Huxley (Los Angeles, 1944), 197–219 and 320–41.

[41] Mircea Eliade, *Shamanism: Archaic Techniques of Ecstasy*, trans. Willard R. Trask (London: Arkana, 1989).

c) Incubation as a literary device: There is still another level that needs to be taken into consideration in the definition of incubation, namely, incubation as a literary motif. The question that concerns us is how we discern incubation in a literary text. While the first two levels of definition concern incubation as an actual practice in the real world, the third concerns incubation as a literary motif employed by the author or redactor and recognized by the reader.[42] Incubation as a literary device does not necessarily correspond to its actual practice behind the text,[43] just as the later report of a dream, which is bound to be conditioned by social conventions regulating such a report, is to be distinguished from the content of an actual dream. Hitherto, discussions of incubation in biblical, as well as ancient Near Eastern studies, have generally failed to differentiate incubation as an actual practice from incubation as a literary device. When it comes to the subject of incubation, they assume a single encompassing definition.[44] The approach of this book will be to distinguish incubation as an actual practice from incubation as a literary device, and the primary focus will be on the latter.

3. Statement of Purpose

This book attempts to fill a lacuna in the previous studies of incubation through a consistently literary analysis of incubation. The focus of this book, hence, is not on incubation as a religious ritual *per se* as practiced at a certain point in time, but on incubation as a literary device both employed by the author or the redactor and recognized as such by the intended listener/reader in ancient Near Eastern literary texts, including the Hebrew Bible.[45] Incubation as a literary device is a

[42] See excursus 2 below for details.

[43] Ann M. Vater, in her study of commissioned message and oral communication, makes a similar point: she says, "One cannot argue on the basis of the story for 'what really happened.'" Ann M. Vater, "Story Patterns for a Sitz," *JSOT* 11 (1979): 49.

[44] One example may be found in Margalit's definition of the incubation scene (Margalit, *The Ugaritic Poem of Aqht: Text, Translation, Commentary*, 260–66). Margalit's definition is based on Hamilton's descriptions of the Greek therapeutic incubation reports.

[45] This does not mean that incubation as a social *realia* behind its literary representations has no relevance in this study. On the contrary, this literary study of incubation assumes that incubation was known and practiced in the ancient Near East including ancient Israel. See further chapter two.

much more complicated phenomenon than has often been assumed. It entails many elements (or motifs) such as sacrifice, dream, theophany, healing, oracle, etc. To be more specific, in this book I will examine three literary texts, from the vantage point of the concept of type-scene, two from the Ras Shamra texts in the Ugaritic language (KTU 1.14 I–15 III and KTU 1.17 I–II) and one from the Hebrew Bible (1 Samuel 1:1–2:11a). Various elements or sub-motifs of the incubation type-scene will be identified and explained in detail with reference to these three literary texts. Further, their narratological functions will also be examined.

4. Defining Method: Incubation as a Type-Scene

Incubation as a literary device, by its very nature, does not provide a factual report as actually practiced at a given point in time. Just as a dream report is necessarily influenced by the social conventions regulating such a report,[46] the incubation scene in literary texts too is governed by literary conventions regulating the composition of the text. The criteria for discerning an incubation as a literary device are, therefore, bound to be different from those for a historical reconstruction of the religious practice. This implies that we need a new way of identifying incubation when we approach it as a literary device. This can be paraphrased in the form of the following question: How can we discern an incubation "motif" in a given text?

That said, I propose the use of type-scene as a methodological tool for the definition and identification of an incubation scene in the three literary texts under examination in this book. The appropriateness of the concept of type-scene for discussing incubation as a literary device can be demonstrated for the following two reasons. (1) The type-scene or "motif-sequence"[47] which consists of set of multiple elements

---

[46] Gnuse regards this as the second stage of processing raw dreams. The first stage of processing occurs when "the conscious mind forms the image of the subconscious to an acceptable set of images," namely, when the dreamer simply "remembers" his or her dream image without verbalizing it (Gnuse, "The Dream Theophany of Samuel: Its Structure in Relation to Ancient Near Eastern Dreams and Its Theological Significance," 13–14).

[47] Recurrent narrative blocks in Homeric texts have been referred to in various ways. Beside "Typische Szenen" or "type-scenes" popularized by W. Arend, Homeric scholars, following M. Parry and A. B. Lord, call them "themes." Other scholars use "motif," "motif-sequence," "stock-scene," "story pattern," etc. This terminological confusion

or sub-motifs provides a proper tool for the literary representation of the practice of incubation since it too is likewise multifaceted. (2) Type-scene, the recognition of which is not determined by any one or several essential elements, but operates on the principle of "family resemblance," will give us a flexible tool to discern incubation as a literary motif in ancient Near Eastern literature.

4.1 *Type-Scene as a Multifaceted Motif*

Scholars customarily designate Walter Arend's *Die typischen Scenen bei Homer* of 1933 as the origin of interest in recurrent scenes in the Homeric epics. In his book, Arend noted that there are certain fixed situations which tend to recur in the *Iliad* and the *Odyssey*, and which, each time they occur, are retold with many of the same motifs and many of the same words. Against previous scholarship that had regarded such repetitions simply as interpolations, Arend attempted to prove their literary quality by showing how in each retelling they adapted to the context, through the narrator's art, to fit the purpose of the story as a whole.[48] And he called those recurrent scenes "type-scene (*typische Szenen*)."[49] Arend provides "Schema" for all the

---

has been reflected in the indices of Oxford University Press commentary and Cambridge University Press commentary on *Iliad* and *Odyssey*. In the Cambridge *Iliad* commentary, Volume 1, the main pertinent entry is "theme (motif)," and there is little under "typical scene." In Volume 2 there are entries under both "typical scenes" and "typical motifs and themes." Volume 4 lists "type-scene," under which there are cross-references to other entries, while Volume 5 lists "type-scenes," "story patterns," and "motifs, repeated."

[48] Walter Arend, *Die typischen Scenen bei Homer*, Problemata 7 (Berlin: Weidmannsche Buchhandlung, 1933), 1–27.

[49] Although W. Arend deserves credit for coining the term "type-scene" (*typischen Szenen*) and also for the painstaking taxonomic presentation of major Homeric type-scenes, he was not the first one to note the importance of recurrent patterns used in oral or oral-derived epics. As a matter of fact, Arend did not realize that Homeric type-scenes are connected to the orality of the Homeric epics. In the foreword to *Der Dialect der Kara-Kirgisen* (1885), Vasilii V. Radlov discusses type-scenes in a Turkish epic under the name of "idea-parts (*Bildtheile*)." He defines the singer's art in terms of how artistically he handles the "idea-parts."

> The art of the singer consists only in arranging all of these ready-made "idea-parts" coherently, as the course of events requires, and in joining them together through newly composed verses. The singer is thus able to sing all of the previously mentioned "idea-parts" in very different ways. He knows how to sketch one and the same idea in a few short strokes, or describe it in detail, or enter into an extremely detailed description in epic breadth. The more adaptable to various situations the "idea-parts" are for a singer, the more diverse his song becomes and the longer he can sing without wearying his audience by the monotony of

type-scenes that he discusses in his book, in which he breaks down each type-scene into various elements and shows that they recur in a fixed order (or in a temporal sequence).

Arend's notion of type-scene was accepted without change, albeit under a different name ("theme"), by Milman Parry and has since been modified by subsequent scholars to suit their own purposes and assumptions.[50] Now most scholars, for example, distance themselves from Arend's original rigidity with regard to the order in which motifs occur within a type-scene and the vocabulary employed in each motif.[51] But the fact remains that type-scene is a recurrent sequence of common motifs—each subdivisible into elements and capable of functioning independently—which seem to be united under a common theme. Arend's type-scene of *Ankunft*, for example, includes the following elements: I) a hero sets out; II) he arrives; III) he finds the host sitting, standing, or busy with something; the onlookers are named; IV) he enters; he speaks.[52] Robert Alter who first introduced the notion of type-scene into biblical studies analyzes the type-scene of visit as follows: a guest approaches; someone spots him, gets up, hurries to greet him; the guest is taken by the hand, led into the room, invited to take the seat of honor; the guest is enjoined to feast; the ensuing meal is described.[53] Although there may be variations or deviations, one of

his images. The inventory of "idea-parts" and the skill in their manipulation are the measure of a singer's ability.

Furthermore, in the same year as Arend (1933), Goerge M. Calhoun published a paper ("Homeric Repetitions") discussing a number of repeated scenes in the Homeric epics. Although he did not use the term "type-scene" and his analysis was much briefer than Arend's, he too observed the effects of different examples of the same type-scene.

[50] For the historical survey of type-scene study in Homeric scholarship, see Mark W. Edwards, "Homer and Oral Tradition: The Type-Scene," *Oral Tradition* 7 (1992): 290–98. Also John M. Foley provides an excellent summary of Homeric scholarship on type-scene (John M. Foley, *Traditional Oral Epic* [Berkeley: University of California Press, 1990], 240–45).

[51] Nagler, for example, argues, "In practice...not only are no two passages normally the same verbatim, they need not be of a pattern (an identical sequence of elements) in order to be recognized as the same motif" (Michael Nagler, *Spontaneity and Tradition: A Study in the Oral Art of Homer* [Berkeley: University of California Press, 1974], 82). But other scholars such as A. Lord, B. Peabody and G. Nagy maintain more conservative opinions by stressing the importance of verbal correspondence for the identification of type-scenes. For the discussion of the three scholar's attitude to the type-scene, see Foley, *Traditional Oral Epic*, 244–56.

[52] Arend, *Die typischen Scenen bei Homer*, 28.

[53] Robert Alter, *The Art of Biblical Narrative* (New York: Basic Books, 1981), 50–51.

the definitive characters of type-scene is the narratival movement of multiple motifs.

This book proposes the use of the notion of type-scene as a tool for defining and identifying incubation as a literary device. In view of the fact that the actual practice of incubation itself is a sequence of various acts (e.g. 'going to a temple,' 'offering sacrifice,' 'lying down to sleep,' 'having a dream,' 'meeting with a god,' etc.), the type-scene as a multifaceted motif is expected to function as a particularly effective tool in the identification and analysis of the literary representation of incubation in the texts under consideration in this book.

4.2 *Type-Scene Recognition: Family Resemblance*

The second reason that the Homeric notion of type-scene provides the best tool in our efforts to define incubation as a literary device lies in the principle of "family resemblance" for type-scene recognition.

Arend distinguishes, within a type-scene, essential elements (*notwendige Teile*) from incidental elements (*zufällige Teile*) and accessorial elements (*Ausschmückungen*). Obviously, essential elements are so called because "Wir können den notwendigen typischen Teil nicht entbehren."[54] In other words, Arend works on the assumption that there are a limited number of elements which are definitional of a given type-scene, without which the type-scene would neither be established nor recognized. Robert Alter, whose idea of type-scene is heavily influenced by Arend, follows in his footsteps and divides the ingredients of type-scene into "required" and "free" ones.[55] To the best of my knowledge, all subsequent biblical type-scene studies have not progressed much on this score from the original position of Arend and Alter. In his study of the prophetic concealment type-scene, for instance, Bryan Britt divides typical elements into "basic elements" (crisis, theophany, commissioning, and divine plan) and "other elements" (food or fasting, rival prophets, successor, mention of prophet's death, etc.).[56]

---

[54] Arend, *Die typischen Scenen bei Homer*, 36, footnote 3.

[55] Robert Alter, "How Convention Helps Us Read: The Case of the Bible's Annunciation Type-Scene," *Proof* 3 (1983): 118–19. Apart from this division among elements, Alter, following Arend who unaware of the oral tradition of the Homeric epics ascribed the skillful use of type-scenes in *Illiad* and *Odysseus* to the genius of the author customarily identified as Homer, also ascribed the subtle use of biblical types to the literary genius of the biblical authors (Alter, *The Art of Biblical Narrative*, 106).

[56] Bryan Britt, "Prophetic Concealment in a Biblical Type Scene," *CBQ* 64 (2002): 38.

The problems with this approach, however, have already been noted by Homeric scholars. Should the arming of Ajax ("Ajax armed himself in gleaming bronze," *Il* 7.206b), for example, be called an arming type-scene when it lacks almost all "essential" details of it? As a matter of fact, the history of the Homeric type-scene study may be summed up as the process of loosening the rigidity of the definition of type-scene originally proposed by Arend and subsequently followed by Parry and Lord.[57] The most significant advance, however, was made by Nagler in his 1967 article "Towards a Generative View of the Oral Formula."[58] Although in this article Nagler does not deal with type-scene directly, he argues that his idea of "formula" at a phrase level does apply to other levels of formulaic language, such as motif, type-scene, and story pattern (plot).

Nagler begins his article by reviewing the current state of scholarship on formula. According to him, scholars are divided between "soft Parryists" and "hard Parryists," depending on their attitude to Milman Parry's definition of formula: "a group of words which is regularly employed under the same metrical conditions to express a given essential idea."[59] Although both agree on the essential validity of Parry's definition, soft Parryists allow Parry's definition to be loosened so as to include additional criteria for discerning formulaic resemblance among phrases, whereas hard Parryists would not recognize formulaic resemblance except as defined by Parry's original definition of formula. Nagler finds both of them problematic. If the hardcore position is accepted, one has to regard as coincidence any resemblance among phrases that are not covered by Parry's definition. But, as Nagler puts it, "When does the echoing of one phrase by another indicate that the poet has employed a formula common to both and when is such resemblance to be explained on other grounds, for instance, coincidence?"[60] The soft Parryists attempt to answer this

[57] Essential elements are one of the two aspects that constitute Arend's notion of type-scene. The other definitive feature of type-scene is a fixed order of those elements. Arend observes that "Er (the poet) erkennt in dem Gesamtvorgang die einzelnen wichtigen Teilvorgänge und baut aus ihnen eine organische Darstellung auf, entsprechend der zeitlichen Reihenfolge, so dass ein Teilvorgan den nächsten auslöst, und kein teil fehlen darf, kein Teil vor den übrigen über Gebühr hervortritt." Arend, *Die typischen Scenen bei Homer*, 25.

[58] Michael N. Nagler, "Towards a Generative View of the Oral Formula," *TAPA 98* (1967): 269–311.

[59] Ibid., 270.

[60] Michael N. Nagler, "Towards a Generative View of the Oral Formula," 270.

question by widening the definition of formula and thereby multiply such definitions almost infinitely. In which case, as Nagler points out, formula "means different things to different people."[61]

The genius of Nagler's approach lies in his rejection of the term "formula" in explaining resemblance among Homeric phrases. In the past attempts were made to account for resemblances among Homeric phrases in terms of "standard and variations." They assumed that there was an underlying standard form that the poet worked with and called it the "formula." Nagler, on the other hand, drawing on generative grammar proposes to see resemblance among phrases, not as the result of the application of a rigid definitions or criteria, but instead as owing to their being the "allomorphs" of some pre-verbal central *Gestalt* "which is the real mental template underlying the production of all such phrases."[62] The *Gestalt* itself is characterized as "pre-verbal" because it exists at a pre-verbal or pre-conscious level in the poet's mind. It is only when the poet realizes that *Gestalt* in the form (metrical, lexical, thematic, etc.) appropriate for the moment that we begin to observe its allomorphs in the Homeric epics.[63] Nagler uses the analogy of "an open-ended family" to refer to a group of allomorphs.[64]

In his book *Spontaneity and Tradition*, Nagler applies this insight to different levels of formulaic diction.[65] After covering the basic points made in his 1967 article in the first two chapters, Nagler applies the same ideas to "the motif," "the motif-sequence" (type-scene) and "plot structure" in the subsequent chapters. With regard to "type-scene" Nagler says, "a type-scene is not essentially a fixed sequence...nor even a fixed pattern for the progressive selection of fixed or variable elements...but an inherited pre-verbal *Gestalt* for the spontaneous generation of a 'family' of meaningful details...In practice, therefore, not only are no two passages normally the same *verbatim*, they need not be of a pattern (an identical sequence of elements) in order to

[61] Ibid., 281.

[62] Ibid.

[63] Ibid., 282.

[64] Nagler's *Gestalt* is comparable to Foley's idea of "traditional referentiality." Foley himself understands Nagler's *Gestalt* as "an ideational nexus of traditional meaning which can take a variety of verbal forms" (John M. Foley, *The Theory of Oral Composition: History and Methodology* [Bloomington, IN: Indiana University Press, 1988], 101). For both of them, there is more than what meets the eye in the use of traditional phrases. For Foley's idea of traditional referentiality, see Foley, *Immanent Art: From Structure to Meaning in Traditional Oral Epic*, 39–60.

[65] Michael Nagler, *Spontaneity and Tradition: A Study in the Oral Art of Homer.*

be recognized as the same motifs."[66] According to Nagler, there is no "standard" form of a type-scene from which given examples may be said to deviate more or less. The arming type-scene, for instance, is a "pre-verbal *Gestalt*" in the poet's mind. It could manifest in language as a more or less amplified type-scene (e.g. *Il* 19.364–424) or as a verb alone (e.g. *Il* 7.206b) depending on the poet's intention at that moment. Instances of a type-scene, since they are allomorphs of the same *Gestalt*, bear family resemblance to one another.[67]

Nagler's insistence that there is no "standard form" of type-scene from which given examples may be said to deviate more or less and that those examples of the same type-scene bear family resemblance to one another provides us with a new perspective to approach the textual data under examination in this book. In the past, scholars tended to look for what they perceived as essential to an incubation scene, whether it be 'deliberate seeking,' 'sacrifice,' 'dream,' etc. Since the motif considered essential by one scholar may not have been so for another scholar (e.g. the deliberate seeking, which Gnuse regards as essential, but is not essential for Oppenheim [cf. "unintentional incubation"]), the result has been a wide diversity of opinion among scholars on the question of incubation in ancient Near Eastern texts in general. Nagler's insight will be helpful in eliminating some of these needless questions (e.g. whether or not 'sacrifice' is essential to the incubation type-scene).[68] This study proposes to read the first tablets of the Kirta and 'Aqhatu stories and the first two chapters of 1 Samuel from the perspective of the incubation type-scene which, if we accept Nagler's idea, will be recognized as sharing family resemblances with each other.

---

[66] Ibid., 81–82.

[67] That there is no standard form of a type-scene seems to have met with a wide acceptance among Homeric scholars. This may be inferred from the fact that this feature of type-scene was included as one of the important characteristics of Homeric type-scenes in Mark W. Edwards's 1992 study of type-scene (Edwards, "Homer and Oral Tradition: The Type-Scene," 287). Even Albert Lord gave a favorable review of Nagler's original idea in his 1975 survey article on the state of scholarship on oral literature. Despite the otherwise favorable review, Lord was hesitant to accept Nagler's idea because he felt that "the individual composing poet is lost in its rarified atmosphere" (Albert B. Lord, "Perspectives on Recent Work on Oral Literature," *Forum for Modern Language Studies* 10 [1974]: 195).

[68] I consider these questions time-consuming because these questions can never be settled due to the dearth of data available to us. The process of decision-making is mostly circular: they cull "essential" elements based on the meager data they have, and the data in turn are examined based on the "essential" elements.

Finally, let me enumerate some of the most important characteristics of the type-scene as collected by M. Edwards. Only those which are helpful for our purpose are listed here. 1) Type-scenes may be said to consist of a structure of certain elements in sequence. But there is no "standard" form of a type-scene from which a given example deviates more or less. 2) A type-scene may be used for a special purpose, usually with elaboration and adaptation. 3) Special purpose may be served by "altering" the order of sequence.[69] 4) A type-scene may carry a significance that goes deeper than the surface level, and invoke meaning from the whole tradition of oral-derived texts.[70] As for the last characteristic, Foley's idea of metonymic use of tradition is worth mentioning here. Foley contends that a type-scene carries a significance that goes deeper than the surface level, and invokes meanings inherited from the whole tradition of oral poetry. Foley argues, for example, that the feasting type-scene is "a celebration of community, an affirmation of comity and hospitality near the center of the Homeric world." In the feasting type-scene in *Odyssey* 1, where the celebration of community is conducted by Telemachos and the disguised Athena, while the brazen suitors ingloriously continue their despoiling of Odysseus' household, Homer's representation of the severity of the insult depends directly on realizing not only how boorishly the suitors are behaving, but also how starkly that behavior contrasts with the values metonymically embodied in the conventionality of the feast type-scene.[71]

5. Summary

In this introductory chapter, we have discussed why the history of religions approach to incubation has failed in biblical and ancient Near Eastern studies: it has much to do with the problem of definition. After differentiating three possible levels of definition of incubation, I have

---

[69] Although I do not endorse any "standard" sequence of motifs, some terms, such as "altering the order," "omitting a given component motif," "compensating for the missing motif," etc., may be used in the following discussion of an incubation type-scene. But this apparent confusion exists only at the level of the vocabulary which I have adopted, in part for lack of better terms, in order to explain unique literary features of a given incubation type-scene.

[70] Edwards, "Homer and Oral Tradition: The Type-Scene," 287–90.

[71] John M. Foley, *Immanent Art: From Structure to Meaning in Traditional Oral Epic* (Bloomington, IN: Indiana University Press, 1991), 34–35.

proposed to focus on incubation as a literary device. In particular I have proposed to use the Homeric conception of type-scene in defining and discerning incubation as a literary device. Finally, two points have been made towards the justification of the use of type-scene: 1) Type-scene is a motif-sequence, while incubation is an action-sequence. 2) Just as we needed a flexible definition of incubation for a comparative perspective, so also we need a parallel flexible definition of incubation as a literary device. The conception of type-scene as a pre-verbal *Gestalt* provides such flexibility. Recognition of type-scene is then done by the principle of family resemblance.

Excursus 1: The Type-Scene Study in Biblical Criticism

It was Robert Alter who borrowed the notion of type-scene from Homeric scholarship and first applied it to the study of biblical narratives. In his 1978 article,[72] Robert Alter proposed a type-scene as the basic approach to recurrent patterns in biblical narrative as an alternative to the standard form-critical notion of *Gattung*.[73] Robert Alter's

---

[72] Robert Alter, "Biblical Type-Scenes and the Uses of Convention," *CI* 5 (1978): 355–68. This seminal article is republished in Alter, *The Art of Biblical Narrative*, chapter 3. Also see Alter, "How Convention Helps Us Read: The Case of the Bible's Annunciation Type-Scene," 115–30.

[73] In German, the term *Gattung* denotes a group of things or beings that have certain characteristics in common, namely, type or kind (s.v. "Gattung" in *Oxford-Duden German Dictionary*, ed. O. Thyen [Oxford: Oxford University Press, 2005]). In form-critical studies, its usage is disputed. Although Gunkel popularized the term among form critics, he never bothered to define it other than giving three criteria for discerning it (e.g. moods, linguistic form, *Sitz Im Leben*), since Gunkel himself borrowed the term from other disciplines such as Classics and Germanics so that he may have not found it necessary to define it. It is among later form critics that the German term has acquired the status of a technical term. But even then the exact range of meaning is not fixed. For some, in distinction to form, *Gattung* refers to the classification of a text as a whole. For others, however, it has the same referent as form, namely, smaller literary units which may have arisen in oral tradition. For still others, *Gattung* refers to the typicality of a text while form pertains to the unique formulation of a text. In the following discussion, I propose to use *Gattung* to describe any pattern of language in a text, both small and large, and genre to the classification of a text as a whole. In other words, *Gattung* includes formula, motif, type-scene, narrative pattern, and genre. For the historical background of Gunkel's *Gattung*, see Martin J. Buss, *Biblical Form Criticism in Its Context*, JSOTSup 274 (Sheffield, England: Sheffield Academic Press, 1999), 226–34. For the terminological confusion of genre and form, see Klaus W. Hempfer, *Gattungstheorie: Information und Synthese* (München: W. Fink, 1973), 14ff.; Tremper Longman III, *Fictional Akkadian Autobiography: A Generic and Comparative Study* (Winona Lake, IN: Eisenbrauns, 1991), 9–10; Wolfgang Richter, *Exegese*

objection to the traditional notion of *Gattung*, however, does not lie with the term *Gattung* itself, which, after all, refers to any recurrent pattern in a narrative, but with its organic relationship with *Sitz Im Leben*. The ultimate agenda of Gunkel and his immediate followers was to reconstruct the history of Israelite religion by determining the original oral traditions that stood behind the biblical text, which is, in turn, made possible through the identification of the *Gattungen* of a given pericope.[74] For them, in other words, the study of *Gattung* or a recurring pattern is only of secondary importance: it is nothing more than an instrument to arrive at its *Sitz Im Leben*. Robert Alter, however, suggests that the recurrent patterns in biblical narratives, whether they be called *Gattung* or type-scenes, can be explained not only without recourse to their putative *Sitz Im Leben*, but also better appreciated by noting their literary roles within a story.[75] Thus, while traditional form-criticism has a diachronic focus, Alter's type-scene study begins with an explicitly synchronic interest in the biblical text.

Two developments in recent scholarship, however, caution us not to take too simplistic an approach in this matter. First, recent scholarly debate on the methodology of form criticism[76] seems to bring form criticism more in consonance with Robert Alter's study of type-scene. In his 1968 presidential address to the Society of Biblical Literature,[77] James Muilenburg launched a new era in form-critical scholarship by urging form critics to pay more attention to the structure of the text at hand than to its pre-literary history. Now most form critics agree that the ultimate agenda of form criticism is not historical but hermeneutical, namely, to arrive at the meaning of the text as a whole. Toward that end, form critics engage in the following two tasks: first to identify

---

als Literaturwissenschaft: Entwurf einer alttestamentlichen Literaturtheorie und Methodologie. (Göttingen: Vandenhoeck & Ruprecht, 1971), 125ff.; Gene Tucker, *Form Criticism of the Old Testament* (Philadelphia, PA: Fortress Press, 1971), 12; William G. Doty, "The Concept of Genre in Literary Analysis," in *Society of Biblical Society Seminar Papers 1*, ed. Lane C. McGaughy (Missoula, Mont.: Scholars Press, 1972), 413ff.

[74] Marvin A. Sweeney, "Form Criticism," in *To Each Its Own Meaning: The Introduction to Biblical Criticisms and Their Application*, ed. Steven L. McKenzie and Stephen R. Haynes (Louisville, KY: Westminster John Knox Press, 1999), 61.

[75] Alter, "How Convention Helps Us Read: The Case of the Bible's Annunciation Type-Scene," 118–19.

[76] See Marvin A. Sweeney and Ehud Ben Zvi, eds., *The Changing Face of Form Criticism for the Twenty-First Century* (Grand Rapids, MI: Eerdmans, 2003); Rolf Knierim, "Old Testament Criticism Reconsidered," *Int* 27 (1973): 435–68; Richter, *Exegese als Literaturwissenschaft: Entwurf einer alttestamentlichen Literaturtheorie und Methodologie*.

[77] James Muilenburg, "Form Criticism and Beyond," *JBL* 88 (1969): 1–18.

a literary type (*Gattung*) of a text and to examine its role within the whole narrative structure.[78] Form criticism thus recalibrated has a more synchronic than diachronic interest in the biblical text. The traditional efforts to locate the socio-historical *Sitz Im Leben* have been completely discarded or have found other slightly different venues.[79] In this sense, the type-scene study may be said to be a sub-category of form criticism as thus redefined. The only difference lies in the fact that the former focuses on the narrative unit called "type-scene," whereas the notion of *Gattung* ("literary type") in form criticism includes the entire gamut of literary conventions from a formula to the classification of a text as a whole.

Another development that cautions us not to take too simplistic an attitude toward the relationship between type-scene study and form criticism has occurred in the area of literary criticism, the kind which began with Luis Alonso-Schökel's *Estudio de poetica hebrea* in the sixties, heavily influenced by New Criticism, a dominant trend in English and American literary criticism in the first half of the twentieth century.[80] This transformation finds its most clear articulation in Meir Sternberg's book *The Poetics of Biblical Narrative*. If the publication

---

[78] Anthony F. Campbell, "Form Criticism's Future," in *The Changing Face of Form Criticism for the 21st Century*, ed. Marvin A. Sweeney and Ehud Ben Zvi (Grand Rapids, MI: Eerdmans, 2001), 23–31.

[79] Wolfgang Richter, for example, distinguishes between *Sitz Im Leben* (social setting) in which the original oral tradition functions and *Sitz in der Literatur* (literary setting) in which the larger literary units of the text appear. Although the lack of evidence makes it extremely difficult to recover the original social setting of smaller, self-contained units (*Gattungen*), he contends that it is not impossible to reconstruct the redactional history of a text by examining the historical occasion in which the small units came together into a larger type. *Sitz in der Literatur* refers to the historical occasion in which the redaction took place. For Richter, there is more than one *Sitz in der Literature*. See Richter, *Exegese als Literaturwissenschaft: Entwurf einer alttestamentlichen Literaturtheorie und Methodologie.*, 147–48.

[80] This kind of literary criticism rejects the concept of literature as a means to an end. Instead, it deems each text as self-subsisting aesthetic object. This objective theory of literature may be traced back to T. S. Eliot who insisted upon the text as "something made" (*poesis*) in and of itself (T. S. Eliot, "Tradition and the Individual Talents" in Hazard Adams, ed., *Critical Theory Since Plato* [New York: Harcourt Brace Javanovich, 1971], 783–87). According to this objective theory of text, a text constitutes an intrinsic world of interrelated elements that work together to produce an organic whole. For a historical survey of the literary study of the Bible since 1960s, see Phyllis Trible, *Rhetorical Criticism: Context, Method, and the Book of Jonah* (Minneapolis: Fortress Press, 1994), 73–80.

in 1957 of Frye's *Anatomy of Criticism*[81] marked a decisive turn from New Criticism,[82] Meir Sternberg's book was one of the major attempts within biblical literary criticism to strike a balance between the synchronic orientation of literary criticism and the diachronic orientation of traditional criticisms within biblical criticism, although some critics regarded his attempt as a failure.[83] Understanding the biblical text in terms of communication between author and reader, M. Sternberg argued that a reconstruction of various historical "sources" is indispensable to the interpretation of the text. These historical signals include the Bible's language system, cultural and literary milieu, theology, and so forth. He says, for example, "To determine the meaning of a word in the biblical text...the interpreter should turn to the linguist and/or turn linguist himself.... We thus engage in the reconstruction that delimits what the writer could have meant against the background of the linguistic knowledge that...he must have taken for granted."[84] M. Sternberg saw the same principle operating at a literary level. Just as the interpreter should engage in an analysis of the ancient language system in order to determine the meaning of a word on the page, so does he need to recuperate ancient literary conventions in order to properly interpret biblical literature.[85] Nowadays more and more literary critics try to balance the synchronic aspect and the diachronic aspect in their interpretation of the biblical text.

Such emphasis on the diachronic aspect was also voiced by some scholars who study type-scenes. Ann M. Vater, for example, brings out the diachronic aspect of type-scene study. Regarding the biblical text as a communication event in her study of the type-scene of "communication through commissioned message," Vater argues that

[81] Northrop Frye, *Anatomy of Criticism* (Princeton, NJ: Princeton University Press, 1985). For critical assessment, see, *inter alia*, Frank Lentricchia, *After the New Criticism* (Chicago: University of Chicago Press, 1980), 3–26.

[82] Frye denounced the rubric of "art for art's sake," declaring close readings futile without understanding the literary context in which a given text is situated. Such literary context is variously called "structural principles," "convention," "archetype," and "underlying laws." As Phyllis Trible suggests, Frye's work seems to resonate with the form-criticism as redefined, in other words, the literary side of form criticism (Trible, *Rhetorical Criticism: Context, Method, and the Book of Jonah*, 63). Especially, Frye's emphasis on the literary context is reminiscent of Wolfgang Richter's notion of *Sitz in der Literature*.

[83] Lynn Poland, "Review: Defending Biblical Poetics," *JR* 68 (1988): 429.

[84] Meir Sternberg, *The Poetics of Biblical Narrative Ideological Literature and the Drama of Reading* (Bloomington, IN: Indiana University Press, 1985), 11–12.

[85] Ibid., 12.

traditional-historical criticisms may open up aspects of distinctive artistic medium of the biblical authors, without a knowledge of which interpretation of the ancient text would be impossible.[86]

In sum, the type-scene is best regarded as a sub-category of form criticism. Both of them share not only a synchronic interest in the text at hand, but also a diachronic interest in the ancient conventions shared by the author and the reader. This study will emphasize both aspects (albeit not equally); the diachronic aspect will show itself as we recuperate the ancient convention which I would dub "the incubation type-scene," while the synchronic interest will be revealed as we discuss the narratological role that the ancient convention plays in a wider narrative unit, with a view to arriving at a certain understanding of the narrative as a whole.

Excursus 2: The Communicative-Semiotic Understanding of a Type-Scene or *Gattung*

Both type-scene studies and form criticism recognize convention as a literary device. In type-scene studies, obviously, type-scenes are considered to be conventional, while form critics recognize convention in *Gattung* in all its variations. Although the role of convention as a literary device has long been noted by literary critics, very few scholars have made any serious efforts to examine its meaning and nature at a theoretical level.[87] A major theoretical advance, however, was achieved when literary critics started to apply linguistic theory, particularly, communication theory to the study of literary convention.[88] According

[86] Vater, "Story Patterns for a Sitz," 55. In her article, Ann M. Vater does not use the word 'type-scene.' But her discussion of the story pattern called "communication through commissioned message" bears much similarity to the study of the type-scene.

[87] It is a historical irony that the value of convention was discovered by those who flouted it (e.g. romanticists), while Classicists and Neoclassicists, who embraced it, had done so unconsciously (Harry Levin, "Notes on Convention," in *Refractions: Essays in Comparative Literature*, ed. Harry Levin [New York: Oxford University Press, 1966], 45).

[88] The recent literature on this topic is immense. But the studies I have found most helpful are the following: Steven Mailloux, *Interpretive Conventions: The Reader in the Study of American Fiction* (Ithaca: Cornell University Press, 1982); Wolfgang Iser, *The Act of Reading: A Theory of Aesthetic Response* (Baltimore, MD: Johns Hopkins University Press, 1980); Stanley Fish, *Is There a Text in This Class?: The Authority of Interpretive Communities* (Cambridge, MA: Harvard University Press, 1980), particularly, pp. 301–21; Jonathan Culler, *Structuralist Poetics: Structuralism, Linguistics and*

to this communicative understanding of conventions, they are agreements or contracts between the author and the reader, which allow the possibility of communication in a literary transaction. As traditional conventions, literary conventions are "habits of arts" which provide compositional possibility for authors and raise expectations in their audiences.[89]

The approach emphasizing the communicative nature of literary conventions has also shed light on theoretical questions regarding genre.[90] Genre theorists such as Warren and Wellek, Billson, Todorov and others understand genre as something essential to communication between the author and the reader.[91] According to the communicative-semiotic understanding of genre, a transaction takes place in the act of reading between the author and the reader (in the form of

the Study of Literature (Ithaca: Cornell University Press, 1975); Eric D. Hirsch, *Validity in Interpretation* (New Haven, CT: Yale University Press, 1967); Frye, *Anatomy of Criticism*.

[89] Mailloux, *Interpretive Conventions: The Reader in the Study of American Fiction*, 130. Stanley Fish's concept of "interpretive communities" is worth mentioning in this context, since it accounts for why ancient texts can be understood by numerous people with different philosophical and ideological presuppositions in quite diverse geographic and temporal locations. According to Stanley Fish, how one reads is a matter of shared conventions or "interpretive strategies." But he denies that readers possess a set of shared interpretive strategies which can be triggered by cues or signals in the text. He argues instead that these textual cues or signals only come into view against the background of shared conventions. In other words, these strategies exists (outside the reader) "prior to the act of reading and therefore determines the shape of what is read rather than, as is usually assumed, the other way around" (Fish, *Is There a Text in This Class?: The Authority of Interpretive Communities*, 14). Interpretive communities are made of those who share interpretive strategies which enable readers to discern cues or signals for the interpretation of certain textual features. Membership in an interpretive community is, therefore, based on shared ways of interpretation, not on physical proximity or shared concerns.

[90] The following discussion draws on Longman III, *Fictional Akkadian Autobiography: A Generic and Comparative Study*, 7–9.

[91] These theorists tend to take a realist or conceptualist view of genre, against a nominalist view which is represented by B. Croce and P. Lacoue-Labarthe and J.-L. Nancy. Croce denies the existence of "genres." His primary reason for denying genres is that it disallows an author's originality, genius, or creativity in the composition of a text. "Nominalists" argue that genres are mere names and have no independent reality (See Hempfer, *Gattungstheorie: Information und Synthese*, 38–41 for Croce's position on genre). But as Warren and Wellek well point out, Croce's theory does not reflect the reality. While it is true that the individuality of many compositions must be maintained, the similarities between the form and the content of various texts must not be denied (Rene Wellek and Austin Warren, *Theory of Literature* [San Diego: Harcourt Brace Jovanovich, 1977], 226). This dissertation is informed by the belief that only a realist or conceptualist view of genre adequately explains the value of a genre as a critical tool.

communication). Genre is the enabling context in which such communication occurs: genre both directs the author in the composition of the text and raises expectations in the reader in the reading of the text. To illustrate this communicative nature of genre, genre critics compare genre to various things such as an "institution," "legal contracts," a "game," "basic sentences," and so forth.[92] Billson, for example, illustrates genre by a comparison with a legal contract.[93] Genres are considered to be expectations commonly agreed upon by the author and the reader.[94] Furthermore, by employing an "institution" (similar to the state, university, or church)[95] as a model, Wellek and Warren not only describe the communicative nature of genre, but also point to its fluidity. Although an individual joins an institution and follows its rules and regulations in the main, he or she may opt to fight for change in either a subtle or a radical manner. Genres similarly compel authors, but can be modified subtly or radically by them. These analogies confirm the point that E. D. Hirsch makes in his book, *Validity in Interpretation*, namely, that the meaning of a text is "genre-bound."[96] With regard to Ugaritic literature, Simon Parker argues that progress in interpreting difficult sections of the Ugaritic texts results only from genre identification.[97] Owing to the essential role that genres play in the communication between the author and the reader, genre misidentification leads to misinterpretation.[98] This provides impetus for the researcher to identify the type of literature he is in the process of interpreting.

This communicative-semiotic understanding of literary convention forms the backdrop of type-scene studies, which this study adopts as its method. While emphasizing the importance of recuperating ancient

---

[92] See Longman III, *Fictional Akkadian Autobiography: A Generic and Comparative Study*, 8–9 for the summary and evaluation of these analogies.

[93] M. Billson, "The Memoir: New Perspectives on a Forgotten Genre," *Genre* 10 (1977): 259–82.

[94] A similar conception is found in the works of the eminent structuralist Todorov who refers to genres as "codes" (Tzvetan Todorov, *The Fantastic: A Structural Approach to a Literary Genre* [Ithaca: Cornell University Press, 1975]).

[95] Wellek and Warren, *Theory of Literature*, 226.

[96] Hirsch, *Validity in Interpretation*, 76.

[97] Simon B. Parker, "Some Methodological Principles in Ugaritic Philology," *Maarav* 2 (1979): 7–41.

[98] According to Hirsch, recognition of a faulty interpretation jars the reader into revising his genre identification and therefore his genre expectations as well. Hirsch conceives of the process of reading and/or interpretation as the development of successive genre identifications until the final decisive identification, which determines the reader's interpretation of the whole (Hirsch, *Validity in Interpretation*, 116ff.).

literary conventions for the better understanding of biblical narratives, Alter proposes type-scene as one of those ancient conventions. He further argues that literary conventions are tacit agreements or contracts between the author and the reader and "the enabling contexts in which complex communication of art occurs."[99] Thus the incubation type-scene is not a modern literary invention superimposed on ancient texts, to use B. Croce's term, *pseudo-concetti* (fake concepts),[100] but an ancient literary convention recognized by the ancient readers and used by ancient authors in their composition of texts, as in the case of Homeric type-scenes. This type-scene study, therefore, presupposes that the contemporary audiences of the stories, familiar with the conventions, would find themselves intrigued at how, in each instance, the convention could be, through the narrator's art, both fruitfully followed and renewed for the specific needs of the plot. By recuperating the ancient literary convention of the incubation type-scene, we hope to arrive at a better understanding of the ancient texts under consideration in this book.

[99] Alter, "Biblical Type-Scenes and the Uses of Convention," 355–68, especially 355.
[100] Hempfer, *Gattungstheorie: Information und Synthese*, 40.

CHAPTER TWO

INCUBATION IN THE ANCIENT NEAR EAST

The fact that the focus of this book is on the literary use of incubation does not preclude the necessity of discussing the historical practice of incubation, since it is this practice of incubation that implicitly undergirds the use of incubation as a literary device.[1] Furthermore, the ancient Near Eastern practice of incubation will provide a reference point in our discerning a pool of motifs that would have been used by the poet/narrator composing the incubation type-scene. Hence, it is appropriate to discuss the ancient Near Eastern practice of incubation at this juncture.[2] Since the purpose of this chapter is to investigate the *practice* of incubation which should have influenced its literary use in the ancient Near Eastern texts, more weight will be placed on non-literary sources such as historical texts, letters, ritual texts, etc. than on purely literary texts.

---

[1] According to the most ancient and persistent approach to the relationship between literature and the world, literature mirrors a world external to itself. Aristotle held that *mimesis* (imitation) is characteristic of all art but differs according to the means it uses, the objects it considers, and the manner it exhibits (cf. Hazard Adams, ed., *Critical Theory Since Plato* [Orlando, FL: Harcourt Brace Jovanovich College Press, 1992], 49–66). Especially, speaking of the type-scene of commissioned message and oral communication, Ann M. Vater argues that from real life one can construct a basic logical pattern for narrating the story (Ann M. Vater, "Story Patterns for a Sitz," *JSOT* 11 [1979]: 49).

[2] For the previous studies of this subject, see Richard E. Averbeck, *Preliminary Study of Ritual and Structure in the Cylinders of Gudea* (Ann Arbor, MI: University Microfilms International, 1988), 550–71; S. A. L. Butler, *Mesopotamian Conceptions of Dreams and Dream Rituals*, AOAT 258 (Münster: Ugarit-Verlag, 1988), 217–39; Georges Contenau, *La divination chez les Assyriens et les Babyloniens. Avec 13 figures, 1 carte et 8 gravures hors texte* (Paris: Payot, 1940), 171–78; Robert K. Gnuse, *Dreams and Dream Report in the Writings of Josephus: A Traditio-Historical Analysis* (Leiden: Brill, 1996), 119–26; Jean-Marie Husser, *Dreams and Dream Narratives in the Biblical World*, BS 63 (Sheffield: Sheffield Academic Press, 1999), 46–50, 69–70, 172–175; Baruch Margalit, *The Ugaritic Poem of Aqht: Text, Translation, Commentary*, BZAW 182 (New York: De Gruyter, 1989), 261–64; A. Leo Oppenheim, *The Interpretation of Dreams in the Ancient Near East: With a Translation of an Assyrian Dream-Book*, TAPA 46 (Philadelphia, PA: American Philological Society, 1956), 187–88.

1. Incubation in Mesopotamia

1.1 *The Cylinders of Gudea (Cylinder A 7:9–12:19)*

The Cylinders of Gudea contain a detailed account of Gudea's construction (Cylinder A) and dedication of a new Eninnu temple for the god Ningirsu, the patron deity of Lagash (Cylinder B). Cylinder A states that the Gudea king of Lagash had three dreams (1:17–23; 9:5–12:13; 20:7–11), the first of which gives occasion to the second and the third dreams. Most scholars concur that the second and the third dreams are certainly incubated, but whether or not the first dream is incubated is a matter of debate.[3]

Gudea's second dream incident provides the most detailed description of what incubation may have looked like in Mesopotamia in particular and in ancient Near East in general. Troubled by the enigma of his first dream, Gudea decided to visit Nanshe, the divine interpreteress in Ningin, to have his dream interpreted. Nanshe not only interpreted Gudea's first symbolic dream point by point (CA 5:11–6:13), but also advised him to fashion a chariot and present it to Ningirsu so that he might "disclose to you (i.e. Gudea) in all details the ground plan of his House"[4] (CA 6:14–7:8). Although Nanshe's instructions to Gudea do not provide any further details, we can presume from the lines that follow that Nanshe advised Gudea to incubate a vision from Ningirsu.[5]

Cylinder A 7:9–12:20, which details the actual procedure of incubation, may be divided into three stages marked by a formulaic phrase

[3] The bone of contention is the interpretation of CA 1:14–16. If one understands it as part of Ningirsu's speech to the divine assembly, there is no good reason to assume that Gudea's first dream was induced. But if one reconstructs the scene in such way that Gudea eavesdrops on the divine assembly and prepares to have an oracular dream to enlighten him by bringing sacrificial animals for an incubation rite, then it is easier to assume that Gudea's first dream is incubational. For the latter interpretation see Averbeck, *Preliminary Study of Ritual and Structure in the Cylinders of Gudea*, 595; Victor Hurowitz, *I Have Built You an Exalted House: Temple Building in the Bible in Light of Mesopotamian and Northwest Semitic Writings*, JSOTSup (Sheffield: Sheffield Academic Press, 1992), 38; Thorkild Jacobsen, *The Harps That Once…: Sumerian Poetry in Translation* (New Haven, CT: Yale University Press, 1987), 389.

[4] Dietz O. Edzard, *Gudea and His Dynasty*, Royal Inscriptions of Mesopotamia: Early Periods (Toronto: University of Toronto Press, 1997), 73.

[5] Moreover, the fact that Nanshe does not give any details about the incubation procedure, other than the type of gift needed for a successful incubation of Ningirsu, seems to suggest that Gudea already knew what he was supposed to do to incubate a divine oracle in a temple.

(CA 7:9–10 and CA 12:20) at both ends: (1) Preparation (CA 8:2–9:4); (2) Oneiric theophany (CA 9:5–12:11); (3) Response (CA 12:12–17).[6] The preparation stage begins with Gudea's fashioning a chariot for Ningirsu as per Nanshe's advice. Then it moves on to describe the various cultic observances to prepare the incubant for the impending theophany. Cylinder A 8:2–3 indicates that these observances may have taken place over a period of several days. The cultic observances include silence (CA 8:4–5),[7] animal sacrifice (CA 8:6–9), incense offerings (8:10–12), and finally prayer (CA 8:13–9:4),[8] which not only suggest Gudea's intention for inducing the second dream, but would have also prepared him psychologically for the imminent encounter with his god. The description of oneiric theophany begins with a description of Gudea's reclining position and Ningirsu's standing position at Gudea's head (CA 9:5–6), both of which are conventional motifs of oneiric theophany.[9] This is followed by a message dream in which Ningirsu provides the solution to Gudea's "problems" (CA 9:7–12:11).[10]

---

[6] Averbeck, inspired by Hubert and Mauss (*Sacrifice: Its Nature and Function*, trans. W. D. Halls [Chicago: University of Chicago Press, 1964]), applies the entry-act-exit scheme to Gudea's second dream incident. My stages (preparation-oneiric dream-reaction) happen to be coterminous with Averbeck's three stages. One point that is brought out more clearly by Averbeck's scheme is the liminality of time and space in which incubation occurs. The essence of incubation is the encounter between the divine and the human. This is accomplished especially when an incubant situates himself in a place which stands between the world of men and that of the gods (i.e. temple) at a time which stands between the time of men and that of the gods (i.e. night or dream). Hence liminality in the practice of incubation is doubly established, whereas, for example, the liminality in the sacrifice is established only in spatial terms. Cf. Averbeck, *Preliminary Study of Ritual and Structure in the Cylinders of Gudea*, 510.

[7] For the role of silence in Mesopotamia rituals see Erica Reiner, "Dead of Night," in *Studies in Honor of Benno Landsberger on His Seventy-Fifth Birthday*, ed. Hans G. Güterbock and Jacobsen Thorkild (Chicago: University of Chicago Press, 1965), 247–51.

[8] For a detailed study of animal sacrifice, incense offering, and prayer as preparatory rituals for incubation dream see Annette von Zgoll, "Die Welt im Schlaf sehen: Inkubation von Träumen im antiken Mesopotamien," *WO* 32 (2002): 89–93.

[9] Oppenheim, *The Interpretation of Dreams in the Ancient Near East: With a Translation of an Assyrian Dream-Book*, 212.

[10] How Ningirsu's message in Gudea's second dream "answers" Gudea's problems as expressed in his prayer is not clear. Gudea, despite his awareness of the divine commission given to him to build Eninnu, was at a loss as to how to proceed with the building project. The symbolic dream seemed to him to contain a message about the detailed plan of the project. That is why he sought out Nanshe's aid, which in turned lead Gudea to incubate a further message from Ningirsu. But Nanshe's promise that Ningirsu would reveal the plan of Eninnu (CA 7:6) and Ningirsu's own words to the same effect in the second dream (CA 9:9–10) do not seem to have been fulfilled

This incubation scene ends with a description of Gudea waking from a dream (CA 12:12) and of his reactions to the oneiric theophany, namely, the confirmation through extispicy (CA 12:13–19).

Another definite instance of Mesopotamian incubation concerns Gudea's third dream in Cylinder A 20:4–12 and it may reveal a different type of incubation. Although no preparatory cultic observances are recorded, and the exact motivation of incubation may be debated,[11] Gudea's intention *per se* to incubate an oracle dream is evident from the fact that it stands as the last in a series of three distinct divinatory procedures which, besides incubation, includes extispicy and a rite involving barley and water. The Sumerian phrase *sag-šè-ná* in line 7 may corroborate this observation. The phrase *sag-šè-ná* (literally "one who lies at the head of someone") is identified in a Sumero-Akkadian vocabulary (series "LÚ=*ša*" 2nd Tablet III:22–28) with Akkadian *mupaššir šunāte* (literally "one who performs *pašāru* of dreams"). Based on this identification, most scholars understand the Sumerian phrase in Cylinder A 20:7 as referring to a special kind of oneiromancer, someone capable either of dreaming on request, or of provoking a dream in someone else and of interpreting it afterwards.[12] But scholars part ways on the issue of its reference. Some scholars (e.g. Jacobsen and Oppenheim) take *sag-šè-ná* to be a reference to Gudea

in any meaningful way in the second dream. There is no description of any plan in the second dream. All Ningirsu does is to describe himself and his functions, as they relate to his various temples. The only architectural information one can gather from it is that the temple is to have foundations, a temple terrace, and a house on top, but as Jacobsen points out, "that seems far too general to have been of much help." Cf. Jacobsen, *The Harps That Once..: Sumerian Poetry in Translation*, 399, footnote 44.

[11] According to Averbeck, the third dream was incubated in order to acquire the "sign," namely, the plan of the temple, promised in the second dream (Richard E. Averbeck, "The Cylinders of Gudea," in *Monumental Inscriptions from the Biblical World*, vol. II of *COS*, ed. William W. Hallo and K. Lawson Younger Jr. [New York: Brill, 2000], 423, footnote 23). Suter, however, takes the third dream as verifying the preliminary preparations for the construction of the temple. The dream does so by envisioning the completion of the building (Claudia E. Suter, *Gudea's Temple Building: The Representation of an Early Mesopotamian Ruler in Text and Image*, Cuneiform Monographs 17 [Groningen: Styx Publications, 2000], 92).

[12] See Oppenheim, *The Interpretation of Dreams in the Ancient Near East: With a Translation of an Assyrian Dream-Book*, 223–24; Husser, *Dreams and Dream Narratives in the Biblical World*, 47. Asher-Greve in discussing the lower register of a cylinder seal at the Oriental Institute in Chicago, identifies the supine central figure lying on a bed as *lú-sag-šè-ná*, a female oneiromancer who interprets the dream of the person kneeling at her feet (Julia M. Asher-Greve, "The Oldest Female Oneiromancer," in *La femme dans le proche-orient antique*, comp. Jean-Marie Durand [Paris: Editions Recherche sur les Civilisations, 1987], 27–32).

and translate line 7, "Gudea lay down to sleep as a *sag-šè-ná*."[13] Others (e.g. Falkenstein and Civil) have taken it to refer to a cultic functionary beside whom Gudea lay down, and translate line 7, "Gudea liess 'einen, der zu Häupten liegt' (bei sich) liegen."[14] Grammatically speaking, both interpretations are possible, because the Sumerian verb *mu-ná* could be taken either as an intransitive verb or as a transitive verb.[15] In either case, the presence of the word *sag-šè-ná* in the Cylinders of Gudea seems to indicate that dreams could be sought or experienced by priests or officials on behalf of their kings. This priestly incubation (incubation by proxy) is also attested to in other regions in later periods of ancient Near East.[16]

[13] Oppenheim, *The Interpretation of Dreams in the Ancient Near East: With a Translation of an Assyrian Dream-Book*, 224; Jacobsen reconstructs the stele of the Vultures of Ennatum vi: 19–20 on the basis of the Cylinder A of Gudea 20:7–8. His translation of these lines indicates that he retained Oppenheim's translation of this passage. See Thorkild Jacobsen, "The Stele of the Vultures Col I-X," in *Kramer Anniversary Volume: Cuneiform Studies in Honor of Samuel Noah Kramer*, ed. Barry L. Eichler (Kevelaer: Butzon & Bercker, 1976), 253.

[14] A. von Falkenstein, "Wahrsagung in der Sumerischen Überlieferung," in *La divination en mésopotamie ancienne et dans les régions voisines*, ed. F. Wendel (Paris: Presses universitaires de France, 1966), 55; cf. M. Civil, "The Song of the Plowing Oxen," in *Kramer Anniversary Volume: Cuneiform Studies in Honor of Samuel Noah Kramer*, ed. Barry L. Eichler (Kevelaer: Butzon & Bercker, 1976), 91.

[15] Averbeck, *Preliminary Study of Ritual and Structure in the Cylinders of Gudea*, 540–41.

[16] In his famous prayer occasioned by the ravage of a pestilence, for example, the Hittite king, Murshili II, clearly differentiates between dreams seen by him as a king and dreams experienced by priests during incubation. The incubation reported in Arrian's *Anabasis Alexandri* (7.27.2) was undertaken by Babylonian priests to obtain divine help for Alexander the Great when he was seriously ill. Oppenheim discusses the dream of Samuel (1 Samuel 3) as a special case of priestly incubation (Oppenheim, *The Interpretation of Dreams in the Ancient Near East: With a Translation of an Assyrian Dream-Book*, 188). For a detailed discussion of priestly incubation in the Hebrew Bible, see L. Delekat, *Asylie und Schutzorakel am Zionheiligtum: Eine Untersuchung zu den Privaten Feindpsalmen* (Leiden: Brill, 1967), 70–73. According to C. A. Meier, Aelius Aristides (117–181 C.E.) said about the temple of Asclepius that "the priest..., or else the priest's slave, sometimes slept for him" (Carl A. Meier, "The Dream in Ancient Greece and Its Use in Temple Cures [Incubation]," in *The Dream and Human Societies*, ed. Gustave E. Von Grunebaum and Roger Caillois [Berkeley: University of California Press, 1966], 316). For a modern variation of this ancient incubation by proxy, see Patton, "A Great and Strange Correction: Intentionality, Locality, and Epiphany in the Category of Dream Incubation," 199.

1.2 *Rituals to Obtain a Purussû (ROP Henceforth)*[17]

ROP, otherwise known as *STT* no. 73, distinguishes itself from other Mesopotamian omen texts in three respects: first, the omen expected is an impetrated omen, a rather rare type of Mesopotamian divination; second, prayers and rituals are described and/or prescribed with a view to disposing the gods favorably to give an answer through a stipulated signal; third, we obtain evidence of private divination techniques not found in the canonical omen literature.[18] The impetrated omens include dreams (lines 1–84), shooting stars (lines 84–109), and oxen (lines 110–138). Most relevant for our purpose is the first of these three, namely, impetrated dreams. S. A. L. Butler the editor of *ROP* identifies five instances of incubation in lines 1–84, the fourth one (lines 61–70) of which not only shows one of the most complicated incubation rituals in ancient Near East, but also explicitly states the intention of the incubant to have a dream oracle. Judging from the prayer (lines 61–64), the priest appeals to the constellation Ursa Major (^{MUL}MAR.GÍD.DA), which can be identified with Ishtar,[19] on behalf of the petitioner for recovery, and the motivation for this priestly

[17] This is the title given by Butler when he edited this omen text excavated in Sultantepe on the basis of *STT* no. 73 (O. R. Gurney and J. J. Finkelstein, eds., *The Sultantepe Tablets*, Occasional Publications of the British Institute of Archaeology at Ankara [London: British Institute of Archaeology at Ankara, 1957–64], no. 73), its duplicate copy that was found in Assur, i.e., *LKA* no. 138 (Erich Ebeling, *Literarische Keilschrifttexte aus Assur* [Berlin: Akademie-Verlag, 1953], no. 138), and three other fragments (C. B. F. Walker, ed., *Miscellaneous Texts*, vol. 51 of *Cuneiform Texts from Babylonian Tablets in the British Museum* [London: Trustees of the British Museum, 1972], no. 103; O. R. Gurney, ed., *Middle Babylonian Legal Documents and Other Texts*, vol. 7 of *Ur Excavation Texts* [London: British Museum Publications, 1974], no. 118; J. van Dijk, A. Goetze, and M. I. Hussey, eds., *Early Mesopotamian Incantations and Rituals*, vol. 11 of *Yale Oriental Series, Babylonian Texts* [New Haven, CT: Yale University Press, 1985], no. 75). The title derives from the formulaic phrases—*purussâ amāru* or *purussâ parāsu*—recurring in the subscription of prayers.

[18] Erica Reiner, "Fortune-Telling in Mesopotamia," *JNES* 19 (1960): 24.

[19] Since Ursa Major is a circumpolar constellation, and thus never sets, it could be invoked at any season of the year. According to Reiner, the identification of Ursa Major with the goddess Ištar and with her heavenly manifestation, Venus, is attested to in ancient star lists and commentaries according to which "The Wagon is Venus in the East" (Erica Reiner, *Astral Magic in Babylonia*, TAPA 85 [Philadelphia, PA: American Philosophical Society, 1995], 57. Cf. Wayne Horowitz, "The Akkadian Name for Ursa Minor: mul.mar.gíd.da.an.na = eriqqi šamê/šamāni," *ZA* 79 [1989]: 242–44; P. F. Gössmann, *Planetarium Babylonicum oder Die Sumerisch-Babylonischen Stern-Namen*, Šumerisches Lexikon 4/2 [Rome: Verlag des Päpstlichen Bibelinstitus, 1950], no. 258, 259). Addressing a prayer to stars before incubation is also attested to in Nabonidus's incubation (see 1.6 below).

incubation seems to be the life-threatening illness of the petitioner. The prayer ends with the priest's request for an oracular dream, "May I see a dream (*šutta lūmur*)!"[20] Lines 65–68, then, prescribe the ritual procedure for an incubation dream. It consists in taking barley of one *harbu*, having a virgin boy grind the corn,[21] sweeping and sprinkling the roof with pure water, drawing a circle,[22] offering incense and flour, reciting the prayer three times, and maintaining silence.[23] After these preparations, the incubant is allowed to "lie down (NÁ-ma)" and "to see a dream (MÁŠ.GE IGI)."

The fifth instance of incubation (lines 71–84) seems to consist of two alternative prayers (lines 71–75 and 77–80) and two alternative prescriptions for incubation rituals (lines 81a–d and lines 82–84).[24] Both prayers are addressed by the petitioner himself to the Wain constellation. In one prayer we have evidence of incubation concerning a safe journey: "If I am to succeed in this journey on which I am about to start, let them give me something (in my dream); if I am to fail in this journey on which I am about to start, let them receive something from me (in my dream)."[25] The other prayer however, leaves us in doubt about its purpose (see esp. lines 79–80). The two ritual procedures

[20] According to Zgoll, the Akkadian idiom for incubation substitute *amāru* for *naṭālu* in the verbal slot when it is couched in a cohortative (Zgoll, "Die Welt im Schlaf sehen: Inkubation von Träumen im antiken Mesopotamien," 83). Also see *anāku ina mūši šutta lūmur* "So, I, in the night, do see a dream" (A. R. George and F. N. H. Al-rawi, "Tablets from the Sippar Library VI. Atra-Ḫasīs," *Iraq* 58 [1996]: 182–83).

[21] In the incubation ritual of Paškuwatti, a virgin is mentioned as the one who moves all the ritual items to an inhabited place. See 2.4 for details.

[22] For a magic circle, see Reiner, *Astral Magic in Babylonia*, 37–39, 55, 59.

[23] Cf. Butler, *Mesopotamian Conceptions of Dreams and Dream Rituals*, 355–56, 367.

[24] The ritual in lines 81a-d is not attested in *STT* no. 73. Butler collated it into his edition from Dijk, Goetze, and Hussey, *Early Mesopotamian Incantations and Rituals*, no. 75.

[25] The translation is Reiner's (Reiner, "Fortune-Telling in Mesopotamia," 27). The subscription of this prayer in line 76 confirms this purpose of incubation: "Incantation for seeing a sign when starting [on a journey]." The comparison of this with Genesis 28:10–21 is particularly attractive. Although many scholars (e.g. Susan Ackerman, "The Deception of Isaac, Jacob's Dream at Bethel, and Incubation on an Animal Skin," in *Priesthood and Cult in Ancient Israel*, ed. Gary A. Anderson [Sheffield: JOST Press, 1991], 92–120) recognize an incubation scene in that pericope, they seem to have failed to recognize the connection between the fifth incubation in *ROP* and Jacob's Bethel story. Although the biblical text is silent about the preparatory prayers and rituals for incubation, considering the redactional tendency to get rid of any indication of pagan religions from the text, Jacob's petition for a safe journey after, albeit not before, oneiric theophany at Bethel makes it most compelling to see the scene in Genesis 28:10ff. as a literary representation of incubation.

are prescribed in lines 81b–c and lines 81e–84 respectively. The one consists of sprinkling water and reciting the prayer three times, but the other of staying on the roof in the still of night[26] alone while everybody is asleep, sprinkling water, scattering flour. Both rituals are followed by the statement "You lie down and you will see a dream" (*purussâ tammar*).[27] It is noteworthy that a roof is mentioned as a possible place for incubation.

Finally, it is worth noting that although *ROP* sheds much light on the *processus* of Mesopotamian incubation by giving detailed prescriptions for the preparatory rituals including prayers,[28] it suggests that there may have been no standard incubation procedure, since, as Butler points out, the rituals prescribed for incubation in *ROP* differ from one another.[29]

1.3 *Kassite Texts*

There are two Kassite texts that may have allusions to the practice of incubation. One of them is the Kassite Omen Text published by H. F. Lutz (University of Pennsylvania Museum Number 13517).[30] According to Lutz, we have in section 1 of the text "a case of official incubation, in which the vision of a liver was seen (*tîrânu* 20 in line 7, and *KÀ-É-GAL* and 'swelling' in line 8)."[31] It is the *barû* who saw the oneiric vision of a liver (line 1), and the place where the dream was induced was É-KUR (line 6), which, Lutz argues, is a special shrine for incubation in Babylonian temples.[32] If Lutz's interpretation of the

[26] As in the fourth incubation in *ROP* (cf. line 68), silence occurs here again as one of the preparations for incubation. This act of maintaining silence is reminiscent of the second instance of incubation in the Cylinder A of Gudea, where Gudea silenced all the assemblies before he lay down to have a dream. For the importance of silence in some of the Mesopotamian divinatory techniques see Reiner, "Dead of Night," 247–51.

[27] For the translation of *purussû* as "dream," see Butler, *Mesopotamian Conceptions of Dreams and Dream Rituals*, 36–37.

[28] The rituals prescribed in *ROP* must have taken place in the temple of Gula, since the colophon (lines 139–141) describes the text as copied from an original in Esabad. Butler, *Mesopotamian Conceptions of Dreams and Dream Rituals*, 371.

[29] Butler, *Mesopotamian Conceptions of Dreams and Dream Rituals*, 222–23. Especially note the table there.

[30] H. F. Lutz, "A Cassite Liver-Omen Text," *JAOS* 38 (1918): 77–96.

[31] Ibid., 87.

[32] Lutz's recognition of incubation in this omen text is owing to his ingenuity in explaining the two entities in the text (LAL and É KUR in line 6) in light of the Herodotus' description of É-Sagila in Babylon. After arguing that É-KUR in line 6

text were correct, then we would have a case in which hepatoscopy is embedded in incubation.[33]

The other Kassite text that may have allusion to incubation belongs to a "historical-epic" genre.[34] Although no more than one-quarter of the original tablet survives, this text provides a very interesting example of the Kassite royal incubation.

Parts of the five lines at the bottom of the obverse features a woman (MUNUS *qa-ta-an-tu*$_4$ "a thin woman" or "the Lady Qatantu") who is weeping at the city gate, or perhaps, at the entrance to a temple, prostrating herself with grief, and Bēl hears her lament. In the first ten lines that survive on the reverse, which follows directly on, we read of the protagonist Kurigalzu the Kassite King going into the temple Esagila and falling asleep on his couch.[35] He, then, had a dream in which he saw Bēl, and Nabû standing in front of Bēl seemed to have shown or read out to his father "the Tablet of Sins."[36]

According to Finkel who published this text, the MUNUS *qa-ta-an-tu*$_4$ is Kurigalzu's wife. Her distress, which may be due to her barrenness, made her cry out to Bēl. Since her barrenness may lead to the

---

should be interpreted not as a proper noun, i.e., the É-KUR temple at Nippur, but as a common noun referring to a special shrine that every temple in Babylon used to have, Lutz identifies the function of that shrine as that of νηὸς μέγας (literally 'big temple'; cf. Herodotus' *The Histories*, Book 1, chapter 181, section 5), i.e., an incubation hall, and the function of LAL-priest in line 6 as that of γυνὴ μούνη τῶν ἐπιχωρίων ("a native woman"; cf. Ibid.) who lies down at the shrine during the night. Cf. Lutz, "A Cassite Liver-Omen Text," 86–87.

33 Although it is not uncommon that omens are placed within other omens and despite Oppenheim's endorsement, Lutz's interpretation of "Division 1" of the text as an oneiric hepatoscopy has met with serious challenges. Following the suggestion of Scheil in *Revue d'Assyriologie* 14 (1917) 150, for example, Reiner has proposed to read MÁŠ.GE6 as "nocturnal extispicy," instead of "dream" (Reiner, "Dead of Night," 248). See also F. R. Kraus who has accepted Reiner's proposal (F. R. Kraus, "Mittelbabylonisch Opferschauprotokolle," *JCS* 37 [1985]: 161).

34 If epic is defined as a lengthy poetic narrative, a historical epic may be considered as one in which historical figures appear without mythological themes. Albert K. Grayson, *Babylonian Historical-Literary Texts* (Toronto: University of Toronto Press, 1975), 41–42.

35 We read in line 6 of the *zaqīqū* spirits approaching Kurigalzu, who was lying awake trying to incubate a dream: za-qí-qí iṭ-ḫu-pu-ḫu-ú su? bu x[x (x)] "the spirits approached him and anxiety…" (The transliteration and translation is Finkel's). The function of the *zaqīqū* spirits seem to have been to allay the king's fears in a similar way to that in which *zaqīqū* came from Nabû to Assurbanipal before he fell asleep and made him relax (Irving L. Finkel, "The Dream of Kurigalzu and the Tablet of Sins," *AnSt* 33 [1983]: 76, footnote 5; for *zaqīqū* as a dream god, see Butler, *Mesopotamian Conceptions of Dreams and Dream Rituals*, 80–83).

36 Finkel, "The Dream of Kurigalzu and the Tablet of Sins," 75.

cessation of the royal line, following an old Mesopotamian procedure, Kurigalzu undergoes the so-called incubation, the deliberate soliciting of a dream message from a god by sleeping in his temple.[37] According to Finkel, Kurigalzu was seeking the reason for his wife's distress. The mention of "Tablet of Sins" at the end of the extant text seems to indicate that Qatanu's misfortune may have been divine punishment for some unwitting misdemeanor, the details of which are recorded in the Tablet of Sins.[38]

It is noteworthy that, although the broken state of the tablet leaves any interpretation provisional, Finkel's interpretation has broached an important literary link between the motif of barrenness and the remedy through dream.[39] It is significant that all of the three texts under examination in this book show a similar plot: all protagonists (Kirta, 'Aquatu, and Hannah) suffer from a lack of offspring and find their answer through oneiric or quasi-oneiric experiences.

1.4 *Mari Evidence*

Most of the data for the Mari practice of incubation come from the paleo-Babylonian period. At least 10 dream-incidents are reported in the Mari letters.[40] Some of the dreams were experienced by the senders of the letters and reported directly to the receiver, Zimli-Lim king of Mari (e.g. ARM X 50, 94, 100). Others, however, were experienced by a third person, whether he or she be a professional or a layperson, and relayed to the king through the senders of the letters (e.g. ARM X 10; ARM XIII 112, 113; A. 15, 222). As can be gathered from the fact that the senders felt it necessary to report the dreams, their contents, with the exception of ARM X 100 and 117, were intended for the king, or at least concerned matters of public significance. Hence, while it is interesting to note in these dream reports that the receivers of dream revelations (*Offenbarungsempfänger*) were not the intended recipients

---

[37] Ibid., 76.

[38] Ibid.

[39] Ibid.

[40] Sasson's 1983 paper on Mari dreams was intended to supplement Oppenheim's foundational study on ancient Near Eastern dream-reports (1956), which predated most of the important publications on Mari dream-reports. In his paper, Sasson discussed all of the ten Mari letters that contain dream-reports. Cf. Jack M. Sasson, "Literary Criticism, Folklore Scholarship, and Ugaritic Literature," in *Ugarit Retrospect: Fifty Years of Ugarit and Ugaritic*, Douglas Y. Gordon (Winona Lake, IN: Eisenbrauns, 1981), 81–98.

of the dream message (*Botschaftsempfänger*),[41] the question more pertinent for our purpose is whether or not these dreams were induced by the medium of incubation. If, hypothetically speaking, they were, then they would belong to the category of "priestly incubation" or "incubation by proxy." But this is not likely because most of the receivers of dream revelation were not professional oneiromancers, but lay people. It is hard to imagine that Zimli-Lim King of Mari would have asked multiple obscure lay people[42] to receive a divine oracle on matters of public significance. This may be part of the reason why these dreams have often been categorized as "prophetic" dreams.[43] Furthermore, the dream reports in the Mari letters fail to mention any details concerning the circumstances of the reception of the dream. We are not told, for instance, when or where the theophany happened.[44] Nor are we informed of any predicament that may have necessitated the recourse to incubation, let alone preparatory rituals. All of this makes it extremely difficult to arrive at any conclusion as to whether or not these dreams were induced by way of incubation.

This does not, however, warrant the conclusion that all the Mari dreams were spontaneous.[45] There are some textual allusions to the effect that some of the dreams may have been sought for.[46] The most

---

[41] The German terms are Ellermeier's (Friedrich Ellermeier, *Prophetie in Mari und Israel*, Theologische und Orientalistische Arbeiten 1 [Herzberg: Verlag Erwin Jungfer, 1968], passim).

[42] Some of the recipients of the dream-revelation are not even mentioned by name. Instead they are referred to a young man (*ṣuḫārum* in ARM 13 112) or a man (1 *awīlum* in ARM 13 113).

[43] Cf. William L. Moran, "New Evidence from Mari on the History of Prophecy," *Bib* 50 (1969): 15–86; Herbert B. Huffmon, "Prophecy in the Mari Letters," *BA* 31 (1968): 101–24, especially 116–17; Jean-Marie Durand, "Les prophéties des textes de Mari," in *Oracles et prophéties dans l'Antiquité: actes du Colloque de Strasbourg, 15–17 juin 1995*, Jean-Georges Heintz (Paris, 1997), 115–34; Ellermeier, *Prophetie in Mari und Israel*, 11–14; Husser, *Dreams and Dream Narratives in the Biblical World*, 44–46.

[44] The exception is ARM X 10 in which Kakkalidi is reported to have had a dream in the temple of Itūr: *ša-ni-tam* [mí]*Ka-ak-ka-li-di i-na É* [d]*I-túr-Me-er i-mu-ur um-ma-a-ni* "By the way, Kakkalidi saw the following [vision/dream] in the temple of Itur-Mer" (line 5–7a). According to Ellermeier, Kakkalidi, a lay person, went to the temple in order to receive a revelation (Ellermeier, *Prophetie in Mari und Israel*, 81). But the content of his dream, which was meant to encourage the king, makes Ellermeier's proposal less likely unless Kakkalidi was seeking an answer for his king's problem or King Zimli-Lim had asked him to get an oracle for him, both of which are, in my opinion, less likely.

[45] Edward Noort, *Untersuchungen zum Gottesbescheid in Mari*, AOAT 202 (Neukirchen-Vluyn: Neukirchener Verlag, 1977), 25ff.

[46] ARM X 117, line 9; ARM X 50, lines 23–26; A. 15.

likely case of incubation dream comes from ARM X 100, which is addressed to Zimli-Lim by his female servant Zunana.[47] The dream-report in this letter distinguishes itself from those in other Mari letters, not only because it discloses some of the circumstances pertaining to the reception of the dream, but also because the receiver of the dream revelation (*Offenbarungsempfänger*) is the same as the intended recipient of the dream message (*Botschaftsempfänger*). We are told in the letter that Zunana's daughter was kidnapped on her way to Rubben (line 6). But when Zunana found out about her whereabouts and went to retrieve her daughter from the custody of a certain Sammētar, he refused to release her (line 19–21). For this reason, Zunana sought Dagan's aid through "incubation."[48] The text does not describe the dialogue between Dagan and Zunana as a dream, but phrases in lines 7–9 suggest this possibility: *ù* $^{[d]}$*D[a-ga]n be-el-ka ú-ṣa-al-l[i]-la-am-ma / ma-am-ma-an ú-ul il-pu-t[a]-an-ni /* ^{d}*[D]a-gan ki-a-am iq-bi-im um-[m]a* "And Dagan, your lord, made me fall asleep / no one touched me / Thus Dagan said to me." Although the interpretation of *uṣallilamma* is still debated,[49] the dream-report in ARM X 100 provides the best evidence for the occurrence of private oracular incubation in the Mari corpus.[50]

---

[47] Alternate readings include Dannana (Georges Dossin, *Correspondance Féminine*, ARM 10 [Paris: Geuthner, 1978], 151), Yanana (Jack M. Sasson, "Mari Dreams," *JAOS* 103 [1983]: 283), and X-nana (Moran, "New Evidence from Mari on the History of Prophecy," 54).

[48] It is interesting to note that one of the Epidaurian inscriptions of cures reports a case of incubation through which a father found his lost son (Stela II no. 24). Cf. Edelstein and Edelstein, *Asclepius: A Collection and Interpretation of the Testimonies*, 225–26, 234.

[49] The problem is the verb in line 7, *ú-ṣa-al-l[i]-la-am-ma*. The attested stem for the factitive/causative meaning of *ṣalālu* "to lie asleep" is the Š-stem. The analysis of *uṣallilamma* as the D-stem with the factitive meaning of *ṣalālu* "to lie asleep" (cf. Dossin, *Correspondance Féminine*, 151; Ellermeier, *Prophetie in Mari und Israel*, 73) would be problematic as well, because the expected form would be *uṣallianna* "caused *me* to fall asleep" with the accusative pronominal suffix. For this reason, J.-M. Durand, who does not find *ṣullulu* "to provide shade" particularly fit for the context, takes the verb as the D-stem of ṣalālu, with the technical meaning "voir pendant son sommeil" (Jean-Marie Durand, *Archives épistolaires de Mari I/1*, ARM 26 [Paris: Recherches sur les civilisations, 1988], 472). He goes on to argue that *lapātum* in line 8 to refer to an opening manual act in an incubation ceremony (Ibid., 461). Although Durand's proposal is possible, it would take more attestations to be fully convincing. Cf. Butler, *Mesopotamian Conceptions of Dreams and Dream Rituals*, 219–20.

[50] Husser discusses a paleo-Babylonian letter from the archive at Mari (A. 747)—to the best of my knowledge, it is still unpublished, except for partial translations here and there—as a possible allusion to the practice of a *double* incubation. When the

1.5 *Assurbanipal*

The so-called Rassam Cylinder, which was inscribed and installed in commemoration of the completion of the rebuilding of the royal palace at Nineveh, provides one or two incubation dream reports concerning Assurbanipal.[51] In the face of the threat from Elamite king Teumman, Assurbanipal is reported to have approached (*amḫar*) Ishtar, taken his stand in her presence (*azzima*), crouched down at her feet (*akmiṣ šapalša*).[52] Although there is no explicit mention in the text of the place in which the incubation happened, the language, "approaching Ishtar," "standing in her presence," "crouching down at her feet," seems to indicate that the whole incident transpired in the temple of Ishtar (Column V, lines 27–28).[53] Divine aid was sought in prayers

decision in the matter concerning calumny had to be made, the oracle from the god Aštabi-El was sought with the following instructions: "The god Aštabi-El should take his place on his couch and should be questioned so that his *seer* may speak..." (lines 13–14). These lines seem to suggest a oneiromantic practice which consists in placing a statue of the divinity on a 'couch' or 'bed' while the 'seer' lies down and sleeps (beside him)." Husser interprets this as a *double* incubation: that of both the statue of the god and that of the seer (Husser, *Dreams and Dream Narratives in the Biblical World*, 48). For the discussion of this letter, see Durand, "Les prophéties des textes de Mari," 130–31; Matthias Köckert and Martti Nissinen, *Propheten in Mari, Assyrien und Israel*, Forschungen zur Religion und Literatur des Alten und Neuen Testaments 201 (Göttingen: Vandenhoeck & Ruprecht, 2003), 117.

[51] For the cuneiform text, see Hugo Winckler, *Die Keilschrifttexte Assurbanipals*, vol. III of *Sammlung von Keilschrifttexten* (Leipzig: E. Pfeiffer, 1893–95), 38–48. For transcription and translation, see George Smith, *History of Assurbanipal: Translated from the Cuneiform Inscriptions* (London: Williams and Norgate, 1871), 117ff. For translations, see Daniel D. Luckenbill, *Historical Records of Assyria from Sargon to the End*, vol. II of *Ancient Records of Assyria and Babylonia* (Chicago: University of Chicago Press, 1927), 290–323; Oppenheim, *The Interpretation of Dreams in the Ancient Near East: With a Translation of an Assyrian Dream-Book*, 246, Text no. 10; Robert D. Biggs, "An Oracular Dream Concerning Ashurbanipal," in *ANET*, ed. James B. Pritchard (Princeton, NJ: Princeton University Press, 1969), 606.

[52] The Akkadian verb *kamāṣu* is usually translated as "squat" or "kneel" (cf. CAD K 117; AHw 431). But when it was used in the context of incubation, it seems to refer to a special position that an incubant assumes as he lies down to sleep. Greenfield translates the Akkadian verb and its West-Semitic cognate (*qmṣ*) as "to lie down in a recumbent position" (Jonas C. Greenfield, "Studies in Aramaic Lexicography I," *JAOS* 82 [1962]: 296–97). Notably, the Ugaritic verb *qmṣ* was used to refer to the position that Kirta assumed as he fell asleep in tears. Although the verb *kamāṣu* does not occur in the incubation scene of the *Epic of Gilgamesh*, Gilgamesh is reported to take a rather unnatural position of a person squatting on the ground, his chin touching his knees, which the verb *kamāṣu* may have denoted (Oppenheim, *The Interpretation of Dreams in the Ancient Near East: With a Translation of an Assyrian Dream-Book*, 216).

[53] Husser, *Dreams and Dream Narratives in the Biblical World*, 40; Oppenheim, *The Interpretation of Dreams in the Ancient Near East: With a Translation of an Assyrian*

and in a formal and lengthy prayer by the king himself. Although there was no animal sacrifice or incense involved as a way of preparation, the tears and prayers no doubt functioned as an inducer of this favorable nocturnal theophany.[54] Answering Assurbanipal's tearful prayers, Ishtar manifested herself to him at night (*ina šat mu-ši*) with comforting words "Do not fear" (*la ta-pal-laḫ*!).[55] The text goes on to describe what appears to be a separate incident of incubation: "(And indeed) in the midst of the (very same) night (variant: in the very same night) in which I addressed myself to Ishtar, a *šabrû*-priest went to bed and had a dream (*u-tu-ul-ma i-na-(at)-tal* MÁŠ.GE$_6$)" (Column V, lines 49b–50).[56] Later the priest relayed to Assurbanipal the dream message that he had received, in which Ishtar in her military trappings gave Assurbanipal a specific military order "delay his attack on Elam" and then wrapped him in her baby-sling as a symbol of protection. This dream report ends rather abruptly without mentioning Assurbanipal's reaction.

The text is not clear about the relationship between these two instances of incubation. Do these two theophanies of night refer to two separate incidents of incubation or to one and the same? Some scholars hold that the two dreams—one by Assurbanipal and the other by the *šabrû* priest—were induced by the one and same preparation, namely, Assurbanipal's prayer in tears.[57] Others, on the other hand,

Dream-Book, 200. But see also Contenau who is a bit agnostic about the place where the incubation took place (Contenau, *La divination chez les Assyriens et les Babyloniens. Avec 13 figures, 1 carte et 8 gravures hors texte*, 172).

[54] The function of the tears and sighs becomes perfectly clear when Ishtar says the following, "Do not fear... Because of thy hands which thou hast raised in prayer, and thy eyes which were filled with tears, I have had mercy upon thee" (Column V, lines 47–49a). The translation is Luckenbill's (*Historical Records of Assyria from Sargon to the End*, 293).

[55] Oppenheim sees the vision of the king as a simple theophany. He bases his opinion on a later comparative data where the same divine figure was simultaneously perceived by one person in a dream and by another in a waking vision (Oppenheim, *The Interpretation of Dreams in the Ancient Near East: With a Translation of an Assyrian Dream-Book*, 201). But the mention of *ina šat muši* seems to be a strong indicator that the theophany is at least nocturnal. This, together with the intention of the king to induce a divine message and the place in which the vision took place, seems to speak in favor of taking the king's nocturnal vision as oneiric (cf. Morris Jastrow, *The Religion of Babylonia and Assyria* [Boston: Ginn & Company, 1898], 350).

[56] The translation is Biggs's (Biggs, "An Oracular Dream Concerning Ashurbanipal," 606).

[57] Husser, for example, contends that "the priest's oneiric vision was provoked by the king's prayer, suggesting a kind of incubation by transfer or delegation" (Husser, *Dreams and Dream Narratives in the Biblical World*, 33). But considering that priestly

recognize two separate incidents of incubation in the text.[58] If the text denotes two different incubations, the priestly incubation was no doubt intended both as a confirmation of and as a "follow-up inquiry" to the first incubated dream. The king may have wanted to confirm the verity of the first oneiric message by having an expert in dreams incubate another message dream. At the same time, Assurbanipal may have wanted to know more details about how he, with the help of Ishtar, can deal with the military threat of the Elamites. This seems to be indicated by the fact that the second message dream delivers a very specific military order to Assurbanipal. In this respect, Assurbanipal's incubation has affinity with Gudea's incubation in which the second and third dreams were induced for the purpose of securing more details concerning the building of the Eninnu temple.

1.6 *Nabonidus*

Oppenheim regards the dream-report described in the Stele of Nabonidus (Column VII:1–22) as "one of the few unequivocally described incubation-dreams in cuneiform literature."[59] According to Oppenheim, the preparatory rituals that Nabonidus performed may have been depicted in the lines at the beginning of the tablet that are now lost. But according to Reiner, this does not have to be the case. Reiner, later cited by Butler, recognizes part of the ritual procedure in the extant lines. In contrast to Oppenheim who, following Langdon, reconstructs

---

incubation dream was normally prepared and induced by the priestly incubant, and not by the petitioner, this "incubation by transfer" is eccentric in that the ritual is accomplished by one person—the king—and the oneiric revelation is received by another, without any apparent prior coordination.

[58] Oppenheim, for example, discerns two separate theophanies, one which was induced and the other was not (Oppenheim, *The Interpretation of Dreams in the Ancient Near East: With a Translation of an Assyrian Dream-Book*, 188). Although no mention is made of the preparation for a dream on the priest's part, however, one may gather on the basis of the idiom "*u-tu-ul-ma i-na-(at)-tal* MÁŠ.GE$_6$" that the dream was prepared for according to the then standard procedure regulating the practice of incubation. Considering the established convention of priestly incubation and the fact that its procedure may have been well known to the readers, one may argue that the scribe may have omitted the routine preparations to get to the important part, that is, the message from Ishtar. Furthermore, the detailed description of the king's preparations may have precluded the need to repeat a similar procedure in the immediately following incubation.

[59] Oppenheim, *The Interpretation of Dreams in the Ancient Near East: With a Translation of an Assyrian Dream-Book*, 188. For a similar evaluation see Husser, *Dreams and Dream Narratives in the Biblical World*, 48.

[mu]-kin-nu ra-ab-bu-tim ("exalted witness") in line 4 and interprets it as referring to the stars enumerated in lines 1–3,[60] Reiner reconstructs *[sur]-qin-nu ra-ab-bu-tim* in line 4 and translates lines 4–5 (*[sur]-qin-nu ra-ab-bu-tim aš-tak-kan-šu-nu-ti-ma*) as "I scattered incense to them [the stars]."[61] Be that as it may, the legible part of the tablet begins with a list of star names which are the very gods to whom Nabonidus directs his petition. His petition consists of what may be expected from someone who has just ascended to the throne, namely, longevity, long years of reign, and divine legitimization. The text goes on to describe Nabonidus as lying down to see the goddess Gula in a dream (*a-na-al-ma ina šat mu-ši* ^{ilu}*Bau be-el-ti*, lines 11–12).[62] Although the text does not register Gula's message in a direct speech, one may infer from the subsequent lines (cf. lines 13–22) that Gula's theophany answered all the requests of Nabonidus's prayer.[63]

This incubation scene is preceded by two other dream-incidents (cf. Column VI). The second dream also appears to have been incubated by Nabonidus who became apprehensive of the enigma of his first dream (*a-na ṭi-ḫu-ti kakkabi rabû u* ^{d}*SIN* "Concerning the approaching of the Great Star and the moon" [lines 4–5]).[64] The text does not mention any ritual preparation, nor is there any indication that the dream-incident took place in a temple. But the fact that the oneiric

[60] Oppenheim, *The Interpretation of Dreams in the Ancient Near East: With a Translation of an Assyrian Dream-Book*, 205; Stephen Langdon, *Die neubabylonischen Königsinschriften* (Leipzig: J. C. Hinrichs, 1912), 278–79.

[61] Reiner, "Fortune-Telling in Mesopotamia," 24, foonote 2; Bulter's translation of lines 4–5 is closer to the literal rendition of the lines: "I placed a very large offering before" the stars (Butler, *Mesopotamian Conceptions of Dreams and Dream Rituals*, 233–34).

[62] Literally, "I lied down and there was Gula in the night!" Although Zgoll does not mention this passage as an example of the elliptical use of the idiomatic formula for incubation, it appears plausible that *anâlma ina šāt mūši* DN may be a legitimate variant of Zgoll's formula (cf. *tanâlma šutta tammar* in *ROP*, line 68).

[63] According to Butler, the nature of the theophany is not clear. In other words, it may not have been oneiric. He goes on to argue that if it were oneiric, two things make the incubation scene rather unusual. First, the dream is not reported. Second, no precise message was communicated through the dream, other than a mysterious gesture of Gula in line 22 (Butler, *Mesopotamian Conceptions of Dreams and Dream Rituals*, 233–34). But if the phrase in lines 11–12 is an elliptical expression for a typical incubation dream scene, a reader would have had no difficulty in recognizing the theophany as oneiric, even though there is no mention of "having a dream" (*naṭālu šutta*).

[64] That this astrological phenomenon took place in a dream is evident from the later remarks of Nebuchadnezzar's attendant, "Do speak to Nabonidus that he should report to you the dream he has seen!" (Column VI, lines 20–23).

vision not only comforts the king by announcing that there are no evil portents in the dream, but also interprets it,[65] reminds us of the not uncommon case of incubation in which a second dream is provoked for the purposes of interpreting the first symbolic dream (cf. the dreams of Gudea and of Assurbanipal).[66] It is in this context that Oppenheim's comment that the incubation-incident in Column VII was intended as a confirmation of the interpretation of the preceding dream would make more sense.[67]

1.7 *Summary*

The Mesopotamian sources thus far examined have brought to light various forms in which incubation could take place in ancient Mesopotamia. Incubation could be practiced by anyone, whether a king or an ordinary person, for any kind of problem, such as illness, journey, foreign invasion,[68] enigmatic dreams, etc. Moreover, a proxy, whether professional or layman, could incubate a dream on behalf of a petitioner. As shown in Gudea's incubation and *Rituals to Obtain a Purussû*,

[65] The way Nebuchadnezzar posed a question to Nabonidus—"Tell me what good (signs) you have seen" (*mi-na-a dum-qi ša ta-aṭ-ṭu-lu qi-ba-a*)—suggests that there was more to Nebuchadnezzar's theophany than simply what the man in line 6 had already said in lines 9–10. It appears that Nebuchadnezzar's appearance in a dream was designed to give a detailed interpretation of Nabonidus' symbolic dream. Unfortunately, however, the text is broken at the place where Nebuchadnezzar's interpretation of the dream starts.

[66] Although incubation for the purposes of interpreting a symbolic dream is attested to elsewhere, Nabonidus' second dream is peculiar in several aspects. First, it is the only example among the texts of the ancient Near East of an apparition of a dead person in a dream. Second, the phenomenon wherein a symbolic dream is recounted and interpreted in a dream is not common (cf. Mesopotamian *Dream Book* Tablet X, Oppenheim, *The Interpretation of Dreams in the Ancient Near East: With a Translation of an Assyrian Dream-Book*, 305, foonote 229). Cf. Husser, *Dreams and Dream Narratives in the Biblical World*, 41–42.

[67] Oppenheim, *The Interpretation of Dreams in the Ancient Near East: With a Translation of an Assyrian Dream-Book*, 205; Husser makes the same point (Husser, *Dreams and Dream Narratives in the Biblical World*, 48).

[68] Assurbanipal II erected a temple to the dream god Manu at Balawat (ancient Imgur Enlil), which was later embellished by Shalmaneser III. No extant evidence tells us why the Assyrian king built a temple to Manu in Balawat. However, some scholars, based on the fact that Manu was a dream god and that Balawat was located on the main road of military campaigns, have speculated that the Assyrian king slept in this temple on his first night out of Nineveh in order to receive a dream concerning the future campaign (D. Oates, "Balawat [Imgur Enlil]: The Site and Its Buildings," *Iraq* 36, no. 173–178 [1974]: 175; Cf. Zgoll, "Die Welt im Schlaf sehen: Inkubation von Träumen im antiken Mesopotamien," 87). For a detailed discussion of this temple of Manu see Butler, *Mesopotamian Conceptions of Dreams and Dream Rituals*, 74–76.

incubation dreams were induced by very complex rituals that might include incense offering, animal sacrifice, purification, crying, prayers, gifts, silence, etc. But it appears that there was no standard procedure. The incubation dreams thus induced may take the form of a symbolic dream or a message dream. The latter may occur in the form of a divine-human dialogue. Incubation could be carried out in any temple, not limited to a certain kind of deities.[69] Also noteworthy is that the incubation dreams may be verified by other divination techniques.

2. Incubation in Hatti

2.1 *The Legend of Naram-Sin*

Our oldest evidence comes from the Hittite version of the legend of Naram-Sin (KBo 3.16+), which was probably handed down to the Hittites as a scribal school text.[70] In this version, Ishtar advises the king to carry out what Mouton calls "divinatory" incubation,[71] which consists of purification, imploration to the gods in tears, and sleep in a pure bed.[72] This incubation-incident may have been motivated by Naram-Sin's desire to discern the divine will concerning one of his military

[69] Zgoll, who tends to accept as "incubation texts" any text with the expressions which he sees as idioms for induced dreams, argues on the basis of both literary and non-literary data that any place with a liminal character could serve as the place of incubation. He adduces mountain, cave, magic circle, roof, etc. as examples (Zgoll, "Die Welt im Schlaf sehen: Inkubation von Träumen im antiken Mesopotamien," 86–88).

[70] See Hans G. Güterbock, "Die historische Tradition und ihre literarische Gestaltung bei Babyloniern und Hethitern bis 1200," *ZA* 44 (1937): 45. Güterbock has identified the genre of this story as "narû-literature," i.e., first person narrations by kings of their experiences. Later, Grayson and Lambert gave this genre a more descriptive name, "poetic autobiographies" (Albert K. Grayson and W. G. Lambert, "Akkadian Prophecies," *JCS* 18 [1964]: 8). This genre has also been called "pseudo-autobiographies" (Grayson, *Babylonian Historical-Literary Texts*, 7) or simply "autobiography" (Erica Reiner, "Die akkadische Literature," in *Altorientalische Literaturen*, von Wolfgang Röllig [Wiesbaden: Akademische Verlagsgesellschaft Athenaion, 1978], 176–80).

[71] Alice Mouton divides the Hittite incubation into *incubation divinatoire* and *incubation therapeuticque* and defines the former as the incubation designed to "obtenir un rêve-message" (Alice Mouton, "Usages privés et publics de l'incubation d'après les textes hittites," *JANER* 3 [2003]: 73). But she does not mention the Legend of Naram-Sin as an example of the divinatory incubation when she discusses the subject in her 2003 study of the Hittite incubation (cf. Ibid., 74–83).

[72] I rely on Güterbock's transliteration and translation: "Geh! Reinige dich, Schlafe auf einem reinen Bett! Rufe deine Götter an und klage zu deinen Göttern!" (Colume III, lines 12–14). Cf. Güterbock, "Die historische Tradition und ihre literarische Gestaltung bei Babyloniern und Hethitern bis 1200," 55–57.

campaigns, as is implied in the question which he poses to Ishtar (cf. Column III, lines 2–11). The text goes on to report how Naram-Sin followed Ishtar's advice and obtained the dream that carried the message of the gods. The dream message (Column III, lines 18ff.) is registered as a dialogue between the dreamer and the gods who appeared in his dream, but unfortunately the details of the message elude us because of the broken state of the tablet. Although this text has no Hittite king in view, the fact that the incubation passage under discussion does not have parallel in the Akkadian version of the legend suggests that the Hittite practice of incubation may have been reflected in this passage.[73]

2.2 *The Plague Prayer*

Muršili II (1321–1295)[74] is the source of the most celebrated allusion to Hittite incubation. Near the end of his "second" plague prayer,[75] Muršili II enumerates several channels through which the gods can reveal their wills to mortals: "[Or] if many people are dying because of some other matter, may I see it in a dream! May it be determined by oracle! May 'a man of a god' speak of it, or due to the fact that I gave

[73] This seems to be proven by an excerpt from Muršili II's annals (KBo 2.5: i 13–17) which records a military feat of an anonymous frontier commander from the town of Ištahar (EN *MAD-GAL9-TI ŠA* [URU]*iš-ta-ha-ra*). When Aparruš de Kalašma, the enemy of the Hittites, took the temple *hekur* of Pittalahša, the town within the region of Malatya, the frontier commander was able to recover the temple and the town of Pittalahša by following the instructions communicated in a dream ([N]][A4]*hé-kur* [URU]*pí-it-ta-la-ah-ša-an* MA.MÚ-*az* [...] x *e-ep-ta* "] il prit [...] le temple *hekur* [et] la ville de Pittalahša [selon les instructions] d'un rêve," cf. Alice Mouton, *Rêves hittites*, CHANE 28 [Leiden: Brill, 2007], 87–88). Although there is no mention of any specifics of the incubation practice—this is not uncommon in other incubation texts—and despite of the possibility of the dream having been spontaneous, the context—the trouble that the frontier commander and, for that matter, Muršili II are confronted with, the connection between the defeat of the enemy and the dream message, and the mention of the temple which may be suggestive of the place in which incubation was performed—seems to indicate that we have an allusion, in this text, to the practice of incubation similar to that of Naram-Sin discussed above.

[74] The date comes from Trevor Bryce, *The Kingdom of the Hittites* (Oxford: Clarendon Press, 1998), xiii.

[75] Beckman observes that "the order of the prayers is not indicated in the texts themselves but has been postulated by modern scholars on the basis of the development of Muršili's argumentation over the course of the series" (Gary Beckman, "Plague Prayers of Muršili II," in *Canonical Compositions from the Biblical World*, vol. I of *COS*, ed. William W. Hallo and K. Lawson Younger Jr. [Leiden: Brill, 1997], 156).

order to all priests, they shall lie down in a (con)sacr(at)ed manner! (*šu-up-pa-ya še-e*[(*š-ki-iš-kán-zi*)])."[76]

In the opinion of many scholars,[77] there is at least one assured case of incubation in the passage under discussion.[78] Muršili II recommends the priests to go through collective incubation in order to find out the reason for the plague that has raged in the country for many years. Mouton, in particular, provides a linguistic justification for this interpretation by observing that the Hittite expression *šuppa/šuppaya šeš-* "sleep in a holy place/manner" is an idiom for a divinatory incubation in the Hittite oneiric texts.[79] The question whether the first request in the plague prayer ("May I see it in a dream!") refers to the incubation by the king himself or simply a spontaneous dream-message, however, will remain undecided solely due to the lack of evidence in the text. But the gravity of the situation that presses Muršili may have led him to resort to the ritual of divinatory incubation as Naram-Sin is reported to have done in the Hittite version.[80]

---

[76] The translation is Mouton's (Mouton, *Rêves hittites*, 122–23). A similar request was also made by the prince and high priest Kantuzzili. When struck by illness, Kantuzzili prays to the sun God Ištanu to reveal to him the error that caused his illness: "[Main]tenant, que mon dieu m'ouvre le tréfonds de son âme vec sincérité, et qu'il me [dis]e mes fautes. Je les reconnaîtrai. Soit que mon dieu me parle dans un rêve. Que mon dieu m'ouvre son coeur. Qu'il [me] dise mes [faut]es, je les reconnaîtrai. Soit que l'ENSI les dise. [Soit] que l'AZU du dieu Soleil [me] les dise à l'aide du'un foie…" (KUB 30.10:24–27) (Mouton, *Rêves hittites*, 119). Kantuzzili's request for divine revelation indicates three channels through which God may make his thoughts known to mortals: by means of dream (*zašḫeya*), through the mediation of female diviner ([sal]ENSI), and by means of a hepatoscopic oracle (cf. Husser, *Dreams and Dream Narratives in the Biblical World*, 54).

[77] See Oppenheim, *The Interpretation of Dreams in the Ancient Near East: With a Translation of an Assyrian Dream-Book*, 188. Cf. Beckman, "Plague Prayers of Muršili II," 158; Albrecht Goetze, "Plague Prayers of Mursilis," in *ANET*, ed. James B. Prichard (Princeton, NJ: Princeton University Press, 1969), 396; Gnuse, *Dreams and Dream Report in the Writings of Josephus: A Traditio-Historical Analysis*, 61; Husser, *Dreams and Dream Narratives in the Biblical World*, 78; René Lebrun, *Hymnes et prières hittites*, Homo Religiosus 4 (Louvain-la-Neuve: Centre d'histoire des religions, 1980), 215; Mouton, *Rêves hittites*, 33.

[78] Some scholars such as Vieyra are very reluctant to see the practice of incubation—at least the form, in their opinion, defined by other cultures in ancient Near East—in these two, because the focus of the passage lies in the discernment of the divine will, not in the enforcement of human will. But their argument would have made better sense in the later contexts such as in Greece where incubation was so thoroughly institutionalized that the mechanical process itself seemed to guarantee the result hoped for by the incubants.

[79] Mouton, "Usages privés et publics de l'incubation d'après les textes hittites," 74.

[80] If, as Mouton proposes as one of two possible scenarios for KBo 2.5 (Mouton, *Rêves hittites*, 87), the incubation had been carried out by Muršili II, who transmit-

2.3 *Texts Alluding to the Public Use of Incubation*[81]

In her 2003 study of the Hittite incubation, Mouton observes that some tablets describe religious festivals during which a practitioner retires to the temple to incubate a dream in order to obtain a divine oracle.[82] According to Mouton, this public use of incubation is almost always for a divinatory purpose, not for a therapeutic one. KUB 27.1+, for instance, describes a king, who in the middle of the festival for Šaušga enters the temple of Šaušga, offers a food sacrifice, pours a libation, and then sleeps "where it is good for him (*nu=ššši kuwapi aššu n=aš apiya šešzi*)."[83] During the king's temple-sleep, the singers and the AZU priests stayed awake and the rituals continued.[84] This seems to indicate that the king's temple-sleep was instituted as a regular component of the festival for Šaušga. In this regard, this royal incubation would distinguish itself from those practiced at a time of crisis.

That said, KUB 43.55 provides an interesting case of the public use of incubation. Its colophon reads, "My Sun, Tutḫaliya the great king saw a dream, during the festival for the Sun goddess of the land of Ḫattuša, in the house of the grand-fathers. This was at this time of the year, in that year that the storm god thundered in the town of Urwaza and it was the Thunder Festival."[85] If we accept Mouton's proposal that the royal couple often performed incubation during religious festivals, this colophon appears to make an allusion to the divinatory incubation that Tutḫaliya carried out during the festival of the sun goddess Arinna. What is especially interesting about this group-tablet (*Sammeltafel*) is that the royal practitioner invokes the divine ancestors (or the spirit of

ted the oneiric instruction to the anonymous field officer later, this would show that Muršili II knew how to induce a dream in a time of crisis, thus enhancing the possibility that that Muršili himself may have resorted to incubation in the matter of plague too.

81 The following paragraphs rely upon Mouton, "Usages privés et publics de l'incubation d'après les textes hittites," 73–91.

82 They may or may not include the Hittite idiom referring to incubation, *šuppa/šuppaya šeš*. Mouton, "Usages privés et publics de l'incubation d'après les textes hittites," 83.

83 Ibid., 76.

84 Ibid.

85 The translation is Mouton's: "(Ce fut) lorsqu'il advint (que) mon Soleil Tuthaliya, le Grand Roi vit un rêve lors du rituel de la déesse Soleil de la terre à Hattuša, dans la maison des grands-pères, -ce fut à ce moment-là de l'année-, pendant cette année-là (que) le dieu de l'orage tonna dans la ville d'Urwara (et que ce fut) la fête du tonnerre" (Mouton, *Rêves hittites*, 149).

the dead) for a therapeutic purpose. This seems to be hinted at by the place in which the dream was sought, i.e., the house of great-fathers (É *hu-uh-ha-aš*) and by the answer from the Sun goddess that predicts Tutḫaliya's proper death.[86] If this is the case, KUB 43.55 seems to be the only attestation in ancient Near Eastern cuneiform texts of the employment of incubation for the necromantic purposes (cf. Nabonidus' second dream-incident). Furthermore, it provides a unique case where the public incubation, i.e. incubation during religious festivals, is used for a therapeutic purpose.[87]

2.4 *Texts Alluding to Private Use of Incubation*

An incubation rite was available not only to the members of the royal family, but also to ordinary Hittites. The evidence seems to show that all therapeutic uses of incubation, except for KUB 43.55, took place in private settings, regardless of religious festivals, although one cannot exclude the possibility that the current distribution of the data is owing to an accident of preservation. It is also noteworthy that most therapeutic uses of the Hittite incubation happen without a *dream*. Healings occur more from the magical-curative effects of the sleep at night than from oneiric theophany.[88] The ritual of Zuwi (VBoT 111), for instance, consists of laying the patient down to sleep on a layer of vegetation (column 3, line 12 *nu=wa=kan ḫaḫḫalaš šašti* UḪ$_7$-*aš šešdu*).[89] Hittites may have considered the prolonged contact with the vegetation as possessing a curative power.

The most celebrated Hittite text which describes therapeutic incubation is the ritual of Paškuwatti (KUB 9.27+).[90] This ritual, designed to treat sexual impotence, is particularly interesting because it provides a detailed account of one specific form that the Hittite therapeutic incubation may have taken. After an introductory section in which

[86] See Mouton, "Usages privés et publics de l'incubation d'après les textes hittites," 82, footnote 16.

[87] Ibid., 82. Later in Greece a similar duality is observed: both private healing and public festival are encompassed in the worship of Asclepius (Lynn R. LiDonnici, *The Epidaurian Miracle Inscriptions*, SBLTT 36 [Atlanta, GA: Scholars Press, 1995], 9; Alice Walton, *The Cult of Asklepios*, CSCP 3 [Ithaca: Cornell University Press, 1894], 73–74).

[88] Mouton, *Rêves hittites*, 73.

[89] Mouton, "Usages privés et publics de l'incubation d'après les textes hittites," 86.

[90] For the transliteration and the translation of the text, see Mouton, *Rêves hittites*, 129–41.

the practitioner is identified as Paškuwatti, a Arazawan woman, and the purpose of the ritual is stated (i 1–3), the text begins to describe in minute detail the actual procedure of the therapeutic incubation, which takes place over three or four days. Paškuwatti begins by gathering pharmacopeia such as bread, fruits, hallucinogenic plants,[91] beverages, one of which is clearly alcoholic, that is, wine, the wool of sheep and the garment (i 4–13). A virgin (literally "girl of sacred purity" in i 14) then takes these items away while the patient, who has just been purified physically, follows her (i 14–15). After moving the patient to an uncultivated place, Paškuwatti makes a gate of reeds (i 16–18) and has the patient pass through it. The curative effect of these magical acts is symbolized by the change of items in the hands of the patient from objects of feminity (spindle and distaff) to objects of virility (a bow and arrows). Then follow Paškuwatti's incantations and prayers in which the problem of the patient is identified (cf. KUB 7.5 ii 2–5). The next day,[92] the practitioner and the patient move to the house of the patient for an incubation dream. After the preparatory sacrifices have been made, prayers said, and a bed, a BAR.TE-garment, and a cloak have been spread in front of the table, the patient lies down to have a dream (KUB 9.27 iii 14–iv 1). If he obtains one of the dreams hoped for, namely, if the deity comes and sleeps with him in a dream,[93] he offers a votive offering to the goddess. Otherwise, the ritual continues. It is noteworthy that this incubation takes place in the private residence of the patient, not in a temple. Also of note is the fact that the ritual of Paškuwatti invoked oneiric theophany, unlike other therapeutic incubations in which no dream is induced or mentioned.

---

[91] Güterbock translates the Hittite term *kalaktar* as "pavot," which is later accepted by Mouton (Hans G. Güterbock, "A Hurro-Hittite Hymn to Ishtar," *JAOS* 103 [1983]: 162; Mouton, *Rêves hittites*, 135).

[92] Mouton observes that the whole process so far described (i 1–ii 25) happened within one day (Mouton, *Rêves hittites*, 71).

[93] This recalls one dream reported in the votive texts of the temple of Asclepius in Epidaurus in which a certain Andromache, who suffered from barrenness, had a sexual relation with a young man, an incarnation of the god Asclepius: "Andromache, an Epeirote, for offspring. In her sleep here she had a dream: she dreamt that a blooming young boy uncovered her and then the god touched her with his hand. After that Andromache bore a son to Arybbas" (Naphtali Lewis, *The Interpretation of Dreams and Portents* [Toronto: Samuel Stevens Hakkert, 1976], 44).

2.5 *Summary*

The Hittite evidence shows the variety of forms that incubation could take in the Hittite world: royal, priestly, private, divinatory, therapeutic, multiple-day, and "dream-less" incubations. It also points to the need for a flexible definition while discussing ancient Near Eastern practices of incubation. In fact, none of the reports of therapeutic incubation gathered by Mouton, with the exception of the ritual of Paškuwatti and some birth rituals, mention dreams. The examples of divinatory incubation also seem to present incubation as one component of the rituals held during religious festivals, rather than making the preparatory nature of the rituals explicit. Furthermore, as noted above, some therapeutic incubations, like the ritual of Paškuwatti, took place in private residences, although Mouton admits that those private residences must have been purified to serve as a place for the practice of incubation.[94] In this regard, Mouton's definition of incubation is helpful at least in explaining the Hittite data for incubation. She defines the Hittite practice of incubation as "*l'acte de dormir au cours d'un rituel, ce dernier étant accompagné ou non de telles prières.*"[95] She adds immediately, "*L'incubation n'est pas toujours destinée à faire apparaître un rêve en particulier.*"[96] As per Mouton's definition, the preparatory nature of rituals is not emphasized, let alone the necessity of oneiric theophany or a holy place. Although Mouton's definition of incubation may appear eccentric, it has a great heuristic value when it comes to dealing with the Hittite data. All this simply reminds us of the fluidity that such a history-of-religions concept as incubation could have, and also of the difficulty in balancing between a catch-all definition in the historical study of religions and a more nuanced definition suited to local cultures.

3. Incubation in Egypt

In late dynastic Egypt, dreams were actively sought through the medium of incubation. The evidence is a legion, ranging from papyri and ostraca

[94] Mouton, *Rêves hittites*, 73–74.
[95] Mouton, "Usages privés et publics de l'incubation d'après les textes hittites," 73.
[96] Ibid.

to numerous testimonies of Greek authors.[97] It is in this period that dream incubation was popularized and institutionalized so much so that it could be performed by private individuals at shrines, such as Hermopolis, Karnak, Medinet Habu, Philae, Canobus, Neith, etc.[98] Large numbers of people, many traveling long distances, and others making annual pilgrimages, sought the beneficence of their favorite divinities at these shrines. One could even have a professional incubate a dream vicariously. According to Strabo (*Geography* 17.17), the most educated and important people of the town of Canobus had their men lie down at the temple of Sarapis when they were too busy to do it in person.[99] Although oracular dreams were still incubated,[100] most incubation dreams served therapeutic function, namely, to bring healing to the sick, which included childless couples. One of the most celebrated examples is the story of Satni and his wife Mahituaskhit, which tells of the latter going to the temple of Imhotep in Memphis, praying to the god, then falling asleep in the temple, and receiving from the god in a

[97] For Egyptian evidence for incubation in the Ptolemaic period, see Sauneron Serge Sauneron, "Les songes et leurs interprétation dans l'Égypte ancienne," *SO* 2 (1959): 40–53; Walter A. Jayne, *The Healing Gods of Ancient Civilizations* (New Haven, CT: Yale University Press, 1925), 3–86; George Foucart, "Dream and Sleep (Egypt)," in *ERE: Vol. V*, vol. 5, ed. James Hastings (Edinburgh: T. & T. Clark, 1922), 35–37; Husser, *Dreams and Dream Narratives in the Biblical World*, 69–72; Gnuse, *Dreams and Dream Report in the Writings of Josephus: A Traditio-Historical Analysis*, 62–67; J. D. Ray, *The Archive of Hor* (London: Egypt Exploration Society, 1976), 7–116. The classical authors who make allusions to the practice of incubation in Egypt include Diodorus, Herodotus, Strabo, etc.

[98] In the text of the Dedication of the temple of Thoth at Medinet Habu (ca. the second century B.C.E.), for example, it is said that Thoth (or possibly Teos) was wont to descend on the temple each evening in the form of an ibis, and every morning the god went forth again from the shrine. On the basis of this text, Boylan argues that the temple was looked upon as a center for night-oracles received through incubation and the chief worshipers in the temple were the sick who came to obtain relief for their pains from such dreams that the night-abiding god of healing might send to them. The peculiar epithet of Thoth in this shrine, ŚTM "he who hears," would fit well with the custom at such a temple (Patrick Boylan, *Thoth, the Hermes of Egypt: A Study of Some Aspects of Theological Thought in Ancient Egypt* [Chicago: Ares, 1979], 168; Dominique Mallet, *Le Kasr el-Agoûz* [Le Caire: L'institut français d'archéologie orientale, 1909], 99–101).

[99] Strabo, *Geography*, trans. and ed. Amédée Tardieu (Paris: Hachette, 1867), http://www.mediterranees.net/geographie/strabon/sommaire.html (accessed May 23, 2008).

[100] David A. Rosalie, *Religion and Magic in Ancient Egypt* (London: Penguin Books, 2002), 281; Gnuse, *Dreams and Dream Report in the Writings of Josephus: A Traditio-Historical Analysis*, 64; Robert K. Ritner, "Dream Books," in *The Oxford Encyclopedia of Ancient Egypt*, vol. 1, ed. Donald B. Redford (Oxford: Oxford University Press, 2001), 410.

dream a cure for her infertility.[101] Moreover, if the available evidence is pieced together, it seems to allow us to reconstruct the *processus* of the Egyptian incubation in the temple. The patient enters one of the sanctuaries where the gods are reported to give responses to those who come to sleep within the sacred enclosure. Once inside the temple, the worshiper prays to the deity to reveal himself and beseeches him by his well-known virtues (e.g. "thou who givest children to him that hath none"). After these invocations, the supplicant waits for the god to come and respond to him in his sleep. The god then appears in a dream telling what should be done when morning comes. He does this in a clear language, using no dark or symbolic language. After waking, the patient usually carries out everything according to the oneiric instructions.[102]

The abundant documentation available from papyri and ostraca from this period, in addition to the numerous testimonies of Greek authors, as compared to the near silence of earlier Egyptian sources, led to the formerly widely held view that incubation was introduced into and developed in Egypt under the influence of Hellenism.[103] But, as Husser points out, the truth of the matter is no doubt more complex and scholars still debate whether dream incubation arose early in Egypt or whether it came later with Greek influence in the Hellenistic era.[104] Even those who argue for the latter, however, admit of a few attenuating factors during the pre-Ptolemaic Egypt,[105] to which we will turn now.

---

[101] For the translation see Gaston Maspero, *Popular Stories of Ancient Egypt*, trans. A. S. Johns (New York: University Books, 1967), 115–71; Sauneron, "Les songes et leurs interprétation dans l'Égypte ancienne," 41.

[102] Foucart, "Dream and Sleep (Egypt)," 35.

[103] Husser, *Dreams and Dream Narratives in the Biblical World*, 70.

[104] Scholars such as Françoise Dunand (*Dieux et hommes en Egypte, 3000 av. J.-C.-395 apr. J.-C.* [Paris: A. Colin, 1991], 185) and Sauneron ("Les songes et leurs interprétation dans l'Égypte ancienne," 40) are of the opinion that the practice of incubation arrived in Egypt under Hellenistic influence, whereas Ritner ("Dream Books," 410) and Volten (*Das demotische Weisheitsbuch, Studien und Bearbeitung*, AAeg 2 [Kopenhagen: E. Munksgaard, 1941], 44) believe that there was a long tradition of incubation from earliest periods. Cf. Gnuse, *Dreams and Dream Report in the Writings of Josephus: A Traditio-Historical Analysis*, 64, footnote 127.

[105] Sauneron, "Les songes et leurs interprétation dans l'Égypte ancienne," 40.

3.1 *The Letters to the Dead*

In a letter on a stela of the First Intermediate Period (c. 2206–2041 B.C.E.) the writer, Merirtyfy, wrote to his deceased wife, Nebetiotef, "Remove the infirmity of my body! Please become a spirit for me [before] my eyes so that I may see you in a dream fighting on my behalf."[106] Since the stela would have been situated near the funerary cult of the deceased took place, it is arguable on the basis of the text that Merirtyfy sometimes spent the night there in the hope of seeing his deceased spouse in a dream.[107] This would then be the first known allusion to incubation in Egypt. According to Ritner, the Letters to the Dead from the Old through the New Kingdoms request information and assistance "that were probably to be visualized through dreams."[108] In contrast, the Execration Texts of the Old and Middle Kingdoms include sections designed to combat "every evil dream in every evil sleep" which may have been provoked by personal enemies or demons. This seems to alludes to an abusive form of incubation.[109]

3.2 *Pharaonic Inscriptions*

The Memphis Stela of Amenhotep II (1454–1419)[110] and the Karnak Stela of Merenptah (1237–1226)[111] tells of the pharaohs having oracular dreams in the middle of battles against foreigners. Amon and Ptah,

---

106 Edward Wente, trans. and ed., *Letters from Ancient Egypt* (Atlanta, GA: Scholars Press, 1990), 215.

107 Husser, *Dreams and Dream Narratives in the Biblical World*, 71. Also see Edward Wente, "Correspondence," in *The Oxford Encyclopedia of Ancient Egypt*, ed. Donald B. Redford (New York: Oxford University Press, 2001), http://www.oxfordreference.com/views/ENTRY.html?subview=Main&entry=t176.e0154 (accessed April 10, 2008); J. F. Borghouts, "Witchcraft, Magic, and Divination in Ancient Egypt," in *Civilizations of the Ancient Near East*, vol. III & IV, ed. Jack M. Sasson (Peabody, MA: Hendrickson, 1995), 1783.

108 Ritner, "Dream Books," 410.

109 Ibid.

110 The chronology of pharaohs in this paragraph follows that of Donald Redford, ed., *The Oxford Encyclopedia of Ancient Egypt* (New York: Oxford University Press, 2001). For the translation of this stela, see John A. Wilson, "The Asiatic Campaigning of Amen-Hotep II," in *ANET*, ed. James B. Prichard (Princeton, NJ: Princeton University Press, 1969), 245–47; A. M. Badawi, "Die neue historische Stele Amenophis' II," *ASAE* 42 (1943): 1–23.

111 For the translation, see James Breasted, H., ed. and trans., *The Nineteenth Dynasty*, vol. III of *Ancient Records of Egypt: Historical Documents from the Earliest Times to the Persian Conquest* (Chicago: University of Chicago Press, 1906–7), 245; Oppenheim, *The Interpretation of Dreams in the Ancient Near East: With a Translation of an Assyrian Dream-Book*, 251.

respectively, appeared in their dreams and encouraged them to go on with the battles by promising divine protection and victory. The dream reported in the Sphinx Stela of Tuthmosis IV (1419–1410)[112] occurs in the context of a royal hunting expedition. When the prince falls asleep in the shadow of the Sphinx, the god Harnakhis-Khepri-Re-Atum appeared in a dream and promised kingship to him in return for a favor. But for its hunting context (as opposed to that of war), which is understandable from the fact that Tuthmosis IV was still a prince, his dream can be compared to the dreams of Amenhotep II and Merenptah in that the gods revealed themselves to the royalty, their earthly sons, at one of those critical moments and announced to them divine support. None of these stelae, however, tell us whether or not the dreams were incubated with a formal ritual or a prayer. A similar story is told of a certain Sethos,[113] an Egyptian king, by Herodotus (*Histories* 2:139). Distressed by the invasion of Sennacherib "the king of Arabians and the Assyrians," Sethos "entered into the inner sanctuary and... bewailed the fate... fell asleep, and dreamed that the god came and stood at this side bidding him to be of good cheer, and go boldly forth to meet the Arabian host..."[114] Scholars do not doubt that this story is a Hellenized account of the event, but the degree of Hellenization is a moot point.[115]

3.3 *The Stela of Qenherkhepeshef*

One may find a Ramesside example for private incubation in the Stela of Qenherkhepeshef, who was a sculptor and a servant in the palace of truth. In his thanksgiving hymn to the goddess Hathor, Qenherkhepeshef alludes to his incubation experience: "I have walked in

[112] For the translation, see James Breasted, H., ed. and trans., *The Eighteenth Dynasty*, vol. II of *Ancient Records of Egypt: Historical Documents from the Earliest Times to the Persian Conquest* (Chicago: University of Chicago Press, 1906–7), 323; Oppenheim, *The Interpretation of Dreams in the Ancient Near East: With a Translation of an Assyrian Dream-Book*, 251.

[113] It is generally assumed that Herodotus made a mistake. Sethos, a Greek name for Seti I (1321–1304 B.C.E.), cannot be contemporary with Sennacherib (705–681 B.C.E.) the king of Assyria.

[114] Oppenheim, *The Interpretation of Dreams in the Ancient Near East: With a Translation of an Assyrian Dream-Book*, 252.

[115] Foucart argues that the story remains a faithful, albeit Hellenized, account of what the classical Pharaohs would have done at a time of crisis (Foucart, "Dream and Sleep [Egypt]," 35). If he is right, we may assume that Amenhotep II and Merenptah performed the practice of incubation just as Sethos did at a time of crisis.

the palace of Beauty (the Valley of the Queens). I have spent the night in this forecourt. I have drunk the water sent of the cliff channel (?).... My body has spent the night in the shadow of your face. I have slept in your forecourt."[116] Although nothing in the text tells us that he actually had a dream, it is certain that his temple sleep was a manifestation of his personal piety.[117] The fact that he was the very owner of the oldest dream books in ancient Near East may speak in favor of the explanation that Qenherkhepeshef's temple sleep was an incubation.[118]

3.4 *Amuletic Decrees*

Incubation by proxy is attested to already in the amuletic decrees of the Twenty-first and Twenty-second Dynasties in very cursive hieratic: "We (i.e. the deities) shall make her dreams good, those which every other male or other female will see for her (we shall make them) good likewise."[119] This amuletic decree seems to indicate that the practice of sending a delegate into the temple to receive a dream for a person who cannot be physically present existed already at the end of New Empire.

3.5 *Summary*

Although the practice of incubation in Egypt proliferated among private individuals and was done within the context of established institutions only in late dynastic period, it is arguable on the basis of the data discussed above that the practice *per se* dates back to as far as the First Intermediate Period, if not earlier. But there is no doubt that

---

[116] Stephen Quirke, *Ancient Egyptian Religion* (London: British Museum Press, 1992), 136.

[117] Dunand, *Dieux et hommes en Egypte, 3000 av. J.-C.-395 apr. J.-C.*, 186.

[118] Ibid.; Butler, *Mesopotamian Conceptions of Dreams and Dream Rituals*, 218; Rosalie, *Religion and Magic in Ancient Egypt*, 281. For a translation of this dream book, see Lewis, *The Interpretation of Dreams and Portents*, 7–15. For the discussion of this dream book, see Oppenheim, *The Interpretation of Dreams in the Ancient Near East: With a Translation of an Assyrian Dream-Book*, 243–45; Gnuse, *Dreams and Dream Report in the Writings of Josephus: A Traditio-Historical Analysis*, 65–69; Scott B. Noegel, *Nocturnal Ciphers: The Allusive Language of Dreams in the Ancient Near East*, AOS 89 (New Haven, CT: American Oriental Society, 2007), 95–99; Ritner, "Dream Books," 400–411.

[119] The translation is Edward's which is found as an appendix in Battiscombe Gunn, "The Decree of Amonrasonthēr for Neskhons," *JEA* 41 (1955): 98–99; Cf. Sauneron, "Les songes et leurs interprétation dans l'Égypte ancienne," 41.

some of the details pertaining to the practice may have undergone changes under the influence of Greek incubation.[120]

4. Incubation in Ancient Greece

It should be noted at the outset that the purpose of this section is to put what has been discussed so far in a comparative perspective by describing the general features of the Greek incubation, and not to undertake an exhaustive study of the subject, which has been done thoroughly by others. Toward this end, we will treat the cult of Asclepius as *partem pro toto*, or better, as a representative sample. I take the Epidaurian inscriptions of cures[121] as well as a few classical authors[122] to illustrate what went on at an Asklepieion.

The earliest attestation to the Asclepian cult[123] occurs in the *Plutus* of Aristophanes (445–385) that gives an accurate, albeit satirical, picture of the practice of incubation at the beginning of the fourth century B.C.E. The details that Aristophanes provides, though set in a comedic context, confirm other testimonies of the practice of incubation that will be treated more thoroughly below. According to the story of Karion, Plutus the god of riches, who had been deprived of his sight by Zeus so that he could not distinguish between the just and unjust, decides to go to the temple of Asclepius to lie down for a therapeutic dream. As part of his incubation ritual, Plutus has a purificatory bath at the sea

[120] Ray, *The Archive of Hor*, 130; Foucart, "Dream and Sleep (Egypt)," 35; Husser, *Dreams and Dream Narratives in the Biblical World*, 71. Especially, Husser points out Aramaic influence on the Egyptian practice of incubation on the basis of a fifth-century B.C.E. Aramaic ostracon found in Elephantine.

[121] Cf. Hamilton, *Incubation or The Cure of Disease in Pagan Temples and Christian Churches*, 17–27; LiDonnici, *The Epidaurian Miracle Inscriptions*, 85–131; Edelstein and Edelstein, *Asclepius: A Collection and Interpretation of the Testimonies*, Text No. 423–424.

[122] E.g. The *Plutus* of Aristophanes (445–385 B.C.E.) and the *Sacred Orations* of Aristides (AD 117–181). For the latter, see Edelstein and Edelstein, *Asclepius: A Collection and Interpretation of the Testimonies*, Text no. 302, 324, 400, 403, 408a, 411a, 412, 417, 435, 449a, 460, 485a, 491b, 484, 485a, 486, 492a, 497, 498, 504, 518, 569a, 570, 597, 602, 604, 605, 605a, 806, 808, 812. Cf. Hamilton, *Incubation or The Cure of Disease in Pagan Temples and Christian Churches*, 44–62; Aelius Aristides, *The Complete Works*, ed. and trans. Charles A. Behr (Leiden: Brill, 1981–86).

[123] By the Asclepian cult is meant here the dream incubation. The first testimony to the Asclepius festival at Epidauros, during which incubation may have occurred, is found in the *Nemeae*, V, 95–97 of Pindar (520–442 B.C.E.) which relates the victor of a boxing match at the Asclepius festival (Edelstein and Edelstein, *Asclepius: A Collection and Interpretation of the Testimonies*, 312).

before entering the temple. In the temple, he offers cakes and incense at the altar and then goes to the sleeping hall to sleep on the makeshift bed that he had brought with him. Although Asclepius is known to heal during *dreams*, and although Plutus is *asleep* when he is healed, another character named Karion spies on the god's appearance and the healing activities while *awake*. Thus, this comedic episode clearly demonstrates the fine boundary between a dream apparition and real theophanies in Greek thought.[124]

The description in *Plutus* of the incubation practice is confirmed by the Epidaurian inscriptions of cures. Although the stelae containing the healing stories can be dated back to the second half of the fourth century on the basis of orthography and the form of the letters,[125] the majority of the stories date much farther back than the time of their inscription on the tablets, which took place as part of a long-term and massive expansion of the Epidaurian sanctuary, essentially an architectural transformation from a local to a pan-Hellenic shrine.[126] The fact that Aristophanes was able to make a parody of the practice at the beginning of the fourth century seems to indicate that the Asclepian healing cult had already been well established by that time. Forty-three stories of cures are inscribed on the two stelae uncovered in a porticoed building near the temple of Asclepius.[127] A survey of these stories reveals a certain uniform pattern characteristic of the practice of incubation in Epidauros and probably in Greece as a whole. The patient, seeking a god's help in his trouble, lies down to rest in the appointed hall after certain preparatory rituals, and during the night there comes to

---

[124] Frances L. Flannery-Dailey, "Standing at the Heads of Dreamers: A Study of Dreams in Antiquity Second Temple Period" (Ph.D. diss., University of Iowa, 2000), 104.

[125] Hamilton, *Incubation or The Cure of Disease in Pagan Temples and Christian Churches*, 27; Edelstein and Edelstein, *Asclepius: A Collection and Interpretation of the Testimonies*, 221.

[126] LiDonnici, *The Epidaurian Miracle Inscriptions*, 4.

[127] The existence of these stelae is also noted by Strabo and Pausanias. Strabo, speaking of Epidauros, says (ii 53): "The Temple is always full of patients and of stelae that have been set up with the cures inscribed on them, just as in Kos and Trikka." And Pausanias, also referring to Epidauros (ii 27): "Stelae have been erected within the precincts...On them were inscribed the names of men and women, cured by Asklepius, and also the diseases from which they suffered, and the method of cure." The purpose of the stelae was obviously to impress suppliants with the divine wonders, thus increase the supplicant's faith, and dispose him to be in an impressionable frame of mind, before incubation. Cf. Hamilton, *Incubation or The Cure of Disease in Pagan Temples and Christian Churches*, 13.

him a visitation from the god. In majority of the cases, the god appears in person, and by some simple act effects the cure. Next morning the patient leaves the Abaton healthy. Subsequently he pays a certain fee and/or offers thanks-offering.

Among the cases marked by this uniformity of the practice, however, there occur a few of singular characteristics. In the story of Sostrata (Stela II, No. 25) the incubatory healing takes place outside the temple. On his way back home after a dreamless night in the temple, Sostrata meets with Asclepius in the form of a man of fine appearance, who, there at Kornoi, performs an operation on Sostrata and makes him well. A case of incubation by proxy is reported in the story of Arata (Stela II, No. 22) who suffered from edema. Since she was not able to move herself, her mother slept in the temple in her lieu and had a dream. When the mother came back home from the temple she found her daughter in good health. In some cases, the god does the work by proxy, his agents being some of the sacred animals maintained in the temple. The incubation dream was also sought for non-therapeutic purposes. A man who lost his son "went to Asclepius and slept in the Abaton...and saw a dream."[128] In the dream, the god led him to the place where his son was (Stela II, no. 24). It is not only a sick person but a broken vessel too could benefit from an incubation dream (cf. Stela I, no. 10). Moreover, the practice of incubation sometimes occurred without a dream. Stela I, no. 20 reads: "Lyson of Hermione, a blind boy. While wide-awake (ὕπαρ) he had his eyes cured by one of the dogs in the Temple and went away healed." In some cases, the votive offerings were suggested or demanded by Asclepius in a vision, as in the story of Ambroisa (Stela I, no. 4), who was ordered to dedicate a silver pig in exchange for divine healing. These offerings, however, were usually made at the suggestion of priests, who would advise them as a means of winning divine favor or of showing gratitude for benefits already received. This is reminiscent of the Hittite votive stelae in which the king or the queen vows to offer a gift in exchange for healing.

As to the preparatory rituals, the Epidaurian inscriptions of cures do not provide many details. Most of the inscriptions do not even mention them. This could be for the same reason why so many ancient

[128] Edelstein and Edelstein, *Asclepius: A Collection and Interpretation of the Testimonies*, 234.

Near Eastern incubation texts either omit it completely or mention it only in passing: first, the focus of the inscriptions was on the effect, not on the process. Second, the process would be already well known to the reader, thus making it unnecessary to elaborate on it. But it is undoubted, judging from the temple buildings and the number of priests and temple-servants, that the incubation dream was preceded by complex rituals accompanied by rites and sacrifices and entailed considerable expenses to the patients. The story of a voiceless boy (Stela I, no. 5) is the only case where there is mention of these ceremonies: Παῖς ἄφωνος. | [οὗτος ἀφί]κετο εἰς τὸ ἱαρὸν ὑπὲρ φωνᾶς· ὡς δὲ προεθύσατο καὶ | [ἐπόησε τὰ] νομιζόμενα, ("A voiceless boy. He came as a suppliant to the Temple for his voice. When he had performed the preliminary sacrifices and fulfilled the usual rites…"). We have no knowledge, however, as to the specific sacrifices performed at Epidauros.

In sum, although most of the Epidaurian inscriptions of cures corroborate the traditional picture of the Greek incubation—private and therapeutic temple-sleep effecting instant healing, prepared by various rituals—as described in Aristophanes' *Plutus*, various deviations are attested as well. If we take into account the data from other temples and other cults, the number and the kind of deviations become greater. Incubation thus might be tried personally or by proxy in case of difficulties (not limited to the case of sickness), over one night or several nights, in any liminal place, with or without a dream. These "deviations" seem to bring the Greek incubation more in line with that of the ancient Near East, although the origin of the practice still remains unsolved.

5. Conclusion

The discussion of the ancient Near Eastern evidence for incubation has not only confirmed the pre-Hellenistic existence of the practice in the ancient world, but has also demonstrated various *avatars* that incubation could assume in different cultures within the ancient Near East. The fluidity characterizing the ancient Near Eastern practice of incubation will exert a significant influence on the discussion of its literary use as type-scene in the remainder of this book. The practice of incubation in Syria-Palestine has been deliberately neglected thus far, partly because there is no definite non-literary evidence for the practice in pre-Hellenistic Syria-Palestine. What little evidence we have is dubious or gives no helpful details about the practice. It has been suggested, for example, that the temple of Hathor at Serabit al Ḥadim in Sinai was a place where incubation may have been practiced.[129] Especially, Grimme sought to read the sense of incubation into the verb *n-m* "he slumbered" in the enigmatic proto-Sinaitic inscription from Serabit al Ḥadim. But his proposal has not been widely accepted. It has also been suggested that a 5th century B.C.E. Aramaic ostracon, discovered in Elephantine, makes allusion to an oneiric presage which is probably incubated.[130] The writer, probably the head of a family, was detained away from home and, fearing that he would be further delayed in his return, wrote to his wife:[131] כען הלו חלמ1 חזית ומן עדנא הו אנה חמם שׂגא <א>תחזי חזו מלוהי שׂלמ "Now, behold, I saw a dream, and from that time on, I was very feverish. Then I saw a vision. Its words: 'Peace!' "[132] But nothing in the text suggests that the dream or the vision was incubated. But the silence in the data does not warrant the conclusion that the practice of incubation was unknown in Syria-Palestine. Rather, considering the fact that Syria-Palestine was in constant cultural interactions with her neighboring cultures, it stands to reason to assume that the concept of seeking a response from the deity was also known in that part of the ancient Near East, although we do not know any details as to the particular form it might have taken. The following literary analysis of the incubation type-scene occurring in three Northwest-Semitic texts is informed by the assumption that the people in Ugarit and ancient Israel were familiar with the concept of incubation as were other peoples in the ancient Near East.[133]

---

[129] Contenau, *La divination chez les Assyriens et les Babyloniens. Avec 13 figures, 1 carte et 8 gravures hors texte*, 175; W. M. Flinders Petrie, *Personal Religion in Egypt Before Christianity*, Harper's Library of Living Thought (London: Harper & Brothers, 1912), 27; Foucart, "Dream and Sleep (Egypt)," 35.

[130] Husser, *Dreams and Dream Narratives in the Biblical World*, 71.

[131] Baruch A. Levine, "An Aramaic Dream Report From Elephantine," in *Archival Documents from the Biblical World*, vol. III of *COS*, ed. William W. Hallo and K. Lawson Younger Jr. (Leiden: Brill, 2002), 218.

[132] H. Donner and W. Röllig, *Kanaanäische und aramäische Inschriften*, vol. 1 (Wiesbaden: Harrassowitz Verlag, 2002), 65, no. 270.

[133] Even if we assume, for instance, that incubation was no longer an actual practice in the first millennium Israel, the same point may stand, for understanding *realia* is not a necessary assumption for the literary convention to work. In this regard, this literary approach may give a powerful model for how authors and readers can share *vivid* understanding of *fictitious* practices.

CHAPTER THREE

THE INCUBATION TYPE-SCENE: A WORKING DEFINITION

In his seminal work *Die typischen Scenen bei Homer* (1933), Walter Arend observed that certain narrative and descriptive sections in the Homeric epics, sections that he called "typical scenes," recur again and again, and are narrated each time in identical or nearly identical language. He also noted that in each of its occurrence the type-scene is adapted by the poet to fit its particular context, through elaboration, curtailment, negation and omission.[1] About a half century later (1981), Robert Alter applied the principle of Homeric composition as articulated by Arend to certain recurring narrative sections in the Hebrew Bible to underscore the artistic acumen/originality of the biblical narrators in adapting conventional material to fit their narratological purposes.[2] Although they were dealing with different genres of composition, Arend and Alter share an interest in how the poet/narrator uses traditional conventions to invoke meanings inherited from the whole tradition of poetry/narrative,[3] and adapts them to serve a particular poetic/narrative purpose.

Although their basic findings about type-scenes are unassailable, their "original versus derivational," "essential versus accidental," or "standard (*Schema*) versus variation (Veränderung)" approach to different instances of the same type-scene is less convincing in my opinion, because it needlessly creates the problem of definition: namely,

---

[1] Walter Arend, *Die typischen Scenen bei Homer*, Problemata 7 (Berlin: Weidmannsche Buchhandlung, 1933). Cf. Bernard Fenik, *Typical Battle Scenes in the Iliad: Studies in the Narrative Techniques of Homeric Battle Description*, Hermes 21 (Wiesbaden: Franz Steiner Verlag GmbH, 1968), 1; Steve Reece, *The Stranger's Welcome: Oral Theory and the Aesthetics of the Homeric Hospitality Scene*, Michigan Monographs in Classical Antiquity (Ann Arbor, MI: University of Michigan Press, 1993), 2.

[2] Robert Alter, "Biblical Type-Scenes and the Uses of Convention," *CI* 5 (1978): 355–68; Robert Alter, *The Art of Biblical Narrative* (New York: Basic Books, 1981), 47–62; "How Convention Helps Us Read: The Case of the Bible's Annunciation Type-Scene," *Proof* 3 (1983): 115–30.

[3] For the metonymic use of convention, see John M. Foley, *Immanent Art: From Structure to Meaning in Traditional Oral Epic* (Bloomington, IN: Indiana University Press, 1991), 7–10; Mark W. Edwards, "Homer and Oral Tradition: The Type-Scene," *Oral Tradition* 7 (1992): 289.

what defines the "standard" type-scene? This question becomes even more acute, when we consider the limited corpus available to us to recover the ancient conventions. As already indicated in chapter one, I believe that the understanding of type-scene first proposed by Nagler provides a better tool for dealing with various examples of the same type-scene without creating the problem of definition. Nagler substitutes the standard-variation approach in favor of the "spontaneity and tradition" approach, according to which all examples of a type-scene are simultaneously both spontaneous and traditional, in the sense that they are spontaneously generated by the pressure of a certain poetic/narrative moment, but are nonetheless generated not *ex nihilo*, but from a pre-verbal traditional *Gestalt*. According to Nagler, the type-scene is defined and recognized on the principle of 'family resemblance' among different examples of the incubation type-scene, and not by the putative "standard" of the type-scene.

In this chapter, various motifs comprising the incubation type-scene will be enumerated and discussed in detail, not because they constitute essential components of the incubation type-scene, but because they represent a pool of motifs, out of which the author may pull any number of motifs so as to craft his own version of the incubation type-scene. Towards the end of this chapter, a heuristic definition of the incubation type-scene will be given as a way of giving more specificity to the abstract principle of 'family resemblance' for the recognition of the incubation type-scene in the ancient Near Eastern literature.

1. Previous Studies

Oppenheim's literary analysis of message dreams assumes that their literary pattern originated from the experience of incubation.[4] Oppenheim provides a few reasons for such an assumption. He explains, for instance, the towering size of the deity often reported in message dreams as a result of the setting of incubation: "The sleeper in the cella, lying at the feet of an image, conditioned by appropriate ritual

[4] Oppenheim states, "We would like to propose that the incubation dream, the dream experienced in a sanctuary or a sacred locality—whether the dream is sought or not—is to be considered the prototype of most of the dreams discussed so far" (A. Leo Oppenheim, *The Interpretation of Dreams in the Ancient Near East: With a Translation of an Assyrian Dream-Book*, TAPA 46 [Philadelphia, PA: American Philological Society, 1956], 190).

preparations which nourish his apprehensions and by reports which channel his imagination, distorts this image in his dream into towering size..."[5] Another reason is theological: "the pattern of incubation-dreams was considered both theologically acceptable and admissible" for the recording of divine messages.[6] Husser's objections that this suggestion of Oppenheim is "not easily verifiable"[7] does not negate the similarity between Oppenheim's literary pattern of message dreams and the practice of incubation attested to in the ancient Near East and in Greece.

The literary pattern that Oppenheim recognizes in the ancient Near Eastern message dreams is a frame structure. The content of the dream is preceded by a description of the setting of the dream, such as when, where and under what circumstances the dream was experienced and is followed by the final part of the frame, which may include a mention of the end of the dream, the reaction of the dreamer or the actual fulfillment of the prediction or promise contained in the dream.[8] This frame structure seems to nicely fit in with the actual procedure of incubation, which also has a tripartite structure.[9]

A few more attempts at the literary analysis of incubation have been made since Oppenheim. The studies by Robert K. Gnuse and Annette von Zgoll, however, are heavily influenced by Oppenheim's pioneering work. In his 1980 doctoral dissertation Gnuse examined 1 Samuel 3 from the perspective of the various elements of Oppenheim's message dream.[10] Although Gnuse is dubious about seeing 1 Samuel 3 as an incubation scene, because of the absence of what he sees as essential

---

[5] Ibid.

[6] Ibid.

[7] Jean-Marie Husser, *Dreams and Dream Narratives in the Biblical World*, BS 63 (Sheffield: Sheffield Academic Press, 1999), 46.

[8] Oppenheim, *The Interpretation of Dreams in the Ancient Near East: With a Translation of an Assyrian Dream-Book*, 187.

[9] Richard E. Averbeck applies the entry-act-exit structure to the practice of incubation attested in the first Cylinder of Gudea. The tripartite structure, entry-act-exit, was originally devised by anthropologists such as Henry Hubert and Marcel Mauss to apply to the ritual of sacrifice (cf. Henri Hubert, *Sacrifice: Its Nature and Function* [Chicago: University of Chicago Press, 1964]). Averbeck finds the tripartite structure useful in explaining the ritual of incubation also (Richard E. Averbeck, *Preliminary Study of Ritual and Structure in the Cylinders of Gudea* [Ann Arbor, MI: University Microfilms International, 1988], 510).

[10] Robert K. Gnuse, "The Dream Theophany of Samuel: Its Structure in Relation to Ancient Near Eastern Dreams and Its Theological Significance" (Ph.D. diss., Nashville, TN: Vanderbilt University, 1980), 199–216.

to the scene, namely, Samuel's intention to have an oneiric revelation (note that there is no mention of preparatory rituals and also that Samuel was surprised at the theophany),[11] his analysis of 1 Samuel 3 as a message dream provides many helpful insights into various motifs comprising the incubation type-scene. Zgoll, in his 2002 article on Mesopotamian incubation, examines both literary and ritual texts and discusses various components that occur in the Mesopotamian practice of incubation.[12] He also identifies the linguistic formula, both Sumerian and Akkadian, whose presence would strongly suggest the presence of the religious practice in a given text. Zgoll's description of various components of the Mesopotamian incubation, however, is not intended to explain the literary function of those components in an incubation scene nor in a literary work in which the incubation scene occurs.

2. The Structure of an Incubation Type-Scene: Component Motifs

Although there is no fixed sequence of motifs in an incubation type-scene, it may show a tripartite structure roughly corresponding to the actual experience of incubation.[13] The first section may include the description of hero-incubant's predicament, time and location of the incubation, and various ritual observances that may or may not be intended to provoke a dream. These preparatory ritual observances may include prayers, weeping, fasting, feasting, libation, incense, animal sacrifice, silence, putting on a special garment, going naked, suspension of daily routine, etc.[14] The ensuing section culminates in the motif of theophany, the divine appearance to an incubant. This theophany may be oneiric, in which case the text registers indications of sleep. Much of the epiphany scene is occupied by the divine message,

[11] Ibid., 216–212.

[12] The full list of the components include a special place, a special time, preparatory rituals (such as incense, animal sacrifice, bread offering, libation, weeping, prayer, purification), lying down in a special bed in a special posture, the position of head, touching, effect on the incubant (Annette von Zgoll, "Die Welt im Schlaf sehen: Inkubation von Träumen im antiken Mesopotamien," *WO* 32 [2002]: 74–101).

[13] Cf. Averbeck, *Preliminary Study of Ritual and Structure in the Cylinders of Gudea*, 506–50.

[14] See 1.2 in chapter two. For the transliteration, translation and philological notes of this text see S. A. L. Butler, *Mesopotamian Conceptions of Dreams and Dream Rituals*, AOAT 258 (Münster: Ugarit-Verlag, 1988), 349–77.

but there may be a dialogue between the incubant and the deity, or allusions to the visual aspects of the epiphany. The divine messages normally address the problem that brought the incubant to the temple. The final section of the tripartite structure may contain the formal conclusion of the dream ("waking motif"), some literary devices confirming the verity of the divine message in dreams, allusions to the change in the hero's physical or mental state, the fulfillment of the divine promise, the carrying out of the instructions given by the deity, the hero's thanksgiving or oath-fulfilling, etc.

Before discussing these various motifs of the incubation type-scene in detail, one caveat needs to be made. The motifs that will be discussed below under each section of the tripartite structure are transferable from one section to another, namely, they are not fixed in their "original" section. They may occur in any section of the tripartite structure. This is determined by the poetic/narrative context in which the type-scene finds itself. Thus for instance, the mention of time may occur in the epiphany section instead of the introduction section. Also, sacrifice may occur in the conclusion section after the epiphany section. This further reaffirms the argument of this book that motifs of a type-scene may be arranged in any way demanded by the pressure of the poetic/narrative moment.

2.1 *Introduction: Preparation before Epiphany*

2.1.1 *Predicament of a Proponent*

The predicament theme provides an answer as to why one resorts to incubation. In contrast to the Greek incubation, specialized as a healing cult, the reasons for incubation in the ancient Near East were many and variegated. Foreign invasions sent Assurbanipal and Sethos to the temples for an oneiric dream,[15] while Naram-Sin wanted to secure, through incubation, Ishtar's protection before he went on a military campaign.[16] Gudea and Nabonidus availed themselves of incubation in order to solve the enigma of the dream that they had had previously.[17] If Finkel's interpretation is correct, Kurigalzu, the Kassite king, slept

[15] See 1.6 and 3.2 in chapter two.
[16] See 2.1 in chapter two.
[17] See 1.1 and 1.7 in chapter two.

in the temple to find out why his wife was barren.[18] Paškuwatti also underwent the rituals of incubation in order to cure sexual impotence.[19] Moreover, one could appeal to incubation even about his or her missing child.[20] All this seems to suggest that the predicament theme plays a large role in the incubation type-scene and it may be registered in the text as various motifs relating to any human problem, including, but not limited to, illness. The predicament theme may be actualized as an independent motif, but it can simply be alluded to in the prayers of the incubant,[21] or in any other motif comprising the incubation type-scene.

2.1.2 *Time*

The time motif addresses the issue as to when the incubational theophany took place. A deity normally visits an incubant during the night. Ancient Near Eastern dream-reports do not appear to be concerned with the exact hour of the night when the deity makes an appearance. In most of the Neo-Assyrian dream-reports, it is simply stated that the future-revealing dreams occurred in the middle of the night (*ina šat mûši*).[22] When Assurbanipal's *šabrû*-priest slept in a temple on behalf of his king, the divine message came "in the middle of the night."[23] A specific hour of night, however, may be designated as the time of theophany. The Greek dream-reports, for instance, specify early morning hours as the propitious time for the divine-human encounter.[24] The

[18] See 1.3 in chapter two.

[19] See 2.4 in chapter two.

[20] See my discussion on ARM X 100 and the Epidaurian incubation texts in chapter two (sections 1.5 and 4).

[21] The case in point is the second incubation of Gudea. In his prayer to Ningirsu, Gudea clearly indicates his intention to build a temple and also his need for a sign (*giškim*, Gudea Cylinder A. 8:19) as well as a precise plan of the building. The purpose of the second incubation, i.e. the problem of Gudea, had not been clearly stated in the text up to this point.

[22] Oppenheim, *The Interpretation of Dreams in the Ancient Near East: With a Translation of an Assyrian Dream-Book*, 241.

[23] Cf. Zgoll, "Die Welt im Schlaf sehen: Inkubation von Träumen im antiken Mesopotamien," 89; Oppenheim, *The Interpretation of Dreams in the Ancient Near East: With a Translation of an Assyrian Dream-Book*, 249, Text No. 10.

[24] The pertinent evidence has been extensively discussed by J. B. Stearns, *Studies of the Dream as a Technical Device in Latin Epic and Drama* (Lancaster, PA: Lancaster Press, 1927), 51ff. Cf. Gnuse, "The Dream Theophany of Samuel: Its Structure in Relation to Ancient Near Eastern Dreams and Its Theological Significance," 204; Oppenheim, *The Interpretation of Dreams in the Ancient Near East: With a Translation of an Assyrian Dream-Book*, 240–41.

Babylonian righteous sufferer, Shubshi-meshre-Shakkan, also encounters a divine apparition in a dream in the morning hours (MÁŠ.GE$_6$ *mu-na-at-tú*).[25] The people of Mari judged the dream of the first half of the night as being unimportant, while the dream of the second half of the night can carry future-revealing messages.[26] Also the phrase "before the lamp of God went out" in 1 Samuel 3:3 may also refer to "a time just before the dawn when oil was almost consumed in the lamp."[27] Genesis 15:11, on the other hand, specifies young night ("After the sun went down") as the time when the subsequent theophany occurred. The dream-report of Thutmosis IV seems to belabor the point that the dream theophany occurred at noon.[28] Finally, it should be noted that the desired dream may not come for several days, in which case the incubation rituals may last over a number of days. Gudea's incubation and Paškuwatti's rituals are cases in point.[29]

All this concern with the time of incubational theophany, particularly, the nighttime, has to do with the concept of liminality. It was believed that night, which embodies liminality,[30] is the most propitious

25 The logogram of *munattu* in erim.huš = *anantu*, Tab. 2, line 263, gìr.babbar, shows that it was a temporal designation, denoting very early morning (Butler, *Mesopotamian Conceptions of Dreams and Dream Rituals*, 32; Cf. Oppenheim, *The Interpretation of Dreams in the Ancient Near East: With a Translation of an Assyrian Dream-Book*, 250. Here *munattu* is translated as "at dawn"). For the text of *ludlul bēl nēmeqi*, see W. G. Lambert, *Babylonian Wisdom Literature* (Oxford: Clarendon Press, 1960), 21–62; Benjamin R. Foster, *Before the Muses: An Anthology of Akkadian Literature* (Bethesda, MD: CDL Press, 2005), 306–23.

26 Jean-Marie Durand, *Archives épistolaires de Mari I/1*, ARM 26 (Paris: Recherches sur les civilisations, 1988), 456–57; Zgoll, "Die Welt im Schlaf sehen: Inkubation von Träumen im antiken Mesopotamien," 89.

27 Gnuse, "The Dream Theophany of Samuel: Its Structure in Relation to Ancient Near Eastern Dreams and Its Theological Significance," 205.

28 The reference to time is made twice in the account of Thutmosis IV's dream. The second reference to time is explicitly connected to the pharaoh's sleep: "Slumber and sleep overcame him at the moment when the sun was at the zenith" (Oppenheim, *The Interpretation of Dreams in the Ancient Near East: With a Translation of an Assyrian Dream-Book*, 251).

29 A passage from Plutarch provides a Classical example of a multiple day incubation: "Timarchus…greatly wished to know what was really meant by the Divine Sign [*daimonion* in Greek] of Socrates, and so…having taken no one but Cebes and myself [Simmias] into his plan, went down into the cave of Trophonius, after performing the usual rites of the oracle. Two nights and one day he remained below; and when most people had given him up, and his family was mourning for him, at early dawn he came up very radiant…" (Carl A. Meier, *Ancient Incubation and Modern Psychotherapy* [Evanston: Northwestern University Press, 1967], 102).

30 Cf. Francis Landy's explanation of Ruth 3: He compares Ruth's appearance at night to Boaz in the threshing floor to a theophanic event that occurred in liminal

time when the gods may manifest themselves to the human.[31] Night is the time that signifies threshold. Also in a similar vein, it may be argued that any reference to time in the incubation type-scene alludes to the liminal quality that informs the practice of incubation. In the practice of incubation, the concept of liminality operates in two additional aspects of space (a temple) and of consciousness (dream). If the night motif is a verbalization of the concept of liminality with regard to time, the temple motif embodies spatial liminality, and the dream motif, the liminality of consciousness.[32]

2.1.3 *Place*

The incubation type-scene may contain information about the place of incubation. For the Greeks, incubation is a "place-event." Classical incubation is all about sleeping in a particular place. If one wants to be healed by Asclepius, the patient must bring his wounded body to him at his shrine.[33] Although it is not limited to the temples of a few deities, the incubation attested to in ancient Near Eastern texts also concerns itself with a holy place where the divine and human encounter is most likely to occur. Unlike in Greece, in ancient Near East incubation was practiced in various temples,[34] such as temple of Ningirsu (cf. the Cylinders of Gudea), Esabad (cf. *ROP*), temple of Marduk at Babylon (cf. the Kurigalzu text),[35] *E-gal-maḫ* (cf. the Weidner Chronicle), temple of Ishtar (cf. the Rassam Cylinder), temple of Nanshe (cf. the Plow of Ox), temple of Itūr-Mer (cf. ARM X 10), etc. Sometimes, a particular area within a temple was indicated as the location relating to the practice of incubation: Šugalam and Ubšukinna in the temple of Ningirsu, E-KUR in the temple of Marduk, and a roof area in the temple of Esabad (cf. Abaton in the temple of Asclepius).[36]

---

time and space. Francis Landy, "Ruth and the Romance of Realism, or Deconstructing History," *JAAR* 62 (1994): 290.

[31] Ann Jeffers, *Magic and Divination in Ancient Palestine and Syria*, SHCANE 8 (Leiden: Brill, 1996), 176.

[32] For details, see below.

[33] Patton, "A Great and Strange Correction: Intentionality, Locality, and Epiphany in the Category of Dream Incubation," 203–4.

[34] Zgoll, "Die Welt im Schlaf sehen: Inkubation von Träumen im antiken Mesopotamien," 87.

[35] It is mentioned in the Kurigalzu text that he fell asleep on a *majjaltu*. *Majjaltu* does not refer to an ordinary bed that could be denoted by *eršu*. It denotes a resting place for the gods, such as the god Dumuzi (Zgoll, "Die Welt im Schlaf sehen: Inkubation von Träumen im antiken Mesopotamien," 93).

[36] For more examples of the incubation space within a temple, see Ibid.

The place of incubation, however, does not have to be limited to a temple and its inner rooms. As historians of religion have noted, it could take place in any place whose liminality may be recognized by local traditions, such as mountains (cf. Gilgamesh), caves, tombs (cf. Isaiah 65:4), shrines (cf. 1 Kings 3), royal palaces (cf. Ashurnasirpal II's palace in Balawat),[37] or even private residences (cf. Paškuwatti's incubation for impotency). In a similar vein, it can be noted that Thutmosis IV had a dream revelation "in the shadow of the Sphinx."[38] In general, the concern about the place in the practice of incubation was to establish liminality with regard to space. The poet/narrator using the convention of the incubation type-scene, however, would incorporate this "place" motif into his version of the type-scene as he deems appropriate to the poetic/narrative purpose.

2.1.4 *Preparatory Ritual Observances*

The incubational theophany was prepared for by various ritual acts, which include purification (cf. Naram-Sin legend and Paškuwatti's ritual), animal sacrifice (Gudea), grain-offering (cf. *ROP*), libation (cf. *ROP*), incense,[39] crying in tears,[40] prayers,[41] oaths, fasting, silence,

[37] Ashurnasirpal II constructed a temple to Mamu, a dream god, within his palace (cf. BM 90980, obverse line 21 to reverse line 2). So speculations have been made that the Assyrian king slept in this temple built within his palace precincts "on his first night out of Nineveh…in order to receive a dream concerning the future campaign" (D. Oates, "Balawat [Imgur Enlil]: The Site and Its Buildings," *Iraq* 36, no. 173–178 [1974]: 175). However, difficult it may be to substantiate this with evidence, this nonetheless suggests the possibility of a royal palace being the location for incubation. See further 2.1.4 in chapter five.

[38] Oppenheim, *The Interpretation of Dreams in the Ancient Near East: With a Translation of an Assyrian Dream-Book*, 251, Text No. 15.

[39] Zgoll argues that incense offering is "besonders typisch für die Vorbereitungen zur Gottes-bebegnung im Traum" (Zgoll, "Die Welt im Schlaf sehen: Inkubation von Träumen im antiken Mesopotamien," 89). She also notes that the Akkadian *maššakkum* or *muššakum*, which refers to a substance that gives off a sweet smell when burned, was used in the context of various incubations. Atra-ḫasis, for example, offers it to the god Enki (Ibid.).

[40] In addition to various offerings to God, several incubation scenes mention the incubant crying in tears (Assurbanipal and Naram-Sin). The incubant's tears demonstrated his or her genuine need for divine protection and aid, and urge the god for a prompt intervention. Oppenheim suggests that crying may be a ritual required of those seeking a dream visitation (Oppenheim, *The Interpretation of Dreams in the Ancient Near East: With a Translation of an Assyrian Dream-Book*, 200). For a different view on the relation between weeping and incubation, see Choon Leong Seow, "The Syro-Palestinian Context of Solomon's Dream," *HTR* 77 (1984): 147, footnote 24.

[41] Prayer distinguishes itself from weeping in that it is a verbal expression of the incubant's desire for the encounter with a god. Usually it comes in the incubation

drawing a circle on the ground (cf. *ROP* and Gilgamesh),[42] putting on a special clothing,[43] going naked,[44] suspending daily routine (cf. Gudea), etc. It stands to reason to assume that the poet/narrator would turn some of these preparatory rituals into literary motifs comprising the first part of the tripartite incubation type-scene and arrange them to achieve his literary purpose. If the "predicament" theme explains the proponent's motivation for incubation, these preparatory acts underscore his or her intentionality in the provocation of a dream revelation. In other words, the "pre-verbal" concept of intentionality is "verbalized" in various motifs describing the preparatory rituals practiced to induce a divine revelation.

As already noted while discussing *Rituals to Obtain a Purussû* there seems to have been no one standard ritual for inducing a revelatory dream.[45] Rituals appear to have been adjusted according to various

---

scene right before the incubant lies down to sleep (Zgoll, "Die Welt im Schlaf sehen: Inkubation von Träumen im antiken Mesopotamien," 92). The problems of the incubant may be revealed here for the first time in prayer. Also vows may be made in prayers. It is incumbent on the incubant to fulfill the vow he has made once his wish is granted in a dream. The unfulfilled vow may lead to complications in the plot of the story. See further 2.3.2 in chapter five.

[42] When Gilgamesh wanted to induce a dream-vision, Enkidu drew a magic circle within which Gilgamesh sat "with his chin on his knees," whereupon he experienced an apocalyptic dream of the Netherworld (A. R. George, *The Babylonian Gilgamesh Epic: Introduction, Critical Edition, and Cuneiform Texts* [Oxford: Oxford University Press, 2003], 67). *Rituals to Obtain Purussû* also mentions the drawing of a magic circle as part of the ritual for incubation (see 1.2 in chapter two). Interestingly, there seems to be some connection between flour-offering and a magic circle. Gilgamesh made the offerings of *maṣḫatu*-flour before lying down in a circle drawn by Enkidu. *ROP* prescribes the drawing of a circle with pure water, probably to demarcate a holy place and the setting out of scented flour in the same context. Another ritual text from Mesopotamia (for the edition see Butler, *Mesopotamian Conceptions of Dreams and Dream Rituals*, 401–5) prescribes the drawing of a *flour-circle* around a tomb where a substitute figurine was buried. Reiner also informs us of a Mesopotamian herbalist's practice of drawing a circle with flour for magical effect (Erica Reiner, *Astral Magic in Babylonia*, TAPA 85 [Philadelphia, PA: American Philosophical Society, 1995], 37–39).

[43] Ernst L. Ehrlich, *Der Traum im Alten Testament*, BZAW 73 (Berlin: Töpelmann, 1953), 14–15; Frances L. Flannery-Dailey, "Standing at the Heads of Dreamers: A Study of Dreams in Antiquity Second Temple Period" (Ph.D. diss., University of Iowa, 2000), 40.

[44] An incubant who sought Trophonius's apparition lay down half-naked like a child in swaddling clothes (Meier, *Ancient Incubation and Modern Psychotherapy*, 100). Also the depiction of the naked Sumerian priests in Gudea Stela ST 4–5 pouring a liquid before the gods provides circumstantial evidence for nakedness as a possible mode of approaching the gods (cf. Claudia E. Suter, *Gudea's Temple Building: The Representation of an Early Mesopotamian Ruler in Text and Image*, Cuneiform Monographs 17 [Groningen: Styx Publications, 2000], 196).

[45] Butler, *Mesopotamian Conceptions of Dreams and Dream Rituals*, 22–223.

factors including the kind of problem, the kind of deity invoked, etc. When incorporated into the incubation type-scene in a given literary work, this motif may or may not show explicit connection to the ensuing theophany. Part of the reason lies in the fact that the incubation as a literary motif is not identical to the practice of incubation. In other words, the observation that the poet/narrator employs the incubation as a type-scene in a given work does not translate into the claim that the proponent depicted in that type-scene is actually practicing incubation in the text. But the presence of these motifs actualizing the concept of intentionality in the incubation type-scene would be enough for the readers, who were well acquainted with the conventions, to fill in the "missing link."

2.2 *Epiphany*

Incubation reaches its highest point in the long-awaited appearance of a deity or his substitute. Patton characterizes the epiphany as "the fulcrum of all ritual orientation that has preceded it, and all that will ensue afterward."[46] The appearance of a deity or its substitute, human or bestial, is the culmination of the process, without which the incubation dream is not efficacious. Healing is not the only thing a god brings out in dreams. His oneiric apparition begets children, shows the plan of a building, resolves the enigma of a symbolic dream, comforts a king distressed over a crisis in his kingdom, and even informs the whereabouts of a lost child. The problems posed in the motifs actualizing the concept of predicament find their answer in the "theophany" motif. In the following sections, we will examine some literary conventions that apply to the theophany motif in the ancient Near Eastern texts.

2.2.1 *Indication of Sleep*

It is customary to indicate that the incubant is asleep before the oneiric theophany is described.[47] For instance, "Slumber and sleep overcame" Thutmosis IV who then met with a god in a dream.[48] Likewise, "Sleep

---

[46] Patton, "A Great and Strange Correction: Intentionality, Locality, and Epiphany in the Category of Dream Incubation," 207.

[47] Gnuse, "The Dream Theophany of Samuel: Its Structure in Relation to Ancient Near Eastern Dreams and Its Theological Significance," 203.

[48] Oppenheim, *The Interpretation of Dreams in the Ancient Near East: With a Translation of an Assyrian Dream-Book*, 251, text no. 15.

that spills over people fell upon" Gilgamesh.[49] In the Cylinders of Gudea, Gudea is said to be lying down (nú) when Ningirsu stepped up to him at his head.[50] The Kurigalzu text also notes that Kurigalzu "fell asleep (*ṣalālu*) on the couch."[51] A *šabrû*-priest "lay down" (*itūlu*) on behalf of Assurbanipal for a mantic dream. Nabonidus "lay down" (*nâlu*) to see the goddess Gula. This indication of sleep before oneiric theophany is so prevalent that Zgoll considers it as part of a Mesopotamian idiom for incubation: Sumerian, *ma-mu*$_2$*-de*$_3$ *ba-nu*$_2$ "to lie down for a dream"; Akkadian, *utūl-ma inattal šutta* "he laid down to see a dream."[52] The same appears to have been true of the Hittite incubation. According to Alice Mouton, *šuppa/šuppaya šeš-* "to sleep in a holy place/manner" serves as an idiom for the Hittite incubation.[53]

Incubation texts may specify a particular way of lying down. Gilgamesh is said to have "rested his chin on his knees" as he slept to have a dream. Similarly, Assurbanipal is reported to have come to the temple of Ishtar and crouched down at her feet (*akmis šapalša*). This crouched position may reflect the apprehensions of the incubant, but it is more likely that it reflects the fact that the incubant is lying at the feet of divine images, embracing the images of the gods.[54]

2.2.2 *Theophany*

Oppenheim points to the fact that the incubant, generally speaking, is passive in his experience of dream theophany.[55] Gnuse in agreement observes, "In all ancient Near Eastern message dreams the deity

[49] George, *The Babylonian Gilgamesh Epic: Introduction, Critical Edition, and Cuneiform Texts*, 589.

[50] Averbeck, *Preliminary Study of Ritual and Structure in the Cylinders of Gudea*, 625.

[51] Irving L. Finkel, "The Dream of Kurigalzu and the Tablet of Sins," *AnSt* 33 (1983): 78.

[52] Zgoll, "Die Welt im Schlaf sehen: Inkubation von Träumen im antiken Mesopotamien," 80–84.

[53] Alice Mouton, "Usages privés et publics de l'incubation d'après les textes hittites," *JANER* 3 (2003): 73–91.

[54] Virgil reports that Hecuba and his daughter, when they saw the enemies entering the city, gathered at the temples awaiting their destiny, praying to the gods and crouched around the ancient altar, embracing the images of the gods (Andreola F. Rossi, "Battle-Scenes in Virgil: An Analysis of Narrative Techniques" [Harvard University, 1997], 193). Modern pilgrims to incubation temples also curl around the pillars of the temple in order to have a dream (Patton, "A Great and Strange Correction: Intentionality, Locality, and Epiphany in the Category of Dream Incubation," 196).

[55] Oppenheim, *The Interpretation of Dreams in the Ancient Near East: With a Translation of an Assyrian Dream-Book*, 188.

initiates the theophany and addresses the human recipient."[56] This passivity is indicated, first, by the startling shock that incubants often express in encountering a deity in a dream. The ancient Near Eastern idiom "to see (in) a dream" describes a sense of suddenness that the incubant may have felt at the first sight or voice of the god.[57] In the account of Thutmosis IV's dream, for instance, we are told that the pharaoh "found" a god speaking to him. The waking motif within a dream is also to be understood to underscore such startling shock of the dreamer. This waking motif in the middle of a dream is well attested to in Classical sources. There the waking of the sleeping person is always done with the words, "Are you asleep, PN?"[58] When the *šabrû*-priest of Ishtar went to bed and had a dream, he woke up with a start as Ishtar made him see a nocturnal vision. 1 Samuel 3:4–10, where Samuel was called three times with such intensity that he woke up each time, may be understood in a similar vein. Yahweh did not call Samuel's name to wake him up for a message, but the waking up is better understood as Samuel's reaction to Yahweh's voice. The note in verse 1 that the vision of Yahweh was rare in those days would account for a sense of surprise that Samuel must have felt at the divine voice that he had just heard.[59]

The passivity of the dreamer is also indicated by the use of verbs meaning "to come" or "to go" to describe the (dis)appearance of a

---

[56] Gnuse, "The Dream Theophany of Samuel: Its Structure in Relation to Ancient Near Eastern Dreams and Its Theological Significance," 206.

[57] Eric R. Dodds, *The Greeks and the Irrational*, Sather Classical Lectures 25 (Berkeley: University of California Press, 1964), 105.

[58] Oppenheim, *The Interpretation of Dreams in the Ancient Near East: With a Translation of an Assyrian Dream-Book*, 189.

[59] There are a few references to "touching" in the theophany scenes. In the second incubation of Gudea, the divine message is introduced as follows: "Thereafter, (Ningirsu) stepped up to the head of the one who was sleeping, briefly touching him (saying)" (Dietz O. Edzard, *Gudea and His Dynasty*, Royal Inscriptions of Mesopotamia: Early Periods [Toronto: University of Toronto Press, 1997], 74). The theophany of Dagan to Zunana seems to go out of its way to mention something about touching Zunana: "And Dagan, your lord, made me fall asleep. And nobody touched me" (Georges Dossin, *Correspondance Féminine*, ARM 10 [Paris: Geuthner, 1978], 151). Zgoll discusses this motif briefly in her study of the Mesopotamian incubation but remains dubious about seeing it as an independent motif in the incubation scene. Based on the fact that the two occurrences of the touching motif occur in a dream, I would suggest that the touching motif would play the same role as that of waking motif in a dream, namely, underscoring the vividness or the objectivity of the dream theophany (cf. Oppenheim, *The Interpretation of Dreams in the Ancient Near East: With a Translation of an Assyrian Dream-Book*, 191).

deity. When introducing the divine message, biblical dreams frequently use the technical phrase, "God came [בוא] to PN in a dream by night" (Genesis 20:3; 31:24; Numbers 22:20).[60] In the Memphis Stela which records the dream of Pharaoh Amenhotep II, the message of Amon is introduced by the clause "the majesty of his august god, Amon... came before his majesty (i.e. the Pharaoh) in a dream." In one of the dream reports of Assurbanipal, Ishtar is said to "enter (*erēbu*)" and "leave (*aṣû*)."[61] Also in Paškuwatti's ritual, the deity is said to "come" and sleep with the incubant. In Classical dream accounts, the dream comes as messages from the gods: the Greek verb used is ἐπισκοπεῖν "to visit." The person does not have the dream, but the dream visits the person, who "sees the god" in that dream.[62]

There is a visual aspect to the theophany motif. This is registered by the standard phrase meaning that a deity or its substitute "stood at the head" of a dreamer.[63] In the Stela of Vulture, we read "Eannatum lay down as an oneiromancer. His master followed behind him...to the sleeper at the head he stepped up."[64] In 1 Samuel 3:10, the Lord is reported to "come and *take a stand* and call" (וַיָּבֹא יְהוָה וַיִּתְיַצַּב וַיִּקְרָא). The Akkadian reports in similar contexts use the word *zâzu* to mean, "to take a stand." In the third dream of the righteous sufferer in *Ludlul bēl nēmeqi*, a young woman of shining countenance "entered and took a stand" (*i-ru-ba-am-ma i-ta*[*z-zi-iz*]).[65] The dream report of Nabonidus describes Bēl as stepping (*iz-ziz-ma*) into Nabonidus's side.[66] In the "Hunger Stela" Chnum is described by a royal dreamer as "standing

[60] Oppenheim, *The Interpretation of Dreams in the Ancient Near East: With a Translation of an Assyrian Dream-Book*, 188; Gnuse, "The Dream Theophany of Samuel: Its Structure in Relation to Ancient Near Eastern Dreams and Its Theological Significance," 206.

[61] Oppenheim, *The Interpretation of Dreams in the Ancient Near East: With a Translation of an Assyrian Dream-Book*, 188.

[62] Patton, "A Great and Strange Correction: Intentionality, Locality, and Epiphany in the Category of Dream Incubation," 206–7.

[63] Oppenheim argues that this standard phrase occurs in Sumerian, Akkadian, Hebrew and Greek dream-reports (Oppenheim, *The Interpretation of Dreams in the Ancient Near East: With a Translation of an Assyrian Dream-Book*, 189).

[64] Thorkild Jacobsen, "The Stele of the Vultures Col I-X," in *Kramer Anniversary Volume: Cuneiform Studies in Honor of Samuel Noah Kramer*, ed. Barry L. Eichler (Kevelaer: Butzon & Bercker, 1976), 253.

[65] This is Oppenheim's restoration. For a different reconstruction see Lambert, *Babylonian Wisdom Literature*, 50–51.

[66] Stephen Langdon, *Die neubabylonischen Königsinschriften* (Leipzig: J. C. Hinrichs, 1912), 278.

before me."[67] The vision of the dream figure is indicated by the term *epistánai kata* "to stand over the head (of a person)" in the Homeric epics (e.g. *Iliad* 24.683; *Odyssey* 20.32).[68] The visual aspect of theophany may also be registered by the towering size of the deity.[69] This is an essential feature of the dream of Gudea, in which he reports seeing a divine figure reaching from earth to heaven. In his dream, Pharaoh Merenptah saw "as if a statue of Ptah were standing before Pharaoh. He was like the height of [x-cubits]." Here the context requires the assumption that the deity was of extraordinary size.[70] Also in *Ludlul bēl nēmeqi*, the size of the apparition is noted: "(In a) dream as well as (in a) vision at dawn it was shown (?) (MAŠ.GE$_6$ *mu-na-at-tú*). A man (*iš-ta-nu eṭ-lu*), surpassing in size, of glorious form, beautifully (?) clad..."[71] Dodds observes that the anonymous "tall man" appears in Greek dreams.[72] Oppenheim attributes this optical aspect in theophany to the situation of incubation, in which the sleeper lay at the feet of an image in the cella.[73]

2.2.3 *Divine Message/Divine-Human Dialogue*

The divine message in a dream is introduced by an exclamation, an imperative, or a question.[74] Nanshe begins her interpretation of Gudea's dream by addressing "My Shepherd." The gods (DINGIR^{meš}) who appear in Naram-Sin's incubation dream also open with the vocative "Naram-Sin." In Samuel's case, it is also the word of address, "Samuel, Samuel," that begins the divine message (cf. 1 Samuel 3:10). The message of Ishtar to Assurbanipal, on the other hand, begins with an imperative, "Do not fear." Abraham is told, "Fear not" in Genesis 15:1. Gnuse notes that biblical dreams frequently begin with a particle

67 Oppenheim, *The Interpretation of Dreams in the Ancient Near East: With a Translation of an Assyrian Dream-Book*, 251.

68 Ibid., 189.

69 Ibid.

70 Ibid.

71 Ibid.

72 Dodds, *The Greeks and the Irrational*, 109.

73 Oppeneheim points out to the fact that the sleeper, "conditioned by ritual preparations and reports that channel his imagination, distorts this image in his dream into towering size." Oppenheim, *The Interpretation of Dreams in the Ancient Near East: With a Translation of an Assyrian Dream-Book*, 190.

74 Gnuse, "The Dream Theophany of Samuel: Its Structure in Relation to Ancient Near Eastern Dreams and Its Theological Significance," 208.

hinnēh "behold."[75] A rhetorical question may introduce the theophany. Ishtar appears in a dream and says to Hattushili, "Shall I abandon you to a (hostile) deity? Be not afraid!"[76] The question does not have to be rhetorical. Nebuchadnezzar said to Nabonidus in a dream, "What kind of good is this that you see?" Solomon was asked in a dream that followed after he had offered a thousand burnt offerings, "Ask! What shall I give you?"

Often such questions initiate the dialogue between a deity and a man so that the whole divine message is styled as a conversation between a man and a god.[77] When Marduk asked Nabonidus in a dream to rebuild the temple É. ḪÚL. ḪÚL, the latter said in reply, "The *Umman-manda* are laying siege to the very temple which you have ordered to (re)build and their armed might is very strong."[78] The *šabrû*-priest had a dream in which Assurbanipal was engaged in a pious dialogue with Ishtar.[79] Naram-Sin also appears to have conversed with the gods, although the broken state of the tablet does not provide us the details. Hatushili responds twice to lady Danu-Hepa, "I have already before made a golden *zaḫum*-ewer for the Weather-god," and "Why did you not give the *ḫuḫupal*-instruments.... to the Weather god?"[80] One of the Mari letters (ARM X 100) preserves a short dialogue between Zunana and Dagan about Zunana's missing child.[81] The most famous biblical example of the divine-human dialogue in a dream occurs in 1 Kings 3:5–15, where God's initial question "Ask! What shall I give?"

---

[75] Ibid., 209.

[76] Oppenheim, *The Interpretation of Dreams in the Ancient Near East: With a Translation of an Assyrian Dream-Book*, 254.

[77] Oppenheim, followed by Gnuse, notes that dialogue occurs only rarely in theophanic dreams (Oppenheim, *The Interpretation of Dreams in the Ancient Near East: With a Translation of an Assyrian Dream-Book*, 191; Robert K. Gnuse, *Dreams and Dream Report in the Writings of Josephus: A Traditio-Historical Analysis* [Leiden: Brill, 1996], 50).

[78] Oppenheim, *The Interpretation of Dreams in the Ancient Near East: With a Translation of an Assyrian Dream-Book*, 250. Another instance of a divine-human dialogue occurs with Nabonidus. When Nebuchadnezzar asks about the symbolic dream he has had, Nabonidus says in reply, "In my dream I saw with joy the Great Star, the moon and the planet Jupiter high up in the sky and it (the Great Star) called me by my name [ ]" (Ibid.).

[79] Ibid., 249.

[80] Ibid., 255. Cf. Gnuse, "The Dream Theophany of Samuel: Its Structure in Relation to Ancient Near Eastern Dreams and Its Theological Significance," 214.

[81] Wolfgang Heimpel, *Letters to the King of Mari* (Winona Lake, IN: Eisenbrauns, 2003), 265.

brings out a long answer from Solomon.[82] Even Asclepius sometimes engages in a dialogue with his patients. A certain Plemon, being forbidden by Asclepius to drink water, replied, "What would you have prescribed for a cow?" It is noteworthy that a certain Plutarchus who when ordered by Asclepius to eat pork asked, "What would you have prescribed for a Jew?"[83] Asclepius reacted amiably to these waggish objections and altered the treatment accordingly.

The motif of divine message may sometimes provide an instant solution to the problem in question. The miracle stories inscribed near the gate of the temple of Asclepius bear witness to many occasions of instant healings by the deity. Gudea's apprehensions about his enigmatic dream are resolved by the interpretation that Nanshe gives him in an oneiric theophany. Similarly when Nabonidus was worried about the two stars that were approaching each other in a dream, the apparition of the god Bēl assured him that there was nothing ominous about the phenomenon.[84] On the other hand, instead of providing instant relief or solution, a deity may declare something that he will do on behalf of the incubant (a promise). In most of these cases, the fulfillment of the divine promise is registered later in the text. For instance, when Sennacherib invaded Egypt with his vast army, Sethos entered the sanctuary in distress and fell asleep there. The god appeared to him, promising that he would send him help. Later the god made good on his words by sending a multitude of field-mice that devoured the quivers and bowstrings of the enemy and ate the thongs with which they bound their shields (Herodotus, *The Histories* 2.139). Ishtar declares to Assurbanipal's entire army, "I shall go in front of Assurbanipal, the king whom I have created myself." Thutmosis IV receives a divine promise in a dream that he will be made pharaoh. Solomon also receives the promise of wisdom, honor, and wealth in 1 Kings 3:11, the fulfillment of which is registered in the immediately following two pericopes: one pericope about two prostitutes disputing over a baby (wisdom) and another about Solomon's administrative officers (honor and wealth).

---

[82] See also Genesis 20 and Numbers 22 for additional examples of the divine-human dialogue in a dream.

[83] Carl A. Meier, "The Dream in Ancient Greece and Its Use in Temple Cures (Incubation)," in *The Dream and Human Societies*, ed. Gustave E. Von Grunebaum and Roger Caillois (Berkeley: University of California Press, 1966), 316–17.

[84] Langdon, *Die neubabylonischen Königsinschriften*, 278.

Alternatively, a deity may give the incubant a series of instructions that would, if faithfully followed, lead to the solution of the problem. In the story of Satni, for instance, Mahituaskhit visits the temple of Imhotep because of her infertility. When she fell asleep praying, Imhotep appeared to her and gave instructions on how to get pregnant: "When tomorrow morning breaks, go thou to the fountain of Satni, thy husband; there thou shalt find growing a plant of colocasia; pull it up, leaves and all, and with it make a potion which thou shalt give to thy husband; then shalt thou sleep with him, and that very night shalt thou conceive."[85] Ishtar tells Assurbanipal through a *šabrû*-priest to stay in the city because she is going out to fight his enemies for him. Here both command and promise is combined.[86]

2.3 *Reaction: After Epiphany*

The incubation type-scene may include some of the following motifs in this part of the frame. Since individual instances of the type-scene would differ from each other according to the type of predicament facing the incubant and the type of the message given by the deity, the configuration of motifs that occur in this part of the incubation type-scene may vary greatly from one instance to another. The indication of the end of dream, however, is most likely to occur in this part of the frame.

2.3.1 *Indication of the End of Dream ("the Waking Motif")*

The fact that the theophany motif is commonly preceded by an indication of sleep (the sleeping motif) anticipates the "waking motif" that comes after the theophany. The formal termination of dream may be indicated by the continued sleep of the incubant (till the morning), or his sudden arousal, or his rising in the morning.[87] The waking motif indicates to the reader that the revelation has occurred in a dream, which in turn confirms the validity of the revelation.[88] As implied in the Akkadian *negeltû* "to awaken with a start," the suddenness

[85] George Foucart, "Dream and Sleep (Egypt)," in *ERE: Vol. V*, vol. 5, ed. James Hastings (Edinburgh: T. & T. Clark, 1922), 35.

[86] Gnuse, "The Dream Theophany of Samuel: Its Structure in Relation to Ancient Near Eastern Dreams and Its Theological Significance," 213.

[87] Cf. Ibid., 214–15.

[88] This idea was first proposed by Oppenheim, *The Interpretation of Dreams in the Ancient Near East: With a Translation of an Assyrian Dream-Book*, 191.

of the arousal may be emphasized in this motif. In the Table IX of the Gilgamesh Epic, Gilgamesh's dream terminates as "he awoke with a start; it was a dream" (*ig-gél-tu-ma šu-ut-tum*).[89] The second dream of Gudea ends with "he woke up with a start and it was but a dream" (*ì-ḫa-luḫ ma-mu-dam*). The end of Thutmosis IV's dream is announced by a similar remark "and the king's son (himself) awoke when he heard this...he recognized the words of this god." The suddenness of the arousal may also be detected in Solomon's dream which terminates with "And Solomon awoke, and behold, it was a dream" (וַיִּקַץ שְׁלֹמֹה וְהִנֵּה חֲלוֹם) as also in the way that Pharaoh's dream ends in Genesis 41:7 (וַיִּיקַץ פַּרְעֹה וְהִנֵּה חֲלוֹם). The waking with a start is also part of the convention of the Greek dream-reports. In Odyssey 4.839 we read: "But Icarus' daughter, waking with a start, drew a warm sense of comfort from the vividness of the dream."[90] Agamemnon too woke with a start with the divine voice still ringing in his ears, seized by the conviction that he will capture Troy that very night. West considers this feature of Greek dream motif to be an influence of the ancient Near Eastern poetic traditions.[91]

The end of dream (the waking motif) may be indicated by the continued sleep until morning or the passage of time till the morning. 1 Samuel 3:15 marks the end of theophany with "Samuel lay until morning" (וַיִּשְׁכַּב שְׁמוּאֵל עַד־הַבֹּקֶר). The dream of Kurigalzu ends with an indication of time, "In the morning, at sun rise (*ina ṣe-ri ina ṣi-it dšamši*) he made [a report (?)] to his courtiers."[92] In Genesis 20:8, Abimelech rose early in the morning (וַיַּשְׁכֵּם אֲבִימֶלֶךְ בַּבֹּקֶר). The end of Jacob's oneiric experience at Bethel (Genesis 28) is doubly marked: first by the mention of "awaking from sleep" (וַיִּיקַץ יַעֲקֹב מִשְּׁנָתוֹ) and then by the indication of passage of time ("Early in the morning, Jacob..." [וַיַּשְׁכֵּם יַעֲקֹב בַּבֹּקֶר]).

---

[89] The scene in Tablet IX, lines 1–14 appears to be the incubation type-scene. Although the theophany motif is missing, almost all the other motifs are present in the scene, such as the predicament motif (the death of Enkidu, fear of lions), the time motif (night), the place motif (mountain), the prayer motif, the waking motif, the change of mood motif ("he grew happy to be alive"). Cf. George, *The Babylonian Gilgamesh Epic: Introduction, Critical Edition, and Cuneiform Texts*, 666–67.

[90] Oppenheim, *The Interpretation of Dreams in the Ancient Near East: With a Translation of an Assyrian Dream-Book*, 191.

[91] M. L. West, *The East Face of Helicon: West Asiatic Elements in Greek Poetry and Myth* (Oxford: Clarendon Press, 1997), 356.

[92] Finkel, "The Dream of Kurigalzu and the Tablet of Sins," 78.

2.3.2 *The "Change of Mood" Motif*

After describing the climatic event of incubation, namely, the appearance of a deity, the poem/narrative may register in the text a literary device designed to confirm the verity of the oneiric experience. In his second and third incubations, Gudea resorted to other methods of divination (e.g. extispicy) to confirm the verity of the oneiric revelation. The verity of revelation may be confirmed, however, in a more subtle way, namely, by indicating the change of attitude or mood of the incubant ("the change of mood motif"). In the tablet IX of the Gilgamesh Epic, for example, Gilgamesh arrives one night at a mountain in sorrow and fear. He was sad because of the loss of his friend Enkidu and afraid of the dangers lurking on his journey to Uta-Napišti. That night, he prays to Sin and then has a dream. Unfortunately the content of his dream is not recorded. But whatever Gilgamesh saw in the dream, it dispelled his fear and made him happy.[93] The change of mood is registered in line 14: "[...in the] presence of the moon he grew happy to be alive (*iḫ-te-du ba-la-ṭu*)."[94] A similar plot is discernible in the story of Jacob in Genesis 28. Jacob arrives at dusk "at a certain place (וַיִּפְגַּע בַּמָּקוֹם)." He was worried and afraid for many reasons, one of which may have been the fear that Yahweh, the god of Israel, had no influence outside the land of Canaan. He lay down in that place (וַיִּשְׁכַּב בַּמָּקוֹם הַהוּא) and had a dream (וַיַּחֲלֹם). The change of mood in Jacob after having the dream is registered in verse 16b and 17b: "Surely the Lord is in this place, and I did not know it...How awesome is this place (מַה־נּוֹרָא הַמָּקוֹם הַזֶּה)! This is none other than the house of God, and this is the gate of heaven." The change of mood is also noted in the Egyptian dream of Djoser: "Then I woke refreshed (?), my heart determined and at rest."[95] As will be shown in subsequent chapters, the change of mood motifs occur in all of three West Semitic examples of the incubation type-scene.

---

[93] George, *The Babylonian Gilgamesh Epic: Introduction, Critical Edition, and Cuneiform Texts*, 667.

[94] Ibid., 666–67.

[95] Oppenheim, *The Interpretation of Dreams in the Ancient Near East: With a Translation of an Assyrian Dream-Book*, 251–52, Text No. 19.

2.3.3 *Carrying Out of the Divine Command or Fulfillment of the Divine Promise*

It has already been noted above (see 2.2.2.) that the divine message could be a command or a promise. The poet/narrator tends to show how the divine command or promise is carried out or fulfilled in the plot of the story. Hence, this motif serves to connect the incubation type-scene to the larger plot of the story. The reader follows the story with attention as to how the divine promise will be fulfilled or how the hero carries out the divine command. The fulfillment of the divine promise may be delayed, even appear to be thwarted by unexpected turn of the events. The hero may not appear to follow the divine instructions in the strictest manner possible. All these provide the poet/narrator with an opportunity to complicate the plot, thereby increasing the suspense of the story. This motif does not figure prominently in the examples of the ancient Near Eastern incubation we examined in chapter two. Small wonder, since many of the so-called incubation texts have but merely an allusion to the practice, or are historical or ritual documents, and not literary ones. The type-scene study of incubation will provide concrete examples of how this motif will develop in the larger unit of the narrative.

2.3.4 *Carrying Out of a Vow*

This carrying out of a vow motif tends to occur when the incubant had made a specific vow before having a theophany. The delinquency in fulfilling the vow will create tension in the story. The votive offering motif may still occur even when the proponent made no vow at the beginning. This would be simply a thanksgiving offering. The example of a successful incubant giving a votive offering in thanksgiving is a legion in ancient texts. In the Classical practice, the thanksgiving offering is institutionalized as a certain amount of fee ("offering to the snake"),[96] due to the priests serving in the temple. And delinquency in proper payment would result in a return to the previous condition of

[96] The payment was put in a box on which an ornamental serpent was seated. This is why a fee for incubation was called "offering to the snake" (Emma J. Edelstein and Ludwig Edelstein, *Asclepius: A Collection and Interpretation of the Testimonies* [Baltimore, MD: Johns Hopkins Press, 1945], 188).

the incubant.[97] Solomon also offered burnt offering after the successful encounter with God (1 Kings 3:15).

3. A Heuristic Definition of Incubation as a Literary Device: Some Proposals for the Recognition of the Incubation Type-Scene

Thus far we have examined various motifs comprising the incubation type-scene. As is already assumed, the incubation scene is recognized not by the presence of a specific sequence of "essential" motifs, but by the principle of family resemblance that exists among different configurations of the motifs that may allude to any aspect of the practice of incubation. This means that there is no essential motif(s) without which the incubation type-scene is not recognized or established. Further, there is no standard sequence of motifs either. The poet/narrator could constitute a specific configuration of motifs out of the pool of relevant motifs available at that time as per the demands of his poetic/narrative purpose in that specific context.

Having said this, a practical question needs to be dealt with: How does the principle of family resemblance actually work as modern readers recognize the ancient literary convention, here termed the incubation type-scene? How does one recognize the incubation type-scene in a given text? I propose four criteria to identify family resemblances among different instances of the incubation type-scene in Ugaritic and biblical literature. First, the reader should be able to discern a plot movement from problem to solution within the incubation type-scene. Unlike a random agglomerate of motifs, they must manifest a discernable organization with a problem-solving structure. Second, although there is no requirement that there may be an essential motif at verbal and thematic levels, that is, while no single motif at the verbal and thematic level conclusively determines the absence or presence of the incubation type-scene in a given text, it may nonetheless be argued

[97] The Epidaurian inscriptions of Asclepian cult give two instances of blind men, whose sight had been restored, but was lost again, owing to their failure to pay the fee due to the priests. A distinction appears to have been made, in that a boy was allowed by the god to evade payment altogether (Mary Hamilton, *Incubation or The Cure of Disease in Pagan Temples and Christian Churches* [St. Andrews: W. C. Henderson & Son, 1906], 31–32).

that four conceptual elements, abstracted from the verbal expression and assumed to be operating at a deeper level, inform the incubation type-scene: predicament, intentionality, liminality, and epiphany. Borrowing Nagler's terminology, these may be called "pre-verbal *Gestalt*." Each pre-verbal *Gestalt* or concept has the potential to be verbalized or actualized as various motifs in a given instance of an incubation type-scene. The concept of predicament may be actualized in the form of motifs alluding to societal or individual crisis, such as a foreign invasion, lack of a royal heir, illness, etc. The concept of liminality may manifest itself in terms of time, space, and consciousness. Night, a temple or a holy place, and dream, for instance, may indicate such liminality that is the precondition for a divine-human encounter. The concept of intentionality can be verbalized through various motifs alluding to preparatory rituals, such as animal sacrifice, libation, prayer, etc. Finally, the concept of epiphany[98] may be articulated in the form of motifs such as the approaching of the deity or its surrogate to the incubant, ensuing divine-human dialogue, divine blessing/promise, divine command, etc. In particular, the divine promise or command embedded in the incubation type-scene generally addresses the solution to the problem, instead of focusing, for instance, on the extraordinariness of a soon-to-be-born hero. These four conceptual elements, or pre-verbal *Gestalts*, serve as important criteria for recognizing or judging a certain scene as an incubation type-scene. Patton, defining the religious practice of incubation, similarly proposes three important conceptual elements that one should look for in an incubation practice: Intentionality, Holy Place, and Epiphany. She goes on to argue for the presence of at least two out of three elements as being essential for a practice to be judged as incubational. I would not, however, set down the number of conceptual elements that are required for the recognition of an incubation type-scene in any given literature. And this leads us to the third criterion for the recognition of an incubation type-scene in West-Semitic literary texts: the literary function of the incubation type-scene. In some instances of the

[98] I will distinguish "epiphany" from "theophany" in this book. While the former represents the concept of a salvific appearance of a god in a certain setting, the latter specifically refers to a motif that indicates the divine appearance to a human petitioner. Thus it may be said that the motif of theophany "verbalizes" the concept of epiphany.

incubation type-scene, all four concepts may be discerned, while in other instances, the presence of three or even two conceptual elements may be sufficient for the scene to be recognized as an incubation type-scene. This is owing to the fact that the judgment depends less on how many of these conceptual elements are discernable, than on how those elements are verbalized in the text and how the ensuing configuration of verbal or thematic motifs accomplishes the poet/narrator's literary purpose. In other words, the literary function of the component motifs within the type-scene and in turn that of the type-scene within the narrative as a whole will prove crucial for the recognition. Finally, the fourth criterion for recognizing family resemblances among different instances of an incubation type-scene is what Foley calls "metonymic use of tradition." Foley's idea of the metonymic use of tradition contends that a type-scene carries a significance that goes deeper than the surface level, and invokes meanings inherited from the entire tradition of the poetry/narrative.[99] These meanings inherited from the whole tradition of poetry/narrative represent the traditional value system of the society to which the poet and the audience both belonged. This traditional value system that the poet's use of the incubation type-scene invokes entails the piety of the incubant who actively seeks divine help in time of distress and the idea of a benevolent and powerful god who responds favorably to the incubant's appeal. In some instances of an incubation type-scene, these values are endorsed in a straightforward manner, whereas in other instances they may be distorted or overturned by a parodical rendering of some of the component motifs.

All these four criteria may prove to be a useful heuristic tool for recognizing family resemblance among instances of an incubation type-scene and thus discerning the use of an incubation type-scene in West-Semitic literature. Hence the final judgment should be made based on the detailed literary analysis of the type-scene, to which the rest of the book will be devoted. Before we do that, however, one final caveat is in order: The incubation type-scene does not necessarily *describe* the proponent of the story actually practicing an incubation rite. Although the incubation type-scene could be employed to

[99] Foley, *Immanent Art: From Structure to Meaning in Traditional Oral Epic*, 34–35.

describe an incubation practiced by the proponent, it is one thing to say that the poet/narrator employed the incubation type-scene as a literary motif, and another to say that the poet/narrator describes the proponent engaging in incubation. As a literary motif, the incubation type-scene could simply allude to the practice without really describing the practice of incubation by the proponent. For instance, Genesis 28 may allude to the incubation practice,[100] but does not describe Jacob practicing the incubation at least as we know it. Another example comes from Ruth 2 in which, Alter argues, the allusion to the type-scene of betrothal scene is made.[101] In fact, one can find all the motifs that Alter identified as essential to the betrothal type-scene in Ruth 2: (1) Future bridegroom or his surrogate journeying to a foreign land (Ruth journeying to a field belonging to an Israelite [verse 3]); (2) encountering a future bride at a well (Ruth meeting a future bride groom at a field where there is a well [verses 4–8]), (3) drawing water from the well (Boaz's servants drawing water for Ruth from the well [verse 9]), (4) rushing to bring home the news of the arrival (Ruth going home to report her rendezvous with Boaz [verses 18–19]), (5) betrothal arrangement (Naomi informing Ruth of the fact that Boaz is the kinsman redeemer [verse 20]), and (6) a meal (Boaz inviting Ruth to a meal [14]). But the recognition of the betrothal type-scene in Ruth 2 does not allow us to say that betrothal actually took place in Ruth 2. The two examples just discussed simply confirm the previous observation that the incubation as a literary device should be distinguished from incubation as a practice.

Excursus 3: Is There Any Difference?

The subsequent chapters are devoted to the analysis of two Ugaritic texts and one biblical text from the perspective of incubation type-scenes. Since all of them are concerned with a particular type of incubation, namely, incubation for the birth of a child, the following question may be posed: what differentiates the type-scene alluding to the practice of incubation for the birth of a child from, for example,

---

[100] For this interpretation, See Susan Ackerman, "The Deception of Isaac, Jacob's Dream at Bethel, and Incubation on an Animal Skin," in *Priesthood and Cult in Ancient Israel*, ed. Gary A. Anderson (Sheffield: JOST Press, 1991), 90–120.

[101] Alter, *The Art of Biblical Narrative*, 58–60.

Alter's Annunciation type-scene, or Husser's Birth of a Hero story? Although they have a common subject matter, namely, the birth of a child, the incubation type-scene distinguishes itself from the latter in the following respects. First, the Birth of a Hero story/Annunciation type-scene does not require the movement of plot from problem to solution. The story of Jesus' birth, for example, does not register any predicament on the part of his parents. Although some Birth of a Hero stories/Annunciation type-scenes tell of a barren womb, the focus of those stories is not on the resolution of the problem, but on the extraordinary birth of a future hero who will come to prominence later in the narrative. This leads to the second difference: The theophanic speech in the incubation type-scene focuses on the problem of an incubant, whereas the theophanic speech in the Birth of Hero story/Annunciation type-scene is more concerned with the future of a yet-to-be-born baby. Neff also observed the same point earlier in his dissertation:

> We have noted a sharp difference between the assurance of healing and the ABDN [Announcement of Birth, Desity, and Name]. A divine messenger or priest promises the birth of a child to a barren woman or an impotent man within an incubational ritual, but these assurances of healing exhibit no fixed pattern. The ABND does not grant fertility but announces the birth of a child with a special destiny.[102]

In the story of Ishmael's birth in Genesis 16, for example, the focus of the angelic message is more on predicting Ishmael's future than on solving Hagar's problem—there is no reason to believe that Sarah stopped persecuting Hagar after her return from the wilderness, not to mention that she was not barren after all![103] Last, but not least, the Birth of a Hero story/Annunciation type-scene rarely shows motifs verbalizing the concept of intentionality. The theophany occurs without any hint of preparatory rituals in the Birth of a Hero story/Annunciation type-scene. From all this it follows that, if a certain birth story registers trouble to the parents, their sacrifice to the gods, prayer in tears, an allusion to holy space, the divine message

[102] Robert W. Neff, "The Announcement in Old Testament Birth Stories" (Ph.D. diss., Yale University, 1969), 151.

[103] The problem of Hagar, who was not barren, is the jealousy of Sarai, who is barren. The angel's speech clearly reaches its climax in the prediction of Ishmale's future: "He shall be a wild donkey of a man, his hand against everyone and everyone's hand against him, and he shall dwell over against all his kinsmen" (verse 12).

concerned less with predicting the future of the baby but more with promising a child to the distressed parents, etc, one may legitimately consider the possibility that the scene in question is in fact the incubation type-scene, not a simple birth story.

CHAPTER FOUR

HOW DĀNÎ'ILU WAS BLESSED WITH A SON?

The Incubation Type-Scene in KTU 1.17 I–II

1. Previous Studies

1.1 *Incubation*

Any historical review of the study of an incubation scene in the first two columns of KTU 1.17 must begin with Julian Obermann's 1946 monograph, *How Daniel Was Blessed With a Son*, in which he has divided the text of the initial columns into six component scenes: (1) "Incubation rites"; (2) "The incubation period"; (3) "Daniel's supplication"; (4) "His request for intercession"; (5) "El's favorable response"; (6) "Daniel apprised of El's blessing"; (7) "His rejoicing"; and (8) "Finale and transition."[1] As these titles imply, Obermann recognized in the text a typical practice of incubation well attested to in the ancient Near East, namely, the oneiric theophany preceded by a multiday preparatory rites of sacrifice, prayer, and the act of lying down in a temple.[2] Obermann's original efforts, however, were tainted with many faulty philological decisions that were obviously affected by his interests in history of religions. For instance, Obermann's concern to include a prayer as a preparation for oneiric theophany leads him to translate [ ]*yškb bʿl bḥnth* (KTU 1.17 I:16) as "[when] he draws near to perform his supplication."[3] Apart from the implausibility of taking *bʿl* as an alloform of the verb *pʿl*, this understanding totally ignores the literary role that Baʿlu plays later in the narrative. This philological eccentricity is partly owing to his goal of reconstructing the Ugaritic practice of incubation on the basis of its literary rendition in the 'Aqhatu story. Obermann's knowledge of ancient Near Eastern practice of incubation influences his understanding of the text, which in turn provides

[1] Julian Obermann, *How Daniel Was Blessed with a Son*, Suppl. to JAOS 6 (Baltimore, MD: American Oriental Society, 1946), 7.

[2] See 1.7 in chapter two.

[3] Obermann, *How Daniel Was Blessed with a Son*, 11–12. Also, Obermann takes *yd* to mean "besprinkle." Behind such a reading is Obermann's desire to see in Dānî'ilu's incubation the Hebrew ritual of sprinkling of blood, oil, or water for purification (Ibid., 9).

the basis for the reconstruction of the Ugaritic practice of incubation. But this attempt is bound to fail unless a careful distinction is made between the incubation as a practice and the incubation as a literary device. Nevertheless, Obermann should be praised for introducing the subject of incubation into the study of the 'Aqhatu story.

Although Obermann's philological analyses have since met serious challenges, his proposal that the first two columns of the tablet KTU 1.17 describe an incubation scene has been widely accepted among Ugaritic scholars.[4] These scholars have not, however, dealt with the subject of incubation in any detail, but have only mentioned, in passing, their preference for reading KTU 1.17 I–II as an incubation scene.[5] In so doing, they have depended on the generally accepted definition

[4] Marvin H. Pope, "The Cult of the Dead in Ugarit," in *Ugarit in Retrospect: Fifty Years of Ugarit and Ugaritic*, ed. Gordon D. Young (Winona Lake, IN: Eisenbrauns, 1981), 159; J. C. L. Gibson, ed., *Canaanite Myths and Legends.* (Edinburgh: T. & T. Clark, 1978), 24; H. Cazelles, "Review: Canaanite Myths and Legends by G. R. Driver," *VT* 7 (1957): 428; Theodor H. Gaster, *Thespis: Ritual, Myth, and Drama in the Ancient Near East* (New York: Harper, 1961), 330; John Gray, *The Legacy of Canaan: The Ras Shamra Texts and Their Relevance to the Old Testament.* (Leiden: Brill, 1965), 108; Cyrus H. Gordon, *Ugarit and Minoan Crete: The Bearing of Their Texts on the Origins of Western Culture* (New York: Norton and Company, 1966), 120; Michael D. Coogan, ed. and trans., *Stories from Ancient Canaan* (Philadelphia, PA: Westminster Press, 1978), 27–28; Jack M. Sasson, "Literary Criticism, Folklore Scholarship, and Ugaritic Literature," in *Ugarit Retrospect: Fifty Years of Ugarit and Ugaritic*, Douglas Y. Gordon (Winona Lake, IN: Eisenbrauns, 1981), 96; Gregorio del Olmo Lete, *Mitos y leyendas de Canaan: según la tradición de Ugarit*, Fuentes de la ciencia bíblica 1 (Madrid Valencia: Ediciones Cristianidad Institución San Jerónimo, 1981), 332–34; Simon B. Parker, *The Pre-Biblical Narrative Tradition: Essays on the Ugaritic Poems Keret and Aqhat*, SBLRBS 24 (Atlanta, GA: Scholars Press, 1989), 100; Dennis Pardee, "An Emendation in the Ugaritic Aqht Text," *JNES* 36 (1977): 54.

[5] The exception to this is Del Olmo Lete. At the Simposio Biblico Español which took place at Salamanque in 1982, Del Olmo Lete presented the two texts of *'Aqhatu* and of *Kirta* as the Canaanite antecedents of the practice of incubation attested in some OT passages. After defining what an incubation is, Del Olmo Lete extracted from each text those essential elements which combine to form a model of incubation, to which the two scenes of *Kirta* and *'Aqhatu* are compared in the following tablet.

Elementos	Campo semantico	1.14 (Krt)	1.17 (Aqht)
a) lamento/afliccion	*bky, anḥ*	X	(implic.)
b) atendo cúltien	*uzr, mizrt*	. . .	X
c) ofrenda previa	*lḥm, šqy*	. . .	X
d) incubatio	*škb, yšn, ln*	X	X
e) teofania	*qrb*	X	X
f) diálogo teofánico	*šal*	X	(equiv.)
g) banquete-sacrific.	*ḏbḥ, tbḥ, lḥm/šqy*	X	X

of incubation, namely, that of historians of religion, in recognizing an incubation in the initial columns of the 'Aqhatu story. Although some of the anomalies, for instance, the absence of a dream, have been noticed by some scholars in the incubation scene of the 'Aqhatu story, these did not change the scholarly consensus of interpreting the initial scene of the 'Aqhatu story as an incubation.[6]

The first serious attack on the incubation theory comes from Baruch Margalit. In his 1989 commentary on the 'Aqhatu text, Margalit attempted to upset this scholarly consensus.[7] After calling into question the applicability of the ancient Near Eastern data for the practice of incubation adduced by Obermann, Margalit went on to enumerate the elements he perceived to be essential to an incubation scene, most of which were borrowed from Hamilton's observations on the Greek therapeutic incubation practice. After comparing them to the Ugaritic data, he concluded that none of the conditions required are fulfilled in the initial scene of the 'Aqhatu text: chthonian gods are not involved, no illness is involved, there is no reason to think that Dānî'ilu's sleeping is part of the ritual, there is no direct theophany, and no cultic personnel are involved. In other words, Margalit argues that the Ugaritic text in question does not qualify as an incubation scene because it does not dovetail with the Greek incubation practice.[8] But, as I have already argued, it is simply wrong to say that only the

---

Del Olmo Lete observes at the end of this table that although the initial rites of the two stories do not agree in terms of the component motifs and their sequence, they are worthy of being called "an incubation" for they contain the essential elements of the sequence: incubation, theophany, theophanic dialogue, sacrificial banquet. For this explanation of Del Olmo Lete's symposium paper, I depend on Jean-Marie Husser, *Le songe et la parole: Etude sur le rêve et sa fonction dans l'ancien Israël*, BZAW 210 (Berlin: W. de Gruyter, 1994), 48.

[6] Simon Parker, for instance, points out the lack of a dream in the scene but he still considers the scene as an incubation rite: "*Aqht* makes no reference to a dream. Rather mythological scenes and communications seem to replace the dream we would expect in an incubation" (Simon B. Parker, *The Pre-Biblical Narrative Tradition: Essays on the Ugaritic Poems Keret and Aqhat*, 101). Caquot and Sznycer's was "a voice in the wilderness" on this matter in early 1970s. They explicitly reject the reading of the initial scene of the 'Aqhatu story as an incubation. But they understand the scene of sacrifice as therapeutic, rather than as preparatory for a therapeutic dream (André Caquot, Maurice Sznycer, and Andrée. Herdner, *Mythes et légendes: introduction, traduction, commentaire*, vol. 1 of *Textes ougaritiques*, Littératures anciennes du Proche-Orient 7 [Paris: Éditions du Cerf, 1974], 404).

[7] Baruch Margalit, *The Ugaritic Poem of Aqht: Text, Translation, Commentary*, BZAW 182 (New York: De Gruyter, 1989), 260–66.

[8] Ibid.

Hellenistic practice deserves being called "incubation." It is a truism among the historians of religion that incubation is practiced in almost every part of the known world and its *avatar* could vary from culture to culture.[9]

Since the publication of Margalit's book, a few scholars have rallied to his support. Most notable among them is Jean-Marie Husser. He deals with the subject of incubation on three different levels: philological, comparative, and literary. In his 1994 publication, *Le songe et la parole: étude sur le rêve et sa fonction dans l'ancien Israël*, Husser challenges Obermann at every juncture of his philological analysis.[10] One must admit that Husser's philology is much more controlled and a great improvement on that of Obermann, but his conclusion that the first two columns of KTU 1.17 do not include an incubation scene is based on his rigid definition of incubation, as well as on his assumption that a literary text such as the 'Aqhatu story should mimic the *realia* of incubation in its literary presentation. The comparative data on incubation were examined in his 1999 book, *Dreams and Dream Narratives in the Biblical World*.[11] Although Husser, unlike Margalit, arrives at a positive conclusion about the existence of an incubation in the ancient Near East, he does not change his opinion about the initial scene of the 'Aqhatu story: "The words 'dream' or 'vision' never appear in the text, and the internal logic of the narration in columns I and II preclude such allusion. This is strictly a supplication ritual... It is therefore inappropriate to talk of incubation as regards these texts."[12] Finally, in his 1996 article, "The Birth of a Hero: Form and Meaning of KTU 1.17 i-ii," Husser provides the literary basis for his reluctance to see an incubation scene in the initial columns of the 'Aqhatu story.[13] Relying on Oppenheim's definition of message dream and its literary structure, he argues that KTU 1.17 I:23–II:8 does not qualify as what he calls an oneiric theophany, because of its lack of conformity

[9] See section 1 in chapter one.

[10] Husser, *Le songe et la parole: Etude sur le rêve et sa fonction dans l'ancien Israël*, 29–62.

[11] Jean-Marie Husser, *Dreams and Dream Narratives in the Biblical World*, BS 63 (Sheffield: Sheffield Academic Press, 1999), 46–50, 52–58, 69–71, 172–75.

[12] Ibid., 77–78.

[13] Jean-Marie Husser, "The Birth of a Hero: Form and Meaning of KTU 1.17 i–ii," in *Ugarit, Religion and Culture : Essays Presented in Honour of Professor John C. L. Gibson*, ed. Nick Wyatt, Wilfred G. E. Watson, and Jeffrey B. Lloyd (Münster: Ugarit-Verlag, 1996), 85–98.

to the patterns laid out for a message dream by Oppenheim. Husser, for example, cites the absence of words for sleeping and waking which would normally demarcate the dream-report, and argues that the repetitive list of filial duties makes the structure too complex to be called a message dream.[14] Instead, he wants to regard the scene as typical of the Birth of a Hero story.[15]

Margalit and Husser's studies have made some scholars more cautious about recognizing the practice of incubation in the initial scene of the 'Aqhatu story. Recalling Caquot and Sznycer who conceived of Dānî'ilu's rituals as affecting a cure for his impotency, N. Wyatt considers the rituals as a therapy intended to affect conception, and not as a preparation for the oneiric theophany.[16] Dietrich and Loretz regard the six-day rituals as *Trauerriten* ("mourning rites") occasioned by Dānî'ilu's loss of a son, without seeing any connection between the rituals and the following theophany.[17] David Wright, on the other hand, is more positive about the connection between the rituals and the theophany, but due to his espousal of a narrow definition of incubation similar to that of Margalit, he says in conclusion, "I agree with Margalit that this is not an incubation ritual *in the classical sense*" (emphasis is mine).[18]

To sum up, Margalit's excursus on incubation in his 1989 commentary on the 'Aqhatu story seems to have led scholars to rethink an issue which had enjoyed scholarly consensus since Obermann's 1946 monograph. It has inspired some scholars to propose alternate ways of understanding the initial scene of the 'Aqhatu story. But as Wyatt observes, the problem of incubation still remains to be solved in the study of the 'Aqhatu story.[19] It appears to the present writer that the core of the issue revolves around the definition of incubation and

[14] Ibid., 94–95.

[15] Ibid. For the difference between the story of birth of a hero and the incubation type-scene with a similar subject, see Excursus 3 in chapter three.

[16] Nick Wyatt, *Religious Texts from Ugarit*, BS 53 (London: Sheffield Academic Press, 2002), 253, footnote 12.

[17] Manfried Dietrich and Oswald Loretz, "Das Aqhat-Epos," in *Weisheitstexte, Mythen und Epen*, vol. 3 of *TUAT*, ed. Otto Kaiser (Gütersloh: Gütersloher Verlagshaus, 1990), 1258, footnote 13.

[18] David P. Wright, *Ritual in Narrative: The Dynamics of Feasting, Mourning, and Retaliation Rites in the Ugaritic Tale of Aqhat* (Winona Lake, IN: Eisenbrauns, 2001), 29, footnote 39.

[19] Nick Wyatt, "The Story of Aqhat (KTU 1.17–19)," in *Handbook of Ugaritic Studies*, ed. Wilfred G. E. Watson and Nick Wyatt (Leiden: Brill, 1999), 247–48.

the distinction between the practice and its literary manifestation. Any step forward will begin with a recognition of these two aspects of the problem.

1.2 *Type-Scenes in the 'Aqhatu Story*

It has been noted that Ugaritic narrative poetry shares some prosodic features with biblical poetry, such as the use of parallelism.[20] It has also been noted that these two literatures share some of the oral compositional features with the Homeric epics, such as formulae and themes.[21] Formulae and themes, which refer to repetitive words and ideas respectively, constitute the structural units of oral composition delineated by the oral composition theory.[22] While Ugaritic formulae have attracted considerable scholarly attention,[23] much fewer studies have been devoted to themes in general and to type-scenes in particular. Two studies, though they do not use the term "a type-scene," may be presented in summary of the previous studies on Ugaritic type-scenes: Those of Dorothy Irvin[24] and Kenneth T. Aitken.[25]

---

[20] Cf. Dennis Pardee, *Ugaritic and Hebrew Poetic Parallelism: A Trial Cut ('Nt I and Proverbs 2)*, VTSup 39 (Leiden: Brill, 1988); Wilfred G. E. Watson, *Classical Hebrew Poetry: A Guide to Its Techniques*, JSOTSup 26 (Sheffield: JSOT Press, 1984); Berlin, *The Dynamics of Biblical Parallelism* (Bloomington, IN: Indiana University Press, 1985). For stock word-pairs in Semitic languages, see Y. Avishur, *Stylistic Studies of Word-Pairs in Biblical and Ancient Semitic Literatures*, AOAT 210 (Neukirchen-Vluyn: Neukirchener Verlag, 1984).

[21] Coogan, *Stories from Ancient Canaan*, 15.

[22] *S. v.* "Formula," in Alex Preminger and T. V. F. Brogan, eds., *The New Princeton Encyclopedia of Poetry and Poetics* (New York: MJF Books, 1993), 422.

[23] Cf. Richard E. Whitaker, "Ugaritic Formulae," in *Ras Shamra Parallels: The Texts from Ugarit and the Hebrew Bible*, vol. 3, ed. Stan Rummel (Roma: Pontificium Institutum Biblicum, 1981), 208–19; "A Formulaic Analysis of Ugaritic Poetry" (Ph.D. diss., Harvard University, 1969); Wilfred G. E. Watson, *Traditional Techniques in Classical Hebrew Verse*, JSOTSup 170 (Sheffield: JSOT Press, 1994), 414–24, 424–30; Kenneth T. Aitken, "Formulaic Patterns for the Passing of Time in Ugaritic Narrative," *UF* 19 (1987): 1–10; Samuel E. Loewenstamm, *Comparative Studies in Biblical and Ancient Oriental Literatures* (Neukirchen-Vluyn: Neukirchener Verlag, 1980), 192–209, 234–235, 256–261, 362–365, 445–448; Simon B. Parker, *The Pre-Biblical Narrative Tradition: Essays on the Ugaritic Poems Keret and Aqhat*, 46–52.

[24] Dorothy Irvin, *Mytharion: The Comparison of Tales from the Old Testament and the Ancient Near East*, AOAT 32 (Neukirchen-Vluyn: Neukirchener Verlag, 1978), 72–80.

[25] Aitken, "Oral Formulaic Composition and Theme in the Aqhat Narrative," 1–16; *The Aqhat Narrative: A Study in the Narrative Structure and Composition of an Ugaritic Tale*, JSS Monographs 13 (Manchester: University of Manchester, 1990).

Irvin analyzes the narrative structure of ancient Near Eastern texts and the Hebrew Bible utilizing two methodological tools: those of folklore studies and of Homeric studies. Her idea of a motif, namely, "an element that recurs in different tale-types" comes from the former and the idea of what Irvin calls "traditional episodes" is borrowed from the latter.[26] Traditional episodes are comparable to Homeric type-scenes. Referring to a traditional episode, Irvin says that "it is so highly standardized that when the story reaches a point at which an episode can be inserted, the episode tells itself, so to speak, and leaves the story-teller's mind free to think ahead and plan the next part of the story."[27] Most interesting for our purpose are Irvin's categories of the traditional Birth episode and the traditional Epiphany episode. According to Irvin, the traditional Birth episode consists of such elements as childlessness, promise of conception, month-counting, birth, the father informed of the birth, the father's reaction, naming and reason, prediction of the future of the baby. Irvin catalogues all ancient Near Eastern birth stories according to a table of component motifs comprising the traditional episodes and observes that no single story contains all the motifs and that the sequence of motifs may vary from story to story.[28] The traditional Epiphany episode, on the other hand, contains elements such as a distressing situation, or summoning act, a saving manifestation on the part of the rescuer (the rescuer does not have to be visible—he may be only audible), the rescuer's question about what is wrong, the explanation, and the aid, which may take the form of instructions.[29] Interestingly enough, Irvin regards the initial scene of 'Aqhatu text as a mixture of two traditional episodes "Epiphany Episode" and "Birth Episode."[30]

In his 1989 article "Oral Formulaic Composition and Theme in the Aqhat Narrative," Kenneth T. Aitken attempts to demonstrate the orality of the 'Aqhatu story through an analysis of various thematic

[26] Irvin, *Mytharion: The Comparison of Tales from the Old Testament and the Ancient Near East*, 1–13.
[27] Ibid., 10.
[28] Ibid., 11. For the table of the motifs comprising traditional episodes, see the table attached at the end of Irvin's book.
[29] Ibid.
[30] Ibid., 77.

units in the story.[31] Following Lord, Aitken divides themes into "compositional themes" and "type-scenes." The quintessential difference between them, according to Aitken, lies in the degree of verbal correspondence between different instances of "themes" in a narrative. The "compositional theme" of Dānî'ilu's dispensing justice at the city gate, for example, recurs at different points of the narrative (KTU 1.17 V:5–8, 1.19 I:20–25) with a considerable degree of verbal correspondence. But the "type-scene" of the lack of a child, according to Aitken, has no such verbal correspondence (cf. KTU 1.17 I:18–19; KTU 1.14 I:6–25).[32] Moreover, Aitken divides themes into essential and ornamental themes. "The essential themes are those that are absolutely necessary to the telling of the story, whereas ornamental themes are inessential to the basic story."[33] The core idea behind all this is that Ugaritic narrative poetry, just like the Homeric epics, is composed of various traditional blocks of narrative that the poet has arranged in order to construct a story with a point reflecting a traditional value system. Aitken's 1990 book, *The Aqhat Narrative : A Study in the Narrative Structure and Composition of an Ugaritic Tale*, does not introduce any new ideas about the composition of the Ugaritic tale, although this time he uses a structuralist method derived from Russian folklore studies by Vladimír Propp and Alan Dundes.[34] He divides the whole narrative into six "moves," according to which all plots move from "lack of condition" to its "liquidation." Each move, in turn, consists of smaller blocs of narrative, which have been named differently by different structuralists, namely, an allomotif, a motif, or a theme. The earlier distinction between essential motifs/allomotifs/themes and inessential motifs/allomotifs/themes is maintained by Aitken in this study.[35] Finally, Aitken seems to recognize an incubation motif or

---

[31] Aitken's article was inspired by Whitaker's study of Ugaritic formulae ("A Formulaic Analysis of Ugaritic Poetry"), which placed the Ugaritic narratives in the category of written texts which reveal the formulaic characteristics of orally composed poetic narratives. Aitken attempts to corroborate Whitaker's conclusion by an analysis of Ugaritic themes, another major feature of oral composition that Parry and Lord demonstrated to have served in the composition of the Homeric epics and Serbo-Croatian narrative poetry. Cf. Aitken, "Oral Formulaic Composition and Theme in the Aqhat Narrative," 13–14.

[32] Ibid., 4.

[33] Ibid.

[34] Aitken, *The Aqhat Narrative: A Study in the Narrative Structure and Composition of an Ugaritic Tale*, 4–24.

[35] Ibid., 21.

theme in the initial scene of the 'Aqhatu story, but it is considered a simple motif which concerns the rituals before the theophany and its component elements are not discussed.[36]

In sum, scholars have recognized compositional skills at the content level in the Ugaritic narrative poems similar to those which classicists have observed in the Homeric epics.[37] In my opinion, however, although the term "type-scene" or "theme" may be found in the scholarly literature on Ugaritic narrative poems, this element is not always clearly defined in relation to other thematic units in the narrative. As has already been suggested in chapter three, the term "type-scene" in this book shall refer to a configuration of motifs with a discernible plot. Component motifs may operate at a verbal level, much like formulae, or at a content level. A motif operating at a content level can also function as a type-scene which has a sequence of its own sub-motifs. Another point to be made with regard to the previous studies of the type-scene in Ugaritic studies is that the typicality of a type-scene has been emphasized over its individuality. Irvin, for instance, delineates a group of motifs comprising the Epiphany episode and catalogues various ancient Near Eastern stories according to the various elements of the episode. But she falls short of discussing the literary or narratological role of an individual instance of the traditional episode in the narrative in which it is embedded. Finally, when it comes to the initial scene of the 'Aqhatu story, the incubation theme is treated as a simple motif describing the rituals. Or, the aggregate of various motifs in the scene is explained as an anomaly, namely, a mixture of two different traditional episodes (Birth episode and Theophany episode), when a better way of explaining the convergence of all various motifs in the first two columns of KTU 1.17 is, in my opinion, to posit an incubation type-scene.

---

[36] Ibid., 81.

[37] The following studies may also be noted for their attention to the thematic structure of the 'Aquatu story: Wright, *Ritual in Narrative: The Dynamics of Feasting, Mourning, and Retaliation Rites in the Ugaritic Tale of Aqhat*; Jeffrey B. Lloyd, "The Banquet Theme in Ugaritic Narrative," *UF* 22 (1990): 169–94; D. R. Hillers, "The Bow of Aqhat: The Meaning of a Mythological Theme," in *Orient and Occident: Essays Presented to Cyrus H. Gordon on the Occasion of His Sixth-Fifth Birthday*, ed. Harry A. Hoffner (Neukirchen-Vluyn: Neukirchener Verlag, 1973), 71–80. In particular, Hillers' article examines the story narrated in the KTU 1.17 IV–1.18 from the perspective of "a story pattern."

2. The Incubation Type-Scene in KTU 1.17 I–II: Component Motifs

Obermann noted in his study of KTU 1.17 I–II that several prenatal narratives in the Bible take place in a sanctuary and they include various motifs such as barrenness, sacrifice, supplication, divine intervention, and the prediction of an exceptional status for a child. But he admits his ignorance as to how these various motifs came to be fused in the prenatal pattern of a hero. A similar puzzlement may be discerned when Irvin argues that the initial scene of the 'Aqhatu story is a mixture of two traditional episodes: Birth episode and Epiphany episode. But such fusion of various motifs in the first two columns of KTU 1.17 is best explained as the incubation type-scene with a plot around the birth of a child. Since the incubation in question concerns the birth of a son, some motifs comprising the incubation type-scene at the beginning of the 'Aqhatu story may overlap with those characteristic of Alter's Annunciation type-scene or Husser's Birth of a Hero story. But the configuration of motifs that occurs in the initial scene of the 'Aqhatu story leaves little doubt as to its being an incubation type-scene, rather than a simple birth story. Now let us turn to the motifs comprising the incubation type-scene in KTU 1.17 I–II.

2.1 *Before Epiphany*

KTU 1.17 I:1–15: Transliteration and Translation[38]

(about 10 lines are missing)

(0)	[...apnk] (1) [dnil . mt . rp]⌜i⌝	[Thereupon, as for Dānî'ilu, the man of Rapa'u],
	ap<h>n . ǵ⌜zr⌝ (2) [mt . hrnmy .]	Thereupon, as for the valiant one, [the Harnamite man],
	uzr ⌜.⌝ ilm . ylḥm .	Girded, he gave the gods food,

[38] The transliteration of KTU 1.17 I is based on the photograph and hand copy made available by Bordreuil and Pardee (Pierre Bordreuil and Dennis Pardee, *Grammaire: Fac-Similés*, vol. 1 of *Manuel d'ougaritique* [Paris: Geuthner, 2004], 122; *Choix de Textes: Glossaire*, vol. 2 of *Manuel d'ougaritique* [Paris: Geuthner, 2004], 22–27), while the transliteration of column II is based on the pencil-copy prepared and supplied as class material by Dennis Pardee. Although largely following the translation by Pardee (Dennis Pardee, "The Aqhatu Legend," in *Canonical Compositions from the Biblical World*, vol. I of *COS*, ed. William W. Hallo and K. Lawson Younger Jr. [Leiden: Brill, 1997], 343–45), I have made some changes that I judge to be appropriate.

(3)	[uzr . yšqy .] bn . qdš .	[Girded, he gave drink] to the sons of the Holy One.
	yd (4) [ṣth yʿl .] ⸢w⸣yškb .	He cast down [his cloak, went up] and lay down,
	yd (5) [mizrth] . ⸢p⸣ yln! .	He cast down [his girded garment] so as to pass the night.
	hn . ym (6) [w ṯn .	Voici! A day, [and two,
	uzr .] ilm . dnil	Girded,] Dānî'ilu to the gods,
(7)	[uzr . ilm] ⸢.⸣ ylḥm .	[Girded,] he gave [the gods] food,
	uzr (8) [yšqy . b]n . qdš	Girded, [he gave drink to the s]ons of the Holy One.
	ṯlṯ . rbʿ ym	A third, even a fourth day,
(9)	[uzr . i]⸢l⸣m . dnil .	[Girded,] Dānî'ilu to the gods,
	uzr (10) [ilm . y]lḥm .	Girded, he gave the gods food,
	uzr ⸢.⸣ yšqy bn (11) [qdš .]	Girded, he gave drink to the sons of the Holy One.
	⸢ḫ⸣mš . ṯdṯ ⸢.⸣ --- ⸢.⸣ ym .	A fifth, even a sixth day,
	uzr (12) [il]⸢m⸣ . dnil .	Girded, Dānî'ilu to the gods,
	uzr . ilm . ylḥm	Girded, he gave the gods food,
(13)	[uzr] . yšqy . bn. qdš .	[Girded,] he gave drink to the sons of the Holy One.
	yd . ṣth (14) [dn]⸢i⸣l .	[Dānī]'ilu cast down his garment,
	yd . ṣth . yʿl . wyškb	He cast down his cloak, went up, and lay down,
(15)	[yd .] mizrth p yln .	He cast down his girded garment so as to pass the night.

The extant text begins by portraying Dānî'ilu as offering food and drink to the gods, who must have included Baʿlu and 'Ilu. As scholars speculate, the missing 10 lines at the beginning may have contained a description of why Dānî'ilu ended up in a temple offering sacrifice to the gods.[39] The scene of Dānî'ilu's preparatory ritual is couched in a seven-day formula. Although the formula may be purely literary, namely, with no corresponding reality, the attested practice of the multiday incubation in the ancient Near East seems to enhance the possibility of its being a faithful reflection of what Dānî'ilu went

[39] Aitken, *The Aqhat Narrative: A Study in the Narrative Structure and Composition of an Ugaritic Tale*, 82; Margalit, *The Ugaritic Poem of Aqht: Text, Translation, Commentary*, 250–51; Wyatt, *Religious Texts from Ugarit*, 250, footnote 3; Wright, *Ritual in Narrative: The Dynamics of Feasting, Mourning, and Retaliation Rites in the Ugaritic Tale of Aqhat*, 20. Especially Margalit argues that another tablet would have existed because he does not find enough space in the missing 10 lines for all the details of the story that he would wish to see narrated before the extant lines at the beginning of KTU 17 I.

through before he experienced a theophany. As to the purpose of the ritual, scholars are divided. But the peculiar chiastic structure of a seven-day formula,[40] however, seems to tip the scale in favor of the proposal that the ritual, quite apart from the simple act of lying down, was meant to induce a divine revelation.

2.1.1 *The Motif of Sonlessness*

While a motif verbalizing the concept of predicament may have been described in the ten missing lines at the beginning of KTU 1.17 I, the predicament that confronts Dānî'ilu is certainly articulated in the words of the narrator later in the theophanic scene: *d in bn lh km aḫh / w šrš km aryh*[41] ("Who had no son like his brothers, no scion like his kinsmen," KTU 1.17 I:18–19). One may even argue that the Ugaritic poet delays the actualization of the concept of predicament until the theophanic scene for a literary effect, for instance, in order to increase the listener's tension. I would call this literary technique "delayed identification," which will reoccur with regard to other motifs.[42] It is certain, however, that the predicament that forced Dānî'ilu to resort to incubation is verbalized in the motif of sonlessness (*in bn*). But it is not just the lack of a son, it is the lack of a legitimate heir. This is indicated by the four-fold repetition of the list enumerating various duties expected of an ideal son/heir. Whether Dānî'ilu is a territorial king or not, the lack of a legitimate son or a proper heir would be a deplorable state that begs to be rectified.[43]

One may also note the literary function that the motif of sonlessness serves within the incubation type-scene (see Table 4.1 below). The motif of sonlessness, first encountered in the narrator's mouth (KTU 1.17 I:18–19), is alluded to in three additional occasions, namely, in the petition of Ba'lu (KTU 1.17 I:20–21, 25–26), in the blessing of 'Ilu

[40] For details, see below.

[41] Throughout this chapter, Ugaritic will be quoted without indicating a word divider or a line division of a tablet. The slash / indicates the division of a poetic line.

[42] The poet's delaying identification or explication for a climactic effect is not unknown in Ugaritic and Hebrew poetry. See Watson, *Traditional Techniques in Classical Hebrew Verse*, 336–38.

[43] For "Quest for an Heir" as a literary plot in Ugaritic and biblical narratives, see J. David Schloen, *The House of the Father as Fact and Symbol: Patrimonialism in Ugarit and the Ancient Near East*, Studies in the Archaeology and History of the Levant (Winona Lake, IN: Eisenbrauns, 2001), 48, 350.

(KTU 1.17 I:42–43) and in Dānî'ilu's reaction to the theophany (KTU 1.17 II:14–15), each time moving closer to the solution of the predicament. If the narrator directly states Dānî'ilu's lack of a son (*in bn lh km aḫh* / *w šrš km aryh* "Who had no son like his brothers, no scion like his kinsmen"), Baʿlu intends to eliminate such a lack by interceding with 'Ilu on behalf of Dānî'ilu (*bl iṯ bn lh km aḫh* "Should he not have a son like his brothers?" and *ykn bnh bbt* "Let him have his son in his house"). 'Ilu *de facto* effects the change of Dānî'ilu's fortune by pronouncing a promise-blessing upon him (*ykn bnh bbt* / *šrš bqrb hklh* "He shall have a son in his house, a scion within his palace"). Finally, 'Ilu's promise-blessing is confirmed in the words of Dānî'ilu himself (*yld bn ly km aḫy* / *w šrš km aryy* "A son will be born to me as [in the case with] my brother / and a scion, as [in the case with] my kinsmen"). It is worth noting here that Dānî'ilu's words, which are part of his joyous reaction to the theophany, shows verbal correspondence with the motif of sonlessness except that the negative particle *in* is replaced by the verb *yld* "beget."[44] Such a verbal correspondence belies the contrast of mood between the stages of the plot, while the change from *in* to *yld* reveals the movement of plot from predicament to solution. Furthermore, one may note that Baʿlu's petition and 'Ilu's blessing, in which the motif of sonlessness is mentioned, do not show verbal correspondence except for the parallelism between *bn* and *šrš*.[45] The negative particle is replaced by the verb denoting existence (*ykn*) and the parallelism of *aḫ* and *ary* is replaced by that of *bt* and *hkl*. This and their sandwiched position seem to indicate the pivotal importance of Baʿlu's petition and 'Ilu's blessing in the plot of reversing Dānî'ilu's fortunes.

---

[44] The motif of sonlessness is formed by the following formula: negative particle + *bn* + preposition *l* with pronominal suffix + *km* + *aḫ* with pronominal suffix // *w* + *šrš* + *km* + *ary* with pronominal suffix.

[45] The word *šrš*, "root," is a common metaphor for a male offspring. Cf. KAI 14:11; 222:C.24–25; Daniel 11:7; Isaiah 5:24; 11:1, 10; 53:2.

Table 4.1: The Development of the Predicament Motif

The Narrator	Lack of a Son	*in bn lh km aḫh / wšrš km aryḫ*	KTU 1.17 I:18–19
Ba'lu	A Son Petitioned	*bl iṯ bn lh km aḫh / wšrš km aryh* *ykn bnh bbt / šrš bqrb hklh*	KTU 1.17 I:20–21, 25–26
'Ilu	A Son Promised	*ykn bnh bbt / šrš bqrb hklh*	KTU 1.17 I:42–43
Dānî'ilu	A Son Confirmed	*kyld bn ly km aḫy / wšrš km aryy*	KTU 1.17 II:14–15

2.1.2 *The Offering Motif*

The offering motif, which consists of the two verbs *ylḥm* and *yšqy* and their indirect objects *ilm* and *bn qdš*, verbalizes the concept of intentionality that informs the incubation type-scene. The four-fold repetition before the theophanic scene (KTU 1.17 I:2–3, 6–8, 9–11, 11–13) seems to indicate that the motif of offering has importance not only within the incubation type-scene, but also in the narrative as a whole. Despite the unmistakable importance of the offering motif in the 'Aqhatu story, however, the basic interpretation of the poetic line containing the motif has been subject to much scholarly debate. The bone of contention resides in the interpretation of the three Ugaritic words, *uzr*, *ylḥm*, and *yšqy*. The right understanding of these three terms is crucial because it often affects the understanding of the scene as a whole. For instance, Caquot and Sznycer, who translate *uzr ilm ylḥm / uzr yšqy bn qdš* as "Danel mange le stimulant divin, il boit le stimulant des saints," interpret this scene as a curative ritual where Dānî'ilu's impotence is healed by the consumption of a stimulant.[46] Dietrich and Loretz, who interpret the scene in question as a mourning-meal (*Trauermahl*) for the deified ancestors, translates it as "Das Weihegeschenk der Götter aß er, Das Weihegeschenk trank der Sohn des Heiligen."[47] So it is necessary to arrive at some philologically

[46] Caquot, Sznycer, and Herdner, *Mythes et légendes: introduction, traduction, commentaire*, 419.

[47] "Der Sohn des Heiligen" refers to deified ancestors. According to Dietrich and Loretz, Dānî'ilu is described as sharing a meal with them. Cf. Dietrich and Loretz, "Das Aqhat-Epos," 1259, footnote 22.

sound conclusions about these words, before we discuss their literary significance.

Some scholars interpret both *ylḥm* and *yšqy* in a non-causative sense.[48] The occurrence of the Š-stems of √lḥm and √šqy in the banquet scenes for the Kôṯarātu and for Kôṯāru-wa-Ḫasīs seems to support such an understanding, not to mention that they are not manifestly couched in causative forms, i.e., with preformative Š-. According to this understanding, what Dānî'ilu eats and drinks is the *uzr* of the gods, which corresponds either to offerings presented to them and eaten by Dānî'ilu (cf. Dietrich and Loretz), as an Israelite would eat portions from a sacrifice given to Yahweh, or to some materials imbued with the gods' power such that eating them would help Dānî'ilu overcome his impotence (cf. Caquot).[49] But, as Pardee and Wright point out, a syntactic difficulty makes this interpretation implausible.[50] If one understands *yšqy* in a non-causative sense, it is necessary to accept an aberrant syntactic structure, i.e., the breaking up of the construct chain "*uzr* of the Holy Ones," for the verb is placed between *uzr* and *bn qdš*. Although the discontinuous construct chain does exist, it is rare and usually involves smaller elements, such as an enclitic *mem*.[51] Moreover, the summary phrase *uzrm yšqy bn qdš* in KTU 1.17 I:22 seems to break up the construct chain not only by the verb *yšqy* but

[48] Cf. Caquot, Sznycer, and Herdner, *Mythes et légendes: introduction, traduction, commentaire*, 419–20; Dietrich and Loretz, "Das Aqhat-Epos," 1259; Cyrus H. Gordon, *Ugarit and Minoan Crete: The Bearing of Their Texts on the Origins of Western Culture*, 121; Joseph Tropper, "Ugaritisch *šqy*: 'trinken' oder 'tränken'?" *Or* 58 (1989): 233–42.

[49] Wright, *Ritual in Narrative: The Dynamics of Feasting, Mourning, and Retaliation Rites in the Ugaritic Tale of Aqhat*, 23.

[50] Pardee, "The Aqhatu Legend," 343, footnote 2; Wright, *Ritual in Narrative: The Dynamics of Feasting, Mourning, and Retaliation Rites in the Ugaritic Tale of Aqhat*, 23.

[51] Joseph Tropper, *Ugaritische Grammatik*, AOAT 273 (Münster: Ugarit-Verlag, 2000), 828; Cyrus H. Gordon, *Ugaritic Textbook*, AnOr 38 (Roma: Pontificium Institutum Biblicum, 1965), 104. For a similar phenomenon in Biblical Hebrew, see Bruce K. Waltke and M. O'Connor, *An Introduction to Biblical Hebrew Syntax* (Winona Lake, IN: Eisenbrauns, 1990), 140; D. N. Freedman, "The Broken Construct Chain," *Bib* 53 (1972): 534–36. Although Caquot cites Isaiah 19:8 as an example where the construct chain may be broken by a prepositional phrase, a better analogue would be found in Hosea 6:9; 14:3 where the construct chain is broken by a finite verb. See also Wright, *Ritual in Narrative: The Dynamics of Feasting, Mourning, and Retaliation Rites in the Ugaritic Tale of Aqhat*, 23.

also by the enclitic *mem*.[52] All this leads us to construe *ylḥm* and *yšqy* as having a causative sense.

Scholars are evenly divided on the interpretation of *uzr*: some understand it to be related to the Semitic root √ʾzr 'to gird,' while others take it to refer to a type of offering.[53] This division in scholarly opinion is, however, based less on the precise semantics of *uzr*, which is unknown to us, than on its presumed syntactic role. If one analyzes *uzr* as the object of the verbs *ylḥm* and *yšqy*, it is plausibly a type of offering. If one sees *uzr* functioning as an adverbial, however, it is plausibly a special garment that Dānîʾilu puts on in the course of the rite (cf. *mizrt*).

The most obvious problem with the "offering" approach of *uzr* is that *uzr*, whatever it may denote, has to be something that is both food and drink. Since it is difficult to think of anything that is both solid and liquid, commentators tend to translate *uzr* in terms of its function, namely, as "(consecrated) oblations," "offerings," "Weihegeschenk," or in terms of *how* it is offered, namely as "a girded-offering," and yet they do not tell us what *uzr* is made of. Some scholars, such as Obermann and Cazelles, understand *uzr* as referring to the special offering of the incubation rite. This is, however, unlikely because the ancient Near Eastern practice of incubation, unlike the more institutionalized practice of incubation in Greece,[54] does not seem to have

---

[52] Wright, *Ritual in Narrative: The Dynamics of Feasting, Mourning, and Retaliation Rites in the Ugaritic Tale of Aqhat*, 23.

[53] For the "garment" interpretation, Pardee, "The Aqhatu Legend," 343; Simon B. Parker, trans., "Aqhat," in *Ugaritic Narrative Poetry*, ed. Simon B. Parker (Atlanta, GA: Scholars Press, 1997), 51; Wyatt, *Religious Texts from Ugarit*, 251; Olmo Lete, *Mitos y leyendas de Canaan: según la tradición de Ugarit*, 367; Husser, *Le songe et la parole: Etude sur le rêve et sa fonction dans l'ancien Israël*, 36; Margalit, *The Ugaritic Poem of Aqht: Text, Translation, Commentary*, 143; Gaster, *Thespis: Ritual, Myth, and Drama in the Ancient Near East*, 330; C. Virolleaud, *La légende phénicienne de Danel*, Mission de Ras-shamra 1 (Paris: Geuthner, 1936), 190. For the "offering" interpretation, see Wright, *Ritual in Narrative: The Dynamics of Feasting, Mourning, and Retaliation Rites in the Ugaritic Tale of Aqhat*, 21; Dietrich and Loretz, "Das Aqhat-Epos," 1259; Coogan, *Stories from Ancient Canaan*, 32; Cyrus H. Gordon, *Ugarit and Minoan Crete: The Bearing of Their Texts on the Origins of Western Culture*, 121; J. C. de Moor, *An Anthology of Religious Texts from Ugarit*, Nisaba 16 (Leiden: Brill, 1987), 225; Harold L. Ginsberg, "The Tale of Aqhat," in *ANET* (Princeton, NJ: Princeton University Press, 1969), 149.

[54] The Greek incubant had to prepare a specific sacrifice to propitiate the god whom he wants to invoke in a dream. The incubant consulting Trophonius, for instance, had to offer honey cake (μάζας μεγαγμένας μέλιτι) (cf. Carl A. Meier, *Ancient Incubation and Modern Psychotherapy* [Evanston: Northwestern University Press, 1967], 100). The Greek incubant offers cakes in the temple of Asclepius and a ram in the temple

had any established standard for preparatory offerings. This is hinted at by the fact that the rituals prescribed for incubation in *Rituals to Obtain a Purussû* differ from one another even though they are practiced in the same temple of Gula.[55]

A more sophisticated argument for the "offering" interpretation of *uzr* comes from David Wright, who proposes to translate it as "a girded-offering," that is to say, an offering performed while wearing the *mizrt*-garment. Wright finds support for this "offering" understanding of *uzr* in the difference in nuance between the two double-transitive stems (D-stem and Š-stem) of √lḥm and √šqy. According to Wright, Dānî'ilu's offering to the gods, which is couched in the verbs *ylḥm* and *yšqy*, focuses on the *presentation* of the specific mentioned object, the *uzr*-offering, while the feasts for the Kôṯarātu and for Kôṯaru-wa-Ḫasīs, which are couched in the Š-stems of the same roots, is more concerned with the guests' *eating and drinking*.[56] Although Wright's insight into the difference in nuance of the two double-transitive stems is commendable, it does not necessitate the presence of the direct object for the "factitive" usage of the verbs in question. The direct object, for instance, is omitted in the "factitive" use of √šqy in KTU 1.17 VI:31: *ḥwy yʿšr w yšqynh* "They feast the living one, give him drink." Furthermore, the direct object of the "causative" stem of √lḥm is explicitly indicated in KTU 1.17 II:29–30: *alp yṭbḫ l kṯrt yšlḥm kṯrt* "A bull he slaughtered for the Kôṯarātu, he caused the Kôṯarātu to eat (it)."

---

of Amphiaraus (Fritz Graf, "Incubation," in *Brill's New Pauly: Encyclopaedia of the Ancient World*, vol. 6, ed. Francis G. Gentry [Leiden: Brill, 2006], 766–67).

[55] S. A. L. Butler, *Mesopotamian Conceptions of Dreams and Dream Rituals*, AOAT 258 (Münster: Ugarit-Verlag, 1988), 222–23.

[56] Interestingly, Wright's proposal is already anticipated by Obermann, when he says, "...while *šlḥm* is used in the strictly causative sense of "to make someone eat," the intensive *laḥḥama* conveys the expansive-distributive sense of "to give, to offer, to invite, someone to eat," thus closely corresponding with the meaning of *šqy*" (Obermann, *How Daniel Was Blessed with a Son*, 8). Tropper, in his 1989 article, identifies three stems for Ugaritic √šqy and gives slightly different meanings to each stem: "austrinken" (G), "einschenken" or "ein Getränk versetzen" (D), "trinken lassen" (Š) (Tropper, "Ugaritisch *šqy*: 'trinken' oder 'tränken'?" 233–42). Although Wright does not accept a simple transitive meaning for Ugaritic √šqy "to drink," he applies Tropper's insight concerning the semantic difference between the D- and Š-stem of √šqy to the context of KTU 1.17 I 1–16. It appears to me that the meaning of *ylḥm* "to provide food" and *yšqy*, "to provide drink," puts the emphasis on the act of the presenter, while that of *yšlḥm* "cause to eat" and *yššq* "to cause to drink" focuses on the act of those who eat and drink.

All these considerations tip the scale in favor of the "garment" interpretation of *uzr*. According to this interpretation, the word *uzr* can be parsed as a passive participle (the *qatūl* pattern) of √ʾzr "to gird." The first alep *u* is explained by vowel harmony with the second vowel: /ʾuzūru/ ← /*ʾazūr/.[57] The word *uzr* is then understood to function substantivally as the subject of the verbs *ylḥm* and *yšqy*, thus describing Dānîʾilu in full ritual robe or loincloth, depending on one's understanding of *mizrt* that is also derived from √ʾzr "to gird." As will be shown later (2.1.3), the "garment" understanding of *uzr* provides various literary links, not only within the incubation type-scene, but also within the narrative as a whole.

The offering motif, which verbalizes the pre-verbal concept of intentionality, is couched in the frame of a seven-day sequence.[58] Although the seven-day formula could be purely literary, namely, the seven-day formula may not reflect the actual duration of the incubation rituals, the practice of a multiday incubation attested in the ancient Near Eastern texts enhances the possibility of it being present in our passage. The offering motif is repeated four times before the event on the seventh day is described. On the seventh day, the motif is not presented as a daily routine, but it is registered in the text as part of Baʿlu's speech (KTU 1.17 I:21–22). The first attestation of the offering motif (lines 2–3), which describes the nature of the action that is about to occur, is couched in a bicolon that is preceded by the full description of Dānîʾilu (lines 0–2),[59] while during the six days of the ritual the offering motif is registered in a tricolon preceded by a monocolon date formula.[60] This numeric increase (from bicolon to tricolon and from day one to day six) seems to reflect the crescendo in Dānîʾilu's feeling of desperation

[57] Tropper, *Ugaritische Grammatik*, 174–75.

[58] For the seven-day formula in Ugaritic epic literature, see Samuel E. Loewenstamm, "The Seven-Day-Unit in Ugaritic Epic Literature," *IEJ* 15 (1965): 121–33. Reprinted in Samuel E. Loewenstamm, *Comparative Studies in Biblical and Ancient Oriental Literatures* (Neukirchen-Vluyn: Neukirchener Verlag, 1980), 192–209.

[59] Cf. D. N. Freedman, "Counting Formulae," *JANESCU* 3 (1970–71): 77.

[60] Wyatt finds the repetition of the offering motif to be problematic and, following Jirku, Caquot and Sznycer, regards the first occurrence of the motif as an instruction/a command and the rest as its fulfillment (Wyatt, *Religious Texts from Ugarit*, 252, footnote 9). The survey of the seven day formula in the Ugaritic literature, however, shows that the seven-day sequence is typically preceded by the passage describing the nature of the action that is about to occur (Loewenstamm, *Comparative Studies in Biblical and Ancient Oriental Literatures*, 193). This is also the case with the description of the seven-day feast for the Kôṯarātu that forms the other end of the *inclusio* structure of the first two columns of the KTU 1.17 I.

and his focusing on attaining a revelation. Furthermore, the tricolon describing Dānî'ilu's incubation offering has a staircase structure,[61] in which the full description of Dānî'ilu in KTU 1.17 I:0–2 is telescoped into "the grammatical subject" slot of the "staircase" structure. Finally, it is noteworthy that the offering motif occurring within Baʿlu's petition (lines 21–22) is couched in a bicolon and has the function of summarizing what has occurred during the past six days. This forms a nice *inclusio* with the bicolon introducing the offering motif in KTU 1.17 I:2–3 (see Table 4.2 below).

Table 4.2: The Offering Motif

A	Introduction (ll 2–3)	*uzr ilm ylḥm / [uzr yšqy] bn qdš*	bicolon
B	Day 1–2 (ll 6–8)	*[uzr] ilm dnil / [uzr ilm] ylḥm / uzr [yšqy b]n qdš*	tricolon-staircase
B	Day 3–4 (ll 9–11)	*[uzr i]lm dnil / uzr [ilm y]lḥm / uzr yšqy bn [qdš]*	tricolon-staircase
B	Day 5–6 (ll 11–13)	*uzr [il]m dnil / uzr ilm ylḥm / [uzr] yšqy bn qdš*	tricolon-staircase
A′	Summary (ll 21–22)	*uzrm ilm ylḥm / uzrm yšqy bn qdš*	bicolon

What is the literary significance of the motif of multiday offering in the incubation type-scene? Margalit argues that the frame of the seven-day sequence is indicative of divine neglect, namely, 'Ilu's failure to notice Dānî'ilu's week-long devotion, not out of his ill-will but simply out of his seniority.[62] But Margalit's assertion seems to be based on an idiosyncratic translation of *abyn* ⸢*at*⸣ *dnil* "Art thou indifferent to Dan'el" (KTU 1.17 I:16–17).[63] The motif of multiday offering is better understood in the context of the incubation type-scene. It does triple duty within the type-scene. First, it builds up sympathy for Dānî'ilu's plight.

[61] Greenstein summarizes the three characteristics of the "staircase" parallelism as follows: "(1) the initial two words of the first line are reproduced initially in the second line; (2) the last word(s) of the first line is (are) either the grammatical noun-phrase (NP) of the first two lines or a vocative; (3) the second and third lines are parallel either synonymously or synthetically" (Edward L. Greenstein, "One More Step on the Staircase," *UF* 9 [1977]: 77). The poetic verse uzr ilm dnil / *uzr ilm ylḥm / uzr yšqy bn qdš* in KTU 1.17 I 6–8, 9–11a, 11c–13 fits Greenstein's definition perfectly.

[62] Margalit, *The Ugaritic Poem of Aqht: Text, Translation, Commentary*, 266–67.

[63] Ibid., 144.

The repetition of the scene describing Dānî'ilu making sacrifice in mourning garb creates tension in the narrative. It reminds the readers of Dānî'ilu's predicament and they are thereby led to sympathize with Dānî'ilu. Second, it creates the expectation that something critical is about to happen. The tension, generated by the repetition, is not static, but builds toward the summit of the seventh day, when Dānî'ilu's fortunes begin to reverse.[64] Third, the motif describing Dānî'ilu's offering in grief anticipates another multiday offering later in the type-scene. Although the two offering motifs share the characteristic vocabulary (√lḥm and √šqy) and seven-day formula, their different narrative context (before and after the theophany) accounts for a variety of differences: the change in mood, the change of verbal stems, the *uzr-alp* change, and the change in the internal structure of the seven day formulae.[65] Although there are no "verbal" connections between the offering motif and the following scene of theophany,[66] the seven-day offering motif may have created, in the mind of the readers who were aware of the convention of incubation, an association strong enough for them to recognize Dānî'ilu's offering as preparatory for the revelation to come. Freedman captures this point in the following remark: "The seven day activity here is the result of the actions on the other six days and is an abrupt—note the lack of parallelism—transition to new material."[67] In this sense, it may be said that the offering motif verbalizes the pre-verbal concept of intentionality which informs the incubation type-scene. Wright seems to confirm this by arguing that the offering "seeks to induce the gods to act on his behalf...that it is a serious and urgent petition to rectify a lamentable condition."[68]

[64] In the seven-day formula, a new event occurs on the seventh day. This is reflected by the fact that often the description of the seventh day does not repeat the daily routine of the past six days. Cf. Loewenstamm, "The Seven-Day-Unit in Ugaritic Epic Literature," 121–33.

[65] See below for details.

[66] There is, for instance, no Ugaritic equivalent to the Akkadian idiom for incubation *ūtul-ma inaṭṭal šutta* ("lie down to have a dream"). Cf. Annette von Zgoll, "Die Welt im Schlaf sehen: Inkubation von Träumen im antiken Mesopotamien," *WO* 32 (2002): 82.

[67] Freedman, "Counting Formulae," 77.

[68] Wright, *Ritual in Narrative: The Dynamics of Feasting, Mourning, and Retaliation Rites in the Ugaritic Tale of Aqhat*, 36.

2.1.3 *The Motif of Ritual Clothing and Ritual Nakedness*

According to E. L. Ehrlich, putting on special clothing or going completely naked could be part of an incubation rite.[69] Ovid's *Fasti* describes the incubation by Numa who was required to put on a rough garment and take off the rings from his fingers before he lay down on the fleece to sleep.[70] The incubants who seek an answer from Trophonius were required to be clothed in white linen and wrapped in swaddling-bands like a child.[71] These data, albeit late in date, may provide a clue to understanding the incubational context in the use of the word *uzr* and the phrase *yd mizrt* and *yd ṣt* (KTU 1.17 I:3–5, 13–15). If the analysis of *uzr* as expressing the subject of the verbs *ylḥm* and *yšqy* is legitimate (thus translated "girded"), and its etymological association with *mizrt* is not a pure coincidence, it may be argued that Dānî'ilu was clothed in the *mizrt* and the *ṣt* while performing the offering. The motif of ritual (dis)robing verbalizes the pre-verbal concept of intentionality in the incubation type-scene.

Although the precise meaning of Ugaritic *mizrt* is uncertain,[72] its use in KTU 1.5 VI:17 and 31 suggests that Ugaritic *mizrt* refers to an article of clothing suited to mourning. KTU 1.5 VI:12–25 describes 'Ilu's reaction to the news of Ba'lu's death. After descending from his throne at the sad news, 'Ilu "pours dirt of mourning on his head, dust of humiliation on his cranium, for clothing, he is covered with a girded garment" (*⸢yṣ⸣q ʿmr un l ⸢ri⸣šh / ʿpr pl<u>t</u>t l qdq⸢dh⸣ / lpš yks mizrtm*) (lines 14–17). The pericope that immediately follows records 'Anatu's acts of

[69] Ehrlich says, "Als Vorbereitung dienten Reinigungsriten, Fasten, sexuelle und alkoholische abstinenz, verschiedenartige Opfer, besondere Bereitung der Schlafstelle, *Anlegung besonderer Kleider (oder völlige Nacktheit)*, Gebet, selbsterniedrigung und kultisches Weinen" (Ernst L. Ehrlich, *Der Traum im Alten Testament*, BZAW 73 [Berlin: Töpelmann, 1953], 14–15).

[70] Susan Ackerman, "The Deception of Isaac, Jacob's Dream at Bethel, and Incubation on an Animal Skin," in *Priesthood and Cult in Ancient Israel*, ed. Gary A. Anderson (Sheffield: JOST Press, 1991), 106.

[71] The incubant dressed like an infant exemplifies the symbolism of death and birth in the rites of Trophonius. This symbolism is also manifested in the process of the incubant being thrust in and out through the hole. Also noteworthy in connection with the statue of Asclepius at Titane is that the god himself there has the character of an infant in swaddling clothes and thus of an incubant. Cf. Meier, *Ancient Incubation and Modern Psychotherapy*, 100, 110.

[72] Pardee states the problem as follows: "The basic question here is whether the garment is only a loin-cloth, which would imply that he served the gods half naked (as some have argued) and that he lay down naked, or whether it implies a full garment held in place by a belt" (Pardee, "The Aqhatu Legend," 343, foonote 3).

mourning for the death of Baʿlu. In this pericope, the bicolon describing ʾIlu pouring dirt and dust on his head is absent, but a monocolon [*lpš*] *tks miz*[*rtm*] "for clothing, she is covered with a girded garment" (lines 31) begins a series of typical acts of mourning in the next tablet after the superscription (KTU 1.6 I:2ff). If the omission of the bicolon describing ʾIlu pouring dust on his head were not a scribal error, it suggests that the *mizrt*-clothing may have served no less as a symbol of mourning than did the dirt on the head.[73] Furthermore, if Ugaritic *mizrt* refers to a loincloth, it would imply that Dānîʾilu served the gods half-naked. This also goes well with a figure of the mourner in KTU 1.16 II:31 (*lbl sk* "without a vest"), in Micah 1:8 (*ʾēylkāh šîlāl wəʿārôm ʾeʿěśeh mispēd* "I will go stripped and naked; I will make lamentation").[74] All this goes to show that the term *mizrt* may be associated with the ambiance of mourning, which draws attention to the predicament of Dānîʾilu. Also, although a specific mention may have been made about Dānîʾilu's sonlessness in the missing lines at the beginning of the column, the description of Dānîʾilu in the *mizrt*-garment (and the *ṣt*)[75] certainly anticipates the explicit disclosure of Dānîʾilu's problem in lines 18b–19 (*d in bn lh km aḫh / w šrš km aryh* "who has no son like his brothers, no scion like his kinsmen"). Furthermore, it may be argued that the motif describing Dānîʾilu in the *mizrt*-garment ("the motif of ritual clothing") not only recalls his predicament, but also registers his intention to enlist divine help.[76]

The term *yd* (KTU 1.17 I:3, 4) indicates that Dānîʾilu removes his *mizrt*- and *ṣt*-garment before lying down to sleep. The term can be interpreted as a verb from √ndy or √ydy "cast down, cast off; remove." This understanding is better than construing the term as the preposition 'with' and viewing Dānîʾilu as ascending his bed wearing (in other words, "with") the clothing in question.[77] If *mizrt* were understood

---

[73] Cf. Moor, *An Anthology of Religious Texts from Ugarit*, 226, footnote 11.

[74] See Isaiah 32:11. For iconic representations of professional mourning women in seminude or nude state from the ancient Near East, see James B. Pritchard, *ANES* (Princeton, NJ: Princeton University Press, 1954), no. 459, 634, 638.

[75] Based on the parallelism of *mizrt* and *ṣt*, Wright argues that the *ṣt*-garment had the same character as the *mizrt*-garment (Wright, *Ritual in Narrative: The Dynamics of Feasting, Mourning, and Retaliation Rites in the Ugaritic Tale of Aqhat*, 31).

[76] For the importance of a special garment in approaching to the deity, see Gaster, *Thespis: Ritual, Myth, and Drama in the Ancient Near East*, 330–31.

[77] For the latter interpretation, see Coogan, *Stories from Ancient Canaan*, 32; Moor, *An Anthology of Religious Texts from Ugarit*, 225. Other idiosyncratic suggestions include Obermann's that *yd* is derived from √ndy (< √nḏy) "to sprinkle" and those

to be a loincloth, as suggested by some scholars,[78] Dānî'ilu would have retired for the night in complete nudity, not to mention that he would have been half-naked when performing the ritual. Although scholars like Wyatt do not like the idea of a naked ritual performer,[79] Wyatt's disposition against the nudity of the ritual performer may be offset by the fact that Sumerian priests were naked during cultic performances. Gudea Stela (ST. 4–5)[80] depicts a libation scene where a shaved male figure pours a liquid rendered by three wavy lines from a spouted jug into a vase. Although only the upper body and part of one foot of the libator remain, he was probably nude, since libators with this kind of jug ware were always depicted nude.[81] Also there are ample Early Dynastic images that show a nude priest pouring liquid from a sprouted jug to a conical vessel.[82] This circumstantial evidence, together with the fact that incubants often went naked or half-naked in preparation for the revelation,[83] enhances the possibility that Dānî'ilu performed preparatory rituals half or fully nude.

Be that as it may, it is certain that the text portrays Dānî'ilu as constantly changing in and out of his ritual clothing. This is thrown into relief by the head position of *uzr* and *yd* in the two poetic units at both

of Gordon and Gaster that *yd* is derived from √ndd 'to flee, away.' Cf. Obermann, *How Daniel Was Blessed with a Son*, 9; Theodor H. Gaster, "Dream in the Bible," in *Encyclopaedia Judaica*, vol. 6, ed. Fred Skolnik (New York: Keter, 2007), 331; Cyrus H. Gordon, *Ugarit and Minoan Crete: The Bearing of Their Texts on the Origins of Western Culture*, 121; Tropper J. and Verreet E., "Ugaritische NDY, YDY, HDY, NDD und D(W)D," *UF* 20 (1988): 345.

[78] Wright, *Ritual in Narrative: The Dynamics of Feasting, Mourning, and Retaliation Rites in the Ugaritic Tale of Aqhat*, 21ff; Husser, "The Birth of a Hero: Form and Meaning of KTU 1.17 i–ii," 88, 93; Dietrich and Loretz, "Das Aqhat-Epos," 1259; M. Dijkstra and J. C. de Moor, "Problematical Passages in the Legend of Aqhatu," *UF* 7 (1975): 174.

[79] Wyatt (*Religious Texts from Ugarit*, 254, footnote 19) points to the long ceremonial robe with thick hem illustrated on the Ba'lu au Foudre Stela and argues that the *mirzt-* and *ṣt*-clothing refer to such ritual garments appropriate to the occasion.

[80] For the images, see Claudia E. Suter, *Gudea's Temple Building: The Representation of an Early Mesopotamian Ruler in Text and Image*, Cuneiform Monographs 17 (Groningen: Styx Publications, 2000), 342, 344.

[81] Ibid., 195.

[82] Ibid., 196. Also see the Seal of UrDun (Fig. 21) in Ibid., 197.

[83] Frances L. Flannery-Dailey, "Standing at the Heads of Dreamers: A Study of Dreams in Antiquity Second Temple Period" (Ph.D. diss., University of Iowa, 2000), 40; Ehrlich, *Der Traum im Alten Testament*, 14–15. *Scholia to Aristophanes' Nubes*, for instance, reports that the participants in the incubation rite of Trophonius received their vision while being naked (Dijkstra and Moor, "Problematical Passages in the Legend of Aqhatu," 174, footnote 27).

ends of the six-day sequence of preparatory ritual. The word for robing (*uzr*) heads off each lines of the first poetic unit, while the word for "disrobing" (*yd* [*ṣth/mizrt*]) leads each lines of the second poetic unit, thus concentrating focus on the binary opposition that informs the six-day sequence of ritual preparation. Wright, citing Catherine Bell's study of binary opposition in ritual, avers that if wearing regular clothing or being clothed is the normal social state, then wearing a ritual garment (*mizrt* and *ṣt*) and being unclothed marks deprivation. He goes on to argue that Dānî'ilu's ritual "was able to maintain and highlight an atmosphere of mourning by moving back and forth between the two modes of deprivation (half-naked and naked), without ever returning Dānî'ilu to a normal state."[84] This seems to reinforce the impression that Dānî'ilu's ritual is motivated by a certain lack in his life and charged with an expectation of a solution.

The motif of ritual clothing and nakedness also has a literary echo in the rest of the 'Aqhatu narrative. The story of 'Aqhatu etched in three clay tablets (KTU 1.17–19) centers around the birth and death of 'Aqhatu, son of Dānî'ilu. Both the beginning (KTU 1.17 I–II) and the end (KTU 1.19) of the story transpire in the absence of a proper son-heir. This contextual agreement is matched by the echoing of certain literary motifs at both ends of the story. One such example is the motif of a ritual clothing and nakedness, in other words, the motif of wearing special clothing and being unclothed. In order to acquire a legitimate heir, Dānî'ilu offers sacrifice to the gods while wearing the *mizrt*- and *ṣt*-garments. When he lies down to have a dream, however, he takes them off. Pūǵatu, when she sees the effects of drought on the land, strips Dānî'ilu of his clothing by rending it.[85] Since the well-known custom is that of tearing off one's own clothing as an expression of grief, scholars are uncertain about the social implication of Pūǵatu's action and Margalit, for instance, proposes an alternate reading.[86] Be that as it may, it is arguable that the scene of Dānî'ilu's going naked

[84] Wright, *Ritual in Narrative: The Dynamics of Feasting, Mourning, and Retaliation Rites in the Ugaritic Tale of Aqhat*, 32.

[85] It is also possible to take the subject of the verb *tmz*ʿ to be *kst* "clothing." In this case, *tmz*ʿ would be parsed as a passive verb. But, to the best of my knowledge, the traditional expression of grief, namely, rending one's own clothes, is never couched in a passive verb with the clothing as a subject.

[86] Margalit takes Ugaritic √mzʿ to mean "to bound, prance (like a gazelle)" and renders *tmz*ʿ as "(The garment of Dānî'ilu, the Rapian) fluttered" (Margalit, *The Ugaritic Poem of Aqht: Text, Translation, Commentary*, 158, 368).

at the beginning of the story echoes the scene where he again had to go, albeit involuntarily, naked again. If the former is in order to procure a son, the latter is a proleptic reaction to the news of his son's death. The motif of putting on ritual clothing at the beginning of the story, on the other hand, similarly reverberates with the later scene of Pūġatu's putting on a man's garment as a way of disguising herself as the goddess 'Anatu, thus gaining access to the one who is responsible for her brother's death. It is noteworthy that the motifs of wearing and removing a garment forms a chiasm. The chiastic structure may be schematized as follows:

Table 4.3: The Motif of Ritual Clothing and Ritual Nakedness

A	*uzr*	Wearing clothing
B	*yd ṣth, yd mizrth*	Removing clothing
B′	*tmzʿ kst*	Removing clothing
A′	*tlbš npṣ ġzr*	Wearing clothing

In conclusion, the motif of ritual clothing and nakedness, which may reflect a practice of incubation known both to the reader and the poet, verbalizes the pre-verbal concept of intentionality. The scene of wearing the *mizrt-* and *ṣt*-garments not only recalls Dānî'ilu's deprivation, but also speaks volumes of his intention to seek divine help, since wearing a mourning garb in the presence of the gods often indicates the incubant's desire to make his voice heard aloud. Furthermore, the motif of ritual clothing and nakedness anticipates Dānî'ilu's and Pūġātu's reactions to the loss of 'Aqhatu. This gives the narrative a sense of unity and connection.

2.1.4 *The Sleeping Motif*

Although there is no explicit mention of *šnt* "sleep" in the text under discussion, almost no one doubts that *yʿl wyškb…wyln* "(Dānî'ilu) went up and lay down…and spent the night" (KTU 1.17 I:4–5 and its parallel lines) implies sleeping.[87]

[87] Even Husser does not deny that Dānî'ilu engages in sleep ritual, but he goes on to say, "[T]he sleep ritual of the supplicant does not necessarily imply that he expected a visit from the divinity in his dream" (Husser, "The Birth of a Hero: Form and Meaning of KTU 1.17 i–ii," 95). Although Husser may have wanted to see a clear textual evidence that links the sleep ritual to the incubant's intention to have a dream, which appears to me to be an imposition of modern assumption on ancient

The three verbs composing the sleeping motif provide little semantic difficulty. The spelling *wynl* in line 5 is most likely a simple mistake for *wyln*, which is confirmed by the appearance of the latter form in line 15. The exact nuance of *yʿl*, however, needs some discussion. Dānîʾilu is said to "go up (*yʿl*) and lie down" after removing his clothing. Two interpretative possibilities present themselves immediately. First, the use of Ugaritic √ʿly may be elliptical and the prepositional phrase, *l ʿršh* "to his bed", may have been omitted but assumed by the poet and the audience.[88] The collocation of the very prepositional phrase and the verb √ʿly later in the text (1.17 I:38) makes this analysis plausible. The problem, however, is that the context of the collocation of the verb √ʿly and the propositional phrase *l ʿršh* in 1.17 I:38 is the sexual intercourse, and not the act of sleeping *per se*. Furthermore, the idiom of "going up on a bed" attested to in other northwest Semitic literature (mainly the Hebrew Bible) appear in the context of copulation or sickness, and not in the context of sleep (cf. Genesis 49:4; 2 Kings 1:4;[89] Isaiah 57:7–8).[90] This makes the first interpretative possibility of *yʿl* less likely, although one cannot completely exclude it from consideration. The second explanation is also based on the elliptical use of √ʿly. The place to which Dānîʾilu goes up, however, is not the assumed bed but the clothing (cf. *mizrt* and *ṣt*) that he has just taken off. Some biblical passages bear witness to mourners who spread sackcloth and use it as a makeshift bed, although not in context of incubation (cf. 2 Samuel 21:10; Esther 4:3; 1 Kings 21:27; Isaiah 58:5). Also the Hittite evidence for incubation attests to a similar act, namely, lying down on a garment (cf. Paškuwatti's therapeutic incubation).[91] All this leads us to believe that the second option is a better interpretation of *yʿl* in lines 5, 6, and its parallel lines. If this interpretation were correct, Dānîʾilu would then have spread the ritual clothing as a makeshift bed and lay

texts, the incubation type-scene has many other motifs that may verbalize the concept of intentionality.

[88] A variation of this interpretation is that of Husser who thinks that Dānîʾilu slept on a raised place, perhaps, a terrace (Husser, "The Birth of a Hero: Form and Meaning of KTU 1.17 i–ii," 93).

[89] Cf. Robert L. Cohn, *2 Kings*, Berit Olam (Collegevillle, Minnesota: The Liturgical Press, 2000), 6.

[90] Cf. Joseph Blenkinsopp, *Isaiah 56–66: A New Translation with Introduction and Commentary*, AB 19B (New York: Doubleday, 2003), 161.

[91] Cf. Alice Mouton, *Rêves hittites*, CHANE 28 (Leiden: Brill, 2007), Text no. 29.

down on it to have an oneiric revelation. Dānî'ilu's act of lying on his ritual clothing is also reminiscent of the act of drawing a magical circle before the incubant lies down within it.[92] All of these may reflect a desire to lie down in the "holy of holies," namely, the spot most propitious for theophany.[93]

Although the sleeping motif is not registered in the text from day one through day four of the ritual, it does not preclude the possibility that the incubant may have lain down every night until he receives a divine revelation on the seventh day. The absence of the motif during the first four days may be explained by the chiastic composition in which the six-day sequence of the ritual is couched.

Table 4.4: The Chiastic Structure of Dānî'ilu's Preparatory Ritual

A	Introduction (1.17 I 2–3; 3–5)	*uzr ilm ylḥm / [uzr yšqy] bn qdš* *yd [ṣth y'l] wyškb / yd [mizrth] p yln!*	C + O (2) Ć + S (2)[94]
B	Day one and two (1.17 I 6–8)	*[uzr] ilm dnil / [uzr ilm] ylḥm / uzr [yšqy b]n qdš*	C + O (3)
B	Day three and four (1.17 I 9–11)	*[uzr i]lm dnil / uzr [ilm y]lḥm / uzr yšqy bn [qdš]*	C + O (3)
A'	Day five and six (1.17 I 11–13; 13–15)	*uzr [il]m dnil / uzr ilm ylḥm / [uzr] yšqy bn qdš* *yd ṣth [dn]il / yd ṣth y'l wyškb / [yd] mirzth p yln*	C + O (3) Ć + S (3)

*C=Ritual Clothing Motif, Ć=Nakedness Motif, O=Offering Motif, S=Sleeping Motif, (2)=Bicolon, (3)=Tricolon.

[92] When Gilgamesh wanted to induce a dream-vision, Enkidu drew a magic circle within which Gilgamesh sat "with his chin on his knees" (S. Dalley, "The Tale of Bulūqiyā and the Alexander Romance in Jewish and Sufi Mystical Sources," in *Tracing the Threads: Studies in the Vitality of Jewish Pseudepigraphia*, ed. J. C. Reeves [Atlanta, GA: Scholars Press, 1994], 254; cf. Husser, *Dreams and Dream Narratives in the Biblical World*, 49).

[93] When the ceremonies of *Rituals to Obtain a Purrusû* were performed for a private individual, they may have taken place at a private residence, even on the roof. In such a case, a sacred area was demarcated by a circle of pure water (Butler, *Mesopotamian Conceptions of Dreams and Dream Rituals*, 236).

[94] D. Wright, following Margalit, makes this poetic verse into a tricolon (Wright, *Ritual in Narrative: The Dynamics of Feasting, Mourning, and Retaliation Rites in the Ugaritic Tale of Aqhat*, 21). But there is no prosodic reason to justify such an emendation.

The above chiastic structure concentrates focus on the sleeping motif by placing it at both the ends of the chiastic composition, thus deliberately omitting it in the middle part of the structure and also by placing the sleeping motif right before the theophany of the seventh day. This is a literary focus and does not necessarily mirror what "really happened." This literary focus on the act of sleeping is fitting to the importance it has in the definition of incubation widely accepted by historians of religion.

The sleeping motif foreshadows 'Ilu's blessing within the incubation type-scene. The verb √ʿly that occurs in the sleeping motif also occurs in the message of 'Ilu with regard to Dānîʾilu's copulation with his wife, which would lead to the birth of an heir. Dānîʾilu engages in ritual "sleep" in order to enlist divine help in solving his problem of sonlessness. In response, 'Ilu commands Dānîʾilu to "sleep" with his wife with the divine promise that she will conceive. The human means of invoking divine help becomes the divine means to bring about salvation. The sleeping motif of the incubation type-scene plays a literary role also in the narrative as a whole. The theme of sleep, which is related to the birth of 'Aqhatu in the initial incubation type-scene, is used later in the context of the death of the son acquired through incubational "sleep." After collecting the pieces of 'Aqhatu's body from Ṣamlu, the mother of the vultures, Dānîʾilu curses the tomb-robbers who would disturb 'Aqhatu from his sleep (cf. *tšḫ̣tann b šnth*). Here the term 'sleep' becomes the euphemistic term denoting the death of the son acquired through "sleep." This is simply another example that shows that the initial type-scene of incubation provides a literary key to understanding the story as a whole.

2.1.5 *The Motif of Prayer*

There seems to be no aural element in Dānîʾilu's preparatory ritual: Neither incantation nor prayer is explicitly registered in the text. Yehezkel Kaufmann once proposed the idea that all temple cultic acts were performed in silence in ancient Israel: "P makes no reference to the spoken word in describing temple rites. All the various acts of the priest are performed in silence."[95] He goes on to argue that the silence of P's cult is rooted in the wish to make a clear break from paganism

[95] Yehezkel Kaufmann, *The Religion of Israel* (Chicago: University of Chicago Press, 1960), 303.

in which prayer, incantation, or spell were integral parts of the cult. If Kaufmann were right,[96] it is arguable that the Ugaritic version of incubation rite may have had a "verbal" element to it. In this regard, although there is no direct citation of Dānî'ilu's prayer in the section describing the preparatory ritual, the issue is not as simple as it may first appear.

Obermann is the first scholar who argued that the preparatory ritual includes Dānî'ilu's prayer: "It is only now, when the narrative turns to the events during the seventh day—again, we should rather say, seventh night—that we learn that the incubation ritual did include prayer."[97] He goes on to say, "In all probability, it [prayer] was offered together with the *uzr* sacrifice" throughout the week.[98] The reason that prayer was mentioned only in the seventh day is, according to Obermann, "to keep the interest of his listeners in suspense by reserving any reference to Danel's prayer and, by the same token, to the purpose of the incubation, until his narrative reached the description of the seventh night."[99] The problem, however, does not lie in his insight into the possible presence of prayer in the apparently silent preparatory ritual but in his philological basis for it. He translates *mk b šbʿ ymm [k] yqrb bʿl bḥnt abyn dnil mt rpʾ anḫ ǵzr mt hrnmy* (KTU 1.17 I:15–18) as "But on the seventh day [when] he draws near to perform his supplication, Danel, Man of Rapi, begs, The Hero, Man of Harnamiya, sighs."[100] As is obvious from this translation, Obermann takes *bʿl* to be a by-form of the verb *pʿl* "to make, do" and *ḥnt* to be a Ugaritic equivalent to Hebrew *təḥinnāh* "supplication." Moreover, he takes *abyn* as a quadriliteral verb meaning "to beg."[101] No serious scholar, however, accepts his philological conclusions.

A more philologically sound argument for the presence of prayer in the preparatory ritual is advanced by David Wright. He admits that the 'Aqhatu text does not cite any prayer spoken by Dānî'ilu. But it does not prevent him from arguing that the preparatory ritual may have included an aural element. Wright singles out the word *anḫ* "the

---

[96] Kaufmann's basic point was later accepted by scholars like Nahum Sarna, Menahem Haran and Moshe Greenberg. Cf. Israel Knohl, "Between Voice and Silence: The Relationship Between Prayer and Temple Cult," *JBL* 115 (1996): 18.

[97] Obermann, *How Daniel Was Blessed with a Son*, 11.

[98] Ibid.

[99] Ibid.

[100] Ibid., 5.

[101] Ibid., 11–13.

moaning one" (KTU 1.17 I:17)[102] as the basis for his assertion that Dānî'ilu may have accompanied his offerings with expressed lamentation.[103] As for the content of the prayer of lament, he provides two items of circumstantial evidence. The first relates to the fact that Ba'lu's supplication has three major elements of a classic lament.[104] Wright argues that Ba'lu's speech, which can be categorized as a lament, is a faithful reflection of Dānî'ilu's prayer of lament. The second circumstantial evidence comes from the ancient Near Eastern texts that attest to the mediation of a prayer by one god to another.[105] Putting these pieces of evidence together, one may argue that Ba'lu functions as a mediator of Dānî'ilu's prayer to 'Ilu. If this is the case, Ba'lu's speech may in fact summarize what Dānî'ilu is imagined to have spoken.

The question then arises: why was the poet silent about Dānî'ilu's prayer when he described his preparatory ritual? The easy answer might be that Dānî'ilu's prayer of lament that accompanied the ritual was omitted because Ba'lu's intercessory prayer provided its basic content (cf. Wright). But why did the poet make no allusion whatsoever to this important aspect of the preparatory ritual in his description of Dānî'ilu's preparatory ritual? The text is silent, although the reality behind the text may not have been so. The answer to this question may be found in the poet's recurrent technique of "delayed identification." In other words, the poet deliberately delayed an aural element until the seventh day. Dānî'ilu prayer is deliberately silenced by the poet in order to keep the interest of the readers in suspense until the seventh day, thus maximizing its climactic effect. This is shown in relief by the contrast between the scene of preparatory ritual and the scene of theophany. The former is narrated by the poet's visual description, whereas

---

[102] The Ugaritic verb occurs only here but its meaning seems to be solidly established by its cognates in other semitic languages (Hebrew אנח, Akkadian anāḫu, Arabic 'nḥ!), all of which can have the translation value "to sigh, moan." Note that the Arabic cognate is *'nḥ*, not the expected *'nḫ*.

[103] Wright, *Ritual in Narrative: The Dynamics of Feasting, Mourning, and Retaliation Rites in the Ugaritic Tale of Aqhat*, 39. It is interesting that Pardee translates the parallel term *abynn* as "lamenting" instead of the more traditional translation "poor, wretched" (Pardee, "The Aqhatu Legend," 344). But see also "du dépouillé" in Bordreuil and Pardee, *Choix de Textes: Glossaire*, 25.

[104] Ibid., 40: "(a) a complaint, describing Dānî'ilu's unfortunate state (lines 16b–21a); (b) a rationale for divine aid, that is, Dānî'ilu gave the gods food offerings (21b–22); and (c) a petition, a call for 'Ilu to remedy Dānî'ilu's hapless condition (23–24)."

[105] Ibid, 39, footnote 84. Cf. David P. Wright, *Disposal of Impurity: Elimination Rites in the Bible and in Hittite and Mesopotamian Literature*, SBLDS 101 (Atlanta, GA: Scholars Press, 1987), 82 and footnote 27.

the latter is carried out by a series of direct speeches. In the former, the characters are silent, while in the theophanic scene the characters are loud. Also, Dānî'ilu's effective silence, a sign of mourning, stands in stark contrast to his later bursting into speech, a sign of joy (cf. KTU 1.17 II:12–23). Furthermore, Dānî'ilu's initial silence may form a contrast to the emphasis on his prayers-curses later, in the context of the loss of his son. Dānî'ilu's prayer-curse serves as a major motif that moves the plot later in the narrative. His prayer-curse is recorded twice. When he sees the effects of the drought, which may portend the death of his son, he utters a spell (*yṣly*)[106] upon the clouds (*'rpt*), the rain (*yr*), and the dew (*ṭl*) (cf. KTU 1.19 I:39–42).[107] As an interesting side note, this prayer is preceded by Pūġatu's "silent" weeping (*tbky pġt bm lb*, line 34) and the scene of Pūġatu tearing Dānî'ilu's garment (lines 36–37), just as Dānî'ilu's speech of joy is preceded by his "silent" prayer and lying down naked in the incubation type-scene. Dānî'ilu's speech of prayer-curse also occurs when he tries to retrieve the remains of his son's body. He prays to Ba'lu to break the wings of the avian culprits so that he may examine their innards for the remnants of his son's dead body. Unlike in the incubation type-scene, Ba'lu's response seems instantaneous this time. These later emphases on Dānî'ilu's loud prayer form a contrast to the initial "silent" prayer in the incubation type-scene.[108]

2.1.6 *Place and Time*

The practice of incubation normally took place in a temple or a sanctuary in ancient Near East, not unlike in Greece. Even a special room within the temple precincts was designated for incubation.[109] If the rite had to be done in private residences, those private residences must have been purified to serve as a place for the practice of incubation.[110] Sometimes a sacred area was delineated, for example, by a magic circle

[106] For the interpretative problem of this word, see Pardee, "The Aqhatu Legend," 351, footnote 95.
[107] For details, see section 3 below.
[108] For the role of "silence" in the practice of incubation, see *Rituals to Obtain a Purrussû*, line 68 (Butler, *Mesopotamian Conceptions of Dreams and Dream Rituals*, 367). Also for the role of silence in the Mesopotamian rituals, see Erica Reiner, "Dead of Night," in *Studies in Honor of Benno Landsberger on His Seventy-Fifth Birthday*, ed. Hans G. Güterbock and Jacobsen Thorkild (Chicago: University of Chicago Press, 1965), 247–51.
[109] Cf. Šugalam and Ubšukinna in the temple of Ningirsu, E-KUR in the temple of Marduk, and Abaton in the temple of Asclepius.
[110] Mouton, *Rêves hittites*, 73–74.

drawn with water.[111] All this attention to the place of incubation may be accounted for by the liminal nature of theophanic experience. Such theophany required a liminal place that provides a link between the natural and supernatural worlds.

Where then did Dānî'ilu perform his rituals? In fact we have such words as *bt bʿl* "Baʿlu's house" and *bt ʾil* "ʾIlu's house" (lines 31–32 and their parallel lines) within the incubation type-scene (KTU 1.17 I–II) but they do not tell us where Dānî'ilu performed his ritual. The only textual hint to the place of incubation is found in lines 24–25 of column II: *dnil bth ymǵyn / yštql dnil lhklh* "Dānî'ilu comes to his house, Dānî'ilu arrives at his palace." This implies that Dānî'ilu was at another location for the incubation rite. Scholars who take the initial scene of the ʾAqhatu story as incubation tend to infer from the line just mentioned that Dānî'ilu's ritual took place in a temple.[112] Some scholars such as del Olmo Lete and Gaster specify it as the temple of Baʿlu.[113] Scholars who are explicitly opposed to the incubation interpretation of the scene, on the other hand, take an agnostic stance on the issue.[114] But, as Wright points out, the complexity and duration of the ritual seems to point to a temple as the logical place where Dānî'ilu performed his ritual.[115] Considering that the reader may have recognized that Dānî'ilu performed incubation at the temple without being told, it appears to me that the motif of a temple hinted at only later in the type-scene is another example of "delayed identification."

The motif of a temple contributes to the development of the plot of the ʾAqhatu story by dint of its symbolic significance. The temple serves as a symbol of divine sovereignty. The architecture and decoration of temples embodies the exaltedness and remoteness of the gods which remind the human of their place in the hierarchical order of

---

[111] Butler, *Mesopotamian Conceptions of Dreams and Dream Rituals*, 236.

[112] Simon B. Parker, *The Pre-Biblical Narrative Tradition: Essays on the Ugaritic Poems Keret and Aqhat*, 100; Olmo Lete, *Mitos y leyendas de Canaan: según la tradición de Ugarit*, 334; Coogan, *Stories from Ancient Canaan*, 27–28; Gaster, *Thespis: Ritual, Myth, and Drama in the Ancient Near East*, 316; John Gray, *The Legacy of Canaan: The Ras Shamra Texts and Their Relevance to the Old Testament.*, 108; Obermann, *How Daniel Was Blessed with a Son*, 7.

[113] Olmo Lete, *Mitos y leyendas de Canaan: según la tradición de Ugarit*, 334; Gaster, *Thespis: Ritual, Myth, and Drama in the Ancient Near East*, 316.

[114] Margalit, *The Ugaritic Poem of Aqht: Text, Translation, Commentary*, 261; Husser, *Le songe et la parole: Etude sur le rêve et sa fonction dans l'ancien Israël*, 49.

[115] Wright, *Ritual in Narrative: The Dynamics of Feasting, Mourning, and Retaliation Rites in the Ugaritic Tale of Aqhat*, 34.

the universe.[116] In this regard, Dānî'ilu's act of offering in a temple shows in relief his piety, namely, the knowledge of his own place in the universe. Dānî'ilu is acting according to the existing order of the universe. He is not upsetting it. This piety towards higher beings easily translates into respect for (fore-)fathers in human relations. The list of filial duties serves to reinforce such an ideology by showing where 'Aqhatu fits into the hierarchical scheme of things and how he is expected to behave.[117] He is subordinate to his father, which means the son is subordinate to the gods, to whom Dānî'ilu is subordinate.[118] Later in the narrative, the motif of a temple is utilized to show the hierarchy-upsetting act of 'Aqhatu which stands in stark contrast with the piety of his father shown at the beginning of the story. After giving a bow to 'Aqhatu, Dānî'ilu made a vow that 'Aqhatu must offer the first-fruits of the game killed with the bow to a temple.[119] Since the text breaks at that moment, we do not know what happened next. But the later plot of the story seems to imply that 'Aqhatu may not have fulfilled the vow made by his father, upsetting both the father-son and the divine-human order. Although the extant text seems to attribute 'Aqhatu's death to the envy of ʿAnatu—'Aqhatu being an innocent victim of divine whim, one cannot exclude the possibility that the poet tries to show 'Aqhatu to be in the wrong: 'Aqhatu did not respect the

---

[116] John Baines, "Palaces and Temples of Ancient Egypt," in *Civilizations of the Ancient Near East*, ed. Jack M. Sasson (New York: Charles Scribner's Sons, 1995), 315.

[117] John Gray, *The Legacy of Canaan: The Ras Shamra Texts and Their Relevance to the Old Testament.*, 111.

[118] Wright, *Ritual in Narrative: The Dynamics of Feasting, Mourning, and Retaliation Rites in the Ugaritic Tale of Aqhat*, 69.

[119] Here I follow Pardee's interpretation (Pardee, "The Aqhatu Legend," 346, footnote 31). Lines 37–38 of KTU 1.17 V are, however, so damaged that the precise understanding is impossible. Most scholars align themselves along one of the following two lines. First, scholars such as Dietrich and Loretz, Wright, and Moor hear in the line the echo of the biblical story of Esau and Jacob in which Isaac asks his son to hunt game for him (Dietrich and Loretz, "Das Aqhat-Epos," 1270 and footnote 95; Wright, *Ritual in Narrative: The Dynamics of Feasting, Mourning, and Retaliation Rites in the Ugaritic Tale of Aqhat*, 94–96; Moor, *An Anthology of Religious Texts from Ugarit*, 235). These scholars take the previous verse (lines 35–36) as Dānî'ilu's (magical) naming or designating of the bow for 'Aqhatu. Scholars like Ginsberg, Pardee, Gaster, del Olmo Lete, and Wyatt, on the other hand, find there the motif of the offering of first-fruits which is attested throughout ancient Near East (Ginsberg, "The Tale of Aqhat," 151, footnote 20; Gaster, *Thespis: Ritual, Myth, and Drama in the Ancient Near East*, 344; Olmo Lete, *Mitos y leyendas de Canaan: según la tradición de Ugarit*, 339; Wyatt, *Religious Texts from Ugarit*, 270 and footnote 87; Cf. Rainer Albertz, *A History of Israelite Religion in the Old Testament Period: Volume 1: From the Beginnings to the End of the Monarchy*, OTL [Louisville, KY: Westminster John Knox Press, 1994], 102; Gregorio del Olmo Lete, *Canaanite Religion* [Winona Lake, IN: Eisenbrauns, 2004], 39).

vow made to the gods, nor did he treat ʿAnatu with respect later. If this interpretation is legitimate, one may appreciate the role that the motif of a temple, a reminder of proper hierarchy of the universe, plays in the development of the narrative plot.

The motif of night, which also exhibits liminality, is assumed in the incubation type-scene in KTU 1.17 I–II. The text does not tell us when the theophany took place. But it does tell us that the incubant spent several days lying down daily for a revelation. The use of the sleeping motif, especially, Ugaritic *yln* may imply the nocturnal aspect of the ritual. David Wright simply says that it is not certain whether the ritual took place during the day, at evening, or at night. This is noteworthy because other incubation texts from the ancient world not only mention the time of oneiric theophany but sometimes go as far as to specify the hour of the night.[120]

The motif of time does not seem to serve any significant role in the ʾAqhatu story as a whole. There seems to be no reference to a time that would play a significant role in developing the plot of the narrative. The motif of place, on the other hand, plays an important role in the structure of the plot. Major junctures of the plot coincide with change of location (See Table 4.5 below).

Table 4.5: The Development of Plot according to Locations

Temple	Incubation for a legitimate son-heir	KTU 1.17 I:1–15
Dnil's home	Visit of the Kôṯarātu (conception of a son)	KTU 1.17 II:24ff.
Dnil's home	Visit of the Kôtāru-wa-Ḫasīs (receiving of a bow)	KTU 1.17 V:9–33
Dnil's home	ʿAnatu's request for a bow and ʾAqhatu's refusal	KTU 1.17 VI:16ff.
ʾIlu's abode	ʿAnatu's plot to kill ʾAqhatu	KTU 1.18 I:1–20
Abilūma	ʿAnatu and Yaṭipānu kill ʾAqhatu	KTU 1.18 IV
Dnil's home	Visit of Pūġatu and Lament for the effects of drought	KTU 1.19 I:29–48
Field	Dānîʾilu's agriculture rites	KTU 1.19 I:49–II:25
Dnil's home	News of ʾAqhatu's death and Conjuration of the Vultures	KTU 1.19 II:26ff.
KNRT	Burial of ʾAqhatu	KTU 1.19 III:39–45
Qrmym etc.	The Curse on the Locals	KTU 1.19 III:46ff.
Dnil's home	Visit of the Weepers, Dānîʾilu's *dbḥ*-sacrifice	KTU 1.19 IV:8–27
YṬPN's tent	Pūġatu's avenge on her brother	KTU 1.19 IV:40ff.

[120] See 2.1.2 in chapter three above.

2.2 *Epiphany*

Text: Transliteration and Translation

The Theophany Motif

Ba'lu Appears to Dānî'ilu (Narrative)

	mk [.] b šbʿ . ymm	Then on the seventh day,
(16)	[w] yqrb . bʿl . b ḥnth .	Baʿlu approached, in his mercy,
	abyn⸢n⸣ (17) [d]nil . mt . rpi ⸢.⸣	The poor one, Dānî'ilu, the man of Rapau,
	anḫ . ǵzr (18) ⸢m⸣t . hrnmy .	The groaning one, the valiant one, the Harnamite man,
	d in . bn . lh (19) km . aḫh .	Who had no son like his brothers,
	w . šrš . km . aryh	No scion like his kinsmen.

Ba'lu's Petition to 'Ilu (Direct Speech)

(20)	bl . iṯ . bn lh . km[121] aḫh .	Should he not have a son like his brothers?
	w šrš (21) km . aryh .	A scion like his kinsmen?
	uzrm . ilm . ylḥm	For girded, he has given the gods food,
(22)	uzrm . yšqy . bn . qdš	Girded, he has given drink to the sons of the Holy One.
(23)	l tbrknn . l ṯr . il aby	Please bless him, O Bull 'Ilu, my father!
(24)	tmrnn . l bny . bnwt	Pronounce a benediction, O creator of creatures!
(25)	w ykn . bnh . b bt .	So that he may have his son at home,
	šrš . b qrb (26) hklh .	A scion within his palace:

The First Occurrence of the List of Filial Duties[122]

	nṣb . skn . ilibh .	Someone to raise up the stela of his father's god,
	b qdš (27) ztr . ʿmh .	In the sanctuary the votive emblem of his clan;

[121] {wm}

[122] This list, which is put in the mouth of Baal, is part of Baal's petition.

	l arṣ . mšṣu . qṭrh	To send up from the earth his incense,
(28)	l ʿpr . ḏmr . aṯrh .	From the dust the song of his place;
	ṭbq . lḥt (29) niṣh .	To shut up the jaws of his detractors,
	grš . d . ʿšy . lnh	To drive out anyone who would do him in;
(30)	⸢a⸣ḫd . ydh . b šk⸢r⸣n .	To take his hand when he is drunk,
	mʿmsh (31) [k] šbʿ . yn .	To carry him when he is full of wine;
	spu . ksmh . bt . bʿl	To eat his grain-offering in the temple of Baʿlu,
(32)	[w] ⸢m⸣nth . bt . il .	His portion in the temple of ʾIlu;
	[ṭ]ḫ . ggh . b ym (33) [ṯi]ṭ .	To plaster his root on a day of mud,
	rḥṣ . npṣh . b ym . rṯ	To wash his outfit on a day of filth.

ʾIlu Blesses Dānîʾilu (Narrative)

(34)	[ks .] ⸢y⸣iḫd . il <. Bdh	[A cup] ʾIlu took <in his hand,
	krpn . bm . ymn	A goblet in the right hand,
	brkm . ybrk .> ʿbdh .	He did indeed bless> his servant,
	ybrk (35) [dni]l . mt . rpi .	He blessed Dānîʾilu the man of Rapaʾu,
	ymr . ǵzr (36) [mt . h]⸢r⸣nmy ⸢.⸣	He pronounced a benediction on the valiant one the Harnamite [man]:

ʾIlu's Benediction on Dānîʾilu: Instruction and Promise

	npš . yḥ . dnil (37) [mt . rp]i .	As for life, may Dānîʾilu the man of Rapaʾu live,
	brlt . ǵzr . mt hrnmy	As for vitality, the valiant one the Harnamite man,
(38)	[…]⸢-⸣ . hw . mḫ .	As for [life?], may he be successful!
	l ʿršh . yʿl (39) [w yšk]⸢b⸣ .	To his bed he shall mount [and lie down],
	bm . nšq . aṯth (40) [w hr .]	As he kisses his wife [there will be conception],
	b ḥbqh . ḥmḥmt	As he embraces her there will be pregancy;
(41)	[hr . tš]⸢k⸣n . ylt .	A child-bearer will [have conception],
	ḥmḥmt (42) [l mt . r]pi .	Pregancy [for the man of] Rapaʾu.
	w ykn . bnh (43) [b bt .	He shall have his son [at home
	šrš] ⸢.⸣ b qrb hklh	A scion] within his palace.

The Second Occurrence of the List of Filial Duties[123]

(44)	[nṣb . skn . i]libh .	[Someone to raise up the stela of] his father's god,
	b qdš (45) [ztr . ʿmh .	In the santuary the votive emblem of his clan;
	l a]⸢r⸣ṣ . mšṣu (46) [qṭrh .	To send up from the [earth his incense,
	l ʿpr . ḏ]mr . aṯr⸢h⸣	From the dust the] song of his place;
(47)	[ṭbq . lḥt . niṣh .	To shut up the jaws of his detractors,
	gr]š . d . ʿšy (48) [lnh .]	To drive out anyone who would do him in.
	(about 10 lines are missing)	…

Baʿlu speaks to Dānî'ilu? (Narrative?)

Baʿlu's Benediction on Dānî'ilu: Instruction and Promise? (Direct Speech)[124]

1.17 II

	(about 11 lines are missing)	…

The Third Occurrence of the List of Filial Duties

(1)	⸢z⸣ [tr . ʿmk .	The votive [emblem of your clan;]
	l arṣ . mšṣu . qṭrk]	[To send up from the earth your incense,]
(2)	l . ʿp⸢r . ḏm⸣ [r . aṯrk .	From the dust the song [of your place;]
	ṭbq] (3) lḥt . niṣk .	[To shut up] the jaws of your detractors,
	g⸢r⸣ [š . d ʿšy . lnk]	To drive out [anyone who would do you in;]
(4)	spu . ksmk . bt . [bʿl .	To eat your grain-offering in the temple of [Baʿlu,
	w mntk] (5) bt il .	Your portion] in the temple of 'Ilu;
	aḫd . ydk [.] ⸢b⸣ [škrn]	To take your hand when [you are drunk],
(6)	mʿmsk . k šbʿt . yn .	To carry you when you are full of wine;
	⸢ṭḫ⸣ (7) ggk . b . ym . ṭiṭ .	To plaster your roof on a day of mud,
	rḥs (8) npṣk . b ym . rṯ .	To wash your outfit on a day of filth.

[123] This, which is put in 'Ilu's mouth, is part of 'Ilu's blessing on Dānî'ilu. The incubation of the list in Baʿlu's petition makes this repetition necessary to the plot.

[124] See the discussion below.

2.2.1 *The Theophany Motif*

The motif of theophany verbalizes the pre-verbal concept of divine-human salvific encounter (Epiphany) that forms the climax of the incubation type-scene. It comes as a culmination of the seven-day preparatory ritual, which consists of the offering of meat,[125] libation, wearing special clothes, ritual nakedness, "silent" prayer, and sleeping in a temple. This can be demonstrated at a literary level. The final day in the seven-day formula usually witnesses a new event, something that serves to move the plot in a new direction—in our passage, the appearance of Baʿlu, Dānîʾilu's patron god.[126] Also, as is customary of the seven-day formula, the text does not repeat any of these ritual acts in its description of the seventh day. But this literary convention does not necessarily mean that Dānîʾilu ceased from doing anything on the seventh day, as if he had observed a "Sabbath."[127] It is logical to reason that Dānîʾilu went through the same routine on the seventh day but with a different result. The non-repetitive description that characterizes the final day of the formula simply throws into sharp relief the new aspect of the day which otherwise would have been similar to the others. The connection made by dint of the seven-day formula between preparatory ritual and theophany drives home the point that the appearance of Baʿlu comes as a culmination of a week-long process of incubation. Through the six-day long repetition of the ritual, the poet builds up sympathy for Dānîʾilu's predicament and creates an expectation that something critical must soon happen.[128] In this

---

[125] This is assumed by the larger context. When Dānîʾilu regales the Kôṯarātu and Kôṯaru-wa-Ḫasīs, animal meat is provided as food (*alp* and *imr*). But Wright would not call these sacrifices, because their focus does not lie in the killing but in the presentation of food (Wright, *Ritual in Narrative: The Dynamics of Feasting, Mourning, and Retaliation Rites in the Ugaritic Tale of Aqhat*, 32–33).

[126] Cf. U. Cassuto, *The Goddess Anat: Canaanite Epics of the Patriarchal Age*, Translated from the Hebrew by Israel Abrahams (Jerusalem: Magnes Press, 1971), 43. For a study of the seven-day formula from a comparative perspective, see Loewenstamm, "The Seven-Day-Unit in Ugaritic Epic Literature," 121–33. According to Loewenstamm, Ugaritic scribes inherited the convention from Akkadian counterparts. One of the isoglosses between the two is the enumeration of days in pairs. This characteristic has disappeared in the biblical examples of the formula.

[127] Cf. Loren R. Fisher, "Literary Genres in the Ugaritic Texts," in *Ras Shamra Parallels: The Texts from Ugarit and the Hebrew Bible*, vol. 2, ed. Loren R. Fisher (Roma: Pontificium Institutum Biblicum, 1975), 141.

[128] Aitken, *The Aqhat Narrative: A Study in the Narrative Structure and Composition of an Ugaritic Tale*, 135.

regard, it is noteworthy that the mood of the scene changes drastically with the theophany motif as a watershed.

The theophany motif begins with the typical introduction of the seventh day in the seven-day formula, *mk b šbʿ ymm* "Then on the seventh day" (KTU 1.17 I:15b)[129] and ends with the third repetition of the list of filial duties (KTU 1.17 II:8). The theophany motif may be divided into three sections, all being marked by direct speeches by Baʿlu, 'Ilu, and Baʿlu successively. Each direct speech is preceded by a short narrative note about the speaker. Baʿlu's petition (KTU 1.17 I:20–33) is, for instance, preceded by a narrative description of Baʿlu "approaching in his mercy" the wretched incubant, Dānî'ilu (cf. *[w] yqrb*[130] *bʿl bḥnt abynn dnil*, lines 16–17a). 'Ilu's blessing (KTU 1.17 I:34ff.) is also introduced by a narrative description of 'Ilu holding a cup in his hand.[131] The narrative introduction to Baʿlu's mediation of 'Ilu's blessing to Dānî'ilu is unfortunately missing due to the damage at the end of the first column and at the beginning of the second column of KTU 1.17. But the pattern observed in the previous two sections makes it plausible to postulate a similar narrative introduction to Baʿlu's final speech.[132] Another element creating a sense of pattern that characterizes the theophany motif is the repetition of the list of filial duties and its strategic placement within the theophany motif. It recurs at the seam of different sections, closing one section and opening another.

---

[129] For the expression of *b šbʿ ymm*, see Loewenstamm, *Comparative Studies in Biblical and Ancient Oriental Literatures*, 194, footnote 4a; Tropper, *Ugaritische Grammatik*, 367; Dennis Pardee, "Review," Ugaritische Grammatik, Josef Tropper, *AfO* Online Version 50 (2003/2004): 200.

[130] The pun on *qrb* seems to bring a sense of closure to the theophany motif: The verb √qrb opens the theophany scene (*wyqrb* "and he approached," line 16 of KTU 1.17 I) and the noun *qrb* in effect closes Baʿlu's petition to 'Ilu (*bqrb hklh* "in the midst of his palace," line 25), 'Ilu's blessing (cf. line 43), and perhaps Baal's speech to Dānî'ilu.

[131] For an iconographical explanation of this gesture, see Jared J. Jackson and Harold H. P. Dressler, "El and the Cup of Blessing," *JAOS* 95 (1975): 99–101; Cf. James B. Pritchard, *The Ancient Near East in Pictures Relating to the Old Testament* (Princeton, NJ: Princeton University Press, 1954), n. 493, 826 and relevant commentaries. Also see the discussion by D. Wright (Wright, *Ritual in Narrative: The Dynamics of Feasting, Mourning, and Retaliation Rites in the Ugaritic Tale of Aqhat*, 71–72).

[132] D. Pardee proposes the narrative framework for transmitting the message of 'Ilu's blessing to Dānî'ilu (Pardee, "The Aqhatu Legend," 344, footnote 15).

The theophany motif concerns the salvific encounter between the incubant, Dānî'ilu and his patron god, Ba'lu. According to the convention, the text registers a visual image of Ba'lu: he approaches (cf. *yqrb*) Dānî'ilu who, in distress, had been seeking divine aid in a manner that is reminiscent of a dutiful son who tries to appease his angry father, namely, with the right food and with the right attitude. Some scholars, however, attempt to disconnect Dānî'ilu's ritual from divine revelation. Husser, for instance, says, "The ritual sleep of the supplicant does not necessarily imply that he expected a visit from the divinity in his dream."[133] But the fact that divine theophany comes as a culmination of the seven-day ritual and a succession of the literary motif of sleeping (*y'l w yškb...yln*, KTU 1.17 I:14–15) and that of divine revelation (*wyqrb b'l*, KTU 1.17 I:16) strongly suggest Dānî'ilu's intention to induce an oneiric revelation. Or it may be said that the author intended a causal relation between the two motifs. This becomes even more plausible when one considers the fact that the sleeping motif is not mentioned in the description of the first four days' ritual, although Dānî'ilu may have lain down every night for divine revelation. The author deliberately placed the sleeping motif in the last unit of the seven-day formula so that the theophany may be seen as the result of the ritual sleep. So it may be said that the ancient audience who could appreciate such literary emphasis must have recognized that Ba'lu appeared to Dānî'ilu as an answer to his week-long offering.[134]

The problem, however, is that, in the "speech" lines following the poet's introductory narration, Ba'lu does not appear to address Dānî'ilu. Ba'lu's speech is directed to 'Ilu, the chief deity of the Ugaritic pantheon. For this reason, some scholars assume that Ba'lu approached 'Ilu, not Dānî'ilu, on the seventh day. On the surface level, they are right. But a closer examination of the literary structure of the theophany motif will prove that Ba'lu did approach Dānî'ilu.

First, a textual difficulty needs to be noted. The last word at the end of line 16 (KTU 1.17 I) is anything but certain. The suggestions

[133] Husser, "The Birth of a Hero: Form and Meaning of KTU 1.17 i–ii," 95.
[134] Wright, *Ritual in Narrative: The Dynamics of Feasting, Mourning, and Retaliation Rites in the Ugaritic Tale of Aqhat*, 36.

proposed include *abyn*,[135] *abynt*,[136] *abyn at*,[137] *abynn*,[138] and *abynm*.[139] The variety of proposals seems to show that the matter is hard to settle at an epigraphical level. This would mean that one's contextual understanding of the text is most likely to determine the reading. An interesting example comes from Dietrich and Loretz. In their *Ugarit Forschungen* (1972) article, they proposed the reading *abynm* and took line 16 as the beginning of Ba'lu's direct speech to 'Ilu: "Unglücklich ist Dnil, der Mann von Rpu."[140] In another *Ugarit Forschungen* (1978) article, however, they deemed *abyn at* as epigraphically superior to *abynm*, and yet asserted that, since "you" is not appropriate in the context of Ba'lu's addressing 'Ilu, the *at* may be a scribal error.[141] Although they changed their epigraphic reading, they adhered to their original interpretation of the passage. But later in their edition (1990) of the 'Aqhatu story, Dietrich and Loretz changed their original interpretation of the passage and adopted the *at* as the correct reading both epigraphically and contextually.[142] They now understand line 16 as Ba'lu's direct speech to Dānî'ilu, not to 'Ilu: "Bist du elend, Danil...."[143] Owing to the epigraphical difficulty involving {abyn--} at the end of line 16, we cannot judge which reading is superior to others, but we are still able to evaluate various contextual understandings resulting from different epigraphic decisions, especially when they affect the "incubation" understanding of the text.

---

135 Obermann, *How Daniel Was Blessed with a Son*, 4.

136 Andrée Herdner, "La légende cananéenne d'Aqhat d'après les travaux récents," *Syria* 26 (1949): 80; John Gray, *The Legacy of Canaan: The Ras Shamra Texts and Their Relevance to the Old Testament.*, 108; Gibson, *Canaanite Myths and Legends.*, 103; Virolleaud, *La légende phénicienne de Danel*, 186; Husser, *Le songe et la parole: Etude sur le rêve et sa fonction dans l'ancien Israël*, 37; Wyatt, *Religious Texts from Ugarit*, 253, footnote 17.

137 Dietrich and Loretz, "Das Aqhat-Epos," 1261; Olmo Lete, *Mitos y leyendas de Canaan: según la tradición de Ugarit*, 368; KTU[1 and 2]; Cf. Simon B. Parker, "Aqhat," 52; Margalit, *The Ugaritic Poem of Aqht: Text, Translation, Commentary*, 118.

138 Bordreuil and Pardee, *Choix de Textes: Glossaire*, 23.

139 Dijkstra and Moor, "Problematical Passages in the Legend of Aqhatu," 174; Manfried Dietrich and Oswald Loretz, "Zur Ugaritischen Lexikographie (V)," *UF* 4 (1972): 34; Cf. Gibson, *Canaanite Myths and Legends.*, 103, note to line 17.

140 Dietrich and Loretz, "Zur Ugaritischen Lexikographie (V)," 34.

141 Manfried Dietrich and Oswald Loretz, "Bemerkungen Zum Aqhat-Text: Zur Ugaritischen Lexikographie (XIV)," *UF* 10 (1978): 67. David Wright also considers the possibility of the *at* being a scribal error. In other words he does not see a second person pronoun in line 16 of KTU 1.17 I. Cf. Wright, *Ritual in Narrative: The Dynamics of Feasting, Mourning, and Retaliation Rites in the Ugaritic Tale of Aqhat*, 37, 38.

142 Dietrich and Loretz, "Das Aqhat-Epos," 1261.

143 Ibid.

We may isolate three interpretative possibilities for lines 16b–19 in the first section of the theophany motif. And they are directly related to the question where Ba'lu's direct speech begins. First, one may accept the reading *abyn at* and take the whole passage in question as Ba'lu's direct speech to Dānî'ilu: "You are a wretched one, Oh Dānî'ilu..."[144] This is the interpretation adopted by Dietrich and Loretz and Del Olmo Lete.[145] This understanding seems to fit with the "incubation" understanding of the passage, because it would easily translate into the confirmation that Ba'lu appeared to Dānî'ilu in response to his practice of incubation ritual. It is even more so when one considers the fact that many ancient Near Eastern reports of theophany begin the divine speech with a similar exclamation.[146] This interpretation, however, has to explain the shift of person in the immediately following verse, which is syntactically connected to the preceding lines by dint of Ugaritic relative pronoun *d*. This problem does not seem insurmountable. Akkadian and Hebrew poetry give examples where there is a shift of person as part of a poetical technique. For example, one of Inanna's love songs reads as follows: "You will become a water-skin for fresh water, a 'thing' of the steppe, Her son Girgire together with her."[147] According to Samuel N. Kramer, since Inanna is still addressing Bilulu, the last part should have read: "Your son Girgire together with you."[148] In other words, the shift of person has occurred without changing its referent. A similar example can be found in Song of Songs 1:2: "Let him kiss me with the kisses of his mouth! For your love is better than wine." Although some commentators want to emend the

---

[144] The exceptions are Margalit and Parker. Margalit accepts the reading *abyn at* but considers the second person pronoun *at* to refer to 'Ilu, and not Dānî'ilu: "Are you indifferent to Danel...?" (Margalit, *The Ugaritic Poem of Aqht: Text, Translation, Commentary*, 144). Parker reads *abynat* as the abstract noun "longing" (Simon B. Parker, "Aqhat," 52).

[145] Cf. Olmo Lete, *Mitos y leyendas de Canaan: según la tradición de Ugarit*, 368: "¡Qué miserable estás, Daniilu..." Also Gregorio del Olmo Lete and Joaquín Sanmartín, *A Dictionary of the Ugaritic Language in the Alphabetic Tradition*, Handbook of Oriental Studies 67 (Leiden: Brill, 2003), 15: "What a wretched you are, PN!" For Dietrich and Loretz's translation, see above.

[146] See 2.2 in chapter three above. Cf. Judges 13 where the angel starts with *hinne-nā' at-'ăqārāh*, 'behold, you are barren'.

[147] Samuel N. Kramer, *The Sacred Marriage Rite: Aspects of Faith, Myth, and Ritual in Ancient Sumer* (Bloomington, IN: Indiana University Press, 1969), 132.

[148] Ibid., 157, footnote 38.

text, M. Pope does not because "Enallage (shift in person) is common in poetry: cf. Deut 32:15; Is 1:29; Jer 22:24; Micah 7:19; Psalm 23."[149]

Second, those who feel uncomfortable with the shift of person between syntactically connected poetic verses may go for another philologically feasible option: that is to read *abyn, abynn, abynm,* or even *abynt* and take lines 16b–19 as Ba'lu's direct speech to 'Ilu: "Dānî'ilu.... is miserable..."[150] The *n* and *m* are taken as enclitic particle attached to an adjective *abyn*, while the *t* would make *abynt* as a abstract noun "misery." Scholars who belong to this category include Gibson, Husser, Wright, and so forth.[151] The problem with this approach, however, is the repetition of the almost identical poetic verse (Lines 18–19 and 20–21). Explaining his preference for seeing the beginning of Ba'lu's speech at line 20, Wyatt argues that if Ba'lu's speech to 'Ilu begins at line 16b, he would indulge "in a gratuitous repetition."[152] Moreover, the interpretation that begins Ba'lu's direct speech to 'Ilu at line 16b, does not seem favorable to the "incubation" interpretation of the text under investigation, because it seems to make the theophany disappear from the text. This interpretation implies that the phrase *wyqrb b'l bḥnth* "Ba'lu approached in his mercy" in line 16a cannot be taken to refer to the theophany to Dānî'ilu. Ba'lu "approached" (*yqrb*) to 'Ilu in line 16a and started to address him in 16b. Husser, for example, argues that even if Dānî'ilu was allowed to be privy to the divine council as an observer, the scene of divine council which the text seems to describe would not qualify as theophany.[153] Theophany in the ancient world is defined as the gods visiting humans, and not vice versa. Moreover, Husser eliminates any possibility of the

---

[149] Marvin H. Pope, *Song of Songs: A New Translation with Introduction and Commentary*, AB 7C (Garden City, N.Y.: Doubleday, 1977), 297.

[150] Gray and Wyatt are an exception. The latter takes the reading *abynt* but, according to his translation, Baal's direct speech does not begin until line 20: "Baal drew near...at the misery of [Da]nel..." (Wyatt, *Religious Texts from Ugarit*, 253: Cf. John Gray, *The Legacy of Canaan: The Ras Shamra Texts and Their Relevance to the Old Testament.*, 108).

[151] Gibson, *Canaanite Myths and Legends.*, 103; Husser, *Le songe et la parole: Etude sur le rêve et sa fonction dans l'ancien Israël*, 37; Wright, *Ritual in Narrative: The Dynamics of Feasting, Mourning, and Retaliation Rites in the Ugaritic Tale of Aqhat*, 38, footnote 73; Cf. Gaster, *Thespis: Ritual, Myth, and Drama in the Ancient Near East*, 332; Ginsberg, "The Tale of Aqhat," 150.

[152] Wyatt, *Religious Texts from Ugarit*, 254, footnote 19.

[153] Simon B. Parker, "The Birth Announcement," in *Ascribe to the Lord: Biblical Studies in Memory of Peter C. Craigie*, ed. Lyle Eslinger and Glen Taylor, JSOTSup 67 (Sheffield: Sheffield Academic Press, 1988), 95.

salvific theophany in the matter of the birth of ʾAqhatu by arguing that Dānîʾilu's joyful reaction following the theophany motif was not to the news of ʾIlu's blessing communicated by Baʿlu or divine messengers, but to the news of the recent birth of his son conveyed by human messengers.[154] Husser's observation that, wherever Baʿlu's speech begins in the text, Baʿlu's petition and ʾIlu's blessing are ingredients of the divine council, and not a theophanic scene, is justified. But that does not lead to the conclusion that there was no theophany let alone incubation. If so, it would not do justice to all the other elements that combine to index the basic concept of incubation, nor to the literary artifice that the poet crafted into the text—patterning, foreshadowing, delayed identification, intensification, contrast and echoes, etc.—to elaborate the incubation type-scene and make it an effective tool for the message of *ʾAquatu* as a whole.

The third interpretative possibility of KTU 1.17 I:16b–19 is to accept the reading *abynn*, advocated by Bordreuil and Pardee,[155] and to take *abynn dnil mt rpi / anẖ ǵzr mt hrnmy* as an object phrase of the infinitive *bḥnth*: thus the translation, "Baʿlu approached, having mercy on the lamenting one, on Dānîʾilu the man of Rapaʾu, the moaning one, on the valiant Harnamite man." This translation is based on the transitive sense of Hebrew/Ugaritic √ḥṇṇ,[156] and the analysis of *abynn* as appositional to *dnil mt rpi*.[157] Although syntactically less likely, one cannot exclude the possibility that *abynn dnil mt rpi* and its parallel line may serve as an object of the verb √qrb or as an adverbial accusative complementing the verb √qrb. If this interpretation is adopted, we would have a strong textual support for Baʿlu's theophany to Dānîʾilu in lines 16–19 of KTU 1.17 I. The issue of unintroduced direct speech in line 20 is shared by the other two approaches, according to Moor a frequent phenomenon in the literature of Ugarit.[158] The more serious

[154] Note that Husser translates *ʿrb* in KTU 1.17 II 26 as a pluperfect in order to justify this interpretation (Ibid., 91–92).

[155] Bordreuil and Pardee, *Choix de Textes: Glossaire*, 26, note to line 16.

[156] Cf. *ḥnny l pn lmlk* "have mercy on me before the king" KTU 2.15:3. For the analysis of *ḥn* (G-imperative) + *n* (personal pronomial suffix) + (enclitic particle), see Tropper, *Ugaritische Grammatik*, 675. Cf. KTU 1.16 II:17: *tqrb aẖ[h]* "She approached her."

[157] Bordreuil and Pardee adequately vocalize *abynn dnil*... *anẖ* gzr... as */ʾabyānana dānīʾila*... *ʾāniẖa ǵazra*... / (note accusative) (Bordreuil and Pardee, *Choix de Textes: Glossaire*, 25).

[158] Moor, *An Anthology of Religious Texts from Ugarit*, 227, footnote 16. Also see 1 Samuel 20:16.

issue with the third option is, however, a literary one: if lines 16–19 describe Ba'lu's appearance to Dānî'ilu, why does the ensuing speech of Ba'lu (KTU 1.17 I:20ff) not address Dānî'ilu? As Husser points out, the text in lines 20–33 clearly registers Ba'lu's petition to 'Ilu. Why do we have Ba'lu's speech to 'Ilu right after we are told that Ba'lu appeared to Dānî'ilu in response to his incubation ritual? This needs to be answered. In fact the answer to this question also helps us answer some of the challenges posed by Husser.

The answer to the question may be found in the poet's literary technique of "delayed identification." We have already seen this technique with respect to the motif of sonlessness and the motif of "silent" prayer, and the motif of a temple, all of which are registered in the text later than they are expected to occur. Similarly, by the time the reader gets to the part saying, "Then on the seventh day, Ba'lu approached having mercy on Dānî'ilu...," the reader may have expected Ba'lu's salvific speech to Dānî'ilu to follow immediately. But such an expectation is thwarted when they find Ba'lu petitioning 'Ilu on behalf of Dānî'ilu. Strictly speaking, however, the fulfillment of the reader's expectation is "suspended" for the moment. Ba'lu's theophanic speech to Dānî'ilu is delayed until later by the insertion of the scene of the divine council. And this insertion is not without authorial intent: the author attempts to show us the proper hierarchy of decision making in the heavenly court. Dānî'ilu had been appealing to the *ilm*, the gods of the pantheon. Hence, it stands to reason that the answer Dānî'ilu received would represent the decision of the heavenly court. Although Ba'lu is Dānî'ilu's patron god, he cannot take a decision on his own. He also has to go through the proper chain of command to get Dānî'ilu blessed.[159] Ba'lu is also part of the world order, and not an exception. This insertion therefore speaks volumes about the theme of the 'Aqhatu story as a whole: the honorable hierarchy of the divine and human world and the proper behavior of its denizens. Notice that later in the narrative we read that intractable 'Anatu has to go through a similar chain of command to get 'Aqhatu killed (KTU 1.18 VI:49ff). After 'Ilu's acquiescence to Ba'lu's petition, we finally, albeit belatedly,

[159] As a side note, the seven-days that took Dānî'ilu to get a divine answer reflect not only the pious insistency of Dānî'ilu, but also the time that may have taken Ba'lu to go through the proper change of command. But it is less likely that, as Margalit suggests, 'Ilu's seniority led to divine indifference to Dānî'ilu's predicament (Margalit, *The Ugaritic Poem of Aqht: Text, Translation, Commentary*, 266–67).

hear Baʿlu speaking to Dānîʾilu. Unfortunately, only the tail end of the speech is extant (cf. KTU 1.17 II:1–8). In sum, the appearance of Baʿlu, which is couched in the verb *yqrb* is to none other than Dānîʾilu, but Baʿlu's salvific speech is "delayed" by the insertion that is intended to underscore the didactic theme of the ʾAqhatu story as a whole, namely, the code of conduct expected of any member who dwells in the divine and human world.

Most of Baʿlu's theophanic speech to Dānîʾilu falls in the broken part of the tablet.[160] But one may plausibly assume that Baʿlu's speech to Dānîʾilu may have shown affinities with ʾIlu's benedictory proclamation on Dānîʾilu.[161] Just as Baʿlu had served as the mediator of Dānîʾilu's prayer to ʾIlu,[162] now he fulfills the function of the mediator of ʾIlu's blessing to Dānîʾilu. So it is crucial to examine ʾIlu's speech in order to get a glimpse of Baʿlu's theophanic speech to Dānîʾilu.

2.2.2 *The Motif of Divine Message: Divine Blessing, Command, and Promise*

The motif of Divine Message also starts with the poet's narrative note (KTU 1.17 I:34–36a) and moves on to ʾIlu's direct speech (lines 36bff). The narration in line 34 is clearly defective. Homoioteleuton has occurred when Ilimilku's eye skipped from *bdh* "in his hand" to *ʿbdh* "his servant."[163] A similar blessing that ʾIlu gives to Kirta allows the following reconstruction: [*ks*] ⸢*y*⸣*iḫd il* <*bdh / krpn bm ymn / brkm ybrk*> *ʿdbh / ybrk* [*dni*]*l mt rpi / ymr*[164] ǵzr [*mt h*]⸢*r*⸣*nmy* "[A cup] ʾIlu

[160] According to KTU's counting, there are at least 21 lines missing between the last visible sign of column 1 and the first visible sign of column 2. If one takes away 4 lines which would continue the list of filial duties, one is left with at least 19 lines for the third section of the theophany motif. This should give enough space for a short narrative introduction and Baʿlu's direct speech of blessing to Dānîʾilu along with the list of filial duty.

[161] Aitken, *The Aqhat Narrative: A Study in the Narrative Structure and Composition of an Ugaritic Tale*, 154.

[162] For a similar mediatory role of Aṯiratu for Baal, see KTU 1.4 IV 40–57.

[163] Pardee, "An Emendation in the Ugaritic Aqht Text," 53–56. Pardee's emendation is based on KTU 1.15 II 16b–20. Following Jackson and Dressler, however, Parker emends *ʿbdh* to *bdh* on the basis of a misreading of a word-divider as an *ʿayin* (Simon B. Parker, "Aqhat," 79, footnote 10: Jackson and Dressler, "El and the Cup of Blessing," 99–101). See also Caquot who, following Virolleaud, restores {byd} at the beginning of the line and reads it "El prend son serviteur [par la main]" (Caquot, Sznycer, and Herdner, *Mythes et légendes: introduction, traduction, commentaire*, 422, footnote w; Virolleaud, *La légende phénicienne de Danel*, 187).

[164] Pardee argues that the Ugaritic word *ymr*, which is a parallel word to *ybrk*, may be taken to stem from the biconsonantal root √mr, meaning "to bless," rather

took <in his hand, a goblet in the right hand, he did indeed bless> his servant, blessed Dānî'ilu the man of Rapa'u, pronounced a benediction upon the valiant Harnamite [man]."[165] Just as the poet's narrative note for Ba'lu's theophany has a visual aspect, so does the narrative note for 'Ilu. The poet portrays 'Ilu raising a cup in his hand. According to Jackson and Dressler, this gesture is reminiscent of the famous stela depicting a worshiper standing before a seated, bearded and horned god, which has been interpreted by the excavator as a representation of the King of Ugarit adoring the god 'Ilu. The latter raises his left hand in a gesture of blessing, while his right hand, palm extended and up, holds a bowl-shaped object."[166] Although they identify the bowl-shaped object as a cup, they do not bother to explain what that particular gesture may signify. Wright, noting the scene of 'Anatu spilling her cup down (...*ksh tšpkm* [*l'pr*]) later in the 'Aqhatu story (KTU 1.17 VI:15–16), proposes that holding up a cup in a hand is a kind of toast, symbolic of acceptance.[167]

Be that as it may, the poet's narrative note is followed by 'Ilu's direct speech. Although in 'Ilu's speech Dānî'ilu is referred to in the third person, he must have been addressed in the second person later in the same blessing mediated by Ba'lu. This is implied by the use of second person pronouns in the list of filial duties concluding Ba'lu's theophanic speech at the beginning of column II (KTU 1.17). Unlike many theophanic speeches which start with a question about the dilemma in which the incubant finds himself,[168] 'Ilu's speech does not start with

---

than from the geminate root √mrr 'to be strong' (<'to be bitter'). Pardee's assertion is expressed in terms of Tropper's new reading, *nmrt* in line 33. Cf. Pardee, "Review," 271, 335.

[165] Wright observes that the scene of 'Ilu's blessing with a cup in one hand occurs in a similar context in both the Kirta story and the 'Aqhatu story. For details, see Wright, *Ritual in Narrative: The Dynamics of Feasting, Mourning, and Retaliation Rites in the Ugaritic Tale of Aqhat*, 71.

[166] Jackson and Dressler, "El and the Cup of Blessing," 100.

[167] Wright, *Ritual in Narrative: The Dynamics of Feasting, Mourning, and Retaliation Rites in the Ugaritic Tale of Aqhat*, 72.

[168] The Hittite story of Appu, for instance, has it that when Appu came to meet with the Sun god with a lamb sacrifice, the Sun-god appeared in human form to Appu and asked, "What is your problem, that I [may solve] it for you." After hearing his reply, he offered to help. This is a pattern also followed in Genesis 21, where God asks Hagar, מה־לך הגר "what troubles you, Hagar?" and promises and gives help. Cf. Harry A. Hoffner, "Appu and His Two Sons," in *Canonical Compositions from the Biblical World*, vol. I of *COS*, ed. William W. Hallo (Leiden: Brill, 1997), 153; Irvin, *Mytharion: The Comparison of Tales from the Old Testament and the Ancient Near East*, 59.

such a question, perhaps because Ba'lu has already made it clear in his petition. 'Ilu's blessing proper manifests a structure of intensification: it creates a sense of focus and intensification as it moves from a general blessing (KTU 1.17 I 36–38a) to a specific promise and instructions (KTU 1.17 I:38b–43).[169] The tricolon *npš yḫ dnil [mt rp]i / brlt ǵzr mt hrnmy / [ ] hw mḫ* "As for (his) throat, may Dānî'ilu, the man of Rapa'u, live, as to (his) gullet, the valiant Harnamite man, ... may he be successful" (lines 36–38a) seems to express a general wish for success. Its application is not limited to a successful copulation, namely, conception. This point becomes obvious when one considers that Dānî'ilu gives a similar blessing[170] to his daughter, Pūǵatu, on her journey to avenge her brother's murderer, Yaṭipānu. The terms *npš* and *brlt* must not be related to sexual desire in this context as some might argue.[171]

After a general blessing, a more specific blessing follows. It directly addresses Dānî'ilu's problem. This is an important characteristic of divine speech in the incubation type-scene. In contrast to the theophanic speech in the story of the Birth of a Hero, which puts more focus on prophecy about the future hero in the womb,[172] 'Ilu's blessing in lines 38b–43 consists of divine instruction (lines 38a–41) and promise (lines 42–43), both of which aim at solving Dānî'ilu's problem of sonlessness. The poetic verse *l 'rš y'l [wyškb]* ...[173] in lines 38–39a clearly echoes Dānî'ilu's act of lying down to sleep in lines 4–5 and

[169] According to Wright, the structure of intensification can be recognized throughout the Aquat story: Cf. Wright, *Ritual in Narrative: The Dynamics of Feasting, Mourning, and Retaliation Rites in the Ugaritic Tale of Aqhat*, 16, 155–156.

[170] Cf. *npš tḥ pǵt*...*n⌈pš⌉ hy mḫ* (KTU 1.19 IV 36, 39). Notice the line containing *brlt* is omitted.

[171] Cf. Obermann, *How Daniel Was Blessed with a Son*, 20a. If the blessing formula in question may be used on any occasion, and in that sense may be called "general," we have a similar structure of intensification in Dānî'ilu's blessing on Pūǵatu in KTU 1.19 IV, which also moves from a general blessing to a specific one: *npš tḥ pǵ[t]*.... *n⌈pš⌉ hy mḫ // tmḫṣ mḫṣ [aḫh] / tkl mkly 'l umt[h]* "May [Pūǵatu] live... As for her throat, may she be successful // May she strike down the one who struck down [her brother], May she finish off him who finished off her family" (lines 36–40).

[172] Husser enumerates three characteristics of the Birth of a Hero story, the birth by divine help, "initial prophecy" indicating the destiny of the hero, and the naming of the new born (Husser, "The Birth of a Hero: Form and Meaning of KTU 1.17 i–ii," 89). Obviously, the theophanic speech in the incubation type-scene occurring in the 'Aqhatu story lacks the second and the third elements. This dovetails with the role of 'Aqhatu in the story as a whole. He is no hero!

[173] The restoration is Wright's (Wright, *Ritual in Narrative: The Dynamics of Feasting, Mourning, and Retaliation Rites in the Ugaritic Tale of Aqhat*, 70). Considering the context and CTA's comment that "the last sign before *bm* is probably *b*, *d*, or *u*," Wright's proposal is very plausible (Cf. Andrée Herdner, *Corpus des tablettes en*

14–15. But the context has changed: Now the act of lying down is not to sleep, but for copulation[174] and it is part of a divine answer to his supplication through incubation.

The following verse is striking in terms of its graphic details: *bm nšq aṯth [hr] bḥbqh ḥmḥmt* "As he kisses his wife [there will be conception,] as he embraces her there will be pregnancy" (lines 39–40). According to some scholars, Ugaritic *ḥmḥmt* may refer to sexual orgasm.[175] What is significant to our study of incubation type-scene, however, is not the graphic details that 'Ilu goes into about this "vulgar" matter,[176] but the fact that these details are omitted later in the motif describing the fulfillment of 'Ilu's command-promise.[177] Just as ancient Near Eastern reports of the practice of incubation often registers the aftermath of a theophanic experience, the incubation type-scene may also include those motifs that reflect the after-effects of the climactic event. One of them is the fulfillment motif. This motif describes how the incubant carries out divine instructions or how the divine promise is fulfilled in the incubant's life. Therefore, when Dānî'ilu went home after his successful encounter with a deity, the reader may have expected Dānî'ilu to carry out everything that he was told to do. The poet, however, instead of describing how faithfully Dānî'ilu carried out 'Ilu's instruction, tells of the visit of the Koṯarātu. How does this relate to the graphic details in 'Ilu's command? 'Ilu's message, first, shows the

cuneiformes alphabetiques decouvertes a Ras Shamra-Ugarit de 1929 à 1939, Mission de Ras Shamra 10 [Paris: Geuthner, 1963], 80, footnote 6).

[174] *l ʿrš yʿl wyškb* is a metonymic euphemism for sexual intercourse. For more details, see Dijkstra and Moor, "Problematical Passages in the Legend of Aqhatu," 179. On euphemistic metonym, see David P. Wright, "David Autem Remansit in Hierusalem: Felix Coniunctio!" in *Pomegranates Golden Bells: Studies in Biblical, Jewish, and Near Eastern Ritual, Law and Literature in Honor of Jacob Milgrom*, ed. David P. Wright, Freedman David N., and Hurvitz Avi (Winona Lake, IN: Eisenbrauns, 1995), 221, footnote 22.

[175] Cf. Moor, *An Anthology of Religious Texts from Ugarit*, 229, footnote 41; Margalit, *The Ugaritic Poem of Aqht: Text, Translation, Commentary*, 282; Wright, *Ritual in Narrative: The Dynamics of Feasting, Mourning, and Retaliation Rites in the Ugaritic Tale of Aqhat*, 79.

[176] In the story of Satni, the god who appeared to a barren Satni in a dream also instructs her to have intercourse with her husband in a graphic way: "receive the fluid of conception from him [your husband]." Cf. Miriam Lichtheim, *The Late Period*, vol. III of *Ancient Egyptian Literature: A Book of Readings* (1980), 138.

[177] Wright was hitting the nail on the head when he observed that "this description provides information that the narrative does not give later on." Cf. Wright, *Ritual in Narrative: The Dynamics of Feasting, Mourning, and Retaliation Rites in the Ugaritic Tale of Aqhat*, 79.

conception scene in advance, thus freeing up some narrative space for the poet to be "creative" in composing the motif of fulfillment. Instead of employing the expected command-fulfillment scheme, the poet inserts the scene describing the visit of the Koṯarātu. By so doing, the poet achieves three things at the same time. First, through the visit of the Kôṯarātu, namely, the goddesses of birth and conception, the poet euphemistically shows that the acts leading to conception, namely, the acts represented by √ʿly, √škb, √nšq, and √ḥbq were achieved. Second, by inserting the visit of the Kôṯarātu, which features Dānîʾilu offering food and drink to the goddesses for seven days, at the end of the incubation type-scene, the poet brings a sense of closure to the type-scene as a whole, which also began with a seven-day long offering. Finally, the visit of the Kôṯarātu once again brings Dānîʾilu's piety to the foreground, thus providing a practical lesson that appropriate behavior with regard to the hierarchical order of the universe brings about a felicitous result.[178]

ʾIlu's command is followed by the promise that Dānîʾilu will have a son (cf. *w ykn bnh [b bt / šrš] b qrb hklh*, lines 42–43).[179] The son who will be born to him is just not any son, but a son who stays at home fulfilling his duties toward his father. This seems to be communicated by two textual hints. The obvious one is the immediately following list of filial duties. Not only is this list a continuation of ʾIlu's promise of a son, but it is also given in a series of asyndetic relative clauses, each beginning with a participle, all of which refer back to *bn* and *šrš* in lines 42–43. To put it in another way, the nature of the son-heir promised by ʾIlu is fleshed out in the list of filial duties. A more subtle hint about the nature of the promised son is the use of the third person pronominal suffix in the lines cited above. In the first colon, the third person pronomial suffix is attached to the noun *bn* "son," and yet in the second colon, it is attached to the word *hkl* "house, palace." In both cola, the suffix refers to Dānîʾilu. From a formal point of view, this use may be designed to inject variation into the poetic verse that otherwise would have become a bit monotonous. But one may argue also that the poet wanted to communicate the nature of the promised

[178] Interestingly, the text describing the visit of the Kôṯarātu says nothing about "conception," although that is the purpose of their visit. Is it then arguable that in contrast to the purpose of Dānîʾilu's seven-day ritual, which is belatedly identified, the purpose of the seven-day offering for the Koṯarātu is "anticipated" in ʾIlu's speech?

[179] The restoration is based on its parallel in lines 25–26 of KTU 1.17 I.

son by artfully placing the third pronominal suffix at the two different points of authorial emphases: The promised son will be "his" son, namely, the son by birth, and the son will stay in "his" house, namely, the heir.

In sum, the motif of theophany forms a climax in the plot of the incubation type-scene. 'Ilu's blessing, in particular, marks the critical and decisive point of divine intervention in Dānî'ilu's situation, and it advances the plot to the point where the birth of a son is assured through the efficacy of divine blessing.[180] The internal structure of the theophany motif reveals the exquisite literary artifice which not only makes the theophany motif aesthetically pleasurable, but also serves to advance the plot by pattern, foreshadowing, echoing, etc, and effectively communicates the theme of the 'Aqhatu story. Although there is no word for "dream" in the text, it is very plausible that the theophany was oneiric. The text not only registers terms that strongly suggest Dānî'ilu's sleep, namely, √škb and √ln, but also places them in close proximity with the language of divine appearance, thus creating an impressionistic connection between Dānî'ilu's sleeping and Ba'lu's theophany in the reader's mind. This is corroborated by the fact that the motif of lying down for the night is mentioned only in the last pair of days, while Dānî'ilu may have lain down every night. Furthermore, the narrative technique of delayed identification may explain why Ba'lu does not address the incubant right away, after he appears to have mercy on him. The divine speech proper is composed of divine instructions and promise which awaits its surprising fulfillment later in the type-scene. Finally, unlike the theophanic scene in the story of Birth of a Hero, Ba'lu's theophanic speech in the incubation type-scene is concerned more with the solution of the predicament of the incubant than with the prediction of the future of a new-born.

Excursus 4: The Divine Oath in KTU 1.17 I:36–38?

One controversial feature of the theophany motif is the possible presence of divine oath in 'Ilu's blessing. The bone of contention is the poetic verse *npš yḥ dnil* [*mt rp*]*i* / *brltǵzr mt hrnmy* / [ ]*ḥ/ṭ hw mḫ̮* (KTU 1.17 I:36b–38a). Scholars are divided roughly into the two

[180] Aitken, *The Aqhat Narrative: A Study in the Narrative Structure and Composition of an Ugaritic Tale*, 83–84.

groups on the interpretation of this verse. One group of scholars such as Gordon, Moor, Dietrich and Loretz, Margalit, Parker and Wright[181] seem to take the verse in question as an oath. All of them, for example, translate the Ugaritic words *npš* and *brlt*[182] as something along the line of "by my life" and "by my soul." Moor and Margalit are more direct in saying that *npš* is an abbreviated formula introducing an oath.[183] There are three items of circumstantial evidence that may be used in favor of such an interpretation. First, the full oath formula is indeed, albeit only once, attested in the Ugaritic text: *ḥnpšk . wḥn[pšy?] hm 'yṯ d ytn l[y]* "(By) your life and (by) my life, if there was (anyone) who gave (anything) to [me], (may I be cursed) (RS 94.2284:12–13).[184] Second, Dijkstra and Moor note that the abbreviated formula is attested in other Semitic languages such as Arabic, Hebrew, and Akkadian.[185] For example, *bənapšô* in Amos 6:8 functions as an abbreviated authenticating element. Also in a letter from the King of Carchemish to the King of Ugarit in the 13th century we can find its Akkadian equivalent: *na-na-a na[p-]ša-ta ša šarri li-it-ma-a-mi* "Nana should swear (by) the life of the king" (RS 8.333 [PRU III, p. 8]).[186] The Akkadian cognate *napšatu* to the Ugaritic *npš* occurs here without *nīš*.[187] Third, Blane W.

[181] Cf. Cyrus Herzl Gordon, *Ugaritic Literature; A Comprehensive Translation of the Poetic and Prose Texts*, Scripta Pontificii Instituti Biblici 98 (Roma: Pontificium Institutum Biblicum, 1949), 86; Moor, *An Anthology of Religious Texts from Ugarit*, 229; Dietrich and Loretz, "Das Aqhat-Epos," 1263, footnote 55; Margalit, *The Ugaritic Poem of Aqht: Text, Translation, Commentary*, 145; Simon B. Parker, "Aqhat," 53; Wright, *Ritual in Narrative: The Dynamics of Feasting, Mourning, and Retaliation Rites in the Ugaritic Tale of Aqhat*, 72–79.

[182] For Ugaritic *brlt*, see Kjell Aartun, *Studien zur ugaritischen Lexikographie: mit kultur- und religionsgeschichtlichen Parallelen* (Wiesbaden: O. Harrassowitz, 1991), 58; Fred Renfroe, *Arabic-Ugaritic Lexical Studies*, ALASP 5 (Munster: UGARIT-Verlag, 1992), 84; Dennis Pardee, "The Ba'Lu Myth," in *Canonical Compositions from the Biblical World*, vol. I of *COS*, ed. William W. Hallo and K. Lawson Younger Jr. (Leiden: Brill, 1997), 264, footnote 203; Marvin H. Pope, "An Arabic Cognate for Ugaritic Brlt?" *UF* 13 (1981): 305–6; B. Cutler and J. Macdonald, "An Akkadian Cognate to Ugaritic Brlt," *UF* 5 (1973): 67–70.

[183] Moor, *An Anthology of Religious Texts from Ugarit*, 229, footnote 38; Margalit, *The Ugaritic Poem of Aqht: Text, Translation, Commentary*, 282, footnote 3.

[184] Conklin's translation and Bordreuil and Pardee's reconstruction. Cf. Blane W. Conklin, "Oath Formulae in Classical Hebrew and Other Semitic Languages" (Ph.D. diss., Chicago: University of Chicago Press, 2005), 221; Bordreuil and Pardee, *Choix de Textes: Glossaire*, 97.

[185] Dijkstra and Moor, "Problematical Passages in the Legend of Aqhatu," 178 and see especially footnotes 70, 71 and 72 for examples.

[186] Conklin, "Oath Formulae in Classical Hebrew and Other Semitic Languages," 222.

[187] According to Conklin, the authenticating element is diversified in the Akkadian texts. The most common formula is *nīš* X. But in many cases, *nīš* is omitted. Cf. Ibid., 200–220.

Conklin argues in his University of Chicago dissertation on oath formulae in Classical Hebrew and Semitic languages that oath formulae have a binary structure: the first element is "the authenticating element" such as the verb of swearing, the "life of X" formulae, the gesture of raising hand, etc. The second element is the actual content of the oath which may or may not be headed by conditional conjunctions *'m*, *'m-l'* or the conjunction *ky*.[188] Accepting Conklin's basic thesis, the Ugaritic verse in question may be argued to be a legitimate oath formula with a binary structure, as long as Ugaritic *npš* alone can form a legitimate abbreviation of a fuller form *ḥnpš*+PN, since the actual content of the oath can be introduced without any marker.[189]

However, the "oath" interpretation of KTU 1.17 I:36b–38a poses several problems. First, those who take the Ugaritic *npš* as an abbreviated formula of *ḥnpš*+PN have to explain the form *npš*. The *npš* in *ḥnpš* is the *nomen rectum* which should be couched in the genitive. Then the expected form with the first person pronominal suffix would be *npšy* in our text. Second, the abbreviated uses of "Life of X" formula in comparative evidence seem to be accompanied by the verb of swearing (cf. *nišbaʿ* and *li-it-ma-a-mi* in the Hebrew and Akkadian examples cited above). It may be owing to these difficulties that scholars such as Coogan, Caquot, Gibson, Pardee, Gaster, Del Olmo Lete, et al., have adhered to a non-oath interpretation of the passage:[190] "May Dānî'ilu, [the man] of Rapa'u, live indeed / may the valiant Harnamite man live to the fullest."[191] But in spite of these difficulties the view of taking the passage in question as an oath makes good literary sense. The motif of a vow may be one of those motifs that verbalize the pre-verbal concept of intentionality. But clearly the incubation type-scene in the 'Aqhatu story lacks the motif of a vow. The motif of an oath, which may have been present in 'Ilu's speech, could have served to compensate for such

---

[188] Ibid., 1.

[189] Conklin devotes chapter 5 to the oaths in which no marker heads the actual content of the oath. According to him, there are 14 oaths which neither use *ky* or *'m* or *'m-l'*. Out of 14, ten oaths have no former marker to introduce the oath. Cf. Ibid., 178.

[190] Coogan, *Stories from Ancient Canaan*, 33; Caquot, Sznycer, and Herdner, *Mythes et légendes: introduction, traduction, commentaire*, 423, footnote x; Gibson, *Canaanite Myths and Legends.*, 104; Bordreuil and Pardee, *Choix de Textes: Glossaire*, 24; Gaster, *Thespis: Ritual, Myth, and Drama in the Ancient Near East*, 355; Olmo Lete, *Mitos y leyendas de Canaan: según la tradición de Ugarit*, 34.

[191] This is Pardee's translation ("The Aqhatu Legend," 344).

lack. Wright, alluding to Milgrom's distinction between the difference between oath and vow, says the followings:

> Given the fact that vows can be made for securing blessings pertaining to family, Dani'il could easily have made a vow. This might have been the easier route because, if the gods did not grant his request, he would not have expended his means in vain. (Of course he might have created more trouble for himself, as Kirta did, by not fulfilling the vow after he received the blessing!) Dani'il presented his offering first, however, thus laying himself open to loss through the gods' rejection. In this way, Dani'il's performance appears more devout. It is a sign of his trust as well as his need. It responds with equal determination by formulating the blessing in the context of an oath, which assures the promise. This oath with attending blessing, then, can be viewed as the specific high point of the initial offering.[192]

It is not unusual to read in other incubation texts that an incubant makes a vow before or after he lies down for an oneiric theophany. Hence, the motif of a vow may be taken to belong to a pool of motifs which verbalize the pre-verbal concept of intentionality. If one could find the motif of an oath in 'Ilu's blessing, one can make a plausible case that the absence of the vow motif is compensated for by the divine oath within the theophany motif. Furthermore, if Wright's observation has any value, one may even say that such configuration of motifs may be intended in order to put an emphasis on Dānî'ilu's piety as demonstrated by his approach to the deity and also on the divine satisfaction at the pious incubant.

2.3 *After Epiphany*

Text: Transliteration and Translation

Dānî'ilu Rejoices

	b dni[l] (9) pnm . tšmḫ̮ .	Dānî'ilu's face lit up with joy,
	w ʿl . yṣhl pi⸢t⸣	(His) temple(s) above shone.
(10)	yprq . lṣb . w yṣḥq	His forehead unforrowed and he laughed.
(11)	pʿn . l hdm . yṯpd .	As he put his feet on the footstool,
	yšu (12) gh . w yṣḥ .	He raised his voice and shouted:

[192] Wright, *Ritual in Narrative: The Dynamics of Feasting, Mourning, and Retaliation Rites in the Ugaritic Tale of Aqhat*, 79. Cf. Jacob Milgrom, *Numbers [Ba-Midbar]: The Traditional Hebrew Text with the New JPS Translation, Commentary by Jacob Milrom* (Philadelphia, PA: Jewish Publication Society, 1990), 488–90.

Dānî'ilu's Expression of Joy

	aṯbn . ank (13) w anḫn .	I will sit and rest,
	w tnḫ . b irty (14) npš .	My soul will rest in my breast.
	k yld . bn . ly . km (15) aḫy .	For a son will be born to me, as to my brothers,
	w šrš . km . aryy	A scion, as to my kinsmen:

The Fourth Occurrence of the List of Filial Duties.

(16)	nṣb . skn . iliby .	Someone to raise up the stela of my father's god,
	b qd⸢š⸣ (17) ztr . ʿmy .	In the sanctuary the votive emblem of my clan;
	l ʿpr[.]ḏmr . aṯr[y]	From the dust the song of my place;
(18)	ṭbq . lḥt . niṣy .	To shut up the jaws of my detractors,
	grš (19) d ʿšy . ln .	To drive out anyone who would do me in;
	aḫd . ydy . b š(20)krn .	To take my hand when I am drunk,
	mʿmsy . k šbʿt y⸢n⸣	To carry me when I am full of wine;
(21)	spu . ksmy . bt . bʿl .	To eat my grain-offering in the temple of Baʿlu,
	w m⸢n⸣ [t](22)y . bt . il .	My portion in the temple of 'Ilu;
	ṭḫ . ggy . b ym . ṯi⸢ṭ⸣	To plaster my roof on a day of mud,
(23)	rḥs . npṣy . b ym . rṯ	To wash my outfit on a day of filth.

Execution of Divine Instruction

(24)	dn . il . bth . ymǵyn	Dānî'ilu arrived at his house,
(25)	yštql . dnil . l hklh	Dānî'ilu came to his palace.
(26)	ʿrb . b bth . kṯrt .	The Kôṯarātu entered his house,
	bnt (27) hll . snnt .	The daughters of brightness, the pure ones.
	apnk . dnil (28) mt . rpi .	Thereupon, as for Dānî'ilu the man of Rapa'u,
	ap . hn . ǵzr . mt (29) hrnmy .	Thereupon, as for the valiant one the Harnamite man,
	alp . yṭbḫ . l kṯ(30)rt .	A bull he slaughtered for the Kôṯarātu,
	yšlḥm . ⸢k⸣ṯrt .	He caused the Kôṯarātu to eat,
	w y(31)ššq . bnt . [h]ll . snnt	He caused the daughters of brightness the pure ones to drink.
(32)	hn . ym . w ṯn .	Voici! A day, even two,
	yšlḥm (33) kṯrt .	He had the Kôṯarātu eat,

	w . yš⸢š⸣q . bnt . hl⸢l⸣ (34) snnt .	He had the daughters of brightness the pure ones drink.
	ṯlṯ . ⸢rb⸣ ʿ ym .	A third, even a fourth day,
	yšl(35)ḥm kṯrt .	He had the Kôṯarātu eat,
	w yššq (36) bnt hll . snnt .	He had the daughters of brightness the pure ones drink.
	ḫmš (37) ṯdṯ . ym .	A fifth, even a sixth day,
	yšlḥm . ⸢k⸣ṯrt (38)	He had the Kôṯarātu eat,
	w yš[šq .] ⸢b⸣nt hll . snn⸢t⸣	He had the daughters of brightness the pure ones drink.
(39)	mk . b šb[ʿ] . ymm .	Then, on the seventh day,
	tbʿ . b bth (40) kṯ⸢r⸣t .	The Kôṯarātu left his house,
	bnt . hll . snnt	The daughters of brightness the pure ones.
(41)	⸢m⸣d⸢d⸣t . nʿmy . ⸢ʿ⸣r⸢š⸣ . ⸢y⸣ld	The dispensers of the goodness (on) the bed of a child,
(42)	⸢y⸣smsmt . ʿrš . ḫll⸢t⸣	of the beauty of the bed of birthing.

Fulfillment of Divine Promise

(43)	yṯb . dnil . [ls]⸢p⸣r ⸢yr⸣ḫh	Dānîʾilu sat down [to count] her months,
(44)	yrḫ . y⸢rḫ⸣ [...]	A month, [a second?] month...
(45)	ṯlṯ . rbʿ [...]	A third, a fourth [month...]
(46)	yrḫm . ymǵy[...]	The months came [...]
(47)	⸢-⸣ [-]⸢-⸣ [...]	

(About ten lines are missing from the bottom of the column)

2.3.1 *The Change-of-Mood Motif: Expression of Joy*

Component motifs of an incubation type-scene are not a random aggregation. They are in such a relationship that they advance the plot from problem to solution, from the predicament of the incubant to the salvific appearance of a patron deity. The change-of-mood motif may be said to verbalize the concept of epiphany in the sense that it is a direct consequence of—thus can be used as circumstantial evidence for—the genuine salvific theophany. In other words, if other means of divination such as extispicy in the Mesopotamian practice of incubation might provide a direct and objective evidence for the genuineness of oneiric theophany, the change-of-mood motif in the incubation type-scene may have fulfilled a similar function by giving circumstantial and subjective confirmation of the efficacy of the theophany.[193] Moreover, if the mood for the first part of the tripartite structure of incubation is determined by the motifs actualizing the concept of predicament, the motif of joy sets the mood in the post-theophany part of the incubation type-scene.

In registering the change of mood motif as part of the incubation type-scene, the poet of *'Aqhatu* describes the joy within Dānî'ilu in terms of the outward reactions of Dānî'ilu's body parts such as face (*pnm*), temple (*pit*), forehead (*lṣb*),[194] and feet (*p'n*) (KTU 1.17 II:8b–11). The poet's descriptive narration then gives way to Dānî'ilu's direct speech, which is also expressive of the changing mood in Dānî'ilu (lines 12b–15). Noteworthy in Dānî'ilu's speech is the use of *anḫn* "I will rest" to express his new mood, since a similar looking, but lexically distinct word, *anḫ* "the moaning one" was used by the poet (in KTU 1.17 I:17) to express exactly the opposite mood.[195] The *k*-clause in lines 14–15 does a double duty: it not only states the reason for Dānî'ilu's new mood but also introduces the list of filial duties for the fourth time. The use of the parallel words *bn* and *šrš* in that clause recalls the other verses that introduce the list of filial duties in the theophany motif, but the *k*-clause introducing the fourth list of filial duties after theophany distinguishes itself from them by substituting *ykn* for *yld*

---

[193] According to the Cylinder of Gudea (CA 12:13–19), the oneiric theophany often had to be confirmed by other means of divination, such as extispicy. For other incubation reports registering the change of mood of the incubant after theophany, see 2.3.2 in chapter three above.

[194] Three of the word's five occurrences are found in the phrase *yprq lṣbh*, an action which precedes laughing (KTU 1.4 IV:28; 1.6 II:16; 1.17 II:10). Ever since Ullendorff suggested an Arabic root √lṣb "narrowness, tightness" as a possible cognate to Ugaritic *lṣb*, scholars' efforts have centered on the identification of what the narrow thing might be that can be "split" prior to laughing. But none of the proposals—Ullendorff's "space between the teeth," Loewenstamm's "space between the lips," Moor's "deep frown as *pars pro toto* for the brow," Dietrich and Loretz's "temples,"—are satisfactory. Furthermore, the attestation in KTU 1.114 (the cure for divine hang over) and KTU 1.103 (deformed fetus omen) suggests that it refers to some part of the head. See more details, Renfroe, *Arabic-Ugaritic Lexical Studies*, 125–26. For the translation "forehead," see Caquot, Sznycer, and Herdner, *Mythes et légendes: introduction, traduction, commentaire*, 204, footnote f; Kevin J. Cathcart and Wilfred G. E. Watson, "Weathering a Wake: A Cure for a Carousal," *PIBA 4*, no. 35–58 (1980): 40; Dennis Pardee, "Ugaritic: The Ugaritic Šumma Izbu Text," *AfO* 33 (1986): 133.

[195] Consider also the consonantal assonance between *abyn⸢n⸣* (KTU 1.17 I:16) and *aṯbn* (KTU 1.17 II:12).

and the *bt-hkl* parallelism for the *aḫ-ary* parallelism. This variation may reflect different speech contexts and different levels of reality.[196]

As is often the case with motifs comprising a type-scene, the change of mood motif in question is expanded and elaborated to the extent that it forms a type-scene of its own. The "expression of joy" motif contains several word-based or phrase-based motifs that tend to occur together whenever such a theme is expressed in the Ugaritic narrative. I was able to find six occurrences of that motif in the Ugaritic literature: Three of them qualify as a full-fledged type-scene (1.17 II:9–23; 1.6 III:14–21; 1.4 IV:28–39), while a single verb *šmḫ* comprises the others (1.4 V 35:20; 1.10 III:37). Table 4.6 compares the former three.

The motifs comprising the theme of "expression of joy" are not identical in the three instances presented above. The motif of "Temple-shining" is not registered in KTU 1.6 III:14–21, nor in KTU 1.4 IV:28–39. The example in KTU 1.4 IV:28–39 even lacks the motif of "Rejoice" and Direct Speech I. But interestingly, it has the motif of "Finger-snapping," that the other two, more complete, examples omit. The order in which those motifs occur is not identical either. The motif of "Feet on the footstool," which occur in the fifth slot in the example in KTU 1.17 II:9–23, occupies the second slot in the example in KTU 1.6 III:14–21. Some of the peculiarities featuring an individual example of this type-scene may be explained in terms of its literary function. For instance,

[196] A few comments should be made on Jean-Marie Husser's suggestion that the *k*-clause in lines 14–15 (*k yld ly bn km aḫy / w šrš km aryy*) should be taken to refer to a birth that has already happened, not to the prospect of a birth (Husser, "The Birth of a Hero: Form and Meaning of KTU 1.17 i–ii," 90–92; cf. Simon B. Parker, "The Birth Announcement," 133–49). In order to justify his case, he interprets the following scene of the visit of the Kôtarātu as a flashback within the narrative, which, by the way, does not fit well with what we know about the style of the poet of *'Aqhatu*. The literary basis to which he anchors his argument is the assumption that the formula represented in the *k*-clause (a passive form of *yld* + *bn* [or parallel words] + l + PN [usually a father]) always announces the birth that has already taken place. This assumption is, however, based on a limited number of examples in the Ugaritic and biblical literature: one in the former and three in the latter (ibid., 90, footnote 9). Furthermore, one of the biblical examples, namely, Isaiah 9:5, is controversial. A number of scholars take *kî-yeled-lānû bēn* as prophetic, namely, referring to a future birth (e.g. George B. Gray, *A Critical and Exegetical Commentary on the Book of Isaiah, I–XXXIX*, ICC [New York: C. Scribner's Sons, 1912], 166; Brevard S. Childs, *Isaiah*, OTL [Louisville, KY: Westminster John Knox Press, 2001], 81). Even if the formula originated in the *Sitz-im-Leben*, where a birth that has already happened is announced to a father, that does not prevent the formula from being used in different literary circumstances (*Sitz im Literatur*, cf. the formula of a prophetic message [*hāyāh dəbar-YHWH 'el-PN bammaḥăzeh lē'mōr*] used of Abram in Genesis 15).

Table 4.6: The Expression of Joy Motif

	KTU 1.17 II:9–23	KTU 1.6 III:14–21	KTU 1.4 IV:28–39
Rejoice	*bdnil pnm tšmḫ* (1)*	*šmḫ lṭpn il* (1)	n/a
Temple shines	*ʿl yṣhl pit* (2)	n/a	n/a
Brow unfurrows	*yprq lṣb* (3)	*yprq lṣb* (3)	*yprq lṣb* (1)
Laugh	*yṣḥq* (4)	*yṣḥq* (4)	*yṣḥq* (2)
Feet on the footstool	*p ʿn l hdm yṯpd* (5)	*p ʿn l hdm yṯpd* (2)	*p ʿn l hdm yṯpd* (3)
Shout aloud	*yšu gh wṣḥ* (6)	*yšu gh wṣḥ* (5)	*yšu gh wṣḥ* (5)
Direct Speech I**	*aṯbn ank w anḫn / w tnḫ birty npš* (7)	*aṯbn ank w anḫn / w tnḫ birty npš* (6)	Lines 31–39 (6)[197]
Direct Speech II**	*"A son shall be given": Lines 14–23 (8)*	*"Baʿlu is alive": Lines 20–21 (7)*	n/a
Finger Snapping	n/a	n/a	*wykrkr uṣbʿth* (4)

* The number in brackets represent the order in which the motif in question occur in the type-scene.
** Direct Speech is divided into two on the basis of its content: Direct Speech I contains the 1st-person expression of joy/mood change, while Direct Speech II gives the reason for such joy/mood change.

the unique occurrence of the "Finger(*uṣbʿt*)-snapping" motif in KTU 1.4 IV:28–39 may foreshadow the mention of *yd* (an euphemism for the male sexual organ) in 'Ilu's direct speech (*yd il mlk ḫssk* "Is it the hand of 'Ilu the king that aroused you?" [line 38]).

As the above table shows, the change-of-mood motifs in KTU 1.17 II:9–23 and KTU 1.6 III:14–21 show close similarity to each other in terms of the kind of motifs included and their sequence. Furthermore, the change-of-mood motif is given in both cases after favorable dreams. Direct Speech II, which gives the reason for the mood change, reflects the difference in content of the two oneiric incidents: the divine promise of a son and the natural portent that Baʿlu is alive. More interesting to our purpose, however, is that, in both KTU 1.17 II:9–23 and KTU 1.6 III:14–21, the change of mood motif occurs right after the description of oneiric incidents, without any textual hint to the change from dream to reality, namely, without the waking motif.[198] But the context

[197] The content in lines 31–39 does not advance the plot. The verbosity of 'Ilu there simply shows how excited he is at the surprising visit of 'Aṯiratu. This seems to be corroborated by the following words of 'Aṯiratu, who does not answer any of 'Ilu's questions, as if she did not hear them, but goes on to make a petition for Baʿlu.

[198] Cf. P. A. Kruger, "Some Further Indicators of Rank Symbolism in Baal Epic," *UF* 27 (1995): 175.

makes it relatively clear that both Dānî'ilu in KTU 1.17 II:9–23 and 'Ilu in KTU 1.6 III:14–21 rejoice in a real world, not in their dreams. Husser denies that the theophany in KTU 1.17 I–II is oneiric simply because there is no mention in the text of Dānî'ilu's waking up from a dream. He goes on to argue that the non-oneiric nature of theophany makes it difficult to regard the initial scene in the 'Aqhatu's story as an incubation scene.[199] Several incubation reports where the change-of-mood motif is registered do note the waking of the proponent before describing his joyful reaction to a new reality after theophany.[200] But one must be very careful not to make it into a rigid rule, when only a few instances are available to us and furthermore when KTU 1.6 III:14–21 clearly shows the change of mood motif without any explicit textual note that 'Ilu awoke from his dream.

Although the change of mood motif is composed of "traditional" Ugaritic phrases that may be used to express joy elsewhere in the Ugaritic epic texts, the embedment in the Incubation type-scene in KTU 1.17 I–II indicates that the motif has a literary role to play, not only within the incubation type-scene, but also in the 'Aqhatu narrative as a whole. First, notice that the change-of-mood motif is couched in the same structure as the sections comprising the theophany motif: the poet's narration (KTU 1.17 II:8–11), a direct speech (lines 12–15), and the list of filial duties (lines 16–23). This not only signals that Dānî'ilu was reacting to the divine speech which has the same tripartite structure, but also yields a stylistic symmetry within the incubation type-scene and highlights 'Ilu's blessing as the pivot in the plot of reversing Dānî'ilu's misfortune, which, by the way, is symbolically implied in the wordplay between *anḫ* "the groaning one" before divine blessing (KTU 1.17 I:17) and *anḫn* "I will rest" after divine blessing (KTU 1.17 II:13). Furthermore, the change of mood motif finds an echo later in the narrative. When Dānî'ilu heard the news of 'Aqhatu's death, the poet describes the mood of sadness in Dānî'ilu in terms of the reaction of his body parts:

---

199 Husser, "The Birth of a Hero: Form and Meaning of KTU 1.17 i–ii," 94–95.

200 Cf. Tablet IX of the Gilgamesh epic and the Egyptian dream of Djoser. See 2.3.2 in chapter three above.

[bh . pʿnm] (45) ṭṭṭ .	[His feet] totter
ʿl[n . pnh . tdʿ .	above, [his face perspires,
bʿdn] (46) ksl . yṯ[br .	behind,] his back muscles [snap,
yǵṣ . pnt . kslh (47)	his vertebrae rattle
anš . d[t ẓrh .	his spine goes week
yšu . gh] (48) w yṣ[ḥ...]	[raising up his voice], he shouts[...]
(49) mḫ̮ṣ [...]	[...]has smitten[...][201]
(KTU 1.19 II:44–49)	

It is hardly accidental that these two motifs expressing Dānî'ilu's mood are occasioned by the news conveyed by messengers, one divine and the other human, and that the first message pertains to the birth of Dānî'ilu's son, while the second concerns the death of 'Aqhatu. The two motifs themselves thus draw a contrast between birth of a son/rejoicing and death of a son/distress and thereby highlight the dramatic and less happy reversal in Dānî'ilu's fortunes.[202]

2.3.2 *The Fulfillment Motif*

Contrary to our expectation of the command-fulfillment pattern, the poet does not describe the copulation between Dānî'ilu and his wife, Dānatay, in the way 'Ilu instructs (cf. KTU 1.17 I:38–41).[203] The details of love-making in 'Ilu's instruction are not translated into Dānî'ilu's actions in this fulfillment motif. What is described instead is the visit of the Kôṯarātu, the goddesses of conception and childbirth,[204] during

---

[201] Notice that the description of physical reaction is followed by the direct speech of Dānî'ilu, as in the case of the expression of joy motif in KTU 1 17 II. But unfortunately, the direct speech is lost in the broken tablet.

[202] Aitken, *The Aqhat Narrative: A Study in the Narrative Structure and Composition of an Ugaritic Tale*, 155.

[203] KTU 1.17 II:41–42 cannot be taken as such description: (41) ⌈*m*⌉*d*̉⌈*d*⌉*t . nʿmy .* ⌈*ʿr*⌉*š .* ⌈*y*⌉*ld (42)* ⌈*y*⌉*smsmt . ʿrš . ḫ̮ll*⌈*t*⌉ "dispensers of the goodness of the bed of conception / of the beauty of the bed of childbirth." Although scholars disagree on the restoration of the first word in line 41, the bicolon verse in lines 41–42 is no doubt part of the description of the Kôṯarātu in their capacity of helping conception and birth. For different restorations and translations, see Gibson, *Canaanite Myths and Legends.*, 106; Olmo Lete, *Mitos y leyendas de Canaan: según la tradición de Ugarit*, 373, 426, footnote g, h, i, j; Dijkstra and Moor, "Problematical Passages in the Legend of Aqhatu," 180; Wright, *Ritual in Narrative: The Dynamics of Feasting, Mourning, and Retaliation Rites in the Ugaritic Tale of Aqhat*, 82, footnote 4, 6.

[204] For the goddesses, see Dennis Pardee, "Kosharoth," in *Dictionary of Deities and Demons in the Bible*, ed. Karel van der Toorn (Leiden: Brill, 1999), 491–92; Alan Cooper, "Divine Names and Epithets in the Ugaritic Texts," in *Ras Shamra Parallels: The Texts from Ugarit and the Hebrew Bible*, vol. 3, ed. Stan Rummel (Roma: Pontificium

which Dānî'ilu's sexual union must have occurred and led to conception. As Wright points out, the visit of the Kôṯarātu can be seen "as a metonymical means of signaling that conception occurs at approximately this point in the narrative."[205] A close reading of the text would not only reveal that the visit of the Kôṯarātu is the poet's creative way of indicating the fulfillment motif, but also that it forms a better conclusion to the incubation type-scene than the scene describing a literal carrying-out of 'Ilu's instructions.

The fulfillment motif is marked off by the note on the change in location: *dnil bth ymǵyn yštql dnil l hklh* "Dānî'ilu arrived at his house, Dānî'ilu came to his palace" (KTU 1.17 II:24–25). This implies that the incident described thus far happened in some place other than Dānî'ilu's house. Although there is no direct evidence in the text, most scholars agree that it took place in a sanctuary or a temple.[206] The original reader might have assumed from the beginning that the whole process of incubation took place in a temple, but the text corroborates such assumption only later in the narrative by giving away that Dānî'ilu had not been at home during the seven-day ritual. This is another example of the literary technique of "delayed identification" that the poet has been using often in this particular instance of the incubation type-scene. When Dānî'ilu returned to his house, the Kôṯarātu arrived. The manner in which Dānî'ilu gives them food and drink recalls Dānî'ilu's offering to the gods when he was seeking divine revelation. There are some points of similarity between the two motifs. First, it is Dānî'ilu who serves the deities in both motifs. Accordingly, the description of the feast also begins with a full introduction of Dānî'ilu (*apnk dnil mt rpi / aphn ǵzr mt hrnmy* [KTU 1.17 II:27–29]) as in the preparatory ritual. Second, the description of the feast for the Kôṯarātu is couched in the seven-day formula, which also

Institutum Biblicum, 1981), 387–88; Wright, *Ritual in Narrative: The Dynamics of Feasting, Mourning, and Retaliation Rites in the Ugaritic Tale of Aqhat*, 84, footnote 8 and the bibliography there.

[205] Wright, *Ritual in Narrative: The Dynamics of Feasting, Mourning, and Retaliation Rites in the Ugaritic Tale of Aqhat*, 85.

[206] Simon B. Parker, *The Pre-Biblical Narrative Tradition: Essays on the Ugaritic Poems Keret and Aqhat*, 100; Olmo Lete, *Mitos y leyendas de Canaan: según la tradición de Ugarit*, 336; Wright, *Ritual in Narrative: The Dynamics of Feasting, Mourning, and Retaliation Rites in the Ugaritic Tale of Aqhat*, 7, 43; Gaster, *Thespis: Ritual, Myth, and Drama in the Ancient Near East*, 316; Dietrich and Loretz, "Das Aqhat-Epos," 1258, footnote 13. Del Olmo Lete goes further to argue that the sanctuary must be the extension of Dānî'ilu's palace.

begins with a general statement about making offerings to the deities and is then broken down into pairs of days describing Dānî'ilu feeding and giving drink to the gods. This structural and contextual similarity between the scene of preparation and that of conclusion gives the sense of closure to the incubation type-scene as a whole and also, by bracketing the theophany motif, it sets the revelation and promise in relief and highlights them.[207]

Despite its structural and contextual similarity to the preparatory ritual, the visit of the Kôṯarātu reveals its individuality in many respects. The location is different: while the preparatory ritual was performed in a temple, the feast for the Kôṯarātu was held in Dānî'ilu's home. The mood is also different. If the mood of the ritual before theophany was that of "introspection, loneliness, melancholy, deficiency, and uncertainty," the mood of the post-revelation feast is one of "hope, prosperity and confidence."[208] The initiator of the situation is also different. In the preparatory ritual, Dānî'ilu is the initiator of the ritual. Dānî'ilu's intention to induce a revelation is thrust at the forefront. But in the later feast, the visit of the Kôṯarātu prompted Dānî'ilu to serve the hospitality meal. Wright confirms this by saying, "In the first example, the offering leads to the god's action; in the second, the god's action leads to the offering."[209] But the most significant difference relates to the seven-day formula. Although the preparatory ritual and the hospitality meal both begin with the full introduction of Dānî'ilu's epithet and both share a six-day itemization, which is broken down into pairs of days, one may observe several dissimilarities that may have a significant effect on the interpretation of the scene as a whole.

The general statement about regaling the goddesses occurs in a tricolon verse. Its first colon (*alp yṭbḫ lkṯrt* "[Dānî'ilu] slaughtered an ox for the Kôṯarātu" [KTU 1.17 II:29–30a]), however, gets omitted in the following six-day repetition of the same theme, thus turning a tricolon verse into a bicolon. This decrease in the verse size seems to coincide with the fact that the momentum of the feast decreases with the passing of days. On the seventh day, one may feel almost betrayed, because nothing significant seems to have happened. The text simply records, "On the seventh day, they departed from his house" (*mk⌜b šb⌝ ymm tbʿ*

[207] Cf. Wright, *Ritual in Narrative: The Dynamics of Feasting, Mourning, and Retaliation Rites in the Ugaritic Tale of Aqhat*, 83.
[208] Ibid.
[209] Ibid., 85.

b bth [KTU 1.17 II:39]). The theme of Dānîʾilu's regaling the goddesses seems to have lost its momentum completely on the seventh-day. In contrast, the seven day formula of the preparatory rituals begins with two bicolon verses, and in the following six-day repetition the bicolon verses are expanded into tricolon verses. Furthermore, the last pair of days in the preparatory ritual registers the ritual with the most elaborate literary craft: Two tricolon verses describe Dānîʾilu's offering and his ritual sleep respectively. The momentum of the ritual actions increases as it moves on to the seventh day and prepares the reader for the climax on the seventh day. It may be argued that the theme of offering is thrown into foreground in the seven-day formula of the preparatory ritual.[210]

If this comparison is legitimate, one may conclude that the theme of feast, which seems to stay in the background of the scene, is not the main focus of the poet's description of the visit of the Kôṯarātu. The main focus of the scene may be hinted at by the emphasis on the epithets of the Kôṯarātu in the seventh-day formula. In fact, what stands out in the scene of the feast for the Kôṯarātu is the repetition of their epithets. All the poetic verses, except the one introducing Dānîʾilu with his full epithets (KTU 1.17 II:27b–29a), contain the goddesses' full appellation: *kṯrt*…*bnt hll snnt* "the Kôṯarātu…the daughters of purity/Hulel, the pure ones." It is especially noteworthy that the poet saves the epithets of the goddesses explicitly descriptive of their role as the harbingers of conception until the seventh day: *⸢m⸣ḏ⸢ḏ⸣t n‘my ⸢‘r⸣š ⸢y⸣ld ⸢y⸣smsmt ‘rš ḫll⸢t⸣* "dispensers of the goodness on the bed of child, of the beauty of the bed of birthing" (KTU 1.17 II:41–42).[211] This may show that the focus of the scene is on the role of the Kôṯarātu as the goddesses of conception. If the original reader was familiar with the function of the Kôṯarātu, whether from acquaintance with the tradition

[210] This contrast between the scene of Dānîʾilu's incubation offering and that of his regaling the goddesses may be shown in the use of different stems of the same verbs for "eating" and "drinking." The initial offering scene is couched in the D-stem of the verbs *lḥm* and *šqy*, while the feast for the Kôṯarātu employs the Š-stem of the same verbs. As we suggested before, this difference may reflect that in the offering scene, the emphasis is put on the act of "presentation" and its "offerer," while in the feast scene the act of eating and drinking itself is under spotlight as well as the consumers. This may partly explains the reason why in the initial offering scene there is no mention of what is offered (*uzr* is not an offering!), whereas in the later feast scene the food is specified as "ox" (*alp*).

[211] The transliteration is based on Pardee's pencil copy, which he has made available to the present author.

preserved in KTU 1.24 (the marriage of Nikkal text) or not, we may have another example of delayed identification: the poet waits until the last climactic day before he reveals the pertinent identity of the goddesses. In other words, the climactic element on the seventh day does not lie in the verb *tbʿ* "they left," but in the identification of the ones "who left the house." In this regard, the impression that the seventh day creates an anti-climax—nothing happens except that the goddesses have left the house—belies the significant fact that ʾAqhatu has now been conceived as a result of the very visit of the goddesses of conception and birth. It is also arguable that the focus of the feast for the Kôṯarātu lies less on Dānîʾilu's piety or hospitality than on how the divine promise for a son is fulfilled through divine agents. Therefore, the visit of the Kôṯarātu may be the poet's creative way of filling the fulfillment motif of the incubation type-scene. By doing so, the poet not only alludes to the theme of the story, namely, the proper behavior within the traditional social order, but he also evinces that the divine promise has been fulfilled without fail.

This function is confirmed by the subsequent scene in which the months of gestation are counted. The text presents the matter as if pregnancy began immediately after the Kôṯarātu left. The motif of counting the months of pregnancy is not uncommon in a birth story. According to Hoffner's translation,[212] Appu's wife becomes pregnant after Appu has met with the Sun-god in a temple through incubation. The text goes on to describe the counting of the months of gestation: "Appu's wife became pregnant. The first month, the second month, the third month, the fourth month, the fifth month, the sixth month, the seventh month, the eighth month, the ninth month passed, and the tenth month arrived. Appu's wife bore a son."[213] Also, in another Hittite story entitled "Kingship in Heaven,"[214] it appears that Kumarbis's months of pregnancy is counted when the birth is narrated. An

[212] Hoffner, "Appu and His Two Sons," 153–54. Also see Irvin, *Mytharion: The Comparison of Tales from the Old Testament and the Ancient Near East*, 60; Hans Ehelof, "Das Motif der Kindesunterschiebung in einer hethitischen Erzählung," *Orientalische Literaturzeitung* 29 (1926): col. 766–69; Hans G. Güterbock, *Kumarbi, Mythen vom Churritischen Kronos aus den Hethitischen Fragmenten Zusammengestellt, Ubers, und Erklart*, Istanbuler Schriften 16 (Zurich-New York: Europaverlag, 1946), 119–22; Johannes Friedrich, "Churritische Sagen und Märchen in Hethitischn Sprache," *ZA* 49, no. 213–241 (1949): 214–23.

[213] Hoffner, "Appu and His Two Sons," 154.

[214] Albrecht Goezte, "Hittite Myths, Epic, and Legends," in *ANET*, ed. James B. Pritchard (120–128, 1969), 120. For other translations, see the bibliography in Irvin,

Egyptian Story ("Doomed Prince") also registers the counting of gestation months, when it tells of a king who had no son but acquired one through a divine aid.[215] Since the incubation type-scene at the beginning of the 'Aqhatu story pertains to the acquisition of a son, it is no wonder that some motifs that are frequent in the traditional birth story are present in it. Here the motif of counting the months of pregnancy is used in the 'Aqhatu text as part of describing how the divine promise is fulfilled.

3. The Narratological Role of the Incubation Type-Scene: Echoing and Foreshadowing

The poet begins the 'Aqhatu Story with an incubation type-scene consisting of various motifs, which verbalize pre-verbal concepts—predicament, intentionality, liminality and epiphany—characteristic of incubation as known in the ancient Near East. These motifs are configured not only to contribute to the internal plot of the incubation, but also to foreshadow the subsequent plot of the 'Aqhatu story.[216] One can find various echoes of the component motifs of the initial type-scene later in various points of the narrative. Some of those echoes are straightforward while others put a twist on original motifs. But all in all, it is clear that the motifs and themes that comprise the initial type-scene contribute to the advance of the plot by way of foreshadowing and echoing. This narratological function of the type-scene has been touched on only briefly in the previous discussion. It is now time to deal with it on its own terms. But one caveat needs to be made before we discuss the narratological significance of the initial incubation type-scene in the 'Aqhatu story. Considerable portions of the 'Aqhatu story are missing. Wyatt describes the status of preservation thus:

Mytharion: The Comparison of Tales from the Old Testament and the Ancient Near East, 61, footnote 1.

[215] Here the motif of the reckoning of the months of gestation occurs in a shortened form: "When her months were completed, she bore a son." Irvin, *Mytharion: The Comparison of Tales from the Old Testament and the Ancient Near East*, 86.

[216] Speaking of the initial feast, for example, Wright says "It thereby becomes a lens for viewing the other feasts in the story" (Wright, *Ritual in Narrative: The Dynamics of Feasting, Mourning, and Retaliation Rites in the Ugaritic Tale of Aqhat*, 44).

> KTU 1.17 is a tablet originally of six columns, of which two are entirely missing, while the beginning and end of the four surviving columns are missing (an estimated twelve or so lines in all on the recto, and on the verso, with a shearing break down the upper surface, perhaps twenty or so), with the wedge-shaped breaks on columns i and iv resulting in even further loss. KTU 1.18 is a tablet of four columns originally, of which two are entirely missing. Again, the beginning and end of the surviving columns are missing (some twenty-five lines or so), and wedge-shaped breaks further reduce the surviving text, with no complete lines in col. i, and only nine complete in col. iv. KTU 1.19 is the best reserved of the three; the only substantial losses here result from friable edges along the three sections into which the tablet has broken, with the additional loss of a central section in col. i, the bottom right hand corner of col. ii, the top corner of col. iii, and a small vertical section in the lower part of col. iv. The surface is also eroded at the beginning of col. i and in the upper central section of col. iv.[217]

According to Wyatt's calculation, approximately 430 out of original 830 lines are missing. The missing lines amount to about 51 percent of all the lines. The fact should serve as a warning to anyone who claims to a "canonical" interpretation of *'Aqhatu*. Any adequate interpretation of the text must remain provisional, and so is mine in the following paragraphs.

That said, the incubation type-scene at the beginning of *'Aqhatu* finds a number of thematic correspondences in the last tablet (KTU 1.19) of the story where the problem that advances the plot is also the lack of a proper son-heir. If KTU 1.17 I–II resolves the crisis of sonlessness by turning to the gods for help (incubation), the proponents in KTU 1.19 seem to resolve the problem by, so to speak, taking matters into their own hands (the vengeance by Pūġatu on the murderer of 'Aqhatu). This is made even more clear when Pūġatu asks for a blessing on her journey for vengeance. It is not *'Ilu* who blesses Pūġatu on her journey, but Dānî'ilu. Significantly, Dānî'ilu's words of blessing are reminiscent of 'Ilu's blessing at the beginning. But on a deeper level, whether or not 'Aqhatu is resuscitated in the missing fourth tablet, the poet may be presenting Pūġatu as a substitute heir, who would perform all the filial duties that 'Aqhatu had failed to perform.[218] This reversal

[217] Wyatt, "The Story of Aqhat (KTU 1.17–19)," 235.

[218] This would be more convincing if one could interpret *grš d 'šy lnh* ("To drive out anyone who would do him [a father] in") to include an avenger of blood. But there is no certainty on this matter.

of sexual roles is hinted at by the reversal of roles between male and female deities. The goddesses Kôṯarātu served as auxiliaries for the two male deities, Baʿlu and ʾIlu, in the initial incubation type-scene: They made sure that ʾIlu's command-promise was fulfilled without fail. But later in the story the role is reversed: the male deity ʾIlu serves as a means to the goddess ʿAnatu's goal of acquiring the coveted bow by killing ʾAqhatu. In a similar vein, it is noteworthy that the goddess ʿAnatu hires male Yaṭipānu to ensure that her will is accomplished.

Several motifs comprising the incubation type-scene find their echoes in KTU 1.19. The motif of weeping in Dānîʾilu's incubation ritual, for example, may be reflected in Pūġatu's silent weeping over the effects of the drought (KTU 1.19 I:34–35). Three points of similarity may be discerned between Dānîʾilu weeping (cf. *anḫ*) and Pūġatu's weeping. First, although Pūġatu's weeping is not prompted by the news of her bereavement, it certainly anticipates it, for infertile land may be symbolic of the shedding of innocent blood.[219] Dānîʾilu similarly lamented the lack of a legitimate heir in the family. Second, both Dānîʾilu and Pūġatu are described as having wept "silently." After seeing the barrenness of the land, Pūġatu "began to weep inwardly, to shed tears silently (*tbky pġt bm lb / tdmʿ bm kbd* [KTU 1.19 I:34–35])." This description of Pūġatu's silent weeping recalls the poet's literary description of Dānîʾilu's weeping. Although Dānîʾilu may have made some moaning sounds, although no articulate words, during the ritual, the poet does not give any hint about any audible aspect of the ritual, until later in the theophanic scene where Dānîʾilu is belatedly identified as "the lamenting one" (cf. *anḫ*)—an example of delayed identification. It may be said that Dānîʾilu's weeping is "silenced" for a literary effect in the text. Third, in the incubation type-scene, the poet removes all aural elements from the scene of preparatory ritual and yet couches the theophanic scene in three direct speeches: notice the transition from "seeing" to "hearing." A similar transition seems to be present in the weeping of Pūġatu. If *bkm* in KTU 1.19 II:8–9 can be

[219] The idea that shedding innocent blood pollutes the soil and renders it infertile recurs in the Bible story of Cain (Genesis 4:11–12; Cf. Numbers 35:33; Deuteronomy 21:1–9). For the literary dependence between 2 Samuel 1:21 and KTU 1.19 I:44–45, see T. L. Fenton, "Comparative Evidence in Textual Study: M. Dahood on 2 Sam. I 21 and CTA 19 (1 Aqht), I, 44–45," *VT* 29 (1979): 162–70. Fenton argues that in both passages, reference is made to the failure of the sources of irrigation, whether dew, rain, or spring water, and such a failure is connected with the shedding of (innocent) blood.

understood as deriving from the root √bky "to weep," one may discern an increase of the volume of Pūǵatu's weeping (from "the weeping inwardly" [*tbky*...*bm lb*] to the bona fide weeping [*bkm*]), which may in turn reflect the increasing importance of her role in the narrative.

The motif of ritual clothing and nakedness in the incubation type-scene also reverberates later in the story.[220] Pūǵatu is said to rend Dānî'ilu's garment when she sees the effects of the drought (*tmzʿ kst dnil*...[KTU 1.19 I:35]). The idea of Pūǵatu rending Dānî'ilu's clothing has puzzled many commentators, because there is no other attestation of such a practice.[221] But there is no doubt that the unusual act of Pūǵatu is a literary variation of the more common motif of rending one's own garment as an expression of grief. The reason the poet describes Pūǵatu rending Dānî'ilu's garment may be of a literary nature and it may be related to the episode later in the plot where the daughter Pūǵatu, an unlikely avenger of blood, volunteers to fulfill the very role of killing the enemy of the family. Watson connects the name YṬPN with Akkadian naṭāpu "tear out" and gives it the meaning "Render, Ripper."[222] If Watson's proposal is accepted, one may see an analogy in their roles as "render" or "killer": Just as Yaṭipānu

[220] See 2.1.3 and Table 3 above.

[221] Dijkstra and Moor regard it as unlikely that Pūǵátu is the subject of the verb *tmzʿ*, because mourners normally rend their own garments (Dijkstra and Moor, "Problematical Passages in the Legend of Aqhatu," 201). An impressive list of scholars have been of the same mind (Caquot, Sznycer, and Herdner, *Mythes et légendes: introduction, traduction, commentaire*, 444, Moor, *An Anthology of Religious Texts from Ugarit*, 250; Dietrich and Loretz, "Das Aqhat-Epos," 1287; Gaster, *Thespis: Ritual, Myth, and Drama in the Ancient Near East*, 358; Ginsberg, "The Tale of Aqhat," 153; U. Cassuto, *Bible and Ancient Oriental Texts*, vol. II of *Biblical and Oriental Studies*, trans. Israel Abrahams [Jerusalem: The Magnes Press, 1975], 193–94; Wright, *Ritual in Narrative: The Dynamics of Feasting, Mourning, and Retaliation Rites in the Ugaritic Tale of Aqhat*, 162). Either they take the word *kst* as the subject of the verb *tmzʿ*, or, they postulate unlikely grammatical forms such as a third person masculine singler *tqlt*-form (Cassuto, *Bible and Ancient Oriental Texts*, 194; cf. "internal deponent" in Caquot, Sznycer, and Herdner, *Mythes et légendes: introduction, traduction, commentaire*, 444, footnote d). But, as Wyatt points out, Pūǵatu and Dānî'ilu are not in mourning yet: they have not been informed of 'Aqhatu's death except in the form of Pūǵatu's premonition (Wyatt, *Religious Texts from Ugarit*, 295, footnote 200). Also, to the best of my knowledge, there is no example of grief-expression in which the garment occurs as the subject of the verb "to rend." Furthermore, in this scene Dānî'ilu is described as acting very calmly, not expressing his emotion, whereas Pūǵatu is described as expressing her emotions not only through tears, but through the act of rending the garment. The act for rending her father's garment should be interpreted in terms of its literary role.

[222] Wilfred G. E. Watson, "Puzzling Passages in the Tale of Aqhat," *UF* 8 (1976): 373.

"rent" 'Aqhatu for the goddess 'Anatu, so Pūġatu who rent Dānî'ilu's garment will "rend" the killer of 'Aqhatu on behalf of Dānî'ilu. With respect to the motif of changing in and out of ritual clothes, one may again observe a similar pattern when Pūġatu went out on a journey of revenge: She puts on the outfits of a warrior and over it she puts on a woman's garb. This reverses the procedure that Dānî'ilu went through at the beginning of the story: Dānî'ilu first took off the outercoat, leaving himself half naked clothed only in a loincloth, and then at night went completely naked for the encounter with the deity.[223]

As we have already mentioned, the prayer motif does not figure prominently, if ever, in the incubation type-scene in the 'Aqhatu story. Such non-prominence of prayer is, however, balanced out by its prominent role in the subsequent plot of the story. First, the motif of prayer plays a plot-advancing role in the scene describing Dānî'ilu's pro-action and re-action to the loss of his son 'Aqhatu. Before Dānî'ilu is informed of the death of his son, he prays (*yṣly*) for the rain clouds and dew to remedy the death-like situation caused by the seven-year long drought. Since Dānî'ilu is unaware of his bereavement at this point in the narrative, it is hard to imagine why he would curse the land with drought, as some scholars may suggest. Rather, the reader would know that the barrenness of the land symbolically announces the death of 'Aqhatu and recognize Dānî'ilu's unsuspecting prayer for rain as being proleptic of his positive role in rectifying the deplorable situation. This seems to be corroborated by his subsequent circumambulation through the fields (cf. *palt*, *aklt*). Dānî'ilu does not curse these fields as he would do with the three towns that are located near the scene of the murder. He "spied something green... hugged it... kissed (it and said...)," his plea being that the shoot may increase abundantly to fill the storehouse. Owing to the loss of the fourth tablet of this story, however, we are simply left with no information on specific actions Dānî'ilu's positive role would entail. The motif of prayer is also alluded to in the poet's description of the events that occur after Dānî'ilu has heard the news of 'Aqhatu's death. Dānî'ilu asks Ba'lu to break the pinions of the hawks (*nšrm*) in order that he may recover 'Aqhatu's remains. In this case, although no word of prayer is used, except for

[223] Furthermore, we can assume that Dānî'ilu in distress may not have managed without personal hygiene, such as shaving or applying cosmetics, it is noteworthy that Pūġatu, before she goes on to avenge, washes herself and puts on cosmetics.

the typical speech introduction formula ([*yšu gh*] *wyṣḥ* “he raises his voice and shouts”), the context makes it clear that Dānî’ilu is praying to Ba‘lu who answers him immediately. Ba‘lu’s instant reaction stands in contrast to the seven days that it took Dānî’ilu to get an answer. It is interesting to note that the nature of Dānî’ilu’s prayer, in contrast to his prayer before the news of his bereavement, is more destructive, that is, closer to a curse on those responsible for his son’s death. Although the torn bodies of the first two suspects (*nšrm* and *hrgb*) are restored to wholeness after they are proven innocent, the body of Ṣamlu mother of the hawks, who devoured the body of ’Aqhatu, is not restored. The negative nature of Dānî’ilu’s prayer seems to be corroborated by his subsequent visit to the three towns that are near the scene of murder. Unlike his earlier circumambulation through the fields, Dānî’ilu curses each town with a different curse. Finally, the slight twist on the motif of prayer is found in the scene where Pūǵatu asks her father Dānî’ilu for a blessing (KTU 19 III:28–33).

(28)	⌜w⌝ t‘n . pǵt . ṯk⌜m⌝t . ⌜my⌝m	Pūǵatu, she who bore water on (her) shoulders, responded;
(29)	qr⌜y⌝m . ⌜a⌝b . dbḥ . ⌜l⌝ ilm	My father has offered sacrifice to the gods,
(30)	š⌜‘l⌝y . dǵ⌜ṯh⌝ (?) . ⌜b⌝ š⌜m⌝ym	Has caused his *dǵṯ*-sacrifice to ascend (as smoke) to the heavens,
(31)	dǵṯ . ḫ̮r⌜nmy . ⌜d⌝ kb⌜kbm⌝	The Harnamien *dǵṯ*-sacrifice of the stars.
(32)	l tb⌜rk⌝n . a⌜lk⌝ . ⌜b⌝r⌜kt⌝m(?)	Now bless me so that I may go in state of blessedness,
(33)	tm⌜rn⌝ . ⌜a⌝l⌜k⌝ . nm⌜rt⌝[224]	Pronounce benediction upon me that I may go beautified.

There is some ambiguity as to whom Pūǵatu addresses in her request for blessing in lines 32–33. In lines 29–30, she refers to her father in the third person as if she were addressing her request to a third party, rather than her father. The readers would then easily take the second person in lines 32–33 to be the gods to whom Dānî’ilu offered a sacrifice and *dǵṯ*-incense: they will reward Dānî’ilu’s family again for

[224] For the reading *nmrt*, instead of KTU’s *nmrrt*, see Tropper, *Ugaritische Grammatik*, 540. If Tropper’s reading were correct, the only explicit basis for deriving the verb *mr*, that occurs in parallel with the verb *brk*, from a root √mrr would disappear. Cf. Pardee, “Review,” 271.

their piety just as they did at the beginning of the story. But the verses that immediately follow thwart this expectation, for it is Dānî'ilu who blesses Pūǵatu in response to her request in the verses cited above.[225] Thus one may say that Pūǵatu addresses her "prayer" to Dānî'ilu. The motif of prayer alluded to in this scene would become more explicit, if one considers the structural similarity between Pūǵatu's petition here and Baʿlu's petition in the theophany motif (KTU 1.17 I:20–23). Both petitioners provide the reason why 'Ilu or Dānî'ilu should bless Dānî'ilu or Pūǵatu: Notice that even the enclitic *m* is attached to the first words that begin the respective motivation clauses: *uzrm* in KTU 1.17 I:21 and *qrym* in KTU 1.19 III:29. The language of Pūǵatu's request for blessing is also reminiscent of Baʿlu's petition for blessing: the *brk/mr* parallelism. Furthermore, Dānî'ilu's blessing and 'Ilu's blessing both use the same formula: *npš yḥ/tḥ* PN, *(brlt* PN), *npš/rḥ hw/hy mḥ*. All these permit us to argue that Pūǵatu's request for blessing is a legitimate variation of the prayer motif.

The sacrifice motif ("eating and drinking"), which is very prominent at the beginning of the first column of KTU 1.17, shows up later at the important junctures of the plot, namely, at the visit of the Kôṯarātu leading to conception, at the receiving of a bow from Kôṯaru-wa-Ḫasīsu, in ʿAnatu's desire and request for the bow, at the scene of 'Aqhatu's murder, at the end of the mourning period for 'Aqhatu, and finally at the scene of Pūǵatu's vengeance. As regards the significance of the initial offering in the plot of the whole narrative, Wright says in his book that is devoted to this very topic: "The initial offering is also paradigmatic because it sets up the basic human-divine relationships that underlie the entire story... Establishing the relationships between characters at the beginning of the story through ritual is necessary and significant because the rest of the story will deal with the upheaval of these relations."[226]

---

[225] This shift in person, if Pūǵatu is in fact addressing her father in lines 32–33, is reminiscent of the same problem in KTU 1.17 I 16–19. Since the last two signs may be read as *at* instead of *n*, one may consider the possibility that a similar shift of person has occurred there. If so, Baal is addressing directly Dānî'ilu the incubant in KTU 1.17 I 16–19 with the shift in person from the second person in lines 16–18 to the third person in lines 18–19. For a similar shift of person in biblical poetry see Pope, *Song of Songs: A New Translation with Introduction and Commentary*, 297.

[226] Wright, *Ritual in Narrative: The Dynamics of Feasting, Mourning, and Retaliation Rites in the Ugaritic Tale of Aqhat*, 46.

The theophany motif, particularly, the appearance of Baʿlu as a tutelage, finds its echo in the scene where Dānî'ilu was in deep grief after hearing the news of his son's death. Just as Baʿlu helped Dānî'ilu in the acquisition of a son-heir, Baʿlu helps him, once again, in recovering 'Aqhatu's dead body. Unlike the first time, Baʿlu does not wait until the seventh day, for his theophany is almost instantaneous and needs no permission from the higher authority. Baʿlu's mediatory role in the theophany motif, on the other hand, finds its reverse in ʿAnatu's visit to 'Ilu seeking permission to kill 'Aqhatu. The necessity for ʿAnatu to go all the way to 'Ilu's abode to obtain permission to have him eradicated seems to corroborate the existing hierarchical organization of the divine and human orders. Although, as one soon realizes, ʿAnatu is not really asking for a permission but extorting it out of "old" 'Ilu,[227] it does not change the fact that she has to make the trip to 'Ilu and has to submit the formal request.

4. Conclusion

In this chapter, we have examined, from the perspective of the incubation type-scene, various motifs that occur together in the first two columns of the 'Aqhatu story: sonlessness, offering, ritual clothing, nakedness, sleeping, theophany, divine speech, change of mood, and fulfillment of promise-command. These motifs cannot be a random aggregate. The *inclusio* structure seen in the seven-day formula at the beginning and the end of the unit speaks against it. Rather, they are arranged in a relationship that serves to form and develop the plot. Such plot development is best illustrated by two different moods that define the first and final parts of the scene, which are symbolically encapsulated in the wordplay between *anḫ* "the moaning one" and *anḫn* "I will rest."

Individual motifs verbalize the pre-verbal Gestalt—namely, predicament, intentionality, liminality, and epiphany—that informs the incubation type-scene. The motif of sonlessness, for instance, verbalizes the concept of predicament. The concept of intentionality is actualized in motifs such as offering, ritual clothing, nakedness, etc. Although there is no explicit mention of "temple," "night" or even "dream," the

---

[227] Cf. KTU 1.18 I:11–12: *ašhlk [šbtk dmm] / šb[t dq]nk mmʿm* "I will [make your gray] hair flow [with blood,] your [gray] beard with gore.

concept of liminality can be discerned by legitimate inferences from the text (e.g. the note that Dānî'ilu returns to his home after the successful incubation rite).

The configuration of motifs occurring in our text not only represents the tradition upon which the poet draws, but also reveals the poet's high degree of literary artifice. For instance, the poet registers the preparatory ritual in a seven-day formula which goes way beyond traditional clichés and is creatively adapted for its literary effect in the current text. Also the poet deliberately delays the identification of certain motifs in the text in order to increase suspense for a climactic effect. Furthermore, the fulfillment motif does not simply repeat the divine command in an indicative mood, for the poet inserts the visit of the Kôṯarātu not only to show that the divine command-promise is fulfilled without fail, but also to corroborate the theme of the story as a whole. Further, the visit of the goddesses, which is couched in a seven-day formula, gives a sense of closure to the whole type-scene. Finally, it should be noted that the incubation type-scene also anticipates the future plot of the story by foreshadowing and patterning. The motif of offering, for instance, reoccurs at important junctures in the story. The motif of prayer and weeping, which was expected in the incubation practice, but did not make it into the incubation type-scene, also figures prominently later in the plot. This simply illustrates that even the absence of a particular motif may not be without reason but has a role intended by the poet. All these considerations notwithstanding, I am not arguing that it is the intention of the author to describe the practice of incubation by Dānî'ilu, and much less that we can reconstruct the Ugaritic practice on the basis of this text. Rather, I am suggesting that the best way to explain the concurrence of those various motifs in a relatively clear literary unit is to postulate the use of incubation as a literary device, namely, the incubation type-scene.

CHAPTER FIVE

HOW KIRTA WAS BLESSED WITH A SON?
The Incubation Type-Scene in KTU 1.14 I–1.15 III

1. Previous Studies

A majority of scholars believe that Kirta resorted to the practice of incubation at the prospect of the total destruction of his family.[1] Many of them mention it only in passing without justifying such belief. F. M. Cross, for example, states without further explanation that 'Ilu "instructs Kirta in an incubation to prepare and conduct a campaign

[1] Gregorio del Olmo Lete, *Mitos y leyendas de Canaan: según la tradición de Ugarit*, Fuentes de la ciencia bíblica 1 (Madrid Valencia: Ediciones Cristianidad Institución San Jerónimo, 1981), 44, 248; Frank M. Cross, *Canaanite Myth and Hebrew Epic; Essays in the History of the Religion of Israel* (Cambridge, MA: Harvard University Press, 1973), 40, 153; Jonas C. Greenfield, "Studies in Aramaic Lexicography I," *JAOS* 82 (1962): 296, footnote 62; "Some Glosses on the KRT Epic," *ErIsr* 9 (1969): 62; "Aspects of Aramean Religion," in *Ancient Israelite Religion: Essays in Honor of Frank Moore Cross*, ed. Patrick D. Miller, Paul D. Hanson, and McBride S. Dean (Philadelphia, PA: Fortress Press, 1987), 73; "Keret's Dream: 'Ḏhrt' and 'Hdrt'," *BSOAS* 57 (1994): 87, 90; Robert K. Gnuse, *Dreams and Dream Report in the Writings of Josephus: A Traditio-Historical Analysis* (Leiden: Brill, 1996), 55; E. Theodore Mullen, *The Divine Council in Canaanite and Early Hebrew Literature*, HSM 24 (Chico, Calif.: Scholars Press, 1980), 248; Ann Jeffers, *Magic and Divination in Ancient Palestine and Syria*, SHCANE 8 (Leiden: Brill, 1996), 128, footnote 21; Cyrus H. Gordon, *Ugarit and Minoan Crete: The Bearing of Their Texts on the Origins of Western Culture* (New York: Norton and Company, 1966), 100; John Gray, "Canaanite Kingship in Theory and Practice," *VT* 2 (1952): 205; Ivan Engnell, *Studies in Divine Kingship in the Ancient Near East* (Oxford: Basil Blackwell, 1967), 152; Margaret G. Robinson, "Dreams in the Old Testament" (Ph.D. diss., Manchester University, 1987), 123; Susan Ackerman, "The Deception of Isaac, Jacob's Dream at Bethel, and Incubation on an Animal Skin," in *Priesthood and Cult in Ancient Israel*, ed. Gary A. Anderson (Sheffield: JOST Press, 1991), 110; Julian Obermann, *How Daniel Was Blessed with a Son*, Suppl. to JAOS 6 (Baltimore, MD: American Oriental Society, 1946), 10, footnote 13; Ernst L. Ehrlich, *Der Traum im Alten Testament*, BZAW 73 (Berlin: Töpelmann, 1953), 42; Michael D. Coogan, ed. and trans., *Stories from Ancient Canaan* (Philadelphia, PA: Westminster Press, 1978), 52; Isaac Mendelsohn, "Dream," in *The Interpreter's Dictionary of the Bible*, vol. 1, ed. George A. Buttrick (Nashville, TN: Abingdon Press, 1961), 868; A. van Selms, *Marriage & Family Life in Ugaritic Literature* (London: Luzac & Company, 1954), 15; Edward L. Greenstein, "Kirta," in *Ugaritic Narrative Poetry*, ed. Simon B. Parker (Atlanta, GA: Scholars Press, 1997), 10.

of "holy war" in order to secure a bride."[2] In his discussion about how Ugaritic men chose a wife, A. van Selms obliquely refers to Kirta as the one who sought an incubation oracle in order to get married.[3] Scholars like Gordon, Ehrlich, Coogan, and Mendelsohn have also made similar points without going into much detail.[4] Some scholars, however, provide justification for their interpretation of the initial scene of the Kirta story as an incubation scene, thus revealing the presupposition behind their reasoning.

The presupposition, shared by those who recognize incubation at the initial scene of *Kirta* and by those who do not, is that the practice of incubation should be characterized by at least two out of three major elements, namely, intentionality, locality, and epiphany.[5] Since there is no doubt whatsoever as to the presence of oneiric theophany in the initial scene of *Kirta*,[6] philological efforts have been poured onto establishing whether there is intentionality on Kirta's part to invoke divine revelation and whether the location of Kirta's theophanic experience deserves the rubric "a holy place." To be more specific, scholars have debated whether or not Kirta's weeping qualifies as a preparatory ritual that is intended to invoke a theophany, whether or not the term *qmṣ* denotes a special position of an incubant or not, whether or not the room (*ḥdr*) which Kirta enters in tears has any cultic connotation. All these questions are oriented toward establishing or tearing down the three "columns" of an incubation rite defined by historians of religion like Patton.[7]

Those scholars who recognize the practice of incubation in the initial scene of *Kirta* have attempted to answer positively at least some, if not all, of those philological questions in order to make their case. Ann

---

[2] Cross, *Canaanite Myth and Hebrew Epic; Essays in the History of the Religion of Israel*, 40.

[3] van Selms, *Marriage & Family Life in Ugaritic Literature*, 15.

[4] See footnote 1 for bibliography.

[5] For the history of religions definition of incubation see Kimberley C. Patton, "A Great and Strange Correction: Intentionality, Locality, and Epiphany in the Category of Dream Incubation," *HR* 43 (2004): 194–223.

[6] One philological question that may relate to oneiric theophany is whether or not the term *hdrt* connotes a revelatory dream. For this, see Josef Tropper, "Ugaritic Dreams: Notes on Ugaritic D̲(h)Rt and Hdrt," in *Ugarit, Religion and Culture: Essays Presented in Honour of Professor John C. L. Gibson*, ed. Nick Wyatt, Wilfred G. E. Watson, and Jeffery B. Lloyd, Ugaritisch-biblische Literatur 12 (Münster: Ugarit-Verlag, 1996), 305–13; Greenfield, "Keret's Dream: 'D̲hrt' and 'Hdrt'," 87–92.

[7] Patton, "A Great and Strange Correction: Intentionality, Locality, and Epiphany in the Category of Dream Incubation," 194–223.

Jeffers, for instance, argues that the tears shed by Kirta recall ritual weeping in times of crisis of the community and may have been meant to induce an oneiric theophany.[8] But she does not admit that 'Ilu's oneiric theophany took place in a sanctuary, adding immediately "I do not think that incubation has to be taken so strictly that the dream must necessarily take place at a sanctuary."[9] J. Obermann, however, finds cultic significance in the room where Kirta lay down to sleep, in the bed and couch on which Kirta's tears fell, but he is ambivalent about the cultic nature of Kirta's weeping by saying, "...incubations...without specification of the ritual details involved are not infrequent."[10] E. Mullen, on the other hand, by answering positively almost all of the philological questions that relate to the issue of incubation, finds all the major elements of the practice of incubation at the initial scene of the Kirta story.[11] Besides the obvious one such as the 'Ilu's oneiric revelation, Mullen discerns a cultic significance in the Ugaritic word *ḥdr* by associating it with a royal sanctuary. He also sees an element of intentionality in Kirta's tearful retreat to his room by arguing that Kirta's tearful prayers (cf. *bṯn* [*r*]*gmm ydmʿ* in KTU 1.14 I:27) "constituted the liturgical part of the ritual."[12] He goes further and speculates that "although not recorded, it [incubation] included offerings to the gods."[13] It is arguable that, while Jeffers and Obermann operate on a flexible definition of incubation in explaining the initial scene of *Kirta* as incubational, Mullen seems to have forced the text into his rigid definition of incubation to achieve the same goal as Jeffers and Obermann. Finally, the contribution of Greenfield to the discussion of incubation in the Kirta text must not go without mention. He was the first to propose the term *qmṣ* as a referent to a recumbent position that an incubant took in order to induce a dream.[14] Moreover, Greenfield's proposal of the term *hdrt* as a cognate of Hebrew and Aramaic *hdr* "glory, majesty" and as a functional equivalent of

[8] Jeffers, *Magic and Divination in Ancient Palestine and Syria*, 135.
[9] Ibid.
[10] Obermann, *How Daniel Was Blessed with a Son*, 10, footnote 13.
[11] The possible exception is *qmṣ* of which the meaning is debated. He does not discuss this word. Cf. Mullen, *The Divine Council in Canaanite and Early Hebrew Literature*, 248–53.
[12] Ibid., 249.
[13] Ibid., 248.
[14] Greenfield, "Some Glosses on the KRT Epic," 60–65.

Akkadian *melammu* "royal radiance"[15] leads him to argue that Kirta's dream was not only *ḥlm* "a dream," but also *hdrt* "a theophanic majesty," namely, that Kirta's dream was not "a fantasy or a phantasma, but a divine behest upon which he was to act immediately."[16] Thus, in Greenfield's opinion, Kirta does not enter his inner chambers (*ḥdr*) just to be able to cry in private but rather to invoke the gods through incubation.[17]

A handful of scholars remain either skeptical[18] or dubious about the opinion of the majority of scholars.[19] But even those who do not see any allusion to the incubation rite in the initial scene of the Kirta story assume the same presupposition about incubation as their opponents in the debate. But though they agree in coming down on the other side of the debate, they differ on some philological and hermeneutical issues mentioned above. Bergman, for example, remains dubious about the "incubation" interpretation of the initial scene of the Kirta story, because he finds an element of a holy place lacking in the scene; He says, "*Ḥdr* probably does not refer to a room in a temple."[20] Husser follows a similar line of reasoning when he says that the room where Kirta fell asleep is "la chambre privée du roi," and not a sanctuary for incubation.[21] He goes further and denies any cultic connotation to Kirta's weeping.[22] He says that it is difficult to "considérer les pleurs de Keret comme un rite préparatoire à l'incubation."[23] Although admitting the possibility of the term *qmṣ* being a special posture of an incubant, Husser argues that "mais s'il [yqmṣ] s'agit d'un terme technique de l'incubation, on s'étonne alors de ne pas le retrouver à propos de

---

[15] Greenfield, "Keret's Dream: 'Ḏhrt' and 'Hdrt'," 87–92.
[16] Ibid., 92.
[17] Greenfield, "Some Glosses on the KRT Epic," 62.
[18] Manfried Dietrich and Oswald Loretz, "Das Keret-Epos," in *Weisheitstexte, Mythen und Epen*, vol. 3 of *TUAT*, ed. Otto Kaiser (Gütersloh: Gütersloher Verlagshaus, 1990), 1218, footnote 33.
[19] Cf. J. Bergman, M. Ottosson, and J. Botterweck, "Chālam," in *TDOT*, ed. J. Botterweck and H. Ringgren (Grand Rapids, MI: Eerdmans, 1977), 426; Choon Leong Seow, "The Syro-Palestinian Context of Solomon's Dream," *HTR* 77 (1984): 141–52; Jean-Marie Husser, *Le songe et la parole: Etude sur le rêve et sa fonction dans l'ancien Israël*, BZAW 210 (Berlin: W. de Gruyter, 1994), 48–51; André Caquot, "Les songes et leur interpretation selon Canaan et Israel," *SO* 2 (1959): 104–6.
[20] Bergman, Ottosson, and Botterweck, "Chālam," 426.
[21] Husser, *Le songe et la parole: Etude sur le rêve et sa fonction dans l'ancien Israël*, 49.
[22] Ibid.
[23] Ibid.

Danil dont le texte abonde pourtant en expressions de ce genre."[24] All this goes to show that even those who refuse to accept the initial scene as incubational do so because of the presupposition that they share with their opponents in the debate about the nature of incubation, often influenced by the Hellenistic definition of incubation.[25]

A quick survey of previous studies points again to the problem of definition. For some scholars, a temple is an essential element without which incubation does not occur, whereas for others incubation does not have to take place in a temple. For some scholars, preparatory ritual is essential to the idea of incubation, but for others an incubational dream may come about without specific rituals (cf. Oppenheim's "unintentional incubation").[26] The above survey also reveals the failure to distinguish the practice of incubation and its literary rendition. In general, scholars seem to have failed to understand that the poet does not have to describe the practice of incubation in order to employ it as a literary device. The literary rendition of incubation is, however, already at some remove from its original circumstances. The incubation type-scene used in the initial scene of the Kirta story is a case in point. In the following paragraphs, the first episode of the Kirta story (KTU 1.14 I–1.15 III) will be analyzed in light of an incubation type-scene in order to show how the religious practice of incubation was employed as a literary device in narrative poetry.

---

[24] Ibid., 50.

[25] Often the Hellenistic definition of incubation has influenced scholarly opinion on this issue. Seow, for instance, says with reference to Kirta's initial dream, "However, I do not think that this qualifies as an "incubation" in the classical sense of the term" (Seow, "The Syro-Palestinian Context of Solomon's Dream," 24). Caquot also seems to subscribe to the Hellenistic definition of an incubation when he argues that "...aussi me paraît-il préférable d'éviter le terme technique d'incubation évoquant les pratiques bien connues des temples helléniques d'Asclépios et d'autres héros" (Caquot, "Les songes et leur interpretation selon Canaan et Israel," 105). It is interesting to note that Caquot, who takes the same position as Jeffers on the two issues, namely, whether or not Kirta's weeping provoked divine intervention and whether or not the room Kirta lay down in was a sanctuary, has come to a different conclusion about the nature of the first scene of the Kirta story. This difference in conclusion results from different definitions of an incubation rite subscribed to respectively by Jeffers and Caquot. Unlike Jeffers, Caquot appears to subscribe to the Hellenistic definition of incubation.

[26] A. Leo Oppenheim, *The Interpretation of Dreams in the Ancient Near East: With a Translation of an Assyrian Dream-Book*, TAPA 46 (Philadelphia, PA: American Philological Society, 1956), 187.

2. The Incubation Type-Scene in KTU 1.14 I–1.15 III: Component Motifs

I contend that the first episode of the Kirta story (KTU 1.14 I–1.15 III) is wholly informed by the incubation type-scene. To put it differently, the incubation type-scene in *Kirta* stands alone as a narrative complete in itself. This distinguishes it from biblical birth stories of heroes that often lack a clear movement of plot and that serve only as an introduction to the heroes' life. The plot of the first episode of *Kirta*, however, clearly shows a movement from problem to solution. It begins, for example, with a rather long description of the total destruction of Kirta's family (KTU 1.14 I:6–25) and ends on the short note of its full restoration (KTU 1.15 III:20–25). The first episode of *Kirta*, like many other reports of the practice of incubation, has a tripartite structure ("Before Epiphany," "Epiphany" and "After Epiphany") with 'Ilu's oneiric encounter with Kirta at the center as a turning point of Kirta's fortune. This divine-human encounter not only constitutes a pivotal point in the flow of the storyline but also provides a structural backbone to the first episode, most of which is occupied by 'Ilu's oneiric instruction and Kirta's faithful observance.[27] More importantly, the plot of the first episode of *Kirta* advances through a succession of various motifs that combine to form a family resemblance to many other instances of the incubation type-scene. As will be discussed below, however, the poet arranges traditional motifs rather freely to fit his narrative purpose instead of depicting the normal procedure of the practice in reality. Such adaptations, in turn, work toward underscoring the moral or the message of the Kirta story.

[27] Scholars find the amount of space devoted to the oneiric message and its fulfillment in the Kirta story to be a bit unusual. Cf. Murray Lichtenstein, "A Note on the Text of I Keret," *JANESCU* 2 (1969): 92; Simon B. Parker, *The Pre-Biblical Narrative Tradition: Essays on the Ugaritic Poems Keret and Aqhat*, SBLRBS 24 (Atlanta, GA: Scholars Press, 1989), 158.

2.1 *Before Epiphany*

2.1.1 *The Motif of a Complete Destruction of a Family and the Motif of Wifelessness*

KTU 1.14 I:7–25[28]

A

(7)	bt (8) [m]lk . itbd!	The house of the king perished,
	d šbʿ (9) [a]ḫm . lh .	Who had seven brothers,
	ṯmnt . bn um	Eight sons of a mother.[29]
(10)	krt . ḥtkn . rš	Kirta, as to (his) family, was ruined,
(11)	krt . grdš . mknt	Kirta was destroyed as to (his) dwelling.

B

(12)	aṯt . ṣdqh . l ypq	His rightful woman he did not acquire,
(13)	mtrḫt . yšrh	(Nor did he) his legitimate wife.
(14)	aṯt . trḫ . w tbʿt	He married a woman but she left,
(15)	ṯ⌈a⌉r[30] um . tkn lh	A relative of a mother who became his.[31]
(16)	mṯlṯt . kṯrm . tmt	A third wife died in health,
(17)	mrbʿt . zblnm	A fourth (died) in illness.
(18)	mḫmšt . yitsp (19) rš⌈p⌉ [.]	A fifth Rašap gathered to himself,
	mṯdṯt . ǵlm (20) ym .	A sixth the lad(s) of Yammu,
	mšbʿthn . b šlḥ (21) ttpl .	The seventh of them fell by the sword.

---

[28] The transliteration and translation are mine, based on the handcopy prepared for by Beudreuil and Pardee (cf. Pierre Bordreuil and Dennis Pardee, *Grammaire: Fac-Similés*, vol. 1 of *Manuel d'ougaritique* [Paris: Geuthner, 2004], Fac-similés 03 RS2[003]+).

[29] I agree with many others who take *bn um* as a parallel to *aḫm* to refer to Kirta's brothers (cf. Dennis Pardee, "The Kirta Epic," in *Canonical Compositions from the Biblical World*, vol. I of *COS*, ed. William W. Hallo and K. Lawson Younger Jr. [Leiden: Brill, 1997], 333; J. C. de Moor and K. Spronk, "Problematical Passages in the Legend of Kirtu [I]," *UF* 14 [1982]: 154). Hebrew *bn(y)-'m* often occurs in parallelism with Hebrew *'ḥ* (Genesis 27:29; 43:29; Deuteronomy 13:7; Judges 8:19; Psalm 50:20; 69:9). But there are some scholars who take *bn um* as a designation of Kirta's children. Cf. Nick Wyatt, *Religious Texts from Ugarit*, BS 53 (London: Sheffield Academic Press, 2002), 180, footnote 9.

[30] For the epigraphical problem of this word, see Josef Tropper, "Die sieben Frauen des Königs Keret," *UF* 27 (1995): 530–31.

[31] A number of scholars who take the following numerals as designations of Kirta's children take line 15 as the beginning of a new poetic unit and translate *tar um* as something along the line of "offspring of one mother." Cf. John Gray, *The Legacy of Canaan: The Ras Shamra Texts and Their Relevance to the Old Testament* (Leiden: Brill, 1965), 7, 27; Nick Wyatt, *Religious Texts from Ugarit*, 181.

A′

	y‘n . ḥtkh . (22) krt [.]	Kirta saw his family,
	y‘n . ḥtkh rš	He saw his family ruined,
(23)	mid . grdš . ṯbth	His dwelling entirely destroyed.
(24)	w b klhn . špḥ . yitbd	In its totality the family perished,
(25)	w b . pḫyrh[32] . yrṯ	In its entirety the heirs.

The motif that verbalizes the pre-verbal *Gestalt* of predicament in the incubation type-scene of *Kirta* concerns a total destruction of a family. This motif is epitomized in lines 24–25, where the totality of the disaster that had befallen Kirta is articulated by two prepositional phrases *bklhn* and *bpḫyrh*, while the idea of destruction is summed up in the verb *yitbd*,[33] which forms an *inclusio* with the verb of the same root, *’itbd!*,[34] earlier in line 7, giving a sense of closure to the motif as a whole. Although Kirta's predicament involves the whole house of Kirta, the focus of the poet's description, however, seems to be centered on the loss of wives, which is centrally located in the *inclusio* structure (A-B-A′). This focus on Kirta's wives is visualized in the text not only by the number of poetic lines devoted to the subject but also by the numeric sequence formula that informs the motif of "wifelessness." The focal attention drawn to this motif of "wifelessness" in the section describing Kirta's predicament is not without a purpose; the poet may have intended it as a portent of the future plot of the narrative, namely, Kirta's quest to obtain the hand of Ḥurray.

[32] Tropper, along with many others, take *y* of *pḫyr* as a *mater lectionis* (Joseph Tropper, *Ugaritische Grammatik*, AOAT 273 [Münster: Ugarit-Verlag, 2000], 53). Other suggestions include an "internal plural" (L. Badre, et al., "Notes ougaritiques," *Syria* 53 [1976]: 103) and a diminutive *quttayil* pattern (Eddy Verreet, "Der Keret-Prolog," *UF* 19 [1987]: 333).

[33] Tropper explains the semantic of *yitbd* as having "besteigerter Bedeutung." He proposes to translate the G-stem of the root √’bd as "zugrunde gehen" and yet its Gt-stem as "vollkommen zugrunde gehen." But the added nuance "vollkommen" is better taken to come from the prepositional phrase that qualifies *yitbd* in lines 24. Furthermore, the use of the Gt-stem of the root √’bd in line 7 seems to invalidate Tropper's suggestion. Cf. Joseph Tropper, *Ugaritische Grammatik*, 519. The reason for the poet choosing the Gt-stem of the root remains elusive to the present writer.

[34] Note a similar metathesis at the beginning of the ’Aqhatu story (*yln*! in KTU 1.17 I:5) and also note that both the words in metathesis happen to be a *leitmotif*, or a key word, in respective sections: *itbd*! ("He perished") in the section describing the destruction of Kirta's family and *yln*! ("He lay down") in the section describing ’Aqhatu's practice of incubation. Moreover in both cases, the fact of metathesis is made obvious to the reader by later repetitions of the words.

The motif describing Kirta's predicament is couched in the *inclusio* structure in which the motif of wifelessness (B [lines 12–21a]) is enveloped by two symmetric rings (A [lines 7b–11] and A′ [21b–25]) depicting the total destruction of Kirta's family. These symmetric rings are informed by three *leitwörter*[35] relating to the idea of destruction (√'bd, √ršš, √gdrš) and by various words denoting Kirta's "house" or "family" (cf. *umt*, *bt*, *ḥtk*, *yrṯ*, *špḥ*, *mknt*, *ṯbt* and *yrṯ*).[36] The verbs connoting destruction in particular form a chiasmus (['bd]-[rš//grdš]-[rš//grdš]-['bd]). Also interesting to note is that the mood governing the motif of the destruction of Kirta's family becomes intensified in the latter end of the *inclusio* structure. This is indicated by the prosodic change between two poetic verses of identical content from a simple bicolon verse earlier in lines 7–10 to a staircase verse later in lines 21b–23.[37] Also the additon of the verb of perception (*y'n* "he saw") in the latter lines (21b–23) seems to intimate the intensification of mood in the latter end of *inclusio*. The verb *y'n* "he saw" seems to effectively communicate the psychological impact of the misfortune on Kirta by personalizing the event as witnessed with Kirta's own eyes. This escalation of mood is matched by the variation that the poet creates in the text by using a variety of terms all denoting, rather generally, Kirta's house-family.[38] The use of a whole gamut of vocabulary—*umt*, *bt*, *ḥtk*,

[35] For the definition of *leitwort*, see Robert Alter, *The Art of Biblical Narrative* (New York: Basic Books, 1981), 93 and Tremper Longman III, *Literary Approaches to Biblical Interpretation*, Foundations of Contemporary Interpretation 3 (Grand Rapids, MI: Academie Books, 1987), 96.

[36] Those scholars who understand the numerals in lines 16–21 as designations of Kirta's children prefer to render *ḥtk* and *špḥ* and *yrṯ* in such a way that they refer specifically to Kirta's lost children. But note that *ḥtk* forms a parallelism with *mknt* and *ṯbt* in lines 10–11 and 21–23. Thus, it is better rendered generally as "family" than specifically "offspring." Furthermore, the *inclusio* structure of the motif of Kirta's predicament strongly suggests that *špḥ* and *yrṯ* in lines 24–25 should be understood along the same line as *umt* and *bt* in lines 6 and 7, namely, as the abstract notion referring to Kirta's family. The word *špḥ* occurs three more times later in the story all in the sense of "offspring" denoting Ḥurray in KTU 1.14 III:40, Kirta's offspring in 1.14 III:48 and Kirta himself in 1.16 I:10. This intimates that *špḥ* may have a *double entendre* whose deeper meaning foreshadows the conclusion of the incubation type-scene, the birth of Kirta's offspring through Ḥurray. The theme of the loss of Kirta's brothers in lines 8–10, on the contrary, seems to go nowhere in the story.

[37] This is reminiscent of the first scene of the 'Aqhatu story where two bicolon verses introducing a seven-day sequence describing Dānî'ilu's sacrifice is expanded into two tricolon verses in the seven-day sequence (cf. KTU 1.17 I:2–15).

[38] With the exception of the word *ḥtk* (cf. lines 10 and 20–21), the poet introduces new words in the other end of the *inclusio* structure that denotes Kirta's house-family: the words *umt* and *bt* in lines 6–7 change to *špḥ* and *yrṯ* in the corresponding lines in

yrṯ, *špḥ*, *mknt*, *ṯbt* and *yrṯ*—that may be subsumed under the rubric "house-family" remotely reflects the extent of the destruction that has befallen Kirta's house-family. Furthermore, the two prepositional phrases (*bklhn* and *bpḫyrh*) in lines 24–25 leave no doubt in the mind of the readers about the extent of the disaster that has befallen Kirta's family: it is total and complete.[39]

The motif of the total destruction of Kirta's family narrows its focus on the loss of child-bearing wives in the middle portion of the *inclusio* structure (lines 12–21). The theme of "wifelessness" is couched in a numeric sequence formula that culminates in the falling by the sword of Kirta's seventh wife (*mšbʿthn*). This interpretation of the numerals in lines 16–21a stands opposed to that of a number of scholars who see designations of Kirta's children in those numerals.[40] But any interpretation taking the numerals as designations of Kirta's children is complicated by the circumstance that the sequence of numerals does not start with "one" and "two," but with the numeral relating to three (*mṯlṯt*).[41] Although many ingenious proposals have been made to solve

the latter end of *inclusio* (lines 24–25), while the word *mknt* in line 11 is replaced by *ṯbt* in line 23 of the same content.

[39] This motif of destruction of a family is reminiscent of two biblical episodes: one in Job and the other in Ruth. For an insightful comparative study, see Parker, *The Pre-Biblical Narrative Tradition: Essays on the Ugaritic Poems Keret and Aqhat*, 146–71.

[40] David T. Tsumura, "The Problem of Childlessness in the Royal Epic of Ugarit: An Analysis of KRT[KTU 1.14I]:1–25," in *Monarchies and Socio-Religious Traditions in the Ancient Near East*, ed. Prince T. Mikasa, Bulletin of the Middle Eastern Culture Center in Japan 1 (Wiesbaden: Otto Harrassowitz, 1984), 11–20; Greenstein, "Kirta," 42, note 3; Verreet, "Der Keret-Prolog," 328–29; Manfried Dietrich and Oswald Loretz, "Der Prolog des KRT-Epos (CTA 14 I 1–35)," in *Wort und Geschichte: Festschrift für Karl Elliger zum 70. Geburtstag*, H. Gese and Rüger H., Alter Orient und Altes Testament (Neukirchen-Vluyn: Verlag Butzon & Bercker Kevelaer, 1973), 32; Nick Wyatt, *Religious Texts from Ugarit*, 181, footnote 19; Joshua Finkel, "A Mathematical Conundrum in the Ugaritic Keret Poem," *HUCA* 26 (1955): 109–49; Jack M. Sasson, "The Numeric Progression in Keret I: 15–20: Yet Another Suggestion," *SEL* 5 (1988): 181–88; André Caquot, Maurice Sznycer, and Andrée. Herdner, *Mythes et légendes: introduction, traduction, commentaire*, vol. 1 of *Textes ougaritiques*, Littératures anciennes du Proche-Orient 7 (Paris: Éditions du Cerf, 1974), 505, footnote k; Harold L. Ginsberg, *The Legend of King Keret: A Canaanite Epic of the Bronze Age* (New Haven, CT: American Schools of Oriental Research, 1946), 33; Anton Jirku, *Kanaanäische Mythen und Epen aus Ras Schamra-Ugarit* (Gütersloh: Gerd Mohn, 1962), 85; Coogan, *Stories from Ancient Canaan*, 58; Olmo Lete, *Mitos y leyendas de Canaan: según la tradición de Ugarit*, 290; F. C. Fensham, "Remarks on Certain Difficult Passages in Keret," *JNSL* 1 (1971): 19; John Gray, *The Krt Text in the Literature of Ras Shamra: A Social Myth of Ancient Canaan*, DMOA 5 (Leiden: Brill, 1955), 27.

[41] J. C. de Moor, "Contributions to the Ugaritic Lexicon," *UF* 11 (1979): 643.

this puzzle, none has succeeded in garnering scholarly consensus.[42] Probably no satisfactory solution is likely to result because the numbers in a numeric sequence formula were never intended to be read literally. Put differently, the numerals are never intended to give the exact number of Kirta's children, or to add up to the whole number one.[43] Although the understanding of the numerals as designations of Kirta's children may be appealing to some in the sense that it would make the text in question look more similar to the first chapter of Job with the loss of children clearly mentioned in the text, the lack of the satisfactory explanation about the numerals tips the scale in favor of the "wives" interpretation.[44] Besides, the fact that the numerals from *mṯlṯt* to *mšbʿt* are formed in imitation of Kirta's first wife *mtrḫt* in line 13[45] strongly suggests the "wife" interpretation of the numerals. If lines 14–15 can be taken to concern Kirta's second wife, we have a "seven-wife" sequence in the middle portion of the *inclusio* structure. The unconventional structure of this numeric sequence may be explained in part by the fact that numeric formulae in the Kirta story have tendency to deviate from traditional forms.[46] After all, the sense of

[42] For instance, the explanation as a multiplicative would make the number of Kirta's sons widly out of proportion, while the "fraction" understanding of numeric progression does not add up to the whole number one. Although some argue that the total 153/140 (=1.09) is good enough for a poet (cf. Tsumura, "The Problem of Childlessness in the Royal Epic of Ugarit: An Analysis of KRT[KTU 1.14I]:1–25," 15; Ginsberg, *The Legend of King Keret: A Canaanite Epic of the Bronze Age*, 33; Finkel, "A Mathematical Conundrum in the Ugaritic Keret Poem," 3), Sasson correctly argues that "its poet would not be so sloppy as to merely approximate a whole digit" (Sasson, "The Numeric Progression in Keret I: 15–20: Yet Another Suggestion," 182).

[43] Dietrich and Loretz, "Das Keret-Epos," 1217, footnote 24.

[44] The "wife" interpretation seems to have been first suggested by Cassuto (U. Cassuto, "Seven Wives of King Keret," *BASOR* 119 [1950]: 18–21. Reprinted in *Bible and Ancient Oriental Texts*, vol. II of *Biblical and Oriental Studies*, trans. Israel Abrahams [Jerusalem: The Magnes Press, 1975]). Cf. Pardee, "The Kirta Epic," 333, footnote 8; Josef Tropper, "Die sieben Frauen des Königs Keret," 531; Baruch Margalit, "Studia Ugaritica II: Studies in *Krt* and *Aqht*," *UF* 8 (1976): 144; J. C. de Moor, *An Anthology of Religious Texts from Ugarit*, Nisaba 16 (Leiden: Brill, 1987), 192; "Contributions to the Ugaritic Lexicon," 643–44; Moor and Spronk, "Problematical Passages in the Legend of Kirtu (I)," 156; Joseph Aistleitner, *Die mythologischen und kultischen Texte aus Ras Schamra*, BOH 8 (Budapest: Akadémiai Kiadó, 1959), 87.

[45] Pardee, "The Kirta Epic," 333.

[46] In addition to the lack of the numeral referring to the "second wife," the numeric formula in question assigns an entire poetic verse to the first wife and to the second wife. This is contrary to the tradition concerning the numeric sequence of seven that organizes the first six into three pairs with the seventh one as a stand-alone climax. This idiosyncrasy relating to the numeric sequence under discussion is comparable to other idiosyncratic seven-day sequence formulae that occur later in the Kirta story.

awkwardness coming from the lack of the numeral "the second wife" in lines 14–15 is much easier to bear than the sense of puzzlement coming from the so-called mathematical conundrum.[47]

The motif of wifelessness which is informed by this rather unconventional form of numeral sequence seems to register all conceivable circumstances in which one could fail to produce offspring. First, one cannot have an heir without a legitimate wife. Kirta does not acquire his lawful and legitimate wife (cf. lines 12–13). Second, one will be left heirless if the wife whom he marries deserts him for whatever reason without bearing a child. Likewise, the second best woman whom Kirta marries (cf. *ṯar um*)[48] deserts him apparently without leaving a child.[49] Finally, one cannot have offspring if his wife dies prematurely. This scenario is dealt with rather thoroughly over the space of three poetic verses (lines 16–21a), although interpretative difficulty prohibits us from arriving at definitive answers as to how each of Kirta's wives dies.[50]

For the detailed study of the seven day formulae in Ugaritic epics see Samuel E. Loewenstamm, "The Seven-Day-Unit in Ugaritic Epic Literature," *IEJ* 15 (1965): 121–33, reprinted in Samuel E. Loewenstamm, *Comparative Studies in Biblical and Ancient Oriental Literatures* (Neukirchen-Vluyn: Neukirchener Verlag, 1980), 192–209.

[47] Finkel, "A Mathematical Conundrum in the Ugaritic Keret Poem," 109–49.

[48] Pardee explains *ṯar um* as Kirta's first cousin on his mother's side, who is less desirable than the first cousin on the father's side, the first projected bride (*aṯt ṣdqh // mtrḫt yrṯ*). Cf. Pardee, "The Kirta Epic," 333, footnote 7. For other interpretation of this phrase, see footnote 29 above.

[49] A number of scholars take the verb *tbʿt* as a euphemism for the premature death of Kirta's wife (cf. Dietrich and Loretz, "Das Keret-Epos," 1217, footnote 22; Caquot, Sznycer, and Herdner, *Mythes et légendes: introduction, traduction, commentaire*, 505, footnote i; Gray, *The Krt Text in the Literature of Ras Shamra: A Social Myth of Ancient Canaan*, 27; Ginsberg, *The Legend of King Keret: A Canaanite Epic of the Bronze Age*, 33; J. C. L. Gibson, ed., *Canaanite Myths and Legends.* [Edinburgh: T. & T. Clark, 1978], 83, footnote 4; Verreet, "Der Keret-Prolog," 323; Badre, et al., "Notes ougaritiques," 99). But it is not necessarily so, especially considering that the immediately following verses delve into the death of Kirta's wives. The following scholars understand the word *tbʿt* as a reference to a simple desertion, not a figurative "departure.": Cassuto, *Bible and Ancient Oriental Texts*, 207; Nick Wyatt, *Religious Texts from Ugarit*, 181; Moor and Spronk, "Problematical Passages in the Legend of Kirtu (I)," 155–56. One may go further and argue that the reason for the second wife's desertion is her infertility, although the desertion by marital unfaithfulness cannot be excluded (cf. Levite's wife in Judges 19). Barrenness was one of the seven reasons that a wife should leave her husband voluntarily or forcibly in ancient China.

[50] Lines 16–21a seem to describe various manners in which a woman in ancient times could have died prematurely without leaving behind any offspring. Cf. Parker, *The Pre-Biblical Narrative Tradition: Essays on the Ugaritic Poems Keret and Aqhat*, 146.

Finally three observations on the narratological role of the motif verbalizing Kirta's predicament are in order. First, the focus on the problem of acquiring a wife at the beginning of the Kirta's story not only provides a better literary connection with a later plot of Kirta's journey in quest of a new wife, but also makes the Kirta story *sui generis* in the ancient Near Eastern literature. According to Kugel, the theme of childless parents visited by a deity to bestow fertility is authentically Israelite, if not ancient Near Eastern, but the theme of a man in quest of a beauty belongs to Greek tradition.[51] If Kugel's observation is correct, the first episode of the Kirta story constitutes an interesting mixture of different traditions: it shows the theme of loss and restoration of Kirta's family-offsrping (cf. *ḥtk*) through divine visitation, while its plot revolves around the acquisition of a wife. Second, the motif of the complete destruction of a family anticipates a complete restoration of a family at the conclusion of the story. The idea of completeness is symbolically carried by the number seven/eight in both motifs. Since Kirta had lost seven/eight brothers and seven wives, he is given seven/eight sons and seven/eight daughters (KTU 1.15 II:23–25). The idea of completeness in the motif of destruction of Kirta's family may also be echoed in the command-action sequence that serves as a backbone the narrative. Not only should *everyone* in Kirta's city participate in his campaign but Kirta is expected to follow 'Ilu's detailed instructions *to the letter*. Third, the ambiguous role of the gods in the Kirta story may have been prefigured in the motif of wifelessness that describes how Kirta's wives die one after another in a numeric sequence. In the story as a whole, Kirta is described as having a special relationship with 'Ilu, but his relationship with other gods including 'Aṯiratu is ambiguous:[52] for example, at Kirta's wedding banquet the gods—variously called *'dt ilm* in KTU 1.15 II:11, *ilm* in 1.15 III:17–18, and *dr 'il* in 1.15 III:19—appear as beneficent ones who pronounce blessing on Kirta (KTU 1.15 III:17–19), but in the divine assembly convened by 'Ilu through 'Ilšu and his wife, they seem unwilling, if not unable, to heal Kirta.[53] This

[51] James L. Kugel, *How to Read the Bible: A Guide to Scripture, Then and Now* (New York: Free Press, 2007), 400–401.

[52] Baʿlu is an exception. Although he maintains a low profile, he is different from the other gods in the pantheon in that he along with 'Ilu maintains a positive relationship with Kirta throughout the story.

[53] Klaas Spronk, "The Legend of Kirtu (KTU 1.14–16): A Study of the Structure and Its Consequences for Interpretation," in *The Structural Analysis of Biblical and Canaanite Poetry*, Willem van der Meer and Johannes C. de Moor (Sheffield: Sheffield

ambiguity may be remotely prefigured in the numeric sequence formula that describes the progressive and complete loss of Kirta's wives. There the deaths of Kirta's five wives are associated with words such as *kṯr, zbl, ršp, ǵlm ym* and *šlḥ* respectively. Although it is not necessary to discern references to divine names or epithets in all those words, the fact that they may be read as divine names or epithets, not to mention that *kṯr*, *zbl*, and *ršp* occur in the broken text that enumerates divine participants in Kirta's wedding banquet (KTU 1.15 III:3–7), indicates that the way the poet describes the deaths of Kirta's five wives may be intended as a subtle foreshadowing of the ambiguous, if not hostile, nature of relationship between Kirta and certain of the gods, which will be developed more explicitly later in the narrative.

2.1.2 *The Motif of Weeping*

KTU 1.14 I:26–30

(26)	yʿrb . b ḥdrh . ybky	He enters his room, he weeps,
(27)	b ṯn⸢h⸣[54] gmm . wydmʿ	Repeating his groans, he sheds tears.
(28)	tntkn . udmʿth	His tears gush forth,
(29)	km . ṯqlm . arṣh	Like one-shekel weights to the ground,
(30)	k mḫmšt . mṭth	Like five-shekel weights to the bed.

Immediately after the description of the pre-verbal *Gestalt* of Kirta's predicament, the motif of weeping that verbalizes the pre-verbal *Gestalt* of intentionality is introduced. The beginning of this motif is marked off by a brief note on the change of location (*yʿrb bḥdrh*).[55] The succession of these two motifs leads the listeners to make a connection between Kirta's weeping and the disaster that has befallen him; Kirta weeps in reaction to the total destruction of his family. This connection is reinforced by the following two literary artifices crafted into the two motifs.

Academic Press, 1988), 81. See also Tony W. Cartledge, *Vows in the Hebrew Bible and the Ancient Near East* (Sheffield: JSOT Press, 1992), 114.

[54] The reading of {h} has been disputed. Virollead restores it as {r}, thus producing *rgmm* "words." Herdner, however, leaves it blank, saying "Le texte n'est pas très favorable à cette lecture [*r*]*gmm*." My reading is based on Bordreuil and Pardee's handcopy (cf. Pierre Bordreuil and Dennis Pardee, *Choix de Textes: Glossaire*, vol. 2 of *Manuel d'ougaritique* [Paris: Geuthner, 2004], 20 and Handcopy number 3).

[55] For the discussion of *ḥdr*, see 2.1.4 below.

The first literary finesse that glues together the motif of Kirta's predicament and that of weeping has to do with the visual aspect of both motifs. The motif of weeping occurs in two poetic verses, one in a bicolon (lines 26–27) and the other in a tricolon (lines 28–30). Although the bicolon registers aspects of Kirta's weeping that are visible (*ydm*ʿ "he shed tears") and audible (*bṯnh gmm* "repeating voices"), the tricolon verse focuses on the visual aspect: by comparing the falling of tear drops to that of shekel-weights (*ṯqlm* and *mḫmšt*)[56] it conjures up a most vivid image of a profusion of tears.[57] This emphasis on the visual aspect in the motif of Kirta's weeping may be reminiscent of the verb *yʿn* "He saw" introduced near the end of the *inclusio* structure that informs the motif of Kirta's predicament. The verb *yʿn* in lines 21 and 22 could have been impressed on the short-tem memory of the audience due to its absence in the other end of the *inclusio* structure (cf. lines 10–11). Then the audience could have made connection between the image of a profusion of Kirta's tears and the verb *yʿn* that intimates the psychological impact of the disaster on Kirta, by visualizing the "tears" continuously welling up in Kirta's eyes when he "saw" his family totally destroyed (cf. *yʿn ḥtkh krt* / *yʿn ḥtkh rš*).

Second, the word *mḫmšt* may also serve as a literary link between the motif of weeping and the theme of Kirta's predicament, particularly, the premature death of Kirta's wives. The chunk *kmḫmšt* is often analyzed into *km* + *hmšt* on two bases, first on the basis of *km rbʿt* "like a quarter-shekel weight" occurring in a similar context, whose word-division is made obvious by different line-placement (KTU 1.19 II:33–34),[58] and second on the basis of the preceding parallel phrase *km*

[56] The two parallel words, *ṯqlm* and *mḫmšt*, must be plural. Kirta's tears must have had many drops. The image is, then, that of increase in the weight of shekel ingots. The word *ṯqlm* refers to many one-shekel ingots, while *mḫmšt* denotes as many five-shekel ingots. In addition, Bordreuil and Pardee consider the possibility that the image in lines 29–30 is that of increase in the number of tiny weights if *ḫmšt* is translated as "one fifth": "et l'image serait celle de l'augmentation du nombre de très petites unités de poids" (Bordreuil and Pardee, *Choix de Textes: Glossaire*, 22). But, in my view, the latter possibility is less likely than the former one.

[57] Although in a broken context, KTU 1.19 II:34 that features the verb *ntk* "pour out," the noun *dmʿt* "tear" and a simile of shekel-weights (*kmrbʿt*) seems to indicate that the simile represents a tradition that Ugaritic readers may have been familiar with.

[58] Note that Gordon reads *k mrbʿt* and takes *mrbʿt* as spanning over two different lines (Cyrus H. Gordon, *Ugaritic Textbook*, AnOr 38 [Roma: Pontificium Institutum Biblicum, 1965], 7.59).

ṯqlm.[59] But if the image in lines 29–30 is that of increase comparable to the formula "thousand…ten thousand" (cf. KTU 1.4 I:25b–28),[60] the numeral *ḫmšt* seems problematic, because it is more likely to be a fraction, "one fifth (shekels)" (cf. *rbʿt ṯqlm* "one fourth shekels" in KTU 1.19 II:34 and *šəlišît haššeqel* "one third shekel" in Nehemiah 10:33) than a multiplicative, "fivefold, five times."[61] Although Bordreuil and Pardee consider the possibility of the image still being that of increase in "nombre de très petites unités de poids" even if *ḫmšt* is understood as a fraction, I find the possibility to be very slim, particularly, compared with the other option that they consider, namely, the image of increase in "poids."[62] Besides, as Wyatt points out, the division *km ḫmšt* leads to an unusual, if not erroneous, sequence of the ballast forms, *km*… // *km*…[63] Furthermore, the poet of *Kirta* may reverse the usual sequence, k… // km…for a literary effect as is shown in KTU 1.14 IV:29–31: *km irby*…*k ḥsn*… "Like locusts…, like grasshoppers…"[64] So agreeing with KTU²,[65] I prefer to analyze *kmḫmšt* as *k* + *mḫmšt*, taking the latter as a multiplicative "fivefold" either on the pattern of Arabic *muqatal*-multiplicative or on that of D-passive participle. That said, one may notice that the word *mḫmšt* "five-shekel weights" immediately recalls the homonym *mḫmšt* "the fifth wife." Then *mḫmšt* serves as a pun that links the motif of weeping to the premature death of Kirta's wives. It is interesting to note that the poet places the verb *npl* "*to fall*" at the last of the three verses describing how Kirta's wives died, thus bridging the motif of the death (cf. *npl*) of Kirta's wives (one of them being *mḫmšt*) to the motif of Kirta's weeping that is visualized as the image of five-shekel weights (*mḫmšt*) *falling* to the ground. All this not only shows that the poet of *Kirta* embedded various literary artifices in the incubation type-scene in order to establish a web of relations among its component motifs, but also helps the reader to pull together

---

[59] Cf. Moor and Spronk, "Problematical Passages in the Legend of Kirtu (I)," 157.

[60] Nick Wyatt, *Religious Texts from Ugarit*, 183, footnote 27.

[61] Tropper cites other attestations of *ḫmšt* as a fraction as well. Cf. Joseph Tropper, *Ugaritische Grammatik*, 347, 374; Moor and Spronk, "Problematical Passages in the Legend of Kirtu (I)," 157. Verreet, "Der Keret-Prolog," 328–29.

[62] Bordreuil and Pardee, *Choix de Textes: Glossaire*, 21–22.

[63] Nick Wyatt, *Religious Texts from Ugarit*, 183, footnote 27. But see KTU 1.16 II:27–28.

[64] Note that its parallel in KTU 1.14 II:50–III:1 has the ballast forms *k irby*….*km ḥsn*.

[65] M. Dietrich, O. Loretz and J. Sanmartín, *The Cuneiform Alphabetic Text from Ugarit, Ras Ibn Hani and Other Places* (Münster: Ugarit-Verlag, 1995).

otherwise independent motifs into a closely-knit literary unit, which I call a type-scene in this book.

Also important for the question of incubation is the relationship between Kirta's weeping and 'Ilu's oneiric appearance. As has already been mentioned at the beginning of this chapter, many scholars have asked the following questions to prove or disprove the presence of an incubation rite in the Kirta text: Did Kirta intend to induce divine help with his tears? Would Kirta's tears have constituted a legitimate cultic preparation for oneiric theophany? But these questions cannot be answered by the present text since it does not purport to describe what an incubation rite should have looked like in Late Bronze Ugarit. Nor does the poet of the Kirta story describe Kirta as engaging in the act of incubation, although he is employing the practice as a literary device. Therefore the text under discussion has nothing to say about Kirta's intention, let alone about the role of weeping in the practice of incubation in Late Bronze Ugarit. Having said that, one may note one textual clue that might create a connection in the minds of the audience between the motif of weeping and the motif of theophany, thus establishing "intentionality" in the motif of Kirta's weeping: 'Ilu's oneiric speech begins with a fatherly attention to Kirta's tears (*mat kirt wybky / ydmʿ nʿmn ǵlm il* "Who is Kirta that he should weep, should shed tears, the goodly land of 'Ilu? [KTU 1.14 I:39–41a]). Parker correctly observes that the mention of the weeping motif in 'Ilu's initial question to Kirta "emphasizes the continuity of El's speech with the preceding, and the directness of El's response to Keret's condition."[66] Furthermore, incubation reports from other parts of the ancient Near east may provide circumstantial evidence that the ancient audience may have taken Kirta's weeping to be preparatory for an oneiric theophany. In the Hittite version of the legend of Naram-Sin (KBo 3.16+), we read that "Naram-Sin purified himself, went through incubation on

[66] Parker, *The Pre-Biblical Narrative Tradition: Essays on the Ugaritic Poems Keret and Aqhat*, 149. Some scholars go further and see a cultic significance in Kirta's tears. Jeffers, for instance, says that the weeping of Kirta "may have been induced with the intention of reminding us of ritual weeping in times of crisis. If so, it is provoked and may be part of an incubation ritual" (Jeffers, *Magic and Divination in Ancient Palestine and Syria*, 135). Jeffers is not alone in this assessment of the role of weeping in an incubation rite. See also Robert K. Gnuse, "The Dream Theophany of Samuel: Its Structure in Relation to Ancient Near Eastern Dreams and Its Theological Significance" (Ph.D. diss., Nashville, TN: Vanderbilt University, 1980), 57; Robinson, "Dreams in the Old Testament," 123; Shaul Bar, *A Letter That Has not Been Read: Dreams in the Hebrew Bible* (Cincinnati, OH: Hebrew Union College Press, 2001), 229.

a pure bed, cried out to his gods and bewailed to his gods" (Column III, lines 14–17).[67] Here weeping appears as an integral part of incubation. In the face of a dangerous invasion by the Elamites, Assurbanipal's apprehensions sent him to Ishtar's temple where in incubation he received a dream. Ishtar's speech made it clear that her theophany is in response to Assurbanipal's tears.[68] Another Assyrian king named Sethos was in a dire distress because of the invasion of the Arabians. He "entered into the inner sanctuary and, before the image of the god, *bewailed* the fate which impended over him" (emphasis is mine).[69] The text goes on to report a successful incubation by Sethos. It is interesting to note here that there is no textual hint that may indicate Setho's intention of provoking divine theophany. The text simply juxtaposes the theme of Setho's distress, his weeping and theophany without necessarily connecting them as a modern interpreter would wish. This underscores the common literary milieu that informs the way the ancient poet communicates with his audience.[70] Although scholars like Husser argue on the basis of lack of evidence that Kirta's weeping is not a preparatory ritual for incubation, contemporary audiences of the Kirta story may have been well aware of the details of an incubation rite, thus making it unnecessary for the poet to express a causal connection between Kirta's weeping and the theophany. The simple succession of motifs, from Kirta's predicament to his weeping and to divine theophany, would have been sufficient for the audience to associate the text with the practice of incubation and thus to recognize and appreciate the incubation type-scene that the poet had put together as a structural device for the first episode of the Kirta story.

Just as the motif of Kirta's predicament anticipates a future plot in terms of its focus on a child-bearing wife, the motif of weeping also has a narratological role to play as a *leitmotif* in the Kirta story as a whole. One encounters the motif of weeping throughout the narrative

[67] Hans G. Güterbock, "Die historische Tradition und ihre literarische Gestaltung bei Babyloniern und Hethitern bis 1200," *ZA* 44 (1937): 57. For the details of this text, see 2.1 in chapter two above.

[68] Oppenheim, *The Interpretation of Dreams in the Ancient Near East: With a Translation of an Assyrian Dream-Book*, 200.

[69] Ibid., 252.

[70] Classical literature also bears witness to the role of tears in inducing divine help. In *Iliad* (Book 1, lines 362–5), Achilles' divine mother answers his son's tearful prayer by asking, "My child, why do you weep? What grief has got to your heart?" Cf. M. L. West, *The East Face of Helicon: West Asiatic Elements in Greek Poetry and Myth* (Oxford: Clarendon Press, 1997), 351.

(cf. Table 5.1).[71] Kirta's weeping is not only mentioned repeatedly by 'Ilu (cf. KTU 1.14 I:39, 40; II:7, 8) but also anticipates, for instance, the noise of domestic animals in the city of Ḫubur. Just as Kirta's noisy weeping in a sense "waked" 'Ilu into paying a visit to Kirta in his room,[72] so did the cry of animals literally waked Pabil into sending messengers to Kirta in his camp. The motif of weeping pervades the second episode of the Kirta story as well. Although the broken state of tablets makes any literary analysis remain provisional, it is noticeable that the motif of weeping used in the scene of the mourning by 'Iluha'u and Ṯitmanatu for their fatally ill father (KTU 1.16 I:12–14, II:35–36) focuses on the aural perception of weeping (bky "weep" // yšnn "grind one's teeth"// ytn g "give a voice") rather than a visual aspect. This emphasis on the aural aspect of weeping may constitute a proper introduction to their long verbal lamentations for their father that follow.

Table 5.1: The Motif of Weeping

Text	Key words	Context
KTU 1.14 I:26–30	bky, dmʿ, ṯn g, ntk udmʿ	Kirta's lament for the loss of his family
KTU 1.14 I:31–32	bky, dmʿ	Kirta falling asleep
KTU 1.14 I:39–41	bky, dmʿ	'Ilu's question in theophany
KTU 1.14 II:7–8	bky, dmʿ	'Ilu's oneiric instruction
KTU 1.14 III:16–19 and its parallel	qr ṯigt, ql nhqt, gʿt, zǵt	Pabil's insomnia
KTU 1.15 V:12	bky	Ḥurray asks unidentified visitors to weep for Kirta
KTU 1.15 VI: 6	bky	Ḥurray asks unidentified visitors to weep for Kirta
KTU 1.16 I:6	bky	In 'Iluha'u's lamentation for Kirta
KTU 1.16 I:12–14	bky, šnn, ytn g	'Iluha'u mourns for Kirta
KTU 1.16 I:25, 30	bky, dmm	Kirta's command to 'Iluha'u not to weep
KTU 1.16 1:54	bky	Ṯitmanatu's reaction to the sight of 'Iluha'u
KTU 1.16 II:35–36	bky, šnn, ytn g	Ṯitmanatu mourns for Kirta
KTU 1.16 II:41	bky	In Ṯitmanatu's lamentation
KTU 1.16 VI:4	bkt, nṣrt	Šaʿtiqatu enters Kirta's house in tears

[71] Greenstein, "Kirta," 11.

[72] Although the passages register no motif of 'Ilu's "waking up" from sleep in the text in question, Elijah's taunt in 1 Kings 18:27 is suggestive: "And at noon Elijah mocked them, saying, 'Cry aloud, for he is a god. Either he is musing, or he is relieving himself, or he is on a journey, or perhaps he is asleep and must be awakened.'"

2.1.3 *The Motif of Sleeping*

KTU 1.14 I:31–35

(31)	bm . bkyh . w yšn	As he weeps, he falls asleep,
(32)	b dmʿh . nhmmt	As he sheds tears, there is slumber.
(33)	⸢š⸣nt . tlun!n (34) ⸢w⸣ yškb	Sleep overpowers him and he lies down,
	nhmmt (35) ⸢w⸣ y⸢q⸣mṣ .	Slumber and he curls up.

The motif of sleeping consists of two bicolon verses and its theme is made exceedingly clear by the dominant use, in the lines under discussion, of the words all connoting "sleep" (cf. *yšn*, *nhmmt*, *šnt*, *yškb*, *nhmmt* and *yqmṣ*). By introducing the motif of sleeping with two prepositional phrases (cf. lines 31–32) that recall the motif of weeping (*bm bkyh* and *bdmʿh*), the poet seems to make Kirta's sleeping part of the chain reaction that ties together Kirta's predicament, his change of location (*yʿrb bḥdrh*), his weeping, and finally his lying down to sleep. If the connection between Kirta's predicament and the motif of weeping is made by subtle literary artifices as well as by the simple juxtaposition of the two motifs, Kirta's weeping and sleeping is directly linked by the propositional phrases that express temporal simultaneity.

The motif of sleeping shows ideational movement from the general idea of lying down to sleep to the idea of sleeping for a specific purpose. The usual words for sleep (*yšn*, *šnt* and *nhmmt*) in lines 31–32 make way for rather technical words for incubation (*yškb* and *yqmṣ*) in lines 33–35. Early commentators explained *nhmmt* on the basis of Hebrew *hāmam* "to make a noise, to confuse"[73] and translated it as, for instance, "l'agitation,"[74] "Aufregungen"[75] or "humming, sighing."[76] But most scholars in recent years take *nhmmt* as a noun derived from the root √nwm "to slumber" (cf. Hebrew *nûm*).[77] The attestation of the

[73] Gray proposes an Arabic etymology "to groan" (Gray, *The Krt Text in the Literature of Ras Shamra: A Social Myth of Ancient Canaan*, 29).

[74] C. Virolleaud, *La légende phénicienne de Keret, roi de Sidoniens*, Mission de Rasshamra 2 (Paris: Geuthner, 1936), 37.

[75] Aistleitner, *Die mythologischen und kultischen Texte aus Ras Schamra*, 89.

[76] Ivan Engnell, *Studies in Divine Kingship in the Ancient Near East* (Oxford: Basil Blackwell, 1967), 151–52.

[77] Gregorio del Olmo Lete and Joaquín Sanmartín, *A Dictionary of the Ugaritic Language in the Alphabetic Tradition*, Handbook of Oriental Studies 67 (Leiden: Brill, 2003), s.v. nhmmt; Joseph Tropper, *Ugaritische Grammatik*, 163; Caquot, Sznycer, and Herdner, *Mythes et légendes: introduction, traduction, commentaire*, 508, footnote v.

pair *šēnâ* and *tənûmâ* in the Hebrew Bible (Psalm 132:4, Proverbs 6:4, 10) not only endorses the more recent scholarly consensus on Ugaritic *nhmmt*, which by the way forms a parallelism with *yšn* and *šnt* in the present motif,[78] but also corroborates the fact that the Ugaritic words *yšn*, *šnt*, and *nhmm* in line 31–32 serve as general terms for sleep. The words *škb* and *qmṣ* in line 33–35, however, denote the act of lying down for a particular purpose, thus underscoring a particular aspect of Kirta's sleep. McAlpine, who did a lexical study on all the Hebrew words that can be subsumed under the semantic rubric "sleep" (√yšn, √nwm, √rdm and √škb), concludes that only the verb *šākab* is used for activities other than sleep and its metaphorical counterpart, death. Thus only the word *šākab* is employed in biblical Hebrew to denote the ideas of the bedridden ("lying in bed"), sexual intercourse, and a nocturnal activity such as an incubation.[79] A quick survey of all the attestations of Ugaritic *škb* seems to show that Ugaritic *škb* is also more or less reserved for the act of lying down for a specific purpose. In KTU 1.5 V:19, the verb *škb* is used to indicate Baal's intercourse with a heifer in a field. In KTU 1.17 I:14 the verb *škb* denotes Dānîʾilu's nightly lying down for a dream. In two economic texts (KTU 4.163 and RS 88.2016) the sleeping, expressed by the verb *škb*, appears to have a specific purpose: it certainly does not refer to a nightly rest at home, since KTU 4.163 talks about a group of people sleeping in the house of a king (*b bt mlk*) and RS 88.2016 speaks of sleeping in the deep (*ʿl thm*).[80] It would be then no philological leap to assume that the word *škb* in line 33 may denote sleep for a special purpose, and this is corroborated by another word for lying down for a special purpose: *qmṣ* in line 35. According to Greenfield, Ugaritic *qmṣ* is cognate to Babylonian Aramaic *qəwāṣ* and Akkadian *kamāṣu*, both of which, if applied to the body, may refer to a contracted, curled

---

These scholars explain *h* as being formed secondarily due to the triconsonantalization of √nwm.

[78] S. J. Dahood, "Ugaritic-Hebrew Parallel Pairs," in *Ras Shamra Parallels: The Texts from Ugarit and the Hebrew Bible*, vol. 2, ed. L. Fisher (Roma: Pontificium Institutum Biblicum, 1975), 215.

[79] Thomas H. McAlpine, *Sleep, Divine & Human, in the Old Testament*, JOSTSup 38 (Sheffield: JSOT Press, 1987), 65–71. Particularly, see the summary and the table (2.13) in pp. 70–71.

[80] M. Yon, et al., "Fouilles de la 48e campagne (1988) à Ras Shamra-Ougarit," *Syria* 67 (1990): 20; Cf. Olmo Lete and Sanmartín, *A Dictionary of the Ugaritic Language in the Alphabetic Tradition*, 814.

up posture.[81] Moreover, he connects the posture to the way in which an incubant lies down for a theophanic dream by arguing that "lying in the crouched, curled-up position" is "usual in incubation."[82] Zevit seems to provide circumstantial evidence for the association of *qmṣ* with an incubation rite when he argues that people may have lain down around a *maṣṣēbâ* stone in a curled-up position to incubate a dream in some cultic centers in ancient Israel.[83] The most famous example of this posture in the context of an incubation comes from the Epic of Gilgamesh. Gilgamesh is told to lie with his chin upon his knees while seeking a dream during incubation (Gilgamesh Tablet IV:14).[84] Kirta's posture denoted by *yqmṣ* is also reminiscent of Elijah's posture of putting his face between his knees in 1 Kings 18:42, although the immediate context of the latter is not an incubation.[85] Greenfield's analysis of Ugaritic *qmṣ* as the posture of an incubant has been widely accepted among scholars. Even Husser who is adamantly opposed to seeing the

---

[81] Mishnaic Hebrew *qamṣūṣ* "a contracted position" has also been invoked in a similar vein. For a detailed philological justification, see Greenfield, "Studies in Aramaic Lexicography I," 297.

[82] Greenfield, "Keret's Dream: 'Ḏhrt' and 'Hdrt'," 87.

[83] Ziony Zevit, *The Religions of Ancient Israel: A Synthesis of Parallactic Approaches* (London: Continuum, 2001), 259.

[84] Cf. A. R. George, *The Babylonian Gilgamesh Epic: Introduction, Critical Edition, and Cuneiform Texts* (Oxford: Oxford University Press, 2003), 589. In a similar vein, Oppenheim explains Gilgamesh's "rather unnatural position of...squatting on the ground" as a possible imitation of 'contracted' burial position, and perhaps necessary to induce prognostic dreams (Oppenheim, *The Interpretation of Dreams in the Ancient Near East: With a Translation of an Assyrian Dream-Book*, 216).

[85] The so-called "Elijah's posture" (cf. M. Idel, *Kabbalah: New Perspectives* [New Haven, CT: Yale University Press, 1988], 78–96) is widely attested in the ancient Near East. The symbolic meaning of this posture may be different from culture to culture. The Egyptian idiom "head on lap," for instance, expresses the act of mourning (Mark S. Smith, *The Ugaritic Baal Cycle*, VTSup 55 [Leiden: Brill, 1994], 297). The act of putting one's head between one's knees symbolizes the deep absorption in God in an Arabic ascetic order (Carl F. Keil, *Commentary on the Books of Kings* [Edinburgh: T. & T. Clark, 1867], 192). Even within the same culture, the crouching posture may possess different meanings in different socio-religious contexts. If Kirta's posture under discussion is for the sake of incubation, the lowering (*tǵly*) of the heads in KTU 1.2 II:22 when the members of the divine council saw Yammu's messengers coming may symbolize fear (Cross, *Canaanite Myth and Hebrew Epic; Essays in the History of the Religion of Israel*, 93). Also Elijah's posture in 1 Kings 18:42 may have a different significance from that of the Jerusalem girls in Lamentation 2:10 where the act of bowing one's head on the ground clearly symbolizes mourning (J. C. de Moor, *An Anthology of Religious Texts from Ugarit*, 32, footnote 141). Having said that, Elijah's posture in 1 Kings 18:42 where "eating and drinking," "going up to the summit of a mountain," the act denoted by *ghr*, and the crouching posture all succeed one another, may be interpreted as foreshadowing his incubation in 1 Kings 19.

initial scene of the Kirta story as an incubation admits that *qmṣ* may refer to the position of an incubant.[86] Thus the motif of sleeping is not only connected to the preceding motif of weeping by two prepositional phrases but also makes way for the motif of theophany by its internal ideational movement from the general idea of sleeping to the technical idea of sleeping for a revelatory dream.

The motif of sleeping is answered by the waking motif later in the type-scene (KTU 1.14 III:50–51). This stands in contrast to the lack of the waking motif in the incubation type-scene of *ʾAqhatu*. The clear demarcation of a dream in the Kirta story may have something to do with the importance of the command-fulfillment structure in the incubation type-scene of *Kirta*. However, the narratological function of the sleeping motif in the Kirta story is not as clear as in the ʾAqhatu story where the sleeping motif in the incubation type-scene serves as a portent for the sexual intercourse of ʾAqhatu with his wife at both the vocabulary and thematic levels.[87] One may postulate a thematic connection of the motif of Kirta's lying down to Kirta's illness that would have made him bedridden and would have rendered his kingly functions dormant, but this connection exists only at the thematic level and is not supported at the vocabulary level.

2.1.4 *Time and Place*

In the incubation type-scene, the pre-verbal *Gestalt* of liminality may be articulated by the motif of a temple or any place of a liminal nature that was considered fit to provide a liaison between the divine and human. The chamber (*ḥdr*) where Kirta enters to weep, however, is more likely to be his private room in the palace than it is to be a room in a temple.[88] This is corroborated by the fact that Kirta's room where Ṯitmanatu enters to weep for her sick father is also called *ḥdr* (KTU

---

[86] Husser, *Le songe et la parole: Etude sur le rêve et sa fonction dans l'ancien Israël*, 33–34.

[87] See 2.1.4 in chapter four above.

[88] Cf. Karel van der Toorn, *Family Religion in Babylonia, Syria, and Israel: Continuity and Changes in the Forms of Religious Life*, SHCANE 7 (Leiden: Brill, 1996), 169; Gnuse, "The Dream Theophany of Samuel: Its Structure in Relation to Ancient Near Eastern Dreams and Its Theological Significance," 50; Husser, *Le songe et la parole: Etude sur le rêve et sa fonction dans l'ancien Israël*, 49; Jeffers, *Magic and Divination in Ancient Palestine and Syria*, 135; Bergman, Ottosson, and Botterweck, "Chālam," 426. For the interpretation of *ḥdr* as a cultic space, see Mullen, *The Divine Council in Canaanite and Early Hebrew Literature*, 248.

1.16 II:50–51) if Ginsberg's restoration is correct.[89] King Kirta may have sought a place to weep where he would not be seen by others, just as Joseph had to hurry to his private room (*haḥadrāh* in Genesis 43:30) to weep without being noticed by his brothers. Although in order to prove Kirta's performance of an incubation rite some scholars have asserted that the room where Kirta enters to weep is indeed part of his royal sanctuary,[90] their assertion cannot be substantiated by the text as we have it, not to mention that it is based on incorrect presupposition.[91] Hence it may be better to admit that the incubation type-scene under discussion does not register the motif of a temple. Kirta does not go to the temple for incubation as Dānî'ilu may have done. The poet, however, may have composed the incubation type-scene without the motif of a temple or a sanctuary as the place of the protagonist lying down for a dream. The poet may omit, delay, or even substitute the motif of a temple in accordance to the narrative need of a story. The reason that the poet makes Kirta's chamber, not a temple, as a place of weeping and incubational sleep may be identified in ideology of kingship. Although Ugaritic *ḥdr* most likely refers to Kirta's private room within his palace, the socio-religious position of Kirta as a priestly king makes it both quasi-public[92] and quasi-religious.[93]

[89] *bkm tʿr[b abh] / tʿrb ḥ[dr krt]* "And she enters into her father's presence / she enters the chamber of Keret." Ginsberg, *The Legend of King Keret: A Canaanite Epic of the Bronze Age*, 28.

[90] See Mullen, *The Divine Council in Canaanite and Early Hebrew Literature*, 248; cf. Mullen, *The Divine Council in Canaanite and Early Hebrew Literature*, 221.

[91] Dietrich and Loretz, "Das Keret-Epos," 1218, footnote 33. Biblical Hebrew *ḥeder* may refer both to a private bedroom and to a room in a temple. When it refers to a bedroom, however, it is either qualified by words like *miškāb* (cf. Exodus 7:28) and *miṭṭâ* (cf. 2 Kings 11:2) or suffixed with a pronoun referring to its owner (cf. Song of Solomon 1:4). Ugaritic *ḥdr* under discussion is not only suffixed with the 3rd person pronominal suffix referring to Kirta (KTU 1.14 I:26) but also apparently has a bed in it (KTU 1.14 I:31). This seems to tip the scale in favor of the interpretation of *ḥdr* as a private bedroom.

[92] When Biblical *ḥeder* appears in court contexts, it does not simply refer to the place where one sleeps, but a place where business was conducted (McAlpine, *Sleep, Divine & Human, in the Old Testament*, 81). Consider also English 'chamberlain.'

[93] There are several passages in the Hebrew Bible which hint at a secondary function of the bedroom (*ḥeder*) as sanctum of the household. According to van den Toorn, *tərāpîm* were installed inside the *ḥeder*, the dim bedroom at the back of the house (Toorn, *Family Religion in Babylonia, Syria, and Israel: Continuity and Changes in the Forms of Religious Life*, 221). Isaiah 26:20 tells that the Israelites were to go to their *ḥădārîm* for prayer. In Isaiah 57:8, it is said that some people had placed their *zikkārôn* (memorial for the dead?) "behind the door and the doorpost" (cf. Ibid.).

'Ilu's oneiric visit to Kirta's private room corroborates the ideology of ancient kingship by portraying King Kirta as the favored channel of divine communication. What is noteworthy in this regard is the fact that Kirta's palace features prominently as a *mise-en-scène* in major junctures of the story (see Table 5.2). Various characters of the story are described as "entering" (*'rb*) Kirta's "house" (*bt*), "court" (ḥẓr), "presence" (*'l abh*) and "room" (*ḥdr*), not only to incubate a dream, as in the case of Kirta, but also to bless (the gods: KTU 1.15 II:9–10), to get married (Ḥurray: KTU 1.15 IV:40–41), to mourn (the nobles: KTU 1.15 IV:16–17; 'Iluha'u: KTU 1.16 I:12–13; Ṯitmanatu: KTU 1.16 II:50–51), and to claim kingship (Yaṣṣubu: KTU 1.16 VI:39–40). Especially KTU 1.15 II presents Kirta's house as the *mise-en-scène* of the encounter between the gods (including 'Ilu and Ba'lu) and Kirta. All this seems to intimate the reason why the poet substitutes Kirta's palace for a temple in his configuration of the incubation type-scene.

At the same time, however, Kirta's withdrawal to his private room in tears may serve as a subtle allusion to Kirta's apathy in matters of religion. The way Kirta invokes a divine apparition stands in stark contrast to that of Dānî'ilu, who, as a paragon of religious piety, goes through multiple-day rituals in a temple in order to induce divine revelation. Although Kirta's weeping in his room may reflect his spontaenous response to an overwhelming difficulty, a comparison with Dānî'ilu seems to suggest that Kirta either did not know how to approach the gods for help or did not care much about cultic protocols of his days. The aural aspect of Kirta's weeping may be understood from this perspective. His inarticulate murmurings (*bṯnh gmm*) stands in contrast to an articulate or even scripted prayer of a pious petitioner. All this begs a rather big question as to what becomes of a priestly king who is not as pious as he should be. The entire story of Kirta seems to confront this problem.

But one must be careful not to extrapolate too much about Ugaritic *ḥdr* from biblical *heder*. It is better to find the narratological significance of Ugaritic *ḥdr* in the fact that Kirta is the king than in the assumption that Ugaritic *ḥdr* may have the same range of meaning as Hebrew *ḥeder*.

Table 5.2: The Motif of "Entering Kirta's House"

Text	Who enters?	Purpose
1.14 I:26, *yʿrb bḥdrh*	Kirta	To weep and to incubate a dream
1.14 IV:41–42, *ašʿrb ǵlmt ḥẓry*	Ḥurray	To marry and bear children
1.15 II:9–10, *ʿrb bth*	The assembly of gods	To bless Kirta's marriage
1.15 IV:16–17, *ʾlh ṯrh tšʿrb*	The nobles of Ḫubur	To be informed of Kirta's illness
1.16 I:12–13, ʿl abh yʿrb	'Iluha'u	To lament Kirta's immanent death
1.16 II:50–51, *tʿrb ʿl ḥdr krt*	Ṯitmanatu	To lament Kirta's immanent death
1.16 VI:39–40, *ʿl abh yʿrb*	Yaṣṣubu	To claim kingship in rebellion

The concept of liminality may also be verbalized in the motif of nighttime. The motif of nighttime, however, exists only in Held's ingenious rendering of ⌜*t*⌝*mḫ mšt mṯth* in KTU 1.14 I:30: "His bed is soaked at night."[94] A better reading of the text may not tell us exactly when Kirta lay down to have an oneiric theophany.[95] Neverthless there are two circumstantial evidences that hint at the nocturnal context of Kirta's incubational sleep. First, as is reported in the dream of Tuthmosis IV ("at the time of the midday...slumber and sleep overcame him"), the unusual time of a dream would have had been noted in the text.[96]

---

[94] Moshe Held, "Mḫṣ/*Mḫš in Ugaritic and Other Semitic Language (A Study in Comparative Lexicography)," *JAOS* 79 (1959): 173, footnote 79.

[95] Held's reading stands in the tradition of reading the first letter in KTU 1.14 I:30 as *t* instead of *k*. This reading, which was first proposed by Virolleaud and later followed by many others, produces the reading *tmḫmšt* in the first half of line 30. After dividing the chunk into *tmḫ* and *mšt*, Virolleaud rendered *tmḫ* as "Elle est mouillée" on a conjecture and yet left *mšt* unrendered (Virolleaud, *La légende phénicienne de Keret, roi de Sidoniens*, 36–37, 60). Whereas Obermann and Driver derived *mšt* from Hebrew *šīt* "clothing," Held proposed Akkadian *mūšū* or *mušītu* "night" as a cognate of Ugaritic *mšt* (Held, "Mḫṣ/*Mḫš in Ugaritic and Other Semitic Language [A Study in Comparative Lexicography]," 173, footnote 79). If Held's suggestion is accepted, we might have a clear textual evidence for the time when Kirta lay down to sleep, namely, nighttime. However, the correct reading of the first letter in KTU 1.14 I:30 is most likely *k*. Although the first letter in line 30 appears to be one horizontal wedge, it is possible that the two shorter horizontal wedges may have been weathered out. This is corroborated by the same sign right above it in line 29, one of whose horizontal wedge is completely weathered out. Furthermore, a similar phrase *km rbʿt* in KTU 1.19 II:33–34 seems to provide additional confirmation of the reading *k*. Although the text is a bit fragmentary there, the context is unmistakably that of weeping: running tears are likened to shekel-weights falling to the ground.

[96] Oppenheim, *The Interpretation of Dreams in the Ancient Near East: With a Translation of an Assyrian Dream-Book*, 251.

Second, if the practice of incubation had been well-known to the ancient audience, which was probably the case, the poet would not have had to tell everything about it to his readers especially when he intended it purely as a literary device. Thus, nighttime may be assumed to be the most logical time for Kirta's withdrawal to his room for an incubational dream. This being the case, one may go further and discuss the possible narratological role of the motif of nighttime in the rest of the story, especially, in the part where Pabil could not sleep at night and decided to send a delegation to Kirta in his "night-quarters" (*mswn* in KTU 1.14 III:21):[97] the nocturnal negotiation between Pabil and Kirta is reminiscent of the oneiric dialogue between 'Ilu and Kirta. In both of the nocturnal incidents, Kirta remained in his private place (*ḥdrh* "room" and *mswnh* "night-quarters") while 'Ilu and Pabil proposed the same list of tributes either in person or through messengers. Both nocturnal interactions are triggered by the noises created by Kirta's weeping (*bṯnh gmm*) and by the domestic animals in the city of 'Udumu respectively.

2.1.5 *The Missing Motifs in the Pre-Epiphany Section: Prayer, Vow, and Sacrifice*

Kirta seems to have offered neither a prayer, let alone a vow, nor sacrifice, before he lay down to have a dream. In this respect Kirta stands in stark contrast to Dānî'ilu who undertakes an elaborate seven-day ritual to induce divine revelation. This difference is even reflected in the way that the patron gods react to the problems of Kirta and Dānî'ilu. In the theophany section of *'Aqhatu*, Ba'lu bases his mediatory petition for Dānî'ilu on the latter's seven-day long sacrifice and libation (cf. KTU 1.17 I:21–22), whereas 'Ilu's oneiric theophany in the Kirta story is a working out of 'Ilu's fatherly love toward his despondent son in tears rather than a response to a prayer or a sacrifice of a pious individual

[97] The meaning "night-quarters" was first suggested by Moor and Spronk on the basis of Arabic *mumsīn* "night-quarters" (Moor and Spronk, "Problematical Passages in the Legend of Kirtu [I]," 168). Their proposal has been accepted by Tropper, Greenstein, Dietrich and Loretz (Joseph Tropper, *Ugaritische Grammatik*, 191; Greenstein, "Kirta," 16; Dietrich and Loretz, "Das Keret-Epos," 1225). An alternative rendering is "a camp" which is based on Akkadian *maswatu* in an Akkadian text discovered at Ras Shamra (J. Nougayrol, *Textes accadiens des archives sud*, PRU IV [Paris: Impr. nationale, 1970], 95: Wolfram von Soden, *Akkadisches Handwörterbuch* [Wiesbaden: Ott Harrassowitz, 1965], s.v. *maswatu*). The word *maswatu* is given in the text as a raw material for the production of wooden objects (cf. F. C. Fensham, "Remarks on Keret 114b–136a [CTA 14:114b–136a]," *JNSL* 11 [1981]: 77). The rendering "camp" is based on the extrapolation that the *maswātu*-wood was used for Kirta's living quarters.

(cf. *ab adm* "father of mankind" in KTU 1.14 I:37, *abh* "his [Kirta's] father" in KTU 1.14 I:41). Hence it may be said that the incubation type-scene that the poet composed for the first episode of *Kirta* lacks the preparatory rituals that figure prominently in the incubation type-scene of *'Aqhatu*, not to mention in the actual practice of incubation. The motifs missing in the pre-epiphany section, however, occur belatedly in the theophany section and in the post-epiphany section of the type-scene. The motif of sacrifice is embedded in the motif of divine command, while the motif of prayer-vow in the fulfillment motif. This illustrates the fact that the poet has the freedom of arranging component motifs of the incubation type-scene according to his narratological and/or "theological" purpose, which will be discussed below in section 3.

That said, however, it is necessary to recall that the motif of Kirta's weeping has not only a visual aspect but also an aural aspect. Kirta makes an inarticulate sound as he sheds tears (*bṯnh gmm w ydmʿ* in KTU 1.14 I:27). Could the act denoted by *ṯny gm* ("repeating voices") be a satirical allusion to a prayer?[98] Or is it simply a reference to a howling of a mourner as is attested to in the scene of 'Iluha'u's and Ṯitmanatu's lamentations (KTU 1.16 I:13 and II:36)? Although we may not know the exact nature of the noise made by Kirta, we do know that the poet has changed the conventional formula for howling or wailing, *ytn gh*, "giving one's voice,"[99] attested to twice later in the story (cf. KTU 1.16 I:13; II:36), to his original phrase, *ṯny gm*, "repeating voices"

[98] In the latter case, one may make a case for "delayed identification" a literary device that is often employed in the story of 'Aqhatu. If one may discern an allusion to Kirta's prayer in the phrase *bṯnh gmm*, then what is lacking in the pre-epiphany section is the content of his prayer. The readers are not privy to the content of Kirta's prayer at this point of the narrative. Only later in the theophany scene, the content of Kirta's prayer is revealed to the readers: Kirta prays that he may acquire a son and multiply his offspring (*[b]nm aqny…[ṯa]rm amid*, KTU 1.14 II:4–5). Some may object that if Kirta offered a prayer before theophany and yet its content was belatedly identified in the theophany section, 'Ilu, albeit not the readers, must have known Kirta's prayer request. But 'Ilu's initial question to Kirta seems to show 'Ilu's ignorance of what Kirta wants. However, 'Ilu's knowledge of Kirta's problem would not have prevented him from asking the question about his problem. The motif of a deity asking of a petitioner in a theophany is one of those traditional materials that a poet could insert in his composition without creating theological tension. Yahweh, for example, asks Solomon what he wants, although he is certainly omniscient. The reason that the allusion is satirical is that the text seems to present it as a hint to Kirta's impiety, rather than as an act of faith.

[99] The formula for mourning, *ntn g*, is distinguished from message formula, *nš' gh* "raising his or her voice" in the Kirta story (KTU 1.16 IV:15; IV:40).

in the motif of Kirta's weeping. This change looks deliberate because it foreshadows one of the most important turns of the plot in the Kirta story. Right after the completion of the first episode of Kirta's loss and restoration, the text makes a transition to the second episode of *Kirta* with the following note: *wtḫss aṯrt ndrh...wtšu gh w[tṣh]...ph m' ap k[rt...] uṯn ndr...apr*..."Then 'Aṯiratu remembered his vow...and she raised her voice and [cried out], 'Look, O K[irta]...or has repeated the vow...I will annul...'" (Emphasis is mine). Most scholars have taken this passage as the description of 'Aṯiratu's accusation against Kirta for the latter altering his vow. But Pardee points out that the root √ṯny "repeat" should not be confused with the root √šny "to be different, to change."[100] If Pardee is right, we may remain ignorant of how Kirta angers the goddess with regard to his vow, but we come to a better knowledge of how component motifs of an incubation type-scene relate to one another. Kirta's inarticulate murmuring or prayer in the pre-epiphany section of the incubation (*ṯny gm*) is not only compensated for by Kirta's articulate vow in the post-epiphany section but, more importantly, also finds its echo in Kirta's apparent failure to fulfill his vow to 'Aṯiratu (*ṯny ndr*). The connection in the latter is both verbal and theological. The use of the verb √ṯny "repeat" in close proximity with the phrase *nš' g* "to raise a voice" in the scene of 'Aṯiratu's claiming the vow clearly recalls the only other use of the root √ṯny in the poet's original phrase *ṯny gm* "repeating voices." Also, since Kirta's inarticulate murmurings present a contrast to the articulate or scripted prayer that is used in an incubation ritual,[101] it may be arguable that Kirta's "repeating voices" (*bṯnh gmm*) is reminiscent of the scene of Kirta's "repeating his vow" (*uṯn ndr*) in terms of his lackadaisical approach to matters of religion.

---

[100] Pardee, "The Kirta Epic," 338, footnote 53.

[101] The incubation rite attested in *Rituals to Obtain a Purussû*, for example, consists of an articulate incanation, a prescription of sacrifice and libation, and the lying down to dream. Cf. S. A. L. Butler, *Mesopotamian Conceptions of Dreams and Dream Rituals*, AOAT 258 (Münster: Ugarit-Verlag, 1988), 349–77. Also in the *Maqlu* ceremony which took place during the night and morning of an important calendrical occasion, formulaic incantations and prayers were recited. Cf. Tzvi Abusch, *Mesopotamian Witchcraft: Toward a History and Understanding of Babylonian Witchcraft Beliefs and Literature*, AMD V (Leiden: Brill, 2002), 97, 185–216.

2.2 *Epiphany*

2.2.1 *The Motif of Dream*

KTU 1.14 I:35b–37a

(35)	w b ḥlmh (36) ⌜i⌝l . yrd .	In his [Kirta's] dream 'Ilu descended,
	b ḏhrth (37) ⌜ab . a⌝dm .	In his vision, the father of mankind.

The motif of dream verbalizes the pre-verbal *Gestalt* of liminality with regard to human consciousness. The oneiric setting of 'Ilu's appearance to Kirta is made explicit by the two parallel references to dream (*bḥlmh* and *bḏhrth*) that preface the motif of divine appearance. The explicit mention of dream makes this incubation type-scene stand in stark contrast to that of the 'Aqhatu story which lacks not only the motif of a dream but also its corresponding motif, i.e., the waking motif. In the incubation type-scene of the Kirta story, parallel references to dream clearly demarcate the beginning and the end of oneiric theophany and in the latter they are connected epexegetically with the waking motif: *krt . yḫṭ . wḥlm ʿbd . il . whdrt* "Kirta woke up and it was a dream, the servant of 'Ilu, it was a theophany" (KTU 1.14 III:50–51). The prominence given to the motif of dream corresponds to the importance of the content of Kirta's dream in the unfolding of the plot in the first episode of Kirta. 'Ilu's oneiric instruction to Kirta is replayed almost word for word in the motif of fulfillment so that any deviation from it would be immediately picked up by the audiences as a possible portent of a future event in the story. In this regard it would have been important to the poet, let alone to the audience, to have a clearly demarcated "dream" section in the type-scene of *Kirta*.[102]

[102] On the other hand, the incubation type-scene of the 'Aqhatu story features the fulfillment motif that is very creative in its composition: Instead of repeating 'Ilu's instruction for sexual intercourse in the fulfillment motif, the poet of 'Aqhatu describes the visit of the Koṯarātu goddesses (see 2.3.2 in chapter four). Such creativity serves the purpose of underscoring the piety of Dānî'ilu's wife, just as the pre-epiphany sacrifice underscores Dānî'ilu's piety. More interesting, however, is that in the incubation type-scene of 'Aqhatu divine beings appear both in oneiric theophany ('Ilu and Baʿlu) and in reality, namely, in the fulfillment motif (Kôtarātu), whereas no god features as a character, at least in the expedition of Kirta to 'Udumu as it is recounted. A clear demarcation of oneiric theophany is not as crucial to the advancement of the plot in the incubation type-scene of 'Aqhatu as it is in the incubation type-scene of Kirta.

A variety of Ugaritic terms are employed to denote "dream" in this incubation type-scene. Besides *ḥlm*, the standard word for "dream" in Northwest Semitic languages,[103] words like *ḏhrt*, *ḏrt* (KTU 1.14 III:47) and *hdrt* (KTU 1.14 III:51) occur as a parallel term for *ḥlm*. Although their general meaning is firmly established by virtue of parallelism, their exact nuances are still moot due to uncertain etymologies. To make things worse, *ḏhrt* and *hdrt* are *hapax legomena* occurring only here in this incubation type-scene. This interpretive difficulty, as well as the variety, of the "dream" terms utilized in this incubation type-scene seems to warrant discussion. Since parallelism is about "sharpening" an apparent emphatic construction[104] rather than simple repetition, the study of these words may shed some light on the role of a dream in this incubation type-scene, as well as on the ancient Near Eastern concept of a dream in general.

There seems to be scholarly consensus that *ḏhrt* and *ḏrt* are etymologically related, although which one of the two is etymologically original is moot. Of various etymologies proposed for Ugaritic *ḏhrt* and *ḏrt*,[105] only two of them are worthy of mentioning here. Both of them assume that *ḏrt* is a phonetic variant of *ḏhrt*.[106] Following

---

[103] Although *ḥlm* is the most common word for a dream in Northwest Semitic languages, its etymology is not certain. According to Koehler, Baumgartner and Stamm (contra Brown-Driver-Briggs), two different meanings of the root √ḥlm, namely, "to become strong" and "to dream" are etymologically connected (Ludwig Koehler and Walter Baumgartner, *The Hebrew and Aramaic Lexicon of the Old Testament*, subsequently revised by Walter Baumgartner and Johann Jakob Stamm [Leiden: Brill, 1994–2000], s.v. *ḥlm*). What brings them together is likely to be a sexual dream that occurs at puberty. A more general meaning "dream" may have grown out of this specific meaning. Cf. Ehrlich, *Der Traum im Alten Testament*, 1; Josef Tropper, "Ugaritic Dreams: Notes on Ugaritic Ḏ(h)Rt and Hdrt," 306.

[104] James L. Kugel, *The Idea of Biblical Poetry: Parallelism and Its History* (Baltimore, MD: Johns Hopkins University Press, 1981), 99.

[105] Tropper summarizes five important proposals: 1. Connection with Hebrew *šwr*, 'to see, look.' 2. Connection with Hebrew *zhr*, Arabic *zahira/zāra*, 'to gleam, shine.' 3. Connection with Aramaic *šhr*, Arabic *sahira*, 'to be awake.' 4. Connection with Arabic *zawr*, a phantom that is seen in sleep. 5. Connection with Arab. *ẓahara*, 'to be manifest.' Josef Tropper, "Ugaritic Dreams: Notes on Ugaritic Ḏ(h)Rt and Hdrt," 307.

[106] A number of scholars take *ḏhrt* as original and explain *ḏrt* as a secondary form with *h* elided before *r* (Cf. Gray, *The Krt Text in the Literature of Ras Shamra: A Social Myth of Ancient Canaan*, 29; Caquot, Sznycer, and Herdner, *Mythes et légendes: introduction, traduction, commentaire*, 509, footnote x; Josef Tropper, "Ugaritic Dreams: Notes on Ugaritic Ḏ(h)Rt and Hdrt," 311; *Ugaritische Grammatik*, 117, 160). But some scholars explain *ḏhrt* as an incorrect spelling of *ḏrt* because the former occurs only once in the Ugaritic corpus (Cf. Ginsberg, *The Legend of King Keret: A Canaanite Epic of the Bronze Age*, 35).

Driver, Gray and Aistleitner, Greenfield connects *ḏhrt* to Aramaic *šhr* "to be awake" and Arabic *sahira* "to be awake" and renders it as "a vision in the state of wakefulness."[107] Going beyond his predecessors, however, Greenfield supports his rendering by a hitherto unrecognized Aramaic noun *šhrt*. According to Greenfield, Aramaic *šhrt* is cognate with Ugaritic *ḏhrt* and is best rendered as "(wakeful) vision" due to its occurrence as a parallel term for *ḥylm'* "dream" in two Jewish incantation texts.[108] As Tropper points out, however, Greenfield's proposal presents two difficulties. First, Greenfield's identification of Aramaic *šhrt* with Ugaritic *ḏhrt* is based on an irregular phoneme correspondence of Ugaritic *ḏ* and Aramaic *š*.[109] Second, Greenfield's interpretation of *šhrt* as "wakeful vision" is untenable, not only because Mandaic *šhar* "to slumber" provides a better etymology than Arabic *sahira* "to be awake," but also because in two parallel texts the word *šnyt* "sleep" replaces *šhrt* in the same context as a parallel word for *ḥylm'* "dream."[110] For this reason, Tropper connects Ugaritic *ḏhrt* to the West Semitic root √ḏhr "to be visible, evident; to appear; to disclose, to instruct" that takes the form of *ẓhr*$_2$[111] "to disclose, to reveal" in Arabic and *zhr* "to warn, to instruct" in Hebrew.[112] If Tropper is right, we find in *ḏhrt* a Ugaritic word for dream that may reveal the ancient ideology of dream, that is, the dream as a vehicle of divine message to humans.[113] It would then be no wonder that the poet employed *ḏhrt*

[107] Greenfield, "Keret's Dream: 'Ḏhrt' and 'Hdrt'," 92. Cf. Gray, *The Krt Text in the Literature of Ras Shamra: A Social Myth of Ancient Canaan*, 29; Aistleitner, *Wörterbuch der ugaritischen Sprache*, 321; G. R. Driver, *Canaanite Myths and Legends.* (Edinburgh: T. & T. Clark, 1956), 149.

[108] Greenfield, "Keret's Dream: 'Ḏhrt' and 'Hdrt'," 89–90.

[109] For the irregular correspondence of Hebrew *š* and Ugaritic *ḏ*, see Dennis Pardee, "The New Canaanite Myths and Legends," *BO* 37 (1980): 285.

[110] Josef Tropper, "Ugaritic Dreams: Notes on Ugaritic Ḏ(h)Rt and Hdrt," 307–8.

[111] Tropper argues that Arabic *ẓhr* has two different groups of meanings that suggest two different roots. What he calls *ẓhr*$_1$ has the meaning of "back, top, noon" (Josef Tropper, "Ugaritic Dreams: Notes on Ugaritic Ḏ[h]Rt and Hdrt," 309).

[112] For a similar view, see Baruch Margalit, *A Matter of "Life" and "Death": A Study of the Baal-Mot Epic (CTA 4-5-6)*, AOAT 206 (Kevelaer: Butzon und Bercker; Neukirchen-Vluyn: Neukirchener Verlag, 1980), 167.

[113] The use of *ḏrt* in KTU 1.6 III:5 seems to bear this out. In his dream/vision (ḥlm/ḏrt) 'Ilu foresees the return of Baal. The ancient Near Eastern concept of a dream as a vehicle of divine message to humans seems to be confirmed also in the biblical Aramaic use of *ḥlm*. Biblical Aramaic *ḥlm* is always used with the verb *ḥzy*, instead of its cognate verb, *ḥlm*. On this basis Ehrlich suggests that "im bibl. aram. nur weissagende Träume vorkommen" (Ehrlich, *Der Traum im Alten Testament*, 1).

and *ḏrt* as a parallel term for *ḥlm* in the context of oneiric revelation of the incubation type-scene.

Just as *ḏhrt*, Ugaritic *hapax* for dream, opens the section of oneiric theophany, so does another Ugaritic *hapax* for dream, *hdrt*, close the section of oneiric theophany. In fact, the word *hdrt* as the last word in the section of oneiric theophany is situated at the seam of dream and reality. Since it occurs in parallelism with *ḥlm*, no one doubts its contextual reference to Kirta's dream. But its etymology is no less problematic than that of *ḏhrt*. A majority of scholars including Greenfield connect Ugaritic *hdrt* to Hebrew/Aramaic *hādār* or *hădārāh* "glory, majesty" and take it as a reference to the manifestation of divine majesty.[114] Husser goes further and says, "on peut même parler, à propos de *hdrt*, de <<théophanie>>, au sens d'une révélation de la majesté divine."[115] Tropper, however, takes *hdrt* as a variant of *ḏhrt*. In other words he does not postulate a different root to explain the word in question. For him Ugaritic *hdrt* is formed by two consecutive processes: a consonantal metathesis and a subsequent sound change from /ḏ/ to /d/. He attributes such phonetic changes to the pausal position it takes and the author's literary intention for wordplay.[116] In my view, the etymology suggested by, for instance, Greenfield and Husser is as good as that suggested by Tropper. Although Tropper tries to invalidate the suggested cognation between Ugaritic *hdrt* and Hebrew *hādār* by observing that Hebrew *hādār* never appears as a parallel term for Hebrew *ḥălôm*, he himself depends on the Hebrew root √zhr "to warn, instruct" to explain Ugaritic *ḏhrt* when the Hebrew word does not occur in an oneiric context either, let alone form a parallelism with *ḥălôm*. Whichever suggestion one accepts, it does not change the poetic message that Kirta's dream is not a psychological phenomenon of human origin but a channel of divine communication. Whether one accepts Greenfield's understanding of *hdrt* as the manifestation of divine majesty (theophany) or Trooper's understanding of it as divine

[114] Greenfield, "Keret's Dream: 'Ḏhrt' and 'Hdrt'," 90–92; C. Cohen, "Biblical Hebrew-Ugaritic Comparative Philology: The Comparison BH Hdrt/hdr = Ug. Hdrt," *ErIsr* 26 (1999): 71–77; cf. Cross, *Canaanite Myth and Hebrew Epic; Essays in the History of the Religion of Israel*, 151–56; Gordon, *Ugaritic Textbook*, 389; J. C. L. Gibson, *Canaanite Myths and Legends.*, 86, footnote 4.

[115] Husser, *Le songe et la parole: Etude sur le rêve et sa fonction dans l'ancien Israël*, 34.

[116] Josef Tropper, "Ugaritic Dreams: Notes on Ugaritic Ḏ(h)Rt and Hdrt," 310–11. For a similar view, see Manfried Dietrich and Oswald Loretz, "Zur ugaritischen Lexikographie, II," *Orientalische Literaturzeitung* 62 (1967): 538.

revelation, he or she may discern the poet's intention of deliberately placing the very rare word for dream at the seam of dream and reality as the last word of the theophany section: the poet seems to be saying in effect that Kirta's dream is not a fantasy but a divine behest upon which he is to act and which, according to the story, he does immediately.[117]

2.2.2 *The Motif of Theophany*

KTU 1.14 I:35b–38a

(35)	w b ḥlmh (36) ⸢i⸣l . yrd .	In his [Kirta's] dream 'Ilu descended,
	b ḏhrth (37) ⸢ab . a⸣dm .	In his vision, the father of mankind,
	wyqrb (38) bšal . krt .	He approached, asking Kirta:

One of the stylistic features of divine appearance in ancient Near Eastern dream reports is the description of a deity's "coming in" or "going out" by means of verbs of motion.[118] This stylistic feature not only underscores the passivity of the dreamer who does nothing but "see" the deity approaching but also indicates that the initiative comes from the deity in the divine-human encounter.[119] The Ugaritic verbs of motion used in the motif of divine appearance under discussion are *yrd* and *qrb*. Del Olmo Lete singles out the verb *qrb* as the word that determinatively informs the element of theophany (*teofania*) in an incubation scene.[120] Although Husser thinks that Del Olmo Lete over-reads the verb, the use of the verb in another theophany scene in the 'Aqhatu story makes Ugaritic *qrb* as a likely candidate for a functional equivalent to Akkadian *erēbu* and Hebrew *bō'* that inform Akkadian

[117] Greenfield, "Keret's Dream: 'Ḏhrt' and 'Hdrt'," 92. For a similar interpretation, see Olmo Lete, *Mitos y leyendas de Canaan: según la tradición de Ugarit*, 253–54: *Kirta despierta de su sueño sagrado y, sabiendo que se trata de una revelación divina, la pone por obra.*

[118] See 2.2.2 in chapter three above.

[119] Husser, *Le songe et la parole: Etude sur le rêve et sa fonction dans l'ancien Israël*, 35; Oppenheim, *The Interpretation of Dreams in the Ancient Near East: With a Translation of an Assyrian Dream-Book*, 188.

[120] Note Del Olmo Lete's table enumerating the elements of incubation in *Kirta* cited in Husser, *Le songe et la parole: Etude sur le rêve et sa fonction dans l'ancien Israël*, 48. This usage of Ugaritic *qrb* stands in contrast to Hebrew *qārab* and Akkadian *qerēbu*, both of which rarely occur in the context of theophany (cf. Lamentation 3:57 and Oppenheim, *The Interpretation of Dreams in the Ancient Near East: With a Translation of an Assyrian Dream-Book*, 330:67).

and Hebrew reports of oneiric theophany.[121] Another Ugaritic verb of motion that characterizes the motif of divine appearance is *yrd*. Generally speaking, Ugaritic *yrd*, unlike Hebrew *yārad*, is rarely used to refer to a deity coming down to meet humans.[122] It is used either in the context of a kingly figure, divine or human, abdicating from his throne or in the context of the gods descending into the netherland.[123] In fact the use of *yrd* in context of theophany is unique to the passage under discussion. This is why Husser says, "c'est le contexte seul qui détermine sa [*yrd*'s] valeur sémantique particulière íci."[124] Of course, one should be careful not to make a mechanical association of the Ugaritic verbs *qrb* and *yrd* with oneiric theophany as if their presence in a text would automatically create a theophany scene. But the context in which the two verbs occur places it beyond doubt that they are playing the same role as other verbs of motion in ancient Near Eastern dream reports (e.g. Akkadian *erēbu* "to enter" and Hebrew *bô* "to enter").

The motif of divine appearance is reutilized later in the incubation type-scene. First, the idea of divine "coming down" is repeated with Baal as a contextual subject. In his oneiric speech, 'Ilu commands Kirta to bring down (*šrd*) Ba'lu with a sacrifice. Since Kirta executes

---

[121] For the examples where Akkaidan *erēbu* is used in context of theophany, see Oppenheim, *The Interpretation of Dreams in the Ancient Near East: With a Translation of an Assyrian Dream-Book*, Text No. 10, 14 and 19. For the use of Hebrew *bō'* in oneiric theophany, see Fensham, "Remarks on Keret 26–43," 49; Husser, *Le songe et la parole: Etude sur le rêve et sa fonction dans l'ancien Israël*, 35; Moor and Spronk, "Problematical Passages in the Legend of Kirtu (I)," 157.

[122] In contrast to Ugaritic *yrd*, the theophanic usage of Hebrew *yārad* is common. Hebrew *yārad* is often used with Yahweh as subject in connection with divine theophany in the Hebrew Bible. Behind this fact seems to lie the mythical idea that the dwelling of Yahweh is in heaven (Cf. Jörg Jeremias, *Theophanie: Die Geschichte einer alttestamentlichen Gattung* [Neukirchen-Vluyn: Neukirchener Verlag, 1977], 12, 15, 36; Fensham, "Remarks on Keret 26–43," 47–49; Husser, *Le songe et la parole: Etude sur le rêve et sa fonction dans l'ancien Israël*, 50–51; Moor and Spronk, "Problematical Passages in the Legend of Kirtu [I]," 157). In Exodus 19, for example, Yahweh is said to "come down" on Mount Sinai to appear to the assembly of Israel amidst lightening and thunder. Also in Psalm 18:10 Yahweh's theophany is couched in the verb *yārad* and connected with natural phenomena. Fensham argues that the divine theophany introduced by the verb *yārad* may occur without natural phenomena by citing Genesis 11:5. But Genesis 11:5 is not a theophany in a strict sense of the term, because there are no human witnesses to that "coming down" of Yahweh. It is noteworty that the divine "coming down" never happens in a dream in the Hebrew Bible. Instead the verb *bô* is used and always in conjunction with the phrase *baḥălôm* (cf. Genesis 20:3; 31:24; 1 Kings 3:15).

[123] Cf. examples in Olmo Lete and Sanmartín, *A Dictionary of the Ugaritic Language in the Alphabetic Tradition*, s.v. *yrd*.

[124] Husser, *Le songe et la parole: Etude sur le rêve et sa fonction dans l'ancien Israël*, 35.

'Ilu's command faithfully later, one may imagine the scene where Ba'lu appears to Kirta on the rooftop of his palace, but Ba'lu's role is not clear in the Kirta narrative in general and in the incubation type-scene in particular.[125] Another reutilization of the motif of divine appearance is found in the scene of Kirta's wedding banquet (KTU 1.15 II). The gods, including 'Ilu and Ba'lu, visit Kirta's house to bless his marriage. The verb used for divine appearance in this scene is *'rb* "to enter" as in Mesopotamian dream reports. Although Kirta's wedding banquet features the gods, elements of liminality are all eliminated from the scene: it does not happen in a temple, neither in a dream nor at night. This may be owing to the fact that the scene is closer to a mythological-anthromorphic story-stelling than to a description of theophany.[126] It is still arguable, however, that the divine appearance at Kirta's wedding banquet is reminiscent of the scene of oneiric theophany in that both of them are oriented toward solving the problem of the person in whom the deity finds great interest. At the same time, however, the scene of Kirta's wedding banquet compensates the oneiric theophany of the incubation type-scene for the latter's lack of the element of divine promise-blessing. Finally, a subtle allusion to the motif of divine appearance may also be discerned in the scene of Pabil's dispatch of his messengers to Kirta. As is discussed below, Pabil's dispatch of messengers to Kirta is portrayed in a way that strongly recalls 'Ilu's oneiric visit to Kirta.

---

[125] Ba'lu's presence in Kirta's military campaign may also be alluded to in the description of the marching of Kirta's army: *hlk lalpm ḫdd / wlrbt kmyr* "They will go by thousands like *storm-clouds* / by myriads like *rain*" (KTU 1.14 II:39–40, emphasis added). For a detailed discussion of this passage, see 2.2.4.2 below. Loewenstamm, by the way, finds the reason for Ba'lu's appearance to Kirta in his traditional role as the god of war par excellence attested to in the prayer appended to a sacrificial ritual in KTU 1.119: "Zum verständis der Erwähnung Baals in diesen Zusammenhange trägt eine ugaritische Urkunde bei, in der das Volk von Ugarit aufgefordert wird, sich in den Bedrängnissen einer Belagerung an Baal zu wenden, der dort somit als der Kriegshelfer par excellence gekenzeichnet ist" (Samuel E. Loewenstamm, "Zur Götterlehre des Epos von Keret," *UF* 11 [1979]: 509). But it does not change the fact that in the Kirta story, 'Ilu, not Ba'lu, is presented as directing the battle. For this point, see Mullen, *The Divine Council in Canaanite and Early Hebrew Literature*, 31ff.

[126] Lindblom distinguishes the motif of theophany and the mythological-anthropological style in the biblical narrative. The divine appearance to Hagar in Genesis 21, for instance, belongs to a thoephanic scene whereas the divine appearance to Lot in Genesis 19 is a stylistic feature of a mythological-anthropological story-telling. Johannes Lindblom, "Theophanies in Holy Places in Hebrew Religion," *HUCA* 32 (1961): 96.

2.2.3 *The Motif of Divine-Human Dialogue*

KTU 1.14 I:38b–II:5

'Ilu's Introductory Question

	mat (39) krt . kybky	Who is Kirta that he should weep?
(40)	ydmʿ . nʿmn .ǵlm (41) il .	Should shed tears, the goodly lad of 'Ilu?
	mlk[.] ṯr abh (42) yarš .	The kingship of the Bull, his father, would he ask?
	hm . d*rk*[t] (43) k ab .adm	Or dominion like (that of) the father of mankind?
	....[127]	

Kirta's Request in Response

(51)	lm (52) [ank . ksp .	What need have I of silver,
	w yrq (Col II.1) ḫrṣ]	And of yellow gold,
	*y*d . mq⌜m⌝h	Along with its place.
	[w ʿb]*d* . ʿlm .	And of a perpetual slave,
	ṯlṯ (3) [ssw]m .	Of three horses,
	mrkbt btrbṣ	A chariot in a courtyard,
	bn . amt	The son of a handmaid?
(4)	[...b]nm . aqny	Let me acquire sons...
(5)	[...n]ʿrm . amid	Let me multiply children...

The motif of divine-human dialogue starts with 'Ilu posing a question to Kirta. 'Ilu's investigative question may have been needed due to the omitted motif of articulate prayer in the pre-epiphany section of the type-scene that usually reveals the wish of an incubant. 'Ilu's initial question does not necessarily indicate that 'Ilu is all-powerful but not omniscient, because the theme of a deity asking about the wish of a petitioner is one of the traditional formats that a poet could employ in his composition without creating theological tension. Yahweh, for example, asks Solomon what he wants although he is certainly understood to be omniscient (*šəʾal māh ʾetten-lāk* "Ask, what shall I give to

[127] Lines 44–51 in KTU 1.14 I are too broken to allow any translation. But on the basis of Kirta's answer that begins KTU 1.14 II one may gather that 'Ilu must have offered a list of wealth in those missing lines.

you?" [1 Kings 3:5b]). Similarly, the same god asks Hagar "What troubles you, Hagar?" (*mah-lāk hāgār*, Genesis 21:17), although he is the ultimate cause of Hagar's trouble (cf. Genesis 21:12). These examples may indicate that the investigative question posed by a deity is less a sign of divine ignorance than an expression of divine love and concerns for a devotee.[128] Such a question in a theophany always provokes an answer from the devotee, which in turn leads to a rather lengthy divine speech that purports to solve the devotee's problem (cf. 1 Kings 3).[129] The motif of divine-human dialogue in the incubation type-scene of *Kirta* closely follows this pattern.

The exact nuance of 'Ilu's first question (*mat krt k ybky*) is uncertain. The bone of contention is the word *mat*. Some scholars understand *mat* as the crasis of an interrogative (*mh*,[130] *my*,[131] or *m*[132] "what, who") and the 2nd person pronoun (*at* "you.").[133] Others who feel uncomfortable with the shift of person in the following verb *ybky* prefer to emend *mat* to *mn*.[134] Still others, Tropper in particular, take *mat* as a variant form of *mh* with an enclitic *t*.[135] Tropper's proposal in particular seems to aim at removing the problem of the shift in person without emending the text. Although all of these analyses make no difference in the understanding that 'Ilu's question purports to discover the nature of Kirta's predicament, the "crasis" interpretation of *mat* has some merits from a literary point of view. First, 'Ilu's question, "what you?" (*m(h) at*),[136]

---

[128] Similar questions have been attested to in the Homeric corpus. In response to Achilles' prayer (*Iliad*, Book 1, lines 362–5), for instance, his divine mother comes and asks, "My child, why do you weep? What grief has got to your heart?" Cf. West, *The East Face of Helicon: West Asiatic Elements in Greek Poetry and Myth*, 351.

[129] In some cases the petitioner responds not by answering the deity's question directly. In *Iliad*, Book 1, lines 362–5, for instance, Achilles says to his divine mother in reply, "You know, why must I tell you all this when you know it?" Cf. Ibid.

[130] Ginsberg, *The Legend of King Keret: A Canaanite Epic of the Bronze Age*, 35.

[131] Cf. *mî 'at* in Ruth 3:16. Gray, *The Krt Text in the Literature of Ras Shamra: A Social Myth of Ancient Canaan*, 30.

[132] Moor and Spronk, "Problematical Passages in the Legend of Kirtu (I)," 158.

[133] For another example of the crasis, see *mhy* "what she" in KTU 2.14:9.

[134] For an epigraphical justification of the emendation, see Bordreuil and Pardee, *Choix de Textes: Glossaire*, 22, note 38. For a similar view, see Engnell, *Studies in Divine Kingship in the Ancient Near East*, 152; Gordon, *Ugaritic Textbook*, 124. For the impossibility of the reading *mn*, see Andrée Herdner, *Corpus des tablettes en cunei-formes alphabetiques decouvertes a Ras Shamra-Ugarit de 1929 à 1939*, Mission de Ras Shamra 10 (Paris: Geuthner, 1963), 62, note 10.

[135] Joseph Tropper, *Ugaritische Grammatik*, 240.

[136] Most scholars have translated Ugaritic *mat* idiomatically as "what is the matter with you?" in analogy to Hebrew *māh-ləkā* in Judges 8:18 that is also followed by a *kî*-clause (Ginsberg, *The Legend of King Keret: A Canaanite Epic of the Bronze Age*,

seems to echo Kirta's answer, "For what I?" (*lm ank*).[137] This draws attention, among other things, to Kirta's trouble and wish that is encapsulated in the interrogative *m* in *mat* and *lm ank*. The divine-human dialogue then gets focused on finding out "what" Kirta needs. After a detour (offer and rejection of a list of wealth), Kirta's "what" is finally verbalized by Kirta himself: "Let me have sons... let me acquire children" (KTU 1.14 II:4–5). Second, the shift in person may be part of the poet's literary artifice.[138] The poet seems to move back and forth between the second person and the third person references to Kirta in 'Ilu's direct speech to Kirta in which the latter is supposed to be addressed in the second person. For instance, Kirta is referred to in the third person in KTU 1.14 II:26–27 and 30–31, but the rhetorical purpose of that shift is not clear. Be that as it may, the general meaning of 'Ilu's first question in lines 38b–41a is relatively clear: 'Ilu has noticed Kirta's tears and asks him what trouble and/or wish he has. Also note that the mention of Kirta's tears using a recurrent pair of verbs (*bky* "to weep" // *dm*ʿ "to shed tears") corroborates a causal relationship between Kirta's tears and 'Ilu's theophany.[139]

'Ilu's second question looks problematic theologically. Why would 'Ilu offer his own kingship to a mere human like Kirta? Why did 'Ilu think in the first place that his own kinship was what Kirta wanted? This interpretive difficulty has made some scholars argue that what 'Ilu offered was not his own kingdom but a kingdom like his own.

14; Olmo Lete and Sanmartín, *A Dictionary of the Ugaritic Language in the Alphabetic Tradition*, 220; Moor and Spronk, "Problematical Passages in the Legend of Kirtu [I]," 158; Nick Wyatt, *Religious Texts from Ugarit*, 184; J. C. L. Gibson, *Canaanite Myths and Legends.*, 83; Greenstein, "Kirta," 13; Jirku, *Kanaanäische Mythen und Epen aus Ras Schamra-Ugarit*, 86; Aistleitner, *Die mythologischen und kultischen Texte aus Ras Schamra*, 89). But note Dietrich and Loretz's translation, *Was wünschest du*? (Dietrich and Loretz, "Das Keret-Epos," 1219).

[137] The analogy between *mat* and *lm ank* is also noted by Ginsberg, *The Legend of King Keret: A Canaanite Epic of the Bronze Age*, 35; Moor and Spronk, "Problematical Passages in the Legend of Kirtu (I)," 158.

[138] For enallage (switch in person as a poetic device) see Marvin H. Pope, *Song of Songs: A New Translation with Introduction and Commentary*, AB 7C (Garden City, N.Y.: Doubleday, 1977), 297. For a Sumerian example of enallage, see Samuel N. Kramer, *The Sacred Marriage Rite: Aspects of Faith, Myth, and Ritual in Ancient Sumer* (Bloomington, IN: Indiana University Press, 1969), 132. Also note a possible shift in person in KTU 1.17 I:16–19 (*abyn at... d in bn lh km aḫh* "You are a lamenting one... who had no son like his brother").

[139] For a similar connection of oneiric theophany and a petitioner's weeping, see Text No. 10 in Oppenheim, *The Interpretation of Dreams in the Ancient Near East: With a Translation of an Assyrian Dream-Book*, 249.

Ginsberg, for instance, reads *mlk <k> ṯr* instead of *mlk ṯr* in KTU 1.14 I:41 and explains the lack of *k* as resulting from haplography.[140] Other scholars such as Spronk take 'Ilu's question as a rhetorical one. According to Spronk, 'Ilu is in effect saying that "Kirta should not set his demands too high, that he should rather enjoy those riches which are within his grasp."[141] Still other scholars take 'Ilu's offer of his own kingdom as a literary hyperbole that is designed to underscore how much Kirta desires offspring: Kirta would not trade it even for 'Ilu's kingship. The frequent use of hyperbole later in the story[142] makes the last hypothesis certainly attractive. But in employing such hyperbole at this point of the narrative, the poet seems to be making a point: The poet may be providing a subtle hint to Kirta's indiligence in matters of religion. Why did 'Ilu think of Kirta as someone who would covet his own kingship? Is he really faithful to 'Ilu? Furthermore, if, as Spronk's suggests, 'Ilu's question is rhetorical, it seems to intimate that Kirta would dare to step over his boundary to claim 'Ilu's kingship. It is interesting to note in this regard that 'Ilu's second question—Would he want the kingship (*mlk*) of the Bull, his father, or dominion (*drkt*) like the father of mankind?—seems to foreshadow another incident where a son defiantly demands his father's kingship, namely, Yaṣṣubu's demand, "Step down from (your) kingship (*mlk*), I will be the king / From your dominion (*drktk*), I, yes I will sit [on the throne]" (*rd lmlk amlk / ldrkt aṯb an* [KTU 1.16 VI 52–54]).

After line 43 of KTU 1.14 I the tablet is completely broken. But seeing that KTU 1.14 II begins with Kirta's answer that includes a partial list of wealth, one may gather that after posing two questions, 'Ilu offers Kirta a list of wealth, which by the way serves as a *Leitmotif* in this story (Cf. KTU 1.14 III:22–25; 34–37; VI:4–8; 17b–22a). But Kirta refuses 'Ilu's offer of wealth and then verbalizes his wish in no ambiguous words. Although the relevant lines are only partly preserved, the

---

[140] Ginsberg, *The Legend of King Keret: A Canaanite Epic of the Bronze Age*, 36. Also see Dietrich and Loretz, "Das Keret-Epos," 1219, footnote 39.

[141] Spronk, "The Legend of Kirtu (KTU 1.14–16): A Study of the Structure and Its Consequences for Interpretation," 64.

[142] Examples of hyperbole used in the story include weights of tears, the length of Kirta's expedition (five months), the number of Kirta's army (three million), the full conscription, the silver and gold along with its mine, Kirta's vow to return twice of 'Aṯiratu's weight in silver and thrice in gold and the birth of Kirta's seven sons and seven daughters in seven years.

gist of Kirta's wish is unmistakable: He wants an heir ("Let me acquire [sons]..., let me multiply [chil]dren" [KTU 1.14 II:4–5]).[143] Kirta's wish made known belatedly in the motif of divine-human dialogue compensates for the lack of the articulate prayer motif that normally reveals the wish of an incubant in the pre-epiphany section of this incubation type-scene. Now having been informed of Kirta's ultimate wish, the audience's focus will be on the question how 'Ilu would grant Kirta's wish, that is, how Kirta would acquire offspring so as to rebuild his house. This focus on offspring in the motif of divine-human dialogue finds a subtle echo later in the way the poet ends the motif of 'Ilu's oneiric instruction. 'Ilu's oneiric speech ends on the note of the child-bearing potential of Kirta's new wife: *wld šp̣ḥ l krt / w ǵlm l ʿbd il* "She might bear a scion to Kirta / a lad for the servant of 'Ilu" (KTU 1.14 III: 48–49). This ending reminds the audience that 'Ilu's oneiric instruction, which on the surface aims at the acquisition of Kirta's wife, has a larger goal in view, that is, the rebuilding of Kirta's house through a legitimate heir.

2.2.4 *The Motif of Divine Command*

The oneiric dialogue between 'Ilu and Kirta carries over to 'Ilu's long speech in which 'Ilu gives Kirta detailed instructions on how to procure a new wife. As is expected of the motif of divine command in the incubation type-scene, 'Ilu's instructions are narrowly focused on the solution to Kirta's problem articulated in the motif of wifelessness at the beginning of the story. The problem of childlessness and its solution is only alluded to in the way the poet ends 'Ilu's oneiric speech. However, the issue of childlessness comes to the foreground in the motif of divine blessing in the post-epiphany section. 'Ilu visits Kirta's house and pronounces blessing upon him with specific regard to Kirta's offspring. Having said that, it is interesting to note that the subjects of "wife" and "offspring" appears in the A-B-A-B pattern throughout the incubation type-scene of the Kirta story (See Table 5.3 below).

[143] This is reminiscent of Hannah who refuses to be comforted by anything other than a male heir. Neither Elkanah's "double portion" (*mānâ 'aḥat appāyim*, 1 Samuel 1:5) nor his own person (*hălô' 'ānōkî tôb lāk mēʿăśārâ bānîm* in v. 8) do not satisfy her.

Table 5.3: The Structure of the Movement of Plot from Problem to Solution in *Kirta*

Motif of Predicament before Epiphany	Motif of Divine-Human Dialogue during Epiphany	Motif of Divine Command during Epiphany	Motif of Divine Blessing after Epiphany
Focus on Wife A	Focus on Offspring B	Focus on Wife A	Focus on Offspring B

The motif of divine command is divided into three segments:[144] ritual preparation (2.2.4.1, KTU 1.14 II 9–27), logistical preparation (2.2.4.2, KTU 1.14 II:28–50a) and military expedition (2.2.4.3, KTU 1.14 II:50b–III:49). Ritual preparation may be further divided into several sections: ritual washing (KTU 1.14 II: 9–11), animal sacrifice (lines 13–18a), libation (lines 18b–19), enlisting divine help (lines 22b–26a), and finally change of location (lines 12, 20–22a, 26a–27a). Logistical preparation is also divided into two sections: food provision (KTU 1.14 II:28–31) and full conscription (lines 32–50a). Finally, the military expedition is subdivided into military march (KTU 1.14 II:50b–III:5), sacking daughter towns and cities (lines 6–10a), a siege of 'Udumu (lines 10b–19a), and negotiation (lines 19b–49). This chain of military actions bears a resemblance to the Assyrian military tactic of terrorizing the enemy into submission.[145] But unlike the Assyrian expedition, Kirta's purpose was not to obtain booty but to receive the hand of the daughter of Pabil, the king of 'Udumu, who will bear him an heir.

2.2.4.1 Ritual Preparation

KTU 1.14 II 9–27

Ritual Washing

(9)	t⌈rt⌉ḥṣ . w tadm	Wash and redden yourself,
(10)	rḥ⌈ṣ⌉ [. y] ⌈d⌉k . amt	Wash your hand to the elbow,
(11)	uṣb[‘tk .] ⌈ ‘⌉d[.]⌈ṯ⌉k⌈m⌉	Your fingers to the shoulder.

[144] The introduction to 'Ilu's instruction (KTU 1.14 II:6–9a) mentions for the fourth time the pair of verbs *bky* "to weep" and *dm‘* "to shed tears." This corroborates the causal relationship between Kirta's many tears and 'Ilu's theophany.

[145] Marc van de Mieroop, *A History of the Ancient Near East, Ca. 3000–323 B.C.*, Blackwell History of the Ancient World (Malden, MA: Blackwell Pub., 2004), 218.

Change of Location

(12)	ʿrb[. b ẓl . ḫmt]	Enter the shade of the tent,

Animal Sacrifice

(13)	qḥ . im[r . b yd]⸢k⸣	Take a lamb in your hand,
(14)	imr . ⸢d⸣ [bḥ . b]*m* . ymn	A sacrifical lamb in a right hand,
(15)	lla . k⸢l⸣ [atn]⸢m⸣	A kid in both hands,
(16)	klt . l[ḥm]⸢d⸣ nzl[146]	All your best food.
(17)	qḥ . ms[rr .][147] ʿṣr (18) dbḥ	Take a fowl, a sacrificial bird.

Libation

	ṣ⸢q⸣ [. b g]⸢l⸣ . ḥtṯ (19) yn	Pour wine into a silver cup,
	b gl . [ḫ]⸢r⸣ṣ . nbt	Honey into a golden bowl.

Change of Location

(20)	ʿl . l ẓr . ⸢m⸣ [g]dl	Ascend to the summit of the tower
(21)	w ʿl . l ẓr . ⸢mg⸣dl .	Yea, ascend to the summit of the tower,
	rkb (22) ṯkmm . ḥm⸢t⸣ .	Mount the shoulders of the wall.

[146] Ugaritic *nzl* is difficult. Most scholars derive it from an Arabic cognate *nuzl* "food offerred to a guest" and assume that the word means "best, choicest." Such an assumption is based on an extrapolation from the fact that the food prepared for a guest must be of fine quality. But apart from the probability of the extrapolation, according to Renfroe, the meaning "food offered to a guest" is a tertiary derivation from the original meaning of the root √nzl "to descend" and a similar semantic deveopment from "to descend" to "food for a guest" did not occur in other Semitic cognate words (Fred Renfroe, *Arabic-Ugaritic Lexical Studies*, ALASP 5 [Munster: UGARIT-Verlag, 1992], 137). For various translations proposed for this word, see Olmo Lete and Sanmartín, *A Dictionary of the Ugaritic Language in the Alphabetic Tradition*, s.v. *nzl*.

[147] L-stem participle of √srr "to fly." The L-stem here has the nuance of habitual or repetitive acts. For the etymology, see Ethiopic √srr "to fly" (Joseph Tropper, *Ugaritische Grammatik*, 581; Moor and Spronk, "Problematical Passages in the Legend of Kirtu [I]," 161). Other translations proposed for this word include "Abgezogenes" (Kjell Aartun, "Neue Beiträge zum Ugaritischen Lexikon I," *UF* 16 [1984]: 49–50), "entrails" (Olmo Lete and Sanmartín, *A Dictionary of the Ugaritic Language in the Alphabetic Tradition*, s.v. *mrss*); cf. "turtle dove" (Gordon, *Ugarit and Minoan Crete: The Bearing of Their Texts on the Origins of Western Culture*, 103); "a knife" (Aistleitner, *Wörterbuch der ugaritischen Sprache*, 224).

Prayer

ša . ydk . (23) šmm .	Raise your hands to the heavens.

Enlisting Divine Help

db⌈ḥ⌉ . ltr (24) abk . il .	Sacrifice to the Bull, your father 'Ilu,
šrd . bʿl (25) b dbḥk	Bring down Baʿlu with your sacrifice
bn . dgn (26) b mṣdk	The Son of Dagan with your game.

Change of Location

w yrd (27) krt . ⌈l⌉ ggt .	Then Kirta must descend from the rooftops.

The lack of preparatory rituals in the pre-epiphany section of the incubation type-scene is compensated by the description of various rituals within the motif of divine command. 'Ilu's prescription of rituals for Kirta is structurally divided into three stages by three verbs of motion: *ʿrb* "enter" in KTU 1.14 II:12, *ʿl* "ascend" in lines 20–21, and *yrd* "he shall descend" in line 26 (see Table 5.4 below). These three stages demarcated by verbs of motion seem to correspond to three spaces with different degrees of sacrality through which Kirta proceeds in carrying out the rituals. He must purify himself before "entering" a sacred place (*ẓl ḫmt* "tent-shrine") where he will offer animal sacrifice and libation, and then he must "ascend" to the 'holy of holies' (cf. *ggt* "rooftops") to bring down Baʿlu with prayer, and finally he must "descend" back to his profane palace to launch the preparations for the military expedition to 'Udumu. These steps of the cultic procedure are reminiscent of the Hellenistic practice of incubation in which an incubant washes himself in the springs within the *temenos* of the temple of Asclepius, offers sacrifice and libation in the temple, and finallly lies down for a dream in a special place called *abaton* within the temple.[148]

[148] See section 4 in chapter two above. There was a gradation of sacred space in Greek temples, from the space of the *temenos* that was a god's possession to the space where access was limited most often to the priests. Even further out were spaces where a god really touched human space. This was the case where lightning, Zeus's divine form, hit the ground: this space was cut off from the rest of the ground, marked as "inaccessible" (*abaton*). Cf. Vedia Izzet, "Sacred Times and Spaces: Greece," in *Religions of*

Table 5.4: The Structure of Kirta's Ritual Preparation

Motion verbs		*ʿrb* "to enter"	*ʿly* "to go up"	*yrd* "to descend"
Place	(*bt*/*ḥẓr*/*ḥdr krt*)	*ẓl ḫmt* "tent-shrine"	*ẓr mgdl*/*ṯkmm ḥmt*/*ggt*	(*bt*/*ḥẓr*/*ḥdr krt*)
Rituals	Purification	Animal Sacrifice and Libation	Prayer, Enlisting Divine Help	End of Rituals

Kirta is first commanded to purify himself by washing and "reddening himself" (*tadm*) before he can offer animal sacrifice and pour libation in "a shade of a tent" (*ẓl ḫmt*).[149] The context makes it clear that Kirta's washing and reddening is not hygienic but cultic; Kirta must be ritually clean before administrating sacrifice to the gods.[150] This is corroborated by the ritual of hand-washing, the subject of lines 10–11, that is widely attested to in the ancient Near East as an act preliminary to sacrificial meals (cf. *dbḥ* and *mṣd*).[151] The motif of change of location (line 12), consisting of a motion verb (*ʿrb*) and a designation

the Ancient World: A Guide, ed. Sarah I. Johnston (Cambridge, MA: Belknap Press, 2004), 270.

[149] The contextual meaning of "a shade" (ẓl) may be gathered from Lot's words in Genesis 19:8b: *bāʾû bəṣēl qōrātî* "they have come under the shadow of my roof." Cf. Ginsberg, *The Legend of King Keret: A Canaanite Epic of the Bronze Age*, 37.

[150] As far as "reddening oneself" (*tadm* in line 9) is concerned, Moor and Spronk understand redness as a result of scrubbing (Moor and Spronk, "Problematical Passages in the Legend of Kirtu [I]," 160). Similarly Pedersen takes *tadm* as a description of Kirta recovering his normal complexion through washing after a period of grief (Johannes Pedersen, "Die KRT-Legende," *Ber* 6 [1941]: 73). Others argue that a sort of cosmetic is responsible for the redness. Wyatt, for instance, takes *tadm* as the application of red ochre widely attested in antiquity (Nick Wyatt, *Religious Texts from Ugarit*, 186, footnote 44). For similar views, see also Dietrich and Loretz, "Das Keret-Epos," 1221, footnote 50; Ginsberg, *The Legend of King Keret: A Canaanite Epic of the Bronze Age*, 36. Still others like Gray connect *tadm* to the use of blood as a means of consecration of the king for his priestly functions (Gray, *The Krt Text in the Literature of Ras Shamra: A Social Myth of Ancient Canaan*, 31). Similarly, Fensham understands *tadm* in the context of 1 King 18:28, where the priests cut themselves until blood gushed out upon them (F.C. Fensham, "Remarks on Keret 59–72," *JNSL* 4 [1977]: 12). But this interpretation of *tadm* cannot explain Pūġatu who also reddens herself not to consecrate herself for a priestly function, but to avenge her brother's death (Caquot, Sznycer, and Herdner, *Mythes et légendes: introduction, traduction, commentaire*, 512, footnote j).

[151] W. G. Lambert, *Babylonian Wisdom Literature* (Oxford: Clarendon Press, 1960), 323–24; Mark W. Edwards, "Homer and Oral Tradition: The Type-Scene," *Oral Tradition* 7 (1992): 306. For a ritual of hand-washing for an ordalist, see *Archives royales de Mari* 25, text 254. Hand-washing is one of the preparations for a bull sacrifice in *Odyssey*, book III, lines 440–460.

of a place (*ẓl ḫmt*), marks a new step in the ritual procedure that 'Ilu enjoins upon Kirta. Here in a "tent-shrine"[152] Kirta must offer animal sacrifice and pour out a libation. Just as the animal sacrifice consists of domesticated animals (*imr* and *llu*) and a non-domesticated bird (*msrr*), so libation consists of wine and wild honey (*yn* and *nbt*).[153] The purpose of Kirta's sacrifice is clarified in the third and final step of the ritual procedure that begins with another indication of change of location in lines 20–22 and culminates in lines 23b–26a where, in order to secure the granting of his wish, Kirta enlists divine help "with his sacrifice (*dbḥ*) and his game (*mṣd*)."[154] Ugaritic *dbḥ* and *mṣd* certainly refer back to Kirta's sacrifice offered in a tent-shrine.[155] The climactic character of this step of the ritual procedure is borne out not only by the number of poetic lines devoted to the motif of change of location (cf. a tricolon verse here as opposed to a mono-colon in the other steps)[156] but also by the location, the parapet of the wall or the rooftops (*ggt* in line 27), which was one of thr favored places for cultic

---

[152] It is Wyatt's translation of *ḫmt* (Nick Wyatt, *Religious Texts from Ugarit*, 186). Gray, followed by Caquot, translates *ḫmt* as "pen" on the basis of an Arabic cognate *ḫumm* "a coop for hens or domestic animals" (Gray, *The Krt Text in the Literature of Ras Shamra: A Social Myth of Ancient Canaan*, 31; Caquot, Sznycer, and Herdner, *Mythes et légendes: introduction, traduction, commentaire*, 513). But Gray's translation is unacceptable because of his wrong assumption that *ḫmt* denotes a place out of which Kirta is to get (*qḥ*) sacrificial animals, not a place of sacrifice. First, the wild bird designated by *msrr* cannot be "taken" out of *ḫmt*, but it has to be hunted (cf. *mṣd* "a game"). Second, considering the recurrence of the change of location motifs, it better fits the context to interpret *ḫmt* as the place in which Kirta administers animal sacrifice including domesticated animals, a non-domesticated bird, and libation.

[153] According to Neufeld, there is no allusion to beekeeping or beehives in the Ugaritic texts (Edward Neufeld, "Apiculture in Ancient Palestine [Early and Middle Age] Within the Framework of the Ancient Near East," *UF* 10 [1978]: 221).

[154] Spronk argues that the offering is made to enlist the help of the gods (Spronk, "The Legend of Kirtu [KTU 1.14–16]: A Study of the Structure and Its Consequences for Interpretation," 65). But I don't see any role of the gods in Kirta's expedition to Udum. The gods play their roles in the predicament scene, in the wedding banquet scene and in the divine assembly convened to deal with Kirta's illness. Note the contrast between the gods and Ilu-Baal. The former are not faithful in their relationship to Kirta, but Ilu and Baal prove themselves to be unchanging in their commitment to Kirta.

[155] Moor and Spronk connect *mṣd* "a sacrifice of game" in line 26 to *msrr* in line 17 and consider the latter as a wild bird. Cf. Moor and Spronk, "Problematical Passages in the Legend of Kirtu (I)," 112.

[156] Line 21 does not have to be a dittography. First, tautological parallelism was normal in ancient poetry. Second the later appearance of this verse in a bicolon simply illustrates the general principle of "shortening" in the motif of fulfillment (for this principle, see discussion on the fulfillment motif below). Cf. Moor and Spronk, "Problematical Passages in the Legend of Kirtu (I)," 161.

activity (cf. Mesha's sacrifice of his oldest son on the wall in 2 Kings 3:27, rituals on the rooftops in *Rituals to Obtain a Purussû* 81e–84 and in Ugaritic Ritual Text RS 1.003:50–55). From a narratological point of view, 'Ilu's command in lines 20–22 foreshadows his command to 'Ilšu and his wife: "Ascend to the shoulders of a building" (KTU 1.16 IV:13). Just as Kirta's mission at the summit is to bring down Baʿlu to deal with Kirta's problem of wifelessness, the mission of the divine couple is to summon the assembly of gods to deal with the matter of Kirta's fatal illness.

The word *šrd* in line 24 is better parsed as a Š-stem imperative of *yrd* than a D-stem imperative of the hypothetical verb *šrd*.[157] It anticipates the appearance of Baʿlu to Kirta later in the text (KTU 1.15 III:3, 12). It is not clear whether Baʿlu's descent amounts to the scene of theophany, an apparent climax of the ritual preparation for Kirta's expedition to 'Udumu, because the appearance of the gods may simply be a function of a mythological-anthromorphic telling of the narrative (cf. the divine appearance at Kirta's wedding banquet). It suggests, however, Baʿlu's role in Kirta's quest to win the hand of Ḥurray: he may have served as a guardian deity who accompanies Kirta's army on campaign. This may be subtly alluded to in lines 39–40: *hlk lalpm ḫdd / w lrbt km yr* "They shall go by thousands like storm-clouds, by myriads like rain."[158] Baʿlu's role in Kirta's expedition, however, should not be overemphasized. As a patron deity of Kirta and a mastermind of Kirta's campaign, 'Ilu still plays a major role in Kirta's efforts to rebuild his house through Ḥurray while Baʿlu is nothing more than 'Ilu's auxiliary hand. This stands in stark contrast to the respective roles of 'Ilu and Baʿlu in the 'Aqhatu story, in which Baʿlu plays a major role as the patron deity of Dānî'ilu and stays faithful to Dānî'ilu throughout the narrative, while 'Ilu stays in the background as a helping hand of

[157] Some scholars argue for the existence of Ugaritic root √šrd. Tropper, for instance, takes Ugaritic *šrd* as a cognate with Hebrew *šārat* and explains the phonetic discrepancy as a sonorization of a dental, which is very rare (Joseph Tropper, *Ugaritische Grammatik*, 140; for Pardee's critique of Tropper on this point, see Dennis Pardee, "Review," Ugaritische Grammatik, Josef Tropper, *AfO* Online Version 50 [2003/2004]: 73). Gray connects Ugaritic *šrd* to a hypothetical Hebrew root √*śrd* "to serve" (Gray, *The Krt Text in the Literature of Ras Shamra: A Social Myth of Ancient Canaan*, 32). But the fact that the meaning of the Hebrew root is based on the extrapolation from the LXX translation of *bgdy śrd* in Exodus 31:10, namely, στολὰς τὰς λειτουργικὰς "garment worn while ministering," makes the connection with Ugaritic *šrd* extremely unlikely.

[158] For the explanation of these poetic lines, see 2.2.4.2 below.

Ba'lu, if not as an accomplice with 'Anatu in the murder of 'Aqhatu. Just as Ba'lu's faithfulness to Dānî'ilu is demonstrated in the episode where Ba'lu helps Dānî'ilu collect the torn pieces of 'Aqhatu's body, so not only does 'Ilu appear later to Kirta to pronounce blessing upon him at his wedding banquet (KTU 1.15 II:16–28), but he also creates the healer goddess Ša'tiqatu to cure Kirta of his fatal illness when the council of the gods have failed him (KTU 1.16 V).

The motif of ritual preparation ends on another indication of change of location: "Kirta shall come down from the rooftops" (lines 26b–27). The shift in person from the second to the third in reference to Kirta coincides with a transition point from ritual preparation to logistical preparation.[159] Note the poet's use of the verb *yrd* in describing Kirta as moving from a consecrated sphere to a profane one. This certainly makes the idea of "coming down" a *leitmotif* in the theophany section of the type-scene: 'Ilu comes down (*yrd*) to Kirta and commands him to "bring down" (*šrd*) Ba'lu. Then Kirta comes down (*yrd*) to carry out 'Ilu's command. Moreover, if Renfroe is correct in observing that Arabic root √nzl, from which many scholars derive Ugaritic *nzl* in line 16, has the basic meaning "to descend,"[160] we may not only find a subtle allusion to the *leitmotif* in that word but it may also corroborate that Kirta's sacrifice has the specific purpose of enlisting Ba'lu's help (*šrd b'l*) under 'Ilu's auspices.[161] In addition, considering that the verb *yrd* has been so far used in describing the divine appearance to humans, its use with Kirta as the subject may have the effect of portraying Kirta as endowed with a divine aura in his relationship to his people.[162]

As was already mentioned above, the motif of Kirta's elaborate rituals embedded in the motif of theophanic instruction compensates for

159 Spronk, "The Legend of Kirtu (KTU 1.14–16): A Study of the Structure and Its Consequences for Interpretation," 66.

160 Renfroe, *Arabic-Ugaritic Lexical Studies*, 137.

161 Ba'lu distinguishes himself from other gods in that he is always associated with 'Ilu to the extent that one may think that one's piety to Ba'lu is the same as one's piety to 'Ilu. In the Kirta story Ba'lu and 'Ilu are in the same side and 'Ilu takes an active role toward Kirta while Ba'lu takes an axiliary role in that relationship. This stands in contrast to the situation in the 'Aqhatu story where Ba'lu takes a more active role while 'Ilu is auxiliary. Even the role of 'Ilu is ambiguous. He gave permission to 'Anatu to kill 'Aqhatu.

162 Knopper argues that the institution of kingship traverses both divine and human spheres. In this regard the king represents humanity to the gods but at the same time he manifests divine attributes to his people. Cf. Gary N. Knopper, "Dissonance and Disaster in the Legend of Kirta," *JAOS* 114 (1994): 582.

its absence in the pre-epiphany section of the type-scene.[163] But the important question is what purpose such a configuration of component motifs might serve. To put it differently, why does ʾIlu command Kirta to go through elaborate rituals to enlist Baʿlu's help after theophany? Why would Kirta need extra divine assurances when ʾIlu is the one who masterminds the entire campaign plan? Is ʾIlu's theophany not enough for Kirta? I propose two tentative suggestions. First, the scene of Kirta going through elaborate rituals with the successful result of enlisting divine help has the effect of presenting Kirta as a priestly king. Gray argues that an important aspect of the priestly function of the king at Ugarit was that of conferring or restoring fertility.[164] When something like a drought occurs in the land, a priestly king is supposed to administer sacrifice to rectify the situation and be able to "bring down rain" (*šrd bʿl*) through rituals. This role of Kirta as a priestly king is intimated later in the second episode of the Kirta story, where Kirta's absence from the throne due to his illness coincides with a period of extended drought in the land (cf. KTU 1.16 III).[165] The invocation of Baʿlu's rain in the context of drought caused by Kirta's illness (cf. KTU 1.16 III:7–8) recalls Kirta's role of bringing down Baʿlu through rituals for the successful expedition to ʾUdumu. In the former Baʿlu is wanted for a fertile land, whereas in the latter Baʿlu is wanted for a fertile womb.[166]

[163] The motif of ritual preparation as described above strongly recalls an incubation rite. Of course, the motif is given not as preparatory for an incubational theophany but for a military expedition. But the embedding of the motif of ritual preparation in divine speech may serve to help the reader to recognize the poet's use of incubation as a literary device in the Kirta story.

[164] Gray, "Canaanite Kingship in Theory and Practice," 207.

[165] Knopper, "Dissonance and Disaster in the Legend of Kirta," 579.

[166] In this regard, the scene of Kirta's successful administration of elaborate rituals places the next segment of the motif of divine command in perspective. The destruction of the priestly king's family is no personal matter. Without Kirta and his heirs functioning properly as a priest-king, the equilibrium of the universe would be in danger and so would be the well-being of the city as a whole. The people in Kirta's kingdom have a lot at stake in Kirta's person. The full mobilization for a military campaign in quest of a wife for Kirta must be understood in this context. It cannot be a political satire, as Margalit would have us believe (Baruch Margalit, "The Legend of Keret," in *Handbook of Ugaritic Studies*, ed. Wilfred G. E. Watson and Nick Wyatt [Leiden: Brill, 1999], 219–33). The full mobilization of the people of Ḫubur for Kirta's quest foreshadows the general meeting of the gods summoned by ʾIlu for Kirta's illness in KTU 1.16 III. Just as the former is preceded by the successful role of Kirta as a priestly King, so is the latter preceded by Kirta's failed role as a priestly King, namely, an extended drought.

Second, 'Ilu's instructions for elaborate rituals for enlisting divine help seem to contain another allusion to the nature of Kirta's religiosity. After all, Kirta in the pre-epiphany section of the incubation does not go through any cultic procedures, as if he either did not know how to approach the gods for help or did not care much about proper cultic protocol. He shuts himself up by withdrawing into his private room instead of going to the temple to seek divine help.[167] 'Ilu's detailed instructions show the paradigmatic example of the cult for enlisting divine help, if not of an incubation ritual: three different types of rituals in three places of different degrees of sacrality. It is as if 'Ilu is giving Kirta an extra-curriculum lesson on the proper rituals to follow when invoking divine help. Ilu's methodical instructions, which seem designed to educate Kirta in cutlic matters, may subtly allude to Kirta's lack of diligence in matters of religion.

2.2.4.2 Logistics Preparation

KTU 1.14 II:28–31

Food Provision for Kirta's City

	ʿdb (28) akl . ⸢l⸣ qryt	Prepare food for the city,
(29)	ḥṭt . ⸢l⸣ bt . ḫbr	Wheat for Daughter Ḫubur.
(30)	yip . ⸢l⸣ḥm . d ḫmš	He must bake bread for the fifth,
(31)	mǵd[.]ṯdṯ . yrḫm	Fine foods for the sixth month.

Mobilization for Campaign

Army Provided and Dispatched

(32)	⸢ʿ⸣dn[.] ngb . w yṣi	A throng will be provisioned and go out,
(33)	ṣb⸢u⸣ . ṣbi . ngb	A mighty army will be provisioned,
(34)	w ⸢y⸣ṣi . ʿdn . mʿ	A mighty throng will go out.

Numerous Army Marching

(35)	ṣ⸢b⸣uk . ul . mad	Your army will be a numerous force,
(36)	ṯlṯ . mat . rbt	Three hundred myriads,
(37)	ḫpṯ . d bl . spr	Soldiers without number,

[167] Margalit seems to be going too far in his characterization of Kirta as "a pathetic king crying himself to sleep like a baby." Cf. Margalit, "The Legend of Keret," 221.

(38)	ṯnn . d bl . hg	Archers without count.
(39)	hlk . lalpm . ḫdd	They will go by thousands like storm-clouds,
(40)	w l rbt . km yr	By myriads like rain.

Full Military Draft

(41)	⸢a⸣ṯr . ṯn . ṯlṯ . hlk	After two, two will go,
(42)	aṯr . ṯlṯ . klhm	After three, all of them.
(43)	yḥd . bth . sgr	The only son must shut up his house,
(44)	⸢a⸣lmnt . škr (45) ⸢t⸣škr .	The widow must hire herself out.
	zbl . ʿršm (46) ⸢y⸣šu .	The invalid must take up his bed,
	ʿwr . mzl (47) ymzl .	The blind man must grope his way along.
	w yṣi . trḫ (48) ḥdṯ	The newly-wed must go out,
	ybʿr . l ṯn (49) ⸢a⸣ṯth	He must entrust his wife to someone else,
	lm . nkr (50) ⸢m⸣ddth .	To a stranger, his beloved.

General Remarks The segment on the logistical preparation for Kirta's campaign consists of one section describing food provision for Kirta's city (KTU 1.14 II:28–31) and another describing a full mobilization of human resources for Kirta's military campaign (KTU 1.14 II:32–50a). The latter is further divided into three sub-sections ("Army Provided and Dispatched," "Numerous Army Marching," and "Full Military Draft")[168] which are interlinked with one another by two key words: *ṣbu* "army" joins the first and second sub-sections, while *ṯlṯ* "three" links the second and the third sub-sections. A similar role is played by the word *ngb* "provided" (KTU 1.14 II: 32) at the juncture of the section of "Food Provision for Kirta's City" and that of "Mobilization for Campaign." The former section belies the expectation of a long military campaign, while the latter presupposes the seriousness of Kirta's military mission, whose outcome will determine the fate of everyone within the kingdom. Finally, in both sections, one can recognize the use of hyperbole and irony as dominant literary devices.

Food Provision for Kirta's City Immediately after coming down from the rooftops, Kirta is now commanded to prepare food and to bake bread for his city (qryt // bt ḫbr "daughter Ḫubur").[169] Since the

[168] Similar themes occur in a summary fashion in 1 Kings 20:27a: "And the people of Israel were mustered [military draft] and were provisioned [provision] and went against them [marching out]" (*ûbənê yiśrāēl hotpāqədû wəkolkəlû wayyēləkû liqrā'tām*).

[169] Although some scholars understand *qryt* and *bt ḫbr* as "granaries" on grounds of Akkadian cognates ([*bīt*] *qarītu* "storeroom, granary" and *bīt ḫubūri* "house of the beer vat," cf. CAD q:132–133; ḫ:220; Nick Wyatt, *Religious Texts from Ugarit*, 188,

part that remains behind is able to prepare their own food and bake their own bread, the *qryt* and *bt ḫbr* is most likely to refer to the part of Kirta's city that goes on campaign.[170] Otherwise, 'Ilu specific instruction "to bake" bread for the fifth/sixth month would not make much sense. Be that as it may, Kirta's city shall be sufficiently provisioned, which stands in contrast to the shortage of food in Pabil's city later in the story. Some scholars take the ordinals, *ḫmš* and *ṯdṯ* (lines 30–31),[171] as referring to particular months of the year, a barley-harvest month and a wheat-harvest month.[172] But the ordinals are better taken to refer to the fifth and sixth month since the departure of Kirta's army for expedition.[173] Having said that, the numbers should be regarded as a hyperbole, a literary device not only used in the immediately following section, but also throughout this incubation type-scene,[174] because in antiquity no expedition lasted six months. But it must be noted that the chronological indication in KTU 1.14 III:2–4 and 1.14 III:10–12 seems to belie the initial expectation about the length of Kirta's

footnote 55, 56; Caquot, Sznycer, and Herdner, *Mythes et légendes: introduction, traduction, commentaire*, 515, footnote x; Ginsberg, *The Legend of King Keret: A Canaanite Epic of the Bronze Age*, 15), *qryt* is better taken as a variant form of *qrt* as that in KTU 1.3 II:6–7a (*tḫtṣb bn qrytm* "she battles between the two towns") and *bt ḫbr* as a reference to Kirta's city-state as is attested to in KTU 1.15 IV:8 (*tr ḫbr [rb]t* / ḫbr tr[r]t "the bulls of Ḫubur the Great, of Ḫubur the Little") (Cf. Moor and Spronk, "Problematical Passages in the Legend of Kirtu [I]," 163; Badre, et al., "Notes ougaritiques," 107; Dietrich and Loretz, "Das Keret-Epos," 1222; J. C. L. Gibson, *Canaanite Myths and Legends.*, 84). The first element of *bt ḫbr* may be then explained either as "a house" or as "a daughter." Whichever one opts for, the phrase as a parallel to *qryt* seems to refer to the whole city-state, without its being limited to Kirta's palace in Ḫubur. The problem with the first option ("Bêtu-Ḫubur") as a place name is that a place name with that structure always needs the first element for it to function as such. For this reason Pardee considers the possibility of its being an unknown place name that may be different from Kirta's city Ḫubur, along with the other possibility of its being a circumstantial title for Kirta's city, "a house of union." But taking *bt* as a personification of a town or country (cf. *genitivus epexegeticus*, Wilhelm Gesenius, *Gesenius' Hebrew Grammar* [Oxford: Clarendon press, 1910] §128k) as in biblical Hebrew may solve the problem. Cf. *bat ṣiyyōn* "daughter Zion" in Isaiah 1:8, *bat 'ammî* "daughter (of) my people" in Isaiah 22:4, *bat 'edōm* "daughter Edom" in Lamentation 4:21, *bat miṣrāyim* "daughter Egypt" in Jeremaiah 46:24, etc. Cf. Koehler and Baumgartner, *The Hebrew and Aramaic Lexicon of the Old Testament s.v.* בת.

[170] Dennis Pardee (personal communication).

[171] Caquot takes *ḫmṯ* as a cardinal and *ṯdṯ* as an ordinal by saying "*Mais ne peut on admettre qu'un oridnal soit mis en parallèle avec un cardinal?*" Caquot, Sznycer, and Herdner, *Mythes et légendes: introduction, traduction, commentaire*, 516, footnote y.

[172] Cf. Gray, *The Krt Text in the Literature of Ras Shamra: A Social Myth of Ancient Canaan*, 32; J. C. L. Gibson, *Canaanite Myths and Legends.*, 84, note 8.

[173] Pardee, "The Kirta Epic," 334, footnote 20.

[174] Ibid.

campaign. Although the mention of the fifth and sixth months' bread anticipates a long period of campaign and reflects a fear of food shortage in case the campaign dragged on longer,[175] the expedition comes to an end in a much shorter time than anticipated and thus the fear of food shortage does not materialize except in two different contexts later in the story. First, Kirta's extended siege causes food shortage in the city of 'Udumu, which is symbolically indicated in the text by the hungry cries of plowing oxen and hunting dogs, bringers of the two staple diet for humans (bread and meat). In this regard, Kirta's city, which is well provisioned, stands in contrast to Pabil's city which suffers from food shortage during the campaign. Second, an extended period of drought caused by Kirta's illness and the consequent absence from royal throne creates food shortage in the land (cf. *kly lhm bm'dnhm / kly yn . bḥmthm* "the food has run out from its storage / the wine has run out from its skins" in KTU 1.16 III:13–16).[176]

Mobilization for Campaign After preparing his city for an extended period of a foreign campaign, Kirta is to call up an army of a size that befits the importance of the mission. Neither Kirta nor his people can afford to fail in this mission. The outcome of the campaign not only determines the fate of Kirta's dynasty but also affects every family living under his reign. This has to do with Kirta in his capacity as a priestly king who is described in the preceding scene of ritual preparation as capable of summoning Ba'lu through sacrificial rituals. Not surprisingly, therefore, Kirta's military campaign, which interests and involves everyone in the city, needs an army of an impressive size in order not to fail in its mission.

The description of the size of Kirta's army begins in line 35, but the poet prefaces it with a tricolon (KTU 1.14 III:32–34) that describes the process of a group of city-dwellers turning into a mighty expeditionary force. In this verse, the two verbs in the first colon (*ngb* and *yṣi*) recur in the second and the third cola respectively in a reversed order, while the subject of the two verbs in the first colon (*'dn*) is augmented in terms of both form and meaning in the second and third cola (cf. *ṣbu ṣbi* and *'dn m'*). In KTU 1.14 III:32, 'Ilu commands "a community of

[175] It may even create the anticipation in the reader's mind that Kirta's mission is not an easy one, thus providing a good justification for a full conscription of human resources in the immediately following section.

[176] This motif may be dimly reflected in the scene where the animals suffer from hunger in the city of Udumu as a result of the passive siege by Kirta's army.

settlers" (*ʿdn*) to be provisioned/armed (*ngb*)[177] and to go out (*yṣi*) for Kirta's campaign. Ugaritic *ʿdn* has often been explained on grounds of Arabic *ʿadānat* "a company of men."[178] Renfroe, however, argues that Arabic *ʿadānat*, whose root √ ʿdn has the connotation of stationariness, is "ill-suited to the description of some sort of expeditionary force" which Ugaritic *ʿdn* seems to allude to.[179] Although Renfroe is correct in seeing the nuance of settlement in the word *ʿadānah*, he fails to discern, in my view, the poet's literary intention in using the word with that nuance in the verse under discussion: the poet shows us the process by which a community of settlers (*ʿdn*) turns into a mighty expeditionary force (*ṣbu ṣbi*).[180] The phrase *ʿdn mʿ* in the third colon (line 34) should be understood in a similar vein. Ugaritic *mʿ* is best taken as a substantive deriving from Semitic root √mʿʿ "be strong/great/many"[181] that modifies the word *ʿdn*. To put it differently, the *ʿdn* that is provisioned/armed (*ngb*) and dispatched (*yṣi*) in the first colon is nothing less than "a mighty army provisioned/armed" (*ṣbu*

[177] Ugaritic *ngb* in KTU 1.14 II:32–33 has often been interpreted as "provisioned" on the basis of the usage of Mari Akkadian *nagāpu* in a Mari letter, *ṣābušu ṣidītam na-ig-ib* "His [Hammurapi's] army are provided with travel provisions" (cf. *Chicago Assyrian Dictionary*, s.v. *nagāpu*). But in this Mari text, as Fensham argues, "the idea of "provisions" does not form part of the meaning of *nagābu*, but is represented by *ṣidītum* in the text. This is borne out by an Akkadian text of Boghazkeui cited by Herdner. There *nagābu* denotes "to provide" and every time in Akkadian texts it is used in connection with an army, exactly like our text under discussion (F. C. Fensham, "Remarks on Keret 79[b]–89 [CTA 14:2 79[b]–89]," *JNSL* 7 [1980]: 23). So strictly speaking, Ugaritic *ngb* may not be necessarily limited to the idea of provisioning the army, either. The previous verses about food provision, however, make it plausible to see the idea of provisioning in Ugaritic *ngb* that predicate Kirta's army. In this sense, *ngb* may be said to serve as a semantic link between the section of food provision for the city and the section of military conscription. But it should not be forgotten that Ugaritic *ngb* may also mean "to provide" an army in any other way, for instance, with weapons.

[178] Edward W. Lane, *An Arabic—English Lexicon* (Beirut: Librairie du Liban, 1968), 1976.

[179] The principal manifestations of the Arabic root √ʿdn—for instance, *ʿadān* "a dwelling place," *maʿdān* "a place of origin", *maʿādinu* "sources, or origins"—have to do with "remaining, staying, dwelling, abiding in a place." Renfroe takes *ʿadānat* to refer to a group of men in the sense of settlement, the community of men. Fred Renfroe, "The Transition from 'Army' to 'Enemy'," *UF* 19 (1987): 232.

[180] From this perspective, one may even suggest that the verb *yṣi*, which is used twice with *ʿdn* as the only subject (in the first and second cola), has an illocutionary sense. In other words, the jussive verb *yṣi* "let them [*ʿdn*] go out" uttered by ʾIlu himself not only commands and describes the marching out of an army, but indeed turns a group of city-*settlers* [*ʿdn*] into a *expeditionary* force [*ṣbu*].

[181] Joseph Tropper, *Ugaritische Grammatik*, 813.

ṣbi ngb) in the second colon and "a mighty expeditionary force" (*wyṣi ʿdn mʿ*) in the third colon. All this may be linked to the scene in KTU 1.14 II:43–50 where even those who normally *stay* in town in time of a war are *mobilized* for this important mission of acquiring a wife for Kirta.

The next sub-section, consisting of three poetic verses in KTU 1.14 II:35–36, 37–38 and 39–40, focuses on the size of Kirta's expeditionary force, the size required by the importance of the mission that Kirta's army undertakes. This sub-section is connected to the previous sub-section by the key word *ṣbu* that thematically defined the previous section and is picked up at the beginning of this section (cf. *ṣbuk ul mad* "Your army shall become a numerous force" in line 35). Although the exact nuance of some military categories such as *ḫpṯ* and *ṯnn* remains uncertain,[182] the overall theme of this sub-section is clear: Kirta's army, provisioned/armed and dispatched, has now become a numerous force (*ul mad*). The number of soldiers will amount to "three hundred myriads" (*ṯlṯ mat rbt*).[183] The *ḫbṯ*-soldiers and *ṯnn*-soldiers will be too

[182] Scholarly consensus has it that *ḫpṯ* and *ṯnn* denote two different military categories in the passage under discussion (Pardee, "The Kirta Epic," 334, footnote 22; Caquot, Sznycer, and Herdner, *Mythes et légendes: introduction, traduction, commentaire*, 517, footnote b; Dietrich and Loretz, "Das Keret-Epos," 1222–23; Gregorio del Olmo Lete, "Notes on Ugaritic Semantics I," *UF* 7 [1975]: 100–101). But their exact nuance is only a matter of educated guess on the basis of their suggested etymologies. There is little Ugaritic data that may shed light on this issue. Both *ḫpṯ* and *ṯnn* occur in KTU 1.103 along with still another term of military category, *ḫrd*. As far as *ḫpṯ* is concerned, Hebrew (*ḥopšî*), Amarna Akkadian (*ḫubšu*), and Egyptian cognates (*ḫpšy*) are proposed. Although a number of scholars translate it as "mercenaries" (Nick Wyatt, *Religious Texts from Ugarit*, 190; William A. Ward, "Two Unrecognized Ḫupšu-Mercenaries in Egyptian Texts," *UF* 12 [1980]: 441–42; Gray, *The Krt Text in the Literature of Ras Shamra: A Social Myth of Ancient Canaan*, 40; Gray, *The Legacy of Canaan: The Ras Shamra Texts and Their Relevance to the Old Testament.*, 138, 235), Pardee takes the rendering "mercenaries" as not doing justice to Ugaritic *ḫpṯ*. According to Pardee, it is a subservient class (or a non-permanent category) that consists of not fully free men who sell their services (personal communication). The etymology of Ugaritic *ṯnn* is uncertain too. Suggested proposals include Akkadian *šanannu* whose meaning is not certain either ("archer(?)" cf. *Chicago Assyrian Dictionary*, š1:366), Egyptian *snn* "the second man" in a chariot (cf. Nick Wyatt, *Religious Texts from Ugarit*, 190, footnote 64), Ethiopic *snn* "sharpen, poke with a lance" (cf. Joseph Tropper, *Ugaritische Grammatik*, 110), and Hebrew *šinʾān* whose meaning is uncertain (cf. Olmo Lete, "Notes on Ugaritic Semantics I," 101).

[183] Some scholars take *ṯlṯ* here and in the list of wealth as a reference to a charioteer. Cf. Olmo Lete, "Notes on Ugaritic Semantics I," 100; Nick Wyatt, *Religious Texts from Ugarit*, 190, footnote 62. Dietrich and Loretz takes *ṯlṯ* here as "three" and *ṯlṯ* in the list of wealth as a charioteer (Dietrich and Loretz, "Das Keret-Epos," 1222, footnote 68; M. Vervenne, "Hebrew Šālîš—Ugaritic Ṯlṯ," *UF* 19 [1987]: 371–73).

numerous to be counted (*bl spr* and *bl hg*). They will march like storm-clouds by thousands (*b aplm*) and by myriads (*b rbt*). Interesting to note is that the idea of numerousness is expressed by the alternation of abstract nouns connoting numerousness and concrete numerals in a symmetric order: A (*ul mad*) B (*ṯlṯ mat rbt*) A′ (*bl spr//bl hg*) B′ (*alpm/rbt*). Some scholars translate *ṯlṯ* as "a charioteer." But such a translation not only breaks the symmetric pattern just mentioned but also makes the use of hyperbole less effective, because literary hyperbole generally works better with concrete concepts.[184] "Three million soldiers" makes a better hyperbole than "hundreds of myriads of charioteers," since no army of three million warriors ever marched the roads of the ancient Near East.[185] This sub-section ends with a bicolon verse comparing Kirta's army to *ḫḏḏ* "storm-clouds" and *yr* "early rain."[186] The marching out of countless soldiers is here likened to the figure of storm-clouds coming in from a distance. Albeit not many, there is at least one biblical passage that employs the figure of clouds to express a numerous army approaching in the distance (Jeremiah 4:13) and another passage that connects the image of clouds to the idea of countlessness (Job 38:37). But narratologically more important is the observation that the poet of *Kirta* uses here the rather unusual image of storm-clouds, when he knew and did use more common images for a numerous army, such as *irby* and *ḥsn*, later in KTU 1.14 II:50 and III:1. The poet's use of the storm images (*ḫdd* and *yr*), therefore, suggests that they may function as a clue to the role of Ba'lu in Kirta's expedition to 'Udumu and the acquisition of Ḥurray who will produce

[184] Wilfred G. E. Watson, "An Unrecognized Hyperbole in Krt," *Or* 48 (1979): 117.

[185] This is also true of the use of "the fifth month" and "the sixth month" as a hyperbolic way of expressing the long period of Kirta's expedition. Here, the force of hyperbole lies in the common knowledge that no expedition could possibly last six months in antiquity. J. C. de Moor, *An Anthology of Religious Texts from Ugarit*, 195, footnote 21. Vervenne ("Hebrew Šālîš—Ugaritic Ṯlṯ," 373) argues in a similar vein that the lexeme *ṯlṯ* in the expression *ṯlṯ mat rbt* is a numeral, which functions in an over exaggerated description of the numerical strength of Keret's army.

[186] The ellipsis of preposition *k* before *ḫdd* in line 39 is not problematic: cf. KTU 1.19 I:13–14 *k ap‘ il bgdrt / klb lḫṯh imḫṣh* "Like a vicious viper in a wall / (like) a dog on its stake did I smite him."; KTU 1.6 II:22–23, *‘dbnn ank imr bpy / k lli bṯbrn qny ḫtu hw* "I took him (as I would) a lamb in my mouth / he was destroyed as a kid (would be) in my crushing" (Caquot, Sznycer, and Herdner, *Mythes et légendes: introduction, traduction, commentaire*, 517, footnote c; Cynthia L. Miller, "Patterns of Verbal Ellipsis in Ugaritic Poetry," *UF* 31 [1999]: 354).

offsprings for Kirta.[187] The role of Baal in this type-scene will become manifest again later when Baʿlu makes a petition to ʾIlu to bless Kirta's marriage.[188] If the presence of Baʿlu brings success to Kirta's campaign and Kirta's marriage in the first episode of the Kirta story [fertility of the womb], the absence of Baʿlu in the second episode coincides with Kirta's ill-health that leads to the failure of nature [fertility of the land] (cf. KTU 1.16 III) and to disorder in the life of the community (cf. Yaṣṣubu's accusations in KTU 1.16 VI:29ff.).

The last sub-section in the "Mobilization for Campaign" (KTU 1.14 II: 41–50) concerns full military draft. The first verse in this sub-section (lines 41–42) serves as a hinge in that it picks up the word "three" (*ṯlṯ*) from the previous sub-section about the size of Kirta's army and anticipates the following seven poetic cola describing full military draft. The word *aṯr* has been variously interpreted.[189] Although

---

[187] As we have already mentioned, the scene of ritual preparation for expedition entails the "bringing down" of Baʿlu through Kirta's sacrifice. This begs the question as to the role of the "son of Dagan" in the subsequent expedition and if there is any hint of that role in the extant text, that would be *ḫdd* and *yr*. If KTU 1.14 II:39–40 describe Kirta's vast army as being accompanied by Baʿlu, this recalls the manner in which Marduk accompanied Cyrus' army on its way to Babylon. According to the Cyrus Cylinder, Marduk orders Cyrus to march to the city of Babylon. Marduk is described to have accompanied Cyrus's army "like a companion and friend," and Cyrus's vast army, "whose number, like the water of the river, cannot be known," is described as going by Marduk's side. Cf. Mordechai Cogan, "Achaemenid Inscriptions: Cyrus Cylinder," in *Monumental Inscriptions from the Biblical World*, vol. II of *COS*, William W. Hallo (Leiden: Brill, 2000), 314–15.

[188] Kirta's expeditionary force escorted by Baʿlu distinguishes itself from, for instance, the Israelite army of conquest under the auspices of Yahweh in that the goal of Kirta's expedition is apparently to acquire love, to put it differently, the fertile mother who will make Kirta's family flourish once more. In this regard *Kirta* bears a resemblance to the Homeric motif of "a face launching a thousand ships." There is no such thing in the Hebrew Bible. The only candidate for such a motif is the story of Samson, but many scholars see that story as originating among the Philistine people whose origin is widely considered to be from the Greek world (cf. Kugel, *How to Read the Bible: A Guide to Scripture, Then and Now*, 400–401).

[189] Its suggested interpretations include a geographical designation ("Asher" in Virolleaud, *La légende phénicienne de Keret, roi de Sidoniens*, 76), the verb "to go" (Nick Wyatt, *Religious Texts from Ugarit*, 191, footnote 67), the adverb "afterwards" (Jirku, *Kanaanäische Mythen und Epen aus Ras Schamra-Ugarit*, 88), "one another" (Dietrich and Loretz, "Das Keret-Epos," 1223), a preposition "after" (Caquot, Sznycer, and Herdner, *Mythes et légendes: introduction, traduction, commentaire*, 518, footnote d; Harold L. Ginsberg, "The Tale of Aqhat," in *ANET* [Princeton, NJ: Princeton University Press, 1969], 143; Joseph Tropper, *Ugaritische Grammatik*, 770–71; Aistleitner, *Die mythologischen und kultischen Texte aus Ras Schamra*, 91; Pardee, "The Kirta Epic," 334; Greenstein, "Kirta," 15; J. C. L. Gibson, *Canaanite Myths and Legends.*, 84; Gray, *The Krt Text in the Literature of Ras Shamra: A Social Myth of Ancient Canaan*, 35; J. C. de Moor, *An Anthology of Religious Texts from Ugarit*, 195), a relative adverb

most recent translators take *aṯr* as a preposition "after," the sense of the hinge verse "after two, two will go / after three, all of them" is not immediately clear. Is this indicative of some kind of military march formation, as Wyatt suggests that the infantry marches in twos and the chariots ride in threes?[190] Probably not, since the use of *klhm* "all of them" in place of "three" in line 42 and the subsequent context of full military draft seem to militate against such an interpretation. The numbers two and three are better taken as a poetic device (x // x+1 formula) for creating a sense of completeness and thus giving expression to the thought that everyone should join Kirta's military expedition. The reason why the numbers two and three were used in the "x // x+1" formula may be found in the literary significance of the number three in the development of the Kirta story.[191] The number three appears at many important junctures of the narrative. For instance, it is on the third day after two days of journey that Kirta stops at Sidon and Tyre to make a vow to 'Aṯiratu; King Pabil offers Kirta, among other things, three horses as a peace gift; for three months Kirta falls sick; and it is on the third day after Kirta's miraculous cure that his impudent son Yaṣṣubu, ignorant of what has happened, comes forward to claim the throne.[192] In sum, the word *klhm* along with a poetic device "x // x+1" serves to underscore the idea of full conscription, an idea that is fleshed out in the subsequent seven cola in a hyperbolic way.

The idea of full military draft is fleshed out in a hyperbolic style in KTU 1.14 II: 43–50a, which may be divided into three poetic verses, namely, a bicolon in lines 43–45a, another bicolon in lines 45b–47a, and a tricolon in lines 47b–50a. The first and second verses seem to have more in common than with the third verse. Besides, being bicolonic, both of them deal with two entities: the first verse concerns

"where" (H. Sauren and G. Kestemont, "Keret, Roi de Ḫubur," *UF* 3 [1971]: 197). See also the discussion in F. C. Fensham, "Note on Keret in CTA 14:90–103a," *JNSL* 8 [1981]: 41).

[190] Nick Wyatt, *Religious Texts from Ugarit*, 191, footnote 68. Also see Joseph Tropper who also sees "two" and "three" as a reference to military formation (*Ugaritische Grammatik*, 771).

[191] The use of "three" that is in an immediate relation with the one under discussion is found in the phrase referring to the size of Kirta's army, *ṯlṯ mat rbt* "three hundred myriads." Pardee explains the use of "three" in this phrase by virtue of its being the first of the plural numbers used for underscoring the vast number. Pardee, "The Kirta Epic," 334, footnote 21.

[192] Theodor H. Gaster, *The Oldest Stories in the World* (Boston: Beacon Press, 1959), 203–4.

people socio-economically unfit to serve in military duty, the second one deals with people physically incapable of discharging the duty. Moreover, the second cola of the first and second verses has the same syntactical construction: subject + a cognate complement + a verb. The third verse stands out not only by its tricolonic form dealing with only one entity, i.e. a newly-married man, but also by its verb-initial syntax, as opposed to the verb-final syntax characteristic of the first and second verses. This seems to call special attention to this verse which, in my view, provides a clue to the *double entendre* that the poet has crafted into this subsection. On a surface level, KTU 1.14 II:43–50a enumerates the kinds of people who were normally exempted from military duty or not even considered for it. But at a deeper or narratological level, it may allude to the person of Kirta in different stages of the narrative.

The tricolon in lines 47b–50a, reminiscent of Deuteronomy 20:7,[193] seems to say at a surface level that even the newly-wed (*trḫ ḥdṯ*)[194] who were usually exempted from military duty should "go out" (*yṣi*) as part of Kirta's expeditionary force. The military nuance of *yṣi* in line 47 cannot be missed here because of its use in the preceding section, i.e., lines 32–34: *ʿdn . ngb . w yṣi*...*w yṣi ʿdn mʿ* "A throng will be provisioned and go out...a mighty throng will go out." The force of hyperbole that informs the tricolon verse in question lies in the fact that ʾIlu seems to command a "preemptive" measure that would prevent the hypothetical situation assumed in Deuteronomy 20:7 from happening. ʾIlu seems to command a young bridegroom to divorce his wife, albeit temporarily, so that he may fight to the death without worring about his bride being taken by another man: "he should abandon his wife to

[193] *ûmî-hāʾîš ʾăšer-ʾēraš ʾiššâ wĕlōʾ lĕqāḥāh yēlēk wĕyāšōb lĕbêtô pen-yāmût bāmmilĕḥāmâ wĕʾîš ʾāḥēr yiqqāḥennâ* "And is there any man who has betrothed a wife and has not taken her? Let him go back to his house, lest he die in the battle and another man take her."

[194] Van Selms, followed by Caquot and Sznycer, argues that *trḫ ḥdṯ* should be translated as "the husband of the new moon" rather than "a newlywed husband" on grounds that "the meaning "new" for *ḥdṯ* has not so far been found in Ugaritic (van Selms, *Marriage & Family Life in Ugaritic Literature*, 45; Caquot, Sznycer, and Herdner, *Mythes et légendes: introduction, traduction, commentaire*, 518, footnote g). But the meaning "new" is attested for *ḥdṯ* (Olmo Lete and Sanmartín, *A Dictionary of the Ugaritic Language in the Alphabetic Tradition*, s.v. ḥdṯ(I)). Besides it, Deuteronomy 24:5 which deals with a military exemption of a newlywed husband includes the expression *iššāh ḥădāšāh* "a newlywed wife." These two data seem to support the translation "the newly wed."

someone else, his beloved to a stranger" (*yb'r l ṯn aṯth lm nkr mddth*).[195] At a deeper level of meaning, however, *trḫ ḥdṯ* "the newly-married" may refer to Kirta himself.[196] The word *trḫ* "to marry, pay the bride price" is a key term that may summarize the first episode of *Kirta*. It is used with regard to Kirta's previous marriage in KTU 1.14 I:14 (*aṯt trḫ w tb't* "He married a woman but she left"), while his first wife is called *mtrḫt* "the girl for whom the bride price is paid" in KTU 1.14 I:13.[197] Moreover, the successful campaign will get Kirta a new wife (cf. *aṯth* in line 49 and *mddth* in line 50), thus turning him into a new bridegroom (*trḫ ḥdṯ* in lines 47–48).[198] Van Selms argues that Kirta's

[195] On the basis of § 45 of Tablet A of the Middle Assyrian Laws, Finkel surmises that the text does not imply a final dissolution of the marriage-tie. He argues that "the bridegroom simply cedes his marital rights to another individual, but only temporarily." Nonetheless, Finkel takes a young bridegroom's act of leaving his wife to another man as a de-facto divorce (Joshua Finkel, "The Expedition of the Ugaritan King Keret in the Light of Jewish and Kindred Traditions," *PAAJR* 23 [1954]: 21–22). Wyatt's interpretation of *ṯn* and *nkr* as a reference to Pabil, which is based on the assumption that there would have been no male to take care of the bride as a result of full conscription, is a result of the misunderstanding of the poetic composition of lines 43–50a (Nick Wyatt, *Religious Texts from Ugarit*, 197, footnote 75).

[196] Gray has taken what I would consider as the "deeper" meaning as the surface meaning of the verse and translated it as follows: "Then let the bride-groom bring forth the bride-price, / Burning to claim his wife, / Yea, to acquire his beloved" (Gray, *The Krt Text in the Literature of Ras Shamra: A Social Myth of Ancient Canaan*, 9). According to Gray, this verse does not continue the theme of full conscription but starts a new subject, that is, the purpose of Kirta's expedition. But Gray's translation is based on an idiosyncratic, if not wrong, meaning of *ṯny* "to claim" and *nkr* "to acquire" (Ibid., 36–37). Besides, the change of *yṣi* to *ybl* in the parallel verse (KTU 1.14 IV:26) does not necessarily support Gray's translation. Scholars have had different takes on *ybl*. Pardee, for instance, takes it as an active verb, translating it as "[the newlywed] conducted (his bride)" (Pardee, "The Kirta Epic," 335). Caquot, Sznycer and Gibson take *ybl* as a passive, translating it along the line of "the newlywed was led away" (Caquot, Sznycer, and Herdner, *Mythes et légendes: introduction, traduction, commentaire*, 528; J. C. L. Gibson, *Canaanite Myths and Legends.*, 87). Scholars like Ginsberg simply consider it a scribal error (Ginsberg, *The Legend of King Keret: A Canaanite Epic of the Bronze Age*, 40). In my view, although Gray's translation is wrong, his insight that the verse may concern Kirta himself may be retained (cf. Fensham, "Note on Keret in CTA 14:90–103a," 46–47). The *double entendre* of this verse should be sought in literary and narratological terms.

[197] van Selms, *Marriage & Family Life in Ugaritic Literature*, 29.

[198] If Ugaritic *trḫ* retains the nuance of "paying the bridal price," the repetition of a list of wealth may be understood as a bride-price that Kirta would have paid to Pabil. The extant tablets do not preserve a section where Kirta paid a bride-price. If he did not pay a bride-price, the list of wealth that he was entitled to by virtue of conquest would have replaced the bridal price. This would add to the significance of the word *trḫ* in the first episode of the Kirta story.

rejection of Pabil's gift amounts to paying the bride price for Ḥurray, making Kirta deserve to be called *trḫ*.

> To the offer of tribute Krt replies by asking for the hand of the king's daughter. This means that he will have the lady Ḥry instead of the tribute offered by her father. In this way, however, he may be said to pay a *mōhar*; the tribute which Pbl pays to him is rendered immediately by Krt to Pbl as a compensation gift for getting his daughter as a wife. In a sense Krt may therefore be considered *trḫ* in the full sense of the word: he has paid the sum required by giving up the claim to tribute.[199]

The *double-entendre* of the tricolon verse in question reveals the irony which has something to do with the fact that the ultimate reason for the exemption of a newly-wed from military duty was to give him opportunity to build his family by siring offspring.[200] The irony is that all the newly-weds in Kirta's kingdom were ordered to "abandon their wives" and to risk "the destruction of their own family" in order to help Kirta "to acquire a new wife" and "to rebuild his own family."[201]

The Ugaritic word *yḥd* in line 43 is cognate to Hebrew *yāḥîd*. Although the latter is usually applied to a child (Genesis 22:2, 12, 16 and Judges 11:34), it may refer to a grown-up (cf. Psalm 22:21; 35:17). Most germane to the interpretation of Ugaritic *yḥd* in line 43 is Psalm 68:6–7, in which the person designated as *yāḥîd* occurs in parallel with people with special needs, such as orphans (*yətômîm*) and widows (*almānôt*). The special need of the *yāḥîd* is said to be met by having a "family" (literally "house" *bayt*). This seems to indicate that Ugaritic *yḥd* may denote a man who has neither brothers nor wives nor children in his house. Furthermore the substitutive use of Ugaritic *aḥd* in the parallel colon (KTU 1.14 IV:21) corroborates this conclusion. It is in these terms that the act of "shutting up his house" (*bth sgr*) should be understood: there is no one else to run his house if he joins the army. This man would normally have been exempted from military duty, but Kirta is ordered to recruit even *yḥd* "a solitary man." This is the surface meaning communicated in a hyperbolic style. The deeper meaning, however, lies in the similarity of this solitary man to Kirta himself. Kirta himself is a solitary man. He is left without brothers,

---

199 van Selms, *Marriage & Family Life in Ugaritic Literature*, 31–32.

200 Ibid., 45.

201 Finkel calls what I would call "irony" here "sarcasm" (Finkel, "The Expedition of the Ugaritan King Keret in the Light of Jewish and Kindred Traditions," 22).

child-bearing wives, and children (cf. the motif of Kirta's predicament). The hyperbole in the surface meaning turns into irony at the deeper level of meaning: To ask a solitary man to shut up his house to join the army certainly goes beyond the ordinary protocol concerning military draft in antiquity, but precisely because Kirta is a solitary man (*yḥd*), he should shut up his house and go on an expedition in quest of a wife.

A more subtle example of *double entendre* may be found in line *zbl ʿršm yšu* "Let the invalid take up his bed." Although the exact nature of illness is not specified in the verse, it may be assumed that the sick person in question would have been considered too much a distraction, let alone a help, to be conscripted for war. The surface sense of this line is that even a very sick person should participate in Kirta's expeditionary force. And this is being said not as a satire of ancient ideology of kingship (contra Margalit),[202] but rather as a serious engagement with it: the role of a king is so crucial that the fate of everyone in his city depends on the success of Kirta's mission to acquire a child-bearing wife.[203] At a deeper level, however, this verse may point us to the bedridden Kirta in the second episode of the story. It is noteworthy in this regard that Yaṣṣubu, Kirta's eldest son, describes the sick Kirta in terms recalling the poetic cola under discussion: *km aḫt ʿrš mdw / anšt ʿrš zbln* "Illness has become (your) bedfellow / sickness (your) companion in bed" (KTU 1.16 VI: 35–36).

2.2.4.3 The Military Expedition

KTU 1.14 II:50b–III:49

The Seven-Day Journey to 'Udumu

	k irby (51) ⸢t⸣škn . šd	Like locusts they will settle on the field,
(1)	⸢k⸣m . ḫsn . pat . mdbr	Like grasshoppers the edges of the steppe.
(2)	l⸢k⸣ . ym . w t̲n	Go a day, a second,
	t̲lt̲ . rbʿ ym	A third, a fourth day,
(3)	⸢ḫm⸣š . t̲dt̲ . ym .	A fifth, a sixth day.
	mk . špšm (4) ⸢b⸣šbʿ .	Then at sunset on the seventh day,

[202] Margalit, "The Legend of Keret," 203–33.

[203] N. Wyatt, *Word of Tree and Whisper of Stone: And Other Papers on Ugaritic Thought* (Piscataway, NJ: Gorgias Press, 2007), 184.

	wtmǵy . ludm (5) rbt! .	You will arrive at ’Udumu the Great,
	wludm. ṯrrt	At ’Udumu the Small.[204]

Attacking Daughter Towns

(6)	wgr . nn. ‘rm .	Now attack the cities,
	šrn (7) pdrm .	Advance against the towns.
	s‘t[205] . bšdm 8) ḥṭbt! .	The women gathering wood will flee from the field,
	bgrnt . ḥpšt	From the threshing-floor the women gathering straw.
9)	s‘t . bn<p>k . šibt .	The women drawing water will flee from the spring,
	b⸢m⸣qr 10) mmlat .	From the fountain the women filling (jugs).

Seven-Day Siege of ’Udumu

	dm . ym . wṯn	Remain quiet, a day, a second,
	11) ṯlṯ . rb‘ . ym .	A third, a fourth day,
	ḫ!mš 12) ṯdṯ . ym	A fifth, a sixth day.
	ḥẓk . al . tš‘l (13) qrth .	Do not shoot your arrows at the city,
	abn . ydk 14) mšdpt	Your slingstones at the citadel.[206]

[204] There have been at least three translations proposed for this word: “powerful” (cf. Ginsberg, *The Legend of King Keret: A Canaanite Epic of the Bronze Age*, 38; Jonas C. Greenfield, “The Epithets RBT//ṮRRT in the Krt Epic,” in *Perspectives on Language and Text: Essays and Poems in Honor of Francis I. Andersen’s Sixtieth Birthday*, E. Conrad and Newing E. [35–37: Eisenbrauns, 1987], 35–37) “well-watered” (cf. Caquot, Sznycer, and Herdner, *Mythes et légendes: introduction, traduction, commentaire*, 519; Pardee, “The Kirta Epic,” 334) and “small.” I prefer to “small,” because it seems to best fit the following description of Kirta’s two-stage attack on Udum, which, as is typical of a Middle and Late Bronze city-state, consists of a capital city and daughter cities that surrounds it. For this translation, see Moor and Spronk, “Problematical Passages in the Legend of Kirtu (I),” 166; J. C. de Moor, *An Anthology of Religious Texts from Ugarit*, 196, footnote 28; S. J. Dahood, “J. C. L. Gibson, *Canaanite Myths and Legends*. Originally Edited by G. R. Driver in 1956. Edinburgh 1978. T. & T. Clark,” *Bib* 62 (1981): 277.

[205] Three verbs, *gr*, *šrn*, and *s‘t* appear in the self-same form later in the motif of fulfillment. As far as the verbs *gr* and *šrn* are concerned, I follow Pardee in taking them in the current context as imperatives, while their repetitions later in the motif of fulfillment as “narrative” infinivive (Pardee, “Review,” 133). The verb *s‘t*, however, can be explained either as a verbal noun that functions as an imperative or as a 3rd femine singular G perfective verb. I assume that the verb is derived from the the Arabic root √s‘y “to flee.” Cf. Joseph Tropper, *Ugaritische Grammatik*, 488.

[206] My translation is based on the assumption that Ugaritic *mšdpt* forms a parallel to *qrth*. For the Arabic etymology suggested for *mšdpt* see Nick Wyatt, *Religious Texts from Ugarit*, 194, footnote 86; J. C. L. Gibson, *Canaanite Myths and Legends.*, 85; cf.

	whn . špšm 15) bšbʿ .	Then at sunset on the seventh day,
	wl . yšn . pbl 16) mlk	Pabil the king will not (be able to) sleep.
	lqr . ṯigt . ibrh	For the sound of the roaring of his bulls,
	17) lql . nhqt . ḥmrh	For the noise of the braying of his donkeys,
	18) lgʿt . alp . ḥrṯ .	For the lowing of his plough-oxen,
	zǵt 19) klb . ṣpr .	For the howling of his hunting dogs.

Negotiation

	wylak 20) mlakm . lk .	Then he will send messengers to you,
	ʿm . krt 21) mswnh	To Kirta at his night-quarters:[207]
	tḥm . pbl . mlk	Message of Pabil the king:
22)	qḥ . ksp .	Take silver,
	wyrq . ḫrṣ	And yellow gold,
23)	yd . mqmh .	Along with its place;
	wʿbd . ʿlm	A perpetual servant,
24)	ṯlṯ . sswm .	Three horses,
	mrkbt 25) btrbṣ	A chariot in a courtyard,
	bn . amt	The son of a handmaid.
26)	qḥ . krt . šlmm 27) šlmm	Take, Kirta, many gifts of peace,
	wng . mlk 28) lbty .	Leave, king, my house,
	rḥq . krt (29) l ḥẓry .	Go away, Kirta, from my court.
	al . tṣr (30) udm . rbt .	Do not besiege ʾUdumu the Great,
	w udm ṯrrt	And ʾUdumu the Small.
(31)	udm . ytnt! . il .	ʾUdumu is the gift of ʾIlu,
	w ušn (32) ab . adm .	And a present of the father of mankind.
	wṯṯb 33) mlakm . lh .	Then, send the messengers back to him:
	lm . ank 34) ksp .	What need have I of silver,
	wyrq . ḫrṣ	And of yellow gold,
35)	yd . mqmh	Along with its place;
	wʿbd 36) ʿlm	Of a perpetual servant,
	ṯlṯ . sswm .	Of three horses,

Pardee, "The Kirta Epic," 335; Gray, *The Krt Text in the Literature of Ras Shamra: A Social Myth of Ancient Canaan*, 9. Other scholars analyze *mšdpt* as a Š-stem feminine participle of the verb *ndp* "to hurl." It can either be passive or active. If it is passive, *mšdpt* would qualify *abn*, which results in the translation "stones thrown from your hand" (cf. Olmo Lete and Sanmartín, *A Dictionary of the Ugaritic Language in the Alphabetic Tradition*, 621). If it is active, *mšdpt* would qualify *yd*, which yields the translation "stones of your throwing-hand" (cf. J. C. de Moor, *An Anthology of Religious Texts from Ugarit*, 197; Joseph Tropper, *Ugaritische Grammatik*, 477).

[207] The meaning "night-quarters" was first suggested by de Moor and Spronk on the basis of Arabic *mumsīn* "night-quarters" (Moor and Spronk, "Problematical Passages in the Legend of Kirtu [I]," 168). Their proposal has been accepted by Tropper, Greenstein, Dietrich and Loretz (Joseph Tropper, *Ugaritische Grammatik*, 191; Greenstein, "Kirta," 16; Dietrich and Loretz, "Das Keret-Epos," 1225).

	mrkbt 37) btrbṣt .	Of a chariot in a courtyard,
	bn .amt	Of the son of a handmaid?
38)	p d . in . bbty . ttn	Rather, you must give what my house lacks,
39)	tn . ly . mṯt . ḥry	Give me maid Ḥurray,
40)	nʿmt . špḥ . bkrk	The fair one, your first born offspring.
41)	⸢d⸣k . nʿm . ʿnt . nʿmh	Whose fairness is like ʿAnatu's fairness,
42)	km . tsm . ʿṯtrt . ts⸢mh⸣	Whose beauty is like ʿAṯtartu's beauty.
43)	dʿqh . ib . iqni .	Whose eyes are lapis-lazuli,
	ʿp[ʿp]⸢h⸣ 44) sp . ṯrml	Whose pupils are alabaster bowls,
	tḥgrn . [s]⸢d⸣m[208]	That are girded with eye-shadow.
45)	ašlw . bṣp . ʿnh	That I might repose in the gaze of her eyes,
46)	dbḥlmy . il . yt⸢n⸣	Whom 'Ilu gave in my dream,
47)	bḏrty . ab . adm	In my dream, the father of mankind.
48)	wld . špḥ . lkrt	That she might bear offspring for Kirta,
49)	wǵlm . lʿbd . il	And a lad for the servant of 'Ilu.

The Seven-Day Journey to 'Udumu The change of location from Kirta's city of Ḫubur to the steppe-land (*šd* in KTU 1.14 II:51 and *mdbr* in 1.14 III:1) serves to indicate the beginning of a new segment in the motif of divine command. The parallel words *irby* and *ḥsn* make the transition smooth by taking up the idea of Kirta's vast army that figures prominently in the previous segment.[209] The armed forces of Kirta that have departed (*yṣi*) from the city of Ḫubur are now on their way (*tškn*) to the city of 'Udumu. If the verb *yṣi*, which encloses the section dealing with the "Mobilization for Campaign" (KTU 1.14 II:32–50a; cf. lines 32 and 47), denotes specifically the departure of Kirta's army from Ḫubur, the Ugaritic word that represents Kirta's journey to 'Udumu is *tškn*. Kirta's army on the road to 'Udumu is visualized by the image of a swarm of locusts descending on a field (*irby tškn šd*). The journey of Kirta's army to 'Udumu is couched in a seven-day formula, a literary device for a climax. Loewenstamm argues that seven-day formulae in the Kirta story represent "the last stage of evolvement of the numerical scheme in Ugaritic literature."[210] Although the traditional barebone structure is maintained (namely, the division of six days into three pairs with the seventh day standing alone), the

208 The restoration and the translation are Wyatt's (Nick Wyatt, *Religious Texts from Ugarit*, 197, footnote 103).

209 For "locusts" as the image for a multitude, see KTU 1.3 ii 10–11; Judges 6:5, 7:12; Joel 2:3–9; Nahum 3:15–17.

210 Loewenstamm, *Comparative Studies in Biblical and Ancient Oriental Literatures*, 200.

seven-day formula informing Kirta's journey to 'Udumu has many idiosyncrasies. Among other things, for instance, it lacks one of the definitive features of the seven-day formula, that is, the fourfold repetition of the six-day routine.[211] This idiosyncratic form of the seven-day unit may allude to a narrative function different from that of the more traditional form. If the traditional form of the seven-day unit, by virtue of its fourfold repetition of the routine, accumulates narratival tension to such a pitch that the event on the seventh day may be presented as a climactic or surprising conclusion of the routine repeated in the formula, a much truncated form of the seven-day formula employed in *Kirta* may reduce, if not completely eliminate, the climactic effect of the seventh-day event. What happens on the seventh day after six-days of "walking" (*lk*) is, to no one's surprise, the arrival of Kirta's army at 'Udumu. If a traditional form of the seven-day formula slows down the narration time through repetitions of a routine, a truncated form has the effect of telescoping a rather long event time into a short narration time. The seven-day journey to 'Udumu is presented only over the space of two poetic verses. It appears as if the poet wanted to hurry on to a "better" part of the story by skipping a "boring" part. Nonetheless, the fact that Kirta's journey to 'Udumu, during which nothing significant seems to happen, is couched in a seven-day sequence formula, a literary device that certainly demands attention, was certainly meaningful. As it turns out later, the most surprising turn of event in the story occurs during Kirta's journey to 'Udumu: Kirta's visit to a shrine for 'Aṯiratu. That visit would not have come across to the audience as so serious a breach of 'Ilu's command if Kirta's journey had not been couched in a seven-day sequence formula in the first place. The very unusual four-day sequence, which results from Kirta's stopover, throws Kirta's breach of faith into a sharp relief.

Attacking Daughter Cities The seven-day long march leads Kirta's army to 'Udumu the Great (*udm rbt*), 'Udumu the Small (*udm ṯrrt*). The strategy of Kirta's army appears similar to that of the Assyrian

---

[211] The imperative verb *lk* "to go" seems to describe the six-day routine. But no routine is repeated after each pair of days. Other idiosyncratic features include the omission of *hn* "Behold" that usually introduces the first pair of days, *ym wṯn*, and the substitution of *špšm bšb*ʿ for *bšb*ʿ *ymm* that introduces the seventh day's routine. Moreover, the word *mk* that usually introduces the seventh day in the sequence is replaced by *hn* (KTU 1.14 III:14) and *aḫr* (KTU 1.14 IV:32) in the seven-day formulae used in the Kirta story.

army, which is to terrorize the enemy into submission.[212] By attacking smaller cities and villages that present easy targets, the Assyrian army tried to convince the capital city to give in. If they did not yield, a siege was laid. The purpose of the attack by Kirta, however, was neither to acquire booty as a way of accumulating wealth nor to topple a sitting king to rule in his stead, but to receive the hand of the daughter of Pabil, the king of 'Udumu, who will bear him an heir.

The verbs *grnn* and *šrn* in KTU 1.14 III:6 are best taken as belonging to the semantic range of active siege, rather than of passive siege.[213] The object of this active siege attack is the daughter cities and towns (*udm ṯrrt*) that surround the capital city of Udum (*udm rbt*).[214] Although the word *ṯrrt* has been taken variously as "well-watered," "small," or "grand or powerful"[215] the rendering "small" seems to best fit the context where Kirta's attack is waged on two stages, active and passve sieges against two different parts of the city. 'Udumu seems to be one of the typical second millennium city-states that consist of a capital city (*udm rbt*) and its sattelites that surround it (*udm ṯrrt*).[216] Although the translation of *udm ṯrrt* as "'Udumu the well-watered city" may be etymologically plausible, considering the attestation of *ṯrrt* in the charm

[212] Van de Mieroop, *A History of the Ancient Near East, Ca. 3000–323 B.C.*, 218.

[213] Scholars who interpret the scene as a passive siege translate *grnn* as something like "stay" (cf. √gwr) and *šrn* as something along the line of "watch (cf. √šwr)" (cf. Gray, *The Krt Text in the Literature of Ras Shamra: A Social Myth of Ancient Canaan*, 37–38; Jirku, *Kanaanäische Mythen und Epen aus Ras Schamra-Ugarit*, 88; J. Sawyer and J. Strange, "Notes on the Keret-Text," *IEJ* 14 [1964]: 96). But following Tropper, I take *grnn* and *šrn* as deriving from III-weak roots √gry "(Streit) erregen" and √šry "Streiten." There is no chance of the daughter cities waging a pitched battled with Kirta's army. They must have stayed in the castles while Kirta attacked them with arrows, slingshots, missiles, etc.

[214] Cazelles argues on the basis of the toponym list of Tuthmosis III that *udm ṯrrt* designates the the cities outside the wall, that is, the low city as opposed to the high city (H. Cazelles, "Review: Canaanite Myths and Legends by G. R. Driver," *VT* 7 [1957]: 422). Following Cazelles, Caquot and Sznycer also considers the possibility that *le terme de <<petite>> désignât la banlieue quie se développe autour de toute grande ville* (Caquot, Sznycer, and Herdner, *Mythes et légendes: introduction, traduction, commentaire*, 519, footnote j).

[215] For the survey of this philological issue see Greenfield, "The Epithets RBT//ṮRRT in the Krt Epic," 35–37.

[216] Cazelles cites from the toponym list of Thutmossis III the pair of cities "'*pr grand*" and "'*pr petit*" (Greenfield, "The Epithets RBT//ṮRRT in the Krt Epic," 422). Dahood cites from Pettinato's geographical atlas the pair of cities "Iltanum the Great" and "Iltanum the Small" (Dahood, "J. C. L. Gibson, *Canaanite Myths and Legends*. Originally Edited by G. R. Driver in 1956. Edinburgh 1978. T. & T. Clark," 277).

against snakebite (RS 24.244),[217] the use of the term "well-watered" for a city remains quite unique, not to mention that it does not form a good parallel to *udm rbt*. Moreover, the motif of "a well-watered city" appears to have no narratological point of contact with the story. In other words, it is a "dead motif."[218] The rendering "grand, powerful" may form a good parallelism but it does not integrate with the story. The understanding of *udm ṯrrt* as daughter towns, however, does not only make a good parallel with *udm rbt* but also integrates well with the plot of the story. For instance, Kirta's attacks (*grnn, šrn*) on "cities" (*ʿrm*) and "towns" (*pdrm*) begins after they arrive at 'Udumu the Great and 'Udumu the Small. This would imply that the "cities" and "towns" under attack should be within the perimeter of the city-state of 'Udumu. Moreover, Pabil demands that Kirta should stop "besieging (*tṣr*) 'Udumu *rbt* and 'Udumu *ṯrrt*"[219] in concluding his speech (1.14 III:29b–30). The context seems to show that Pabil is asking for a complete withdrawal of Kirta's army from his kingdom in exchange of handsome tributes, rather than only for a lifting of the passive siege on the capital city.[220]

The scene of women fleeing from the field is located between the scene of attacking daughter cities and besieging the capital city of 'Udumu. This scene seems to depict the effect the attack of Kirta's

---

[217] On the basis of Arabic *ṯarr* Aistleitner translates *ṯrrt* as "*wasserreich*" (Aistleitner, *Wörterbuch der ugaritischen Sprache*, 344). A number of scholars have accepted his translation. Furthermore, the reference to *Arsẖ* as *ṯrrt* in the charm against the snakebite (RS 24.444) is taken to support the translation, for *Arsẖ* is apparently a Hurrian name for the Tigris (Michael C. Astour, "Two Ugaritic Serpent Charms," *JNES* 27 [1968]: 23). For the criticism against this translation, see Greenfield, "The Epithets RBT//ṮRRT in the Krt Epic," 36.

[218] The "leg" of the chair and the "foot" of the mountain apply, by analogy, parts of the human body to parts of inanimate objects. These extensions, however, have become assimilated into the language, and are commonly no longer felt as metaphorical. They are 'dead' metaphors (Rene Wellek and Austin Warren, *Theory of Literature* [San Diego: Harcourt Brace Jovanovich, 1977], 196). Likewise the motif that plays no role in the narrative may be called a "dead" motif.

[219] Tropper and Fensham note two possible interpretations of Ugaritic *tṣr* in KTU 1.14 III:29: "to vex" and "to besiege." In Hebrew it is sometimes difficult to distinguish between *ṣrr* "attack" and *ṣwr* "to besiege." In the current context, one can apply either "do not harass" or "do not besiege." Cf. Joseph Tropper, *Ugaritische Grammatik*, 105, 674; Fensham, "Remarks on Keret 114b–136a (CTA 14:114b–136a)," 77–78.

[220] Note that in the scene of passive siege against the capital city of 'Udumu, the word *ṣr* was *not* used. The use of the word at the conlcusion of Pabil's message seems to indicate the broader usage of the term; namely, it refers both the active siege against 'Udumu the Small and the passive siege against 'Udumu the Great.

army has on the common people of 'Udumu. Kirta's army may have struck awe into the hearts of the people of 'Udumu, which is part of Kirta's strategy in threatening Pabil to surrender. This scene also makes a good transition from the active siege of 'Udumu the Small to the passive siege of 'Udumu the Great, by demonstrating Kirta's intention of blockade. He would block every traffic, material and human, in and out of the city so that the city-dwellers could not get their daily necessities such as wood, straw and water. It is interesting to note here the prominence of female figures in this scene (*ḥṭbt*, *ḥpšt*, *šibt*, and *mmlat*). Although gathering fire-wood and drawing water may have been women's work, this seems to indicate at a deeper level the purpose of Kirta's siege of 'Udumu,[221] that is to receive the hand of Ḥurray from her father Pabil. In particular, the women who came out of the walled-city to draw water and fill jugs strongly recalls what Alter calls the type-scene of betrothal which describes a future bridegroom encountering his future wife at the well.[222]

The Seven-Day Siege of 'Udumu Kirta's passive siege is also couched as a seven-day formula. As in the section dealing with the "Journey to 'Udumu" above, it is far from a traditional form of the formula. The first pair of days (*ym wṯn*) are preceded by a verb *dm* "Remain quiet"[223] that apparently replaces a more extended introduction to the formula as well as the particle *hn*. But unlike the seven-day unit describing Kirta's journey, the seven-day unit under discussion registers a detailed routine of six days, although it is not repeated after every pair of days and recorded only once after the third pair of days: *ḫmš ṯdṯ ym* / *ḥẓk al tšʿl qrth* / *abn . ydk mšdpt* "a fifth, a sixth day / do not shoot your

[221] The poet of *Kirta* describes the food-shortage caused by the siege in terms of the hungry noises of plough-oxen and hunting dogs (KTU 1.14 III:18–19). This is rhetoric of *part for the whole*. The use of feminine figures may be explained in a similar way. The blockade of traffic in and out of the city is represented by these women fleeing from the field. Cf. Gray, *The Krt Text in the Literature of Ras Shamra: A Social Myth of Ancient Canaan*, 38.

[222] Alter, *The Art of Biblical Narrative*, 52.

[223] Pardee ("The Kirta Epic," 335) suggests *dm* as a particle, but the fact that another seven-day sequence formula in *Kirta* starts with an imperative *lk* "go" tips the scale for the rendering "be silent." The word *dm* heads the seven-day unit with no change in spelling in the fulfillment motif. This may be explained in terms of a majority of verbs used in the motif of divine command that appear exactly in identical forms in the fulfillment motif. Moreover, all the verbs (*grnn*, *šrnn*, *sʿt*, *yšn*) that occur in the vicinity of *dm* retain the same form in the fulfillment motif.

arrows at the city / the slingstones at the citadel."[224] This makes the formula a little closer to a traditional form of formula. And this may have to do with the fact that the event on the seventh day forms a quasi-climactic conclusion to the six-day routine. On the seventh day, which is introduced by *hn*, not by the more traditional *mk*, Pabil will not be able to sleep because of the noise from the hungry and thirsty animals in the city.[225] Although Pabil's insomnia is not the climactic goal of Kirta's siege attack, it is certainly one important step toward that goal. The noise forces Pabil to initiate a negotiation with Kirta.

It is noteworthy that the noise made by animals takes up four poetic lines. They seem to form two bicola rather than one tetracolon. Both verses give the reason why Pabil could not sleep, but they have different line structures as well as different thematic emphases. In the first bicolon, the volume of sound is brought to the foreground. This is shown by the construct chain that expresses the idea of noise (*ql ṯigt* and *ql nhqt*). The second bicolon, on the other hand, seems to emphasize the effect of Kirta's siege on the city more than on the volume of noise. This is shown, again, by the construct chain that denotes the animals affected by the siege (*alp ḥrṯ* and *klb ṣpr*). The affected animals are none other than plowing oxen and hunting dogs.[226] They are the providers of two main food sources, bread and meat. This seems to show metonymically that the siege does not only affect Pabil's sleep, but that the whole town suffers from a shortage of food. The seven-day siege, like Kirta's seven-day journey, is a literary device to cover the

[224] The bow and the sling were two long-range weapons available in antiquity. Both were used mainly in a siege attack. When they were used in a siege attack, the slingmen always served close to the archers. Cf. Yigael Yadin, *The Art of Warfare in Biblical Lands* (New York: McGraw-Hill Book, 1963), 6, 64.

[225] Cf. 2 Kings 3:9 where the lack of water affects animals.

[226] There are at least two etymological explanations proposed for the meaning of *klb ṣpr* "hunting dogs." A number of scholars derive *ṣpr* from various Semitic cognates meaning "bird" and take *klb ṣpr* to refer to a hunting dog (literally, "a dog of a bird"). Cf. Olmo Lete and Sanmartín, *A Dictionary of the Ugaritic Language in the Alphabetic Tradition*, s.v. *ṣpr* and various cognates there). Gibson, however, proposes Arabic *ṣafara* "to whistle" as the etymology of *ṣpr* and translates *klb ṣpr* as "the dog (to which) he whistled" namely "his hunting dogs" (J. C. L. Gibson, *Canaanite Myths and Legends.*, 85, footnote 7). There are other translations proposed for *klb ṣpr*. Weippert, for instance, translates it as "*Wachhund*," while Aistleitner proposed the translation "hungrigen Hunde." Caquot and Sznycer, however, take it as "*chien de berger*." Cf. Manfred Weippert, "Mitteilungen zum Text von Ps 19:5 und Jes 22:5," *ZAW* n.s. 32 (1961): 98, footnote 14; J. C. de Moor, *An Anthology of Religious Texts from Ugarit*, 197; Aistleitner, *Die mythologischen und kultischen Texte aus Ras Schamra*, 91; Caquot, Sznycer, and Herdner, *Mythes et légendes: introduction, traduction, commentaire*, 523.

lapse of the siege and should not be taken literally.[227] The protestations of the animals that are associated with food production imply that Kirta's siege was long enough to deal a severe blow to the local economy. And this forms a nice contrast to that of Kirta's city, Ḫubur, where food provisions were more than enough.

Negotiation Pabil initiates negotiation by sending messengers to Kirta in reaction to Kirta's siege.[228] Although Kirta's passive siege remains a fundamental reason for Pabil's dispatch of messengers, the text seems to present the noise made by the animals as the immediate cause of Pabil's sleepless nights. Noteworthy in this regard is that the poet devotes four poetic lines to the theme of noise (cf. lines 15–19a). Why is so much attention paid to the theme in the text? At a surface level, one may recall the annoyance of noise that is attested to in the story of Atraḫasis, in which the noise that humans make vexes the chief god Enlil so much that he persuades the divine assembly to vote for the destruction of man by the deluge.[229] Noise was no small nuisance both for gods and humans in antiquity! But, at a deeper level, the scene of noisy protestations of animals seems to be intended as one of those links that connect the scene of the visit of Pabil's messengers and that of 'Ilu's oneiric visit to Kirta. From this perspective one may discern in the noise made by animals Kirta's weeping that was not silent either (cf. *bṯnh gmm* in KTU 1.14 I). To put it differently, just as the noises of the animals in need force Pabil to send messengers to Kirta, 'Ilu's theophany appears to be a direct response to Kirta's weeping who too is in deep trouble.[230] Moreover, the recurrent list of wealth provides another

---

[227] Gray, *The Krt Text in the Literature of Ras Shamra: A Social Myth of Ancient Canaan*, 37.

[228] This seems to be corroborated by several points of contrast between the scenes of Kirta's blockade and Pabil's reaction. First the contrast is created by two different adverbial phrases, *qrth* "to the city [of 'Udumu]" in KTU 1.14 III:13 and *'m krt mswnh* "to Kirta at his camp" in line 20–21, which respectively indicate the direction of Kirta's "silent treatment" and that of Pabil's dispatch of messengers. Second, the six-day silence (*dm*) of Kirta's army stands in contrast with the unbearable noises made by hungry and thirsty animals within Pabil's city. It almost sounds like an irony to say that the six-day silence on the part of Kirta's army has the effect of keeping King Pabil awake at night.

[229] Benjamin R. Foster, "Atra-Ḫasis," in *Canonical Compositions from the Biblical World*, vol. I of *COS*, ed. William W. Hallo and K. Lawson Younger Jr. (Leiden: Brill, 1997), 450.

[230] The connection between 'Ilu's theophany and Kirta's weeping, by the way, seems to be corroborated by repeated mentions of the word-pair *bky* and *dm'* in the context of oneiric theophany (KTU 1.14 I:31–32, 39–40; 1.14 II:7–9).

link that connects the visit of Pabil's messengers and that of 'Ilu to Kirta: Pabil's messengers offer the same list of gifts to Kirta as the one that 'Ilu had offered to Kirta previously. Furthermore, both visits may have been nocturnal. Although there is no direct evidence indicating the hour of 'Ilu's theophany or that of Pabil's dispatch of messengers, the context makes it plausible to assume nighttime for both events. Especially as far as the hour of Pabil's dispatch of messengers, one may adduce *špšm* "sunset"[231] in line 14 and *mswn* "night-quarters"[232] in line 21 as circumstantial evidences for the nocturnal visit of Pabil's

[231] Ugaritic *špšm* appears always as part of a numeric unit (KTU 1.14 III:3, 14; 1.14 IV:33, 36; 1.14 V:6; 1.20 II:5; 1.22 II:24). On the evidence available it is difficult to decide whether it means "at sunrise" or "at sunset." Loewenstamm prefers the former rendering on the basis of a passage in the Gilgamesh Epic (Tablet I:IV:21; XII:199), but the passage he cites is not conclusive as Moor and Spronk correctly points out (Loewenstamm, *Comparative Studies in Biblical and Ancient Oriental Literatures*, 200, footnote 22; Moor and Spronk, "Problematical Passages in the Legend of Kirtu [I]," 165). In my judgment, the context seems to point to the rendering "at sunset." First, the context does not necessarily postulate the nightly march of Kirta's army, nor does it suggest the nightly journey of Rāpi'ūma for that matter. Second, the mention of Pabil's insomnia at the time designated by *špšm* on the seventh day points to the rendering "at sunset." Some scholars such as Dietrich and Loretz parse *špšm* as a dual on the basis of *byn h'rbym* (cf. Exodus 12:6; Manfried Dietrich and Oswald Loretz, "Die ugaritischen Zeitangaben *ṣbu špš // 'rb špš* und *špšm*," *UF* 22 [1990]: 77). But Pardee and Tropper correctly refuse to see any connection between Ugaritic *špšm* and the Hebrew phrase: it is better to be taken as *špš* plus an enclitic *mem* (Dennis Pardee, *Les textes rituels: fascicule 1: Chapitres 1–53*, RSOu XII [Paris: Éditions Recherche sur les Civilisations, 2000], 202, footnote 241; Joseph Tropper, *Ugaritische Grammatik*, 332). For the rendering "at sunrise," see Olmo Lete and Sanmartín, *A Dictionary of the Ugaritic Language in the Alphabetic Tradition*, 836; Nick Wyatt, *Religious Texts from Ugarit*, 193 and footnote 78.

[232] It is not completely clear whether Pabil waited until sunrise to dispatch messengers or dispatched them in the middle of the night. If the word *mswn* is rendered as "night-quarters," it adds weight to the latter possibility. The word *mswn* has been subject to much debate. I have adopted the proposal, first suggested by Moor and Spronk and later accepted by Tropper, Greenstein, and Dietrich and Loretz, that *mswn* is cognate to Arabic *mumsīn* "night quarters," that is in turn derived from Arabic √msw IV "to spend the night" (Joseph Tropper, *Ugaritische Grammatik*, 191; Greenstein, "Kirta," 16; Dietrich and Loretz, "Das Keret-Epos," 1225). But I have to admit that there are a number of scholars who derive *mswn* from Ras-shamra Akkadian *maswātu*, which seems to refer to a raw material for the production of wooden objects. This identitication was first proposed by Jirku (*Journal of Northwest Semitic Languages* 3 [1973]:34) who rendered the word as *Zeltlager*. Jirku's proposal has been accepted by many commentators who render Ugaritic *mswn* as "camp" (Badre, et al., "Notes ougaritiques," 113; Ginsberg, *The Legend of King Keret: A Canaanite Epic of the Bronze Age*, 39; Caquot, Sznycer, and Herdner, *Mythes et légendes: introduction, traduction, commentaire*, 523, footnote x; Nick Wyatt, *Religious Texts from Ugarit*, 195; Pardee, "The Kirta Epic," 335). This rendering, however, is based on the extrapolation that the *maswātu*-wood was used for Kirta's living quarters.

messengers. The nocturnal dispatch of Pabil's messenger would point to the degree of Pabil's distress caused by Kirta's extended siege.[233] All this goes to show that the motif of divine appearance in this incubation type-scene is far from being a dead motif, but rather continues to play a role in the development of the story.

Pabil's offer of wealth does not come unconditionally. Pabil demands Kirta to reciprocate by halting his siege attack and by completely withdrawing his troops from the city of 'Udumu (cf. lines 26–30).[234] The form of his message to Kirta is interesting: he seems to assert his inalienable right for 'Udumu: "'Udumu is a gift of 'Ilu, a present of the father of mankind (*udm ytnt il / wušn ab adm* in KTU 1.14 III:31–32)." Here Pabil appeals to 'Ilu, Kirta's patron god, as the final court of appeal. Later in the fulfillment motif, however, Pabil ends his message on a different note. Instead of asserting his inalienable right over the city, he ends his message with an exhortation for Kirta to withdraw completely from his city (KTU 1.14 V:44–45). This underscores the poet's ability to rearrange traditional materials to serve various narratological purposes in the story. The change in question reflects the change of speakers as well as the change of narrative contexts. In the motif of divine command, the audience hears Pabil's message from the mouth of 'Ilu, whereas in the fulfillment motif Pabil himself is the speaker. It seems fitting therefore that 'Ilu's version of Pabil's message ends with a theological claim, that is, the inalienability of 'Ilu's gift, while Pabil's version should end with the demand that best illustrates his own interest, that is, the pragmatic demand that Kirta should leave the city in peace.[235]

Kirta rejects Pabil's offer of wealth. He instead demands the hand of Pabil's daughter Ḥurray. In order to persuade Pabil to give his daughter

---

[233] In a similarly dire situation caused by the siege of the Syrians, King Joram of Israel gets up in the night and decides to send out two scouts to see if the words of lepers were true (cf. 2 Kings 7). It is interesting to note that both the Syrians besieging Samaria and the besieged King Joram are described as getting up "in twilight" (verse 7) and "at night" (verse 12) respectively. These references to nighttime seem to underscore the sense of *angst* that they have.

[234] Pabil may have assumed that Kirta was demanding his own kingdom, just as 'Ilu himself wondered if Kirta wanted his kingdom. So as 'Ilu did, he offers a tribute that may settle Kirta for less than his kingdom of 'Udumu. Cf. Loewenstamm, "Zur Götterlehre des Epos von Keret," 507.

[235] Later in the fulfillment motif, Pabil's message is conveyed through human messengers. So we have even there Pabil's *ipsissima verba* and the messengers' version of them. But as expected, both are identical (cf. KTU 1.14 V:33–45 and 1.14 VI:3–15).

to him, Kirta picks up the language of a gift (*ytnt*) used by Pabil himself: "You must give (*ttn*) what my house lacks, give (*tn*) maid Ḥurray...[236] whom 'Ilu gave (*ytn*) in my dream, in my vision, the father of mankind." (cf. KTU 1.14 III:38–40, 46–47).[237] In other words, Kirta appeals to Pabil's faith in 'Ilu as the final court of appeal in their negotiation. Here Kirta's mention of his dream (*hlmy* and *ḏrty*) is noteworthy: it may reflect the poet's intention not only to remind the audience of the oneiric context of Pabil and Kirta's speeches, namely, their being uttered by 'Ilu in Kirta's dream, but also to anticipate the end of the theophany section of the incubation type-scene which is couched in the *inclusio* structure informed by the words for "dream."[238,239] Finally it may be noted that Kirta's reply to Pabil ends with the child-bearing aspect of Ḥurray, which is an appropriate ending considering the fact that the long speech made by 'Ilu was given in answer to Kirta's very specific request concerning his offspring. Moreover, it also anticipates the conclusion of the story in KTU 1.15 III:20–25. Thus, as Parker

[236] Three poetic verses about Ḥurray's beauty (lines 41–45) are inserted between Kirta's demand of Ḥurray and his assertion of Ḥurray as 'Ilu's gift to him. They show a literary pattern "from general to specific." After generally comparing Ḥurray's beauty (*n'm* and *tsm*) to two goddesses, 'Anatu and 'Aṯtartu, the poet narrows focus on the beauty of Ḥurray's eyes (cf. Nick Wyatt, *Religious Texts from Ugarit*, 197, footnote 103). According to West, a common way of praising a woman's beauty was to say that she resembles or is equal to a goddess. The comparison may be to the goddesses in general. Alternatively a woman may be compared to a particular goddess. For example, Homer can speak of "Hermione, who had the form of golden Aphrodite." Moreover, as in the Ugaritic verses in question, different aspects of the person may be compared to different deities. So Agamemnon, as he marshals his army, is described as "in eyes and head like Zeus whose sport is thunder, like Ares as to his baldric, his chest like Poseidon." Cf. West, *The East Face of Helicon: West Asiatic Elements in Greek Poetry and Myth*, 243.

[237] Parker, *The Pre-Biblical Narrative Tradition: Essays on the Ugaritic Poems Keret and Aqhat*, 211; Loewenstamm, "Zur Götterlehre des Epos von Keret," 507.

[238] Parker, *The Pre-Biblical Narrative Tradition: Essays on the Ugaritic Poems Keret and Aqhat*, 154.

[239] Puzzling to the audience, however, is that 'Ilu does not seem to have promised Ḥurray as a gift to Kirta up to this point of his dream. Where in his dream did 'Ilu promise to give Ḥurray to Kirta? Although some scholars find the allusion in Kirta's very specific wish about offspring (KTU 1.14 II: 4–5), a better answer may be found, in my view, in the fact that Kirta's speech about Ḥurray as 'Ilu's gift is part of 'Ilu's own speech. To put it differently, 'Ilu's oneiric prescription of Kirta's message for Pabil may have performative power by virtue of its being divine words. The descriptive sentence *dbḥlmy il ytn* "Ilu has given [Ḥurray] in my dream" (KTU 1.14 III:46), when it is uttered by 'Ilu, may not simply describe a fact, but it does things, namely, makes a promise to Kirta. When the same sentence is later uttered by Kirta, however, it does nothing but describe a fact about Ḥurray being 'Ilu's gift to Kirta.

points out, it functions "as a kind of fulcrum in the total structure of this first section of the poem" of Kirta.[240]

2.2.5 *Conclusion: Absent Motif in the Section of Oneiric Theophany*

As a way of concluding the long discussion of the theophany section of the incubation type-scene, it must be emphasized that the theophany section in the incubation type-scene of *Kirta* does not register the motif of divine blessing-promise. Divine speech normally includes the element of promise and blessing as well as instructions. But the divine message in this type-scene registers only 'Ilu's instruction. Indeed, 'Ilu's speech ends with the words that Kirta is supposed to return to Pabil, and does not "promise" the success of the negotiation, let alone bless the marriage that would produce offspring for Kirta. This abrupt interruption of 'Ilu's speech not only makes the motif of fulfillment more interesting by virtue of its unpredictability, but also creates a free space in the motif of fulfillment where the poet creatively arrange materials to fit his narratological and ideological purposes. The lack of divine promise in the theophany section is compensated later in the post-epiphany section of the incubation. One may even say that the motif of divine promise-blessing is belatedly identified in the post-epiphany section of this incubation type-scene.[241]

2.3 *After Epiphany*

2.3.1 *The Waking Motif*

KTU 1.4 III:50–51

(50)	krt . yḫt . w ḥlm	Kirta awoke and it was a dream,
(51)	ʿbd . il . w hdrt	The servant of 'Ilu and it was a theophanic vision.

[240] Parker, *The Pre-Biblical Narrative Tradition: Essays on the Ugaritic Poems Keret and Aqhat*, 154.

[241] We have already seen several examples of this literary device in the 'Aqhatu story. Also in 2 Kings 20, we may find an example of "delayed identification." Hezekiah, after being told that he will die of illness, prayed earnestly to Yahweh for healing. Yahweh appears (not to Hezekiah but) to his prophet Isaiah, and gives some instructions as well as the promise of healing. But the text does not repeat Yahweh's answer through Isaiah's mouth. So at this point the reader would not know whether or not Isaiah communicated Yahweh's answer to Hezekiah faithfully. But we are informed belatedly in verse 8 through Hezekiah's question (verse 8) that Isaiah faithfully communicated Yahweh's words to Hezekiah.

This bicolon, which registers the waking motif, serves as a milestone that punctuates the incubation type-scene of the Kirta story. It not only testifies to the dream's vividness and thus its validity[242] but it also marks the beginning of the post-epiphany section of the type-scene. It is significant that at this point, where the waking motif ends the oneiric theophany, Kirta is referred to as *'bd 'il* "a servant of 'Ilu." It may intimate that the image of Kirta as an obedient servant of 'Ilu will dominate the narrative from this point on. Indeed in the subsequent section on fulfillment, Kirta as the servant of 'Ilu is described to follow 'Ilu's instructions almost to the letter. A pair of "dream" words (*ḥlm* and *hdrt*) take the audience back to another milestone that described the initial moment of Kirta's dream: *w b ḥlmh il yrd* / *b ḏhrth ab adm* "In a dream 'Ilu descended, in a vision, the father of mankind" (KTU 1.14 I:35–37). There, however, 'Ilu was described as *ab adm* "father of mankind" (cf. KTU 1.14 I:37) and correspondingly Kirta was called *ǵlm 'il* "the lad of 'Ilu" in the immediately following verse (cf. KTU 1.14 I:40–41). These epithets befit the context where 'Ilu, moved by Kirta's profusely shed tears, makes a move toward him in good will.

Just as Kirta's new epithet *'bd il* serves as a portent of the future plot of the story, an Ugaritic *hapax* for dream may play a similar role in the narrative. As is already discussed above (cf. 2.2.1), the etymology of the word *hdrt* is subject to debate, although its meaning has been approximated as "vision" on the basis of its parallel *ḥlm*. Whether one takes *hdrt* as a variant of *ḏhrt* "a revelatory dream,"[243] or as a cognate of Hebrew *hādār* "adornment, splendor,"[244] the word *hdrt*, which begins the fulfillment motif, underscores the revelatory nature of a dream. Kirta's dream is not a fantasy that can be disregarded, but a divine revelation that needs to be fulfilled with sincerity. By placing the word *hdrt* at the seam of dream and reality, the poet prepares the audience for what is in store in the subsequent section. From this point on, the audience's focus will be on how thoroughly Kirta will carry out divine instructions that he has received in an oneiric revelation. This may account for the length of the fulfillment section that follows. The poet does not cut it short to get to more "interesting" parts, namely, the scenes of wedding banquet and the birth of children.

---

[242] Diana Lipton, *Revisions of the Night: Politics and Promises in the Patriarchal Dreams of Genesis*, JSOTSup 288 (Sheffield: Sheffield Academic Press, 1999), 15.

[243] Josef Tropper, "Ugaritic Dreams: Notes on Ugaritic Ḏ(h)Rt and Hdrt," 305–12.

[244] J. C. L. Gibson, *Canaanite Myths and Legends.*, 86, footnote 4.

2.3.2 *The Motif of Fulfillment*

As soon as Kirta wakes up from his dream, he goes about carrying out 'Ilu's instructions and does so to the letter. Kirta as a servant of 'Ilu (*'bd 'il*) takes great care to faithfully, if not literally, translate his oneiric instructions (cf. *hdrt*) into practice. The great care taken by Kirta in executing 'Ilu's command is intimated by the way the poet composes the fulfillment motif. With some important exceptions, which will be discussed below, all of 'Ilu's words, i.e., all the poetic lines in the motif of divine command, are reproduced in the fulfillment section. This stands in stark contrast to the incubation type-scene of the 'Aqhatu story where the poet describes the visit of the Kôṯarātu goddesses without reproducing the divine words when recounting the fulfillment. Only necessary changes are made in the repetition of 'Ilu words in the fulfillment section of *Kirta* such as verbal mood (from imperative to narrative) or pronominal suffix (from 2nd to 3rd person). Moreover, in a number of cases where the change of verbal mood is not reflected in the consonantal spelling, the poetic lines in the fulfillment section appear identical to those in the motif of divine command.[245] All this may subtly allude to the rigor that is demanded of Kirta as 'Ilu's servant in the execution of divine command and thus may create the impression that the success of Kirta's mission depends on how literally Kirta translates 'Ilu's commands into practice.[246]

The fulfillment section is, however, not a simple translation of 'Ilu's words from an imperative mood to a narrative mood. A closer comparison of the two sections will reveal somewhat significant variations that can be organized into four patterns of change. Some lines are

[245] The imperative *'rb* "enter" in divine speech, for instance, has the same form as the perfect *'rb* "he entered" in the fulfillment motif. The jussive *yrd* "he shall descend" in the motif of divine command has the same form as the perfect or the preterite *yrd* "he descended" in the fulfillment motif. Interesting to note is that in the section where 'Ilu's instructions are directed not to the person of Kirta but to his army, almost all the verbs used in divine instructions appear with the same spelling (cf. *ngb* "to be provisioned," *yṣi* "to go out," *hlk* "to walk," *tškr* "to hire," *yšu* "to take up," *ymzl* "to grope," *tškn* "to settle," *grnn* "to attack," *šrn* "to advance against," *s't* "to sweep," *dm* "be silent").

[246] Some changes are purely stylistic or suspect of being errors: *amt* (1.14 II:10) > *amth* (1.14 III:53); *'l* (1.14 II:20) > *w'ly* (1.14 IV:2); *šmm* (1.14 II:23) > *šmmh* (1.14 IV:5); *yḥd* (1.14 II:43) > *aḥd* (1.14 IV:21); *lm nkr* (1.14 II:49) > *w l nkr* (1.14 IV:28); *k irby* (1.14 II:50) > *km irby* (1.14 IV:29); *km ḥṣn* (1.14 III:1) > *k ḥṣn* (1.14 IV:30); *udm rbm* (1.14 III:5) > *udm rbt* (1.14 IV:47); *w ludm* (1.14 III:5) > *w udm* (1.14 IV:48); *ḥṭbh* (1.14 III:8) > *ḥṭbt* (1.14 IV:51); *zǵt* (1.14 III:18) > *lzǵt* (1.14 V:11); *btrbṣt* (1.14 III:37) > *btrbṣ* (1.14 V:21).

expanded (Expansion), while other lines are shortened or omitted (Contraction and Omission). There are still other lines that describe something that Kirta does that is not included in 'Ilu's detailed instructions (Addition). Finally, some lines concern something that should have been included in 'Ilu's oneiric speech that occurs belatedly in the fulfillment section (Compensation).

Expansion When 'Ilu's oneiric instructions are translated into narrative reality in the fulfillment section, some of them expand. This is most clearly indicated by the recurrent list of gifts in the speeches of Pabil and Kirta. Although it occurs only twice in the oneiric negotiation between Kirta and Pabil, it is quoted four times in the fulfillment section. The full-blown list of gifts is quoted at every stage of communication: from Pabil to his messengers, from the messengers to Kirta, from Kirta to the messengers and from the messengers to Pabil. Considering that the motif of divine command fails to guarantee the success of Kirta's expedition through promise-blessing, this expansion, which has the effect of delaying the scene of Kirta's successful acquisition of Ḥurray, seems designed to increases narratival tension to the maximum. Whereas the motif of oneiric theophany, oriented toward the solution of an incubant's problem, does not waste space in getting to the point, namely, 'Ilu's advice about Ḥurray, the fulfillment motif tends to add details to the story in order to provide a high degree of verisimilitude. What needs to be emphasized, however, is that this expansion is not detrimental to the overall idea of Kirta's obedient observance of 'Ilu's instruction in the fulfillment section.

The event on the seventh day of the siege is also expanded. What appears to be a dialogue between Pabil and his wife (KTU 1.14 V:13–21?) is inserted. All we can say for sure is that the first thing Pabil does after a disturbed sleep is to address his wife "listen closely" (*šmʿ mʿ*). Since the remainder of Kirta's words to his wife or the possible reply of his wife are too damaged to be reconstructed, the literary purpose of this insertion remains a mystery,[247] let alone its effect on the overall image of Kirta as a faithful servant of 'Ilu.

[247] Merill takes Pabil's address to his wife as "a stylistic device of the narrator to inject some variation into a portion where the narrative is very repetitious." But he adds immediately, "The conversation plays no apparent role in any succeeding incident." Cf. Arthur L. Merrill, "The House of Keret: A Study of the Keret Legend," *SEÅ*, no. 33 (1968): 9.

Contraction and Omission The fulfillment section shortens or omits some poetic verses without detriment to the idea of Kirta's faithful observance of 'Ilu's command. The bicolon in KTU 1.14 II:13–14 (*qḥ im[r b yd]k / imr d[bḥ b]m ymn* "Take a lamb in your hand / a sacrificial lamb in your right hand") is shortened to a monocolon in KTU 1.14 III:55b–56 (*lqḥ imr dbḥ bydh* "He took a sacrificial lamb in his hand"). Also the tricolon in KTU 1.14 II:20–22 (*'l lẓr m[g]dl / w 'l lẓr . mgdl / rkb ṯkmm ḥm*t "Ascend to the summit of the tower / yes, ascend to the summit of the tower / mount the top of the wall"), which may take its form owing to dittography, is shortened to a bicolon in KTU 1.15 III:2b–4 (*w'ly lẓr mgdl / rkb ṯkmm ḥmt* "And ascend to the summit of the tower / mount the top of the wall"). These two examples of contraction show that contraction does not change the overall sense of the poetic verses in which contraction happens, nor does it make Kirta's obedience any less desirable.[248] The monocolon in KTU 1.14 III:56 captures the gist of 'Ilu's command expressed in the bicolon verse in KTU 1.14 III:55b–56. 'Ilu would not have commanded Kirta to take a lamb in one hand and another lamb in the other hand in the bicolon verse. In a similar way, the emphatic, if not dittographic, repetition of *'l lẓr mgdl* in the divine speech no longer appear in the fulfillment section.

Three poetic verses that appear in the divine instruction disappear completely in the fulfillment section. One of the verses that express the idea of Kirta's numerous army (*ḫpṯ d bl spr / ṯnn d bl hg* "soldiers without number / archers without count" in KTU 1.14 II:37–38) is omitted later in the section describing Kirta's word-for-word execution of 'Ilu's command. Also the six-days routine in the seven-day formula of Kirta's siege (*ḥẓk al tš'l qrth abn ydk mšdpt* "Do not shoot your arrows at the city / your sling-stones at the towers" in KTU 1.14 III:12b–14a) is left out completely in the corresponding section on fulfillment. Even a part of Kirta's message that must be relayed to Pabil *ipsissimis verbis* is omitted in the fulfillment section: the omitted verse concerns the beauty of Ḥurray's eyes (*tḥgrn [s]dm / ašlw bṣp 'nh*, KTU 1.14 III:44b–45).[249] What do these examples of omission imply on the nature of

[248] For contraction and expansion as an art of Ugaritic versification, see J. C. de Moor, "The Art of Versification in Ugariti and Israel II: The Formal Structure," *UF* 10 (1978): 187–217.

[249] Van Selms takes the word *tḥgrn* as having sexual connotation on the basis of its obscure use in the myth of Dawn and Dusk (van Selms, *Marriage & Family Life*

Kirta's piety? Do they serve as an allusion to Kirta's lackadaisical attitude toward matters of religious piety by showing Kirta's failure to execute 'Ilu's command? The omission of the verse concerning Kirta's numerous army (KTU 1.14 II:37–38) may not be so detrimental to the image of Kirta as a pious servant of 'Ilu. After all, the verse is more of a predictive description than of a command. Its poetic message is already made in the preceding, as well as subsequent, verses. Hence, as in the case of contraction, the omission of KTU 1.14 II:37–38 may not damage the image of Kirta as a faithful follower of 'Ilu's words. A similar point can be made about the second example of omission (KTU1.14 III:12b–14a), too. At first glance, the omission of a verse containing 'Ilu's command ("Do not shoot...") may appear to wreak havoc on Kirta's image as a faithful servant of 'Ilu. But on a closer examination of the text, the apparent non-compliance is not as bad as it may appear at first. First, the fact that the seven-day formulae used in the Kirta story is idiosyncratic both in terms of structure and literary function serves as a mitigating factor. The structure of seven-day formulae in the Kirta story is a much truncated one where the six-day routine is not repeated. Furthermore, if the literary function of the formula is to delay the flow of narrative through repetitions of a routine in order to maximize the climactic effect that the event on the seventh day has on the audience, the seven-day formulae used in the Kirta story serve as a device for summary rather than for climax by telescoping a long narrated time into a short narration time. The omission of the verse describing the six-day routine befits the idiosyncratic features of seven-day units in the Kirta story (cf. a seven-day unit of Kirta's journey to 'Udumu). The second mitigating factor is that the omitted routine concerns a negative command. The command does not demand any act on the part of Kirta's army. Since this command may have already been given in a positive form at the beginning of the seven-day formula (cf. *dm* "remain silent"), the omission of the negative command in the fulfillment motif does not necessarily mean any active violation of 'Ilu's command. Most importantly, the omission brings the poet's literary artifice to the foreground. The literary artifice crafted into the scene of Kirta's siege revolves around the idea of sound and silence.

---

in Ugaritic Literature, 42–44). But as Wyatt correctly points out, it has something to do with the beauty of Ḥurray's eyes. I tentatively accept Wyatt's restoration *tḫgrn [s] dm* "they are surrounded by [eye-shad]ow" (Nick Wyatt, *Religious Texts from Ugarit*, 197, footnotes 102 and 103).

The imperative *dm* "remain silent" stands in contrast to the sounds made by domestic animals within the city. It is an irony that what causes Pabil's insomnia is not the war-cries of Kirta's army, but their silence. It is a surprise from the traditional viewpoint of the seven-day formula that the six-day silence does not culminate in the climactic war-cries of Kirta's army on the seventh day but is followed by the noises made by hungry and thirsty animals.[250] All these factors seem to indicate that the omission of the bicolon mentioning Kirta's military non-attack is intended by the poet to present more clearly the literary contrast between "silence" and "noise," thereby creating a sense of irony in Pabil's reaction on the seventh day. But it does not necessarily expose Kirta's indifference toward matters of religious piety. The third example of omission, however, seems to point us in a different direction. It is owing to the fact that the omitted verse concerns the words that 'Ilu himself entrusted for Kirta to speak in response to Pabil's message. Kirta as a servant of 'Ilu is supposed to communicate them without compromise. Kirta's compromise stands in stark contrast to the faithfulness of his human messengers. Although their speech that relays Kirta's message is not preserved (KTU 1.14 40ff), their meticulousness in dealing with their master' message may be confirmed by their communication of Pabil's message. There is no difference between Pabil's own words and the messengers' version of them (cf. KTU 1.14 V:33–45 vs. 1.14 VI:3–15). Kirta's failure to be a perfect mouthpiece of 'Ilu is also thrown into relief by the fact that although 'Ilu never entrusted Pabil with any message, Pabil is presented in the text as a faithful deliverer of what 'Ilu predicted him to say: Pabil's message in the fulfillment section is identical with Pabil's message in the section recounting the divine instruction.[251] In the Hebrew Bible, the discrepancy between God's *ipsissima verba* and its human version may play an important role in the advancement of a plot. Many Jewish com-

---

[250] This is one of the characteristics of the seven-day formulae used in the Kirta story. The event on the seventh day is a temporal and logical consequence of the six-day long routine, instead of something extraordinary as in the case of the seven-day formula in the 'Aqhatu story. For example, Kirta's army's journey to 'Udumu is expressed in a seven-day formula in a dream revelation. The six days' marching is concluded with the note that Kirta's army has arrived at 'Udumu on the seventh day. It looks as if the seven-day formula is a device used by the poet to pick up the narrative pace rather than a device to delay the pace of the story to a climax.

[251] Note that the order of the last two verses in KTU 1.14 III:27–32 is reversed in the fulfillment motif. But Pabil's message in the fulfillment motif preserves the entire message that 'Ilu predicted Pabil to say in the motif of divine command.

mentators have found Eve's version of Yahweh's prohibition to be an allusion to her indiligence in matters of religious piety that eventually led to the violation of God's command.[252] The divinely ordained words should not be added as in the case of Eve or subtracted as in the case of Kirta. Although the idea of the beauty of Ḥurray's eyes is already expressed in the immediately preceding verse (KTU 1.14 III:43–44), Kirta's failure to be a perfect mouthpiece of ʾIlu is a subtle but unmistakable hint about the nature of his religious piety.[253]

Addition Most of ʾIlu's commands are faithfully executed by Kirta in the fulfillment section. Some cases of expansion, of contraction, and even of omission do not change or seriously damage the general tenor of the fulfillment motif: Kirta is an obedient servant of ʾIlu. But an unexpected addition to the plot, which breaks off the seven-day unit of Kirta's journey, seriously challenges such an image of Kirta. According to KTU 1.14 IV:32–43, on the third day of journey, Kirta stops at sanctuaries in Sidon and Tyre to make a spontaneous vow to ʾAṯiratu:

(31)	tlkn . (32) ym . wṯn	They went a day, a second,
	⸢a⸣ḫ̮r (33) šp⸢š⸣m . b⸢ṯ⸣lṯ	At sundown on the third day,
(34)	y⸢m⸣ [ǵy . l]qdš (35) aṯrt ṣrm	He arrived at the sanctuary of ʾAṯiratu of Tyre,
	w l ilt (36) ṣd[y]⸢n⸣m .	At (the sanctuary of) the goddess of Sidon.
	ṯm (37) yd⸢r⸣ [.] ⸢k⸣rt . ṯʿ	There noble Kirta took a vow:

[252] James L. Kugel, *The Bible as It Was* (Cambridge, MA: Harvard University Press, 1997), 76–77. See also Jeremiah 26:2 where Yahweh warns Jeremaiah of not "diminishing a word" (*ʾal-tigraʿ dābār*) when serving as a divine messegner. Heller's observation about Samuel's words over against Yahwh's words conveys a similar point. He argues that in contrast to the first bloc of Samuel's material (1 Sameul 1–7) where the oracle either comes from the mouth of a prophet or from Yahweh directly, its second block (chapters 8–16) presents Samuel's prophetic acitiviy in a two-way interplay. The narrator relates both what Yahweh tells Samuel and what Samuel tells the addressees. In no case, however, are the two messages ever identical; in most cases they are significantly different; and in a few cases they are contradictory. Heller then conclues that by means of this repetitive dissonance, the texts rhetorically raise the suspicion of the reader about the character of Samuel. Roy L. Heller, *Power, Politics, and Prophecy: The Character of Samuel and the Deuteronomistic Evaluation of Prophecy*, Library of Biblical Studies (New York: T. & T. Clark, 2006), 46.

[253] The disparity between divine command and its fulfillment may be attributed to different authors. For example, in the story of Noah's flood, Yahweh's command is to take seven pairs of clean animals and two pairs of unclean animals to the ark, but its fulfillment is to take two pairs of animals, both clean and unclean. It is very hard to attribute this to the intention of one author.

(38)	iiṯt . aṯrt . ṣrm	The gift[254] of Aṯiratu of Tyre,
(39)	w ilt ṣdynm	The goddess of Sidon:
(40)	hm . ḥ⸢r⸣y . bty (41) iqḥ	If I take Ḥurray to my house,
	aš‘rb ǵlmt (42) ḥẓry	Bring the girl into my courts,
	ṯnh k!s!pm (43) atn	Twice her weight I will give in silver
	w ṯlṯh hrṣm	And three times her weight in gold.[255]

Although there are some philological difficulties,[256] one cannot deny the presence of the traditional formula of vow-making in lines 38–42, whose components are nicely summarized by Parker as follows: Identification of the deity to which a vow is made (cf. lines 38–39), protasis that normally begins with *hm* or *’m* (cf. lines 40–42a), and apodosis that is normally couched in a first person imperfect verb (cf. lines 42b–43).[257] Furthermore, Kirta's vow shows many contextual similarities to vow-making in ancient Near East, including ancient Israel. For instance, according to Cartledge, a vow usually "grows out of a situation of need, is made by a human to the gods, and is offered at a shrine.... The material object promised is apparently a physical representation of the thing requested and when it is forgotten, the deity is angered."[258] Kirta's vow-making seems to fit Cartledge's description of vow-making in ancient Near East. Kirta's vow grows out of the need for offspring, and is made by Kirta to ’Aṯiratu the goddess at her shrine at Sidon and Tyre. Furthermore, Kirta's avowed gifts are silver

[254] Ugaritic *iiṯt* is difficult. The attestation of *iṯt* in an Ugaritic letter (KTU 2.13) does not determine the matter. The rendering "gift" is based on the root √’ṯ "to give." Alternately, Ugaritic *iiṯt* has been rendered as "by the life of," or "as she lives" on the basis of the existence particle *iṯ*. The difficulty with the latter is that there exists yet no proof that the particle *iṯ* was inflected for person. If the former rendering is accepted, that would refer to silver and gold promised in lines 42–43. Cf. Caquot, Sznycer, and Herdner, *Mythes et légendes: introduction, traduction, commentaire*, 530, footnote w; Pardee, "The Kirta Epic," 336, footnote 34.

[255] In antiquity, a value of person is often measured against the same weight in gold. In *Iliad* (Book 22, line 351), Priam proposes gold in the weight of Hector's body as the ransom for his son's body. In a Hittite ritual (KUB 30.15 + 39.19 obverse 26–28) a dead king who is symbolically weighed (in the form of mortar) against gold and other precious substances. In Lamentation 4:2 we read of "The precious sons of Zion, worth their weight in fine gold..." Cf. West, *The East Face of Helicon: West Asiatic Elements in Greek Poetry and Myth*, 395–96.

[256] For the problematic spellings of two toponyms *ṣrm* and *ṣdnym*, see Nick Wyatt, *Religious Texts from Ugarit*, 200, footnote 114.

[257] Simon B. Parker, "The Vow in Ugaritic and Israelite Narrative Literature," *UF* 11 (1979): 694.

[258] Cartledge, *Vows in the Hebrew Bible and the Ancient Near East*, 114–15.

and gold in the weight of Ḥurray, although the phrase "twice (*t̠nh*) and three times her weight (*t̠lt̠h*)" may be another example of hyperbole.[259]

The literary ingenuity of this scene lies in the fact that the poet makes vow-making, usually an act of piety, into the opposite by placing the motif of vow in the post-epiphany section of the incubation type-scene. The motif of a vow is one of those motifs that the poet may pull out to compose the incubation type-scene. In the incubation type-scene in 1 Samuel 1, for instance, Hanna makes a vow before she has a quasi-theophany experience with Eli the priest (verse 11). The motif of vow-making occurs in Hittite reports of a therapeutic dream, too.[260] In KUB 15.1, Puduhepa makes a vow in her dream: "If you, goddess, my lady, will have made well again His Majesty…, I shall make a statue of gold for Hebat and I shall make her a rosette of gold" (KTU 15.1).[261] Noteworthy in the incubation type-scene under discussion is that the motif of vow is registered neither in the pre-epiphany section as a preparatory ritual (cf. Hanna's vow), nor in the motif of divine-human dialogue as a way of a pious request (cf. Puduhepa's vow), but it appears in the fulfillment motif as an unexpected addition. Although the motif of a vow may, in theory, occur in any section within the incubation type-scene, what makes the use of the vow motif in *Kirta* unique and interesting is that the poet does not use it as a

[259] From an archaeological standpoint, the amount of silver and gold promised by Kirta is unrealistic. A figurine from Minet el Beida, cast in bronze, has its body covered with silver and its head and headdress with god (James B. Pritchard, *The Ancient Near East in Pictures Relating to the Old Testament* [Princeton, NJ: Princeton University Press, 1954], number 481). Two figurines from Ras Shamra itself, dating from a few centuries earlier, are made of silver and dressed in gold loin cloths and torques (Pritchard, *The Ancient Near East in Pictures Relating to the Old Testament*, number 482). The largest of these three is 28 centimeters tall, so that they do not approach the scale proposed in Kirta's vow. However, we may discern a literary evidence in Puduhepa's oneiric vow which comes closer to Kirta's vow. The queen promises "a silver statue of Hattusilis—as tall as Hattusilis himself, with its head, its hands (and) and its feet gold." Even put in comparison with Puduhepa's unusually handsome gift, Kirta's vow to offer silver and gold twice and thrice Ḥurray's weight is best taken as a hyperbole. Cf. Parker, *The Pre-Biblical Narrative Tradition: Essays on the Ugaritic Poems Keret and Aqhat*, 73.

[260] Most of this dream accounts date to the reign of Hattušili III and Puduhepa. In those accounts often dubbed "votive texts," the queen makes a vow for, or the gods asks for a gift in exchange of healing. Cf. Alice Mouton, *Rêves hittites*, CHANE 28 (Leiden: Brill, 2007), 24; Oppenheim, *The Interpretation of Dreams in the Ancient Near East: With a Translation of an Assyrian Dream-Book*, 254.

[261] Oppenheim, *The Interpretation of Dreams in the Ancient Near East: With a Translation of an Assyrian Dream-Book*, 254, text 30.

device to underscore the incubant's piety but to expose it in such way as to anticipate the second episode of the Kirta story.

From the perspective of command and execution, Kirta's vow to 'Aṯiratu exposes his lack of reverence for 'Ilu since it is a clear departure from 'Ilu's oneiric instructions. The number of details in 'Ilu's instructions and Kirta's almost literal execution of them make such breaking of the scheme of command and execution not only conspicuous to the audience but also an undeniable breach of faith toward 'Ilu. From a formal standpoint, Kirta's visit to the shrine breaks up the seven-day formula into a three-day sequence and a four-day sequence. Although a three-day sequence of journey is attested to elsewhere in Ugaritic literature (KTU 1.22 II:24–25), the four-day sequence is outside the scope of Ugaritic literary convention.[262] This idiosyncratic structure that results from Kirta's vow symbolically shows the idiosyncratic nature of Kirta's act. Overall, the text clearly presents Kirta's vow as a violation of 'Ilu's command. It is also noteworthy in a similar vein that Kirta's vow is presented in the text as a set-up for a later breach of faith against 'Aṯiratu, rather than as a demonstration of his piety toward the goddess. Thus the inculsion of Kirta's vow in the fulfillment motif serves to intimate not only Kirta's unfaithfulness toward 'Ilu the father of the gods (*ab ilm*) but also his "flawed" piety toward 'Aṯiratu the creatress of the gods (*qnyt ilm*). Especially the goddess's anger incited by Kirta's failure to fulfill the vow functions as a bridge betweem the first and the second episodes of the Kirta story.

[262] Scholars like Loewenstamm and Parker argue that the four day sequence unit is *ad hoc* formulation resulting from a later insertion of the motif of vow (Loewenstamm, "Zur Götterlehre des Epos von Keret," 510; Parker, *The Pre-Biblical Narrative Tradition: Essays on the Ugaritic Poems Keret and Aqhat*, 207–8. Cf. Dietrich and Loretz, "Das Keret-Epos," 1241). The idiosyncratic four-day sequence, however, may have been the poet's literary artifice not only to underscore the aberrance of Kirta's behavior in this "received form" of the text, but also to garner the maximum attention of readers at this point in the narrative. Considering that the seven-day formula in the Kirta story is a device more of summary than of a climax, one may see that this interruption actually slows down the pace of narrative when it is supposed to proceed quickly to the scene of siege. This slowing down in narrated time (For the definition of narrated time, see Shimon Bar-Efrat, *Narrative Art in the Bible* [London; New York: T. & T. Clark, 2004], 143) has the effect of garnering the readers' attention on the motif of vow and prepares them for a surprising turn of event that comes later in the plot. Cartledge, for instance, argues that the resulting four-day sequence is an indication of the poet's ingenuity that has made the motif of a vow an integral part not only of the immediate structure but also of the later plot of the epic. Cf. Cartledge, *Vows in the Hebrew Bible and the Ancient Near East*, 109.

Finally, it is interesting to put in a comparative perspective the motif of a vow used in the Kirta story. The Jacob story in Genesis shows many similarities to the first episode of the Kirta story.[263] Both Jacob and Kirta went on a journey for a wife. Both have a divine revelation in a dream. Both stop at a certain shrine to make a vow to the effect that they would return with a gift if their journeys are successful. Germane to our discussion, however, is the narratival function of a vow in both stories. In the Kirta story, a major transition is made when 'Aṯiratu remembers the vow Kirta made to him. In fact the bicolon "Then 'Aṯiratu remembers his vow, the goddess...." (*wtḫss aṯrt ndrh* / *wilt . p*[...], in KTU 1.15 III:25–26) begins a new episode in the Kirta story. In a similar fashion, it is when the angel of God reminds Jacob of the vow he made to the God of Bethel that Jacob decides to leave Laban for his homeland (cf. Genesis 31:13). Thus in both the stories, remembering a vow serves as a major transitional point in the plot of the narrative. But the reminder of the vow by the messenger of God is for the purpose of informing Jacob of the fact that the conditions of his vow have been met and for the purpose of encouraging him to go back home to fulfill his vow, whereas the remembering of the vow by 'Aṯiratu leads to the accusation against Kirta who neglected to fulfill the vow (cf. *uṯn ndr*) when the conditions of his vow were met and to a subsequent punishment on him.

Compensation (The Motif of Divine Promise and Blessing) The poet of *Kirta* seems to compensate for the lack of divine promise and blessing in the section of theophany by embedding it in the fulfillment section. In Kirta's dream, 'Ilu gives him detailed instructions on how to acquire a child-bearing wife, Ḥurray, but does not guarantee the success of Kirta's mission through blessing, let alone promise him to give him children through Ḥurray. This puts the motif of divine speech in the Kirta story in stark contrast with the selfsame motif in the incubation type-scene of *'Aqhatu*, where 'Ilu not only commands 'Aqhatu to sleep with his wife (*l'ršh y'l* "May he go up to his bed" in KTU 1.17 I:38), but also guarantees through promise and blessing that the copulation leads to conception.[264] Since the motif of divine promise and blessing is relocated from the section of oneiric theophany to

[263] On the comparison of Keret and Jacob, see Loren R. Fisher, "Two Projects at Claremont," *UF* 3 (1971): 25–31.

[264] *bm nšq aṯth [ḥr] / bḥbqh ḥmḥmt....wykn bnh [bbt] / [šrš] bqrb hklh* "As he kisses his wife, there will be [conception], as he embraces his wife there will be preg-

the post-epiphany section of the type-scene in *Kirta*, a new setting for divine promise-blessing is required: the poet uses Kirta's wedding banquet as the occasion for divine blessing.[265] Also noteworthy is that the motif of divine promise and blessing is composed in mythological-anthromorphic style of narrative, rather than as a theophany scene.

The assembly of the gods (*ʿdt ʾilm*) including Baʿlu and ʾIlu are invited to what looks like a wedding banquet for Kirta and Ḥurray.[266] After the badly damaged first 10 lines of KTU 1.15 II preserving several divine names, we come to a summary reference in line 11 to the arrival of all the gods (*ʿdt ilm*), which in turn leads to Baʿlu's petition to ʾIlu to bless Kirta (line 12).[267] In several respects, the scene of divine blessing in *Kirta* is reminiscent of a similar scene in the ʾAqhatu story. First, both scenes of divine blessing involve Baʿlu as an intermediary between ʾIlu and his human devotees.[268] The language used in Baʿlu's petition is also identical (*tmr // tbrk*) in both scenes. But there is a point of dissimilarity as well: in the Kirta story, Baʿlu's petition is limited to a minimum, namely, the traditional blessing formula. His petition does not mention any specific circumstances concerning Kirta. In the ʾAqhatu story, however, Baʿlu's petition goes beyond the traditional minimum to allude to ʾAqhatu's problem and even suggests a solution to ʾIlu. This difference may be explained by Baʿlu's narratological role in respective stories. Baʿlu plays a significant role in the

nancy...He will have a son [in his house], [a scion] within his palace" in KTU 1.17 I:39–40, 42–43.

[265] KTU 1.15 II:1–11 is badly broken. We can discern, however, several divine names and a term for the gods viewed as a group, i.e., *ʿdt ilm*, "the assembly of gods." Pardee correctly observes that "the crucial words for what it is that Kirta prepared for the gods having disappeared from lines 8–10, the assumption of a type of banquet or feast is based on the fact that in the following section drinking vessels are mentioned" (Pardee, "The Kirta Epic," 337). Mullen's assertion that the setting for divine blessing is the divine council (Mullen, *The Divine Council in Canaanite and Early Hebrew Literature*, 248) should be rejected because the presence of the phrase "the assembly of gods" does not necessitate the setting of the divine council in the heavenly court.

[266] Parker, *The Pre-Biblical Narrative Tradition: Essays on the Ugaritic Poems Keret and Aqhat*, 162; J. C. L. Gibson, "Myth, Legend, and Folk-Lore in the Ugaritic Keret and Aqhat Texts," in *Congress Volume, Edinburgh 1974* (Leiden: Brill, 1975), 62; Robert W. Neff, "The Announcement in Old Testament Birth Stories" (Ph.D. diss., Yale University, 1969), 37; Spronk, "The Legend of Kirtu (KTU 1.14–16): A Study of the Structure and Its Consequences for Interpretation," 69; Margalit, "The Legend of Keret," 223.

[267] Parker, *The Pre-Biblical Narrative Tradition: Essays on the Ugaritic Poems Keret and Aqhat*, 162.

[268] Mullen, *The Divine Council in Canaanite and Early Hebrew Literature*, 248.

story of ʾAqhatu as the latter's patron deity, while in the Kirta story Baʿlu's role remains only in the background.[269] The second similarity between the two scenes of divine blessing is that ʾIlu's blessing in both scenes consists of a traditional gesture of blessing (cf. KTU 1.15 II:16–18a and 1.17 I:34a), a general blessing (1.15 II:18b–20 and 1.17 I:34b–38a), and a specific blessing-promise (cf. 1.15 II:21–III:16 and 1.17 I:38bff.). As typical of the incubation type-scene, the last is geared toward the solution of respective petitioners. ʾIlu promises Kirta and Dānîʾilu with a child-bearing wife and a dutiful son respectively.

Just as the motif of a vow embedded in the fulfillment section serves as a portent for the second episode of the Kirta story, so does the embedded motif of divine blessing seem to foreshadow the third episode of the Kirta story. Although most of ʾIlu's blessing concerns the enumeration of the sons and the daughters that will be born of Kirta's new marriage, ʾIlu decides to go extra miles to add some details about the firstborn and the last born children.

KTU 1.15 II

(26)	tl⸢d⸣ . y⸢ṣb⸣ [.]⸢ǵlm⸣	She shall bear the lad Yaṣṣubu,
(27)	ynq . ⸢ḥl⸣b . ⸢a⸣ [ṯ]rt	Who will drink the milk of ʾAṯiratu,
(28)	mṣṣ . ṯ⸢d⸣ . ⸢b⸣tlt . [ʿnt]	Shall suckle at the breasts of Girl [ʿAnatu].

KTU 1.15 III

(16)	⸢ṣ⸣ǵrthn . abk⸢rn⸣	The youngest of these girls, I shall treat as the firstborn.

The third part of ʾIlu's blessing, namely, a specific blessing-promise (KTU 1.15 II:21–III:16) has an *inclusio* structure. ʾIlu's prediction of the future of Kirta's firstborn son (1.15 II:26–28) and that of Kirta's lastborn daughter (1.15 III:16) encloses ʾIlu's blessing-promise specifically geared to meet Kirta's need. The corresponding part of ʾIlu's blessing in the ʾAqhatu story (KTU 1.17 I:38b–?) registers no prediction about Dānîʾilu son, ʾAqhatu. As it has already been noted in chapter three, an element of a prediction about the future of a new-born is what distinguishes the theophany in the birth story of a hero from the

[269] For discussion of the role of Baʿlu in the narrative, see further below.

theophany in the incubation type-scene. The lack of any prediction about 'Aqhatu therefore may be explained by the fact that the theophany in the 'Aqhatu story forms a part of the incubation type-scene, not to mention that 'Aqhatu is less a hero than a tragic victim. The prediction about Kirta's firstborn son and lastborn daughter, however, may look like a misfit in the theophany scene of the incubation type-scene. But there are several mitigating factors. First, the divine blessing-promise that includes the prediction about a new-born does not occur in the theophany section of the incubation type-scene in *Kirta*.[270] It is embedded in the final section of an incubation type-scene as sort of compensation for the lack of divine promise in the theophany scene. Strictly speaking, the divine speech in the incubation type-scene of the Kirta story registers no prediction about a future hero. Second, the prediction about the last-born daughter may be no prediction at all, at least on the surface level. 'Ilu's words, "The youngest of these girls, I shall treat as the firstborn," may be a simple blessing, indicating that even the youngest of Kirta's children will lead as abundant a life as the eldest.[271] Be that as it may, the motif of divine blessing in the fulfillment motif reflects the poet's intention to use it as a literary adumbration of the future plot. As has been noted, the incubation type-scene in the Kirta story shows more freedom in the arrangement of component motifs. This freedom often entails a literary purpose on the part of the poet. Thus, the prediction registered in KTU 1.15 II:26–28 foreshadows the scene in the second episode of the story where the nobles proclaim Yaṣṣubu as an heir apparent to the ailing king Kirta.[272] The prediction

[270] Neff, "The Announcement in Old Testament Birth Stories," 36.

[271] Nick Wyatt, *Religious Texts from Ugarit*, 212, footnote 157.

[272] When the readers read that Yaṣṣubu grew on the milk of the goddess, they knew that he was marked out for kingship. The motif of a prince sucking the nipples of goddesses is well attested to in ancient Near East as well as in ancient Greece. West summarizes comparative data on this motif as follows: "Erechtheus was born from the earth and 'reared' by Athena. Heracles was sucked by Hera, in one version as an infant, in another as a grown man as a means to immortality. In Mesopotamia this was an ancient idea. Many of the early Sumerian kings claimed to have been nourished by the milk of the mother goddess Ninhursaga, and many reliefes and terracottas show her suckling the royal infant. In *Enūma eliš*...we read of Marduk that "Ea his father created him, Damkina his mother bore him; he sucked the nipples of goddesses".... The motif remained current with the Neo-Assyrian kings. In an oracle to Esarhaddon Ishtar calls herself his good wet-nurse, and in another to Assurbanipal she says 'Like a nurse I carried you on my hip...I placed you between my breats'. Nabu tells him 'You were little, Assurbanipal, when I left you with the Queen of Nineveh; you were a baby, Ashurbanipal, when you sat on the knee of the Queen of Nineveh. Her four

registered in KTU 1.15 III:16, on the other hand, prepares the reader for a surprising turn of events in the missing third episode of the story where Ṯitmanatu replaces Yaṣṣubu on the seat of the throne.[273]

Finally, the literary role of the gods in the motif of blessing may be discussed. According to KTU 1.15 III:17–19, the gods bless Kirta right after 'Ilu's blessing before they return to their dwellings. Some of these gods are even named in the first 10 lines of KTU 1.15 I: [*aliy*]*n b'l*, *yrḫ zbl*, [*kṯ*]*r w ḫss*, *rḥmy*, *ršp zbl*, etc. The whole assembly of the gods seems to cooperate to forward the common goal of rebuilding Kirta's family. Interestingly enough, however, some gods who participated in Kirta's wedding banquet are also associated with various situations that have led to the total destruction of Kirta's family. Kirta's third wife died while "in health" (*kṯrm*) and the fourth wife in illness (*zbln*). The death of the fifth wife is attributed to the god *ršp*, while the demise of the sixth wife is associated with the act of Yammu's lads.[274] These subtle allusions to the gods in the description of Kirta's predicament highlight the ambiguous attitude of the gods toward Kirta throughout the story. The gods who participate in Kirta's wedding banquet, for example, do not remain beneficent toward Kirta. When 'Ilu calls for a healer in the assembly of gods summoned by 'Ilšu to deal with the problem of Kirta's illness, no god replies to 'Ilu's thrice repeated calls. They may have been unable to do the job but their collective silence to 'Ilu's calls seems to make their good will toward Kirta very suspicious. The attitude of 'Aṯiratu toward Kirta is ambiguous, too. In the

---

nipples were set in your mouth; two you were sucking, and two you pulled own to your face." We find the idea at ugarit too. Keret is told that his wife will bear a son "she shall bear the lad yaṣṣib, a sucker of the milk of Athirat, a drainer of the breats of the maiden, the wet-nurse of the gods" (West, *The East Face of Helicon: West Asiatic Elements in Greek Poetry and Myth*, 133). See also Moor and Spronk, "Problematical Passages in the Legend of Kirtu (I)," 175; Neff, "The Announcement in Old Testament Birth Stories," 73; Knopper, "Dissonance and Disaster in the Legend of Kirta," 577. For iconographic evidence for the royal children sucking the breasts of a goddess, see André Caquot and Maurice Sznycer, *Ugaritic Religion*, Iconography of Religions. (Leiden: Brill, 1980), 18–19, Plates XXVIII a, XXVIII b; Carole Roche, "The Lady of Ugarit," *NEA* 63 (2000): 215.

273 Simon B. Parker, "The Historical Composition of KRT and the Cult of El," *ZAW* 89 (1977): 169.

274 If *šlḥ* is a divine name as suggested by Del Olmo Lete, then we have one more evidence that connects Kirta's misfortune to the activity of the deities. Cf. Matitiahu Tsevat, "The Canaanite God Šälaḥ," *VT* 4 (1954): 49; Olmo Lete and Sanmartín, *A Dictionary of the Ugaritic Language in the Alphabetic Tradition*, 816.

incubation type-scene, ʾAṯiratu is supplicated to foster the success of Kirta's mission. ʾIlu himself invokes ʾAṯiratu in blessing Kirta's firstborn child: "May he drink the milk of ʾAṯiratu!" But the second episode of *Kirta* assumes a situation where ʾAṯiratu turns hostile toward Kirta and undoes ʾIlu's blessing by making Kirta fatally ill. This ambiguous, if not hostile, relationship that the gods have with Kirta should be understood in the comparative light of ʾIlu's attitude to Kirta. Both not only corroborate the ideology of ideal kingship in antiquity but also underscore Kirta's religious apathy, the priestly king who ought to have been the paragon of piety. ʾIlu's unconditional favor to Kirta assumes the ancient ideology of kingship whereas Kirta's "flawed" piety is thrown into relief by ʾIlu's unreciprocated faithfulness. ʾIlu's dealings with Kira are intended to portray Kirta as a "flawed" hero-king, rather than to put forward the covenantal relationship between ʾIlu and Kirta. The ambiguous attitude of the other gods to Kirta (beneficent and hostile) is also a function of the two conflicting situations, of Kirta in the role of priestly king who is pivotal to the harmony of divine and human worlds and of Kirta as a man of dubious piety. The gods help Kirta to rebuild his house because the latter's importance as a priestly king, but they are not as forgiving as ʾIlu about Kirta's breach of faith.

2.3.3 *The Motif of Birth*

KTU 1.15 III:20–25

(20)	wtqrb . wld bn lh	Her time came and she bore a son for him,
(21)	wtqrb . wld bnm lh	Her time came and she bore sons for him.
(22)	mk . bšbʿ . šnt	In seven years' time
(23)	bn . krt . km hm . tdr	Kirta's son were as many as they were promised,
(24)	ap . bnt . ḥry (25) km hm	Ḥurray's daughters as many as them.

The motif of birth does triple duty. First it serves as a direct fulfillment of ʾIlu's blessing-promise. Second, it concludes the whole incubation type-scene by providing the ultimate resolution to the plot that began with the motif of the complete destruction of Kirta's family. Third, it serves as a bridge to the second episode of the Kirta story through the *double entendre* of the word *tdr* in line 23.

The motif of child birth used in this type-scene is a truncated one. The element of counting the months of gestation is telescoped into one word *tqrb* "Her time came."[275] But the use of the formulaic word *wld* makes the motif of birth easily recognizable. The use of *bnm* "sons" in line 21, instead of *bnt* "daughters," may be explained by the perceived importance of male offspring.[276] Moreover, *bnm* may be a dual, thus forming a x // x+1 formula referring to the sum of sons born.[277] The following tricolon (lines 22–24) expands on the number of Kirta's new-borns. But it does so not by mentioning a specific number, but by alluding to the numbers mentioned in the motif of 'Ilu's promise-blessing in KTU 1.15 II:23–25. The word *tdr*, which may be parsed as 3rd m.pl., G-passive preformative of √ndr "to vow," not only highlights the fact that the birth of children is the direct result of 'Ilu's promise but also reminds the readers of Kirta's spontaneous vow to 'Aṯiratu. The fact that Kirta's unfulfilled vow is picked up in the immediately following bicolon that begins the second episode of *Kirta* shows that the master poet who is able to make use of every artistic ploy at his disposal employs the motif of birth as a bridge to the second episode of the story. Moreover, the tricolon provides yet another example of hyperbole. It is rare to produce 14 children in seven years' time. It is clearly a literary hyperbole designed to show not only 'Ilu's power but also his favorable disposition toward Kirta (cf. Jacob's children and Job's children).[278]

3. The Narratological Role of the Incubation Type-Scene: Foreshadowing and Reminiscing

The length of the incubation type-scene in *Kirta* and the clear movement of plot from loss to restoration within the type-scene make the

[275] The word *tqrb* has been rendered in three ways. First, it is rendered as "to be approached (by the husband)," thus a euphemism for sexual intercourse (cf. Caquot, Sznycer, and Herdner, *Mythes et légendes: introduction, traduction, commentaire*, 540, footnote n). Second, on the basis of Arabic *'aqraba* "to be near to bringing forth" and *muqribah* "woman near to bringing forth," one may translate it as "(her time to bear) approaches" (J. C. L. Gibson, *Canaanite Myths and Legends.*, 91; Pardee, "The Kirta Epic," 338). Third, *tqrb* has also been translated as "soon" on the basis of Arabic *qāraba* "to make things happen at very short intervals" (Moor and Spronk, "Problematical Passages in the Legend of Kirtu [I]," 176; Dietrich and Loretz, "Das Keret-Epos," 1236). But considering that the element of counting gestation months is missing in the motif of birth, one may discern a very truncated form of it in the word *tqrb*.

[276] Pardee, "The Kirta Epic," 338.

[277] Ibid.

[278] Nick Wyatt, *Religious Texts from Ugarit*, 213, footnote 160.

incubation type-scene in *Kirta* stand alone as a complete narrative in itself. It is no wonder that the incubation type-scene constitutes the entirety of the first episode of the Kirta story, which Merrill and Parker take as the basic story of *Kirta* to which other thematically related episodes were added later.[279] This characteristic of the incubation type-scene in *Kirta* helps us to distinguish Ugaritic type-scenes from classical type-scenes as well as from biblical type-scenes: unlike the latter two, Ugaritic type-scenes may constitute a fully developed story with a plot. Besides, Ugaritic type-scenes consist of theme-based formulae and motifs in contrast to meter-based formulae and motifs as in the classical type-scene, and unlike biblical type-scenes which occur only at important junctures in a hero's life such as birth, marriage, or death,[280] Ugaritic type-scenes may occur anywhere in a poem narrating a hero's life. This difference may be connected to different textures of respective literatures: Classical literature is meter-based poetry while Ugaritic literature is parallelism-based poetry, and biblical type-scenes occur only in prose.

Since Ugaritic poets do not use flashback as a story-telling device,[281] they tends to depend on an elaborate system of literary allusions that not only make the story more pleasurable, but also serve as plot-advancing devices and make the communication of the message more effective. As shown through many examples above, component motifs of the incubation type-scene in *Kirta* are interconnected with one another through a sophisticated web of allusions either through foreshadowing or reminiscing. For instance, the reason that the motif of predicament has the *inclusio* structure that centers its focus on the theme of "wifelessness" may be connected to the later development of the story. Thus, although the ultimate resolution of Kirta's problem lies in procuring of children (cf. the motif of birth), the first episode revolves around the acquisition of a fertile wife for Kirta. As an

---

[279] Merrill, "The House of Keret: A Study of the Keret Legend," 10; Parker, "The Historical Composition of KRT and the Cult of El," 161–75.

[280] Alter, *The Art of Biblical Narrative*, 51.

[281] In biblical narrative flashbacks are sometimes inserted by the narrator when a new character enters the narrative, providing background and details from the past (cf. Introduction of Jephthah in Judges 11:1–3). But as Bar-Efrat correctly points out, this is not customary in biblical narrative. Bar-Efrat observes that time in biblical narrative flows "evenly in the narrative.... The narrative does not include simultaneous events or flashbacks. Time proceeds in one direction, without any deviation from the usual chronological order." Cf. Shimon Bar-Efrat, *Narrative Art in the Bible*, JSOTSup (Sheffield: Almond Press, 1989), 280.

illustration of reminiscing, one may adduce the scene of Pabil's dispatch of messengers to Kirta, where the poet composes the visit of Pabil's messenger in such way that it recalls 'Ilu's oneiric visit to Kirta in his room. Besides the same list of tributes offered by both 'Ilu and Pabil,[282] the poet describes their visit as being directly caused by the "noise" problem, Kirta's weeping and the animals' crying. Also, both visits may have been nocturnal.

The narratological function of incubation type-scene is not only fulfilled by a sophisticated web of allusions, but also by a particular configuration of component motifs that the poet chooses in the composition of the incubation type-scene. Instead of placing the motifs of sacrifice and vow in the pre-epiphany section of the type-scene, the poet of *Kirta* embeds them in the epiphany section and in the post-epiphany section respectively. Furthermore, he embeds the motif of divine blessing not in the epiphany section but in the post-epiphany section. This particular configuration is imbued with narratological significance. By embedding the motifs of vow and divine blessing in the post-epiphany section of the incubation, for instance, the poet prepares the reader for subsequent episodes of the story. The vow made at Sidon and Tyre by Kirta—his failure to fulfill it nearly causes his death—serves as a bridge from the first to the second episode where the plot revolves around Kirta's illness. Likewise, if there was a fourth tablet of the Kirta story, 'Ilu's blessing made at Kirta's wedding banquet may have adumbrated the third episode where the plot may have revolved around the theme of the youngest replacing the oldest on the throne.[283] All this seems to intimate that the Kirta story is not a conflation of three distinct episodes but a unified work of art composed by

[282] Parker wonders why 'Ilu would offer the same list of tributes that he would later command Kirta to reject when it is offered by Pabil. In order to answer this question, Parker speculates that the original list offered by 'Ilu would have included only gold and silver and that the other items are added later. But he does not explain why such addition might have been needed in the narrative except to say that textual corruption and subsequent influence of refrain may have been responsible for the addition. In my judgment, however, the poet deliberately uses the same list of gifts in order to place 'Ilu's visit and the visit of Pabil's messenger in a relation of reminiscent allusion. Cf. Parker, *The Pre-Biblical Narrative Tradition: Essays on the Ugaritic Poems Keret and Aqhat*, 150.

[283] For the hypothetical reconstruction of the third episode see Spronk, "The Legend of Kirtu (KTU 1.14–16): A Study of the Structure and Its Consequences for Interpretation," 79.

a master poet who uses the incubation type-scene as the base story on which to further develop the plot of his story.

Finally, it is noteworthy that all the literary artifices crafted into the composition of the incubation type-scene serve to communicate the message of the Kirta story. Scholars are divided on this matter and scholarly disagreement operates on several levels. Is the Kirta story ultimately political or religious? If it is the former, does it confirm the ideology of ideal kingship (propaganda)[284] or decredit it (satire)?[285] If it is the latter, what is the nature of the relationship between 'Ilu and Kirta? Is it covenantal?[286] Does it reflect the influence of the monotheistic faith of the Amarna religion?[287] All these questions are also related to another unanswerable question whether there is a fourth tablet of *Kirta*, or not.

The analysis of the first episode of *Kirta* through the grid of the incubation type-scene seems to reveal two thematic foci of the Kirta story: ideology of kingship (political focus) and a "flawed" king in matters of religious piety (religious focus). I wish to propose that the failure to consider both foci has resulted in the current division of opinion among scholars. The Kirta story takes, without endorsing explicitly, the ideology of ideal kingship for granted. 'Ilu's oneiric theophany to Kirta, for instance, underscores the favored position of a king in communication with the divine world.[288] The scene of sacrifice embedded in the motif of divine command presents Kirta in the capacity of a priestly king who mediates the divine and human worlds.[289] The mediatory role of

[284] Cf. Nick Wyatt, "Epic in Ugaritic Literature," in *A Companion to Ancient Epic*, ed. John M. Foley (Oxford: Blackwell, 2005), 246–54. Reprinted in N. Wyatt, *Word of Tree and Whisper of Stone: And Other Papers on Ugaritic Thought*, 143–153; Merrill, "The House of Keret: A Study of the Keret Legend," 5–17; Olmo Lete, *Mitos y leyendas de Canaan: según la tradición de Ugarit*, 276–77.

[285] Margalit, "The Legend of Keret," 203–33. Also see Koch who regards the Kirta story as a comic (*apud* Baruch Margalit, *The Ugaritic Poem of Aqht: Text, Translation, Commentary*, BZAW 182 [New York: De Gruyter, 1989], 46).

[286] Cyrus H. Gordon, "The Patriarchal Age," *JBR* 21 (1953): 238–43; F. C. Fensham, "Remarks on Keret 73–79," *JNSL* 6 (1979): 19–24; H. Gottlieb, "El und Krt-Jahwe und David," *VT* 24 (1974): 159–67. Cf. Loewenstamm, "Zur Götterlehre des Epos von Keret," 505–14.

[287] J. C. de Moor, "The Crisis of Polytheism in Late Bronze Ugarit," *OtSt* 24 (1986): 2–3. Parker also considers this possibility (Parker, *The Pre-Biblical Narrative Tradition: Essays on the Ugaritic Poems Keret and Aqhat*, 215).

[288] Knopper, "Dissonance and Disaster in the Legend of Kirta," 575; Seow, "The Syro-Palestinian Context of Solomon's Dream," 144.

[289] Caquot and Sznycer, *Ugaritic Religion*, 18.

Kirta as a priestly king is pivotal to the well-being of people, as well as of the gods, because the divine and human worlds are in a distinct but inseparable relation so that the disturbance of order in one realm affects the other.[290] That is why the gods are interested in Kirta's house, and why the people of Ḫubur have much at stake in Kirta's campaign. Just as everyone in Kirta's kingdom is mobilized for the expedition to 'Udumu, the whole assembly of gods (*'dt ilm* "the assembly of gods" in KTU 1.15 II:11 and *dr il* "the circle of 'Ilu" in 1.15 III:19) attend Kirta's wedding banquet and give their collective blessings on Kirta and Ḥurray (KTU 1.15 III:17–19). Likewise, when drought occurs in the land, owing to Kirta's failure to execute his priestly role, 'Ilu summons the whole assembly of gods through 'Ilšu and his wife to deal with Kirta's illness. All these show that the Kirta story assumes the veracity of the ideology of ideal kingship.[291]

Another focus of the story concerns the "flawed" piety of a king. Kirta as a priestly king who serves as an intermediary between the divine and human worlds is expected to be the paragon of religious piety.[292] The Kirta text, however, seems to be punctuated with subtle allusions to Kirta's lackadaisical attitude toward matters of religion. Among other things, Kirta's vow seems to discredit the true nature of Kirta's religiosity. The fact that Kirta's vow is a breaking of the command and execution structure, the idiosyncratic four-day sequence that results from the insertion of a vow-making scene, and Kirta's failure to fulfill his vow to Aṯiratu, all these show that Kirta's vow-making,

[290] A similar idea appears in the biblical wisdom tradition where the king is described to the one who maintains harmony with the divine order by his just dealings in society (Helen A. Kenik, *Design for Kingship: The Deuteronomistic Narrative Technique in 1 Kings 3:4–15*, SBLDS 69 [Chico, California: Scholars Press, 1983], 88).

[291] For a summary of the ideology of kingship in ancient Near East see John H. Walton, *Ancient Near Eastern Thought and the Old Testament: Introducing the Conceptual World of the Hebrew Bible* (Grand Rapids, MI: Baker Academic, 2006), 278–86.

[292] This idea is most explicitly endorsed by the Deuteronomist Historian who evaluates Israelite and Judean Kings in accordance with their adherence to the cult of Yahweh. A similar idea also occurs in Homeric literature. In the Chryses episode, for instance, king Agamemnon's rejection to return Chryses's daughter incurs the anger of Apollo, placing the Achaean camp in danger of annihilation by plague. This episode underscores the importance of the king's piety in the well-being of his people (Shiroe Yoshikazu, "An Impious King: The Ethics of the Iliad Represented in the Chryses Episode" *Classical Studies* 4 [1988] 14–27 [Japanese]). This idea is not limited to Western civilizations. In Ancient China, the harmony between the divine and human worlds depended on the virtuous behavior of the king in his dutiful reverence to the ancestors (Kelly Bulkeley, *Dreaming in the World's Religions: A Comparative History* [New York: New York University Press, 2008], 55).

usually an act of piety, is depicted by the poet as an act of a flawed piety.[293] This clear mark of Kirta's lackadaisical attitude toward 'Ilu would not have come as a complete surprise to careful audiences who were able to pick up subtle allusions to Kirta's religious apathy in the preceding text. First, although 'Ilu's theophany to Kirta confirms the ideology of ideal kingship, the manner in which Kirta invokes divine apparition is a far cry from what one may expect from a pious king. Kirta invokes divine help by weeping aloud in his private room. This stands in stark contrast to the way Dānî'ilu invokes divine help in a similar situation with a seven-day long series of sacrifices, libations, and prayer at a temple. Although Kirta's weeping in his room may reflect his spontaenous response to an overwhelming difficulty, a comparison with Dānî'ilu seems to suggest that Kirta either did not know how to approach the gods for help or did not care much about cultic protocol. Instead of going through elaborate sacrifices with scripted prayer, he withdraws himself to his own room, and weeps with extemporaneous murmurings. Second, 'Ilu's offer of his own kingdom in Kirta's dream may also be suggestive of the true nature of Kirta's piety. His offer seems to assume that Kirta would want to have 'Ilu's kingship. Although his question may have different literary functions, Yaṣṣubu's claim to throne (KTU 1.16 VI:52–54), which recalls 'Ilu's offer of kingship through the use of the same word-pair, *mlk* "kingship" and *drkt* "domain," corroborate the negative allusion to the nature of Kirta's piety. Third, 'Ilu's detailed instructions of sacrifice may be seen as alluding to Kirta's religious indiligence. The poet places the motif of sacrifice not in the pre-epiphany section of the incubation type-scene, but embeds it in divine instruction. It is as if 'Ilu as a kind father gave a lesson on how to properly invoke divine help to his human son who has just missed sacrifice in invoking 'Ilu's help. Since the details involving the rituals—such as purification before entering the tent-shrine, sacrifice and libation in a tent-shrine, and finally prayer and

[293] One may argue that Kirta's vow itself does not constitute a case of impiety because vow-making is normally a religious act and/or because 'Ilu did not punish Kirta for that vow. Rather, his failure to fulfill it is a serious lapse that is punished with illness. But the broader narratological context puts Kirta's vow in a clearly negative light, let alone the broken seven day unit. The fact that vow-making was an act of piety in antiquity makes Kirta's refraction all the more poignant. Also the fact that 'Ilu did not punish Kirta is consistent with the portrayal of 'Ilu in this story. No matter what Kirta does, 'Ilu continues to show his favor to him. This unconditional love of 'Ilu has the effect of throwing Kirta's irreligiosity into a clear relief.

theophany on the rooftops—strongly recall the standard procedure of an incubation rite, it may be argued that its purpose may have been pedagogical on 'Ilu's part. Finally, Kirta's apathy in matters of religion is alluded to by the way he deals with 'Ilu's *ipsissima verba*. The poet portrays Kirta in the fulfillment motif as omitting some of the words that 'Ilu orders Kirta to speak to Pabil. Although the poetic line missing in Kirta's version does not change significantly its logic, Kirta's failure to obey 'Ilu completely by conveying all of his words to Pabil certainly prepares the readers for the subsequent refraction of 'Ilu's command by making a vow to 'Aṯiratu. All these may have a cumulative effect as subtle, but sure, allusions to Kirta's lackadaisical attitude toward matters of religion. In this regard Kirta's vow may not necessarily be a later addition to the first episode, as Parker would make us believe, but part of the literary artifices crafted into the composition of incubation type-scene.

These two foci provide a consistent perspective in understanding the whole story. The ultimate question is "What if the one who plays such an important role as the king is a man of religious indiligence?" That is one of the questions that the Kirta story tries to answer in matters of Ugaritic religion. The answer that the Kirta story gives as a whole is not positive. Despite unceasing help from 'Ilu and Ba'lu, Kirta ends up being deathly sick. 'Ilu's creation of Ša'tiqatu relieves Kirta of illness, but Kirta is then challenged by his legitimate son, Yaṣṣubu, to come down from his kingship. Yaṣṣubu's claim may be based on his concern for the institution of kingship rather than on his greed for power. Considering that his accusations against Kirta confirm the ideology of ideal kingship that the Kirta story takes for granted, Yaṣṣubu's claim may have been a legitimate one. Nevertheless, Kirta curses his son and thereby loses his legitimate heir given him through the help of and blessed to become an heir by 'Ilu and other gods. And such a tragic conclusion may be the answer to the question "What if a king is irreligious?" In this regard, 'Ilu's unconditional favor needs not be taken as an influence of a monotheistic religion. The poet deliberately contrasts 'Ilu's faithfulness with Kirta's unfaithfulness, thus throwing the latter's inappropriateness as a priestly king into sharper relief. The ambiguous attitude of the gods toward Kirta is also to be understood in a similar vein. Kirta as a king is pivotal to the wellbeing of the gods. So they bless Kirta's marriage to rectify his childlessness. On the other hand, they are not as forgiving as 'Ilu with respect to Kirta's religious apathy. Goddess 'Aṯiratu makes him fatally ill. The assembly of gods would not answer 'Ilu's repeated calls for help in saving Kirta from illness. Both 'Ilu's unfailing love for Kirta and the gods' ambiguous, if not hostile, attitude toward Kirta are really corollaries of the two foci (the ideology of ideal kingship and "flawed" piety of a king) working criss-cross in the story.

4. Conclusion

The incubation type-scene in the Kirta story provides an example of incubation as a literary device that does not necessarily look like the practice of incubation. Although the lack of rituals in the pre-epiphany section of the type-scene and the place where Kirta encountered 'Ilu makes it hard to say that Kirta is in the text resorting to the practice of incubation, one may say that a sequence of component motifs that comprise the first episode of the Kirta story bears a family resemblance to other instances of incubation type-scenes. First, a sequence of motifs that occur in the first episode of *Kirta* not only articulate the four major concepts that underpin the practice of incubation, namely, predicament, intentionality, liminality and epiphany, but they are also arranged so as to serve the poet's narrative purpose. For example, although the pre-epiphany section of the type-scene does not include any rituals, their absence is compensated for by the motifs of sacrifice and of a vow that appear in the post-epiphany section, and their placement makes good sense in terms of the further development of narrative. This simply confirms our hypothesis that the component motifs of incubation type-scene do not have a fixed place in the type-scene, but they can appear anywhere within the type-scene when it better serves the literary purpose of the poet. Second, the incubation type-scene in *Kirta* may stand alone as a story complete in itself with a clear movement of plot from introduction to crisis, to climax, and to denouement. In this regard, the incubation type-scene in *Kirta* distinguishes itself from biblical type-scenes which according to Alter occur only as an introduction to the life of a hero. As will be shown in chapter six, the type-scene in 1 Samuel 1 seems to show a transitional stage in the development of the history of the tradition. It has every mark of an independent incubation type-scene with Hannah as the protagonist but is also used as the introduction to the life of a hero. Third, it is noteworthy that the overall plot and the particular configuration of component motifs contribute to the effective communication of the poet's messages about Ugaritic kingship and religion. Although Margalit objects that the meat of the Kirta story is the second and the third episodes and that the first episode serves only as an introduction,[294] the above analysis proves the critical importance of the first episode in the Kirta story as a whole. Although one can never be sure of the history of the composition of Kirta story, Merrill and Parker may be correct in arguing that the first episode is the basic story of *Kirta* out of which the extant version of the story is developed. This may account for the mixed image of Kirta found in this incubation type-scene. Kirta the incubant proves himself to be pious by executing 'Ilu's oneiric command meticulously. But at the same time, one may discern several subtle allusions that may subject his piety into reasonable doubt. And the latter may also account for other misfortunes in Kirta's life that the subsequent plot of the story revolves around. If the second and third episodes of Kirta are later additions to the first episode of *Kirta*, the textual allusions to Kirta's indiligence in matters of religion may be also said to be secondary.

[294] Margalit, "The Legend of Keret," 214.

CHAPTER SIX

HOW HANNAH WAS BLESSED WITH A SON?
The Incubation Type-Scene in 1 Samuel 1:1–2:11

1. Previous Studies

Despite the paucity of biblical data, the subject of incubation has engaged a number of biblical scholars. The complexity inherent in the concept of incubation has lent itself to various approaches of research. The subject of incubation has been dealt with as part of history-of-religions discussions on dream divination in ancient Israel (1.1), in exegetical studies of those passages that are considered relevant to an incubation rite (1.2), or as part of form-critical discussions of the dream reports in the Hebrew Bible (1.3). However, with regard to the Hannah story (i.e. the story of Samuel's birth), very little has been said in relation to the subject of incubation (1.4).

1.1 *The History-of-Religions Approach*

Did ancient Israel practice an incubation rite? Since the Hebrew Bible contains no explicit reference to this religious practice, the question of its existence in ancient Israel may be posed with legitimacy from the perspective of the comparative study of religions.[1] Those scholars who are convinced of the uniqueness of Israelite religion tend to answer the question in the negative. For them, the very notion of inducing divine revelation through temple-sleep was foreign to the religious thought of ancient Israel. For instance, Resch believes that incubation "...mit der Theologien Israels absolut unvereinbar ist."[2] Although Kaufmann does not even mention, let alone discuss, incubation in his book, *The Religion of Israel*, his separation between revelation and divination and

[1] Jean-Marie Husser, *Dreams and Dream Narratives in the Biblical World*, BS 63 (Sheffield: Sheffield Academic Press, 1999), 167; Robert K. Gnuse, "The Dream Theophany of Samuel: Its Structure in Relation to Ancient Near Eastern Dreams and Its Theological Significance" (Ph.D. diss., Nashville, TN: Vanderbilt University, 1980), 62.

[2] Andreas Resch, *Der Traum im Heilsplan Gottes: Deutung und Bedeutung des Traums im Alten Testament* (Freiburg: Herder, 1964), 115.

the characterization of the latter as paganism, that is, "coercing the gods to do the will of the practitioner," allow us to interpret his silence on the subject as a strong negation.[3]

A number of scholars, however, who see more continuity than discontinuity between the religions of ancient Israel and those of its neighbors, tend to assume, if not assert, the existence of an incubation rite in ancient Israel. Their argument may be summarized thus: Although there is no explicit reference to an incubation rite in the Hebrew Bible, all the necessary ideas for the functioning of this religious practice in ancient Israel may be found in the Bible. First, the Hebrew Bible seems to recognize the revelatory nature of dreams.[4] In various Genesis passages, for instance, the patriarchs are said to have revelatory dreams at major junctures in their lives.[5] Even in the prophetic literature, which is generally taken as expressing a negative attitude toward dreams, there is no absolute rejection of dreams as a legitimate channel for divine revelation. In this regard, Blenkinsopp points out that doubt about the propriety of dreams as a way of obtaining revelations is not justified in light of prophetic history as a whole.[6] Second, the Hebrew Bible seems to affirm the idea that particular spaces, especially

---

[3] Yehezkel Kaufmann, *The Religion of Israel* (Chicago: The University of Chicago Press, 1960), 40.

[4] For instance, Ehrlich says, "Voraussetzung jeder Inkubation is der Glaube an die Wirklichkeit des Traumes" (Ernst L. Ehrlich, *Der Traum im Alten Testament*, BZAW 73 [Berlin: Töpelmann, 1953], 14). Similarly Jeffers states, "The precondition for the incubation is the belief in the reality of the dream" (Ann Jeffers, *Magic and Divination in Ancient Palestine and Syria*, SHCANE 8 [Leiden: Brill, 1996], 136).

[5] Frederick H. Cryer, *Divination in Ancient Israel and Its Near Eastern Environment*, JSOTSup 142 (Sheffield: JSOT Press), 265; Otto Eissfeldt, "Wahrsagung im Alten Testament," in *La divination en Mésopotamie ancienne et dans les régions voisines* (Paris: Presses universitaires de France, 1966), 143–46; Shaul Bar, *A Letter That Has not Been Read: Dreams in the Hebrew Bible* (Cincinnati, OH: Hebrew Union College Press, 2001), 165; André Caquot, "La divination dans l'ancient Israël," in *La divination*, ed. André Caquot and Marcel Leibovici (Paris: Presses Universitaire de France, 1968), 94; Gnuse, "The Dream Theophany of Samuel: Its Structure in Relation to Ancient Near Eastern Dreams and Its Theological Significance," 83.

[6] Joseph Blenkinsopp, *A History of Prophecy in Israel* (Louisville, KY: Westminster John Knox Press, 1996), 156. Grabbe says in a similar vein, "Dreams seem to be treated negatively in Jeremiah (23:27–32; 29:8) and are otherwise seldom mentioned in the prophetic literature. This has led to the conventional assertion that the OT prophets regarded dreams negatively. This sweeping generalization needs to be challenged" (Lester L Grabbe, *Priests, Prophets, Diviners, Sages: A Socio-Historical Study of Religious Specialists in Ancient Israel* [Valley Forge, PA: Trinity Press International, 1995], 145–47). For attitudes toward dreams in prophetic literature, see Bar, *A Letter That Has not Been Read: Dreams in the Hebrew Bible*, chapter 4; Cryer, *Divination in Ancient Israel and Its Near Eastern Environment*, 263–67.

temples, are places where divine-human contact is most easily attainable.[7] Yahweh seems to have had a special connection with the holy places where he was worshipped. In particular, he was believed to be present in the tent-shrine in the desert as well as in the temple of Jerusalem. For this reason, Lindblom takes the element of a holy place as a definitive feature of biblical theophanies.[8] Third, the Hebrew Bible recognizes the legitimacy of "inquiring of YHWH," in other words, of soliciting an oracle from God.[9] Wilson, for instance, argues that before the rise of the monarchy the seer (*rōʾēh*) served as a channel of communication between God and the people, inquiring of God on behalf of the people and delivering oracles from God to the people, although both of these functions were later taken over by the prophet (*nābîʾ*).[10] Thus, for those scholars who recognize the presence in Israel of all the necessary ideas for the functioning of incubation, there is no compelling reason not to assume the existence in Israel of an incubation rite, for after all it is a subcategory of dream divination which was widely attested in the ancient Near East. Delekat, for instance, argues that incubation is one of the three procedures that Israelite priests resorted to in order to derive oracles from Yahweh.[11] In a similar vein, Wilson asserts that in the early period of Israelite history, when the roles of a priest and a prophet had not yet diverged, the prophet (*rōʾēh*) may

[7] Frances L. Flannery-Dailey, "Standing at the Heads of Dreamers: A Study of Dreams in Antiquity Second Temple Period" (Ph.D. diss., University of Iowa, 2000), 52; Jeffers, *Magic and Divination in Ancient Palestine and Syria*, 136; Johannes Lindblom, "Theophanies in Holy Places in Hebrew Religion," *HUCA* 32 (1961): 91–106.

[8] Johannes Lindblom, "Theophanies in Holy Places in Hebrew Religion," *Hebrew Union College Annual* 32 (1961): 92–93.

[9] Ehrlich, *Der Traum im Alten Testament*, 14; Blenkinsopp, *A History of Prophecy in Israel*, 127; L. Delekat, *Asylie und Schutzorakel am Zionheiligtum: Eine Untersuchung zu den Privaten Feindpsalmen* (Leiden: Brill, 1967), 70ff; Cornelis Van Dam, *The Urim and Thummim: A Means of Revelation in Ancient Israel* (Winona Lake, IN: Eisenbrauns, 1997), 109; Roland de Vaux, *The Early History of Israel*, David Smith (Philadelphia, PA: Westminster Press, 1978), 350.

[10] Robert R. Wilson, *Prophecy and Society in Ancient Israel* (Philadelphia: Fortress Press, 1980), 139–40.

[11] Delekat, *Asylie und Schutzorakel am Zionheiligtum: Eine Untersuchung zu den Privaten Feindpsalmen*, 71: "Am Zionheiligtum wurden drei Mittel verwendet, um Omina zu erlagen: Inkubation, Beobachtung des Oferfeues und Losfeile." Delekat goes on to argue that although a priestly or surrogate incubation is the dominant form of incubation in ancient Israel, eventually lay persons were allowed to have their own dream revelations and not only for holy purposes, but also for mundane ones (ibid., 71–72).

have received revelation through dreams.[12] Even after the establishment of the monarchy, according to Blenkinsopp, "central prophets" may have received revelations through dreams. Blenkinsopp adduces Habakkuk 2:1 as an allusion to the incubation practiced by Habakkuk, the central and prebendary prophet, in order to induce divine oracle at a time of crisis.[13] These conclusions derived from the history of religions, however, seem to conflict with the actual data we have in the Hebrew Bible. Concerning the disparity between the picture adduced from the comparative study of religions and that drawn from the Hebrew Bible, Robinson says,

> Whatever the official religious attitude towards incubation, there seems little doubt that it would have continued to be practiced at least at a popular level. It is quite clear that no amount of condemnation or dissuasion could prevent the people from resorting to all sorts of divinatory practices in order to discover what they believed would be the future course of events or to obtain information otherwise hidden from them.[14]

The paucity of biblical data on incubation has often been explained as a result of the Deuteronomistic redaction. Ehrlich, followed by many others, argues that the Deuteronomistic redactor toned down any reference to incubation in the text, not only because incubation occurred at sacred shrines outside of Jerusalem, but also because of the important role that incubation played in the pagan cults.[15] The conclusions drawn from the history of religions should remain tentative, however, because they are almost exclusively based on the analogy from comparative evidence, instead of on internal evidence from ancient Israel, sometimes on indeed tendentious interpretation of biblical "prooftexts."

1.2 *The Exegetical Approach*

In conjunction with the historical question as to the existence of the incubation rite in ancient Israel, biblical scholars have engaged in the

---

[12] Robert R. Wilson, *Prophecy and Society in Ancient Israel* (Philadelphia, PA: Fortress Press, 1980), 135.

[13] Blenkinsopp, *A History of Prophecy in Israel*, 127.

[14] Margaret G. Robinson, "Dreams in the Old Testament" (Ph.D. diss., Manchester University, 1987), 100.

[15] Ehrlich, *Der Traum im Alten Testament*, 18–19. Also see Gnuse, "The Dream Theophany of Samuel: Its Structure in Relation to Ancient Near Eastern Dreams and Its Theological Significance," 62; Robinson, "Dreams in the Old Testament," 152–53.

exegesis of particular passages which are purported to contain incubation scenes. These passages include Genesis 15:1–6; 25:21; 28:10–29:1; 46:1–5, Exodus 38:8,[16] Numbers 22–24, 1 Samuel 3, 1 Kings 3:1–15 (//2 Chronicles 1:2–13); 1 Kings 19, Job 35:10–11, Psalm 3; 6; 16:7; 17:15; 30:2–3; 51; 139:18, Isaiah 38:6; 65:4, Jeremiah 31:26. In this approach, scholars examine a given passage through the grid provided by their explicit or implicit definition of an incubation rite. Unfortunately, however, none of these passages has garnered scholarly consensus as a proof-text for the biblical incubation scene. Even 1 Kings 3:1–15, which Ehrlich describes as "die vollständigste Inkubation im Alten Testament,"[17] has failed to win scholarly consensus.[18]

Two factors contribute to this wide divide in scholarly opinion. First, disparate definitions of what constitutes an incubation rite lead to different exegetical conclusions regarding those passages. A celebrated example is provided by what Oppenheim dubbed "unintentional incubation" to refer to the apparently unsolicited oneiric theophany in Genesis 28 and 1 Samuel 3. Although some scholars[19] have accepted Oppenheim's suggestion, others take the term "unintentional incubation" as an oxymoron. Gnuse says, for instance, that "the phrase is a contradiction in terms, for incubation implies purposes... therefore unintentional incubation is the same as no incubation at all."[20] Second, scholarly disagreement on biblical allusions to the incubation practice

[16] Anton Jirku, "Ein Fall von Inkubation im Alten Testament," *ZAW* 33 (1913): 151–52.

[17] Ehrlich, *Der Traum im Alten Testament*, 19.

[18] Admitting that the overall impression of the narrative in 1 Kings 3 is that of an incubation scene, some scholars argue that there is no direct causal link between the offering of sacrifice and the occurrence of dream. For instance, Caquot concludes that it is hard to prove that it is an incubation scene because "l'initiative de la revelation appartient pleinment à le divinité" (André Caquot, "Les songes et leur interpretation selon Canaan et Israel," *SO* 2 [1959]: 107; cf. Lindblom, "Theophanies in Holy Places in Hebrew Religion," 103). For a detailed discussion of this passage from the perspective of an incubation rite, see Robinson, "Dreams in the Old Testament," 117–21.

[19] For instance, note Jeffers's definition of an incubation dream: "Incubation dreams are dreams which are stimulated through the use of a particular ritual. The main condition, it seems, is that the subject spend the night at a "holy" place. *I would add that incubation is a phenomenon which can be experienced spontaneously* or contrived artificially" (emphasis mine; Jeffers, *Magic and Divination in Ancient Palestine and Syria*, 130).

[20] Gnuse, "The Dream Theophany of Samuel: Its Structure in Relation to Ancient Near Eastern Dreams and Its Theological Significance," 211. See also Shaul-Bar's definition of an incubation dream (Bar, *A Letter That Has not Been Read: Dreams in the Hebrew Bible*, 223).

may be attributed to the composite nature of biblical texts and their complicated editorial history. A number of scholars, frustrated by the apparent disparity between their definitions and the biblical data, resort to the pre-text that is assumed to be historically prior to, thus more pristine than, the final text. Efforts are made to find an incubation rite in the hypothetical, early level of the text in which all the necessary conditions would have been met. Ackerman, for instance, argues that the lack of preparatory ritual in Jacob's incubation at Bethel (Genesis 28) is due to its secondary placement in Genesis 27 which registers two elements with cultic resonance, that is, the animal skins with which Jacob clothed himself and the food that Jacob did not share with Isaac ("untasted sacrifice"). According to Ackerman, "at some juncture in its transmission history... ritual elements properly belonging to the incubation rite were freed from their original" context to meet the narrative requirements of the final text.[21] Speaking of Jacob's dream at Bethel, Ehrlich also maintains that incubation may have been present in an earlier Canaanite level of the narrative.[22]

1.3 *The Form-Critical Approach*

The history-of-religions approach engaging the historical question of an incubation rite in ancient Israel and the exegetical search for biblical allusions to the practice share one objectionable element in their methodology. These studies, although they are not unaware of the literary nature of biblical texts, have not distinguished the practice of incubation from its literary rendition as clearly as they ought to. As a consequence, the subject of incubation as a literary device has been neglected. Although it does not concern incubation *per se*, Gnuse's study of 1 Samuel 3 is noteworthy in its attention to the form-critical structure of a message dream report. In his 1980 doctoral dissertation, Gnuse compares Oppenheim's form-critical structure of ancient Near Eastern message-dream reports with the biblical text that reports

[21] Susan Ackerman, "The Deception of Isaac, Jacob's Dream at Bethel, and Incubation on an Animal Skin," in *Priesthood and Cult in Ancient Israel*, ed. Gary A. Anderson (Sheffield: JOST Press, 1991), 119.

[22] "In unserem alttestamentlichen Texte is von Inkubation nicht die Rede, doch mag auf der kanaanäischen Stufe der Erzählung vielleicht an eine soche gedacht worden sein" (Ehrlich, *Der Traum im Alten Testament*, 32).

Samuel's oneiric experience.[23] Oppenheim proposes that the form-critical structure of the message-dream report shows the following basic elements:

I. Setting
   A. Who—the recipient of the dream
   B. When—the time of the dream
   C. Where—the site, usually a shrine
   D. What conditions—circumstances surrounding the reception of the dream
II. Dream Content—divine message
III. Termination of the Dream—usually a statement that the dreamer awoke.
IV. Fulfillment of the Dream—an account of how the word of the deity came true.[24]

By showing that all these elements, except "Fulfillment of the Dream," may be found in 1 Samuel 3, Gnuse tries to establish that 1 Samuel 3 is better defined as an auditory message dream than as a prophetic call narrative.[25] When it comes to the question of the relationship between Samuel's oneiric experience and incubation, he falls back on the history-of-religions definition of incubation and argues that the lack of preparatory rituals make it unjustified to identify Samuel's oneiric experience as an incubation dream.[26] It is unfortunate, however, that, while adopting Oppenheim's form-critical structure of the message dream, Gnuse pays no attention either to Oppenheim's proposal that the form-critical structure in question may have originated

[23] From an analysis of historical records and epic literature Oppenheim identifies the tripartite form-critical structure of the message-dream report: the setting, the message and the dreamer's reaction.

[24] This is basically Gnuse's summary, to which I have made some adaptations (cf. Robert K. Gnuse, "A Reconsideration of the Form-Critical Structure in 1 Samuel 3: An Ancient Near Eastern Dream Theophany," *ZAW* 94 [1982]: 381). For a full original presentation of the pattern of message dreams, see A. Leo Oppenheim, *The Interpretation of Dreams in the Ancient Near East: With a Translation of an Assyrian Dream-Book*, TAPA 46 (Philadelphia, PA: American Philological Society, 1956), 186–97.

[25] Robert K. Gnuse, "The Dream Theophany of Samuel: Its Structure in Relation to Ancient Near Eastern Dreams and Its Theological Significance" (Ph.D. diss., Nashville, Tennessee: Vanderbilt University, 1980), 188–223.

[26] Ibid., 218–19.

in the practice of incubation[27] nor to Oppenheim's assertion that literary conventions control the way actual reality is recorded, and not the other way around.[28] If Gnuse had paid attention to these, he might not have dismissed so quickly the possibility of 1 Samuel 3 being a literary rendition of Samuel's genuine incubation experience.

Scholars like Jeffers, however, have been more open to Oppenheim's proposal that the form-critical structure of the message dream may have originated in the practice of incubation. Jeffers tries to draw a pattern of an incubation scene from some of the reports that Oppenheim categorizes as message dreams. But Jeffers's concerns are more historical than literary. He tries to establish the historical reality of the practice out of those elements that he discerns in message-dream reports such as Genesis 28 and 1 Kings 3.[29] Also noteworthy is Long's study of "Prophetic Inquiry Schema," although he does not deal with incubation as such. Unlike Gnuse and Jeffers, Long begins with a conscious separation between a divinatory practice and its literary rendition and attempts to show "cases in which divinatory practice has had direct influence in shaping, even creating, specific genres of literature or if not genres, certainly striking literary patterns."[30] According to Long, the institution of prophetic inquiry has left its impression on the form-critical pattern called "Prophetic Inquiry Schema," which also has a tripartite structure: A. Setting (situation) and preparation for inquiry; B. Audience with the Prophet; C. Fulfillment of the Oracle. The form-critical analyses of Jeffers and Long reveal the same problem that plagues the exegetical approach to the subject. They invoke the Deuteronomistic censure whenever their literary patterns, whether it be the pattern of incubation or that of prophetic inquiry, do not fit the textual data that they study. Although the Deuteronomistic redactor may have amended the passages so that they do not appear to support an incubation rite, which were practiced at local shrines and were often associated with pagan religions, scholars are in danger of using the Deuteronomistic redaction as a *Deus-Ex-Machina* whenever there is disparity between their form-critical pattern and the actual textual

[27] Oppenheim, *The Interpretation of Dreams in the Ancient Near East: With a Translation of an Assyrian Dream-Book*, 190.

[28] Hence, Oppenheim argues that the study of literary convention is the only way to learn the dream experiences of the ancient people (Ibid., 184).

[29] Jeffers, *Magic and Divination in Ancient Palestine and Syria*, 134–36.

[30] Burke O. Long, "The Effect of Divination Upon Israelite Literature," *JBL* 92 (1973): 489.

data. The type-scene approach to incubation as a form-critical category is expected to remove some of the arbitrariness in previous form-critical studies of divinatory practices, since the type-scene focuses on the final text, rather than the pre-text, and the idea of family resemblance as a heuristic principle may transform the type-scene approach into a more powerful form-critical tool for analyzing the biblical passages that have indeed gone through a complex redactional history.

1.4 *Studies of the Hannah Story from the Perspective of Incubation*

Only a few passing remarks have been made about the story of Hannah (i.e. the birth story of Samuel) in relation to the practice of incubation. After interpreting a late Babylonian cuneiform text (BM 47749) as describing an incubation rite undertaken by Kurigalzu for his barren wife who prostrated herself and wept at the entrance of a temple (or at the city gate), Finkel connects this tablet to the story of Hannah in 1 Samuel 1.[31] Here the point of similarity is more in the unhappy barren woman weeping at the door of a temple, rather than in her husband actively seeking divine help through a dream. Knowles compares the story of childless Hannah visiting the temple to cure her infertility through divine intervention with the story of Dānīʾilu in Ugarit as well as with a Hittite incubation text (KUB 1.15) where male impotence is cured through an incubation rite.[32] These passing comments relating 1 Samuel 1 to other instances of incubation do not elaborate how the biblical text concerning Hannah reflects an incubation rite. More important to our study of 1 Samuel 1–2 as an incubation type-scene is Obermann's remarks on what he calls "pre-natal narratives extant in Scripture." He defines them as the stories in which the "virility of an aged husband is restored, infertility of a barren wife is cured, by divine intervention."[33] Then he adds a very interesting observation: "In all instances, the child in question is to become an outstanding personage, in some instances the parent is such a personage as well."[34]

[31] Irving L. Finkel, "The Dream of Kurigalzu and the Tablet of Sins," *AnSt* 33 (1983): 75.

[32] Melody D. Knowles, *Centrality Practiced: Jerusalem in the Religious Practice of Yehud and the Diaspora in the Persian Period* (Atlanta, GA: Society of Biblical Literature, 2006), 99, footnote 75.

[33] Julian Obermann, *How Daniel Was Blessed with a Son*, Suppl. to JAOS 6 (Baltimore, MD: American Oriental Society, 1946), 28.

[34] Ibid.

And Obermann takes Hannah as an example of the latter case. Furthermore, he identifies the pre-natal narrative of Samuel as one of the few that take place at a sanctuary with sacrifices being explicitly mentioned. Obermann concludes with the assertion that the pattern of the biblical pre-natal narratives already occurs in the Dānī'ilu story.[35] Obermann's observation that not only the exceptional nature of the child but also that of the parents are emphasized in some of the biblical pre-natal narratives seems to support my hypothesis that what Alter identifies as the so-called annunciation type-scene is an adaptation of the incubation type-scene when the latter is incorporated into the larger story of a hero's life. If the piety of incubants, namely, the parents, is emphasized in the incubation type-scene, the exceptional nature of the newborn comes to the foreground in the biblical annunciation type-scene. This is why the divine message in the incubation type-scene is oriented toward the solution of an incubant's problem, whereas the divine message in the annunciation type-scene focuses on the extraordinariness of the newborn. The Hannah story seems to present a transitional stage from the incubation type-scene to the biblical annunciation story, as will be shown below.

1.5 *Caveats*

Before attempting an analysis of the individual motifs comprising the incubation type-scene in 1 Samuel 1:1–2:11a, a few caveats are in order. First, I do not reconstruct the "original" text for my literary analysis as McCarter does in his Anchor Bible commentary, although I fully recognize the value of textual criticism for the proper understanding of the books of Samuel. I follow Walters in the view that it is best to study the Masoretic Text and the Septuagint on their own terms.[36] Although I do not reconstruct the "original" text, however, I will incorporate assured results from textual criticism, whenever they are appropriate,

---

[35] Obermann (Ibid.) says, "We do not see clearly how these various motifs—sterility or barrenness, sacrifice and supplication, divine intervention, prediction of the exceptional status of the child—had come to be fused in the pre-natal narrative pattern of a hero. But we do know now that the pattern is already consolidated in Ugarit."

[36] According to Walters, neither the Hebrew nor the Greek text of 1 Samuel 1 can be shown to derive from the other. Rather, in his view, they are discrete narratives, each with its own *Tendenz*. Cf. Stanley Walters, "The Greek and Hebrew Texts of 1 Samuel 1," *JBL* 107 (1988): 385–412, especially p. 409.

into my analysis of the incubation type-scene.[37] Second, my literary analysis focuses on the final form of the Masoretic Text, and not on any other particular stage in the history of the text, although I do concede that the first book of Samuel derives from heterogeneous sources or traditions that have a long history of transmission before being arranged in their finally redacted form. This aspect of my study in fact differentiates my form-critical analysis of the incubation type-scene in 1 Samuel 1:1–2:11a from previous form-critical studies of divinatory practices.[38] The heuristic principle of family resemblance in the study of the incubation type-scene allows us to focus on the final text which may or may not preserve an incubation rite as such. So, in the following analysis of the incubation type-scene in the Hannah story, more attention will be paid to the literary features of the final text that the author crafted by forming individual motifs into an organic unit called "the incubation type-scene," rather than to the question of the history of composition of the text. Fortunately, most historical critics agree that the text under discussion (1 Samuel 1:1–2:11a) is a homogeneous unit, except the song of Hannah at the beginning of chapter 2, which is usually taken as late.[39] Third, my analysis of 1 Samuel 1:1–2:11a is

---

[37] For this purpose, I have consulted mainly the following two works: Jürg Hutzli, *Die Erzählung von Hanna und Samuel: Textkritische und literarische Anayse von 1. Samuel 1–2 unter Berüchsichtigung des Kontextes* (Zürich: Theologischer Verlag, 2007), 47–128; P. Kyle McCarter, *I Samuel: A New Translation* (Garden City, N.Y.: Doubleday, 1980), 49–58 and 67–71.

[38] Cf. Gnuse, "The Dream Theophany of Samuel: Its Structure in Relation to Ancient Near Eastern Dreams and Its Theological Significance", 158–236; Murray Lichtenstein, "Dream Theophany and the E Document," *JANESCU* I/2 (1969): 45–54; Robinson, "Dreams in the Old Testament," chapter 7.

[39] Almost all critics agree that 1 Samuel 1:1–28 is a homogeneous unit of tradition that a later editor used as a basic material for his version, whether they call it "E" (K. Budde, *Die Bücher Samuel* [Tübingen: J. C. B. Mohr, 1902], 2), "Samuel source" (G. W. Anderson, *A Critical Introduction to the Old Testament* [London: Gerald Duckworth, 1959], 74), or the "Prophetic source" (McCarter, *I Samuel: A New Translation*, 64). In other words, it has its own integrity and contains some of the earliest materials in the book of Samuel. Hence it is meaningful to treat the unit as a coherent unit. Indeed studies by Willis, Polzin, Fokkelmann, etc., have proved the utility of a literary study of this text (Robert Polzin, *Samuel and the Deuteronomist: A Literary Study of the Deuteronomic History* [New York: Harper & Row, 1989], 18–39; J. P. Fokkelman, *Vow and Desire [1 Sam. 1–12]*, vol. IV of *Narrative Art and Poetry in the Books of Samuel: A Full Interpretation Based on Sylistic and Structural Analyses* [Assen: Van Gorcum, 1993], 1–111; John T. Willis, "An Anti-Elide Narrative Tradition from a Prophetic Circle at the Ramah Sanctuary," *JBL* 90 [1971]: 288–308). For a composition history of the book of Samuel in general, see Georg Fohrer, *Introduction to the Old Testament*, trans. David E. Green (Nashville, TN: Abingdon Press, 1968), 215–27; Wilson, *Prophecy and Society in Ancient Israel*, 169–84; McCarter, *I Samuel: A New Translation*, 12–27;

not intended as a full-scale commentary on the text, but as a demonstration of the narrator's use of the incubation type-scene in the composition of the Hannah story. So my comments will be limited to serving that purpose.

2. The Incubation Type-Scene in 1 Samuel 1:1–2:11a: Component Motifs

2.1 *Before Epiphany*

Text: 1 Samuel 1:1–11

1a וַיְהִי אִישׁ אֶחָד מִן־הָרָמָתַיִם צוֹפִים מֵהַר אֶפְרָיִם
b וּשְׁמוֹ אֶלְקָנָה בֶּן־יְרֹחָם בֶּן־אֱלִיהוּא בֶּן־תֹּחוּ בֶן־צוּף אֶפְרָתִי
2a וְלוֹ שְׁתֵּי נָשִׁים
b שֵׁם אַחַת חַנָּה
c וְשֵׁם הַשֵּׁנִית פְּנִנָּה
d וַיְהִי לִפְנִנָּה יְלָדִים
e וּלְחַנָּה אֵין יְלָדִים
3a וְעָלָה הָאִישׁ הַהוּא מֵעִירוֹ מִיָּמִים יָמִימָה לְהִשְׁתַּחֲוֹת וְלִזְבֹּחַ לַיהוָה צְבָאוֹת בְּשִׁלֹה
b וְשָׁם שְׁנֵי בְנֵי־עֵלִי חָפְנִי וּפִנְחָס כֹּהֲנִים לַיהוָה
4a וַיְהִי הַיּוֹם
b וַיִּזְבַּח אֶלְקָנָה
c וְנָתַן לִפְנִנָּה אִשְׁתּוֹ וּלְכָל־בָּנֶיהָ וּבְנוֹתֶיהָ מָנוֹת
5a וּלְחַנָּה יִתֵּן מָנָה אַחַת אַפָּיִם
b כִּי אֶת־חַנָּה אָהֵב
c וַיהוָה סָגַר רַחְמָהּ
6a וְכִעֲסַתָּה צָרָתָהּ גַּם־כַּעַס בַּעֲבוּר הַרְּעִמָהּ
b כִּי־סָגַר יְהוָה בְּעַד רַחְמָהּ
7a וְכֵן יַעֲשֶׂה שָׁנָה בְשָׁנָה
b מִדֵּי עֲלֹתָהּ בְּבֵית יְהוָה כֵּן תַּכְעִסֶנָּה
c וַתִּבְכֶּה
d וְלֹא תֹאכַל
8a וַיֹּאמֶר לָהּ אֶלְקָנָה אִישָׁהּ
b חַנָּה

Arthur Weiser, *The Old Testament: Its Formation and Development*, trans. B. M. Barton (New York: Association Press, 1961), 157–70; Otto Kaiser, *Introduction to the Old Testament*, trans. John Sturdy (Oxford: Basil Blackwell, 1975), 151–60; Otto Eissfeldt, *Die Komposition der Samuelisbücher* (Leipzig: J. C. Hinrichs, 1931). For the form-critical units and the sources of 1 Samuel 1–3, see Gnuse, "The Dream Theophany of Samuel: Its Structure in Relation to Ancient Near Eastern Dreams and Its Theological Significance," 237–75; Jan Dus, "Die Geburtslegende Samuel 1 Sam. 1: Eine traditionsgeschichtliche Untersuchung zu 1 Sam. 1–3," *RSO* 43 (1969): 163–94.

c לָמֶה תִבְכִּי
d וְלָמֶה לֹא תֹאכְלִי
e וְלָמֶה יֵרַע לְבָבֵךְ
f הֲלוֹא אָנֹכִי טוֹב לָךְ מֵעֲשָׂרָה בָּנִים
9a וַתָּקָם חַנָּה אַחֲרֵי אָכְלָה בְשִׁלֹה וְאַחֲרֵי שָׁתֹה
b וְעֵלִי הַכֹּהֵן יֹשֵׁב עַל־הַכִּסֵּא עַל־מְזוּזַת הֵיכַל יְהוָה
10a וְהִיא מָרַת נָפֶשׁ
b וַתִּתְפַּלֵּל עַל־יְהוָה
c וּבָכֹה תִבְכֶּה
11a וַתִּדֹּר נֶדֶר
b וַתֹּאמַר
c יְהוָה צְבָאוֹת
d אִם־רָאֹה תִרְאֶה בָּעֳנִי אֲמָתֶךָ
e וּזְכַרְתַּנִי
f וְלֹא־תִשְׁכַּח אֶת־אֲמָתֶךָ
g וְנָתַתָּה לַאֲמָתְךָ זֶרַע אֲנָשִׁים
h וּנְתַתִּיו לַיהוָה כָּל־יְמֵי חַיָּיו
i וּמוֹרָה לֹא־יַעֲלֶה עַל־רֹאשׁוֹ

Translation: 1 Samuel 1:1–11

1a There was a certain man from Ramathaim, a Zuphite[40] from the hill country of Ephraim,
b and his name *was* Elkanah the son of Jeroham, son of Elihu, son of Tohu, son of Zuph, an Ephraimite.
2a He *had* two wives.
b The name of the first *was* Hannah,
c and the name of the second *was* Peninnah.
d Now Peninnah had children,
e but Hannah *had* no children.
3a Now this man used to go up annually[41] from his city to worship and to sacrifice to YHWH of hosts at Shiloh;
b there the two sons of Eli, Hophni and Phinehas, *were* priests to YHWH.

---

[40] Wellhausen, Driver, McCarter, et al., take *hrmtym ṣwpym* as grammatically impossible and adopt the Septuagint's reading Seifa which points to *ṣwpy* "a Zuphite." The Masoretic reading *ṣwpym* may be a result of the *mem* of *mhr* having been accidentally written twice (dittography). Hutzli, on the contrary, is in favor of the Masoretic text. This emended reading results in a nice balance between 1a and 1b: in both lines, a genealogical affiliation is followed by a tribal affiliation. Cf. McCarter, *I Samuel: A New Translation*, 51; Hutzli, *Die Erzählung von Hanna und Samuel: Textkritische und literarische Anayse von 1. Samuel 1–2 unter Berüchsichtigung des Kontextes*, 48; S. R. Driver, *Notes on the Hebrew Text and the Topography of the Books of Samuel* (Oxford: Clarendon Press, 1913), 1; J. Wellhausen, *Der Text der Bücher Samuelis* (Göttingen: Vandenhoeck und Ruprecht, 1871), 34.

[41] Literally, "from days to days." Cf. Exodus 13:10; Judges 11:40; Judges 21:19.

4a On any given day
b when Elkanah had sacrificed,
c he would give portions to Peninnah his wife and to all her sons and daughters.
5a But to Hannah he would give one special portion,
b because it *was* Hannah that he loved,
c though YHWH had closed her womb.
6a Her rival used to vex her sore in order to provoke her,
b because YHWH had closed her womb completely.[42]
7a So it went on year by year.
b Whenever she went up to the house of YHWH, so she used to vex her.
c Therefore she wept
d and would not eat.
8a Elkanah her husband said to her:
b   Hannah,
c   why do you weep?
d   And why do you not eat?
e   And why is your heart grieved?
f   Am I not better to you than ten sons?
9a Hannah arose after the eating and drinking in Shiloh.
b Meanwhile Eli the priest was sitting upon the seat by the doorpost of the temple of YHWH.
10a   She *was* in bitterness of soul,
b and prayed to YHWH.
c As she wept bitterly,
11a she vowed a vow,
b and said,
c   O YHWH of hosts,
d   if you will indeed look on the affliction of your servant,
e   and remember me,
f   and not forget your handmaid,
g   but will give to your handmaid a man-child,
h   then I will give him to YHWH all the days of his life,
i   and no razor shall come upon his head.

2.1.1 *The Motif of Childlessness*

As in the other instances of the incubation type-scene that we have examined in *Kirta* and *ʾAqhatu*, the type-scene in the Hannah story constitutes a story complete in itself with a clear movement of plot

[42] The preposition *baʿad* which functions idiomatically with the verb *sgr* seems to stress the totality of Hannah's barrenness: thus the translation "completely." Cf. Lyle M. Eslinger, *Kingship of God in Crisis*, Bible and Literature Series 10 (Decatur, GA: Almond Press, 1985), 73.

from problem to solution.[43] It begins with the problem of Hannah's barrenness and ends with its solution, namely, the birth of Samuel. The problem of Hannah's childlessness, which articulates the pre-verbal *Gestalt* of predicament, is first introduced in lines 2de, immediately after the narrator introduces Elkanah and his wives into the narrative, respectively in verse 1 and lines 2abc. There in lines 2de, Hannah's childlessness is contrasted with Peninnah's fecundity by the narrator without value judgment.[44] The contrast in child-bearing ability between Hannah and Peninnah in lines 2de is what sets in motion the plot of the story. This seems to be intimated by the phrase *wayəhî* in line 2d which seems to express higher salience not only by breaking the chain of the four nominal clauses (1b, 2a, b, c) but also by picking up the main line of the narrative at the same level as the *wayəhî* in verse 1.[45] Also noteworthy is the double chiastic structure of lines 2de (*hyh l*PN vs. *l*PN *ên*) and lines 2bcde (Peninnah-Hannah; Hannah-Peninnah). This chiasmus not only underscores the contrast in child-bearing ability between Hannah and Peninnah but also serves as a metaphoric prediction of the eventual reversal of the two women's fortunes.[46] One may, however, discern the narrator's efforts to make the contrast between Hannah and Peninnah not too overt at this point in the narrative by smoothing it out with alliteration and assonance in lines 2bcde.[47] This smoothing-out of the contrast serves to prepare the

[43] Walter Brueggemann, *First and Second Samuel*, Interpretation (Louisville, KY: John Knox Press, 1990), 12; Roy L. Heller, *Narrative Structure and Discourse Constellations: An Analysis of Clause Function in Biblical Hebrew Prose* (Winona Lake, IN: Eisenbrauns, 2004), 49; Antony F. Campbell, *1 Samuel*, FOTL 7 (Grand Rapids, MI: Eerdmans, 2003), 43.

[44] Note the disjunctive sequence in 2e ("*waw* plus a non-verbal element") right after the *wayyiqtol* form in 2d. Cf. Walter Brueggemann, "1 Samuel 1: A Sense of a Beginning," *ZAW* 102 (1990): 34.

[45] Dennis Pardee, "Hebrew Verbal System in a Nutshell," the 2003 draft of an unpublished paper, 18. Joosten argues, however, that *wayəhî* in line 2d is in the exposition, not on the level of the main line of events as in verse 1, 4, 20 (Jan Joosten, "Workshop: Meaning and Use of the Tenses in 1 Samuel 1," in *Narrative Syntax and the Hebrew Bible*, ed. Ellen van Wolde [Brill: Leiden, 1997], 79–80). But the fact that line 2d sets the plot in motion seems to indicate the high salience of that line which places it on the same story line as verse 1, 4, and 20.

[46] Eslinger, *Kingship of God in Crisis*, 69.

[47] Cf. *šem* ʾaḥat ḥ*annāh* wə *šem* haššēnît pən*innāh* (2d) // wayəhî lipən*innāh* *yəlādîm* û ləḥ*annāh* ʾên *yəlādîm* (2e). The second *yəlādîm* in line 2e may have been the narrator's deliberate choice over the singular *yeled* or *wālād* (cf. Gen 11:30) for the sake of rhyming it with *yəlādîm* in 2d. After all, the Septuagint has the singular παιδιόν "child."

reader for the more dramatic description of the opposition between Elkanah's two wives. The contrast in view in lines 2de, which could be a simple statement of a fact by the narrator without value judgment, later evolves into the emotionally charged opposition between the fertile but unloved wife and the barren but loved co-wife. This escalation in emotional conflict between Hannah and Peninnah corresponds with the narrator charging the simple contrast of have and have-not with religious significance: Peninnah's *yəlādîm* "children" in line 2d is paraphrased as *kōl-bāneyhā ûbənôteyhā* "all her sons and her daughters" in the context of Elkanah's distribution of sacrificial portions (line 4c), namely, a sign of blessing, whereas Hannah's *ên yəlādîm* "childlessness" is paraphrased twice as "YHWH closed her womb" in lines 5c and 6b, a sign of lack of divine blessing.

Since in antiquity the socio-economic worth of women was measured by the number of sons they bore, quite apart from the fact that women were invariably blamed for their childlessness, the psychological, let alone the social, pressure on childless women must have been immense.[48] Hannah was no exception. The narrator elaborates on Hannah's distress on account of her barrenness in four different relational contexts: 1) Hannah and tormenting co-wife, Peninnah; 2) Hannah and loving but obtuse husband, Elkanah; 3) Hannah and corrupt priests, Hophni and Phinehas; 4) Hannah and YHWH who closed her womb. Hannah's distress escalates through these habitual abusive relationships to a boiling point until Hannah's one-time, initiative-taking action is recounted in verse 9.

Peninnah is first introduced into the story as the second wife of Elkanah (cf. line 2c), fertile with many sons and daughters (cf. lines 2d, 3b).[49] Out of what René Girard calls "mimetic desire,"[50] Peninnah

---

[48] Tony W. Cartledge, *1 & 2 Samuel*, Smyth & Helwys Bible Commentary (Macon, GA: Smyth & Helwys, 2001), 27–28.

[49] Fokkelmann speculates that Peninnah had as many children as Leah on the basis of Elkanah's question to Hannah: "Am I not better than ten sons?" Cf. Fokkelman, *Vow and Desire (1 Sam. 1–12)*, 31.

[50] Klein argues that Girard's concept of "mimetic desire" may serve as a tool for exploring jealousy in the context of biblical Hebrew narrative. Mimetic desire is the term coined by René Girard, a French philosopher, for the complex of attitudes and actions arising from imitation of another generated by desire of what the other has. This acquisitive mimetic desire thus subsumes jealousy, rivalry and all the actions taken to gain the object of desire. So, Klein analyzes the relationship of Peninnah and Hannah through the mimetic desire. While taking Peninnah's torment as deriving from her mimetic desire for Elkanah's love, Klein praises Hannah for refusing to enter

made a regular point of harassing Hannah "in order to provoke her."[51] Peninnah's harassment is said to have occurred routinely during Elkanah's annual trips to Shiloh where the whole family would participate in worship and sacrifice. The narrator seems to associate Elkanah's distribution of sacrificial portions with Peninnah's tormenting of Hannah by narrating the two events in sequence. According to Pedersen, in early Israel the sharing of a sacrificial meal prepared from a sacrificed animal had the function of uniting the family members and relatives gathered around the common table in communal spirit.[52] But for Hannah, it became a nightmare that haunted her constantly. Although the exact nuance of the phrase denoting Hannah's portion (*mānāh 'aḥat 'appāyim*) escapes us,[53] a number of scholars detect Elkanah's favoritism

into the subject-rival competition and being victimized. According to Klein, Hannah has chosen to be victimized rather than attempting to get even with Peninnah. Cf. Lillian R. Klein, "Hannah: Marginalized Victim and Social Redeemer," in *A Feminist Companion to Samuel and Kings* (Sheffield: Sheffield Academic Press, 1994), 77–92.

[51] The exact meaning of the phrase *ba'ăbûr har'imāh* escapes us. Most scholars take the preposition *ba'ăbûr* as expressing a purpose. But the verb *har'imāh* has lent itself to many different renditions. The bone of contention is two-fold: one question is whether the Hiphil form is causative or internally transitive, and the other question is whether or not the root behind *har'imāh* is etymologically identical to *r'm* "to thunder." BDB registers only one entry for *r'm*, while HALOT takes the *r'm* in question (*r'm* II) to be etymologically different from *r'm* I "to thunder." My translation "in order to provoke her" assumes HALOT's position to be correct and takes the Hiphil form as causative. If one accepts BDB and takes the Hiphil form as internally transitive, Frymer-Kensky's translation will result: "so that she may cry out." Cf. Tikva Frymer-Kensky, *Reading the Women of the Bible* (New York: Schocken Books, 2002), 302.

[52] Johannes Pedersen, *Israel: Its Life and Culture*, vol. II (Atlanta, GA: Scholars Press, 1991), 334.

[53] The traditional translation "a double portion" is a conjecture based on the dual form *'appāyim*. The later, von Josef Kara's analysis of *py šnym* = *apym* "twice" (prothetic *aleph*) is accepted by many scholars. Cf. Shimon Bar-Efrat, *Das Erste Buch Samuel: Ein narratologisch-philologischer Kommentar* (Stuttgart: Verlag W. Kohlhammer, 1996), 65. Cartledge argues that Peninnah's rancor may be understood from the perspective of the legislation in Deuteronomy 21:15–17 directed to a man who had two wives, and whose oldest son was descended from the less favored wife. The law required him to honor the oldest son as the firstborn by designating a double portion of the inheritance to him. By giving Hannah a double portion that should have been given to Peninnah's first son, Elkanah not only shows his love for Hannah, but also practically makes the son to be born out of Hannah's barren womb as his firstborn. Cf. Cartledge, *1 & 2 Samuel*, 30. A number of others, taking a cue from the Targums (*hwlq ḥd bhyr*), have proposed "one choice portion," assuming that *'appāyim* is somehow related to *pîmāh* "fat." Fokkelman argues that "one special portion" reflects the inner tension between Elkanah's position and his intention. "On the one hand he goes by the book, one portion for one person, on the other hand he wants, within the narrow boundaries of this, to give a sign of consolation, so that the phrase more or less says: 'It is true only one portion, because there was no other way, but nevertheless one of a special

in the portion that he gives Hannah and regard it as the immediate provocation for Peninnah's attacks on Hannah.[54] The intensity of Peninnah's harassment is thrown into relief by the use of a cognate object with an emphatic *gam* in line 6a, as well as by the replacement of Peninnah's name by the term *ṣārātāh* "rival wife" or "enemy," the language underlining Peninnah's rancor against Hannah.[55] Furthermore, Peninnah's harassment was not a one-time event, but a constant one. This is made clear in line 7a, in which *ya'ăśeh*, a Qal imperfect with an impersonal subject, occurs with the time reference, *šānāh bəšānāh*: "And thus it occurred (A) year after year (B)."[56] This general statement is elaborated in line 7b in reverse order: "Every time she would go up

kind." Cf. Fokkelman, *Vow and Desire (1 Sam. 1–12)*, 21, 24. Some others, taking a cue from the Septuagint's reading (πλὴν ὅτι "however"), regard *'pym* as a mistake of *'ps* and translate the phrase in question as "(only) one portion." Cf. Driver, *Notes on the Hebrew Text and the Topography of the Books of Samuel*, 7–8; Yairah Amit, "'Am I not More Devoted to You Than Ten Sons?' (1 Samuel 1.8): Male and Female Interpretations," in *A Feminist Companion to Samuel and Kings* (Sheffield: Sheffield Academic Press, 1994), 69. McCarter conjectures a corruption of the word *kpym* which means "proportionate to," suggesting that Elkanah gave Hannah one portion that was as great as Peninnah's portions combined, thus provoking Peninnah's rancor. Cf. McCarter, *I Samuel: A New Translation*, 52; Frymer-Kensky, *Reading the Women of the Bible*, 302. Finally, Tsumura takes a literalist approach to this. According to him, it seems best to keep the literal meaning "two noses" and to read the Masoretic form as a technical term of the sacrificial ritual. He cites the Ugaritic *ap* "nose" that appears together with *npš* "lung" as an offering to deities in ritual texts. Cf. David T. Tsumura, *The First Book of Samuel* (Grand Rapids, MI: Eerdmans, 2007), 113.

[54] Cf. Bar-Efrat, *Das Erste Buch Samuel: Ein narratologisch-philologischer Kommentar*, 65.

[55] Keith Bodner, *1 Samuel: Narrative Commentary* (Sheffield: Sheffield Phoenix Press, 2008), 15; Klein, "Hannah: Marginalized Victim and Social Redeemer," 82. Birch argues that the term is seldom used in describing family relationships and often used in describing relationships between peoples or nations. The choice of the language suggests that the relationship of Israel without a king taunted by its neighboring kingdoms may be reflected in the family tension between Hannah and Peninnah (Bruce C. Birch, *The First and Second Books of Samuel*, NIB 2 [Nashville, TN: Abingdon Press, 1995–2002], 975).

[56] Paul Joüon, *A Grammar of Biblical Hebrew*, trans. and ed. Muraoka T. (Roma: Pontificio Istituto Biblico, 2003) §155b; Robert Alter, *The David Story: A Translation with Commentary of 1 and 2 Samuel* (New York: W. W. Norton, 1999), 4, footnote 7; Fokkelman, *Vow and Desire (1 Sam. 1–12)*, 27; Bar-Efrat, *Das Erste Buch Samuel: Ein narratologisch-philologischer Kommentar*, 66; Tsumura, *The First Book of Samuel*, 112, footnote 43; Hans W. Hertzberg, *I & II Samuel: A Commentary*, OTL (Philadelphia, PA: Westminster Press, 1964), 21; Karl A. Leimbach, *Die Bücher Samuel*, Die heilige Schrift des alten Testamentes (Bonn: Peter Hanstein Verlag, 1936), 21. Contra those who take the subject as Elkanah: McCarter, *I Samuel: A New Translation*, 49; Eslinger, *Kingship of God in Crisis*, 75; Henry P. Smith, *The Books of Samuel*, ICC (Skokie, IL: Varda Books, 2005), 7.

the house of YHWH (B´), she [Peninnah] would torment her (A´)."[57] Also, the waw-consecutive perfect form *wəki'ăsattāh* at the beginning of line 6a and the imperfect verb *tak'isennāh* at the end of line 7b, which enclose the unit of lines 6a–7b, corroborate the repetitive and habitual nature of Peninnah harassment.[58] Nonetheless, Hannah was not affected by mimetic desire: she not only refuses to enter into the bearing children competition with Peninnah (unlike Rachel), but also remains a passive victim of Peninnah's persecution (unlike Sarah). It is noteworthy in this regard that references to Hannah mostly take the form of the pronominal suffixes on the verbs that predicate Peninnah's actions in verses 6–7. This is significant considering that in the Hannah story as a whole, Hannah is the subject of the verb over three times more often than she is the object.[59] The silence and inaction of Hannah in this part of the story stands in stark contrast to her bold speeches and initiative-taking actions against all odds in the other part of the story.

Hannah's distress from childlessness is further aggravated by her loving but misunderstanding husband. Elkanah, like Saul's father Kish

[57] Note one inclusion formed by *kēn* in lines 7ab and another formed by the root *k's* "to vex" in lines 6a and 7b.

[58] The rivalry between Peninnah and Hannah recalls the birth stories in Genesis where matriarchs find themselves in a similar conflict with their rivals. Although it was through Sarah's initiative that Hagar conceived Abraham's scion, the slave girl "looked with contempt on" her barren mistress "when she saw that she had conceived" (Genesis 16:4). Sarah who could not stand her look began to "deal harshly with her" (Genesis 16:6) after getting a permission from Abraham. Another confrontation comes right after Isaac is weaned. Provoked by Ishmael mocking infant Isaac, Sarah forces Abraham to drive out both Ishmael and his mother. One may notice that in both incidences Sarah does everything within her means to counter the provocation of her rival. So does Rachel. Although she was not provoked like Sarah, she enters into competition with her sister and co-wife, Leah. She says to Jacob, "Give me children, or I shall die" and then gave him her maid Bilhah as concubine (Genesis 30:1–3). Unlike Sarah and Rachel, however, Hannah never responds to Peninnah's torment but takes the matter to YHWH. It is significant to note that Sarah's counteractions always lead to Hagar's friendly encounters with YHWH, who pronounces a blessing on Ishamel. Rachel's counteraction also led to a merely vicarious materinty; eventually she bears two sons, but she is to pay for the second birth with her life, and the future kings of Israel will spring from one of Leah's sons. The examples of Sarah and Leah stand in stark contrast to that of Hannah, who did not react, but instead approached God and gave birth to Samuel, the most influential shaper of Israel's history.

[59] Carol Meyers, "Hannah and Her Sacrifice: Reclaiming Female Agency," in *A Feminist Companion to Samuel and Kings* (Sheffield: Sheffield Academic Press, 1994), 99.

(1 Samuel 9:1), is introduced into the narrative with his genealogy.[60] Although the genealogy itself is not that impressive (cf. verse 1),[61] such an introduction seems to intimate that Elkanah was a well-known and respected man at least within his own clan, thus in part giving a false lead because the principal protagonist of the story turns out to be Elkanah's wife Hannah.[62] Also, considering the fact that he made an annual trip to the sanctuary in Shiloh to worship and offer sacrifice to YHWH (line 3a), Elkanah must have been a pious man in ironical contrast to Eli's two sons of *bəliyaʿal* (cf. line 3b and 2:12).[63] Furthermore, he is the kind of husband who tries to be fair to his less favored wife.[64] Although he loves Hannah more than Peninnah (line 5b),[65] he makes sure that the latter and all of her children get their deserved portions in the post-sacrifice distribution of food.[66] His special affection for Hannah is indicated by his act of giving a special portion to

[60] Both Elkanah and Kish rest on a chain of four forefathers which fill the second half of a line with enumeration. Just as Elkanah's tribal affiliation was noted twice, chapter 9 too makes a double note of the tribal name (Benjamin), at the end of verse 1a and b. What is more striking is that both in 1:1 and 9:1, the substantival tribal names (*eprāyim* and *binyāmîn*) are alternated with the gentilic nouns (*eprātî* and *ben-ʾîš yəmîmî*). These facts seem to suggest that Samuel and Saul may be closely connected. This is corroborated by the name Zuph in 1:1 which also appears as a place name. Zuph features in 1 Samuel 9 as Samuel's town that Saul visits to inquire about the whereabouts of his father's missing donkeys.

[61] Although Brueggemann (*First and Second Samuel*, 12) rates Elkanah's genealogy as "impressive," the persons named in Elkanah's genealogy are all obscure. If the genealogy has the purpose of legitimization, Elkanah's genealogy in 1 Samuel 1:1 does a poor job in contrast to that employed in 1 Chronicles 6:11–13 where the genealogy places Elkanah's family among the Levites. Since 1 Samuel 1 ends in the birth of Samuel, one may even say that Samuel's natural lineage grants him no claim to any important position. In this regard, the explanation of Samuel's name is important. The narrator and Hannah put an emphasis on *myhwh* "from YHWH" by placing it at the beginning of a clause. This intimates Samuel's true genealogy: He is from YHWH. Cf. Eslinger, *Kingship of God in Crisis*, 66–67. Also as Bodner argues, this rather pedestrian genealogy that begins the whole book of Samuel is "a long way from the lists of wars and court officials that will inundate the narrative in the not too distant future" (Bodner, *1 Samuel: Narrative Commentary*, 13).

[62] Alter, *The David Story: A Translation with Commentary of 1 and 2 Samuel*; Fokkelman, *Vow and Desire (1 Sam. 1–12)*, 15–16; ackroyd, 19; Bar-Efrat, *Das Erste Buch Samuel: Ein narratologisch-philologischer Kommentar*, 63;

[63] For Elkanah's annual trip to Shiloh, see footnote 88 below.

[64] Eslinger, *Kingship of God in Crisis*, 71.

[65] The narrator emphasizes Elkanah's love for Hannah in two ways: first, he repeats Hannah's name. Second, he accords the name a special position via the inversion of predicate and subject. Cf. Fokkelman, *Vow and Desire (1 Sam. 1–12)*, 22.

[66] Contra Cartledge who argues that the double portion that was given to Hannah would have been the fair portion for Penninah who was the mother of Elkanah's firstborn (Cartledge, *1 & 2 Samuel*, 30).

Hannah in line 5a, although this provokes Peninnah's tormenting. He must have been aware of the interfamilial conflict and frustrated at his inability to resolve it, because Peninnah, after all, was his legitimate wife, not a slave girl like Hagar,[67] and also because it was YHWH who had closed her womb (cf. Jacob's angry response to Rachel in Genesis 30:2). Elkanah's words to Hannah in verse 8, triggered by Hannah's weeping and not eating in lines 7cd,[68] not only seem to vent Elkanah's frustration, but also show that he does not understand Hannah's true need. Undoubtedly he intended to console her, but Elkanah's words do not seem to have been formulated sensitively enough to achieve their objective. On the contrary, Elkanah's questions sound more like scolding than comforting.[69] The sequence, *lāmāh....lāmāh...hălô'*, occurs mostly in the context of reprimanding in Hebrew prose (cf. Genesis 4:6–7; 1 Samuel 17:8; 2 Samuel 11:21; Numbers 22:37; cf. 1 Chronicles 21:3).[70] In addition, many scholars point out the self-centered worldview that is revealed in Elkanah's fourth question, "Am I not better to you than ten sons?" Jobling, for instance, says, "If you wish to assure someone of your love, the line "Are *you* not more to *me* than...?" seems much more promising than "Am I not more to you...?"![71] Hannah's silence speaks volumes about the ineffectiveness

[67] Frymer-Kensky, *Reading the Women of the Bible*, 303.

[68] The text (8a) clearly registers Elkanah's words as a one-time event, not an iterative act, but the two acts that trigger Elkanah's words may or may not be iterative. This ambiguity comes from the narrator's strategy to mix the two levels of the narration of the past event, iterative and punctual.

[69] Klein, "Hannah: Marginalized Victim and Social Redeemer," 97. Klein categorizes Elkanah as "blamer" who is much more interested in throwing his weight around rather than really finding out anything.

[70] Contra Tsumua (*The First Book of Samuel*, 113) who says, "[T]he four-fold question with three "why's" conveys Elkanah's concern for his beloved wife." But in my opinion, the way the narrator formulates Elkanah's question that recalls other scenes of scolding is intended to convey the actual effect of his utterance on Hannah.

[71] David Jobling, *1 Samuel*, Berit Olam (Collegeville, MN: The Liturgical Press, 1998), 131; Yairah Amit ("'Am I not More Devoted to You Than Ten Sons?' [1 Samuel 1.8]: Male and Female Interpretations," 74) says in a similar vein, "Elkanah's words reveal him to possess the egocentricity of a child who perceives himself as the center of his world...Elkanah's flow of questions is the complaint of a man who never matured, who perhaps enjoys moving back and forth between two women when one is the mother of his children and the other continues to fulfill the oedipal role of his own mother." On the contrary, Bar-Efrat (*Das Erste Buch Samuel: Ein narratologisch-philologischer Kommentar*, 67) takes Elkanah's effort as a sincere one to comfort Hannah by saying, "Er sagt nicht, dass *sie* ihm mehr wert sei als zehn Söhn, sondern dass *er* ihr mehr wert sei als zehn Söhn, denn in seinem Versuch, sie zu trösten, bezieht er sich auf ihre Gefühle."

of Elkanah's well-meaning words.[72] Hannah simply leaves the scene without really engaging Elkanah's questions. The next time we hear Hannah speaking of her true need, it is to YHWH of hosts.

In discussing the motif of Hannah's childlessness that articulates the pre-verbal concept of predicament, one cannot escape discussing the possible role of the Elides. The narrator inserts a piece of information on the priesthood of Eli's two sons in line 3b.[73] Since it is not Eli's two sons but Eli who plays the role of a priest in the subsequent unfolding of the story, scholars have wondered why the redactor decided to insert this bit of information at this point in the narrative. Although some scholars regard it as a blind motif,[74] several point out that the introduction of Eli's two sons in line 3b may foreshadow their priestly activities described in 1 Samuel 2:12–18 and also their fall in the battle against the Philistine in 1 Samuel 4.[75] In addition, in my opinion, it plays a role within the incubation type-scene of 1 Samuel 1. The mention of the Elides in 3b may suggest their unwholesome role in the cultus at Shiloh, in which Elkanah's family participated. What they did to the women working at the entrance of tent of meeting (cf. 1 Samuel 2:22) leads us to suspect the kind of danger they posed to someone like Hannah who is desperate to conceive.[76]

Finally, one may mention YHWH's role in aggravating Hannah's distress from childlessness. Hannah is never said to be "barren" in the text. The narrator never uses the word *'ăqārāh* in relating Hannah's childlessness. This is rather surprising considering that Sarah, Rebecca, and Rachel, even Manoah's wife, receive this adjective in the text when their miraculous conception is recounted. The narrator, however, uses

[72] Bar-Efrat, *Das Erste Buch Samuel: Ein narratologisch-philologischer Kommentar*, 67; Alter, *The David Story: A Translation with Commentary of 1 and 2 Samuel*, 4, footnote 8; Cartledge, *1 & 2 Samuel*, 31.

[73] McCarter (McCarter, *I Samuel: A New Translation*, 64) calls this "invidious juxtaposition" meaning that the two layers of the text may come from different sources. The Elide material and the Hannah-Samuel material run in parallel, never converging. Hannah never speaks to Eli's sons, nor does Samuel. They never even meet in the story although they may have done so in the real world. This invidious juxtaposition seems to serve as a redactional technique to exalt Samuel and to degrade Eli and his sons. For the redactional technique in 3b, see also Reinhard Wonneberger, *Redaktion: Studien zur Textfortschreibung im Alten Testament, entwickelt am Beispiel der Samuel-Überlieferung* (Göttingen: Vandenhoeck & Ruprecht, 1991), 200–201.

[74] Wonneberger, *Redaktion: Studien zur Textfortschreibung im Alten Testament, entwickelt am Beispiel der Samuel-Überlieferung*, 200.

[75] Cf. Eslinger, *Kingship of God in Crisis*, 76.

[76] Jobling, *1 Samuel*, 134.

a euphemistic idiom charged with theological implication: "YHWH closed Hannah's womb." The narrator never tells why YHWH closed Hannah's womb, so one should not assume that Hannah is at fault for her state of being barren.[77] Rather, it may be intended to draw attention to the fact that events on the human plane of the narrative are in fact the consequence of an initiative from the divine plane.[78] What interests us more in terms of Hannah's predicament is, however, that the idea of YHWH's closing of a womb leaves no hope for Hannah, thus maximizing the dramatic effect of the motif of barrenness in the story.[79] In some sense, Hannah's predicament reaches a nadir in the statement that attributes her barrenness to divine agency. It is one thing to say that Hannah is barren and yet another thing to say that YHWH had closed Hannah's womb. The latter leaves no hope, as is shown in Sarah's proposal out of despair, "Behold now, YHWH has prevented me from bearing children. Go in to my servant" (Genesis 16:2). In this regard, Fokkelman's words are worth quoting here: "The hard fact 6b knocks the bottom out of all the glimmers of hope seeking their refuge in the movement of Hannah 'every time when she went up to the house of the Lord.'"[80] YHWH's closing of Hannah's womb is tantamount to his foreclosing her future.

In sum, the motif of Hannah's childlessness, which articulates the concept of predicament, is expanded by the narrator elaborating on Hannah's distress from childlessness in four relational terms. Hannah's distress is exacerbated by a rival's persecution, the husband's insensitivity, the possible danger posed by the corrupt Elides, and finally the divine womb-closure. Given that the annunciation type-scene focusing on the extraordinariness of the baby does not elaborate on the mother's distress from barrenness,[81] the narrator's expansion of the motif of childlessness in the Hannah story indicates that it is better

[77] Although the idiom "YHWH's closing a womb" is used as a punishment for sin to explain the barrenness of Abimelech's wife (Genesis 20:17) and that of Michal, the daughter of Saul (2 Samuel 6:23), one should remember that in these two cases the narrator identifies the sins responsible for their condition. Cf. Joan E. Cook, *Hannah's Desire, God's Design: Early Interpretation of the Story of Hannah*, JSOTSup 282 (Sheffield: Sheffield Academic Press, 1999), 11–12.

[78] Eslinger, *Kingship of God in Crisis*, 73–74.

[79] Brueggemann, *First and Second Samuel*, 13.

[80] Fokkelman, *Vow and Desire (1 Sam. 1–12)*, 25.

[81] For instance, the story of Samson's birth mentions in passing the fact that Manoah's wife was barren (Judges 13:2). It tells nothing about her distress from barrenness. The story quickly moves to the appearance of an angel of YHWH. Likewise,

understood as belonging to the incubation type-scene which focuses on the incubant's overcoming the initial predicament through piety.

2.1.2 *The Motif of Preparatory Sacrifice*

The background against which the story of Hannah unfolds is Elkanah's annual trip to the sanctuary at Shiloh and the sacrifice offered during that trip (3a).[82] It was during one of those trips (4ab) that Hannah had made the fateful move to the temple in order to make a vow and received Eli's blessing. Although no sacrifice was offered with the specific purpose of preparing for Hannah's prayer vigil in the temple, or to make her vow more effective, let alone to induce divine appearance,[83] it is undeniable that Elkanah's annual sacrifice provides the backdrop to Hannah's fateful experience in the temple. This is made clear by Eli's misperception of Hannah as an unworthy woman who had drunk too much wine at the sacrificial meal (lines 13d, 14bc, and 15e).[84]

Mary's barrenness in the story of Jesus' birth poses no problem to her. After all, she is portrayed as a virgin.

[82] The nature of Elkanah's trip to Shiloh has been a subject of some scholarly debate. A number of scholars take one of the *ḥaggîm* imposed on every male in Israel (Exodus 23:14–17) as the occasion for Elkanah's trip to Shiloh. In particular, the feast of Ingathering, the annual *ḥag* of pilgrimage *par excellence*, is proposed as the reference of *zebah hayyāmîm* in 1 Samuel 1:21, on the basis of "the yearly feast of YHWH in Shiloh" (*ḥag-YHWH bəšilōh miyyamîm yamîmāh*) in Judges 21:19 where the yearly feast is associated with the vintage festival (cf. 21:21). Cf. Gnuse, "The Dream Theophany of Samuel: Its Structure in Relation to Ancient Near Eastern Dreams and Its Theological Significance," 248; Cartledge, *1 & 2 Samuel*, 28. In my opinion, however, there are some issues that may point us in another direction. 1 Samuel 1 shows no sign that Elkanah's worship and sacrifice was public as expected of the Feast of Ingathering. Rather, his worship and sacrifice look more like a family event. Furthermore, the day on which Elkanah's family go up to Shiloh does not seem to have been determined by any agricultural calendar, but by family custom or the will of the participants. This seems to be intimated by the scene of Hannah's dedication of Samuel to the temple of Shiloh. The text makes it clear through the repetitive note of Hannah's weaning that the time-point of Hannah's going up to Shiloh is determined by the time when Hannah weans the baby. Cf. M. Haran, *Temples and Temple-Service in Ancient Israel* (Winona Lake, IN: Eisenbrauns, 1985), 304–5; Menahem Haran, "Zebaḥ Hayyamīm," *VT* 19 (1969): 11–22. If this is the case, Elkanah's trip to Shiloh may have been optional, not imposed on the family by any law. Then, his regular trip to Shiloh may be said to underscore his piety. Cf. Bodner, *1 Samuel: Narrative Commentary*, 13; Brueggemann, "1 Samuel 1: A Sense of a Beginning," 34.

[83] Contra Jobling (*1 Samuel*) who says, "Hannah prays close to where Eli the chief priest is standing, and he takes notice of her. Perhaps she intends him to. This man figures in her plans." But, in my opinion, the text does not support his claim.

[84] Why did Eli take Hannah to be a drunkard? The early Israelites, like the Canaanites of Shechem (Judges 9:27), gave themselves to rejoicing and fully enjoyed

What is, however, more relevant to the incubation type-scene is Hannah's refusal to eat and drink. As in the motif of weeping (cf. Section 2.1.3 below), there seems to be a development in the nature of Hannah's fasting from an "everyday" act to a quasi-ritual act.[85] Hannah's "not eating" in line 7d is a reaction to Peninnah's harassment and an expression of the bitterness of her soul. This perspective may be discerned in Elkanah's questions in line 8d: "Why do you not eat? Why is your heart grieved?" Here Elkanah seems to explain Hannah's refusal to eat epexegetically as meaning that "her heart is grieved." Hannah's "not eating," then, seems to evolve into a "fasting," a quasi-cultic act in line 9a, where Hannah finally makes the decisive move from being a habitual victim to raising herself to change the situation once and for all.[86] This seems to be intimated by the awkward syntax in the phrase, "After the eating at Shiloh and the drinking (*'aḥărēy oklāh bəšilōh wəaḥărēy šātōh*)," in line 9a.

The phrase *'aḥărēy oklāh bəšilōh wəaḥărēy šātōh* presents at least two interpretive problems. The first one is whether or not Hannah participated in "the eating and drinking" and the second problem is how one should understand the awkwardly positioned, let alone apparently redundant, *bəšilōh*. However one may interpret *'aḥărēy oklāh*, Hannah's refraining from eating and drinking at this point in the narrative seems to be made clear by line 7d ("she would not eat"), line 15e ("I have drunk neither wine nor strong drink"), and line 18d ("and she ate").[87] That is to say, it is only after having spoken to the priest and

what the sacrificial meal offered. In that meal, not only meat but also bread and wine were provided. Hence it is only natural that some people over drank themselves and wondered around the holy place late at night. Especially considering the corrupt priests who oversaw the *cultus* at Shiloh, some acts of debauchery is all the more likely to have happened. Frymer-Kensky (*Reading the Women of the Bible*, 304) says, "Eli may have been accustomed to the sight of drunkenness." For more details on the sacrificial meals in ancient Israel, see Pedersen, *Israel: Its Life and Culture*, 334–41; Cartledge, *1 & 2 Samuel*, 29; Roland de Vaux, *Ancient Israel: Its Life and Institutions*, trans. John McHugh (New York: McGraw-Hill Book Company, 1961), 427–28.

[85] Peter D. Miscall, *1 Samuel: A Literary Reading*, Indiana Studies in Biblical Literature (Bloomington, IN: Indiana University Press, 1986), 12.

[86] Cf. Fokkelman, *Vow and Desire (1 Sam. 1–12)*, 46–47.

[87] Some scholars, who re-vocalize the Masoretic Text *'aḥărēy 'oklah* "after eating" to *'aḥărēy 'oklāh* (note *mapiq*) "after her eating," argue that Hannah ate and drank together with her family. For instance, Eslinger (*Kingship of God in Crisis*, 75–76) thinks that Hannah obliged Elkanah by eating her portion at the family meal. Frymer-Kensky (*Reading the Women of the Bible*, 304) says in a similar vein, "Eating in this context is a religious obligation, and so we are told that Hannah ate and drank." But other scholars, who take the Masoretic form *'oklāh* as an infinitive form like *šātōh* that

having received his blessing that she resumed eating. More interesting for our purpose, however, is the second problem of the awkward position of the phrase *bəšilōh*. Many scholars take the phrase itself, let alone its inconvenient position, as "superfluous,"[88] "unnecessary,"[89] or "oddly repetitive,"[90] and have proposed several emendations. Wellhausen was the first to propose *bəšēlāh* "boiled meat" which has been recently accepted by Hertzberg.[91] McCarter, on the other hand, has proposed *bəšelî* "privately."[92] But Eslinger, followed by Fokkelman, has demonstrated the literary purpose for the allegedly superfluous phrase. Both Eslinger and Fokkelman take note of the structural similarity between verses 3 and 9, both of which consist of two lines of contrast (ab). Both lines 3a and 9a have the phrase "at Shiloh" while line 3b rephrases it with a monosyllabic word *šām* "there" and the phrase "at the seat near the temple of YHWH" in line 9b give "at Shiloh" a much narrower focus. They both foreshadow the contrast scheme that governs chapters 2–3 by alternating movement with stasis. Elkanah actively goes up to worship and sacrifice at Shiloh (3a) but Eli's sons are simply there (3b). Hannah rises to stand before YHWH (9a), but Eli is sitting at the doorpost (9b).[93] The inconvenient position of *bəšilōh* in 9a intimates Hannah's determination to get an audience with YHWH in the temple, since the break "at Shiloh" of the otherwise connected "eating and drinking" indicates that the eating and drinking will have a different nature from this point on. Fokkelman argues that "she decided to make it [eating and drinking] into the spiritual preparation

---

does not allow a suffix, maintain that Hannah did not eat or drink. Note in this regard that the Septuagint (LXX) has μετὰ τὸ φαγεῖν αὐτοὺς "after their eating..." and also that many English Bibles reflect LXX in their choice of "they" as the subject of the verb "to eat" (cf. NRSV, JPS, ESV, KJV). So Bar-Efrat (*Das Erste Buch Samuel: Ein narratologisch-philologischer Kommentar*, 57) argues that Hannah did not participate in her family meal by saying, "Sie [Hannah] nimmt an den Mal nicht teil..., aber sie wartet still bis zum Ende des Mals, um ihr Familienmitglieder nicht zu verletzen. Dennach steht sie auf, um zu beten..."

[88] Driver, *Notes on the Hebrew Text and the Topography of the Books of Samuel*, 12.

[89] Peter R. Ackroyd, *The First Book of Samuel* (Cambridge: Cambridge University Press, 1971), 23; Smith, *The Books of Samuel*, 9.

[90] McCarter, *I Samuel: A New Translation*, 53.

[91] Cf. W. Nowack, *Richter, Ruth und Bücher Samuelis* (Göttingen: Vandenhoeck und Ruprecht, 1902), 5; Hertzberg, *I & II Samuel: A Commentary*, 22. Cf. Smith, *The Books of Samuel*, 9–10.

[92] McCarter, *I Samuel: A New Translation*, 53.

[93] Eslinger, *Kingship of God in Crisis*, 75.

for the Nazirite, in imitation of the mother of Samson."[94] This seems to corroborate my view that Hannah's refraining from eating and drinking may have originated as an emotional response to Peninnah's harassment (cf. verse 7), but by the time Hannah transformed it into positive energy in order to stand before YHWH in verse 9, the simple act of refraining from eating and drinking out of distress had taken on a quasi-cultic nature, namely, it had become a cultic fasting and abstention from wine for the purpose of winning divine favor.[95]

Furthermore, the eating and drinking aspect of the sacrifice punctuates the whole incubation type-scene. Peninnah's harassment of Hannah happens in the context of a sacrificial meal. Hannah reacts to Peninnah's harassment by refusing to eat her special portion. It is only after Hannah receives Eli's blessing that she begins to eat. Thus the movement from fasting to eating coincides with the movement from a problem to a solution. Not only does the motif of eating and drinking punctuate the incubation type-scene in 1 Samuel 1, but it also figures prominently in chapter 2 where the sins of Eli's sons stand in stark contrast to the piety of Elkanah's family. Eli's sons took (*lāqaḥ*) by force the sacrificial meat even before it was offered to YHWH (2:16). In the first prophecy against Eli, the "man of God" plays with the word *kābad* "to be heavy" in order to drive home his accusation of the Elides of "honoring" not YHWH but their sons (*təkabbēd*, 2:30) as they fatten themselves (*ləhabrî'ăkem*, 2:30) with the choicest parts of the sacrificial offerings that the people of Israel brought to YHWH.[96] Their fortune will soon be overturned and they will ask the new and faithful priest of YHWH for a morsel of bread (*pat-leḥem*, 2:36). This inversion of fortunes is already intoned by Hannah in her song: "Those who were full have hired themselves for bread, but those who were hungry have ceased to hunger" (2:5). The theme of eating and drinking is also repeated at important junctures in the book of Samuel.[97]

---

[94] Fokkelman, *Vow and Desire (1 Sam. 1–12)*, 47.

[95] Miscall also notes that there are two dimensions of meaning in Hannah's refraining from eating and drinking. He calls them "everyday eating" and "ritual fasting" respectively. He says, "She [Hannah] eats and drinks because she is famished and weak or she performs a ritual eating and drinking and then goes to pray to the Lord." Cf. Miscall, *1 Samuel: A Literary Reading*, 12.

[96] Philip Long, "First and Second Samuel," in *A Complete Literary Guide to the Bible*, ed. Ryken Leland and Tremper Longman III (Grand Rapids, MI: Zondervan, 1993), 171.

[97] See section 3 below. Cf. Miscall, *1 Samuel: A Literary Reading*, 11; Cartledge, *1 & 2 Samuel*, 46.

2.1.3 *The Motif of Weeping*

Incubation texts often present the participant as approaching the deity in tears in order to induce a divine appearance. The poet of *Kirta*, for instance, underscores the importance of Kirta's weeping not only through an elaborate description of the act (KTU 1.14:26–30) but also by strategic uses of the pair *bky* and *dmʿ* within the incubation type-scene (KTU 1.14:31–32; 39–40). Likewise, Hannah is portrayed as a woman of tears. The narrator uses the verb *bākāh* "to weep" three times (7c, 8c, and 10c: cf. 6a)[98] and gives it high salience in lines 7c and 10c. If verses 3–8 are taken as the exposition which is punctuated by a sequence of iterative verbs, the waw-consecutive imperfect form *wattibke* in line 7c expresses high salience in that it is markedly a perfective verb within that sequence. Although one may interpret the mixture of imperfect and perfective verbs as the narrator's deliberate interweaving of iterative and punctilear events, the context of the exposition may allow us to translate the form *tattibke* as the iterative; thus Alter's translation "she would weep and would not eat."[99] The imperfect verb *tibke* in 10c, on the other hand, occurs in the middle of the sequence of perfective verbs, namely, in the context of events presented as perfectives. Although a number of scholars take it as constituting a circumstantial clause to the preceding or following verbs, it does not change the fact that the verb *tibke* expresses high salience in the sequence of perfective verbs.[100] And it would not be a coincidence that another verb of high salience *wəhāyāh* in line 12a also introduces

[98] If one takes *harʿimāh* in line 6a as an internal Hiphil of *rāʿam* "to thunder," one may discern the motif of weeping in 6a. And the phonetic similarity between *harʿimāh* in 6a and *raḥmāh* in 6b may serve as a literary link between Hannah's bitter cry and her barren womb. Cf. Frymer-Kensky, *Reading the Women of the Bible*, 302–3.

[99] Alter, *The David Story: A Translation with Commentary of 1 and 2 Samuel*, 4. Note Pardee's translation "and (each time that) she wept." Pardee seems to think of the perfective form *wattibke* as expressing perfective, although it happens within the iterative structure. Pardee also considers the possibility of emending the Massorectic vocalization to *wətibke*, "in order that she weep," or "with the result that she would weep." However that may be, the Masoretic vocalization requires analysis as a perfective, and any non-perfective analysis (as a frequentative or a purpose/result clause) requires emendation (personal communication).

[100] Joosten provides three interpretative possibilities: (a) a frequentative "she used to cry," (b) an expression of the imperfective aspect "as she was crying," (c) as a prospective "she was about to cry." Joosten favors the last possibility. Cf. Joosten, "Workshop: Meaning and Use of the Tenses in 1 Samuel 1," 75. But in my opinion, the second possibility is most feasible in the context in question. Pardee ("Hebrew Verbal System in a Nutshell," a 2003 draft of an unpublished paper, p. 22) also takes the form as "expressing continuousness of weeping during the prayer."

the act of Hannah's long and intense prayer. One may then argue that the narrator intends to place special emphasis on the motif of tearful prayer in his portrayal of Hannah in this incubation type-scene.

Hannah's tears not only give vent to her inner bitterness but also create positive energy to cry out to YHWH for his intervention. As in the case of Hannah's abstinence from eating and drinking, there is an interesting development in the nature of Hannah's tears from line 7c to line 10c. Hannah's weeping in line 7c, along with her fasting in line 7d, is a reaction to Peninnah's habitual harassment in line 7b, whereas line 10c, which is sandwiched between the motif of prayer and that of vow-making, seems to point to Hannah's determination to get an audience with YHWH.[101] In other words, Hannah's "everyday" weeping in line 7d turns to a "once-and-for all" ritual weeping in line 10c. This development coincides with the change of the time frames of the narrative. The weeping as a simple outlet for Hannah's distress occurs in the exposition of the narrative, which is carried on by a sequence of iterative verbs (verses 3–8), whereas the weeping as a means of inducing divine mercy occurs in the context of events expressed perfectively (verses 9–28). Hannah's weeping in the latter instance creates a positive energy within her to stand up against all odds and pray before YHWH and make a vow. This interrelation between weeping and vow-making is iconically expressed in the chiastic structure formed between 10c and 11a: *bākōh* (A: Cognate Supplement): *tibkeh* (B: the verb "to weep") = *tiddōr* (B´: the verb "to vow") : *neder* (A´: Cognate Supplement).[102]

One may observe a similar development in the expressions of Hannah's inner state. Fokkelman argues that the attention the narrator pays to Hannah's inner state is, as far as the standards of Hebrew story telling are concerned, very detailed and leads to three descriptive clauses (8e, 10a, and 15d).[103] If the expressions in lines 8e and 10a are attuned to Hannah's bitterness about her barrenness and its concomitant situation within the family, the description in line 15d, *'iššāh qəšat*

[101] An interesting light may be shed by looking at another barren woman who had a child through miracle in 2 Kings 4. The Shunamite woman in 2 Kings 4 is also desperate to get an audience with a man of God when she loses her miracle boy. In order to do so, she tells a lie twice, the first time to her husband and the second time to Gehashi. Once she gets an audience with Elisha, she shows her determination to get an answer from him by clinging to Elisha's leg.

[102] Fokkelman, *Vow and Desire (1 Sam. 1–12)*, 35.

[103] Ibid., 34. For a similar observation, see Cartledge, *1 & 2 Samuel*, 31.

rûăḥ, seems to indicate Hannah's determination to rise beyond the cyclical feelings of defeat. The expression in line 15d occurs only here. Also the meaning "hard-spirited," "obstinate" (cf. Deuteronomy 2:30) does not seem to fit the context.[104] Hence, many scholars follow the Septuagint's reading γυνή ᾗ σκληρὰ ἡμέρα "a woman for whom this is a hard day,"[105] which seems to reflect the Hebrew expression *qəšēh yôm* "one whose day is hard" (cf. Job 30:25).[106] But this is not necessary. The phrase *ʾiššāh qəšat rûăḥ* appears to be the narrator's choice of words to express Hannah's bitterness of heart (by an implicit reference to the phrase *mārat nepeš* in verse 10) and her dogged determination to put an end to it at the same time.

2.1.4 *The Motif of Prayer and Vow-Making*

One of the features that distinguish Hannah from the other barren women who become mothers through divine intervention is her ability to turn her bitter emotions toward none other than YHWH. Unlike Sarah or Rachel, Hannah in refusing to enter into the subject-rival competition with Peninnah is not affected by mimetic desire. There is nothing in the text that indicates that Hannah wanted children out of envy for Peninnah's children. Hannah's desire arises from within and is maintained as a personal, and yet unfulfilled wish. In this regard, Klein argues that the story of Hannah is the only instance in the Hebrew Bible where female rejection of mimetic desire occurs.[107] Hannah does not even attempt to correct Elkanah's misunderstanding reflected in his four-fold question in verse 8. Even the thought that YHWH is ultimately responsible for her barrenness does not stop her from standing (up for herself) before YHWH asking for a change (cf. line 9a).[108] She turns her bitterness (cf. line 10a) into positive energy to initiate the

---

[104] G. W. Ahlström, "I Samuel 1, 15," *Bib* 60, no. 254 (1979): 254; Alter, *The David Story: A Translation with Commentary of 1 and 2 Samuel*, 6, footnote 15; Eslinger, *Kingship of God in Crisis*, 79.

[105] The English translation is taken from Albert Pietersma and Benjamin G. Wright, eds., *A New English Translation of the Septuagint* (Oxford: Oxford University Press, 2007).

[106] For instance, Dhorme considers the Septuagint's reading as more difficult and therefore original, while the Masoretic reading is an adaptation of the more difficult reading (P. Dhorme, *Les Livres de Samuel*, Études Bibliques [Paris: Librairie Victor Lecoffre, 1910], 21, footnote 15).

[107] Klein, "Hannah: Marginalized Victim and Social Redeemer," 81–82.

[108] The Septuagint's reading of verse 9 makes it clear that Hannah rose "to stand before YHWH" (καὶ κατέστη ἐνώπιον κυρίου).

process of divine intervention: "she prayed to YHWH" (*wattitpallel 'al-YHWH*) in line 10b. Since it is YHWH who had closed her womb, it is only logical to turn to YHWH who can also open it.[109] So she offers a long and fervent prayer to YHWH with a broken heart.

What is interesting to note with regard to Hannah's prayer is the use of the preposition *'al* in line 10b. YHWH is introduced by the preposition *'al*. Since the verb *hitpallel* governs its addressee usually with the prepositions *lə*, *'el*, or *lipnēy*,[110] the use of *'al* begs an explanation. Commentators note that the preposition *'al* is suited to denote the party on whose behalf prayer is being offered, and is then a synonym of *ba'ad*. Although Bar-Efrat explains it away by saying that the narrator of the story uses *'al* and *'el* interchangeably,[111] Fokkelman provides the following reason for the use of *'al* at this particular point in the narrative: "Hannah, having sprung to her feet, relates vitally, directly, and intensely, to God, as if God is not the addressee of her prayer, but the object of her prayer."[112] Furthermore the use of *'al* in line 10b lends itself to the comparison with the double use of the same preposition in line 9b where Eli is portrayed as sitting "on" (*'al*) the seat "beside" (*'al*) the doorpost of the temple of YHWH. This seems to bring out the contrast between Eli and Hannah in terms of their attitudes toward YHWH. The passively sitting Eli seems to relate to YHWH as the institutional God, unlike Hannah who actively rises to engage YHWH as if he were her personal God. Eli almost appears to be separated from YHWH by the objects "on" (*'al*) which he sits, whereas, for Hannah, YHWH is the very object she prays for (*'al*).[113]

---

[109] The narrator's use of the term "womb" (*reḥem*) in the books of Samuel is worth noting. In 1 Samuel 1:5–6 it is twice used in the context of Hannah's barrenness. The only other use of the term occurs in David's confession of his sin to Gad: "....Let me fall into his hand of YHWH, for his mercy (*reḥem*) is great..." (2 Samuel 24:14). Trible has made a compelling case that the root *rḥm*, variously used as "womb" and as "compassion," has a stable meaning that is present in both uses. That stable meaning is something like "womb-like mother love." Then it is no coincidence that the term is used in those two places and nowhere else. "It is an act of Yahweh's graciousness that God should open the womb of Hannah." Cf. Brueggemann, "1 Samuel 1: A Sense of a Beginning," 45, footnote 23. For a discussion of God's control of the womb, see Phyllis Trible, *God and the Rhetoric of Sexuality* (Philadelphia, PA: Fortress Press, 1978), 34–38.

[110] Note verses 10, 12, 26, and 27.

[111] Bar-Efrat, *Das Erste Buch Samuel: Ein narratologisch-philologischer Kommentar*, 68.

[112] Fokkelman, *Vow and Desire (1 Sam. 1–12)*, 35.

[113] Ibid.

The nominal clause in line 10a (*wəhîʾ mārat nepeš*) is significant in this regard. Located between line 9b and line 10b, line 10a informs the reader of Hannah's inner state as she engages in her prayer and thereby corroborates the contrast between Eli and Hannah in attitude to YHWH in their hearts.

Out of Hannah's long prayer (cf. 12a) only the words of the vow are preserved, in verse 11, perhaps because they are important for the unfolding of the plot.[114] Hannah has not been afforded a single syllable of direct speech up to this point in the story. But Hannah's unyielding quest for the ultimate player in all human affairs, not distracted by Peninnah's provocation or by Elkanah's obtuse remarks, finally finds voice when Hannah moves her mouth, breaking years of sorrowful silence, to utter "O YHWH of hosts."

Cartledge proposes the four elements for what he calls the "Vow Account" in the biblical narrative: (1) Narrative Introduction, (2) Address to the Deity, (3) Protasis of the Vow (Condition), (4) Apodosis of the Vow.[115] The language in lines 11ab, *nādar ʾet neder + ʾāmar*, is typical of the narrative introduction of all biblical vows in narrative texts (cf. Numbers 21:2 [Israel's vow], 2 Samuel 15:8 [Absalom's vow], Judges 11:30–31 [Jephthah's vow], Genesis 28:20–22 [Jacob's vow]). The vocative "O YHWH of hosts" in line 11c corresponds to the second element of Cartledge's "Vow Account." Interestingly, Hannah's vow is the only biblical vow account which includes an address to the deity.[116] The third and fourth elements, which deal with a single

[114] Bar-Efrat, *Das Erste Buch Samuel: Ein narratologisch-philologischer Kommentar*, 68; Cartledge, *1 & 2 Samuel*, 33. For the role of vow in the plot of biblical narratives, see Tony W. Cartledge, *Vows in the Hebrew Bible and the Ancient Near East* (Sheffield: JSOT Press, 1992), 162–99. Pardee, however, argues on the basis of the short prayer as quoted and the semantic ambiguity of the root √rbb that it is not possible to determine whether the author wished to say that Hannah kept repeating the words quoted or that these words were to be considered a summary of a much longer prayer (Dennis Pardee, "Hebrew Verbal System in a Nutshell" the 2003 draft, p. 24, footnote 83).

[115] Cartledge, *Vows in the Hebrew Bible and the Ancient Near East*, 145. Fisher also provides a four-part structure on the basis of his analysis of Ugaritic and biblical vows: (1) Introductory Formula, (2) Address to the god, (3) the Condition, (4) the Vow or Gift. Cf. Loren R. Fisher, "Literary Genres in the Ugaritic Texts," in *Ras Shamra Parallels: The Texts from Ugarit and the Hebrew Bible*, vol. 2, ed. Loren R. Fisher (Roma: Pontificium Institutum Biblicum, 1975), 147–52, especially, 149–150.

[116] Cartledge, *Vows in the Hebrew Bible and the Ancient Near East*, 147. In addition, Hannah is the first character who addresses God through the unrivaled epithet, "YHWH of hosts," in the Hebrew Bible according to its canonical order (cf. Bodner, *1 Samuel: Narrative Commentary*, 18). According to Fokkelman, Hannah's use of this divine title distinguishes itself from the other two uses, whose context has to do with

request and promise, are expanded into a four-part conditional protasis in lines 11defg and a two-part promissory apodosis in lines 11hi.[117] Hannah has only one request: YHWH may give her a male child (*zeraʿ ʾănāšîm* in line 11g).[118] But this request is prefaced by three parallel expressions, "see my affliction" (11d) "remember me" (11e) and "not forget me" (11f). These parallel expressions along with a three-time repetition of "your maid-servant" (11d, f, g) not only underscore the intensity of Hannah's supplication but also reveal her character, both humility and brashness, both despair and determination.[119] They are meant to garner God's attention before Hannah finally verbalizes the specific way in which she wants to be remembered (11g).

This request is balanced by a single promise that Hannah makes in the two-part apodosis—to give the child back to YHWH all of his days (11h).[120] The meaning of this promise is clarified later in line 22f: "and he will dwell there [in the temple] forever." The verb *nātan* that forms the backbone of Hannah's vow ("If you will give, I will give") not only stands in contrast to the verb *lāqaḥ* "to take" that characterizes the Elides' wicked behavior in the temple (cf. 1 Samuel 2:16)—Hannah, a barren woman, is willing to give to YHWH whereas the Elides, the

the routine of the *cultus* administered by Eli's sons in verse 3 and the illusion that the Ark of YHWH constitutes an institutional assurance of God's help in chapter 4 (Fokkelman, *Vow and Desire [1 Sam. 1–12]*, 36). Hannah's invocation of God by his full title is an expression of her unadulterated piety, namely, her living and personal relation with the deity, that will initiate a change (Fokkelman, *Vow and Desire (1 Sam. 1–12)*, 36).

[117] The Septuagint's version deletes 11f ("and will not forget your maid servant") from the protasis and adds "and will not drink wine or strong drink" to the apodosis, thus making a nicely balanced structure of two three-part sections.

[118] Literally 'a seed of men'. The immediate context requires the meaning "a male child." Hannah intends a boy in her vow, as her Nazirite vow makes clear. Cf. Alter, *The David Story: A Translation with Commentary of 1 and 2 Samuel*, 5; Fokkelman, *Vow and Desire (1 Sam. 1–12)*, 37. But the expression occurs only here. Also, Hebrew *zeraʿ* may be a collective noun, referring to a plural entity. Furthermore, another birth story in chapter 2 seems to suggest that the narrator may have intended it to be ambiguous, anticipating Hannah's second round of conception and birth. Cf. McCarter, *I Samuel: A New Translation*, 61; Eslinger, *Kingship of God in Crisis*, 438, footnote 12; Frymer-Kensky, *Reading the Women of the Bible*, 304.

[119] Cartledge, *Vows in the Hebrew Bible and the Ancient Near East*, 192.

[120] The overall structure of Hannah's vow is nothing but *si dederis dabo* "if you give, I will give" a reversal of *do ut des* "I give so you will give," the relationship that often informs the sacrificial system. Cf. Cartledge, *Vows in the Hebrew Bible and the Ancient Near East*, 38; Polzin, *Samuel and the Deuteronomist: A Literary Study of the Deuteronomic History*, 135; Alter, *The David Story: A Translation with Commentary of 1 and 2 Samuel*, 84; Fokkelman, *Vow and Desire (1 Sam. 1–12)*, 36.

chosen priests, are ready to use force to take from YHWH—but also makes a smooth transition to a Nazirite vow in line 11i, for, after all, the term δοτόν "granted" seems to have been meant as the Greek translation of the Hebrew term *nāzîr* in verse 11 of the Septuagint.[121] The clause "No razor will come upon his head" in line 11i nuances Hannah's dedication of Samuel in line 11h. Although some scholars[122] are reluctant to give Samuel Naziriteship owing to the lack of the term *nāzîr*,[123] quite apart from the disappearance of the theme of Naziriteship later in the story,[124] the long hair of Samuel, along with the theme

---

121 McCarter, *I Samuel: A New Translation*, 53.

122 Scholars like Miscall and Cartledge argue that it is difficult to speak of Samuel as a Nazirite, because he is characterized as a Nazrite neither in the sense of a charismatic war leader like Samson nor as the *nāzîr* described in Numbers 6. Cf. Miscall, *1 Samuel: A Literary Reading*, 13; Cartledge, *1 & 2 Samuel*, 32–33. However, scholars, such as Hylander, Dus, and McCartner, go further and speculate that the birth story in 1 Samuel 1 originally concerned Saul, who better fits the profile of a Nazirite (I. Hylander, *Der literarische Samuel-Saul-Komplex [1. Sam 1–15]: Traditionsgeschichtlich Untersucht* [Uppsala: Almqvist & Wiksell, 1932], 11–39; Dus, "Die Geburtslegende Samuel 1 Sam. 1: Eine traditions-geschichtliche Untersuchung zu 1 Sasm. 1–3," 167ff; McCarter, *I Samuel: A New Translation*, 26–27, 63, 65). Gnuse, on the other hand, denies the historicity of the story and considers the birth story of Samuel as a literary creation (Gnuse, "The Dream Theophany of Samuel: Its Structure in Relation to Ancient Near Eastern Dreams and Its Theological Significance," 239–40).

123 The variant reading in the Septuagint is dotovn which McCarter identifies with Hebrew *nāzîr*. But the difficulty is that Hebrew *nāzîr* is translated in the Septuagint by five different terms, none of which is dotovn (cf. Hutzli, *Die Erzählung von Hanna und Samuel: Textkritische und literarische Anayse von 1. Samuel 1–2 unter Berüchsichtigung des Kontextes*, 64). Furthermore, 4QSam[a] does not attest to *nāzîr* in the verse in question, except in McCarter's reconstruction (McCarter, *I Samuel: A New Translation*, 53–54). Nevertheless, one cannot deny the presence of some key elements comprising a Nazirite vow both in the Masoretic text and in the Septuagint. After all, we do not know whether the elaborate Nazirite law in Numbers 6 was applied in this early period of Israel's history.

124 Hannah's Nazirite vow in 11i may foreshadow the prophetic office of Samuel later in the story. Although a number of scholars take Samuel's long hair as a sign of his Naziriteship, they are often at a loss about its role in the unfolding of the story. This confusion has led some to suggest that the birth story of Samuel originally belonged to Saul who better fits the profile of a Nazirite as attested to in the Samson story. If a Nazirite is narrowly defined only by Samson's model or by Number 6:1–21, the dedication of Samuel as a Nazirite does seem to be a blind motif going nowhere in the subsequent narratives. In my opinion, however, there is one possible way of understanding the narratological role of the theme in the subsequent story of Samuel. Amos 2:10–11 makes a link between a prophet and a Nazirite and many scholars suspect that early prophets and nazirites were both charismatics active in times of war, and that the two categories were similar and at times indistinguishable (Stanley N. Rosenbaum, *Understanding Biblical Israel: A Reexamination of the Origins of Monotheism* [Macon, GA: Mercer University Press, 2002], 252; Theodorus C. Vriezen, *The Religion of Ancient Israel* [Philadelphia, PA: Westminster Press, 1967], 178;

of dedication in 11h, leaves no doubt about his Naziriteship.[125] It is noteworthy that the same Nazirite vow as in line 11i occurs in the story of Samson's birth (Judges 13:5).[126] It leads the reader to anticipate that Samuel, like Samson, may play a heroic role as the savior of Israel from a foreign hand.[127] However, more interesting from the perspective of the incubation type-scene is that the exceptional nature of the yet-to-be-born child is expressed not in the motif of divine message, but in Hannah's vow-prayer. This may be significant, considering that in other biblical annunciation type-scenes, the exceptional nature of the child is usually announced by a divine messenger. One of the crucial differences between Samson's birth story and that of Samuel is that Samuel's Nazirite vow is imposed by his mother, whereas Samson's vow is divinely initiated. What comes to the foreground in Hannah's Nazirite vow is the initiative-taking character of the mother, rather than Samuel's heroic future. In this regard, one may even say that Samuel was chosen by Hannah, rather than by God, unlike other "divinely chosen" heroes in their birth stories.[128] This peculiarity in Hannah's Nazirite vow fits well with the idea of the incubation type-scene where the character and the piety of an incubant are usually underscored.

The same point can be made by another possible allusion to the future role of the yet-to-be-born child in Hannah's vow. One of the

Blenkinsopp, *A History of Prophecy in Israel*, 46). If the account in 1 Samuel 1 assumes the early period when the distance between a Nazirite and a prophet was not that great, one may argue that Hannah's dedication of Samuel as a Nazirite serves as a foreshadowing of his future role as a prophet, although the latter's role is portrayed not as a leader in battle but as communicating the divine word to the whole of Israel.

[125] Bar-Efrat, *Das Erste Buch Samuel: Ein narratologisch-philologischer Kommentar*, 68; Eslinger, *Kingship of God in Crisis*, 77. For a comparison between Samuel and Samson in terms of a Nazirite vow, see Fokkelman, *Vow and Desire (1 Sam. 1–12)*, 39–40.

[126] The comparison with the story of Samson's birth needs further study. Although almost all scholars discern literary connections between the birth story of Samuel and Samson, only a few have bothered to elaborate on them. The following studies have been helpful to me: McCarter, *I Samuel: A New Translation*, 64–66; Hylander, *Der literarische Samuel-Saul-Komplex (1. Sam 1–15): Traditionsgeschichtlich Untersucht*, 25–33; Robert Alter, "How Convention Helps Us Read: The Case of the Bible's Annunciation Type-Scene," *Proof* 3 (1983): 123–24; Campbell, *1 Samuel*, 43–44; Jobling, *1 Samuel*, 171–72; Fokkelman, *Vow and Desire (1 Sam. 1–12)*, 39–40.

[127] Miscall, *1 Samuel: A Literary Reading*, 1.

[128] Gnuse, "The Dream Theophany of Samuel: Its Structure in Relation to Ancient Near Eastern Dreams and Its Theological Significance," 239; Fokkelman, *Vow and Desire (1 Sam. 1–12)*, 40; James S. Ackerman, "Who Can Stand Before YHWh, This Holy God? A Reading of 1 Samuel 1–15," *Proof* 11 (1991): 3.

conditional clauses, 11d, recalls YHWH's visitation of Israel in the Exodus account. Exodus 3:7–8 associates God's sending of Moses with his "seeing the affliction" of the people of Israel. This is one of those threshold-points in the Hannah story where Hannah's private concerns take on national significance. One may even say that Hannah's vow is a reflex of the bitterness of the Israelites when oppressed by the Egyptians. Likewise, YHWH's subsequent sending of Moses after looking at the people's affliction creates an anticipation in the reader's mind that the same deity would send a second Moses. Thus Samuel is not only to relieve Hannah's personal misery but also to save the nation from the moral and religious chaos described in Judges 17–21 by ushering in the institution of monarchy. But this foreshadowing is very subtle and not conspicuous enough to make Samuel the focus of an incubation type-scene: hence it provides another reason that the story in 1 Samuel 1 is better taken as the incubation type-scene of a pious woman than the story of a hero (i.e., the annunciation type-scene).

To sum up, although Hannah's vow follows the standard form of vow-making in Northwest Semitic literature, its detailed elaborations in the conditional protasis and in the promissory apodosis reveal the depth of feeling and the determination of character, not to mention the piety, of the one undertaking the vow. The allusion to the future of the yet-to-be-born child is not so dominant as to overshadow the spotlight on the incubant.

2.1.5 *The Motif of a Temple*

The incubation type-scene in 1 Samuel 1 is punctuated with cyclical movements of the proponents from one place to another. Elkanah's family is said in line 3a to go up to Shiloh in order to worship and to sacrifice to YHWH and in lines 19cd they are said to return to Ramah. Also the narrator embeds a smaller cycle of travelling within the large cycle of traveling from Shiloh to Ramah. The smaller cycle of travelling within Shiloh is framed by *qûm* "to arise" in line 9a and *hālak* "to go" in line 18c and provides a locative setting for Hannah's decisive, one-time act in the temple of YHWH (*hēykal YHWH* in line 9b). All this seems to underscore the narrator's efforts to make it clear that Hannah's encounter with Eli takes place within YHWH's temple. And this is important from the perspective of the incubation type-scene, because the motif of a holy place is one of the salient elements of the incubation type-scene.

More specifically, the narrator has three ways of registering the space-coordinate of the event that takes place between lines 9a and 18c. We zoom in from "in Shiloh" (9a) to the temple of YHWH (9b), and to "before YHWH" (12b, 15f). The phrase "in Shiloh" in line 9a is further elaborated to indicate the exact location of Eli within the temple of YHWH through the double use of the preposition *'al*: he is "on" (*'al*) the seat—prefiguring the exact image of his death at the end of chapter 4—" 'beside' (*'al*) the doorpost of the temple of Yahweh." The locative detail introduced by the second *'al* provides the proper explanation of how Eli was able to observe Hannah praying.[129] Finally, it is the phrase "before YHWH" (*lipnēy YHWH*) that provides a narrower focus on the location of the singular event that effects a decisive change in Hannah's situation. Hannah prayed "before YHWH" (12b) and poured her heart out "before YHWH" (15f). Bar-Efrat identifies the phrase with "at the entrance to the tent of meeting" (*petaḥ 'ōhel mô'ēd*) on the basis of Joshua 19:51.[130] The phrase "before YHWH" may not only serve as a circumlocution for the temple, but it also seems to connote more than a building where the cultus takes place. It seems to signal direct contact between Hannah and Yahweh.[131] It encapsulates the purpose of Hannah's "arising" in 9a, namely, to seek God's face (*pənēy YHWH*). It is interesting to note that the phrase, "before YHWH," which signifies the closest point where a human can get to the divine realm, throws the sin of Eli's sons into sharp relief, for they committed adultery with the women working before YHWH, namely, "at the entrance to the tent of meeting" (1 Samuel 2:22).

Shiloh seems to be an ambivalent site. It is the place where the ark of YHWH is enshrined, where Joshua parceled out land to most of the tribes (cf. Joshua 18:1–10; 19:51; 21:2), and the place that tradition marks as YHWH's uniquely "chosen place" before Jerusalem. And yet, it is the place where a civil war is prevented only at the last moment (Joshua 22:9, 12), and where subsequently, at the end of Judges, civil war does in fact take place. The abduction, carried out in Shiloh during

---

[129] Alfons Schulz, "Narrative Art in the Books of Samuel," in *Narrative and Novella in Samuel*, ed. David M. Gunn (Sheffield: Sheffield Academic Press, 1991), 129; Bar-Efrat, *Das Erste Buch Samuel: Ein narratologisch-philologischer Kommentar*, 68.

[130] Bar-Efrat, *Das Erste Buch Samuel: Ein narratologisch-philologischer Kommentar*, 65.

[131] Fokkelman, *Vow and Desire (1 Sam. 1–12)*, 45.

a religious festival that recalls *zebaḥ hayyāmîm* in 21a, deals a blow to the prestige of the city and the sanctuary.[132] This negative image is corroborated in the evil acts of Eli's sons, the priests of YHWH at Shiloh. The conflicting double images seem to be reflected in its role in the story of Hannah. The cultus at Shiloh provides a background for Peninnah's habitual torment of Hannah, and yet it is in the temple at Shiloh that Hannah prays the prayer that effects a change in the story. This also coincides with the contrast between Elkanah's habitual sacrifice at Shiloh and Hannah's singular and decisive trip to the temple. And Hannah's purposeful trip to the temple is something that differentiates the incubation type-scene in the Hannah story from other biblical annunciation stories, for instance, the story of Samson's birth, where Samson's mother was suddenly visited by the angel of YHWH.

2.1.6 *The Motif of Night*

The author has crafted into the Hannah story several artifices that orient the reader in terms of the temporal background of the story. By using both imperfective and perfective sequences and mixing them together at times, the narrator embeds the singular events such as the vow-making and the miraculous conception of a barren wife within the habitual circumstances around the national cultus at Shiloh,[133] thus telling the story that begins with Hannah's private predicament but ends with a birth that is of historic significance for the nation of Israel. This is also done by the clever use of the word *yôm*. The particular event is described as happening on "one day" (*hayyôm* in 4a), while the habitual circumstances around the cultus at Shiloh are predicated in the phrase "from days to days" (*miyyāmîm yāmîmāh* in 3a). The end-result of playing the particular off against the habitual is the lifelong (*kōl-yəmēy ḥayyāw* in 11h) dedication of Samuel that will change

[132] Baruch Halpern, "Shiloh," in *ABD*, vol. 5, ed. David N. Freedman (New York: Doubleday, 1992), 1213–15; Miscall, *1 Samuel: A Literary Reading*, 9; Fokkelman, *Vow and Desire (1 Sam. 1–12)*, 19–20.

[133] The transition from the habitual to the punctual is so smooth that one cannot be absolutely sure whether *watibke* in 7c and *wayyo'mer* 8a belong to the habitual or the punctual. Both are couched in the perfective, but both the fact that the weeping in 7c appears to be triggered by Peninnah's torment, which is couched in the imperfective and the fact that the saying in 8c also appears to be triggered by the habitual fasting make it very hard to determine whether the weeping in 7c and the saying in 8a is presented as complete or as a frequentative. Perhaps this ambiguity may have been intended by the narrator, thus making the transition even smoother.

once and for all the *has-been* state of affairs with regard to the cultus at Shiloh. Furthermore, the temporal construction in line 20a, *wayəhî litqupôt hayyāmîm*, expresses the cyclical aspect of the year but at the same time points to that unforgettable coming around of the year which introduces Hannah's delivery, thus providing another case of setting the particular over against the habitual.[134]

This great care that the narrator bestows on the time coordinate of the events leads us to wonder whether there is any indication of when the "theophanic" encounter between Hannah and Eli happened registered in the text. The clause *wayyaškimû babbōker* in 19a may be significant in this regard. The mention of "rising in the morning" comes right after the scene of the encounter between Eli and Hannah, a variation of the motif of divine-human encounter. The question is whether the clause in 19a may serve as a legitimate clue to the nocturnal encounter between Eli and Hannah, namely, to the motif of night in this incubation type-scene. A definitive answer may forever remain beyond our ken, but the comparative survey of the scenes where a divine oracle is solicited in the last chapters of Judges may shed some light on this issue. The scene of the people of Israel inquiring of God/YHWH punctuates the story in Judges 20–21. They are reported to have gone up three times to Bethel to inquire of YHWH concerning the punitive battle against the Benjaminites and one more time to the same place to inquire of YHWH concerning the problem of the genocide of the Benjaminites brought about by their rash oath sworn at Mizpah. Although each scene varies in details, the general configuration of component motifs is similar (see Table 6.1 in Section 3). The procedure of inquiring of YHWH seems to be people going up to Bethel, weeping, fasting, sacrificing until evening, posing a question, a divine answer, rising early in the morning, and finally carrying out the instructions in accordance with the oracle. The third and fourth scenes of inquiring of YHWH have both time indicators, "until the evening" and "tomorrow" or "the next day" that bracket the nocturnal revelation of divine oracle, but the first and second scenes, which show an abbreviated version of the scene, register only one of them. The first scene has only "in the morning" while the second scene has only "until the evening." Since there is no doubt that the first and second scenes describe the same motif of "inquiring of YHWH" as the third and

[134] Fokkelman, *Vow and Desire (1 Sam. 1–12)*, 14.

fourth scenes, one may say that the phrase "in the morning" implies the nocturnal revelation of an oracle. The same point can be made of the inquiry of God by Balaam in Numbers 22. Terrified by the military might of the people of Israel, Balak sends envoys twice to bring the prophet Balaam to curse Israel. When the envoys arrive, Balaam tells them to wait until the next morning when he will give them the answer. The dialogue between God and Balaam is clearly nocturnal. The narrator makes it explicit by saying "And God came to Balaam at night and said..." with respect to Balaam's second attempt to solicit God's answer on this matter (Numbers 22:19). As for Balaam's first conversation with God, however, the narrator registers only "in the morning" as the time indicator of when that conversation took place. But there can be no doubt that the first conversation was also nocturnal.[135] Furthermore, the nocturnal conversation that Samuel had with YHWH in 1 Samuel 3 has "until the morning" (*'ad habbōker*) as the time indicator. Though the clause "The lamp of God had not yet gone out" may serve as a time indicator apart from the context in general, the narrator's use of "until the morning" may be understood in a manner analogous to similar phrases in Judges 20–21 and in Numbers 22. All these suggest that the clause "they rose early in the morning" (*wayyaškimû babbōker*) in line 19a of our text may be the narrator's way of indicating the nocturnal background of the encounter between Eli and Hannah.[136] The time when Hannah retired to the temple privately is most likely to be late at night, considering that it is after she sat through the sacrificial meal that she "arose" to head for the temple of YHWH (line 9a: cf. 1 Samuel 9).

2.2 *Epiphany*

1 Samuel 1:12–18a

12a	וְהָיָה
b	כִּי הִרְבְּתָה לְהִתְפַּלֵּל לִפְנֵי יְהוָה
c	וְעֵלִי שֹׁמֵר אֶת־פִּיהָ
13a	וְחַנָּה הִיא מְדַבֶּרֶת עַל־לִבָּהּ

---

[135] Husser, *Dreams and Dream Narratives in the Biblical World*, 176–77.

[136] A similar point can be made about the nocturnal revelation that Samuel has at major junctures in his career. For details see Section 3. Also see 2.3.1 in chapter three where it is argued that the end of a dream may be indicated not only by an incubant's sudden arousal but also by his continued sleep until the morning or his rising in the morning.

b רַק שְׂפָתֶיהָ נָּעוֹת
c וְקוֹלָהּ לֹא יִשָּׁמֵעַ
d וַיַּחְשְׁבֶהָ עֵלִי לְשִׁכֹּרָה
14a וַיֹּאמֶר אֵלֶיהָ עֵלִי
b עַד־מָתַי תִּשְׁתַּכָּרִין
c הָסִירִי אֶת־יֵינֵךְ מֵעָלָיִךְ
15a וַתַּעַן חַנָּה
b וַתֹּאמֶר
c לֹא אֲדֹנִי
d אִשָּׁה קְשַׁת־רוּחַ אָנֹכִי
e וְיַיִן וְשֵׁכָר לֹא שָׁתִיתִי
f וָאֶשְׁפֹּךְ אֶת־נַפְשִׁי לִפְנֵי יְהוָה
16a אַל־תִּתֵּן אֶת־אֲמָתְךָ לִפְנֵי בַּת־בְּלִיָּעַל
b כִּי־מֵרֹב שִׂיחִי וְכַעְסִי דִּבַּרְתִּי עַד־הֵנָּה
17a וַיַּעַן עֵלִי
b וַיֹּאמֶר
c לְכִי לְשָׁלוֹם
d וֵאלֹהֵי יִשְׂרָאֵל יִתֵּן אֶת־שֵׁלָתֵךְ אֲשֶׁר שָׁאַלְתְּ מֵעִמּוֹ
18a וַתֹּאמֶר
b תִּמְצָא שִׁפְחָתְךָ חֵן בְּעֵינֶיךָ
c וַתֵּלֶךְ הָאִשָּׁה לְדַרְכָּהּ

Translation

12a And as[137]
b she continued to pray before YHWH
c Eli watched her mouth,

[137] The most convenient solution to the problematic form *wəhāyāh* in 12a is to emend it to *wayəhî* as Gesenius suggests (Wilhelm Gesenius, *Gesenius' Hebrew Grammar* [Oxford: Clarendon press, 1910] §112uu; McCarter, *I Samuel: A New Translation*, 54). Then, we have the standard narrative sequence of a temporal clause in lines 12ab: *wayhî + ky (k'šr) + qātal + wayyqitol* (cf. Thomas O. Lambdin, *Introduction to Biblical Hebrew* [New York: Charles Scribner's Sons, 1971], §110). In our text, however, the four nominal and iterative clauses are inserted between *qātal* (12b) and *wayyiqtol* (13d), in order to explain why Eli viewed Hannah a drunk. Some scholars who are opposed to the emendation consider either the possibility that *wəhāyāh* consists of *wə*-conjunctive + perfective verb, thus resulting in the same syntax, or the possibility that *wəhāyāh* is a marked durative, introducing a long series of nominal and iterative clauses. In the latter, the perfective form in 12b may be problematic, but Pardee explains the form as lexically iterative or durative (Dennis Pardee, "Hebrew Verbal System in a Nutshell," the 2003 draft, p. 24; cf. Fokkelman, *Vow and Desire [1 Sam. 1–12]*, 42, footnote 84). In my opinion, however, the possibility of *wəhāyāh* consisting of wə-conjunctive and a perfective verb should be seriously considered. First, in 1 Samuel 1 there is no such sequence as *wayəhî kî* to express a temporal clause. Second, we have the same narrative sequence in 1 Samuel 17:48, where the phrase *wəhāyāh kî* is followed by a perfective verb *qām* "(the philistine) arose" that cannot be a lexically durative or iterative (cf. Christo van der Merwe, "Workshop: Text Linguistics and the Structure of 1 Samuel 1," in *Narrative Syntax and the Hebrew Bible*, ed. Ellen van Wolde [Brill: Leiden, 1997], 164). Hence one may find the reason for the

13a but Hannah[138] was speaking to herself—
b only her lips were moving,
c while her voice could not be heard.
d Thus Eli took her as a drunkard.
14a Eli said to her:
b How long will you behave like a drunkard?
c Remove your wine from you.
15a Hannah answered
b and said:
c No, my lord,
d a woman of determined spirit am I.
e Neither wine nor strong drink have I drunk.
f But I have poured out my soul before YHWH.
16a Do not regard your maidservant as a worthless woman,
b for out of my great distress and vexation have I spoken thus far.
17a Eli answered,
b and said,
c Go in peace,
d May the God of Israel grant your request that you have requested of him.
18a She said,
b May your servant-girl find favor in your eyes.
c The woman went her way.

2.2.1 *The Motif of Divine-Human Dialogue*

The narrator of the Hannah story replaces a deity with a human surrogate in composing the motif of theophany in this incubation type-scene. This is no surprise considering that in the Greek reports of the incubation practice, Asclepius appears even in the form of an animal, let alone human. What is more surprising in the quasi-theophany in this incubation type-scene is that the human surrogate, Eli, does not represent YHWH in a proper manner. For instance, unlike YHWH

narrator using *wəhāyāh*, instead of the more expected *wayəhî*, not merely in grammar but also in the narrator's literary intent. A similar mixture between imperfect and perfect verse also occurs in line 7c where the perfective verb *wattibke* occurs when one expects an imperfect form *wəbakətāh* "she would weep." Both the imperfective form *wəhāyāh* within perfective narrative sequence and the perfective form *wattibke* within the imperfective iterative sequence express high salience. And interestingly, both verbs of such high salience may be related to Hannah's heart-pouring prayer.

[138] The name Hannah is missing both in 4QSam[a] and in the Septuagint. But for the same construction, a proper noun + a personal pronoun + a participle, see Deuteronomy 31:3, *YHWH 'lhyk hw' 'br lpnyk…yhwš' hw' 'br lpnyk*. Cf. Bar-Efrat, *Das Erste Buch Samuel: Ein narratologisch-philologischer Kommentar*, 69; Hutzli, *Die Erzählung von Hanna und Samuel: Textkritische und literarische Anayse von 1. Samuel 1–2 unter Berüchsichtigung des Kontextes*, 67.

who is God of knowledge (1 Samuel 2:3), Eli is described as slow in understanding what is going on: he needs to be informed by Hannah. Also when in verse 17 he piously blesses her and assures her that her petition will be granted, he has no idea as to the content of the petition. Alter argues that the uncomprehending Eli is virtually a parody of the annunciating figure of the conventional type-scene.[139] He goes further and argues that it is an "apt introduction to a story in which the claim to authority on the house of Eli will be rejected."[140] In this regard, Eli's posture in line 9b may be significant. Eli is introduced in this type-scene as "sitting" on a seat. Usually, the deity in the incubation type-scene is introduced as someone who "takes a stand" before an incubant in an imposing way (cf. 1 Samuel 3:10).[141] Eli's posture in line 9b may serve as a subtle allusion to his non-conventional role in the motif of theophany in this incubation type-scene, not to mention the foreshadowing of his literal falling from his seat to death in chapter 4.

Verses 12–13 introduce the motif of divine-human dialogue not only by providing Eli's motive for initiating a conversation with Hannah but also by revealing the difference in point of view between Eli and the narrator/reader. As in many incubation scenes in ancient Near Eastern literature, where the divine regard for and address to the incubant is triggered by the profuse tears shed by the incubant (cf. KTU 1.14 I:38–41), Eli notices and addresses Hannah apparently because of the unusual length and intensity of her prayer (12b).[142] Here it is important to note that line 12b expresses the narrator/reader's point of view. Eli, however, (mis)perceives the same phenomenon as an unusually long stay at the temple after hours and the incomprehensible gibberish

---

[139] Alter, *The David Story: A Translation with Commentary of 1 and 2 Samuel*, 5, footnote 14.

[140] Ibid.

[141] Oppenheim, *The Interpretation of Dreams in the Ancient Near East: With a Translation of an Assyrian Dream-Book*, 190.

[142] The root √rbh that may express both the duration and the ardor (by way of repetition) of Hannah's prayer reverberates in Hannah's own words in 16b: *kî-mērōb śîḥî wəka'sî dibbartî 'ad-hennāh* "For out of much distress and vexation I have spoken thus far." If the phrase *mērōb śîḥî* "out of much distress" indicates the ardor of her prayer, the phrase *'ad-hennāh* "thus far" which is the direct answer to Eli's question *'ad-matay* "How long?" may connote the length of her prayer. Cf. Frymer-Kensky, *Reading the Women of the Bible*, 304; Cartledge, *Vows in the Hebrew Bible and the Ancient Near East*, 187; Bar-Efrat, *Das Erste Buch Samuel: Ein narratologisch-philologischer Kommentar*, 69.

of a drunkard (13d and 14b). The narrator underscores this difference in point of view by couching the root *škr* representing Eli's point of view and the root *pll* representing the narrator/reader's point of view in the same *hitpā'el* form (12b and 14b), thus having them refer back and forth to each other. And this separation in point of view makes this motif of theophany unique, or even ludicrous. Furthermore, the four clauses between lines 12ab and line 13d serve as a parenthetical digression by the narrator in order to provide a circumstantial reason for Eli's misperception. Judging from appearances, Eli may have had good reasons to consider Hannah as a drunkard. But, even in these clauses designed to explain Eli's misperception, the narrator makes a subtle allusion to the sincerity of Hannah's prayer, by mentioning four different organs, all with a pronominal suffix referring to Hannah: "her mouth" (12c), "her heart" (13a), "her lips" (13b), and "her voice" (13c).[143] Thus the narrator makes Eli's misperception all the more poignantly contrastive to the fervor of Hannah's prayer. The narrator's portrayal of Eli as judging by appearance stands in contrast to YHWH who "looks on the heart" (*yir'eh lallēbāb*, cf. 1 Samuel 16:7). And what makes this scene ironical is the fact that Eli works as YHWH's surrogate in this motif of theophany.

The dialogue between Eli and Hannah is initiated by Eli's rebuke in verse 14. As discussed in the Kirta story, it is not unusual in the incubation type-scene for a deity to first ask a question, that is later answered in the negative by the incubant. And such a negation gives occasion to the incubant to state her problem or wish. Eli's question seems to play a similar role, although in a ludicrous way. Eli's first two words *'ad-mātay* "How long?" not only reveals that it was the incessancy of her prayer that provoked him but it is also answered elegantly by the two words with which Hannah's reply ends, namely, *'ad-hennāh* "Thus far" in line 16b. The *hitpā'el* form *tištakkārîn* in line 14b recalls another *hitpā'el* form *ləhitpallēl* in 12b, thus distorting the latter. This rhetorical question in line 14b is followed by a clause commanding an immediate prohibition of the use of wine in line 14c. Interestingly the verb *šākar* in line 14b and the noun *yayin* in line 14c are picked upon by Hannah to correct Eli's misperception of her in line 15e: *wəyayin wəšēkār lō' šātîtî* "I have drunk neither wine nor

[143] According to Fokkelman, these four organs make up the "solid cord of a whole cloud of terms for her person." Cf. Fokkelman, *Vow and Desire (1 Sam. 1–12)*, 43.

strong drink." Considering that the pair "wine and strong drink" often features in a Nazirite vow (cf. Numbers 6:3) and that Samson's mother is prohibited in the context of a Nazirite vow from drinking "wine and strong drink" during pregnancy, one may argue that the lack of this element in Hannah's vow may be compensated for here in Hannah's voluntary abstention of wine and strong drink.

Eli's rebuke elicits a long answer from Hannah, consisting of six clauses (15c, d, e, f, 16a, and b). Hannah's refutation of Eli's accusation becomes longer in each poetic line. Moreover, she alternates a line of negation (15c, e, 16a) which is directly pointed at Eli with a positive line (15d, f, 16b) with reference to herself that reveals her reality.[144] As far as the negative lines are concerned, Hannah begins with a one-syllable word, "No" (15c). Although the immediately following "My lord" softens some of its edge, Hannah's decisive "No" not only speaks volumes about her character, but also serves as a subtle allusion to the unconventional role that the divine messenger is made to play in this incubation type-scene.[145] She then specifies that she has refrained from wine and strong drink (15f). Finally she extends her speech and asserts that she is not a corrupt and sinful woman (16b).[146] In the positive lines that become progressively detailed, Hannah gives the psychological grounds for her action. She is a sad but determined woman, who in her pain pours out her heart. The mention of "wine and strong drink" in line 15e leads to the metaphor of out-pouring of her heart in line 15f. The last phrase, *'ad-hennāh*, puts an end to her refutation of Eli's accusation that starts with *'ad-mātay*.[147]

From the perspective of the incubation type-scene, this motif of divine-human dialogue includes one additional unconventional element. The initial question posed by a surrogate of YHWH does not

---

[144] Bar-Efrat, *Das Erste Buch Samuel: Ein narratologisch-philologischer Kommentar*, 69; Fokkelman, *Vow and Desire (1 Sam. 1–12)*, 45.

[145] The fact that Hannah begins her speech to Eli with a negation may be put in proper perspective when one compares it to the first word that Hannah utters in her prayer: "YHWH of hosts" (11c). The full title of the deity, which reflects divine captaincy, is the first utterance that breaks Hannah's long silence in the narrative. In other words, Hannah starts with the full affirmation of YHWH's power. According to Bodner, the name is used here as a reminder of "divine sovereignty at the outset of Israel's experiment with kingship" (Bodner, *1 Samuel: Narrative Commentary*, 13).

[146] For the interpretation of *bəliya'al* as a proper noun, see Cartledge, *1 & 2 Samuel*, 34; Tsumura, *The First Book of Samuel*, 122–24.

[147] Bar-Efrat, *Das Erste Buch Samuel: Ein narratologisch-philologischer Kommentar*, 15.

lead to the answer that reveals the problem and/or the wish of the incubant. Hannah could have disclosed that she has suffered infertility and consequent harassment for a long time, and that she has just made a vow to God. But she does not do that, so Eli remains ignorant. Her last word *'ad-mātay* in line 16b seems to say "here and no further."[148] This may be significant because of the implication that just as the narrator portrays Eli, a surrogate of YHWH, as ignorant and imperceptive, thus undeserving of his role in the incubation type-scene, he makes Hannah the incubant sound as if she did not expect much from Eli and the cultus that he oversees. This is also shown in her frequent use of "I" in addressing Eli rather than "your servant," which, in contrast, dominates her address to YHWH in verse 11. This ludicrous portrayal of the motif of divine-human dialogue distinguishes the incubation type-scene of Hannah's story from other incubation type-scenes, where a deity or a divine messenger is never trifled with by an incubant. This uniqueness may have been meant by the narrator to serve his narratological purpose, namely, to foreshadow the reversal of fates in the subsequent story.[149]

2.2.2 *The Motif of Divine Blessing*

Hannah's determined but polite refutation of Eli's initial accusation seems to have worked. Eli soon changes his attitude and dismisses Hannah with a blessing. His blessing is significant not because of what Eli meant to say but because of what he says. The most important feature of the divine message in the incubation type-scene is that it ought

---

[148] Fokkelman, *Vow and Desire (1 Sam. 1–12)*, 48.

[149] The expression "*Do not regard* (*nātan*) your servant *as* (*lipnēy*) a worthless woman" seems to be meant as a sarcastic parody of Eli's incompetence to serve as a mediator of YHWH for Hannah. Scholars have correctly observed that citing a few isolated usages of *lipnēy* as "as, like" is not sufficient to establish that *nātan*...*lipnēy*...can mean 'regard...as..." (cf. McCarter, *I Samuel: A New Translation*, 54). Nonetheless, most scholars agree that the context overwhelmingly supports that meaning. Then one may suspect that the narrator had an axe to grind in employing that unique expression at this particular point in the narrative. In my opinion, the use of the idiom is meant to express Hannah's lack of confidence in Eli as an agent of YHWH. Hannah says to Eli, "Do not give..." The verb *nātan* predicates Hannah's pious vow to YHWH (11g, h). Hannah's vow shows the structure, *si dederis dabo*, "If you give...I will give..." Although Hannah asks God "to give," she asks his surrogate "not to give." It is as if Hannah meant to say, "Eli, I expect nothing from you." Furthermore, the use of the phrase *lipnēy* seems to allude to Eli's two sons of *bəliyyā'al*, because the word *pānîm* percolates the names, Hophni and Phinehas, both of which represent an opposition to the piety of Elkanah-Hannah.

to be geared toward the solution of the problem that has brought the incubant before the deity. It is only incidentally that Eli's message accomplishes this aspect of the divine blessing in this incubation type-scene.

There is some debate about the nature of Eli's blessing in verse 17. Is it the courteous wish of a priest who just tries to save face, or a divine prediction from a surrogate of YHWH? The verb form *yitten* does not steer us to a solution and the narrator may have been purposely ambiguous in this matter.[150] Such ambiguity in turn discloses the discrepancy in the points of view between Eli and Hannah. The construction *yitten 'et šēlātēk 'ăšer šā'alt mē'immô* in line 17d is a cliché because the choice of words is so general that the priest could bestow this pronouncement on almost any cult participant. This choice of words results from Eli's ignorance of Hannah's problem of barrenness and her Nazirite vow. But for Hannah, Eli's words are more than a cliché. It is a prophetic blessing from YHWH himself. This is shown not only by her breaking her fast and her changed countenance that are recounted in lines 18de,[151] but also by her use of Eli's "cliché" when she explains the birth of Samuel as a divine gift in line 27b.

The discrepancy in points of view between Eli and Hannah creates not only humor but also a sense of irony. Eli's wish for the divine granting of Hannah's request becomes a pre-figuration of the demise of Eli's own priesthood.[152] Furthermore it is in Eli's unwitting pronouncement that the personal and national dimensions of the story converge. Hannah's private problem of barrenness and her vow when dedicating Samuel are intricately entangled with the problem of the cultus administered by the Eli family and also with their future fate. Eli's use of "God of Israel" in his blessing may be significant in this regard. This is the only occurrence of "God of Israel" in the story of Hannah, where the deity is otherwise always identified by the tetragrammaton YHWH. Fokkelman sees in the phrase the first explicit mention of the national dimension hidden in the story of Hannah. This national dimension will be brought fully to the foreground when

---

150 Alter, *The David Story: A Translation with Commentary of 1 and 2 Samuel*, 5, footnote 14; Cartledge, *1 & 2 Samuel*, 34; Fokkelman, *Vow and Desire (1 Sam. 1–12)*, 51; Pardee, "Hebrew Verbal System in a Nutshell," a 2003 draft, p 26, footnote 89.

151 Brueggemann, *First and Second Samuel*, 14.

152 James S. Ackerman, "Who Can Stand Before YHWh, This Holy God? A Reading of 1 Samuel 1–15," 3.

Hannah picks upon Eli's word *šā'al* "to ask" in her explanation to Eli about her dedication of Samuel to the sanctuary in verse 28. This verb *šā'al* serves to link and contrast, in an extraordinary fashion, the two most important people in 1 Samuel 1–12, the prophet Samuel and King Saul. Without having the faintest idea of their impact Eli has uttered words which touch upon the secret of the future.[153] And if there is one positive role for Eli in this motif of theophany, it would be that Eli's utterance transforms Hannah's personal predicament into a matter of national significance.

The dominant presence of Hannah in the epiphany scene is most clearly indicated by the fact that Hannah, not Eli, has the final say in the motif of divine-human dialogue (18b): "May your slave-girl find favor in your eyes!" The epiphany scene officially ends with the verb of motion, *wattēlek* "She went (on her way)" (18c). This strongly recalls the "waking" motif that usually serves as the termination of the theophanic event in the incubation type-scene. The absence of the dream motif may account for this replacement with the motion verb depicting Hannah's departure from the temple.[154]

2.3 *After Epiphany*

1 Samuel 1:18d–28, 2:11a

18d וַתֹּאכַל
e וּפָנֶיהָ לֹא־הָיוּ־לָהּ עוֹד
19a וַיַּשְׁכִּמוּ בַבֹּקֶר
b וַיִּשְׁתַּחֲווּ לִפְנֵי יְהוָה
c וַיָּשֻׁבוּ
d וַיָּבֹאוּ אֶל־בֵּיתָם הָרָמָתָה
e וַיֵּדַע אֶלְקָנָה אֶת־חַנָּה אִשְׁתּוֹ
f וַיִּזְכְּרֶהָ יְהוָה
20a וַיְהִי לִתְקֻפוֹת הַיָּמִים
b וַתַּהַר חַנָּה
c וַתֵּלֶד בֵּן

[153] Fokkelman, *Vow and Desire (1 Sam. 1–12)*, 51. Cf. Polzin, *Samuel and the Deuteronomist: A Literary Study of the Deuteronomic History*, 18–30; Brueggemann, "1 Samuel 1: A Sense of a Beginning," 11–12.

[154] Many ancient Near Eastern dream reports use the verbs of motion such as "to come/go (בוא)," "to enter (*erēbu*)," "to leave (*aṣû*)," etc., to describe (dis)appearance of a deity in a dream. In Classical dream accounts, the dream "comes" as messages from the god: the Greek verb used is ἐπισκοπεῖν "to visit." All this corroborates the fact that the verb הלך in line 18c may have been intended as an allusion to the waking motif that officially ends the theophany scene. Cf. Section 2.2.2 in chapter three above.

d וַתִּקְרָא אֶת־שְׁמוֹ שְׁמוּאֵל
e כִּי מֵיְהוָה שְׁאִלְתִּיו
21 וַיַּעַל הָאִישׁ אֶלְקָנָה וְכָל־בֵּיתוֹ לִזְבֹּחַ לַיהוָה אֶת־זֶבַח הַיָּמִים וְאֶת־נִדְרוֹ
22a וְחַנָּה לֹא עָלָתָה
b כִּי־אָמְרָה לְאִישָׁהּ
c עַד יִגָּמֵל הַנַּעַר
d וַהֲבִאֹתִיו
e וְנִרְאָה אֶת־פְּנֵי יְהוָה
f וְיָשַׁב שָׁם עַד־עוֹלָם
23a וַיֹּאמֶר לָהּ אֶלְקָנָה אִישָׁהּ
b עֲשִׂי הַטּוֹב בְּעֵינַיִךְ
c שְׁבִי עַד־גָּמְלֵךְ אֹתוֹ
d אַךְ יָקֵם יְהוָה אֶת־דְּבָרוֹ
f וַתֵּשֶׁב הָאִשָּׁה
g וַתֵּינֶק אֶת־בְּנָהּ עַד־גָמְלָהּ אֹתוֹ
24a וַתַּעֲלֵהוּ עִמָּהּ כַּאֲשֶׁר גְּמָלַתּוּ בְּפָרִים שְׁלֹשָׁה וְאֵיפָה אַחַת קֶמַח וְנֵבֶל יַיִן
b וַתְּבִאֵהוּ בֵית־יְהוָה שִׁלוֹ
c וְהַנַּעַר נָעַר
25a וַיִּשְׁחֲטוּ אֶת־הַפָּר
b וַיָּבִיאוּ אֶת־הַנַּעַר אֶל־עֵלִי
26a וַתֹּאמֶר
b בִּי אֲדֹנִי
c חֵי נַפְשְׁךָ אֲדֹנִי
d אֲנִי הָאִשָּׁה הַנִּצֶּבֶת עִמְּכָה בָּזֶה לְהִתְפַּלֵּל אֶל־יְהוָה
27a אֶל־הַנַּעַר הַזֶּה הִתְפַּלָּלְתִּי
b וַיִּתֵּן יְהוָה לִי אֶת־שְׁאֵלָתִי אֲשֶׁר שָׁאַלְתִּי מֵעִמּוֹ
28a וְגַם אָנֹכִי הִשְׁאִלְתִּהוּ לַיהוָה
b כָּל־הַיָּמִים אֲשֶׁר הָיָה הוּא שָׁאוּל לַיהוָה
c וַיִּשְׁתַּחוּ שָׁם לַיהוָה
11a וַיֵּלֶךְ אֶלְקָנָה הָרָמָתָה עַל־בֵּיתוֹ

Translation

18d Then she ate,
e and she did not wear a (former) face any more.
19a They rose up early in the morning,
b worshiped before YHWH,
c returned,
d and arrived at their house in Ramah.
e Elkanah "knew" Hannah his wife,
f and YHWH remembered her.
20a In due time
b Hannah conceived,
c bore a son,
d and called his name Samuel:
e For from YHWH I have requested him.

21 The man Elkanah and all his house went up to offer to YHWH the yearly sacrifice and his vow.[155]
22a But Hannah did not go up,
b for she said to her husband,
c When the child is weaned,
d I will take him,
e and he will appear in the presence of YHWH
f and dwell there forever.
23a Elkanah her husband said to her,
b Do what is good in your eyes.
c Remain until you have weaned him.
d Only, may YHWH establish his word.
f So the woman remained,
g and nursed her son until she weaned him.
24a She took him up with her, when she had weaned him, with a three-year-old bull,[156] an ephah of flour and a skin of wine,
b and she brought him to the house of YHWH at Shiloh.
c Now the child was young.
25a They slaughtered the bull,
b and brought the child to Eli.
26a She said,
b Oh, my lord!
c By your life, my lord!
d I am the woman who once was standing by you here, praying to YHWH.

---

[155] Because the reader is not told of Elkanah's vow in the preceding text, the word *nidrô* "his vow" has puzzled many scholars. McCarter observes that *neder* "vow" occurs as the object of *zbḥ*, "to sacrifice," nowhere else and suggests that the Masoretic Text may be a vestige of an expansive text. So he ends up omitting this problematic word from his reconstruction of the text. Cf. McCarter, *I Samuel: A New Translation*, 50, 55. Some scholars argue that the narrator meant Hannah's vow by "his vow," for, after all, it is the husband who is responsible for the fulfillment of his wife's vow (Deuteronomy 23:22). Cf. Bar-Efrat, *Das Erste Buch Samuel: Ein narratologisch-philologischer Kommentar*, 72. Other scholars consider the possibility that Elkanah made a vow for the safe delivery of the baby or for a good crop that year, which is not mentioned in the text for some unknown reason. Cf. Alter, *The David Story: A Translation with Commentary of 1 and 2 Samuel*, 6, footnote 21; Cartledge, *1 & 2 Samuel*, 32; Campbell, *1 Samuel*, 41.

[156] The Masoretic Text reads *prym šlšh* "three bulls." But in verse 25 only one bull is slaughtered. The Septuagint reads μόσχῳ τριετίζοντι "a three year old bull" and 4QSam[a] (*mšlš*) also supports the Septuagint's reading. A number of scholars, therefore, consider the possibility that during the transmission of Masoretic text, the *mem* of the *mšlš* may have moved to the word *pr*. The reconstructed expression *pr mšlš* is elliptical, omitting the unit of time in question (years) as in Genesis 15:9. Cf. Hutzli, *Die Erzählung von Hanna und Samuel: Textkritische und literarische Anayse von 1. Samuel 1–2 unter Berüchsichtigung des Kontextes*, 81–82; McCarter, *I Samuel: A New Translation*, 63. McCarter, *I Samuel: A New Translation*, 63.

27a For this child I prayed,
b and the Lord has granted me my request that I requested of him.
28a Therefore, as for me, I have lent him to YHWH.
b As long as he lives,[157] he is lent to YHWH.
c She[158] worshipped the Lord there,
11a and Elkanah went to Ramah to his house.

2.3.1 *The Motif of Change of Mood*

If the incubation type-scene is structured as a plot that moves from problem to solution, where the solution begins with the theophany experienced by the incubant, the motif of change of mood serves, like other means of divination used after waking from a dream in Mesopotamian reports of incubation, as a direct and objective confirmation for the genuineness of the theophany in the incubation type-scene. In the case in question, the narrative portrayal of Eli in the epiphany section, along with the ambiguous form *yitten* that may be taken as both a simple wish and a prophetic blessing, incites doubt as to whether Eli's words will be effective or not. The motif of change of mood, however, serves to prove that Hannah's encounter with Eli does correspond with the experience of genuine theophany.

As in the Kirta story, the narrator of the Hannah story describes the joy within Hannah in terms of her exterior demeanor. She breaks her fast and starts to eat. There are no tears in her face any more. Her sad face has disappeared.[159] The grief and despair of lines 7cd are

[157] The Masoretic reading *hyh* is problematic because of its perfective form. The Septuagint reading ζῇ may have Hebrew *ḥy* as a Vorlage. Hutzli argues that the confusion of ḥ with h leads to *hy*, which later became *hyh* (Hutzli, *Die Erzählung von Hanna und Samuel: Textkritische und literarische Anayse von 1. Samuel 1–2 unter Berüchsichtigung des Kontextes*, 87).

[158] The verb in the Masoretic text is marked as 3 m.s., with the contextual subject uncertain (*wyšthw*). The readings of the Septuagint and 4QSam[a] agree as opposed to the Masoretic text in reading *wtšt*a*ḥw*, thus making Hannah the subject of the verb. Although some scholars prefer the Masoretic text for the very reason that it is ambiguous, I accept the reading of the Septuagint and 4QSam[a], because the immediately following song of Hannah may best be introduced by the clause "she worshipped the Lord there."

[159] Although the clause in line 18e is literally translated "she no longer had her face," a number of scholars translate *pāneyhā* as "sad or troubled face" on the basis of Job 9:27. Pardee (personal communication), however, argues that, from context, the phrase need only mean "her (former) face," i.e., the one that the narrator has presented implicitly up to this point. That face was indeed 'sad', but *pānîm* does not in and of itself express sadness. The syntax with *pāneyhā* in the first position is, however, curious, for the noun-initial formulation may be expected to have expressed some form of disjunction (cf. McCarter, *I Samuel: A New Translation*, 55). Pardee suggests

nullified in lines 18de in a chiastic way: *wattibke* (A, 7c): *wəlō' to'kal* (B, 7d) = *wattō'kal* (B′, 18d): *ûpāneyhā lō'-hāyû-lāh 'ôd* (A′, 18e). Also, Hannah's words in line 15e "I have drunken neither wine nor strong drink" make us wonder if she started to drink wine at this point in the narrative. It appears that the narrator is deliberately silent on this issue. Unlike eating in general, drinking wine is more closely associated with a Nazirite vow. So the narrator may have intended to portray Hannah as being abstentious from wine by not mentioning her resumption of drinking. Be that as it may, Hannah's changed mood culminates in her triumphant praise of YHWH's salvation in 1 Samuel 2:1–10: "My heart exults in YHWH...for I rejoice in your salvation."

2.3.2 *The Motif of Fulfillment*

The motif of fulfillment of an incubation type-scene is a counterpart of the motif of the divine message which registers either divine promise-blessing or instruction-command. Thus the fulfillment motif tends to reflect the vocabulary and the subject matter of the divine message. An obvious example is provided by the incubation type-scene in the Kirta story whose fulfillment motif looks like a verbatim repetition of 'Ilu's message to Kirta. But sometimes the poet/narrator deliberately takes the liberty of composing the fulfillment motive in a way that avoids the vocabulary recalling the motif of divine message and thus achieves the narratological purpose of the moment. A fine example of this creative composition of the fulfillment motif is found in the 'Aqhatu story, where the poet, instead of reproducing 'Ilu's language of sexual intercourse, inserts the visit of the Kôṯarātu, goddesses of conception and birth, before reporting the birth of 'Aqhatu. The motif of fulfillment in the incubation type-scene of the Hannah story shows a certain affinity to that of the 'Aqhatu story in that the narrator composes the motif in such a way as to recall Hannah's vow rather than Eli's blessing. This may be a natural corollary of the fact that Eli's pronouncement of blessing on Hannah contains no specific content other than the general reference to Hannah's prayer-request. Since Eli refers to Hannah's prayer-request in his pronouncement of blessing, it is no wonder that the fulfillment motif in this incubation type-scene reflects the vocabulary and the subject matter of Hannah's vow in verse 11.

(personal communication) that the fronting here probably expresses a focusing on the organ wherein the change of mood was visible.

The change of mood in Hannah may have affected the family relations, for we see the Elkanah's family acting in unison for the first time in chapter 1: "They arose early in the morning, worshipped before YHWH, returned and arrived at their house in Ramah" (19abcd). The sequence of four plural verbs conveys a sense of solidarity among the family members.[160] With this note of location change we arrive at one of the most important events in the history of Israel, namely, the birth of Samuel, the king-maker. The report of Samuel's birth starts with a euphemism for sexual intercourse: "And Elkanah knew Hannah his wife." It is noteworthy that not only is Hannah called "the wife" of Elkanah for the first time but also the proper names Elkanah and Hannah appear in the same line, and in the line describing their marital union at that. Noteworthy in the study of the incubation type-scene is Cook's observation that only in the Hannah story among all the biblical stories of a barren wife, or the biblical annunciation stories, is the sexual intercourse registered in the text.[161] This may have to do with the fact that other annunciation stories in the Hebrew Bible always occur as an introduction to the life of a hero, hence the focal point of the birth stories lies in the miraculous birth and the divine choice of a future hero. Thereby, the role of the mother or the parents is minimized to the point of being unnamed as in the case of Samson's birth story. The first chapter of 1 Samuel, on the other hand, throws Hannah's initiative into sharp relief, thus deserving of being called "the Hannah story." It is also proper to recognize the Hannah story as "the incubation type-scene," because it emphasizes the initiative-taking action of an incubant toward the solution of a problem. The registering of intercourse between Elkanah and Hannah may be explained from this perspective. Before the narrator reports the role of the divine in conception and birth, he mentions what Elkanah and Hannah do on their part. The copulation is a part of the problem-solving process. This is corroborated by another report of birth in 1 Samuel 2:20–22, where the initiative is taken by Eli and YHWH simply "visits" Hannah. Needless to say, there is no mention of the intercourse between Hannah and

[160] Bodner, *1 Samuel: Narrative Commentary*, 22. Cf. Eslinger, *Kingship of God in Crisis*, 81; Fokkelman, *Vow and Desire (1 Sam. 1–12)*, 52–53.

[161] Joan E. Cook, *Hannah's Desire, God's Design: Early Interpretation of the Story of Hannah*, JSOTSup 282 (Sheffield: Sheffield Academic Press, 1999), 38. For this reason, Fokkelman refuses to call the birth of Samuel "a miracle." Cf. Fokkelman, *Vow and Desire (1 Sam. 1–12)*, 53.

Elkanah. Hutzli argues that the birth report in 1 Samuel 2:20–22 is a theological corrective to the first chapter of 1 Samuel where it appears as if God is forced to intervene in human affairs by the intermediary of a determined woman.[162] Be that as it may, by registering the intercourse in the text, the narrator brings the role of the incubant into the foreground without detriment to her image as a pious woman.

When Eli says, "May the God of Israel establish your request that you requested of him" (17d), he is unwittingly referring to the two conditions of Hannah's vow: (1) God's remembering Hannah and (2) giving her a son. The narrator registers the fulfillment of the first condition in line 19f where YHWH's memory of her is expressed in the context of conception, whereas the second condition of her vow is fulfilled in verse 20 which concerns the birth and naming of Samuel. The "intercourse" line (19e) with two proper names as the subjects is immediately followed by line 19f predicating the action of YHWH. Thus in the two immediately succeeding lines we have a triangle that contributes to the birth as a solution to Hannah's problem. Copulation may be a necessary but not a sufficient condition for the conception of a life. YHWH is the sufficient condition as is expressed in line 19f: "and YHWH remembered (*zkr*) her." It not only serves as the fulfillment of the first condition of Hannah's vow (11e), but also recalls lines 5c and 6b where YHWH is identified as the one who closed (*sgr*) Hannah's womb.[163] As in the case of Rachel (Genesis 30:22), here YHWH's remembering a woman occurs in the context of opening a womb. One may note here that, unlike other incubation type-scenes, the language of the fulfillment motif in the Hannah story does not reflect a divine message, but the vow of an incubant. The terms of divine blessing seem in some sense predetermined by Hannah, while the surrogate of YHWH, Eli, is relegated to the role of merely pointing back to Hannah's vow. This highlights Hannah's initiative-taking role in this type-scene.

The fulfillment of the second condition of Hannah's vow is reported in verse 20. The narrator reports through a quick succession of three waw-consecutive verbs with Hannah as the subject that "Hannah conceived, bore a son, and called his name 'Samuel'" (20bcd). The phrase *litqūpôt hayyāmîm* "at the coming around of days" in line 20a seems

[162] Hutzli, *Die Erzählung von Hanna und Samuel: Textkritische und literarische Anayse von 1. Samuel 1–2 unter Berüchsichtigung des Kontextes*, 80.

[163] Fokkelman, *Vow and Desire (1 Sam. 1–12)*, 48; Fokkelman, *Vow and Desire (1 Sam. 1–12)*, 48.

to assume a considerable lapse of time between verses 19 and 20. But it may not be what it looks like because the time phrase does not refer to the beginning of pregnancy, but to the time of birth.[164] Many scholars, following the Septuagint, connect the temporal phrase to line 20c, and not to line 20b. Hence, JPS translates, "Hannah conceived, and at the turn of the year bore a son."[165] The common motif of counting the gestation months in birth reports may have been telescoped in that temporal phrase. This motif may occur in a fuller form as in the 'Aqhatu story where the motif of counting gestation months spans several poetic lines (cf. KTU 1.17 II:43ff), or the same motif may be shortened as the phrase *wtqrb* "and her time came (and bore a son)"[166] in the incubation type-scene of the Kirta story (KTU 1.15 III:20).[167] The conception and birth in lines 20bc comes as the fulfillment of the second condition of Hannah's vow (line 11g) that specifies the particular way in which YHWH "remembers" Hannah.

Hannah is not the first woman to name her child. The matriarchs Leah and Rachel also named their children. And Hannah's naming

---

[164] Bar-Efrat, *Das Erste Buch Samuel: Ein narratologisch-philologischer Kommentar*, 71; Fokkelman, *Vow and Desire (1 Sam. 1–12)*, 54.

[165] The reason that the narrator places line 20a one line "too soon" with respect to Hannah's becoming pregnant in 20b may have something to do with his reluctance to break the change of three *waw*-consecutive sequences of 20bcd. By moving the temporal clause one line up, the narrator is able to keep the *waw*-consecutive verbs with Hannah as subject apart from other *waw*-consecutive verbs in verse 19. Cf. Fokkelman, *Vow and Desire (1 Sam. 1–12)*, 55.

[166] Translation is Pardee's. Dennis Pardee, "The Aqhatu Legend," in *Canonical Compositions from the Biblical World*, vol. I of *COS*, ed. William W. Hallo and K. Lawson Younger Jr. (Leiden: Brill, 1997), 338. For more details, see chapter five above.

[167] Further, the use of *wayəhî* and the word for "day" deserve some mention. As for the former, it is the fourth time that the narrator uses it. The first use in verse 1 introduces the presentation of the characters of the story. The second use in verse 2 introduces the problem of Hannah's barrenness and Elkanah's regular trips to Shiloh. The third use in verse 4 breaks the sequence of the iterative verbs, thus introducing one day's event into the events of many days. That is the day when Hannah decisively arose to make a vow at the temple. The final use in verse 20 introduces the solution to Hannah's problem that was itself introduced by the second use of *wayəhî* in verse 2. This coincidence of the use of *wayəhî* with the plot of the story is reconfirmed by the use of the word *yôm*. The problem of Hannah is set in the sequence of iterative verbs [cf. *miyyāmîm yāmîmāh*], while Hannah's efforts to stand up for herself are narrated in sequence of punctual verbs [cf. *hayyôm*]. Now the solution to Hannah's barrenness is set in the interaction of the iterative and the punctual. Although the semantic range of the phrase *litqūpôt hayyāmîm* certainly brings itself close to the iterative, the event for which it serves as a background is the birth of Samuel, which is a one-time event in the history of the nation of Israel, not to mention in Hannah's life.

befits her image as an initiative-taking heroine in this incubation type-scene. What is more interesting, however, is the explanation that Hannah gives for the name "Samuel." First of all, it must be acknowledged that although Hannah's explanation of the name "Samuel" is hard to justify in terms of modern philology, a survey of other biblical name-giving pericopes will confirm that her etymology of the name corresponds well.[168] This means that it is not necessary to postulate a confusion of traditions in the composition of 1 Samuel 1, although the connection of Samuel and Saul by means of the wordplay on *šā'al* may be a literary foreshadowing of a future plot of the narrative.[169] Having said that, it is important to note that Hannah's explanation, "For[170] from YHWH I have asked him," recalls Eli's use of *šā'al* in his pronouncement of blessing on Hannah.[171] If there is any connection between the motif of fulfillment and the motif of divine blessing in this incubation type-scene, it would be the word *šā'al*. Hannah's use of this word that characterizes Eli's blessing would indicate that she accepted his blessing as YHWH's promise. Hannah's fondness of this

[168] Yair Zakovitch, "A Study of Precise and Partial Derivations in Biblical Etymology," *JSOT* 15 (1980): 31–50.

[169] Scholars interested in the compositional history of the text are in agreement that the narrative in chapter 1 originally concerned Saul, although when the change of protagonist from Saul to Samuel occurred is moot. Cf. Marc Brettler, "The Composition of 1 Samuel 1–2," *JBL* 116 (1997): 602. For a good summary of major players such as Dus and Hylander, see Gnuse, "The Dream Theophany of Samuel: Its Structure in Relation to Ancient Near Eastern Dreams and Its Theological Significance," 240–44. However, most scholars interested in the final form of the text focus on the literary and narratological significance of the connection made in 1 Samuel 1 between Samuel and Saul. Cf. Polzin, *Samuel and the Deuteronomist: A Literary Study of the Deuteronomic History*, 18–30.

[170] Note that the use of *kî* is unique because it introduces a different level of narrative, namely, direct speech without a *verbum dicendi* (cf. Joüon, *A Grammar of Biblical Hebrew*, 157c). In other words, the whole line may be called "an unintroduced direct speech," which Moor argues to be a frequent phenomenon in the Ugaritic literature (cf. KTU 1.17 I:20; J. C. de Moor, *An Anthology of Religious Texts from Ugarit*, Nisaba 16 [Leiden: Brill, 1987], 227, footnote 6; see also 1 Samuel 20:16).

[171] Scholars like McCarter and Eslinger observe that the accent of Hannah's explanation lies on "from YHWH" which seems to be hinted at by its emphatic first position in the clause. Both agree that such positioning is redactional or literary. By placing *myhwh* before "I have asked," Hannah (and the narrator) emphasize that Samuel is from Yahweh. Considering that Elkanah's genealogy was not very impressive, thus inappropriate as a legitimization of a hero, Hannah's naming may reveal the real genealogy of Samuel: He is from God. Also considering that Peninnah's children are given no names in the text, while Samuel is the only named child of Elkanah, one may say that the narrator intends to portray Samuel as the firstborn of Elkanah. Cf. Eslinger, *Kingship of God in Crisis*, 83; McCarter, *I Samuel: A New Translation*, 62.

word is made more explicit a few years later, when Hannah brings the child to Eli for dedication. In verses 27–28, Hannah not only uses the root √š'l four times but also couches it in different *binyanim* with different nuances.

We have seen that the fulfillment motif of this incubation type-scene appears to reflect more Hannah's vow than Eli's blessing in terms of both vocabulary and subject matter. This goes against the generic expectation that the fulfillment motif is usually a counterpart of the motif of the divine message.[172] This is owing to the narrator's narratological strategy of contrasting the progressive decline of the Elides with the increasing prominence of Hannah-Samuel. Although the narrator does not portray Eli's blessing as being ineffective, the manner in which he composes the fulfillment motif underscores Hannah's initiative-taking character and piety by wording the fulfillment motif in such a way as to recall the terms that Hannah herself had used in her vow. In other words, the fulfillment motif gives the impression that YHWH has fulfilled the conditions of Hannah's vow, rather than suggesting that YHWH's blessing through Eli has been fulfilled. The rather insignificant role assigned to Eli as a surrogate of YHWH in comparison to the role of Hannah as the heroine, foreshadows the ultimate demise of his family. Hannah's dominant presence continues in the following motif.[173] In verse 24 Hannah would appear to go to Shiloh unaccompanied by Elkanah—in any case his name goes unmentioned. Furthermore, over the next fifteen verses the reader is led to wonder whether or not Elkanah went on the journey and was present at the handing over of Samuel. The plural subject of the verbs in lines 25a and b is ambiguous. The subject of the obeisance in line 28c is most likely Hannah, although the Masoretic text makes that ambiguous too. Only when the reader arrives at 2:11a ("Elkanah went back to Ramah to his house"), does he deduce from Elkanah's return journey that he was present when his son was admitted to the temple.[174] The conclusion that may be drawn from this intricate manipulation of the narrative is that the narrator intended to dedicate the post-epiphany section of this incubation type-scene in its entirety to its heroine,

[172] Line 27b provides the exact language of the fulfillment motif, although that line is embedded in the motif of vow-fulfillment: "And God gave to me my request that I have asked of him."

[173] Jobling, *1 Samuel*, 133.

[174] Fokkelman, *Vow and Desire (1 Sam. 1–12)*, 60.

Hannah. No wonder that this section of the type-scene is punctuated with Hannah's four speeches that become increasingly long and culminate in the ten-verse Song of Hannah.

2.3.3 *The Motif of Vow-Fulfillment*

The presence of the motif of vow-making in the pre-epiphany section of this incubation type-scene makes the motif of vow-fulfillment inevitable in the narrator's composition of the post-epiphany section. But the space devoted to the motif (19 verses including Hannah's song), if the number of verses can serve as an index to the significance of that motif in the composition of this type-scene, needs to be explained. All the more so when the motif of fulfillment usually gets the most space in the post-epiphany section of an incubation type-scene. In the motif describing an incubant's execution of divine commands, an incubant reveals what he is really made of and, in the motif of a deity fulfilling his promise, the deity proves himself to be benevolent and/or powerful toward the incubant. In all this the focus remains on the incubant and his relationship to the deity. Although the incubation type-scene of the Hannah story follows other instances of the type-scene in this respect (cf. section 2.1.3 above), it differentiates itself from others by virtue of its special concern for the child born through "incubation." This special concern seems to have led to the unusual length of the motif of vow-fulfillment in this incubation type-scene, since the subject matter of the motif of vow-fulfillment is the dedication of Samuel as a permanent Nazirite to YHWH. What is noteworthy in this regard is the fact that Hannah's song is occasioned not by the birth of Samuel, which is a simple solution to Hannah's personal problem, but by the dedication of Samuel as a Nazirite at the national center of cultus at that time, which imbues the story of Hannah with national significance. Finally, the motif of vow-fulfillment contains three speeches, one made by Elkanah in verse 23 and two made by Hannah in verses 23 and 26–28. The first speech of Hannah is echoed by Elkanah's response whereas Hannah's second speech does not get a response from the addressee, Eli, but leads to Hannah's poem praising sovereign YHWH who reverses human fortunes in his infinite wisdom (cf. 1 Samuel 2:3). Eli is virtually ignored. This seems to show another purpose that the narrator may have had in mind in his composition of the type-scene, that is, to exalt Hannah-Samuel and denigrate Eli and his sons by contrasting them.

The motif of vow-fulfillment in this incubation type-scene is enclosed by further travels back and forth of Elkanah's family, from Ramah to Shiloh in verse 21 and from Shiloh to Ramah in 1 Samuel 2:11a. The novelty of the trip comes from the fact that the traveling company is no longer in disruptive relations, owing to the birth of Samuel (cf. verse 20). The changed dynamics in family relationships seems to be registered in the text by the explicit mention of both "Elkanah" and "his family" as the subject of the verb *wayya'al* "and...went up" in verse 21. The purpose of the second trip in verse 21 is more than a regular, habitual worship and sacrifice.[175] The word *nidrô* "his vow" in verse 21 seems to point to a specific purpose that Elkanah has in mind as he goes up to Shiloh in accordance with the custom of "yearly sacrifice." Since all textual witnesses agree on the 3rd person, masculine, singular suffix in *nidrô*, scholars have debated the reference to "his vow." Does it refer to the vow that Elkanah made for the safe delivery of his son during the gestation months?[176] Or does it refer to Hannah's vow in verse 11?[177] However one may answer these questions, it remains true that the mention of "his vow" at this point of the narrative is deliberate. Hanna's refusal to go up with Elkanah in line 22a stands in stark contrast to the going up of the whole family in verse 21. Hannah's action seems to disturb the hard-earned family unity, recalling her previous refusal to participate in the sacrificial meal. More importantly for the study of incubation type-scene, Hannah's independent action in line 22a creates suspense not only because her refusal to participate in worship may damage her image as a pious woman, but also because of the narrator's association of Elkanah's visit in verse 21 with a vow. Although "his vow" may not refer to Hannah's vow, the reader is immediately reminded of Hannah's vow when coming to the end of verse 21, "his vow." The disjunctive syntax in line 22a, "But Hannah did not go up," which immediately follows "his vow," is

---

[175] For the literary comparison between verse 3 and verse 21, see Eslinger, *Kingship of God in Crisis*, 84. He enumerates four points of comparison between the two verses.

[176] Alter, *The David Story: A Translation with Commentary of 1 and 2 Samuel*, 6, footnote 21. Cartledge argues that although vows were made in times of distress, they were sometimes made as a matter of course, and suggests that Elkanah's vow belongs to the latter (Cartledge, *1 & 2 Samuel*, 32).

[177] Bar-Efrat argues on the basis of Deuteronomy 23:22 that Elkanah is responsible for the fulfillment of Hannah's vow. Cf. Bar-Efrat, *Das Erste Buch Samuel: Ein narratologisch-philologischer Kommentar*, 72.

enough to lead the reader to suspect that Hannah may be defaulting on the payment of her vow. As Cartledge points out, the dire consequences that may befall those who forget their vows are well attested to in ancient Near Eastern literature.[178] We have seen one of the most celebrated examples of this in our discussion of the Kirta story. Then the following question poses itself to us. Will Hannah end up in the same fate as Kirta?[179] Put differently, does Hannah intend to default on the payment of her vow by keeping the baby at home as long as she can?

In order to answer these questions properly, we need to take a close look at the dialogue between Hannah and Elkanah in verses 22–23. Hannah's speech in verse 22 is enclosed by two time references that start with the preposition *'ad* (cf. lines 22b and f). In between come three waw-consecutive perfect verbs in a quick succession, all of which focus on the action of a child: "I will cause him to go up, he will appear before YHWH and he will stay there" (lines 22def). Line 22f may be taken as having the strongest accent as Hannah intones her words. It not only clarifies what she meant by "Then I will give him to YHWH all the days of his life" in line 11h, but also dissipates any doubt in the reader's mind about her commitment to her vow. Fokkelman may be right in saying that the short period of weaning registered in 22b serves only to throw the perpetuity of Samuel's dedication into relief.[180] Furthermore, line 22f is subtly formulated to upset the state of affairs of the Israelite cultus. The adverb *šām* "there" in line 22f with the tetragrammaton in the preceding line strongly recalls line 3b where Eli's two sons were introduced into the narrative as being "there" as YHWH's priest. Also, the verb *yāšab* in line 22f recalls Eli's "sitting" on the seat of the temple in line 9b. Therefore Hannah's words in line 22f may be argued to contrast the "has been" priests to the "would-be" priest. Samuel will replace the Elides in the role of a mediator between YHWH and the people of Israel. This is why most scholars believe that the text does not portray negatively Hannah's nursing the baby at home

[178] Cartledge, *Vows in the Hebrew Bible and the Ancient Near East*, 135.

[179] Eslinger, by way of emendation, attempts to make this question as serious as possible: "With a vow, Hannah did not go up." Cf. Eslinger, *Kingship of God in Crisis*, 86. But Cartledge argues against Eslinger on the ground that his emendation is a result of the misunderstanding of what a vow was in the ancient Near East. Vow was always conditional in antiquity, unlike the modern usage of the term in English (Cartledge, *Vows in the Hebrew Bible and the Ancient Near East*, 191).

[180] Fokkelman, *Vow and Desire (1 Sam. 1–12)*, 64–65.

for a while.[181] Elkanah's response, however, may reveal the narrator's negative view of Hannah's postponement of the vow-fulfillment.[182] Elkanah's speech is also enclosed by the two idioms that embed the story of Hannah in a wider canonical context. Although Elkanah's speech shows him to be a different person from that which he was in verse 8,[183] the formulation of Elkanah's speech reveals the narrator's view of the weaning period that delays the fulfillment of Hannah's vow. The apparently concessive words in line 23b seem to belie the negative opinion of the narrator on Hannah's weaning period: "Do what is good in your eyes." This line is reminiscent of the formula in the final episodes in the Book of Judges. The cultic and moral chaos of Israel in the last chapters of Judges is punctuated with the narrator's note of "Everyone did what was good/right in his own eyes" (Judges 17:6; 19:24; 21:25). By using a phrase that is strongly reminiscent of the situation described in Judges 17–21—it may even be contemporaneous to that of the initial chapters of 1 Samuel—the narrator of the Hannah story may be putting Hannah's postponement of her vow due to breast-feeding in a negative light. Polzin asks in this regard, "Was the weaning worth it?" Polzin understands Hannah's weaning period as a parable of the period of Saul's reign before David came to throne.[184] The negative evaluation of the narrator, however, is not final. He seems to provide another opportunity for Hannah to prove her faithfulness to YHWH. He does this by changing the Niphal form of the verb *gāmal* in Hannah's speech (cf. line 22c) to a Qal form with Hannah as the subject in line 23c. The narrator's accent in Elkanah's words "stay until you wean him" in line 23b falls on "you." In other words, it is up to Hannah to decide when she will wean her baby and bring him to Shiloh.

---

[181] Alter, *The David Story: A Translation with Commentary of 1 and 2 Samuel*, 7, footnote 22; Baldwin, *1 & 2 Samuel*, 53; Cartledge, *1 & 2 Samuel*, 40; Bar-Efrat, *Das Erste Buch Samuel: Ein narratologisch-philologischer Kommentar*, 72; Ackroyd, *The First Book of Samuel*, 27; Fokkelman, *Vow and Desire (1 Sam. 1–12)*, 65–66.

[182] Cf. Eslinger, *Kingship of God in Crisis*, 86. According to Walter, the Septuagint version of the story seems to portray Hannah as being reluctant to give up Samuel. Unlike the Masoretic text, the Septuagint does not connect Hannah's weaning to her perpetual dedication of Samuel. Cf. Stanley D. Walters, "Hannah and Anna: The Greek and Hebrew Texts of 1 Samuel 1," *JBL* 107 (1988): 399.

[183] The apparently redundant *'iššāh* in line 23a, along with the concessive tone of his speech, clearly tells us of the changed attitude of Elkanah toward Hannah. He is no longer a misunderstanding egotist, but her "husband" who understands well her motherly instinct to nurse the baby.

[184] Polzin, *Samuel and the Deuteronomist: A Literary Study of the Deuteronomic History*, 28.

Although the weaning period in antiquity was known to be much longer than it is now, there was not a standard period of breast-feeding.[185] Ultimately, weaning was the mother's decision. The narrator seems to be saying through Elkanah that, although the immediate fulfillment of a vow is most ideal, her natural desire as a mother to nurse her child is understandable—this is all the more so considering the corrupt priests into whose care the baby will be entrusted.[186] But Hannah should be aware that it is ultimately she that weans the baby. Finally, line 23d forms a proper conclusion to Elkanah's speech. Many scholars emend the Hebrew *dəbārô* to *hayyōṣēʾ mippîkā* on the basis of 4QSam[a] and the Codex Vaticanus of the Septuagint, for the reason that the narrative of 1 Samuel 1 records no words of YHWH.[187] Further, the context seems to support the emendation since the phrase *hayyōṣēʾ mippîkā* is a well-established idiom for a vow (Numbers 30:3, Judges 11:36; Jeremiah 44:17).[188] But one must explain why the redactor responsible for the current Masoretic text has changed it, if other witnesses had the original, to "his [YHWH's] words" that seems to have no reference in the immediate context.[189] The answer is to be found in the fact that just like line 23b ("Do what is good in your eyes"), line 23d ("May YHWH establish his word") also connects the Hannah story to a wider canonical context. The idea of YHWH's word being established plays an important role in the subsequent story about Samuel-Saul-David. The fall of Eli and the raising of a new prophet/priest are described in terms of establishing YHWH's words (1 Samuel 3:12: Cf. 2:35). Saul was rejected because he failed to establish YHWH's words

---

[185] This is why scholars have different opinions on how old child Samuel may have been when he was brought to Shiloh. Cf. Mary J. Evans, *1 and 2 Samuel*, NIBCOT (Peabody, MA: Hendrickson Publishers, 2000), 19 (more than 5 years); Fokkelman, *Vow and Desire (1 Sam. 1–12)*, 61 (2–3 years); Cook, *Hannah's Desire, God's Design: Early Interpretation of the Story of Hannah*, 62 (2 years); Cartledge, *1 & 2 Samuel*, 41; Tsumura, *The First Book of Samuel*, 128; Smith, *The Books of Samuel*, 12; Bar-Efrat, *Das Erste Buch Samuel: Ein narratologisch-philologischer Kommentar*, 72.

[186] Bar-Efrat, *Das Erste Buch Samuel: Ein narratologisch-philologischer Kommentar*, 61; Bodner, *1 Samuel: Narrative Commentary*, 23; Cartledge, *Vows in the Hebrew Bible and the Ancient Near East*, 188.

[187] McCarter, *I Samuel: A New Translation*, 56; Hutzli, *Die Erzählung von Hanna und Samuel: Textkritische und literarische Anayse von 1. Samuel 1–2 unter Berüchsichtigung des Kontextes*, 79.

[188] Hutzli, *Die Erzählung von Hanna und Samuel: Textkritische und literarische Anayse von 1. Samuel 1–2 unter Berüchsichtigung des Kontextes*, 79–80.

[189] The argument that "his words" refers to Eli's words in verse 17 cannot be accepted because Eli's words are already established by the birth of Samuel.

(1 Samuel 15:11), despite his counter-claim (1 Samuel 15:13). Furthermore, David prays for YHWH's words to be established concerning him (2 Samuel 7:25). All this seems to confirm that the dedication of Samuel to YHWH is the very act of establishing YHWH's words. The redactor/narrator may have intended the expression "his word" in line 23d as a threshold between the private story of Hannah and the national history of Israel. Hutzli, who assumes Masoretic "his word" to be secondary, provides a slightly different explanation for the change in the Masoretic text. He argues that the copyist saw that Hannah's story had a national significance, but he did not like the fact that God was portrayed as being passive, since he was portrayed as intervening not because of his own promise in Deuteronomy 18:18 but because he was prompted by Hannah's vow. Hence, according to Hutzli, the copyist had changed the expression for her vow to "his word."[190] Although one may not agree with Hutzli's speculation, there is an element of truth in saying that the story of Hannah in 1 Samuel 1 forcefully underscores Hannah's initiative-taking, independent character, quite apart from her pious humility, to the point that the role of the divine seems to recede into the background. Perhaps, one of the reasons that the motif of theophany is described in such a ludicrous way is to emphasize Hannah's role in the incubation type-scene, which incidentally revolves around the need and initiative of an incubant. This fits well with the narrator's intention to contrast Hannah to Eli. Even YHWH, although he is an important player, stays in the background. He never speaks.

As Elkanah's speech shows, the element of the weaning period does add suspense. But that suspense does not create any real doubt that Hannah will fulfill her vow, because, although the narrator seems not to approve of the postponement of fulfilling of the vow as the best course of action on Hannah's part, he approves of the second best option of leaving the matter of determining the appropriate length of her weaning period to Hannah's religious piety and integrity of character. And she does indeed fulfill her vow *as soon as* she weans the child[191] by bringing him to Shiloh with a three-year-old bull, one

[190] Hutzli, *Die Erzählung von Hanna und Samuel: Textkritische und literarische Anayse von 1. Samuel 1–2 unter Berüchsichtigung des Kontextes*, 80.

[191] Fokkelman, *Vow and Desire (1 Sam. 1–12)*, 60. For a different interpretation, see McCarter, *I Samuel: A New Translation*, 55.

ephah of flour, and a skin of wine.[192] Although scholars find the use of the phrase "when she weaned him" for the fourth time to be redundant in terms of context and to be intrusive in terms of syntax, its use in line 24a which concerns Hannah's execution of her own promise to Elkanah (cf. line 22d) serves to highlight Hannah's initiative in putting an end to the nursing period.[193] This initiative-taking act of Hannah serves to dispense of any doubt about her commitment to her vow to YHWH and to demonstrate her piety and integrity.

The scene of the actual dedication of Samuel is described in verses 24–28. It consists of Hannah bringing the boy to the temple in Shiloh (line 24b) along with thanksgiving offerings (line 24a), slaughtering the bull in the temple (line 25a), and finally presenting the boy to Eli the priest (line 25b). As Samuel is being presented to Eli as a Nazirite,[194] Hannah accompanies her act of dedication with a long speech in verses 26–27. Hannah's speech is couched in a quasi-oath formula. Although the intervening lines (26d, 27a and b) make this "oath formula" less obvious to the reader,[195] one may find an authenticating element in line 26c and the oath content in line 28a and b.[196] Hannah's use of an oath formula may be in order to assure Eli of the seriousness of her action. Eli, who has just been informed of her amazing story, needs to be reassured, perhaps with an oath, of her seriousness in dedicating her hard-won son for permanent temple service. Especially, lines 27b and 28a recalls the structure of Hannah's vow, *si dederis dabo* "if you

---

[192] For the detailed discussion of these offerings, see Tsumura, *The First Book of Samuel*, 129–32; Carol Meyers, "An Ethnoarchaeological Analysis of Hannah's Sacrifice," in *Pomegranates Golden Bells: Studies in Biblical, Jewish, and Near Eastern Ritual, Law and Literature in Honor of Jacob Milgrom*, ed. David P. Wright, Freedman David N., and Hurvitz Avi (Winona Lake, IN: Eisenbrauns, 1995), 77–92.

[193] The verb *wattēyneq* in line 23g points to the close bond between Hannah and the baby. Noteworthy in this regard is that the latter is called "her son."

[194] I tend to agree with Alter and Bar-Efrat that the plural subjects of the two verbs in verse 25 are Elkanah and Hannah. Cf. Alter, *The David Story: A Translation with Commentary of 1 and 2 Samuel*, 8, footnote 25; Bar-Efrat, *Das Erste Buch Samuel: Ein narratologisch-philologischer Kommentar*, 74. For other interpretations, see Eslinger, *Kingship of God in Crisis*, 89–90.

[195] Fokkelman takes Hannah's speech in verse 26–28 as a full-fledged oath formula. Cf. Fokkelman, *Vow and Desire (1 Sam. 1–12)*, 69. But I do not agree with his analysis of line 28b as the only line belonging to oath content. The perfective form *hiš'iltihû* in 28a may be a performative.

[196] For the syntax of the oath formulae attested to in Classical Hebrew and other Semitic languages, see Blane W. Conklin, "Oath Formulae in Classical Hebrew and Other Semitic Languages" (Ph.D. diss., Chicago: University of Chicago Press, 2005).

give... I will give..." (cf. 11gh),[197] although Hannah's giving in this fulfillment motif gets a different vocabulary *hiš'iltīhû* "I have lent him."[198] Thus, lines 27b and 28a demonstrate that Hannah has fulfilled her vow exactly in accordance with the terms that she laid down in verse 11. In this sense, Hannah's speech in verses 26–28 may be said to constitute the official completion of Hannah's vow-fulfilling.

Having said this, one needs to dwell on the change in vocabulary from the verb *nātan* to the Hiphil form of *šā'al* in line 28a.[199] In relation to this, one may also note its Qal passive participle form in line 28b, not to mention the Qal perfective form and a nominal form in line 27b. The narrator employs four different forms of the root √š'l in Hannah's dedication speech in verses 27–28. This concentrated use of the root √š'l in the motif of dedication begs an explanation, especially considering the fact that the narrator could have easily replaced the perfective form *hiš'iltīhû* in line 28a with the Qal perfective form *nətattîw* (cf. 11h) and also the Qal passive form *šā'ûl* in line 28b with the word *nāzîr* that is missing but implied in Hannah's vow. The narrator's use of the root √š'l is often taken as a foreshadowing of the subsequent plot of the story where Samuel and Saul interact with each other at the dawn of the monarchy in Israel's history. The narrator's intention in playing on the verb *šā'al* may be revealed most clearly in the form *šā'ûl* in line 28b. As Polzin, followed by many others, suggests, the narrator may have wanted the reader to read the Hannah story not only as a story of a barren woman who has a son through the determination of her will, as well as divine intervention, but also as a metaphor for the history of nation of Israel. In other words, the story in chapter 1 about how and why God agreed to give Hannah a son,

---

[197] The theme of divine giving and taking back occurs in the story of Abraham and Isaac, here and in the story in 2 Kings 4. Both in the story of Abraham and Isaac and in the story of Elishah and a Shunamite woman, God almost took away the sons whom he had given to the parents, making good on his own words. In the contrast, Hannah asks for a son, and, when God gives a son to her in response to her prayer, she volunteers to give him back to God. The focus of the Hannah story falls on Hannah's initiative.

[198] In addition, the phrase *kōl-hayyāmîm 'ăšer hāyāh* line 28b may recall Hannah's vow that dedicates Samuel for all the days of his life (cf. *kōl-yəmēy hayyāyw* in line 11h).

[199] A number of scholars take the Hiphil form *hiš'iltīhû* in line 28a as performative (cf. Joosten, "Workshop: Meaning and Use of the Tenses in 1 Samuel 1," 78; Tsumura, *The First Book of Samuel*, 132; Bar-Efrat). But Fokkelman takes it as a simple past (Fokkelman, *Vow and Desire [1 Sam. 1–12]*, 69).

Samuel, is an "artistic prefiguring of the larger story in 1 Samuel about how and why God agreed to give Israel a king... the story of Samuel's birth is a the story of Saul's birth as king of Israel" in a metaphoric sense.[200] This is where the incubation type-scene in the Hannah story parts ways with those in Ugaritic epics. The incubation type-scene in 1 Samuel 1:1–2:11a, while, like those in Ugaritic epics, showing all the characteristics of the type-scenes as a story complete in itself, like other biblical birth stories is still part of a larger story about the heroic figure in Israel, Samuel, the king-maker. Many details in the component motifs, for example, details about Eli and his sons, show no role in the immediate plot of the incubation type-scene. The narrator's preoccupation with the word *šāʾal* does not have any immediate role within the incubation type-scene. Rather it serves to foreshadow the unfolding plot of the subsequent story, with focus on the relationship between Samuel and Eli or Samuel and Saul. Having already associated Samuel with the judge-warrior figure of Samson through their parallel birth stories, the narrator seems also to suggest an analogy between the figures of Samuel and Saul by way of wordplay, thus incorporating the story of Samuel's birth into the larger narrative about Samuel who anointed the first two kings of Israel.

3. The Narratological Role of the Incubation Type-Scene in the Book of Samuel

The key role of the Hannah story in the books of Samuel as a whole has already been noticed by many scholars.[201] For example, taking 1 Samuel 1 as a kind of parabolic introduction to the Deuteronomic history of kingship, Polzin argues as follows.

> Hannah was the mother of Samuel, but she also stood for Israel requesting a king. Elkanah was a slighted but loving husband, but he also introduced us to a God rejected by his people. Eli was the scion of a fallen priestly house, but in addition he was a royal figure falling to his death. Samuel himself was a priest, judge, and prophet certainly, but he also

[200] Polzin, *Samuel and the Deuteronomist: A Literary Study of the Deuteronomic History*, 26.

[201] Cf. Brueggemann, "1 Samuel 1: A Sense of a Beginning," 42; Campbell, *1 Samuel*, 42.

represented Saul (chap. 1), a victorious David (chap. 2–4), and an idealized judge who would succeed to leadership in exilic times (chap. 7).[202]

In a similar vein, Green regards the genre of the Hannah story as a *māšāl*, more specifically, a *hugged*, "enigma to be told."[203] Whereas Polzin's interpretation derives from his assumption that the Deuteronomist who is responsible for the books of Samuel is no less than the author who has created a work of art with full integrity,[204] Green bases his interpretation on Bakhtin's literary theory of genre and utterance.[205] Be that as it may, these synchronic, literary, and narratological studies have shown a complex network of meanings that exist between the Hannah story and the subsequent story of Samuel-Saul-David. However, since I am here dealing with the narratological function of the incubation type-scene in the Hannah story, I will not recount what has already been said about the larger narratological role of the Hannah story.[206] My focus will be on two points relating to the incubation type-scene. First, I will discuss how some of the component motifs of the incubation type-scene are further developed in the subsequent chapters of the books of Samuel. Second, I will discuss how the incubation theme is utilized by the narrator in the last chapters of Judges and the first book of Samuel; in particular, the reception of prophetic oracles by the people of Israel in Judges 20–21, by Saul in 1 Samuel 9 and 28, and by Samuel in 1 Samuel 3, 9 and 15.

Some of the component motifs recur at important junctures of the subsequent narrative. The motif of eating and drinking punctuates the Hannah story. It is in the setting of the sacrificial meal that jealous Peninnah makes a regular point of tormenting Hannah who would always receive the special portion from Elkanah. Unlike the rest of the family, however, Hannah neither eats nor drinks. It is during Hannah's fasting that she takes the decisive move toward a solution. After

---

[202] Polzin, *Samuel and the Deuteronomist: A Literary Study of the Deuteronomic History*, 81.

[203] Barbara Green, *How Are the Mighty Fallen? A Dialogical Study of King Saul in 1 Samuel*, JSOTSup 365 (Sheffield: Sheffiled Academic Press, 2003), 55.

[204] Polzin, *Samuel and the Deuteronomist: A Literary Study of the Deuteronomic History*, 13–17.

[205] Green, *How Are the Mighty Fallen? A Dialogical Study of King Saul in 1 Samuel*, 55–83.

[206] Cf. Jobling, *1 Samuel*, 50–76; Polzin, *Samuel and the Deuteronomist: A Literary Study of the Deuteronomic History*, 26–30; Willis, "An Anti-Elide Narrative Tradition from a Prophetic Circle at the Ramah Sanctuary," 288–308; Miscall, *1 Samuel: A Literary Reading*, 1–8.

meeting Eli at the temple, she goes back to eating again. Thus the motif of eating and drinking coincides with the movement of the plot within the incubation type-scene. The contrast between Hannah and the rest of the family in terms of eating and drinking carries over to the contrast between Hannah and the Elides. In contrast to Hannah who was once hungry but later "ceased to hunger" (cf. 1 Samuel 2:5), the Elides once "fattened themselves with the choicest parts of every offering" to YHWH (cf. 1 Samuel 2:29) but later would beg the new and faithful priest for "a morsel of bread" (cf. 1 Samuel 2:36). The motif of eating and drinking also figures prominently in the story of Saul and the female medium at Endor (1 Samuel 28). Saul is in great distress (cf. verse 5 and 15) not only because of the military threat from the Philistines but also because all the regular means of divination have failed. He does not eat all day (cf. verse 20). At night, he pays a visit to the female medium at Endor and encounters Samuel through her channeling. But he comes away even more terrified from this theophanic experience. Saul now eats and drinks at the urging of his servants and the female medium. It is interesting to note that "a morsel of bread" (*pat-leḥem* in verse 22) is mentioned as the food that the female medium sets before Saul. It certainly recalls the only other use in the books of Samuel (1 Samuel 2:36) where the miserable fate in store for the Elides is described in terms of "a morsel of bread."

In 1 Samuel 29, on the other hand, David is in great distress. When he comes back from Aphek, he finds his town ravaged and all the women and children taken captive, including his two wives. Further, the grief of the people was so great that they even contemplate stoning David to death. David therefore inquires of YHWH through the ephod. Unlike Saul in chapter 28, David receives an answer from YHWH that encourages him to pursue the Amalekites. But since David does not know where they have gone, he needs another "oracle." That oracle comes from a hungry and thirsty Egyptian who had not eaten bread or drunk water for three days. The Egyptian, now refreshed with bread and water, leads David's army to the band of Amalekites. When they arrive at the Amalekite camp, David finds them spread abroad all over the land, eating and drinking. He strikes them down and recovers all his people and belongings. Again in this episode of 1 Samuel 30, we find the motif of (not) eating and (not) drinking functioning as a structural backbone of the plot. Particularly interesting is the occurrence of *bəliyaʿal* in verse 22. It refers to the men of David who, although they had crossed the brook Besor and participated in the campaign against the Amalekites, did not wish to share the booty of the battle with their brothers-in-arms who had stayed behind due to physical exhaustion. In other words, they are stingy givers. Just like the word *pat-leḥem* in 1 Samuel 28:22, the word *bəliya'al* seems to recall the Elides who were willing to "take by force" what belonged to YHWH in order to fatten themselves (1 Samuel 2:29). All these examples show how the narrator repeatedly uses the motif of eating and drinking in his composition of the later story.

The incubation type-scene in the Hannah story seems not only to recall the motif of "inquiring of God/YHWH" that punctuates the scene of the people of Israel dealing with the sins of the Benjaminites in Judges 20 and with their own sin of a rash oath sworn at Mizpah in Judges 21, but also to anticipate a particular mode of divination that Samuel resorts to at major junctures in his career as prophet and king-maker, that is, at its beginning in 1 Samuel 3, at the installation of Saul as a king in 1 Samuel 9–10, and finally at the pronouncement of the divine rejection of Saul in 1 Samuel 15. Also Saul's hearing of YHWH's words with regard to his installation as a king and his fatal battle against the Philistine at Gilboa is expressed in a similar configuration of motifs, recalling the incubation type-scene of the Hannah story. In particular, Saul's resort to the female medium Endor in 1 Samuel 28 may be regarded as a parody of the incubation type-scene in 1 Samuel 1–2.

The four scenes of the people of Israel inquiring of YHWH/God concerning the Benjaminites in Judges 20–21 present some important individual motifs and themes that recall the incubation type-scene of the Hannah story.[207] The people of Israel gather together at Mizpah to go to war against the Benjaminites because of the latter's unwillingness to give up the "worthless people" (*bənēy bəliyya'al*, Judges 20:13) of Gibeah who had committed a heinous sin against fellow Israelites. But before they go to war, they decide to go up to Bethel to inquire of God/YHWH. Three times the people of Israel go up to inquire of God/YHWH concerning their upcoming battle against the Benjaminites. The narrator informs us in the account of the third inquiry that "the ark of the covenant of God was there [in Bethel] in those days and Phinehas the son of Eleazar, son of Aaron, ministered before it in those days" (Judges 20:27–28). In the second and third inquiries,

---

[207] Miscall, *1 Samuel: A Literary Reading*, 6.

Table 6.1: The Inquiries of YHWH in Judges 20–21

	Judges 20:18	Judges 20:23	Judges 20:28	Judges 21:3
Problem	War against the Benjaminites	War against the Benjaminites & defeat	War against the Benjaminites & defeat	Loss of one tribe and rash vow
Preparatory Rituals	n/a	weeping	fasting, sacrifice	weeping
Place	Bethel	Bethel	Bethel with the ark of covenant	Bethel
Time	"rose in the morning"	"until evening"	"until evening" & "tomorrow"	"until evening" & "the next day the people rose early"
Intro. to question	"they inquire of God"	"and they inquired of YHWH"	"and they inquired of YHWH"	"and they said,"
Question	"question"	"question"	"question"	"question"
Divine answer	"answer"	"answer"	"answer"	n/a
Post-theophany sacrifice	n/a	n/a	n/a	building an alter and offering sacrifice

we are also informed that the posing of a question was preceded by weeping, fasting, and sacrifice. The fourth inquiry of God deals with the situation of genocide against the tribe of Benjamin that was occasioned by a rash oath sworn by the people of Israel at Mizpah—"No one will give his daughters in marriage to Benjamin" (Judges 21:1). Although the fourth inquiry replaces the narrative introduction "and they inquired of God/YHWH" (*wayyiš'ălû bē'lōhîm*/b*YHWH*, verse 18, 23, 28) with a simpler one "they said," the other elements of the scene lead us to regard it as the same type of divination as the previous incidents of inquiring of YHWH. All of the four inquiries share many elements of the incubation type-scene (see Table 6.1).

The major points of contact between these inquiries of YHWH and the incubation type-scene in 1 Samuel 1:1–2:11a include the theme of the solicitation of a divine answer, the motif of predicament associated with "worthless men" (Judges 20:13), the motif of preparatory rituals, such as weeping, fasting, sacrifice, performed "before the Lord" (Judges 20:23, 26), the holy place where the ark of YHWH is preserved and Phinehas served as YHWH's priest, and the nocturnal setting.

Although these common motifs and themes do not add up to a literary type-scene because of the brevity of the passages in question, they may serve to link the last episodes of Judges to the Hannah story.

The incubation type-scene of the Hannah story foreshadows a particular means of divination that characterizes Samuel's prophecy at major junctures in his career. 1 Samuel 3 describes how the boy Samuel begins his career as a prophet under Eli's apprenticeship. The chapter begins with an observation that the word of YHWH was rare during Eli's tenure at Shiloh (*ûdəbar-YHWH hāyāh yāqār bayyāmîm hāhēm*, cf. verse 1) and ends on a note about the establishment of Samuel as the national prophet to whom YHWH continually manifests himself with his words (*kî-niglāh YHWH 'el-šəmû'ēl bəšilōh bidəbar YHWH*, cf. verses 20–21).[208] The exact nature of Samuel's experience in 1 Samuel 3, however, has been subject to much scholarly debate. Particularly germane to our discussion is the question whether or not the theophanic event in 1 Samuel 3 alludes to an incubation rite. A number of scholars have seen an analogue to an incubation rite in the account of 1 Samuel 3.[209] But some scholars tend to be more cautious in their affirmation of the religious rite being described in 1 Samuel 3, although they agree that the basic situation in that chapter recalls an incubation scene.[210] Perhaps the following remarks of Ehrlich represent the opinion of most of the scholars who have written on this issue:

> Es mag zwar scheinen, daß hier formal ein klassisches Beispiel einer Inkubation vorliege: Die Szene spielt im Heiligtum zu Silo während der Nacht, Samuel liegt im Tempel, und JHWH offenbart sich ihm. Bei näherer Prüfung is jedoch die Annahme einer Inkubation abzulehnen.[211]

---

[208] Thus, it shows how Samuel replaces his master Eli in the role of the mediator between YHWH and the people of Israel. An interesting parallel may be found in Sargon's inscription recounting his biography before he became a king, when he served Uzrababa, the king of Kish. That inscription describes Sargon's dream, in which the deity informs him of the impending doom of his master. Unlike Eli who submitted to the decree, Uzrababa endeavors to get rid of Sargon. See translation in Jerrold S. Cooper and Wolfgang Heimpel, "The Sumerian Sargon Legend," *JAOS* 103 (1983): 67–82. For a detailed comparison, see Bar, *A Letter That Has not Been Read: Dreams in the Hebrew Bible*, 178–79.

[209] For the bibliography, see Gnuse, "The Dream Theophany of Samuel: Its Structure in Relation to Ancient Near Eastern Dreams and Its Theological Significance," 217, footnote 204. Add to that bibliography Michael Fishbane, "I Samuel 3: Historical Narrative and Narrative Poetics," in *Literary Interpretations of Biblical Narratives II*, ed. Gros Louis (Nashville, TN: Abingdon, 1982), 192.

[210] Cf. Smith, *The Books of Samuel*, 27.

[211] Ehrlich, *Der Traum im Alten Testament*, 45.

What Ehrlich attempted in vain to find "bei näherer Prüfung" in the text was any textual detail that might demonstrate Samuel's intention to induce the word of YHWH: thus he concludes that "Obwohl die Traumoffenbarung im Tempel stattfindet, handelt es sich um keine Inkubation," because "es fehlt vollkommen die Absicht, ein Traumorakel zu erlagen."[212] Ehrlich's proposal has been accepted by many scholars.[213] But as we have emphasized many times in this study, the practice of incubation should be differentiated from its literary rendering, especially when we deal with a unit of text whose literary sophistication has been well proven.[214] This means that while the history of religions concept of incubation may not obtain without the intention to acquire an oneiric revelation on the part of an incubant, its literary rendition does not have to register the incubant's intention by revealing his or her psychology. In my opinion, Oppenheim's category "unintentional incubation" should be understood as a literary category, not a term that denotes any practice in reality. And this seems to be demonstrated in Oppenheim's emphasis on the difference between real dream experiences and its literary rendition. He argues that the reference to dreams in the literature is "subject to its own rigid and consistent stylistic conventions.... The censorship exercised by these conventions has reduced the dream-contents to an extremely small number of types which have to be studied as such....the existence of literarily acceptable dream-types has channeled the imaginations of dreamers and poets alike into certain pre-established patterns."[215] It is unfortunate, however, that many scholars have misunderstood Oppenheim's literary type "unintentional incubation" for a historical concept

[212] Ibid., 48.

[213] After surveying the argument both for and against the idea of incubation in 1 Samuel 3, for instance, Gnuse adduces the lack of preparatory rites as the decisive reason for his refusal to call the scene as "incubation" (Gnuse, "The Dream Theophany of Samuel: Its Structure in Relation to Ancient Near Eastern Dreams and Its Theological Significance," 219). In a similar vein, Bar argues that the lack of preparation and Samuel's surprise at the voice of YHWH all point to the infelicity of the term "incubation" for 1 Samuel 3 (Bar, *A Letter That Has not Been Read: Dreams in the Hebrew Bible*, 180). Lindblom arrives at the same conclusion, albeit through a slightly different argumentation. Lindblom argues that the divine message 1 Samuel 3:11–12 came to Samuel not in a dream but in a wakeful theophany (Lindblom, "Theophanies in Holy Places in Hebrew Religion," 100–101).

[214] Fishbane, "I Samuel 3: Historical Narrative and Narrative Poetics," 191–203.

[215] Oppenheim, *The Interpretation of Dreams in the Ancient Near East: With a Translation of an Assyrian Dream-Book*, 184–85.

and have found it to be an oxymoron.[216] Hence, once we realize the fact that whatever the actual experience of Samuel might have been, the text in 1 Samuel 3 contains an ancient literary pattern drawing on the actual practice of incubation, we may leave open the possibility that the nocturnal revelation in 1 Samuel 3 may be something very close to an incubation dream.

With these points in mind, reading 1 Samuel 3 as an incubation type-scene provides much insight into the passage. The plot shows movement from problem to solution as expected in an incubation type-scene. The narrator seems to identify in verse 1 the problem as the rarity in those days of YHWH's words. What makes it interesting is that the problem is not that of an individual but of the nation. This may explain the lack of any incubant. We are not informed of any individual who visits the temple in order to get his personal problem solved through temple sleep. That is why no preparatory rituals are recorded. There is no one who visits the temple with offerings. Instead, we have Samuel who, filling in for Eli, offers sacrifices by day and sleeps by the ark of YHWH, waiting perhaps for the rare word of YHWH. The incubation model on which the narrator may have based his composition of the type-scene is a surrogate incubation, in which a priest sleeps in place of an incubant and the divine oracle concerns not the priest but the (absent) incubant. This explains why the divine word is not expressed in terms of a solution for Samuel's problem. Samuel is not an incubant as such, but a surrogate. The divine message that Samuel receives addresses the problem of the rarity of YHWH's word in the nation by dealing with the source of that problem, namely, the house of Eli. This indirect way of dealing with the problem comports with the narrator's strategy of contrasting Hannah-Samuel and the Elides in order to exalt the former and to disparage the latter. One of the surprises of this incubation type-scene is that Samuel, the surrogate incubant, is himself part of the solution. It is through Samuel's mediatory role that the nation will hear the words of YHWH again. In contrast to the incubation type-scene in the Hannah story where

[216] For instance, see discussion of the Oppenheim's "unintentional incubation" in Gnuse, "The Dream Theophany of Samuel: Its Structure in Relation to Ancient Near Eastern Dreams and Its Theological Significance," 210–211; Cf. Robinson, "Dreams in the Old Testament," 97; Jenny M. Lowery, "The Form and Function of Symbolic Vision Reports in the Hebrew Bible" (Ph.D. diss., The Southern Baptist Theological Seminary, 1999), 14, footnote 16.

Eli plays God to Hannah, Hannah's son, Samuel, plays God to Eli in 1 Samuel 3. The narrator's theological theme, the reversal of fortunes, is iconically demonstrated in the reversal of roles of the surrogates of YHWH in the motif of theophany.

Even those who can never bring themselves to see an incubation in 1 Samuel 3 may agree with Husser that "the initiatory value of this first nocturnal revelation... suggests that it is henceforth by means of nocturnal, oneiric conversations such as this that the prophet [Samuel] will hear the word of God."[217] Indeed, it is plausible to argue that YHWH's words concerning the anointing of Saul as a king and his later divine rejection may have come to Samuel through nocturnal revelation. Although the exact mechanism of Samuel's reception of YHWH's words is not mentioned in the text, one may argue that YHWH's words on the rejection of Saul may have come to Samuel through nocturnal revelation. On the eve of the final confrontation between Samuel and Saul (cf. 1 Samuel 15), Samuel cried out to the Lord all night and in the morning he rose early to meet Saul to pronounce God's rejection of Saul (verse 12). Although the final redactor made YHWH's words in verse 10–11a and Samuel prayer vigil in 11b–12a look like separate incidents, their juxtaposition makes it plausible to argue that Samuel received YHWH's final words on Saul through nocturnal revelation as well.[218] This is confirmed by Samuel's own words in verse 16: "I will tell you what YHWH said to me last night." The fact that YHWH revealed his rejection of Saul to Samuel who cried out all night leads us to wonder whether the same mode of revelation may not have been used at the anointing of Saul in 1 Samuel 9–10. But the text is more complicated here. When Saul visits him on account of his father's lost donkeys, Samuel tells Saul "Today you will eat with me and in the morning... I will tell all that is on your mind" in 1 Samuel 9:19.[219] By "all that is on your mind (*kōl ʾăšer bilbābəkā*)" Samuel does not mean "his father's lost donkeys," because he tells Saul in the next verse that "they had been found." And only after spending the night was Samuel able to announce God's choice of Saul as Israel's

---

[217] Husser, *Dreams and Dream Narratives in the Biblical World*, 177.

[218] Cf. 2 Samuel 7:4, The YHWH came to Nathan at night.

[219] According to Gnuse, the words "Samuel lay until the morning" in 1 Samuel 3:15 serve as an official termination of the dream theophany (Gnuse, "A Reconsideration of the Form-Critical Structure in 1 Samuel 3: An Ancient Near Eastern Dream Theophany," 381).

nāgîd. One may wonder why Samuel had to wait until the next morning to tell what he already knew and, similarly, why the narrator inserts the motifs of sacrificial meal, coming back to town, spending the night on the roof, and waking Saul at the break of dawn between Samuel's words "I will tell you..." (9:19) and his proclamation of Saul's princeship (10:1). This may be a subtle allusion to the particular means that Samuel resorted to for divine message, although the narrator reports through flashback the fact that the revelation about Saul had come to Samuel a few days earlier (1 Samuel 9:16).[220]

Finally, the incubation type-scene in 1 Samuel 1 finds its echo in the two scenes of Saul receiving God's words through Samuel in 1 Samuel 9–10 and 1 Samuel 28.[221] First, the scene in 1 Samuel 9–10 where Saul receives through Samuel God's words on his future kingship is reminiscent of the incubation scene in the Hannah story. Saul visits Samuel at Zuph with a personal problem, namely, the whereabouts of his father's lost donkeys. Samuel, however, takes the moment to reveal YHWH's plan for Saul. As in the case of the incubation type-scene in 1 Samuel 1, the private problem of Saul's family leads to a surprising solution that has an impact on everyone in the nation. As for the mode of revelation, it is interesting to note that Samuel does not reveal God's plan for Saul right away, but he buys time until the next morning. He says to Saul, "For today, you shall eat with me, and in the morning...I will tell you all that is in your mind" (1 Samuel 9:19). The narrator intends to portray the scene of Saul receiving the divine message about his kingship in terms of the incubation type-scene. Saul goes up to *bāmāh* "the high place" where the sacrifice is held, and eats the portion prepared only for him in the *liškāh* "the hall" attached to the *bāmāh*-sanctuary.[222] After the sacrifice and the meal, Saul comes down from the high place to the city and lies down to sleep on the roof, perhaps that of Samuel's residence.[223] At the break of dawn, Samuel calls to

---

[220] According to Bar-Efrat (*Narrative Art in the Bible*, JSOTSup [Sheffield: Almond Press, 1989], 175), the use of "flashbacks" is not customary. If so, one may speculate that the insertion of a flashback in 1 Samuel 9:16 may be the redactor's effort not to make Samuel's reception of revelation appear like pagan divination through a dream.

[221] For the connection between Saul's inquiry of a female medium and incubation, see Nowack, *Richter, Ruth und Bücher Samuelis*, 136.

[222] The Septuagint version of the Hannah story mentions *liškāh* (katavluma in LXX 1 Samuel 1:18) as the place where Elkanah's family participates in the family meal.

[223] I am following the Septuagint. MT does not make sense.

Saul on the roof (verse 26) and reveals that YHWH has chosen him to be *nāgîd* "prince" over the people of Israel. Here Samuel is playing the role of a deity who visits an incubant at dawn. The time coordinate of when Samuel received his first word of God must also have been at the break of the dawn (cf. 1 Samuel 3:3). The place of Saul lying down to sleep was the roof, to be compared with the place of a Mesopotamian incubation scene in *Rituals to Obtain a Purussû* (cf. See 1.2 in chapter two above). The post-epiphany section in 1 Samuel 10:2ff also recalls the incubation type-scene in the Hannah story. After parting from Samuel, Saul meets two men who will confirm Samuel's words about the lost donkeys. Then Saul meets three men who are on their way to Bethel with three goats, three loaves of bread and a skin of wine, the offerings which recalls Hannah's thanksgiving offering for the dedication of her son to the temple. Finally, Saul meets a band of prophets whom he joins in prophesying with harp, tambourine and flute, at which point the Spirit of YHWH rushes on him. Saul's subsequent prophesying may correspond to the Hannah's triumphant song at the end of the incubation types-scene in 1 Samuel 1–2.

In Samuel 28, we are informed that Saul is in great distress not only because of the Philistine threat but also because God does not answer him either through dreams, Urim, or prophets. Saul pays a visit to a female medium in Endor in order to get an answer to these problems. Just as in the incubation type-scenes in 1 Samuel 3 and 9–10, the narrator bases the type-scene on the surrogate incubation model. In contrast to the incubation type-scene in the Hannah story where an obscure woman encounters a male authority figure who plays God to her, a male authority figure goes to an obscure medium who plays God to him in 1 Samuel 28. Saul's fasting is comparable to that of Hannah. Also Saul's resumption of eating food after the "theophanic" experience recalls Hannah's resumption of eating after receiving Eli's blessing. Furthermore, the post-"theophany" scene where the female medium brought out a fattened calf and flour for Saul is reminiscent of the scene where Hannah brings a bull and an ephah of flour and a skin of wine for Eli. The absence of the skin of wine in 1 Samuel 28 has to do with the lack of the motif of drinking in the type-scene in 1 Samuel 28. The *pat-leḥem* that the female medium sets on Saul's table refers us back to the first prophecy against the Elides who will ask the new and faithful priest to hire them for a morsel of bread. The surprising element of this type-scene in 1 Samuel 28 is that the divine message does not solve Saul's problem, but exacerbates it.

The above discussion has shown that the incubation type-scene of the first two chapters of 1 Samuel serves as a fulcrum that allows the reader to go both backward and forward for narratological connections within the canon.

4. Conclusion

I have proposed the incubation type-scene as a literary device that informs the composition of the Hannah story. Although many scholars have followed Alter in taking the Hannah story as belonging to the annunciation type-scene, the above analysis of 1 Samuel 1:1–2:11a has revealed several features that are better understood from the perspective of the incubation type-scene. First, just as in the two Ugaritic instances of incubation type-scene, the Hannah story has a clear movement of plot from problem to solution. She is introduced as "childless" in verse 2 and the narrator reports the birth of Samuel from Hannah's once blocked womb in verse 20.[224] This clear plot movement is often missing in so-called annunciation type-scenes in the Hebrew Bible where the focus lies more on the extraordinariness of a future hero's birth than on the divine solution to the problem. Since the incubation type-scene focuses on the solution of a problem, it tends to include an extended motif that articulates the incubant's problem. But the annunciation type-scene focusing on the extraordinariness of the birth tends to minimize the role of the parents in the story. For instance, the story of Samson's birth in Judges 13 does not mention the mother's distress from childlessness, but quickly moves to the theophanic scene (verses 3–23).

Second, unlike annunciation type-scenes that register no hint for the woman's intention to induce divine intervention, the Hannah story features a woman determined to get a divine audience in the temple. There in the temple, Hannah weeps, prays, and makes a vow that sort of forces the deity to act on her behalf. In fact, Hannah is the only barren wife that went to the temple to seek a solution from

[224] This movement of plot is indicated by word-plays. If Hannah's barrenness is encapsulated in the word *sgr* "close" in verse 5 and 6, the lifting of that predicament is registered in the verb *zkr* "to remember" in verse 19. Note a similar word-play between *anḫ* "the mourning one" and *anḫn* "I will rest" in the ʾAqhatu story. If the former represents Dānîʾilu's mood before theophany, the latter symbolizes his mood after theophany.

YWHW. On the contrary, theophany was surprising to Manoah's wife. The angel of YHWH visited her instead of her visiting YHWH. The third feature that helps us to see the incubation type-scene in the Hannah story is the content of divine message. The divine message in the quasi-theophanic scene of the Hannah story is oriented toward the solution of her problem. In the annunciation type-scene, however, the divine message underlines the extraordinariness of the baby to be born. Although Eli's blessing is not specific enough, it was undoubtedly meant for the solution of Hannah's problem. Fourth, the Hannah story inherits the tradition of celebrating a pious incubant actively seeking divine help. One may enumerate several hints that combine to underscore Hannah's initiative-taking piety: a) Hannah, neither Elkanah nor Eli, makes a Nazirite vow regarding Samuel, not to mention naming him; b) it is Hannah who decides *when* to take the child to the temple; c) her speeches occur six times and culminate in her triumphant song; d) the sexual intercourse is mentioned in the fulfillment motif. Hannah's Nazirite vow stands out especially, because it underlines Hannah's, not God's, volunteering or choosing her son to be a hero. This stands in stark contrast to the story of Samson's birth, where the angel commands the imperceptive parents to raise Samson as a Nazirite and the angel has to repeat it twice because of the obtuseness of the parents.[225] In the Hannah story, however, the parents' character and piety is brought to the foreground, even eclipsing that of Eli the priest. Hannah's initiative-taking character is further demonstrated by the fact that Hannah is the subject of the verb over three times more often than she is the object. This rate may be put in perspective by noting

[225] Neither Manoah nor his wife recognize who the annunciator is, although the latter's awesome appearance leaves no doubt in the reader's mind that he is the angel of God. But, as Alter points out, Manoah is put in a more negative light than her wife, since the divine messenger appears to Manoah's wife first, who had to go fetch her husband when the angel appears the second time. Further, Manoah almost forces the angel to repeat what he had already said about the child's Naziriteship, presses a human meal on the angel, and is obtuse enough to ask for the angel's name. Only after a grand pyrotechnic display on the altar does Manoah understand that he is the angel of God. Samson's fate, on the other hand, is explicitly stated by the angel in verse 5 and the spectacular emphasis on the miraculous altar flame after the moment of annunciation introduces the formal motif of fire that will punctuate the Samson story until he is blind, and may also be meant to reinforce the etymology of his name, "sun-power." Cf. Alter, *The David Story: A Translation with Commentary of 1 and 2 Samuel*, 124.

that a woman in biblical prose is the subject of verbs exactly the same number of times as she is the object of verbal forms.[226]

That said, one may note the creative use of the traditional type-scene in the Hannah story. Several nonconventional elements are introduced to the story so as to embed it in a broader narrative context. Although the Hannah story is a story complete in itself, having its own plot, it is still a part of the larger narrative about Samuel, the heroic king-maker of Israel. This incubation type-scene serves as an introduction to the life of Samuel. This aspect seems to have led the narrator to compose a rather long motif of vow-fulfillment, which culminates in an emphatic exclamation, namely, Hannah's joyous song that in turn climaxes with the announcement of God's anointed. The motif of vow-fulfillment shows how Hannah dedicates Samuel to the sanctuary in Shiloh. This is where the personal problem of Hannah meets a solution of national significance. If any connection can be assumed between a Nazirite and a prophet at this point in Israel's history, Hannah's Nazirite vow seems to foreshadow Samuel's function as YHWH's prophet, although the omission of the word *nāzîr* in the Masoretic text seems to weaken such a connection. Be that as it may, the narrator's composition of the motif of vow-fulfillment indicates the function of this type-scene as an introduction to the larger narrative of Samuel's life as a prophet. And this aspect of the type-scene brings the Hannah story closer to other birth stories in the Hebrew Bible.

Another peculiarity of the incubation type-scene in question is the ludicrous role of a divine messenger, Eli. Not to mention his imperceptiveness of taking praying Hannah as a mumbling drunkard, he fumbles ambiguous words in his blessing when he should have felt most confident as a divine messenger. This is part of the narrator's stratagem of contrasting Hannah-Samuel to Eli and his sons in order to foreshadow the exaltation of the former and the fatal fall of the latter. This illustrates the point that the configuration of component motifs of the type-scene may be adapted to the literary agenda that the narrator has in a larger narratological context: the narrator puts the convention to good expressive use not only through its full-scale

[226] Meyers, "Hannah and Her Sacrifice: Reclaiming Female Agency," 99.

employment but also through ellipsis, truncation, or pointed reversals of the conventional pattern.[227]

Finally, one may note the use of incubation type-scene at the beginning of 1 Samuel as a narratological device that connects the story of Hannah-Samuel to the last days of Judges and to the story of Saul the first King of Israel, because Judges 20–21 and 1 Samuel 9, 28 shows a configuration of motifs that recall the Hannah story. This helps us to read the Hannah story not only as a story of a barren woman in deep distress, but also as a story of the nation of Israel in trouble due to lack of a king. Just as the solution to Hannah's problem is found in her "asking" a son and being given Samuel, so will the solution to her people's problem be found in their "asking" a king and being given one, that is, Saul. The story of Hannah and that of Israel intersects each other at the person of Samuel who represents the solution of Hannah's problem and that of Israel's.

[227] Alter, "How Convention Helps Us Read: The Case of the Bible's Annunciation Type-Scene," 123.

CHAPTER SEVEN

SUMMARY

This book has attempted to break the impasse in Ugaritic and biblical scholarship on incubation by proposing that incubation may have been utilized as a literary device in the West-Semitic literary tradition. Toward that end, I have borrowed the idea of a type-scene from Homeric scholarship, especially one proposed by Nagler. Nagler argues that a type-scene does not consist of a fixed sequence of motifs (contra Arend), but was an inherited *Gestalt* for the spontaneous generation of a 'family' of meaningful details. According to Nagler's conception of a type-scene, therefore, the reader recognizes it through the family resemblance it bears with other instances of the same type-scene. Further, according to Nagler, a type-scene has elements of convention and invention. The conventional element of a type-scene has to do with the fact that the *Gestalt* of a type-scene is inherited, and not created, by the poet. This is best illustrated by Foley's concept of the metonymic use of a type-scene which contends that a type-scene carries a significance that goes deeper than the surface level and invokes meanings inherited from the whole tradition of poetry/story. The inventional element has to do with the idea that the inherited *Gestalt* resides only in the poet's mind, but in order to be recognized by the reader, has to be "verbalized" in various specific motifs in accordance with the poet's narrative need of the moment. This work has applied Nagler's definition of a type-scene to the discussion of incubation type-scenes in two Ugaritic texts and one biblical text.

The incubation type-scene in the 'Aqhatu story registers a sequence of motifs that strongly emulates the religious practice, articulating all the four foundational concepts of the incubation type-scene: the lack of an legitimate heir articulating the concept of predicament, the motifs of the seven-day offering, ritual clothing, nakedness, prayer ("delayed identification" cf. Wright), and lying down, all articulating the concept of intentionality, the motifs of a temple and perhaps a dream articulating the concept of liminality, and the motif of divine blessing/promise and instruction articulating the concept of epiphany. This configuration of motifs is no random aggregate. Rather, they are arranged in a relationship that serves to form the plot that moves from Dānî'ilu's sonlessness to the birth of 'Aqhatu. In addition, the configuration of motifs in this incubation type-scene also displays high degree of literary artifice on the part of the poet, as has been demonstrated above. Moreover, the incubation type-scene in the 'Aqhatu story affirms the tradition upon which the poet of the type-scene draws in a straightforward manner. The elaborate seven-day ritual that Dānî'ilu goes through before the occurrence of theophany underscores his religious piety, portraying him as a paragon of piety. Ba'lu, Dānî'ilu's patron deity, responds positively to Dānî'ilu's pious appeal. All this goes to underscore the theme of the story as a whole: the sacred hierarchy of the divine and human world and the proper behavior of its denizens. The four-fold repetition of a filial duty within the type-scene seems to reinforce the theme of knowing one's place within the hierarchical order of the world. And by inserting the scene of divine council in the theophany scene (Ba'lu's petition and 'Ilu's blessing), the poet shows that even Ba'lu has to go through a proper chain of command before he pronounces blessing upon Dānî'ilu (cf. Anatu's journey to 'Ilu's abode in order to get a permission to kill 'Aqhatu).

The incubation type-scene in the Kirta story provides a good example wherein the poet arranges traditional motifs rather freely to suit his narrative purpose instead of depicting the normal procedure of the practice in reality. A sequence of motifs that informs the first episode of *Kirta*, however, combine to bear a family resemblance to other instances of incubation type-scene. First of all, it shows a clear movement from problem to solution. Thus this incubation type-scene begins with a rather long description of the total destruction of Kirta's family (KTU 1.14 I:6–25) and ends on a short note of its full restoration (KTU 1.15 III:20–25). Further, the configuration of motifs in this incubation type-scene not only shows in relief the poet's literary artifice, but also effectively serves to communicate the theme of the Kirta story as a whole; the story as a whole seems to affirm the ideology of kingship, but examines the possibility that a king in such an important position could turn out to be a "flawed" hero. After all, Kirta appears to be less than perfect in his relationship with the gods, including 'Ilu. In fact, unlike Dānî'ilu, he does not go through any rituals prior to theophany and his weeping may or may not be intended to induce divine help. Furthermore, his spontaneous visit to the shrines at Sidon and Tyre in order to make a vow to 'Aṯiratu provides an occasion that costs him his health and almost his throne even. Although the text seems to connect Kirta's breach of a vow (not the vow-making itself) to his later misfortunes, it is undeniable that the text puts Kirta's vow in a negative light by portraying it as an addition to 'Ilu's original commands in the context of Kirta's otherwise perfect execution of 'Ilu's detailed instructions. And if the faithful execution underscores Kirta's piety, the act of making an oath, which was not explicitly commanded by 'Ilu, seems to point to Kirta's flawed piety toward 'Ilu. In this connection, one may note the poet's artifice in placing the oath motif, which is usually to be expected in the pre-epiphany section, in the post-epiphany section and also in the poet's turning what is generally taken as an act of piety in the ancient Near East (cf. Hannah's vow) into something that is detrimental to Kirta's piety. Finally, it should also be mentioned that the incubation type-scene in *Kirta* may provide a good example of it being able to stand alone as a story complete in itself, without being part of a larger story of a hero yet to be born. Kirta, not the son that he acquired through incubation, figures as the protagonist in the subsequent episodes of the story. The son born to Kirta in the first episode plays only an auxiliary role in the rest of the story: hence it may justifiably be called "the Kirta story."

Although the Hannah story has usually been recognized as a variation of the annunciation type-scene, it bears a family resemblance to the other two instances of incubation type-scene. This particular configuration of component motifs not only shows the movement of the plot from Hannah's barrenness to the birth of Samuel, but also contributes to the narrator's literary purpose of emphasizing Hannah's piety and also her character capable of taking initiative. The surprising element, however, comes from Eli's role as YHWH's surrogate. Eli's behavior and words defeat our expectation of YHWH that figures prominently in the theophanic scene, for Eli not only misperceives praying Hannah as a mumbling drunkard, but he is also ignorant of the desperate need that has brought her to the temple. The parodical description in this incubation type-scene of the divine figure dovetails with the narrator's larger purpose of contrasting Eli's house to Samuel's house in the wider context. If the incubation type-scene in *Kirta* puts a spin on the pious image of the incubant, while maintaining the benevolent and powerful image of the deity, the type-scene in the Hannah's story, on the other hand, plays on the latter image, while maintaining the pious and initiative taking-image of the incubant.

Furthermore, unlike the incubation type-scene in Kirta, this incubation type-scene also serves as an introduction to the life of a national hero, Samuel, and this is indicated by the author composing an unusually long motif of vow-fulfillment, which concerns the dedication of Samuel to the sanctuary at Shiloh.

Finally, I would like to suggest some areas that need further study. I have already mentioned in passing the possibility that the incubation type-scene in the Hebrew Bible may have been a proto-form of biblical stories of the birth of heroes that is usually completely incorporated as an introduction to the heroic life, thus losing some of the characteristics of the incubation type-scene. The story of Hannah seems to provide a case in transition from the one to the other. But this possibility needs to be demonstrated in a separate study. Also, other instances of the incubation type-scene may be studied, especially incubation type-scenes in which the problem of an incubant is other than barrenness/childlessness. For instance, Elijah's encounter with YHWH in 1 Kings 19, Abraham's encounter with YHWH in Genesis 15, Jacob's oneiric experience in Genesis 28, Hagar's experience in the wilderness in Genesis 21, the cure of Hezekiah's illness in 2 Kings 20, etc., may be studied with great promise from the perspective of the incubation type-scene.

BIBLIOGRAPHY

Aartun, Kjell. "Neue Beiträge zum Ugaritischen Lexikon I." *UF* 16 (1984): 1–52.

——. *Studien zur ugaritischen Lexikographie: mit kultur- und religionsgeschichtlichen Parallelen*. Wiesbaden: O. Harrassowitz, 1991.

Abusch, Tzvi. *Mesopotamian Witchcraft: Toward a History and Understanding of Babylonian Witchcraft Beliefs and Literature*. AMD 5. Leiden: Brill, 2002.

Ackerman, James S. "Who Can Stand Before YHWH, This Holy God? A Reading of 1 Samuel 1–15." *Proof* 11 (1991): 1–24.

Ackerman, Susan. "The Deception of Isaac, Jacob's Dream at Bethel, and Incubation on an Animal Skin." In *Priesthood and Cult in Ancient Israel*, edited by Gary A. Anderson, 92–120. Sheffield: JOST Press, 1991.

Ackroyd, Peter R. *The First Book of Samuel*. Cambridge: Cambridge University Press, 1971.

Adams, Hazard, ed. *Critical Theory Since Plato*. New York: Harcourt Brace Javanovich, 1971.

——, ed. *Critical Theory Since Plato*. Orlando, FL: Harcourt Brace Jovanovich College Press, 1992.

Ahlström, G. W. "I Samuel 1, 15." *Bib* 60, (1979): 254.

Aistleitner, Joseph. *Die mythologischen und kultischen Texte aus Ras Schamra*. BOH 8. Budapest: Akadémiai Kiadó, 1959.

——. *Wörterbuch der ugaritischen Sprache*. Philologisch-Historische Klasse 106. Berlin: Akademie-Verlag, 1965.

Aitken, Kenneth T. "Formulaic Patterns for the Passing of Time in Ugaritic Narrative." *UF* 19 (1987): 1–10.

——. "Oral Formulaic Composition and Theme in the Aqhat Narrative." *UF* 21 (1989): 1–16.

——. *The Aqhat Narrative: A Study in the Narrative Structure and Composition of an Ugaritic Tale*. JSS Monographs 13. Manchester: University of Manchester, 1990.

Albertz, Rainer. *A History of Israelite Religion in the Old Testament Period: Volume 1: From the Beginnings to the End of the Monarchy*. OTL. Louisville, KY: Westminster John Knox Press, 1994.

Alter, Robert. "Biblical Type-Scenes and the Uses of Convention." *CI* 5 (1978): 355–68.

——. *The Art of Biblical Narrative*. New York: Basic Books, 1981.

——. "How Convention Helps Us Read: The Case of the Bible's Annunciation Type-Scene." *Proof* 3 (1983): 115–30.

——. *The David Story: A Translation with Commentary of 1 and 2 Samuel*. New York: W. W. Norton, 1999.

Amit, Yairah. "'Am I not More Devoted to You Than Ten Sons?' (1 Samuel 1.8): Male and Female Interpretations." In *A Feminist Companion to Samuel and Kings*, 68–76. Sheffield: Sheffield Academic Press, 1994.

Anderson, G. W. *A Critical Introduction to the Old Testament*. London: Gerald Duckworth, 1959.

Arend, Walter. *Die typischen Scenen bei Homer*. Problemata 7. Berlin: Weidmannsche Buchhandlung, 1933.

Aristides, Aelius. *The Complete Works*. Edited and translated by Charles A. Behr. Leiden: Brill, 1981–86.

Asher-Greve, Julia M. "The Oldest Female Oneiromancer." In *La femme dans le proche-orient antique*, compiled by Jean-Marie Durand, 27–32. Paris: Editions Recherche sur les Civilisations, 1987.

Astour, Michael C. "Two Ugaritic Serpent Charms." *JNES* 27 (1968): 13–36.

Averbeck, Richard E. *Preliminary Study of Ritual and Structure in the Cylinders of Gudea*. Ann Arbor, MI: University Microfilms International, 1988.

——. "The Cylinders of Gudea." In *Monumental Inscriptions from the Biblical World*. Vol. II of *COS*, edited by William W. Hallo and K. Lawson Younger Jr., 417–33. New York: Brill, 2000.

Avishur, Y. *Stylistic Studies of Word-Pairs in Biblical and Ancient Semitic Literatures*. AOAT 210. Neukirchen-Vluyn: Neukirchener Verlag, 1984.

Badawi, A. M. "Die neue historische Stele Amenophis' II." *ASAE* 42 (1943).

Badre, L., P. Bordreuil, J. Mudarres, L. ʿAjjan, and R. Vitale. "Notes ougaritiques." *Syria* 53 (1976): 95–125.

Baines, John. "Palaces and Temples of Ancient Egypt." In *Civilizations of the Ancient Near East*, edited by Jack M. Sasson, 303–17. New York: Charles Scribner's Sons, 1995.

Baldwin, Joyce G. *1 & 2 Samuel*. The Tyndale Old Testament Commentaries. Downers Grove, IL: Inter-Varsity Academics, 2008.

Bar, Shaul. *A Letter That Has not Been Read: Dreams in the Hebrew Bible*. Cincinnati, OH: Hebrew Union College Press, 2001.

Bar-Efrat, Shimon. *Narrative Art in the Bible*. JSOTSup. Sheffield: Almond Press, 1989.

——. *Das Erste Buch Samuel: Ein narratologisch-philologischer Kommentar*. Stuttgart: Verlag W. Kohlhammer, 1996.

——. *Narrative Art in the Bible*. London ; New York: T. & T. Clark, 2004.

Beckman, Gary. "Plague Prayers of Muršili II." In *Canonical Compositions from the Biblical World*. Vol. I of *COS*, edited by William W. Hallo and K. Lawson Younger Jr., 156–60. Leiden: Brill, 1997.

Ben Zvi, Ehud, and Michael H. Floyd, eds. *Writings and Speech in Israelite and Ancient Near Eastern Prophecy*. Atlanta, GA: Society of Biblical Literature, 2000.

Bergman, J., M. Ottosson, and J. Botterweck. "Chālam." In *TDOT*, edited by J. Botterweck and H. Ringgren, 4:421–32. Grand Rapids, MI: Eerdmans, 1977.

Berlin. *The Dynamics of Biblical Parallelism*. Bloomington, IN: Indiana University Press, 1985.

Biggs, Robert D. "An Oracular Dream Concerning Ashurbanipal." In *ANET*, edited by James B. Pritchard, 606. Princeton, NJ: Princeton University Press, 1969.

Billson, M. "The Memoir: New Perspectives on a Forgotten Genre." *Genre* 10 (1977): 259–82.

Birch, Bruce C. *The First and Second Books of Samuel*. NIB 2. Nashville, TN: Abingdon Press, 1995–2002.

Blenkinsopp, Joseph. *A History of Prophecy in Israel*. Louisville, KY: Westminster John Knox Press, 1996.

——. *Isaiah 56–66: A New Translation with Introduction and Commentary*. AB 19B. New York: Doubleday, 2003.

Bodner, Keith. *1 Samuel: Narrative Commentary*. Sheffield: Sheffield Phoenix Press, 2008.

Booth, G., trans. *The Historical Library of Diodorus the Sicilian*. London: W. Taylor, 1814.

Bordreuil, Pierre, and Dennis Pardee. *Choix de Textes: Glossaire*. Vol. 2 of *Manuel d'ougaritique*. Paris: Geuthner, 2004.

——. *Grammaire: Fac-Similés*. Vol. 1 of *Manuel d'ougaritique*. Paris: Geuthner, 2004.

Borghouts, J. F. "Witchcraft, Magic, and Divination in Ancient Egypt." In *CANE*, vol. III & IV, edited by Jack M. Sasson, 1775–85. Peabody, MA: Hendrickson, 1995.

Boylan, Patrick. *Thoth, the Hermes of Egypt: A Study of Some Aspects of Theological Thought in Ancient Egypt*. Chicago: Ares, 1979.

Breasted, James, H., ed. and trans. *The Eighteenth Dynasty*. Vol. II of *Ancient Records of Egypt: Historical Documents from the Earliest Times to the Persian Conquest*. Chicago: University of Chicago Press, 1906–7.

——, ed. and trans. *The Nineteenth Dynasty*. Vol. III of *Ancient Records of Egypt: Historical Documents from the Earliest Times to the Persian Conquest*. Chicago: University of Chicago Press, 1906–7.

Brettler, Marc. "The Composition of 1 Samuel 1–2." *JBL* 116 (1997): 601–12.

Britt, Bryan. "Prophetic Concealment in a Biblical Type Scene." *CBQ* 64 (2002): 37–58.

Brueggemann, Walter. "1 Samuel 1: A Sense of a Beginning." *ZAW* 102 (1990): 33–48.

——. *First and Second Samuel*. Interpretation. Louisville, KY: John Knox Press, 1990.

Bryce, Trevor. *The Kingdom of the Hittites*. Oxford: Clarendon Press, 1998.

Budde, K. *Die Bücher Samuel*. Tübingen: J. C. B. Mohr, 1902.

Bulkeley, Kelly. *Dreaming in the World's Religions: A Comparative History*. New York: New York University Press, 2008.

Buss, Martin J. *Biblical Form Criticism in Its Context*. JSOTSup 274. Sheffield, England: Sheffield Academic Press, 1999.

Butler, S. A. L. *Mesopotamian Conceptions of Dreams and Dream Rituals*. AOAT 258. Münster: Ugarit-Verlag, 1988.

Campbell, Anthony F. "Form Criticism's Future." In *The Changing Face of Form Criticism for the 21st Century*, edited by Marvin A. Sweeney and Ehud Ben Zvi, 15–31. Grand Rapids, MI: Eerdmans, 2001.

——. *1 Samuel*. FOTL 7. Grand Rapids, MI: Eerdmans, 2003.

Caquot, André. "Les songes et leur interpretation selon Canaan et Israel." *SO* 2 (1959): 101–24.

——. "La divination dans l'ancient Israël." In *La divination*, edited by André Caquot and Marcel Leibovici, 83–114. Paris: Presses Universitaire de France, 1968.

Caquot, André, and Maurice Sznycer. *Ugaritic Religion*. Iconography of Religions. Leiden: Brill, 1980.

Caquot, André, Maurice Sznycer, and Andrée Herdner. *Mythes et légendes: introduction, traduction, commentaire*. Vol. 1 of *Textes ougaritiques*. Littératures anciennes du Proche-Orient 7. Paris: Éditions du Cerf, 1974.

Cartledge, Tony W. *Vows in the Hebrew Bible and the Ancient Near East*. Sheffield: JSOT Press, 1992.

——. *1 & 2 Samuel*. Smyth & Helwys Bible Commentary. Macon, GA: Smyth & Helwys, 2001.

Cassuto, U. "Seven Wives of King Keret." *BASOR* 119 (1950): 18–21.

——. *The Goddess Anat: Canaanite Epics of the Patriarchal Age*. Translated from the Hebrew by Israel Abrahams. Jerusalem: Magnes Press, 1971.

——. *Bible and Ancient Oriental Texts*. Vol. II of *Biblical and Oriental Studies*. Translated by Israel Abrahams. Jerusalem: The Magnes Press, 1975.

Cathcart, Kevin J., and Wilfred G. E. Watson. "Weathering a Wake: A Cure for a Carousal." *PIBA* 4, no. 35–58 (1980).

Cazelles, H. "Review: Canaanite Myths and Legends by G. R. Driver." *VT* 7 (1957): 420–30.

Chatman, Seymour B. *Story and Discourse: Narrative Structure in Fiction and Film*. Ithaca: Cornell University Press, 1978.

Childs, Brevard S. *Isaiah*. OTL. Louisville, KY: Westminster John Knox Press, 2001.

Civil, M. "The Song of the Plowing Oxen." In *Kramer Anniversary Volume: Cuneiform Studies in Honor of Samuel Noah Kramer*, edited by Barry L. Eichler, 83–96. Kevelaer: Butzon & Bercker, 1976.

Cogan, Mordechai. "Achaemenid Inscriptions: Cyrus Cylinder." In *Monumental Inscriptions from the Biblical World*. Vol. II of *COS*, William W. Hallo, 314–15. Leiden: Brill, 2000.

Cohen, C. "Biblical Hebrew-Ugaritic Comparative Philology: The Comparison BH Hdrt/hdr = Ug. Hdrt." *ErIsr* 26 (1999): 71–77.
Cohn, Robert L. *2 Kings*. Berit Olam. Collegevillle, Minnesota: The Liturgical Press, 2000.
Conklin, Blane W. "Oath Formulae in Classical Hebrew and Other Semitic Languages." Ph.D. diss. Chicago: University of Chicago Press, 2005.
Contenau, Georges. *La divination chez les Assyriens et les Babyloniens. Avec 13 figures, 1 carte et 8 gravures hors texte*. Paris: Payot, 1940.
Coogan, Michael D., ed. and trans. *Stories from Ancient Canaan*. Philadelphia, PA: Westminster Press, 1978.
Cook, Joan E. *Hannah's Desire, God's Design: Early Interpretation of the Story of Hannah*. JSOTSup 282. Sheffield: Sheffield Academic Press, 1999.
Cooper, Alan. "Divine Names and Epithets in the Ugaritic Texts." In *Ras Shamra Parallels: The Texts from Ugarit and the Hebrew Bible*, vol. 3, edited by Stan Rummel, 333–469. Roma: Pontificium Institutum Biblicum, 1981.
Cooper, Jerrold S., and Wolfgang Heimpel. "The Sumerian Sargon Legend." *JAOS* 103 (1983): 67–82.
Cross, Frank M. *Canaanite Myth and Hebrew Epic; Essays in the History of the Religion of Israel*. Cambridge, MA: Harvard University Press, 1973.
——. "Prose and Poetry in the Mythic and Epic Texts from Ugarit." *HTR* 67 (1974): 1–15.
Cryer, Frederick H. *Divination in Ancient Israel and Its Near Eastern Environment*. JSOTSup 142. Sheffield: JSOT Press.
Culler, Jonathan. *Structuralist Poetics: Structuralism, Linguistics and the Study of Literature*. Ithaca: Cornell University Press, 1975.
Cutler, B., and J. Macdonald. "An Akkadian Cognate to Ugaritic Brlt." *UF* 5 (1973): 67–70.
Dahood, S. J. "Ugaritic-Hebrew Parallel Pairs." In *Ras Shamra Parallels: The Texts from Ugarit and the Hebrew Bible*, vol. 2, edited by L. Fisher, 71–382. Roma: Pontificium Institutum Biblicum, 1975.
——. "J. C. L. Gibson, *Canaanite Myths and Legends*. Originally Edited by G. R. Driver in 1956. Edinburgh 1978. T. & T. Clark." *Bib* 62 (1981): 274–77.
Dalley, S. "The Tale of Bulūqiyā and the Alexander Romance in Jewish and Sufi Mystical Sources." In *Tracing the Threads: Studies in the Vitality of Jewish Pseudepigraphia*, edited by J. C. Reeves, 239–69. Atlanta, GA: Scholars Press, 1994.
Delekat, L. *Asylie und Schutzorakel am Zionheiligtum: Eine Untersuchung zu den Privaten Feindpsalmen*. Leiden: Brill, 1967.
Deubner, Ludwig. *De Incubatione Capita Quattuor Scripsit Ludovicus Deubner. Accedit Laudatio in Miracula Sancti Hieromartyris Therapontis e Codice Messanensi Denuo Edita*. Lipsiae: B. G. Teubner, 1900.
Dhorme, P. *Les Livres de Samuel*. Études Bibliques. Paris: Librairie Victor Lecoffre, 1910.
Dietrich, Manfried, and Loretz, Oswald. "Zur ugaritischen Lexikographie, II." *Orientalische Literaturzeitung* 62 (1967): 533–52.
——. "Zur Ugaritischen Lexikographie (V)." *UF* 4 (1972): 27–36.
——. "Der Prolog des KRT-Epos (CTA 14 I 1–35)." In *Wort und Geschichte: Festschrift für Karl Elliger zum 70. Geburtstag*, H. Gese and Rüger H, 31–36. Neukirchen-Vluyn: Verlag Butzon & Bercker Kevelaer, 1973.
——. "Bemerkungen Zum Aqhat-Text: Zur Ugaritischen Lexikographie (XIV)." *UF* 10 (1978): 65–72.
——. "Das Aqhat-Epos." In *Weisheitstexte, Mythen und Epen*. Vol. 3 of *TUAT*, edited by Otto Kaiser, 1254–1305. Gütersloh: Gütersloher Verlagshaus, 1990.
——. "Das Keret-Epos." In *Weisheitstexte, Mythen und Epen*. Vol. 3 of *TUAT*, edited by Otto Kaiser, 1254–1305. Gütersloh: Gütersloher Verlagshaus, 1990.

——. "Die ugaritischen Zeitangaben *ṣbu špš // ʿrb špš* und *špšm*." *UF* 22 (1990): 75–77.
Dijk, J. van, A. Goetze, and M. I. Hussey, eds. *Early Mesopotamian Incantations and Rituals*. Vol. 11 of *Yale Oriental Series, Babylonian Texts*. New Haven, CT: Yale University Press, 1985.
Dijkstra, M., and J. C. de Moor. "Problematical Passages in the Legend of Aqhatu." *UF* 7 (1975): 171–216.
Dodds, Eric R. *The Greeks and the Irrational*. Sather Classical Lectures 25. Berkeley: University of California Press, 1964.
Donner, H., and W. Röllig. *Kanaanäische und aramäische Inschriften*. Vol. 1. Wiesbaden: Harrassowitz Verlag, 2002.
Dossin, Georges. *Correspondance Féminine*. ARM 10. Paris: Geuthner, 1978.
Doty, William G. "The Concept of Genre in Literary Analysis." In *Society of Biblical Society Seminar Papers 1*, edited by Lane C. McGaughy, 413–48. Missoula, Mont.: Scholars Press, 1972.
Driver, G. R. *Canaanite Myths and Legends*. Edinburgh: T. & T. Clark, 1956.
Driver, S. R. *Notes on the Hebrew Text and the Topography of the Books of Samuel*. Oxford: Clarendon Press, 1913.
Dunand, Françoise. *Dieux et hommes en Egypte, 3000 av. J.-C.-395 apr. J.-C.* Paris: A. Colin, 1991.
Dundes, Alan. *The Study of Folklore*. Englewood Cliffs, New Jersey: Prentice-Hall, 1965.
Durand, Jean-Marie. *Archives épistolaires de Mari I/1*. ARM 26. Paris: Recherches sur les civilisations, 1988.
——. "Les prophéties des textes de Mari." In *Oracles et prophéties dans l'Antiquité: actes du Colloque de Strasbourg, 15–17 juin 1995*, Jean-Georges Heintz, 115–34. Paris, 1997.
Dus, Jan. "Die Geburtslegende Samuel 1 Sam. 1: Eine traditions-geschichtliche Untersuchung zu 1 Sam. 1–3." *RSO* 43 (1969): 163–94.
Ebeling, Erich. *Literarische Keilschrifttexte aus Assur*. Berlin: Akademie-Verlag, 1953.
Edelstein, Emma J., and Ludwig Edelstein. *Asclepius: A Collection and Interpretation of the Testimonies*. Baltimore, MD: Johns Hopkins Press, 1945.
Edwards, Mark W. "Homer and Oral Tradition: The Type-Scene." *Oral Tradition* 7 (1992): 284–330.
Edzard, Dietz O. *Gudea and His Dynasty*. Royal Inscriptions of Mesopotamia: Early Periods. Toronto: University of Toronto Press, 1997.
Ehelof, Hans. "Das Motif der Kindesunterschiebung in einer hethitischen Erzählung." *Orientalische Literaturzeitung* 29 (1926).
Ehrlich, Ernst L. *Der Traum im Alten Testament*. BZAW 73. Berlin: Töpelmann, 1953.
Eissfeldt, Otto. *Die Komposition der Samuelisbücher*. Leipzig: J. C. Hinrichs, 1931.
——. "Wahrsagung im Alten Testament." In *La divination en Mésopotamie ancienne et dans les régions voisines*, 141–46. Paris: Presses universitaires de France, 1966.
Eliade, Mircea. *Shamanism: Archaic Techniques of Ecstasy*. Translated by Willard R. Trask. London: Arkana, 1989.
Ellermeier, Friedrich. *Prophetie in Mari und Israel*. Theologische und Orientalistische Arbeiten 1. Herzberg: Verlag Erwin Jungfer, 1968.
Engnell, Ivan. *Studies in Divine Kingship in the Ancient Near East*. Oxford: Basil Blackwell, 1967.
Eslinger, Lyle M. *Kingship of God in Crisis*. Bible and Literature Series 10. Decatur, GA: Almond Press, 1985.
Evans, John D. *Malta*. London: Thames and Hudson, 1959.
Evans, Mary J. *1 and 2 Samuel*. NIBCOT. Peabody, MA: Hendrickson Publishers, 2000.

Fahd, Taufy. "Les songes et leur interprétation selon l'Islam." In *Les songes et leur interprétation*, edited by A.-M. Esnoul, 125–57. Paris: Édition du Seuil, 1959.

——. "Istikhāra." In *The Encyclopaedia of Israel*, 4:259–60. Leiden: Brill, 1978.

Falkenstein, A von. "Wahrsagung in der Sumerischen Überlieferung." In *La divination en mésopotamie ancienne et dans les régions voisines*, edited by F. Wendel, 45–68. Paris: Presses universitaires de France, 1966.

Fenik, Bernard. *Typical Battle Scenes in the Iliad: Studies in the Narrative Techniques of Homeric Battle Description*. Hermes 21. Wiesbaden: Franz Steiner Verlag GmbH, 1968.

Fensham, F. C. "Remarks on Certain Difficult Passages in Keret." *JNSL* 1 (1971): 11–22.

——. "Remarks on Keret 26–43." *JNSL* 2 (1972): 37–52.

——. "Remarks on Keret 59–72." *JNSL* 4 (1977): 11–21.

——. "Remarks on Keret 73–79." *JNSL* 6 (1979): 19–24.

——. "Remarks on Keret 79(b)–89 (CTA 14:2 79(b)–89)." *JNSL* 7 (1980): 17–25.

——. "Note on Keret in CTA 1-4:90–103a." *JNSL* 8 (1981): 35–47.

——. "Remarks on Keret 114b–136a (CTA 14:114b–136a)." *JNSL* 11 (1981): 69–78.

Fenton, T. L. "Comparative Evidence in Textual Study: M. Dahood on 2 Sam. I 21 and CTA 19 (1 Aqht), I, 44–45." *VT* 29 (1979): 162–70.

Ferngren, Gary B., and Darrel W. Amundsen. "Healing and Medicine: Healing and Medicine in Greece and Rome." In *Encyclopedia of Religion*, edited by Mircea Eliade. New York: Macmillan, 2005.

Finkel, Irving L. "The Dream of Kurigalzu and the Tablet of Sins." *AnSt* 33 (1983): 75–80.

Finkel, Joshua. "The Expedition of the Ugaritan King Keret in the Light of Jewish and Kindred Traditions." *PAAJR* 23 (1954): 1–28.

——. "A Mathematical Conundrum in the Ugaritic Keret Poem." *HUCA* 26 (1955): 109–49.

Finnegan, Ruth H. "How Oral is Oral Literature?" *BSOAS* 37 (1974): 52–64.

——. *Oral Poetry: Its Nature, Significance, and Social Context*. Cambridge: Cambridge University Press, 1977.

Fish, Stanley. *Is There a Text in This Class?: The Authority of Interpretive Communities*. Cambridge, MA: Harvard University Press, 1980.

Fishbane, Michael. "I Samuel 3: Historical Narrative and Narrative Poetics." In *Literary Interpretations of Biblical Narratives II*, edited by Gros Louis, 191–203. Nashville, TN: Abingdon, 1982.

Fisher, Loren R. "Two Projects at Claremont." *UF* 3 (1971): 25–32.

——. "Literary Genres in the Ugaritic Texts." In *Ras Shamra Parallels: The Texts from Ugarit and the Hebrew Bible*, vol. 2, edited by Loren R. Fisher, 131–51. Roma: Pontificium Institutum Biblicum, 1975.

Flannery-Dailey, Frances L. "Standing at the Heads of Dreamers: A Study of Dreams in Antiquity Second Temple Period." Ph.D. diss. University of Iowa, 2000.

Fohrer, Georg. *Introduction to the Old Testament*. Translated by David E. Green. Nashville, TN: Abingdon Press, 1968.

Fokkelman, J. P. *Vow and Desire (1 Sam. 1–12)*. Vol. IV of *Narrative Art and Poetry in the Books of Samuel: A Full Interpretation Based on Sylistic and Structural Analyses*. Assen: Van Gorcum, 1993.

Foley, John M. *The Theory of Oral Composition: History and Methodology*. Bloomington, IN: Indiana University Press, 1988.

——. *Traditional Oral Epic*. Berkeley: University of California Press, 1990.

——. *Immanent Art: From Structure to Meaning in Traditional Oral Epic*. Bloomington, IN: Indiana University Press, 1991.

Foster, Benjamin R. "Atra-Ḫasis." In *Canonical Compositions from the Biblical World*. Vol. I of *COS*, edited by William W. Hallo and K. Lawson Younger Jr., 450–51. Leiden: Brill, 1997.

——. *Before the Muses: An Anthology of Akkadian Literature*. Bethesda, MD: CDL Press, 2005.
Foucart, George. "Dream and Sleep (Egypt)." In *ERE: Vol. V*, vol. 5, edited by James Hastings, 34–37. Edinburgh: T. & T. Clark, 1922.
Freedman, D. N. "Counting Formulae." *JANESCU* 3 (1970–71): 65–81.
——. "The Broken Construct Chain." *Bib* 53 (1972): 534–36.
Friedrich, Johannes. "Churritische Sagen und Märchen in Hethitischn Sprache." *ZA* 49, no. 213–241 (1949).
Frye, Northrop. *Anatomy of Criticism*. Princeton, NJ: Princeton University Press, 1985.
Frymer-Kensky, Tikva. *Reading the Women of the Bible*. New York: Schocken Books, 2002.
Garsiel, Moshe. "Word Play and Puns as a Rhetorical Device in the Book of Samuel." In *Puns and Pundits: Word Play in the Hebrew Bible and Ancient Near Eastern Literature*, edited by Scott R. Noegel, 181–204. Bethesda, MD: CDL Press.
Gaster, Theodor H. *The Oldest Stories in the World*. Boston: Beacon Press, 1959.
——. *Thespis: Ritual, Myth, and Drama in the Ancient Near East*. New York: Harper, 1961.
——. "Dream in the Bible." In *Encyclopaedia Judaica*, vol. 6, edited by Fred Skolnik, 8–9. New York: Keter, 2007.
George, A. R. *The Babylonian Gilgamesh Epic: Introduction, Critical Edition, and Cuneiform Texts*. Oxford: Oxford University Press, 2003.
George, A. R., and F. N. H. Al-rawi. "Tablets from the Sippar Library VI. Atra-Ḫasīs." *Iraq* 58 (1996): 147–90.
Gesenius, Wilhelm. *Gesenius' Hebrew Grammar*. Oxford: Clarendon Press, 1910.
Gibson, J. C. L., ed. *Canaanite Myths and Legends*. Edinburgh: T. & T. Clark, 1978.
——. "Myth, Legend, and Folk-Lore in the Ugaritic Keret and Aqhat Texts." In *Congress Volume, Edinburgh 1974*. Leiden: Brill, 1975.
Ginsberg, Harold L. *The Legend of King Keret: A Canaanite Epic of the Bronze Age*. New Haven, CT: American Schools of Oriental Research, 1946.
——. "The Tale of Aqhat." In *ANET*, 149–55. Princeton, NJ: Princeton University Press, 1969.
Gnuse, Robert K. "The Dream Theophany of Samuel: Its Structure in Relation to Ancient Near Eastern Dreams and Its Theological Significance." Ph.D. diss. Nashville, TN: Vanderbilt University, 1980.
——. "A Reconsideration of the Form-Critical Structure in 1 Samuel 3: An Ancient Near Eastern Dream Theophany." *ZAW* 94 (1982): 379–90.
——. *Dreams and Dream Report in the Writings of Josephus: A Traditio-Historical Analysis*. Leiden: Brill, 1996.
Goetze, Albrecht. "Plague Prayers of Mursilis." In *ANET*, edited by James B. Prichard, 393–96. Princeton, NJ: Princeton University Press, 1969.
——. "Hittite Myths, Epic, and Legends." In *ANET*, edited by James B. Pritchard. 120–128, 1969.
Gordon, Cyrus H. "The Patriarchal Age." *JBR* 21 (1953): 238–43.
——. *Ugaritic Textbook*. AnOr 38. Roma: Pontificium Institutum Biblicum, 1965.
——. *Ugarit and Minoan Crete: The Bearing of Their Texts on the Origins of Western Culture*. New York: Norton and Company, 1966.
——. *Ugaritic Literature; a Comprehensive Translation of the Poetic and Prose Texts*. Scripta Pontificii Instituti Biblici 98. Roma: Pontificium Institutum Biblicum, 1949.
Gottlieb, H. "El und Krt-Jahwe und David." *VT* 24 (1974): 159–67.
Gössmann, P. F. *Planetarium Babylonicum oder Die Sumerisch-Babylonischen Stern-Namen*. Šumerisches Lexikon 4/2. Rome: Verlag des Päpstlichen Bibelinstitus, 1950.

Grabbe, Lester L. *Priests, Prophets, Diviners, Sages: A Socio-Historical Study of Religious Specialists in Ancient Israel.* Valley Forge, PA: Trinity Press International, 1995.
Graf, Fritz. "Incubation." In *Brill's New Pauly: Encyclopaedia of the Ancient World*, vol. 6, edited by Francis G. Gentry, 766–67. Leiden: Brill, 2006.
Gray, Bennison. "Repetition in Oral Literature." *Journal of American Folklore* 84 (1971): 289–303.
Gray, George B. *A Critical and Exegetical Commentary on the Book of Isaiah, I–XXXIX.* ICC. New York: C. Scribner's Sons, 1912.
Gray, John. "Canaanite Kingship in Theory and Practice." *VT* 2 (1952): 193–220.
——. *The Krt Text in the Literature of Ras Shamra: A Social Myth of Ancient Canaan.* DMOA 5. Leiden: Brill, 1955.
——. *The Legacy of Canaan: The Ras Shamra Texts and Their Relevance to the Old Testament.* Leiden: Brill, 1965.
Gray, Louis H. "Incubation." In *ERE: Vol. 7*, edited by James Hastings, 206–7. Edinburgh: T. & T. Clark, 1914.
Grayson, Albert K. *Babylonian Historical-Literary Texts.* Toronto: University of Toronto Press, 1975.
Grayson, Albert K., and W. G. Lambert. "Akkadian Prophecies." *JCS* 18 (1964): 7–30.
Green, Barbara. *How Are the Mighty Fallen? A Dialogical Study of King Saul in 1 Samuel.* JSOTSup 365. Sheffield: Sheffiled Academic Press, 2003.
Greenfield, Jonas C. "Studies in Aramaic Lexicography I." *JAOS* 82 (1962): 290–99.
——. "Some Glosses on the KRT Epic." *ErIsr* 9 (1969): 60–65.
——. "Aspects of Aramean Religion." In *Ancient Israelite Religion: Essays in Honor of Frank Moore Cross*, edited by Patrick D. Miller, Paul D. Hanson, and McBride S. Dean, 67–78. Philadelphia, PA: Fortress Press, 1987.
——. "The Epithets RBT//ṮRRT in the Krt Epic." In *Perspectives on Language and Text: Essays and Poems in Honor of Francis I. Andersen's Sixtieth Birthday*, E. Conrad and Newing E., Winona Lake, IN. 35–37: Eisenbrauns, 1987.
——. "Keret's Dream: 'Ḏhrt' and 'Hdrt'." *BSOAS* 57 (1994): 87–92.
Greenstein, Edward L. "One More Step on the Staircase." *UF* 9 (1977): 77–86.
——. "Kirta." In *Ugaritic Narrative Poetry*, edited by Simon B. Parker, 9–48. Atlanta, GA: Scholars Press, 1997.
Gunkel, Hermann. *The Folktale in the Old Testament.* Translated by Michael D. Rutter. Sheffield: Almond Press, 1987.
Gunn, Battiscombe. "The Decree of Amonrasonthēr for Neskhons." *JEA* 41 (1955): 83–105.
Gunn, David M. "The 'Battle Report': Oral or Scribal Convention?" *JBL* 93 (1974): 513–18.
——. "On Oral Tradition: A Presponse to John Van Seters." *Semeia* 5 (1976): 155–62.
Gurney, O. R., ed. *Middle Babylonian Legal Documents and Other Texts.* Vol. 7 of *Ur Excavation Texts.* London: British Museum Publications, 1974.
Gurney, O. R., and J. J. Finkelstein, eds. *The Sultantepe Tablets.* Occasional Publications of the British Institute of Archaeology at Ankara. London: British Institute of Archaeology at Ankara, 1957–64.
Güterbock, Hans G. "Die historische Tradition und ihre literarische Gestaltung bei Babyloniern und Hethitern bis 1200." *ZA* 44 (1937): 45–149.
——. *Kumarbi, Mythen vom Churritischen Kronos aus den Hethitischen Fragmenten Zusammengestellt, Ubers, und Erklart.* Istanbuler Schriften 16. Zurich-New York: Europaverlag, 1946.
——. "A Hurro-Hittite Hymn to Ishtar." *JAOS* 103 (1983): 155–64.
Halpern, Baruch. "Shiloh." In *ABD*, vol. 5, edited by David N. Freedman, 1213–15. New York: Doubleday, 1992.

Hamilton, Mary. *Incubation or The Cure of Disease in Pagan Temples and Christian Churches*. St. Andrews: W. C. Henderson & Son, 1906.
Haran, M. *Temples and Temple-Service in Ancient Israel*. Winona Lake, IN: Eisenbrauns, 1985.
Haran, Menahem. "Zebaḥ Hayyamīm." *VT* 19 (1969): 11–22.
Heimpel, Wolfgang. *Letters to the King of Mari*. Winona Lake, IN: Eisenbrauns, 2003.
Held, Moshe. "Mḫṣ/*Mḫš in Ugaritic and Other Semitic Language (A Study in Comparative Lexicography)." *JAOS* 79 (1959): 169–76.
Heller, Roy L. *Narrative Structure and Discourse Constellations: An Analysis of Clause Function in Biblical Hebrew Prose*. Winona Lake, IN: Eisenbrauns, 2004.
——. *Power, Politics, and Prophecy: The Character of Samuel and the Deuteronomistic Evaluation of Prophecy*. Library of Biblical Studies. New York: T. & T. Clark, 2006.
Hempfer, Klaus W. *Gattungstheorie: Information und Synthese*. München: W. Fink, 1973.
Herdner, Andrée. "La légende cananéenne d'Aqhat d'après les travaux récents." *Syria* 26 (1949): 1–16.
——. *Corpus des tablettes en cuneiformes alphabetiques decouvertes a Ras Shamra-Ugarit de 1929 à 1939*. Mission de Ras Shamra 10. Paris: Geuthner, 1963.
Hertzberg, Hans W. *I & II Samuel: A Commentary*. OTL. Philadelphia, PA: Westminster Press, 1964.
Hillers, D. R. "The Bow of Aqhat: The Meaning of a Mythological Theme." In *Orient and Occident: Essays Presented to Cyrus H. Gordon on the Occasion of His Sixth-Fifth Birthday*, edited by Harry A. Hoffner, 71–80. Neukirchen-Vluyn: Neukirchener Verlag, 1973.
Hirsch, Eric D. *Validity in Interpretation*. New Haven, CT: Yale University Press, 1967.
Hoffner, Harry A. "Appu and His Two Sons." In *Canonical Compositions from the Biblical World*. Vol. I of *COS*, edited by William W. Hallo, 153–54. Leiden: Brill, 1997.
Horowitz, Wayne. "The Akkadian Name for Ursa Minor: mul.mar.gíd.da.an.na = eriqqi šamê/šamāni." *ZA* 79 (1989): 242–44.
Hubert, Henri. *Sacrifice: Its Nature and Function*. Chicago: University of Chicago Press, 1964.
Huffmon, Herbert B. "Prophecy in the Mari Letters." *BA* 31 (1968): 101–24.
Hurowitz, Victor. *I Have Built You an Exalted House: Temple Building in the Bible in Light of Mesopotamian and Northwest Semitic Writings*. JSOTSup. Sheffield: Sheffield Academic Press, 1992.
Husser, Jean-Marie. *Le songe et la parole: Etude sur le rêve et sa fonction dans l'ancien Israël*. BZAW 210. Berlin: W. de Gruyter, 1994.
——. "The Birth of a Hero: Form and Meaning of KTU 1.17 i–ii." In *Ugarit, Religion and Culture: Essays Presented in Honour of Professor John C. L. Gibson*, edited by Nick Wyatt, Wilfred G. E. Watson, and Jeffrey B. Lloyd, 85–98. Münster: Ugarit-Verlag, 1996.
——. *Dreams and Dream Narratives in the Biblical World*. BS 63. Sheffield: Sheffield Academic Press, 1999.
Hutzli, Jürg. *Die Erzählung von Hanna und Samuel: Textkritische und literarische Anayse von 1. Samuel 1–2 unter Berüchsichtigung des Kontextes*. Zürich: Theologischer Verlag, 2007.
Hylander, I. *Der literarische Samuel-Saul-Komplex (1. Sam 1–15): Traditionsgeschichtlich Untersucht*. Uppsala: Almqvist & Wiksell, 1932.
Idel, M. *Kabbalah: New Perspectives*. New Haven, CT: Yale University Press, 1988.

Irvin, Dorothy. *Mytharion: The Comparison of Tales from the Old Testament and the Ancient Near East.* AOAT 32. Neukirchen-Vluyn: Neukirchener Verlag, 1978.
Irwin, Lee. *The Dream Seekers: Native American Visionary Traditions of the Great Plains.* Norman: University of Oklahoma Press, 1994.
Iser, Wolfgang. *The Act of Reading: A Theory of Aesthetic Response.* Baltimore, MD: Johns Hopkins University Press, 1980.
Izzet, Vedia. "Sacred Times and Spaces: Greece." In *Religions of the Ancient World: A Guide*, edited by Sarah I. Johnston, 266–72. Cambridge, MA: Belknap Press, 2004.
Jackson, Jared J., and Harold H. P. Dressler. "El and the Cup of Blessing." *JAOS* 95 (1975): 99–101.
Jacobsen, Thorkild. "The Stele of the Vultures Col I–X." In *Kramer Anniversary Volume: Cuneiform Studies in Honor of Samuel Noah Kramer*, edited by Barry L. Eichler, 247–60. Kevelaer: Butzon & Bercker, 1976.
——. *The Harps That Once...:Sumerian Poetry in Translation.* New Haven, CT: Yale University Press, 1987.
Jastrow, Morris. *The Religion of Babylonia and Assyria.* Boston: Ginn & Company, 1898.
Jayne, Walter A. *The Healing Gods of Ancient Civilizations.* New Haven, CT: Yale University Press, 1925.
Jeffers, Ann. *Magic and Divination in Ancient Palestine and Syria.* SHCANE 8. Leiden: Brill, 1996.
Jeremias, Jörg. *Theophanie: Die Geschichte einer alttestamentlichen Gattung.* Neukirchen-Vluyn: Neukirchener Verlag, 1977.
Jirku, Anton. "Ein Fall von Inkubation im Alten Testament." *ZAW* 33 (1913): 151–52.
——. *Kanaanäische Mythen und Epen aus Ras Schamra-Ugarit.* Gütersloh: Gerd Mohn, 1962.
Jobling, David. *1 Samuel.* Berit Olam. Collegeville, MN: The Liturgical Press, 1998.
Joosten, Jan. "Workshop: Meaning and Use of the Tenses in 1 Samuel 1." In *Narrative Syntax and the Hebrew Bible*, edited by Ellen van Wolde. Brill: Leiden, 1997.
Joüon, Paul. *A Grammar of Biblical Hebrew.* Translated and edited by Muraoka T. Roma: Pontificio Istituto Biblico, 2003.
Kaiser, Otto. *Introduction to the Old Testament.* Translated by John Sturdy. Oxford: Basil Blackwell, 1975.
Kaufmann, Yehezkel. *The Religion of Israel.* Chicago: University of Chicago Press, 1960.
Keil, Carl F. *Commentary on the Books of Kings.* Edinburgh: T. & T. Clark, 1867.
Kenik, Helen A. *Design for Kingship: The Deuteronomistic Narrative Technique in 1 Kings 3:4–15.* SBLDS 69. Chico, California: Scholars Press, 1983.
Kirkpatrick, Patricia G. *The Old Testament and Folklore Study.* JSOTSup 62. Sheffield: JSOT Press, 1988.
Klein, Lillian R. "Hannah: Marginalized Victim and Social Redeemer." In *A Feminist Companion to Samuel and Kings*, 77–92. Sheffield: Sheffield Academic Press, 1994.
Knierim, Rolf. "Old Testament Criticism Reconsidered." *Int* 27 (1973): 435–68.
Knohl, Israel. "Between Voice and Silence: The Relationship Between Prayer and Temple Cult." *JBL* 115 (1996): 17–30.
Knopper, Gary N. "Dissonance and Disaster in the Legend of Kirta." *JAOS* 114 (1994): 572–82.
Knowles, Melody D. *Centrality Practiced: Jerusalem in the Religious Practice of Yehud and the Diaspora in the Persian Period.* Atlanta, GA: Society of Biblical Literature, 2006.
Koehler, Ludwig, and Walter Baumgartner. *The Hebrew and Aramaic Lexicon of the Old Testament.* Subsequently revised by Walter Baumgartner and Johann Jakob Stamm. Leiden: Brill, 1994–2000.

Köckert, Matthias, and Martti Nissinen. *Propheten in Mari, Assyrien und Israel*. Forschungen zur Religion und Literatur des Alten und Neuen Testaments 201. Göttingen: Vandenhoeck & Ruprecht, 2003.
Köhler, Ludwig H. *Old Testament Theology*. Translated by A. S. Todd. Philadelphia, PA: Westminster Press, 1957.
Kramer, Samuel N. *The Sacred Marriage Rite: Aspects of Faith, Myth, and Ritual in Ancient Sumer*. Bloomington, IN: Indiana University Press, 1969.
Kraus, F. R. "Mittelbabylonisch Opferschauprotokolle." *JCS* 37 (1985): 127–218.
Kruger, P. A. "Some Further Indicators of Rank Symbolism in Baal Epic." *UF* 27 (1995): 169–76.
Kugel, James L. *The Idea of Biblical Poetry: Parallelism and Its History*. Baltimore, MD: Johns Hopkins University Press, 1981.
——. *The Bible as It Was*. Cambridge, MA: Harvard University Press, 1997.
——. *How to Read the Bible: A Guide to Scripture, Then and Now*. New York: Free Press, 2007.
Lambdin, Thomas O. *Introduction to Biblical Hebrew*. New York: Charles Scribner's Sons, 1971.
Lambert, W. G. *Babylonian Wisdom Literature*. Oxford: Clarendon Press, 1960.
Landy, Francis. "Ruth and the Romance of Realism, or Deconstructing History." *JAAR* 62 (1994): 285–317.
Lane, Edward W. *An Arabic-English Lexicon*. Beirut: Librairie du Liban, 1968.
Langdon, Stephen. *Die neubabylonischen Königsinschriften*. Leipzig: J. C. Hinrichs, 1912.
Lebrun, René. *Hymnes et prières hittites*. Homo Religiosus 4. Louvain-la-Neuve: Centre d'histoire des religions, 1980.
Lecerf, Jean. "The Dream in Popular Culture: Arabic and Islamic." In *The Dream and Human Societies*, edited by Gustave E. Von Grunebaum and Roger Caillois, 365–79. Berkeley: University of California Press, 1966.
Leimbach, Karl A. *Die Bücher Samuel*. Die heilige Schrift des alten Testamentes. Bonn: Peter Hanstein Verlag, 1936.
Lentricchia, Frank. *After the New Criticism*. Chicago: University of Chicago Press, 1980.
Levine, Baruch A. "An Aramaic Dream Report From Elephantine." In *Archival Documents from the Biblical World*. Vol. III of *COS*, edited by William W. Hallo and K. Lawson Younger Jr., 218. Leiden: Brill, 2002.
Lewis, Naphtali. *The Interpretation of Dreams and Portents*. Toronto: Samuel Stevens Hakkert, 1976.
Lichtenstein, Murray. "Dream Theophany and the E Document." *JANESCU* I/2 (1969): 45–54.
——. "A Note on the Text of I Keret." *JANESCU* 2 (1969): 92–100.
Lichtheim, Miriam. *The Late Period*. Vol. III of *Ancient Egyptian Literature: A Book of Readings*, 1980.
LiDonnici, Lynn R. *The Epidaurian Miracle Inscriptions*. SBLTT 36. Atlanta, GA: Scholars Press, 1995.
Lindblom, Johannes. "Theophanies in Holy Places in Hebrew Religion." *HUCA* 32 (1961): 91–106.
Lipton, Diana. *Revisions of the Night: Politics and Promises in the Patriarchal Dreams of Genesis*. JSOTSup 288. Sheffield: Sheffield Academic Press, 1999.
Lloyd, Jeffrey B. "The Banquet Theme in Ugaritic Narrative." *UF* 22 (1990): 169–94.
Loewenstamm, Samuel E. "The Seven-Day-Unit in Ugaritic Epic Literature." *IEJ* 15 (1965): 121–33.
——. "Zur Götterlehre des Epos von Keret." *UF* 11 (1979): 505–14.
——. *Comparative Studies in Biblical and Ancient Oriental Literatures*. Neukirchen-Vluyn: Neukirchener Verlag, 1980.

——. *Comparative Studies in Biblical and Ancient Oriental Literatures*. Neukirchen-Vluyn: Neukirchener Verlag, 1980.
Long, Burke O. "The Effect of Divination Upon Israelite Literature." *JBL* 92 (1973): 489–97.
——. "Recent Field Studies in Oral Literature and Their Bearing on OT Criticism." *VT* 26 (1976): 187–98.
Long, Philip. "First and Second Samuel." In *A Complete Literary Guide to the Bible*, edited by Ryken Leland and Tremper Longman III. Grand Rapids, MI: Zondervan, 1993.
Longman III, Tremper. *Literary Approaches to Biblical Interpretation*. Foundations of Contemporary Interpretation 3. Grand Rapids, MI: Academie Books, 1987.
——. *Fictional Akkadian Autobiography: A Generic and Comparative Study*. Winona Lake, IN: Eisenbrauns, 1991.
Lord, Albert B. "Homer and Huso II: Narrative Inconsistencies in Homer and Oral Poetry." *TAPA 69* (1938), 439–45.
——. *The Singer of Tales*. Harvard Studies in Comparative Literature. Cambridge, MA: Harvard University Press, 1960.
——. "Perspectives on Recent Work on Oral Literature." *Forum for Modern Language Studies* 10 (1974): 187–210.
Lowery, Jenny M. "The Form and Function of Symbolic Vision Reports in the Hebrew Bible." Ph.D. diss. The Southern Baptist Theological Seminary, 1999.
Luckenbill, Daniel D. *Historical Records of Assyria from Sargon to the End*. Vol. II of *Ancient Records of Assyria and Babylonia*. Chicago: University of Chicago Press, 1927.
Lutz, H. F. "A Cassite Liver-Omen Text." *JAOS* 38 (1918): 77–96.
Maguire, Jack. *Night and Day*. New York: Simon & Schuster, 1989.
Mailloux, Steven. *Interpretive Conventions: The Reader in the Study of American Fiction*. Ithaca: Cornell University Press, 1982.
Mallet, Dominique. *Le Kasr el-Agoûz*. Le Caire: L'institut français d'archéologie orientale, 1909.
Margalit, Baruch. "Studia Ugaritica II: Studies in *Krt* and *Aqht*." *UF* 8 (1976): 137–92.
——. *A Matter of "Life" and "Death": A Study of the Baal-Mot Epic (CTA 4-5-6)*. AOAT 206. Kevelaer: Butzon und Bercker; Neukirchen-Vluyn: Neukirchener Verlag, 1980.
——. *The Ugaritic Poem of Aqht: Text, Translation, Commentary*. BZAW 182. New York: De Gruyter, 1989.
——. "The Legend of Keret." In *Handbook of Ugaritic Studies*, edited by Wilfred G. E. Watson and Nick Wyatt, 203–33. Leiden: Brill, 1999.
Maspero, Gaston. *Popular Stories of Ancient Egypt*. Translated by A. S. Johns. New York: University Books, 1967.
McAlpine, Thomas H. *Sleep, Divine & Human, in the Old Testament*. JOSTSup 38. Sheffield: JSOT Press, 1987.
McCarter, P. Kyle. *1 Samuel: A New Translation*. Garden City, N.Y.: Doubleday, 1980.
Meier, Carl A. "The Dream in Ancient Greece and Its Use in Temple Cures (Incubation)." In *The Dream and Human Societies*, edited by Gustave E. Von Grunebaum and Roger Caillois, 303–19. Berkeley: University of California Press, 1966.
——. *Ancient Incubation and Modern Psychotherapy*. Evanston: Northwestern University Press, 1967.
Mendelsohn, Isaac. "Dream." In *The Interpreter's Dictionary of the Bible*, vol. 1, edited by George A. Buttrick, 868–69. Nashville, TN: Abingdon Press, 1961.
Merrill, Arthur L. "The House of Keret: A Study of the Keret Legend." *SEÅ*, no. 33 (1968): 5–17.

Meyers, Carol. "Hannah and Her Sacrifice: Reclaiming Female Agency." In *A Feminist Companion to Samuel and Kings*, 93–104. Sheffield: Sheffield Academic Press, 1994.

——. "An Ethnoarchaeological Analysis of Hannah's Sacrifice." In *Pomegranates Golden Bells: Studies in Biblical, Jewish, and Near Eastern Ritual, Law and Literature in Honor of Jacob Milgrom*, edited by David P. Wright, Freedman David N., and Hurvitz Avi, 77–92. Winona Lake, IN: Eisenbrauns, 1995.

Métraux, Alfred. "Le shamanisme chez les Indiens de l'Amérique du Sud tropicale." In *Acta Americana*, edited and translated by Jeremy Narby and Francis Huxley, 197–219 and 320–41. Los Angeles, 1944.

Milgrom, Jacob. *Numbers [Ba-Midbar]: The Traditional Hebrew Text with the New JPS Translation, Commentary by Jacob Milrom*. Philadelphia, PA: Jewish Publication Society, 1990.

Miller, Cynthia L. "Patterns of Verbal Ellipsis in Ugaritic Poetry." *UF* 31 (1999): 333–72.

Miscall, Peter D. *1 Samuel: A Literary Reading*. Indiana Studies in Biblical Literature. Bloomington, IN: Indiana University Press, 1986.

Moor, J. C. de. "The Crisis of Polytheism in Late Bronze Ugarit." *OtSt* 24 (1986): 1–20.

——. *An Anthology of Religious Texts from Ugarit*. Nisaba 16. Leiden: Brill, 1987.

——. "The Art of Versification in Ugariti and Israel II: The Formal Structure." *UF* 10 (1978): 187–217.

——. "Contributions to the Ugaritic Lexicon." *UF* 11 (1979): 639–53.

Moor, J. C. de, and K. Spronk. "Problematical Passages in the Legend of Kirtu (I)." *UF* 14 (1982): 153–71.

Moore, G. Foot. *History of Religions*. New York: Charles Scribner's Sons, 1922.

Moran, William L. "New Evidence from Mari on the History of Prophecy." *Bib* 50 (1969): 15–86.

Mouton, Alice. "Usages privés et publics de l'incubation d'après les textes hittites." *JANER* 3 (2003): 73–91.

——. *Rêves hittites*. CHANE 28. Leiden: Brill, 2007.

Muilenburg, James. "Form Criticism and Beyond." *JBL* 88 (1969): 1–18.

Mullen, E. Theodore. *The Divine Council in Canaanite and Early Hebrew Literature*. HSM 24. Chico, Calif.: Scholars Press, 1980.

Nagler, Michael. *Spontaneity and Tradition: A Study in the Oral Art of Homer*. Berkeley: University of California Press, 1974.

——. "Towards a Generative View of the Oral Formula." *TAPA 98* (1967), 269–311.

Neff, Robert W. "The Announcement in Old Testament Birth Stories." Ph.D. diss. Yale University, 1969.

Neufeld, Edward. "Apiculture in Ancient Palestine (Early and Middle Age) Within the Framework of the Ancient Near East." *UF* 10 (1978): 219–47.

Niditch, Susan. *Oral World and Written Word: Ancient Israelite Literature*. Louisville, KY: Westminster John Knox Press, 1996.

Noegel, Scott B. "Dream and Ideology of Mantics: Homer and Ancient Near Eastern Oneiromancy." In *Ideologies as Intercultural Phenomena: Proceedings of the Assyrian and Babylonian Intellectual Heritage Project*, 143–57. Helsinki: Neo-Assyrian text Corpus Project, 2000.

——. *Nocturnal Ciphers: The Allusive Language of Dreams in the Ancient Near East*. AOS 89. New Haven, CT: American Oriental Society, 2007.

Noort, Edward. *Untersuchungen zum Gottesbescheid in Mari*. AOAT 202. Neukirchen-Vluyn: Neukirchener Verlag, 1977.

Nougayrol, J. *Textes accadiens des archives sud*. PRU IV. Paris: Impr. nationale, 1970.

Nowack, W. *Richter, Ruth und Bücher Samuelis*. Göttingen: Vandenhoeck und Ruprecht, 1902.
Oates, D. "Balawat (Imgur Enlil): The Site and Its Buildings." *Iraq* 36, no. 173–178 (1974).
Obermann, Julian. *How Daniel Was Blessed with a Son*. Suppl. to JAOS 6. Baltimore, MD: American Oriental Society, 1946.
Olmo Lete, Gregorio del. "Notes on Ugaritic Semantics I." *UF* 7 (1975): 89–102.
——. *Mitos y leyendas de Canaan: según la tradición de Ugarit*. Fuentes de la ciencia bíblica 1. Madrid Valencia: Ediciones Cristianidad Institución San Jerónimo, 1981.
——. *Canaanite Religion*. Winona Lake, IN: Eisenbrauns, 2004.
Olmo Lete, Gregorio del, and Joaquín Sanmartín. *A Dictionary of the Ugaritic Language in the Alphabetic Tradition*. Handbook of Oriental Studies 67. Leiden: Brill, 2003.
Olrik, Axel. "Epische Gesetze der Volksdichtung." *Zeitschrift für Deutsches Altertum* 51 (1909): 1–12.
Ong, Walter J. *Orality and Literacy: The Technologizing of the Word*. London: Routledge, 1982.
Oppenheim, A. Leo. *The Interpretation of Dreams in the Ancient Near East: With a Translation of an Assyrian Dream-Book*. TAPA 46, 179–373. Philadelphia, PA: American Philological Society, 1956.
Pardee, Dennis. "An Emendation in the Ugaritic Aqht Text." *JNES* 36 (1977): 53–56.
——. "The New Canaanite Myths and Legends." *BO* 37 (1980): 269–91.
——. "Ugaritic and Hebrew Metrics." In *Ugarit in Retrospect: Fifty Years of Ugarit and Ugaritic*, edited by Douglas Y. Gordon, 113–30. Winona Lake, IN: Eisenbrauns, 1981.
——. "Ugaritic: The Ugaritic Šumma Izbu Text." *AfO* 33 (1986): 117–47.
——. *Ugaritic and Hebrew Poetic Parallelism: A Trial Cut (ʿNt I and Proverbs 2)*. VTSup 39. Leiden: Brill, 1988.
——. "The Aqhatu Legend." In *Canonical Compositions from the Biblical World*. Vol. I of *COS*, edited by William W. Hallo and K. Lawson Younger Jr., 343–56. Leiden: Brill, 1997.
——. "The Baʿ Lu Myth." In *Canonical Compositions from the Biblical World*. Vol. I of *COS*, edited by William W. Hallo and K. Lawson Younger Jr., 241–73. Leiden: Brill, 1997.
——. "The Kirta Epic." In *Canonical Compositions from the Biblical World*. Vol. I of *COS*, edited by William W. Hallo and K. Lawson Younger Jr., 333–42. Leiden: Brill, 1997.
——. "Kosharoth." In *Dictionary of Deities and Demons in the Bible*, edited by Karel van der Toorn, 491–92. Leiden: Brill, 1999.
——. *Les textes rituels: fascicule 1: Chapitres 1–53*. RSOu XII. Paris: Éditions Recherche sur les Civilisations, 2000.
——. "Review." Ugaritische Grammatik. Josef Tropper. *AfO* Online Version 50 (2003/2004): 1–404.
Parker, Simon B., trans. "Aqhat." In *Ugaritic Narrative Poetry*, edited by Simon B. Parker, 49–80. Atlanta, GA: Scholars Press, 1997.
——. "The Historical Composition of KRT and the Cult of El." *ZAW* 89 (1977): 161–75.
——. "Some Methodological Principles in Ugaritic Philology." *Maarav* 2 (1979): 7–41.
——. "The Vow in Ugaritic and Israelite Narrative Literature." *UF* 11 (1979): 693–700.
——. "The Birth Announcement." In *Ascribe to the Lord: Biblical Studies in Memory of Peter C. Craigie*, edited by Lyle Eslinger and Glen Taylor. Journal for the Study

of the Old Testament Supplement Series 67, 133–49. Sheffield: Sheffield Academic Press, 1988.
——. *The Pre-Biblical Narrative Tradition: Essays on the Ugaritic Poems Keret and Aqhat*. SBLRBS 24. Atlanta, GA: Scholars Press, 1989.
Parry, Adam, ed. *The Making of Homeric Verse: The Collected Papers of Milman Parry*. Oxford: Clarendon Press, 1971.
Parry, Milman. "Review of Walter Arend, 'Die Typischen Scenen bei Homer'." *Classical Philology* 31 (1936): 357–60.
Patton, Kimberley C. "A Great and Strange Correction: Intentionality, Locality, and Epiphany in the Category of Dream Incubation." *HR* 43 (2004): 194–223.
Pedersen, Johannes. "Die KRT-Legende." *Ber* 6 (1941): 63–105.
——. *Israel: Its Life and Culture*. Vol. II. Atlanta, GA: Scholars Press, 1991.
——. *Israel: Its Life and Culture*. Vol. I. Atlanta, GA: Scholars Press, 1991.
Person, Raymond F. *Second Zechariah and the Deuteronomic School*. JSOT. Sheffield, England: JSOT Press, 1993.
Petrie, W. M. Flinders. *Personal Religion in Egypt Before Christianity*. Harper's Library of Living Thought. London: Harper & Brothers, 1912.
Petrovich, Avvakum. *La vie de l'Archprêtre Avaakum, ecrite par lui-même*. Translated by Pierre Pascal. Paris: Galimard, 1938.
Pietersma, Albert, and Benjamin G. Wright, eds. *A New English Translation of the Septuagint*. Oxford: Oxford University Press, 2007.
Poland, Lynn. "Review: Defending Biblical Poetics." *JR* 68 (1988): 426–34.
Polzin, Robert. *Samuel and the Deuteronomist: A Literary Study of the Deuteronomic History*. New York: Harper & Row, 1989.
Pope, Marvin H. *Song of Songs: A New Translation with Introduction and Commentary*. AB 7C. Garden City, N.Y.: Doubleday, 1977.
——. "An Arabic Cognate for Ugaritic Brlt?" *UF* 13 (1981): 305–6.
——. "The Cult of the Dead in Ugarit." In *Ugarit in Retrospect: Fifty Years of Ugarit and Ugaritic*, edited by Gordon D. Young, 159–79. Winona Lake, IN: Eisenbrauns, 1981.
Preminger, Alex, and T. V. F. Brogan, eds. *The New Princeton Encyclopedia of Poetry and Poetics*. New York: MJF Books, 1993.
Pritchard, James B. *The Ancient Near East in Pictures Relating to the Old Testament*. Princeton, NJ: Princeton University Press, 1954.
——. *ANES*. Princeton, NJ: Princeton University Press, 1954.
Quirke, Stephen. *Ancient Egyptian Religion*. London: British Museum Press, 1992.
Ray, J. D. *The Archive of Hor*. London: Egypt Exploration Society, 1976.
Redford, Donald, ed. *The Oxford Encyclopedia of Ancient Egypt*. New York: Oxford University Press, 2001.
Reece, Steve. *The Stranger's Welcome: Oral Theory and the Aesthetics of the Homeric Hospitality Scene*. Michigan Monographs in Classical Antiquity. Ann Arbor, MI: University of Michigan Press, 1993.
Reiner, Erica. "Fortune-Telling in Mesopotamia." *JNES* 19 (1960): 23–35.
——. "Dead of Night." In *Studies in Honor of Benno Landsberger on His Seventy-Fifth Birthday*, edited by Hans G. Güterbock and Jacobsen Thorkild, 247–51. Chicago: University of Chicago Press, 1965.
——. "Die akkadische Literature." In *Altorientalische Literaturen*, von Wolfgang Röllig, 176–80. Wiesbaden: Akademische Verlagsgesellschaft Athenaion, 1978.
——. *Astral Magic in Babylonia*. TAPA 85. Philadelphia, PA: American Philosophical Society, 1995.
Renfroe, Fred. "The Transition from 'Army' to 'Enemy'." *UF* 19 (1987): 231–34.
——. *Arabic-Ugaritic Lexical Studies*. ALASP 5. Munster: UGARIT-Verlag, 1992.
Resch, Andreas. *Der Traum im Heilsplan Gottes: Deutung und Bedeutung des Traums im Alten Testament*. Freiburg: Herder, 1964.

Richter, Wolfgang. *Exegese als Literaturwissenschaft: Entwurf einer alttestamentlichen Literaturtheorie und Methodologie.* Göttingen: Vandenhoeck & Ruprecht, 1971.

Ritner, Robert K. "Dream Books." In *The Oxford Encyclopedia of Ancient Egypt*, vol. 1, edited by Donald B. Redford, 410–11. Oxford: Oxford University Press, 2001.

Robinson, Margaret G. "Dreams in the Old Testament." Ph.D. diss. Manchester University, 1987.

Roche, Carole. "The Lady of Ugarit." *NEA* 63 (2000): 214–15.

Rosalie, David A. *Religion and Magic in Ancient Egypt.* London: Penguin Books, 2002.

Rosenbaum, Stanley N. *Understanding Biblical Israel: A Reexamination of the Origins of Monotheism.* Macon, GA: Mercer University Press, 2002.

Rosenberger, Veit. *Griechische Orakel: eine Kulturgeschichte.* Darmstadt: Wissenschaftliche Buchgesellschaft, 2001.

Rossi, Andreola F. "Battle-Scenes in Virgil: An Analysis of Narrative Techniques." Harvard University, 1997.

Sasson, Jack M. "Literary Criticism, Folklore Scholarship, and Ugaritic Literature." In *Ugarit Retrospect: Fifty Years of Ugarit and Ugaritic*, Douglas Y. Gordon, 81–98. Winona Lake, IN: Eisenbrauns, 1981.

——. "Mari Dreams." *JAOS* 103 (1983): 283–93.

——. "The Numeric Progression in Keret I: 15–20: Yet Another Suggestion." *SEL* 5 (1988): 181–88.

Sauneron, Serge. "Les songes et leurs interprétation dans l'Égypte ancienne." *SO* 2 (1959): 17–61.

Sauren, H., and G. Kestemont. "Keret, Roi de Ḫubur." *UF* 3 (1971): 181–222.

Sawyer, J., and J. Strange. "Notes on the Keret-Text." *IEJ* 14 (1964): 96–98.

Schloen, J. David. *The House of the Father as Fact and Symbol: Patrimonialism in Ugarit and the Ancient Near East.* Studies in the Archaeology and History of the Levant. Winona Lake, IN: Eisenbrauns, 2001.

Schulz, Alfons. "Narrative Art in the Books of Samuel." In *Narrative and Novella in Samuel*, edited by David M. Gunn, 119–70. Sheffield: Sheffield Academic Press, 1991.

Seow, Choon Leong. "The Syro-Palestinian Context of Solomon's Dream." *HTR* 77 (1984): 141–52.

Shafton, Anthony. *Dream Reader: Contemporary Approaches to the Understanding of Dreams.* New York: State University of New York Press, 1995.

Smith, George. *History of Assurbanipal : Translated from the Cuneiform Inscriptions.* London: Williams and Norgate, 1871.

Smith, Henry P. *The Books of Samuel.* ICC. Skokie, IL: Varda Books, 2005.

Smith, Mark S. *The Ugaritic Baal Cycle.* VTSup 55. Leiden: Brill, 1994.

Spronk, Klaas. "The Legend of Kirtu (KTU 1.14–16): A Study of the Structure and Its Consequences for Interpretation." In *The Structural Analysis of Biblical and Canaanite Poetry*, Willem van der Meer and Johannes C. de Moor, 62–83. Sheffield: Sheffield Academic Press, 1988.

Srejović, Dragoslav. "Neolithic Religion." In *Encyclopedia of Religion*, edited by Mircea Eliade, 6459–66. New York: Macmillan, 1987.

Sternberg, Meir. *The Poetics of Biblical Narrative Ideological Literature and the Drama of Reading.* Bloomington, IN: Indiana University Press, 1985.

Strabo. *Geography.* Translated and edited by Amédée Tardieu. Paris: Hachette, 1867.

Suter, Claudia E. *Gudea's Temple Building: The Representation of an Early Mesopotamian Ruler in Text and Image.* Cuneiform Monographs 17. Groningen: Styx Publications, 2000.

Sweeney, Marvin A. "Form Criticism." In *To Each Its Own Meaning: The Introduction to Biblical Criticisms and Their Application*, edited by Steven L. McKenzie and Stephen R. Haynes, 58–89. Louisville, KY: Westminster John Knox Press, 1999.

Sweeney, Marvin A., and Ehud Ben Zvi, eds. *The Changing Face of Form Criticism for the Twenty-First Century*. Grand Rapids, MI: Eerdmans, 2003.
Tedlock, Barbara. "Sharing and Interpreting Dreams in Amerindian Nations." In *Dream Cultures: Explorations in the Comparative History of Dreaming*, edited by David Shulman and Guy G. Stroumsa. New York: Oxford University Press, 1999.
Thrämer, Eduard. "Health and Gods of Healing." In *ERE: Vol. VI*, edited by James Hastings, 6:540–56. New York: Charles Scribner's Sons, 1908.
Todorov, Tzvetan. *The Fantastic: A Structural Approach to a Literary Genre*. Ithaca: Cornell University Press, 1975.
Toorn, Karel van der. *Family Religion in Babylonia, Syria, and Israel: Continuity and Changes in the Forms of Religious Life*. SHCANE 7. Leiden: Brill, 1996.
Trible, Phyllis. *God and the Rhetoric of Sexuality*. Philadelphia, PA: Fortress Press, 1978.
——. *Rhetorical Criticism: Context, Method, and the Book of Jonah*. Minneapolis: Fortress Press, 1994.
Tropper J., and Verreet E. "Ugaritische NDY, YDY, HDY, NDD und D(W)D." *UF* 20 (1988): 339–50.
Tropper, Josef. "Die sieben Frauen des Königs Keret." *UF* 27 (1995): 529–32.
——. "Ugaritic Dreams: Notes on Ugaritic Ḏ(h)Rt and Hdrt." In *Ugarit, Religion and Culture: Essays Presented in Honour of Professor John C. L. Gibson*, edited by Nick Wyatt, Wilfred G. E. Watson, and Jeffery B. Lloyd. Ugaritisch-biblische Literatur 12, 305–13. Münster: Ugarit-Verlag, 1996.
——. "Ugaritisch *šqy*: 'trinken' oder 'tränken'?" *Or* 58 (1989): 233–42.
——. *Ugaritische Grammatik*. AOAT 273. Münster: Ugarit-Verlag, 2000.
Tsevat, Matitiahu. "The Canaanite God Šälaḥ." *VT* 4 (1954): 41–49.
Tsumura, David T. "The Problem of Childlessness in the Royal Epic of Ugarit: An Analysis of KRT[KTU 1.14I]:1–25." In *Monarchies and Socio-Religious Traditions in the Ancient Near East*, edited by Prince T. Mikasa. Bulletin of the Middle Eastern Culture Center in Japan 1, 11–20. Wiesbaden: Otto Harrassowitz, 1984.
——. *The First Book of Samuel*. Grand Rapids, MI: Eerdmans, 2007.
Tucker, Gene. *Form Criticism of the Old Testament*. Philadelphia, PA: Fortress Press, 1971.
Van Dam, Cornelis. *The Urim and Thummim: A Means of Revelation in Ancient Israel*. Winona Lake, IN: Eisenbrauns, 1997.
Van der Merwe, Christo. "Workshop: Text Linguistics and the Structure of 1 Samuel 1." In *Narrative Syntax and the Hebrew Bible*, edited by Ellen van Wolde. Brill: Leiden, 1997.
Van de Mieroop, Marc. *A History of the Ancient Near East, Ca. 3000–323 B.C.* Blackwell History of the Ancient World. Malden, MA: Blackwell Pub., 2004.
Van Selms, A. *Marriage & Family Life in Ugaritic Literature*. London: Luzac & Company, 1954.
Van Seters, John. "The Conquest of Sihon's Kingdom: A Literary Examination." *JBL* 91 (1972): 182–97.
——. *Abraham in History and Tradition*. New Haven, CT: Yale University Press, 1975.
——. "Oral Patterns or Literary Conventions in Biblical Narrative." *Semeia* 5 (1976): 139–52.
Vater, Ann M. "Story Patterns for a Sitz." *JSOT* 11 (1979): 47–56.
Vaux, Roland de. *Ancient Israel: Its Life and Institutions*. Translated by John McHugh. New York: McGraw-Hill Book Company, 1961.
——. *The Early History of Israel*. David Smith. Philadelphia, PA: Westminster Press, 1978.
Verreet, Eddy. "Der Keret-Prolog." *UF* 19 (1987): 317–35.
Vervenne, M. "Hebrew Šālîš—Ugaritic Ṯlṯ." *UF* 19 (1987): 375–90.

Virolleaud, C. *La légende phénicienne de Danel*. Mission de Ras-shamra 1. Paris: Geuthner, 1936.
——. *La légende phénicienne de Keret, roi de Sidoniens*. Mission de Ras-shamra 2. Paris: Geuthner, 1936.
Volten, Aksel. *Das demotische Weisheitsbuch, Studien und Bearbeitung*. AAeg 2. Kopenhagen: E. Munksgaard, 1941.
Von Soden, Wolfram. *Akkadisches Handwörterbuch*. Wiesbaden: Ott Harrassowitz, 1965.
Vriezen, Theodorus C. *The Religion of Ancient Israel*. Philadelphia, PA: Westminster Press, 1967.
Walker, C. B. F., ed. *Miscellaneous Texts*. Vol. 51 of *Cuneiform Texts from Babylonian Tablets in the British Museum*. London: Trustees of the British Museum, 1972.
Wallis, W. D. "Prodigies and Portents." In *ERE: Vol. X*, edited by James Hastings. Edinburgh: T. & T. Clark, 1914.
Walters, Stanley. "The Greek and Hebrew Texts of 1 Samuel 1." *JBL* 107 (1988): 385–412.
——. "Hannah and Anna: The Greek and Hebrew Texts of 1 Samuel 1." *JBL* 107 (1988): 385–412.
Waltke, Bruce K., and M. O'Connor. *An Introduction to Biblical Hebrew Syntax*. Winona Lake, IN: Eisenbrauns, 1990.
Walton, Alice. *The Cult of Asklepios*. CSCP 3. Ithaca: Cornell University Press, 1894.
Walton, John H. *Ancient Near Eastern Thought and the Old Testament: Introducing the Conceptual World of the Hebrew Bible*. Grand Rapids, MI: Baker Academic, 2006.
Ward, William A. "Two Unrecognized Ḫupšu-Mercenaries in Egyptian Texts." *UF* 12 (1980): 441–42.
Watson, Wilfred G. E. "Puzzling Passages in the Tale of Aqhat." *UF* 8 (1976): 371–78.
——. "An Unrecognized Hyperbole in Krt." *Or* 48 (1979): 112–17.
——. *Classical Hebrew Poetry: A Guide to Its Techniques*. JSOTSup 26. Sheffield: JSOT Press, 1984.
——. *Traditional Techniques in Classical Hebrew Verse*. JSOTSup 170. Sheffield: JSOT Press, 1994.
Weippert, Manfred. "Mitteilungen zum Text von Ps 19:5 und Jes 22:5." *ZAW* n.s. 32 (1961): 97–99.
Weiser, Arthur. *The Old Testament: Its Formation and Development*. Translated by B. M. Barton. New York: Association Press, 1961.
Wellek, Rene, and Austin Warren. *Theory of Literature*. San Diego: Harcourt Brace Jovanovich, 1977.
Wellhausen, J. *Der Text der Bücher Samuelis*. Göttingen: Vandenhoeck und Ruprecht, 1871.
Wente, Edward, trans. and ed. *Letters from Ancient Egypt*. Atlanta, GA: Scholars Press, 1990.
——. "Correspondence." In *The Oxford Encyclopedia of Ancient Egypt*, edited by Donald B. Redford. New York: Oxford University Press, 2001.
West, M. L. *The East Face of Helicon: West Asiatic Elements in Greek Poetry and Myth*. Oxford: Clarendon Press, 1997.
Whitaker, Richard E. "A Formulaic Analysis of Ugaritic Poetry." Ph.D. diss. Harvard University, 1969.
——. "A Formulaic Analysis of Ugaritic Poetry." Ph.D. diss. Harvard University, 1969.
——. "Ugaritic Formulae." In *Ras Shamra Parallels: The Texts from Ugarit and the Hebrew Bible*, vol. 3, edited by Stan Rummel, 208–19. Roma: Pontificium Institutum Biblicum, 1981.

Willis, John T. "An Anti-Elide Narrative Tradition from a Prophetic Circle at the Ramah Sanctuary." *JBL* 90 (1971): 288–308.
Wilson, John A. "The Asiatic Campaigning of Amen-Hotep II." In *ANET*, edited by James B. Prichard, 245–48. Princeton, NJ: Princeton University Press, 1969.
Wilson, Robert R. *Prophecy and Society in Ancient Israel*. Philadelphia, PA: Fortress Press, 1980.
Winckler, Hugo. *Die Keilschrifttexte Assurbanipals*. Vol. III of *Sammlung von Keilschrifttexten*. Leipzig: E. Pfeiffer, 1893–95.
Wonneberger, Reinhard. *Redaktion: Studien zur Textfortschreibung im Alten Testament, entwickelt am Beispiel der Samuel-Überlieferung*. Göttingen: Vandenhoeck & Ruprecht, 1991.
Wright, David P. *Disposal of Impurity: Elimination Rites in the Bible and in Hittite and Mesopotamian Literature*. SBLDS 101. Atlanta, GA: Scholars Press, 1987.
——. "David Autem Remansit in Hierusalem: Felix Coniunctio!" In *Pomegranates Golden Bells: Studies in Biblical, Jewish, and Near Eastern Ritual, Law and Literature in Honor of Jacob Milgrom*, edited by David P. Wright, Freedman David N., and Hurvitz Avi, 215–30. Winona Lake, IN: Eisenbrauns, 1995.
——. *Ritual in Narrative: The Dynamics of Feasting, Mourning, and Retaliation Rites in the Ugaritic Tale of Aqhat*. Winona Lake, IN: Eisenbrauns, 2001.
Wyatt, Nick. "The Story of Aqhat (KTU 1.17–19)." In *Handbook of Ugaritic Studies*, edited by Wilfred G. E. Watson and Nick Wyatt, 234–58. Leiden: Brill, 1999.
——. *Religious Texts from Ugarit*. BS 53. London: Sheffield Academic Press, 2002.
——. "Epic in Ugaritic Literature." In *A Companion to Ancient Epic*, edited by John M. Foley, 246–54. Oxford: Blackwell, 2005.
——. *Word of Tree and Whisper of Stone: And Other Papers on Ugaritic Thought*. Piscataway, NJ: Gorgias Press, 2007.
Yadin, Yigael. *The Art of Warfare in Biblical Lands*. New York: McGraw-Hill Book, 1963.
Yon, M., J. Gachet, P. Lombard, and J. Mallet. "Fouilles de la 48e campagne (1988) à Ras Shamra-Ougarit." *Syria* 67 (1990): 1–29.
Young, Serenity. "Buddhist Dream Experience: The Role of Interpretation, Ritual, and Gender." In *Dreams: A Reader on the Religious, Cultural, and Psychological Dimensions of Dreaming*, edited by Kelly Bulkeley. New York: Palgrave, 2001.
Zakovitch, Yair. "A Study of Precise and Partial Derivations in Biblical Etymology." *JSOT* 15 (1980): 31–50.
Zevit, Ziony. *The Religions of Ancient Israel: A Synthesis of Parallactic Approaches*. London: Continuum, 2001.
Zgoll, Annette von. "Die Welt im Schlaf sehen: Inkubation von Träumen im antiken Mesopotamien." *WO* 32 (2002): 74–101.

AUTHOR AND SUBJECT INDEX